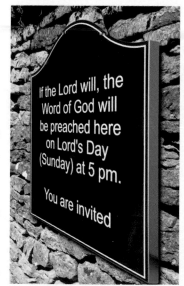

God's heart for the poor hasn't changed. No one is disposable to God, so no one is disposable to us. Today's orphans, widows and strangers are the poor; the powerless; the exploited. Christian Aid's first priority is fighting for their tomorrow because we believe everyone deserves one.

The Church of Scotland is committed to this work by sponsoring Christian Aid.

0131 220 1254
www.christianaidscotland.org.uk

We believe in life before death

Registered charity number SC039150 Registered Company number 5171525

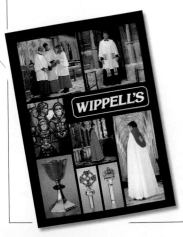

The Right Reverend David W. Lunan MA BD

MODERATOR

The Church of Scotland
YEAR BOOK
2008/2009

Editor
Rev. Ronald S. Blakey
MA BD MTh

Published on behalf of
THE CHURCH OF SCOTLAND
by SAINT ANDREW PRESS
121 George Street, Edinburgh EH2 4YN

THE OFFICES OF THE CHURCH

121 George Street
Edinburgh EH2 4YN

Tel: 0131-225 5722
Fax: 0131-220 3113
Internet: http://www.churchofscotland.org.uk/

Office Hours:
Facilities Manager:

Monday–Friday 9:00am–5:00pm
Carole Tait 0131-240 2214

MISSION AND DISCIPLESHIP COUNCIL

Edinburgh Office	121 George Street, Edinburgh EH2 4YN	0131-225 5722
Glasgow Office	59 Elmbank Street, Glasgow G2 4PQ	0141-352 6946
Inverness Office	Main Street, North Kessock, Inverness IV1 3XN	01463 731712
Perth Office	Arran House, Arran Road, Perth PH1 3DZ	01738 630514

SOCIAL CARE COUNCIL

Charis House	47 Milton Road East, Edinburgh EH15 2SR	Tel: 0131-657 2000
	[E-mail: info@crossreach.org.uk]	Fax: 0131-657 5000

SCOTTISH CHARITY NUMBERS

The Church of Scotland – Unincorporated Councils and Committees	SC011353
The Church of Scotland General Trustees	SC014574
The Church of Scotland Investors Trust	SC022884
The Church of Scotland Trust	SC020269

(For the Scottish Charity Numbers of congregations, see Section 7)

QUICK DIRECTORY

A.C.T.S.	01259 216980
Bridgeton, St Francis-in-the-East Church House	0141-554 8045
Carberry	0131-665 3135/7604
Christian Aid London	020 7620 4444
Christian Aid Scotland	0131-220 1254
Church of Scotland Insurance Co. Ltd	0131-220 4119
Glasgow Lodging House Mission	0141-552 0285
Media Relations Unit (Press Office)	0131-240 2243
Priority Areas Office	0141-248 2905
Safeguarding Office (item 38 in Assembly Committee list)	0131-240 2256
Scottish Churches House	01786 823588
Scottish Churches Parliamentary Office	0131-558 8137
Scottish Churches World Exchange	0131-315 4444
Scottish Storytelling Centre/John Knox House	0131-556 9579/2647
Trust Housing Association Ltd (formerly Kirk Care)	0131-225 7246
Year Book Editor	01899 229226

Pulpit Supply: Fee and Expenses
Details of the current fee and related expenses in respect of Pulpit Supply will be found as the last item in number 3 (the Ministries Council) on page 9.

First published in 2008 by SAINT ANDREW PRESS, 121 George Street, Edinburgh EH2 4YN on behalf of the CHURCH of SCOTLAND

Copyright © The CHURCH of SCOTLAND, 2008

ISBN 978 0 86153 387 9

British Library Cataloguing in Publication Data
A catalogue record for this book is available from the British Library.

Printed and bound by Bell and Bain Ltd, Glasgow

CONTENTS

**All correspondence regarding the *Year Book* should be sent to
The Editor, *Church of Scotland Year Book*,
Saint Andrew Press, 121 George Street, Edinburgh EH2 4YN
Fax: 0131-220 3113
[E-mail: yearbookeditor@cofscotland.org.uk]**

GENERAL ASSEMBLY OF 2009
The General Assembly of 2009 will convene on
Thursday, 21st May 2009

FROM THE MODERATOR

It was Dr Johnson who famously said: 'Knowledge is of two kinds; we know a subject ourselves, or we know where we can find information on it'. Whatever you want to know about the workings of the Church of Scotland, you have found the book. No-one could retain all that is contained in this *Year Book*, except perhaps its remarkable editor, Rev. Ron Blakey, whose encyclopaedic knowledge and caring style are legendary. The Church is much in his debt.

It is not only ministers who delve periodically into the *Year Book*; a wide range of people use it for reference. Presbytery Clerks like myself, however, more than most make regular forays into its pages. It rewards familiarity with its format – lists, numbering, ordering and annotation – and, in searching for what I needed, I was often gently surprised by coming across facts that I didn't even know I didn't know.

The information in the *Year Book* helps us to understand the structures of the Church and to identify many of the people involved with its day-to-day operations. The structures of the Church – the wineskins – in turn facilitate across the nation the worship, witness and service of the Church, and in local communities they nurture the formation of people's lives and the shaping of our Christian faith and character.

We can therefore use the *Year Book* as a prayer book, remembering one another before God, so that the Holy Spirit breathes life into all we say and do. I commend the *Year Book* to you as a source of valuable information, as an accurate historical record of the Church of Scotland in 2008, and as a means of grace.

David W. Lunan
July 2008

Thubhairt an t-Ollamh Somhairle MacIain: 'Tha eòlas ann de dhà sheorsa; tha eòlas againn fhèin air cuspair, no tha fios againn càit an lorg sinn fiosrachadh ma dhèidhinn'. Ge b'e dè a tha thu airson a lorg mun dòigh anns a bheil Eaglais na h-Alba ag obrachadh, seo an leabhar dhutsa. Cha b'urrainn do dh'aon neach na tha de dh'fhiosrachadh anns an *Leabhar Bhliadhnail* seo a chumail air chuimhne, mur e, 's dòcha, am fear-deasachaidh barraichte, an t-Urr. Ron Blakey. Tha an t-eòlas mìorbhaileach farsaing agus an dòigh chùramach anns am bi e ag obair air bilean an t-sluaigh. Tha an Eaglais fada na chomain.

Chan e a-mhàin ministearan a bhios a' ruamhar anns an *Leabhar Bhliadhnail*. Bidh farsaingeachd de dhaoine eile a' lorg fiosrachaidh ann cuideachd. Bidh Clèirich Clèire, mar a tha mi fhèin, nas trice na càch a' toirt roidean am measg a dhuilleagan. Tha cumadh an leabhair gad oideachadh mar as motha a chuireas tu de dh'eòlas air – le liostaichean, àireamhan, nòtaichean agus mìneachadh. Ann a bhith a' sireadh na bha mi ag iarraidh, gu tric ghabh mi beagan iongantais nuair a thàinig mi tarsaing air fiosrachadh air an robh mi aineolach, agus gun fhios gu robh mi aineolach air.

Tha am fiosrachadh anns an *Leabhar Bhliadhnail* gar cuideachadh ann a bhith a' tuigsinn structaran na h-Eaglais agus ann a bhith a' toirt aithne dhuinn air mòran de na daoine a tha an sàs na h-obair o latha gu latha. Tha structaran na h-Eaglais – na searragan, mar gum biodh – a' toirt taic air feadh na dùthcha do dh'adhradh, fianais agus seirbheis na h-Eaglais; anns a' choimhearsnachd gu h-ionadail tha iad a' toirt cumaidh air beatha dhaoine agus a' cur cruth air ar creideamh Crìosdail agus ar buadhan.

Air an adhbhar sin faodaidh sinn an *Leabhar Bliadhnail* a chleachdadh mar leabhar-ùrnaigh, a' cuimhneachadh a chèile an làthair Dhè, agus mar sin bidh an Spiorad Naomh a' sèideadh beatha anns gach nì a bhios sinn ag ràdh agus a' dèanamh. Tha mi a' moladh an *Leabhair Bhliadhnail* dhuibh mar chladhan a tha gar toirt gu fiosrachaidh a tha luachmhor, mar dhealbh mionaideach air suidheachadh Eaglais na h-Alba ann an 2008, agus mar mheadhan gràis.

David W. Lunan
July 2008

FROM THE EDITOR

Whatever other charges may be levelled against the *Year Book*, dull annual repetition hardly fits. Once again, there are several new or substantially revised sections.

There was a ready welcome for constructive suggestions coming from the Gaelic Groups which operate under the auspices of the Council of Assembly, the Mission and Discipleship Council and the Ministries Council. These Groups share a common desire to promote the wider use of Gaelic within the Church of Scotland and believe that the *Year Book* can be of assistance in this. As a first step, there are included this year two new features:

• the Moderator's Introduction to the *Year Book* appears in both English and Gaelic
• there is a section describing both the resources that are currently available in Gaelic and further work that is being envisaged within the wider Church of Scotland.

As has readily been acknowledged in previous years, this Editor owes much to the pawky wisdom of the late and great Andrew Herron, who edited this volume for more than thirty years. He explained once that 'editorial freedom' in the case of the *Year Book* was summed up in the words 'you can print whatever you like as long as it is exactly what the Conveners and Secretaries give you, even to the point where you are printing what you do not fully understand'. That last somewhat wry comment apparently referred to a theological mini-thesis which, in Andrew's view, lacked a certain clarity. 'I took it on trust', he said, 'and printed it.' Memory recalls a third-year essay in Systematic Theology where words were penned which were, to this mind, more than a minor mystery. They were, however, words of the redoubtable Ronald Gregor Smith, and they were reproduced in trust – trust amply rewarded with a pass mark. To the Editor's shame, there is not a word of usable Gaelic in his vocabulary. He is therefore immensely grateful to those who have prepared the Gaelic text and is more than happy to reproduce it in the sure confidence that it contains nothing either scurrilous or libellous.

Saint Andrew Press accepted the suggestion that it could prove helpful to hikers, ramblers and travellers in general if the *Year Book* were to include a section giving for each church listed the appropriate Ordnance Survey National Grid Reference. Accordingly, a new section with this information is included this year, and for this the Church owes a great debt of gratitude to John Hume, who undertook the painstaking research that must have been required. As a musical bonus, there is the lively expectation that, throughout at least the summer months, our tracks and hills will reverberate to the strains of 'The Happy Holy Wanderer':

> 'I love to go a-wandering
> Across the hills and back:
> I never miss a single kirk,
> My *Year Book*'s in my pack.'

All our churches are now required to have 'legal names' to set alongside their recently acquired Charity Numbers. Not all Presbyteries have completed their part in this, but those which have will find their labours reflected in the appropriate appendix. Presbytery Clerks must have had to count to many more than ten as the administrative implications of this imposition sank in. Nor are they alone. The editorial hat is doffed in admiration to the staff of our Law Department, who have had to cope with the Everest of paper generated by this mind-numbing exercise in bureaucratic tedium – a task made more irritating still by the lack of consistency and accuracy in the Legal Names as eventually agreed. For example, the sorely abused apostrophe must even now be in intensive care, sprinkled as it is, without logic and seemingly at random, throughout these names. As one might say, 'some saints have it; others do not'. It will doubtless appear as if the *Year Book* is acquiescing in this further descent into slovenly inexactitude; that is not so. It would appear that these names, down to the last or lost jot and tittle, rank with the Laws of the Medes and Persians for their sacrosanct untouchability.

In regard to this new nomenclature, two questions come to mind:

- Will it hasten or in any way aid the coming of the Kingdom? The only charitable answer has to be 'not in the slightest'.
- Could it in any way impede the coming of that Kingdom? The only possibility might be if the Charity Regulator and the Council of Heaven fail to agree an appropriate Charity Number and Legal Name for the hereafter. If there should be a celestial civil servant with this task languishing in a 'to do' file, the following is offered as a basis for negotiation: HE31130712: St Peter's-by-the-Gate: The Church of the Holy Eternity.

In discussions with the Office of the Scottish Charity Regulator regarding these 'Legal Names', the time-honoured 'normal' names as used by the *Year Book* in the Presbytery Lists and elsewhere were referred to as 'colloquial names'. It is at once stressed that there was nothing either dismissive or disparaging in this, nor any suggestion that these names were less than worthy in their place. It did, however, encourage the intriguing thought that alongside these names could be set the colloquial names of the ministers where these are known and printable. A random and totally unrepresentative enquiry showed what the results might be. Several ministers are known in local shorthand as 'Jehu', such is their alleged speed behind the wheel; there is at least one 'Dibley', reflecting physical shape rather than theological slant; and there are those known by their own catchphrases. We have, for example:

- 's'pose' – the minister's reaction to any idea of which he himself had not thought,
- 'soonas' in token of the speed at which action is promised or required, and
- 'thoughtyouknew' – the catch-all response to any suggestion that the communication skills of the manse have been found wanting.

We were assured that there is a 'skive', a 'Stalin's daughter', two Napoleons and a 'headless chicken', but of course we do not believe it.

By far the most common of such 'names' owes its popularity to the commendable feature of our contemporary Church that sees increasing numbers of our parish ministers continuing their academic studies well beyond their student days. In particular, the DMin courses are attracting encouraging numbers of recruits – and, in a mix of admiration and affection, congregations have not been slow to catch on, as was admirably illustrated in the vestibule of a west-of-Scotland church. Two visitors from Cheltenham enquired of the duty elder who was to be leading worship that morning; they were visibly thrown by the answer: 'it's wur demon'.

Ronald S. Blakey
July 2008

SECTION 1

Assembly Councils,
Committees, Departments and Agencies

INDEX OF ASSEMBLY COUNCILS, COMMITTEES, DEPARTMENTS AND AGENCIES

[Note: Years, where given, indicate the year of appointment]

1. THE COUNCIL OF ASSEMBLY

Remit
1. To implement the plan of reorganisation and structural change of the Agencies of the General Assembly as formulated by the Assembly Council and approved by the General Assembly of 2004.
2. To monitor, evaluate and co-ordinate the work of the Agencies of the General Assembly, within the context of policy determined by the Assembly.
3. To advise the General Assembly on the relative importance of work being undertaken by its various Agencies.
4. To receive reports from, offer guidance to and issue instructions to Agencies of the General Assembly as required from time to time on matters of management, organisation and administration.
5. To bring recommendations to the General Assembly concerning the total amount of the Church's Co-ordinated Budget for the following financial year and the disposition thereof among Local Mission, Parish Staffing and the Mission and Renewal Fund.
6. To determine the allocation of the total budgets for the following financial year for Parish Staffing and the Mission and Renewal Fund among the relevant Agencies of the General Assembly and Ecumenical Bodies.
7. To prepare and present to the General Assembly an indicative Rolling Budget for the following five financial years.
8. To receive and distribute unrestricted legacies and donations among the Agencies of the General Assembly with power to specify the use to which the same are to be applied.
9. To consider and decide on proposals from Agencies of the General Assembly to purchase heritable property or any other asset (except investments) valued in excess of £50,000 or lease any heritable property where the annual rental exceeds £10,000 per annum, declaring that no Agency save those referred to in section 19 hereof shall proceed to purchase or lease such property without prior approval from the Council.
10. To consider and decide on proposals from Agencies of the General Assembly, save those referred to in section 19 hereof, to sell or lease for a period in excess of five years or otherwise dispose of any heritable property, or sell or otherwise dispose of any asset (except investments) valued in excess of £50,000, held by or on behalf of that Agency, with power to allocate all or part of the sale or lease proceeds to another Agency or Agencies in terms of section 11 hereof.
11. To reallocate following upon consultation with the Agency or Agencies affected unrestricted funds held by or on behalf of any of the Agencies of the General Assembly to another Agency or Agencies with power to specify the use to which the same are to be applied.
12. To determine staffing and resourcing requirements of Agencies of the General Assembly, including inter-Departmental sharing or transfer of staff, in accordance with policies drawn up by the Council of Assembly in line with priorities approved by the General Assembly, it being declared that the term 'staffing' shall not include those appointed or employed to serve either in particular Parishes or overseas.
13. To consult with the relative Councils and Agencies in their appointment of Council Secretaries to the Church and Society, Ministries, Mission and Discipleship, Social Care and World Mission Councils, to appoint the Ecumenical Officer, the Director of Stewardship, the Head of Media Relations and the Personnel Manager and to nominate individuals to the General Assembly for appointment to the offices of Principal Clerk of the General Assembly,

Depute Clerk of the General Assembly, General Treasurer of the Church and Solicitor of the Church.

14. To keep under review the central administration of the Church, with particular regard to resolving issues of duplication of resources.

15. To provide an Internal Audit function to the General Assembly Councils, Statutory Corporations and Committees (other than the Social Care Council).

16. To attend to the general interests of the Church in matters which are not covered by the remit of any other Agency.

17. To deal with urgent issues arising between meetings of the General Assembly, provided that:
    (a)   these do not fall within the jurisdiction of the Commission of Assembly or of any Presbytery or Kirk Session,
    (b)   they are not of a legislative or judicial nature and
    (c)   any action taken in terms of this clause shall be reported to the next General Assembly.

18. To encourage all Agencies of the General Assembly to work ecumenically wherever possible and to have regard to the international, evangelical and catholic nature of the Church.

19. For the avoidance of doubt, sections 9 and 10 shall not apply to the Church of Scotland General Trustees, the Church of Scotland Housing and Loan Fund for Retired Ministers and Widows and Widowers of Ministers and the New Charge Development Committee and its successor body, all of which may deal with heritable property and other assets without the approval of the Council.

Membership

(a)   Convener, Vice-Convener and eight members appointed by the General Assembly; the General Treasurer and the Solicitor of the Church; the Principal Clerk as Secretary to the Council; together with:

(b)   the Conveners of the Councils, namely Church and Society, Ministries, Mission and Discipleship, Social Care, Support and Services, and World Mission, together with the Convener of the Panel on Review and Reform, and the Secretaries of the following Councils, namely Church and Society, Ministries, Mission and Discipleship, Social Care and World Mission.

Convener: Rev. Alan Greig BSc BD (2008)
Vice-Convener: Professor Peter Brand BSc PhD DSc FRSE (2008)
Secretary: The Principal Clerk

---

2. THE CHURCH AND SOCIETY COUNCIL

Remit

The remit of the Church and Society Council is to facilitate the Church of Scotland's engagement with, and comment upon, national, political and social issues through:

• the development of theological, ethical and spiritual perspectives in the formulation of policy on such issues;

• the effective representation of the Church of Scotland in offering on its behalf appropriate and informed comment on political and social issues;

• the building, establishing and maintaining of a series of networks and relationships with leaders and influence-shapers in civic society, and engaging long-term in dialogue and the exchange of ideas with them;

- the support of the local church in its mission and engagement by offering professional and accessible resources on contemporary issues;
- the conducting of an annual review of progress made in discharging the remit and the provision of a written report to the Council of Assembly.

Membership
Convener, Vice-Convener, 28 members appointed by the General Assembly, one of whom will also be appointed to the Ecumenical Relations Committee, and one member appointed from and by the Social Care Council and the Guild. The Nomination Committee will ensure that the Council membership contains at least five individuals with specific expertise in each of the areas of Education, Societal/Political, Science and Technology and Social/Ethical. This number may include the Convener and Vice-Convener of the Council.

Convener:	Rev. Ian F. Galloway BA BD (2008)
Vice-Convener:	Rev. Alexander G. Horsburgh MA BD (2008)
Secretary:	Rev. Ewan R. Aitken BA BD

3. THE MINISTRIES COUNCIL
Tel: 0131-225 5722; Fax: 0131-240 2201
E-mail: ministries@cofscotland.org.uk

Remit
The remit of the Ministries Council is recruitment, training and support of recognised ministries for the mission of the Church, and assessment of patterns of national deployment of parish ministries. In pursuance of this remit, the Council is charged with:

- developing patterns of ministry which allow the Church of Scotland to be effective in its missionary calling and faithful to the one ministry of Jesus Christ;
- recruiting individuals of the highest calibre collaboratively to lead the Church through its ordained ministries;
- providing the Church with a range of ministries including the ministry of word and sacrament, the diaconate, auxiliary ministers, readers and specialist workers;
- developing assessment processes which ensure that those who serve the Church in its various ministries do so in response to God's call on their life;
- providing education, initial training, in-service training and personal-development appraisal of the highest quality to ensure that all those engaged in the various ministries of the Church are equipped to engage in Christ's mission and make the Gospel relevant in a rapidly changing society;
- building good relationships with, and offering quality pastoral support and care to, all the ministries of the Church;
- assisting the whole Church in its responsibility to meet the gospel imperative of giving priority to the poorest and most marginalised in our society;
- undertaking all of its local planning and appraisal work in full co-operation with Presbyteries, local congregations and other denominations, in order to ensure that emerging patterns of church life are effective at a local level and are a viable use of the Church's resources;
- evaluating all developments in ministry in order to ensure their effectiveness and relevance to the life of the Church today;

- working transparently and in collaboration with the other Councils in order to ensure the most effective use of the Church's finance, property and human resources;
- conducting an annual review of progress made in discharging the remit and providing a written report to the Council of Assembly.

Membership

Convener, four Vice-Conveners, 36 members appointed by the General Assembly, one of whom will also be appointed to the Ecumenical Relations Committee, and one member appointed from and by the General Trustees, the Housing and Loan Fund, the Committee on Chaplains to Her Majesty's Forces and the Diaconate Council. For the avoidance of doubt, where a representative of these other bodies is a member of staff, he or she will have no right to vote.

Convener:	Rev. Graham S. Finch MA BD
Vice-Conveners:	Rev. Neil J. Dougall BD
	Rev. Barry W. Dunsmore MA BD
	Rev. Lezley J. Kennedy BD ThM MTh
	Rev. Muriel B. Pearson MA BD

Staff

Council Secretary:	Rev. Dr Martin Scott DipMusEd RSAM BD PhD
	(Tel: ext. 389; E-mail: mscott@cofscotland.org.uk)
Pastoral Adviser and Associate Secretary: (Support and Development)	Rev. John P. Chalmers BD (Tel: ext. 309; E-mail: jchalmers@cofscotland.org.uk)
Associate Secretary: (Planning and Deployment)	Mr John Jackson BSc (Tel: ext. 312; E-mail: jjackson@cofscotland.org.uk)
Associate Secretary: (Priority Areas)	Rev. Dr H. Martin J. Johnstone MA BD MTh PhD (Tel: 0141-248 2905; E-mail: mjohnstone@cofscotland.org.uk)
Associate Secretary: (Vocation and Training)	Mrs Moira Whyte MA (Tel: ext. 266; E-mail: mwhyte@cofscotland.org.uk)
Ministries Support Officers:	Mr Ronald Clarke BEng MSc PECE (Tel: ext. 242; E-mail: rclarke@cofscotland.org.uk) Rev. Jane Denniston MA BD (Tel: ext. 204; E-mail: jdenniston@cofscotland.org.uk) Rev. Gavin J. Elliott MA BD (Tel: ext. 255; E-mail: gelliott@cofscotland.org.uk) Rev. Angus R. Mathieson MA BD (Tel: ext. 315; E-mail: amathieson@cofscotland.org.uk) Mrs Suzie Stark (Tel: ext. 225; E-mail: sstark@cofscotland.org.uk) Mr John Thomson (Tel: ext. 248; E-mail: jthomson@cofscotland.org.uk)
Priority Areas Development Worker:	Mr Noel Mathias BA BTh MA (Tel: 0141-248 2905; E-mail: nmathias@cofscotland.org.uk)

Ministries Council
Further information about the Council's work and services is obtainable through the Ministries Council at the Church Offices. Information is available on a wide range of matters including the Consolidated Stipend Fund, National Stipend Fund, endowment grants, travelling and other expenses, pulpit supply, study leave, ministry development conferences, pastoral care services (including occupational health), Enquiry and Assessment, Education and Training, Parish Appraisal, Priority Areas, New Charge Development, Area Team Ministry, Interim Ministry, Readership, Chaplaincies, the Diaconate, Parish Staffing, and all aspects of work connected with ministers and the ministry of word and sacrament.

Committees
It should be noted that two of the committees which previously operated within the Council have merged. The result is that those responsibilities which formerly lay with the Business Committee and the Strategic Advisory Group are now dealt with by the recently formed Strategic Planning Group.

The following Committees are therefore currently responsible for the policy development and implementation of the work of the Ministries Council.

1.   Strategic Planning Group
Convener: Rev. Graham S. Finch MA BD
The Strategic Planning Group comprises the Convener, the Vice-Conveners and senior staff of all five areas (including Finance) of the Council. It is empowered by the Council to engage in broad-ranging thinking regarding the future outlook and plans of the Council. It reports directly to the Council and brings forward to it ideas and consultation papers offering options as to the future strategic direction of the Council's work. Though a key part of the Council's work, it is a consultative and advisory group rather than a decision-making one.

2.   Vocation and Training Committee
Convener: Rev. Lezley J. Kennedy BD ThM MTh
The Vocation and Training Committee is responsible for the development and oversight of policy in relation to the enquiry and assessment process for full-time and auxiliary ministers of Word and Sacrament and for Deacons and Readers, together with the admission and readmission of ministers. It is further responsible for the supervision of those in training for the recognised ministries of the Church and operates with powers in relation to both of these areas of work to make recommendations of suitability for training and readiness to engage in ministries at the end of a training period. Much of the practical work of implementing policy is carried out by the Committee's two main Task Groups – the Assessment Scheme Task Group and the Candidate Supervision Task Group. In addition, the Curriculum Task Group, which carries out regular reviews of the Curriculum for training for the recognised ministries of the Church, reports to the Vocation and Training Committee.

3.   Planning and Deployment Committee
Convener: Rev. Neil J. Dougall BD
The Planning and Deployment Committee is responsible for the overall planning of the deployment of the Church's ministries, primarily through the ongoing monitoring of the development of Presbytery Plans. The Committee also oversees work on emerging ministries (including New Charge Development work) and deals with all issues relating to policy in respect of employment matters. The Committee receives regular reports from the three Task Groups relating to the above remit.

4. Support and Development Committee
Convener: Rev. Barry W. Dunsmore MA BD
The Ministries Support and Development Committee is responsible for overseeing the pastoral care of all recognised ministries, which includes the Occupational Health Scheme and Counselling Service: and for the promotion of lifelong learning and development opportunities for these ministries, which includes study leave and accompanied review. Also included is the work of Interim Ministry, Area Team Ministry and all aspects of Chaplaincy.

5. Finance Committee
Convener: Mr Leslie Purdie
The Ministries Finance Committee operates with powers to deal with the Parish Ministries Fund, the National Stipend Scheme, Vacancy Schedules, Maintenance Allowances, Hardship Grants and Bursaries, Stipend Advances, management of investments, writing-off shortfalls and the granting of further endowments. It also maintains an oversight of the budgets for all recognised ministries.

6. Priority Areas Committee
Convener: Rev. Muriel B. Pearson MA BD
The Priority Areas Committee is responsible for developing, encouraging and overseeing strategy within priority-area parishes, working both to the agenda of the Council and also in response to local congregations. It is empowered to develop resources to enable congregations to make appropriate responses to the needs of people living in poverty in their parishes, and to raise awareness of the effects of poverty on people's lives in Scotland. It also co-ordinates the strategy of the wider Church in its priority to Scotland's poorest parishes.

The Council also has several *ad hoc* Task Groups,which report to the Committees and implement specific policies of the Council, as follows:

Accompanied Review Task Group
Leader: Rev. Karen K. Watson BD MTh

Assessment Task Group
Leader: Rev. Iain M. Greenshields BD DipRS ACMA MSc MTh

Candidate Task Group
Leader: Rev. Donald G.B. McCorkindale BD DipMin

Conference and Development Task Group
Leader: Rev. Joanne Hood MA BD

Interim Ministries Task Group
Leader: Rev. James Reid BD

Chaplaincies Task Group
Leader: Rev. Dorothy Anderson LLB DipLP BD

Communications Task Group
Leader: Rev. Karen K. Watson BD MTh

Curriculum Task Group
Leader: Rev. Peter White BVMS BD

Pastoral and Spiritual Care Task Group
Leader: Rev. John H.A. Dick MA MSc BD

Employment Issues Task Group
Leader: Mr Grant Gordon

Emerging Ministries Task Group
Leader: Rev. Jared Hay BA MTh DipMin DMin

Presbytery Planning Task Group
Rev. H. Taylor Brown BD CertMin

Health and Healing Task Group
Leader: Rev. Gordon MacRae BA BD

Other Related Bodies:
Chaplains to HM Forces
See separate entry at number 10.

Housing and Loan Fund
See separate entry at number 23.

Pulpit Supply: Fee and Expenses
The General Assembly of 1995 approved new regulations governing the amount of Supply Fee and Expenses. These were effective from 1 July 1995 and are as follows:
1. In Charges where there is only one diet of worship, the Pulpit Supply Fee shall be a Standard Fee of £50 (or as from time to time agreed by the Ministries Council).
2. In Charges where there are additional diets of worship on a Sunday, the person fulfilling the Supply shall be paid £10 for each additional Service (or as from time to time agreed by the Ministries Council).
3. Where the person is unwilling to conduct more than one diet of worship on a given Sunday, he or she shall receive a pro-rata payment based on the total available Fee shared on the basis of the number of Services conducted.
4. The Fee thus calculated shall be payable in the case of all persons permitted to conduct Services under Act II 1986.
5. In all cases, Travelling Expenses shall be paid. Where there is no convenient public conveyance, the use of a private car shall be paid for at the Committee rate of Travelling Expenses. In exceptional circumstances, to be approved in advance, the cost of hiring a car may be met.
6. Where weekend board and lodging are agreed as necessary, these may be claimed for the weekend at a maximum rate of that allowed when attending the General Assembly. The Fee and Expenses should be paid to the person providing the Supply before he or she leaves on the Sunday.

4. THE MISSION AND DISCIPLESHIP COUNCIL

Remit

The remit of the Mission and Discipleship Council is:

- to take a lead role in developing and maintaining an overall focus for mission in Scotland, and to highlight its fundamental relationships with worship, service, doctrine, education and nurture;
- to take a lead role in developing strategies, resources and services in Christian education and nurture, recognising these as central to both mission and discipleship;
- to offer appropriate servicing and support nationally, regionally and locally in the promotion of nurturing, worshipping and witnessing communities of faith;
- to introduce policy on behalf of the Church in the following areas: adult education and elder training, church art and architecture, congregational mission and development, doctrine, resourcing youth and children's work and worship;
- to establish and support the Mission Forum with representatives of relevant Councils;
- to encourage appropriate awareness of, and response to, the requirements of people with particular needs including physical, sensory and/or learning disabilities;
- to conduct an annual review of progress made in discharging the remit and provide a written report to the Council of Assembly.

Membership

Convener, three Vice-Conveners and 21 members appointed by the General Assembly, one of whom will also be appointed to the Ecumenical Relations Committee, the Director of Stewardship, one member appointed from and by the General Trustees, the Guild, the Parish Development Fund, the 'Church Without Walls' Planning Committee and the Scottish Churches Community Trust, and the Convener or Vice-Convener of the Committee on Church Art and Architecture as that Committee shall determine. The Nomination Committee will ensure that the Council membership contains at least three individuals with specific expertise in each of the areas of Education and Nurture, Mission and Evangelism and Worship and Doctrine.

Convener: Rev. Angus Morrison MA BD PhD
Vice-Conveners: Mrs Linda Dunnett BA DCS
                                   Rev. Alan D. Birss MA BD
                                   Rev. Mark E. Johnstone MA BD

Staff

Council Secretary: Rev. Douglas A.O. Nicol MA BD
                                   (E-mail: dnicol@cofscotland.org.uk)
Associate Secretary: Mr Steve Mallon
  (Education and Nurture)   (E-mail: smallon@cofscotland.org.uk)
Associate Secretary: Rev. Alex. M. Millar MA BD MBA
  (Mission and Evangelism)   (E-mail: amillar@cofscotland.org.uk)
Associate Secretary: Rev. Nigel J. Robb FCP MA BD ThM MTh
  (Worship and Doctrine)   (E-mail: nrobb@cofscotland.org.uk)

Regional Development Officers

Regional Development Officers work with the Council and Associate Secretaries in developing and delivering quality resources for congregations. Based in Regional Offices in Edinburgh, Glasgow, Inverness and Perth (the addresses of which are on page xviii), the Officers appointed at the time of going to print are:

Mr Steve Aisthorpe BA   Inverness
Mr Graham L. Allison BA   Glasgow

Rev. Andrew B. Campbell BD DPS MTh	Perth
Ms Fiona H. Fidgin BEd	Edinburgh
Mr Dale London	Perth
Rev. Robin J. McAlpine BDS BD	Perth
Rev. Linda Pollock BD MTh	Inverness
Vacant	Glasgow

The Netherbow: Scottish Storytelling Centre: The integrated facilities of the **Netherbow Theatre** and the **John Knox House Museum**, together with the outstanding new conference and reception areas, are an important cultural and visitor centre on the Royal Mile in Edinburgh and provide advice and assistance nationally in the use of the arts in mission, education and worship. 'Story Source', 'Scriptaid' and other resources are available. Contact the Director, The Netherbow: Scottish Storytelling Centre, 43–45 High Street, Edinburgh EH1 1SR (Tel: 0131-556 9579; E-mail; donald@scottishstorytellingcentre.com; Website: www.scottishstorytellingcentre.co.uk). The new Centre also houses the **Scottish Churches Parliamentary Office**.

The Well Asian Information and Advice Centre: The Council provides support and funding for the Presbytery of Glasgow's innovative project that serves the south side of Glasgow by assisting with welfare, housing, immigration, asylum and personal problems. The Well has a strong mission basis on the clear principles that sharing the love of Christ has to include accepting people for who they are and respecting the beliefs of others. A regular prayer letter is available. Contact The Well, 48–50 Albert Road, Glasgow G42 8DN (Tel: 0141-424 4523; Fax: 0141-422 1722; E-mail: the.well@btinternet.co.uk). See further under **Mission and Evangelism Task Group**.

Life and Work
(Tel: 0131-225 5722; Fax: 0131-240 2207; E-mail: magazine@lifeandwork.org)
Life and Work is the Church of Scotland's monthly magazine. Its purpose is to keep the Church informed about events in church life at home and abroad and to provide a forum for Christian opinion and debate on a variety of topics. It has an independent editorial policy. Contributions which are relevant to any aspect of the Christian faith are welcome.
The price of *Life and Work* this year is £1.60. With a circulation of around 32,000, it also offers advertisers a first-class opportunity to reach a discerning readership in all parts of Scotland. See further under **Publishing Committee**.

Saint Andrew Press
(Tel: 0131-240 2253; Fax: 0131-220 3113; E-mail: acrawford@cofscotland.org.uk)
Saint Andrew Press is the Church of Scotland's publishing house. Formed in 1954, it publishes Church resources, Church stationery, *The Church of Scotland Year Book* and a wide and varied catalogue of fascinating books. These explore the Christian faith in thought-provoking and inspiring ways.
Saint Andrew Press aims to help engender a closer relationship with God and Jesus Christ by producing a range of books that place the Church of Scotland's publishing programme right at the heart of the community. It aims to promote the Christian voice in a way that is strong, modern and relevant to today's world.
The publishing programme includes the updated series of New Testament commentaries, *The New Daily Study Bible*, by the late Professor William Barclay, which has been read by many millions of people around the world. Best-sellers include *A Glasgow Bible* by Jamie Stuart, *Outside Verdict* by Harry Reid, *Iona* by Kenneth Steven, *My Father: Reith of the BBC* by Marista Leishman and *Silent Heroes* by John Miller. Other popular titles include *Practical Caring* by

Sheilah Steven, *Will You Follow Me?* by Leith Fisher, Beginners' Guides to the Old and New Testament, *Pray Now* and *Common Order* and *Common Ground* from the Church of Scotland Office for Worship and Doctrine.

Saint Andrew Press is compiling a mailing list for all those who would like to receive regular information on its publications. Up-to-date information on all Saint Andrew Press titles can be found at www.churchofscotland.org.uk/standrewpress

All new proposals for publication should be sent to the Head of Publishing in the form of a two-page description of the book and its readership, together with one sample chapter. Saint Andrew Press staff are always happy to offer help and advice. See further under **Publishing Committee**.

Committee on Church Art and Architecture
Membership
The Committee shall comprise a Convener, Vice-Convener and 15 members appointed by the General Assembly.

Remit
This Committee replaces the Committee on Artistic Matters and will take forward that Committee's remit, which is in the following terms:

The Committee advises congregations and Presbyteries regarding the most appropriate way of carrying out renovations, alterations and reordering of interiors, having regard to the architectural quality of Church buildings. It also advises on the installation of stained glass, tapestries, memorials, furniture and furnishings, and keeps a list of accredited artists and craftsworkers.

Any alteration to the exterior or interior of a Church building which affects its appearance must be referred to the Committee for approval, which is given through the General Trustees. Congregations contemplating alterations are urged to consult the Committee at an early stage.

Members of the Committee are prepared, when necessary, to visit churches and meet office-bearers. The Committee's services are given free.

The Committee seeks the conservation of the nation's heritage as expressed in its Church buildings, while at the same time helping to ensure that these buildings continue to serve the worship and witness of the Church in the present day.

In recent years, the General Assembly has conferred these additional duties on the Committee:
1. preparation of reports on the architectural, historical and aesthetic merit of the buildings of congregations involved in questions of readjustment
2. verification of the propriety of repair and renovation work forming the basis of grant applications to public bodies
3. the offering of advice on the maintenance and installation of organs
4. facilitating the transfer of unwanted furnishings from one church to another through the quarterly *Exchange and Transfer*
5. the compilation of a Register of Churches
6. the processing of applications from congregations for permission to dispose of surplus communion plate, and the carrying out of an inventory of sacramental vessels held by congregations.

Education and Nurture Task Group
Individual Christians motivated and equipped for mission and service
This is the aim of the Task Group, and this ideal underpins all that we do. Our task is to create and to encourage learning opportunities in local churches and to provide national events and programmes alongside these that enhance what's going on in the local situation.

We work in the following areas:

- Children's Ministry (Linda Pollock): lpollock@cofscotland.org.uk
- Youth Ministry (Steve Mallon): smallon@cofscotland.org.uk
- Adult Learning (Fiona Fidgin): ffidgin@cofscotland.org.uk
- Elder Training (Robin McAlpine): rmcalpine@cofscotland.org.uk

In addition, we have the following key areas of concern for which we have established working groups:

- Membership in the Church
- Supporting people with learning difficulties
- Adult learning and spirituality
- Developing educational resources with Saint Andrew Press.

We also seek to continue to support Guild Educational Representatives in their vital role of providing and supporting learning at local Guild meetings around Scotland.

The Task Group is also responsible for the National Youth Assembly which meets each year in September, and supports the Youth Representatives who attend the General Assembly every May.

Recent new programmes include:

- Cosycoffeehouse – a kit for local churches to create an authentic coffee-house experience for younger teenagers
- Digital Witness – new resources created by young people themselves
- Children's and Youth Ministry Trainers – local-resource people to encourage local workers
- Children's Assembly – a forum for children who want to get involved in the life of the Church of Scotland.

Mission and Evangelism Task Group (METAG)

The Mission and Evangelism Task Group, within the Mission and Discipleship Council, operates with the following remit:

- *To encourage* local initiatives;
- *To offer* expertise, research, development and training;
- *To assist* local churches to be mission-focused;
- *To be alert to* new opportunities in today's Scotland; and lastly,
- *To identify* those shifts occurring in theological thinking and reflection that hint at something new, and to consider their appropriateness or otherwise in a Scottish context.

The Task Group has the following priorities:

- **EMERGING CHURCH** (to explore the development of emerging patterns of church in the changing cultural scene that is contemporary Scotland);
- **CONFIDENCE IN SHARING AND SPEAKING ABOUT WHAT WE BELIEVE** (to seek to build confidence in personal witness and faith sharing through resources and training);
- **INTERFAITH** (to promote the development of interfaith relations, supported by the Interfaith Officer, Iain Stewart, and by The Well Asian Information and Advice Centre in Glasgow); and
- **IMPACT** (to sponsor and recommend the locally based children's and youth work that is undertaken through the programme and to develop it further).

Rural Strategy Team

The remit of the Rural Strategy Team is to affirm, support and resource rural churches. It is responsible for planning for a Church presence at the Royal Highland Show and for organising the Rural Church Conference in late October 2008. It seeks to reflect the full extent of rural experience, encompassing farming, fishing, tourism, forestry and other professions/industries that have a bearing on rural life. This will involve collaboration with ecumenical partners and responding periodically to requests for submissions to government consultations.

The Convener is Rev. Bryan Kerr; the Secretary (Rev. Alex. M. Millar) can be contacted by telephone at 0131-225 5722 ext. 307, or by e-mail at amillar@cofscotland.org.uk

Publishing Committee
Membership
Convener, Vice-Convener and eight members appointed by the General Assembly. The Head of Publishing shall act as Secretary to the Committee, and the Editor of *Life and Work* shall also be in attendance, both on a non-voting basis.

Remit
The remit of the Publishing Committee is:
*   to oversee Saint Andrew Press, including the taking of all related commercial decisions, and to receive regular reports on the Press's operation from the Head of Publishing;
*   to monitor pricing and delivery of published materials to Councils of the General Assembly and the use by such Councils of Saint Andrew Press;
*   to monitor the cost of printing and related activities by Councils and Agencies and to make recommendations to the Council of Assembly's Budget Group on whether any or all of these activities should be outsourced;
*   to oversee the publishing of *Life and Work* and *Ministers' Forum* and to take all relevant commercial decisions affecting these publications. For the avoidance of doubt, it is expressly declared that, in order to protect the editorial independence of *Life and Work*, the magazine's Advisory Committee shall come within the aegis of the Council of Assembly through the Council's Communication Committee. The editor of *Ministers' Forum* is Rev. John A. Ferguson of Peterculter (Tel: 01224 735041);
*   to operate within a budget approved by the Council of Assembly and provided by the Mission and Renewal Fund, as augmented by surpluses generated by Saint Andrew Press, and to determine the balance between revenue-earning and subsidised activities within that budget;
*   to report quarterly to the Council of Assembly's Budget Group.

Worship and Doctrine Task Group
The Worship and Doctrine Task Group, within the Mission and Discipleship Council, will have responsibility for the remits of the former Panels on Worship and on Doctrine.

The Panel on Worship existed to witness to the importance of worship as a primary function of the Church. In this, the Panel
*   was concerned with the provision of worship materials for public use, being responsible for the production of *Common Order* and *Pray Now*;
*   encouraged courses and retreats to promote spiritual growth;
*   encouraged new developments in church music and the training of musicians;
*   was engaged in providing materials for worship in Gaelic;
*   was involved in the compilation of new hymn books and supplements;
*   published occasional papers on aspects of the practice of public worship.

The Panel on Doctrine was required to:
*   fulfil remits from the General Assembly on matters concerning doctrine;
*   draw the attention of the Assembly to matters inside the Church of Scotland or elsewhere which might have significant doctrinal implications, with recommendations for action;
*   be available for consultation by other Committees of the General Assembly on any matter which might be of doctrinal significance;
*   communicate and consult in an ecumenical context on matters involving doctrine.

5. THE SOCIAL CARE COUNCIL
SOCIAL CARE (CrossReach)
Charis House, 47 Milton Road East, Edinburgh EH15 2SR
Tel: 0131-657 2000; Fax: 0131-657 5000
E-mail: info@crossreach.org.uk; Website: www.crossreach.org.uk

The Social Care Council, known as CrossReach, provides social-care services as part of the Christian witness of the Church to the people of Scotland.

Remit
The remit of the Social Care Council is:
* as part of the Church's mission, to offer services in Christ's name to people in need;
* to provide specialist resources to further the caring work of the Church;
* to identify existing and emerging areas of need, to guide the Church in pioneering new approaches to relevant problems and to make responses on issues arising within the area of the Council's concern through appropriate channels such as the Church's Church and Society Council, the Scottish Government and the like;
* to conduct an annual review of progress made in discharging the remit and provide an annual written report to the General Assembly;
* to oversee an appropriate corporate management and support service to deliver the above and be responsible for funding all salaries and related costs;
* to set and review terms and conditions of staff and establish appropriate internal governance systems.

Membership
Convener, two Vice-Conveners and 28 members appointed by the General Assembly, one of whom will also be appointed to the Ecumenical Relations Committee. The Council shall have power to appoint such Committees and Groups as it may from time to time determine to be appropriate to ensure that the Council's Remit is fulfilled.

Convener: Rev. David L. Court (2005)
Vice-Conveners: Dr Sally Bonnar (2008)
                       Rev. Sydney S. Graham (2007)

Staff
Chief Executive Officer: Mr Alan Staff
                           (E-mail: alan.staff@crossreach.org.uk)
Executive Director: Mr James Maguire
                           (E-mail: james.maguire@crossreach.org.uk)

Management Structure
The management structure is service-based. There are three Regional Directors, each with geographic and specialist areas of responsibility. They are supported by Heads of Service, who have lead roles for particular types of service and client groups.

Regional Director West and
   Older People: Marlene Smith (marlene.smith@crossreach.org.uk;
                                     tel: 0141-338 6565)
Heads of Service: Brenda Fraser (East)
                           Allan Logan (West)
                           Annie McDonald (North)
                           Helen Thomson (Dementia)

Regional Director East and
   Young People and Families: Paul Robinson (paul.robinson@crossreach.org.uk)
General and Strategic Manager: Chris McNaught

Regional Director North and
   Adult Services: Calum Murray (calum.murray@crossreach.org.uk;
                          tel: 01738 783200)
Heads of Service: Flora Mackenzie
                          Gerard Robson
                          George McNeilly
                          Dave Clark

Director of Corporate Planning: Jeannette Deacon (jeannette.deacon@crossreach.org.uk)
Principal Officers: Greg Dougal
                          Viv Dickenson

Director of Finance: Robert Nelson (robert.nelson@crossreach.org.uk)
Principal Officers: Philip Chan
                          Alastair Purves

Director of Human Resources: Peter Bailey (peter.bailey@crossreach.org.uk)
Principal Officers: Jane Allan
                          Mari Rennie

IT Manager: Yvonne Farrant (yvonne.farrant@crossreach.org.uk)

Director of Estates: David Reid (david.reid@crossreach.org.uk)

Fundraising, Marketing and
   Communications Manager: Pam Taylor (pam.taylor@crossreach.org.uk)

List of Services

CrossReach operates over 80 services across Scotland, and a list of these can be obtained from Charis House on 0131-657 2000, or from the CrossReach website: www.crossreach.org.uk

Fundraising, Marketing and Communications

Manager: Pam Taylor (pam.taylor@crossreach.org.uk)
Volunteer Development Co-ordinator: Maggie Hunt (maggie.hunt@crossreach.org.uk)
Communications Officer: Hugh Brown (hugh.brown@crossreach.org.uk)

The Fundraising, Marketing and Communications department encompasses the functions of fundraising, media and public relations, publicity, congregational liaison and volunteer development. Fundraising aims to increase income development for the Council's work to ensure the long-term sustainability of our valuable care services across Scotland. We want to inform people about our mission, and work with those who are the most needy in our society. We invite people to donate money to support all our work and to volunteer their time – either to fundraise or to help carry out essential tasks of all kinds. We also ask people to pray with us about our services; to help them do that, a free prayer letter is produced three times a year. You can also keep up to date with the latest news about CrossReach by receiving our free newspaper *Circle of Care*, which has a print run of 40,000 copies three times a year. If you would like to know more about any of the above work, or be added to our mailing list, please contact the FM&C team at Charis House on 0131-657 2000.

Congregational Contacts

Congregational Contacts are the link people between CrossReach and local churches. Each church should have an appointed Contact who receives mailings three times a year. There are currently over 1,000 Congregational Contacts. They undertake work in a variety of ways. They provide current, correct and appropriate information to their Church. They often act as distributors for the *Circle of Care* newspaper and act as agents for our calendar, Christmas card and merchandise. Church members are the most important part of the 'Circle of Care' provided by the Church of Scotland. It's the caring work in the communities of Scotland which is our largest area of service provision. Congregational Contacts provide the vital link between the formal services provided by CrossReach and the community work and prayers of the local churches, and we greatly appreciate the work done by these volunteer champions.

Speakers for Guilds and other Groups

Members of CrossReach staff will gladly visit congregations and other Church organisations to talk about our work. To request a speaker, please write to the FM&C team at Charis House, 47 Milton Road East, Edinburgh EH15 2SR.

6. THE SUPPORT AND SERVICES COUNCIL

Remit

The Support and Services Council will provide a network for its component Committees which report direct to the General Assembly. The remit of the Council is:

- to provide opportunities for consultation among its component committees with a view to identifying and eliminating areas of overlap and duplication of work and resources;
- to elect a Convener who will represent the Council on the Council of Assembly;
- to receive and consider annual reports from component committees on progress made in discharging their remits and transmit these to the Council of Assembly.

Membership

The Conveners and Vice-Conveners of the following Committees:

- Assembly Arrangements
- Central Services
- Ecumenical Relations
- Legal Questions
- Stewardship and Finance
- Safeguarding

together with (as non-voting members):

- The Principal Clerk
- The Depute Clerk
- The Solicitor of the Church
- The General Treasurer
- The Director of Stewardship
- The Ecumenical Officer
- The Head of the Safeguarding Office.

Staff
Minutes Secretary: Rev. Marjory A. MacLean LLB BD PhD
The Council shall meet annually within two weeks of the close of the General Assembly to elect
a Convener who shall be one of the constituent committee conveners and a Vice-Convener who
may be drawn from the convener or vice-convener members. Secretarial support will be provided
by an appropriate member of administrative staff from within the area. The Convener may serve
for up to a maximum of four years and the Vice-Convener for up to three years, both positions
to be confirmed annually. Other meetings of the Council may be held as required.
Convener: Mrs Vivienne A. Dickson CA
Vice-Convener: Rev. John C. Christie BSc BD

Assembly Arrangements Committee
See separate entry at number 8.

Central Services Committee
See separate entry at number 9.

Ecumenical Relations Committee
See separate entry at number 18.

Facilities Management Department
See separate entry at number 20.

General Treasurer's Department
See separate entry at number 21.

Human Resources Department
See separate entry at number 24.

Information Technology Department
See separate entry at number 25.

Law Department
See separate entry at number 26.

Legal Questions Committee
See separate entry at number 27.

Principal Clerk's Department
See separate entry at number 34.

Stewardship and Finance Committee
See separate entry at number 36.

7. THE WORLD MISSION COUNCIL
Tel: 0131-225 5722; Fax: 0131-226 6121
Answerphone: 0131-240 2231
E-mail: world@cofscotland.org.uk
Website: www.churchofscotland.org.uk/worldmission

Remit
The remit of the World Mission Council is:
- to give life to the Church of Scotland's understanding that it is part of Jesus Christ's Universal Church committed to the advance of the Kingdom of God throughout the world;
- to discern priorities and form policies to guide the Church of Scotland's ongoing worldwide participation in God's transforming mission, through the Gospel of Jesus Christ;
- to develop and maintain mutually enriching relationships with the Church of Scotland's partner churches overseas through consultation in the two-way sharing of human and material resources;
- to equip and encourage Church of Scotland members at local, Presbytery and national levels to become engaged in the life of the world Church;
- to help the people of Scotland to appreciate the worldwide nature of the Christian faith;
- to keep informed about the cultural, political, social, economic, religious and ecclesiastical issues of relevance to worldwide mission;
- to recruit, train and support paid staff and volunteers to work overseas;
- to direct the work of the Council's centres in Israel;
- to foster and facilitate local partnerships between congregations and Presbyteries and the partner churches;
- to undertake the responsibilities of the former Board of World Mission in regard to the Church's Overseas Charges and the Presbytery of Europe and its congregations as set out in the relevant Assembly legislation;
- to conduct an annual review of progress made in discharging the remit and provide a written report to the Council of Assembly.

Membership
Convener, two Vice-Conveners, 24 members appointed by the General Assembly, one of whom will also be appointed to the Ecumenical Relations Committee, and one member appointed by the Presbytery of Europe.

Convener: Rev. Colin Renwick BMus BD (2006)
Vice-Conveners: Rev. D. Stewart Gillan BSc MDiv PhD (2008)
                      Mr Leon Marshall CA (2006)

Departmental Staff
Secretary: Rev. Prof. Kenneth R. Ross BA BD PhD
Associate Secretaries: Mr Walter Dunlop ARICS (Israel/Palestine)
                      Mr Sandy Sneddon (Centrally Supported Partnerships)
                      Carol Finlay RGN RMN DipCNE MSc (Local Development)

Finance: Post vacant

Personnel: Mrs Angela Ocak (Human Resources Department)

Strategic Commitments: 2006–10
Mission in a New Mode – Local to Local
- **Evangelism** – working with partner churches on new initiatives in evangelism
- **Reconciliation** – working for justice, peace and reconciliation in situations of conflict or threat
- **The Scandal of Poverty** – resourcing the Church to set people free from the oppression of poverty.

Partnership Priorities
Following a consultation with partner churches held in St Andrews in September 1999, the then Board of World Mission identified the following priority areas for partnership in mission:

1. **Theological Education:** developing ministerial and lay training at appropriate levels in all our churches.
2. **Evangelism:** helping one another to create new models and launch new initiatives to take the Gospel to all people.
3. **Holistic Mission:** enabling one another to respond with Christian compassion to human needs in our rapidly changing societies.
4. **Mission in Pluralistic Societies:** strengthening Christian identity in our multi-religious and multi-cultural societies by supporting one another and sharing our experiences.
5. **Prophetic Ministry:** inspiring one another to discern and speak God's Word in relation to critical issues which arise in our times.
6. **Human and Material Resources:** finding new and imaginative ways of sharing our resources at all levels of Church life.

World Mission and World Resources
Sharing in the mission of God worldwide requires a continuing commitment to sharing the Church of Scotland's resources of people and money for mission in six continents as contemporary evidence that it is 'labouring for the advancement of the Kingdom of God throughout the world' (First Article Declaratory). Such resource-sharing remains an urgent matter because most of our overseas work is in the so-called 'Third World', or 'South', in nations where the effects of the widening gap between rich and poor is *the* major issue for the Church. Our partner churches in Africa, most of Asia, the Caribbean and South and Central America are desperately short of financial and technical resources, which we can to some extent meet with personnel and grants. However, they are more than willing to share the resources of their Christian faith with us, including things which the Church in the West often lacks: enthusiasm in worship, hospitality and evangelism, and a readiness to suffer and struggle for righteousness, and in many areas a readiness to sink denominational differences. Mutual sharing in the world Church witnesses to its international nature and has much to offer a divided world, not least in Scotland.

Vacancies Overseas
The Council welcomes enquiries from men and women interested in serving in the Church overseas. Vacancies for mission partner appointments in the Church's centrally supported partnerships, the World Exchange volunteer programme and opportunities with other organisations can all be considered. Those interested in more information are invited to write to the Personnel Manager in the first instance.

HIV/AIDS Project
On the Report of the Board of World Mission, the General Assembly of 2002 adopted an HIV/AIDS Project to run from 2002 to 2007. The 2006 General Assembly extended the Project to 2010. The Project aims to raise awareness in congregations about the impact of HIV/AIDS and

seeks to channel urgently needed support to partner churches. For further information, contact the Co-ordinator, HIV/AIDS Project, 121 George Street, Edinburgh EH2 4YN (E-mail: hivaids@cofscotland.org.uk).

Jubilee Scotland
The Council plays an active role in the coalition which works within Scotland for the cancellation of unpayable international debt. For further information, contact the Co-ordinator, Jubilee Scotland, 41 George IV Bridge, Edinburgh EH1 1EL (Tel: 0131-225 4321; Fax: 0131-225 8861; E-mail: mail@jubileescotland.org.uk).

Christian Aid Scotland
Christian Aid is the official relief and development agency of 41 Churches in Britain and Ireland. Christian Aid's mandate is to challenge and enable us to fulfil our responsibilities to the poor of the world. Half a million volunteers and collectors make this possible, with money given by millions of supporters. The Church of Scotland marks its commitment as a Church to this part of its mission through an annual grant from the Mission and Renewal Fund, transmitted through the World Mission Council which keeps in close touch with Christian Aid and its work.

Up-to-date information about projects and current emergency relief work can be obtained from:
- The National Secretary: Mr Gavin McLellan, Christian Aid Scotland, Pentagon Centre, 36 Washington Street, Glasgow G3 8AZ (Tel: 0141-221 7475)
- The Area Co-ordinators:
  Edinburgh: Mrs Shirley Brown, 41 George IV Bridge, Edinburgh EH1 1EL (Tel: 0131-220 1254)
  Glasgow and West of Scotland: Ms Diane Green/Ms Eildon Dyer, Pentagon Centre, 36 Washington Street, Glasgow G3 8AZ (Tel: 0141-221 7475)
  Perth: Miss Marjorie Clark, Perth Christian Centre, 28 Glasgow Road, Perth PH2 0NX (Tel: 01738 643982)
- The Director: Dr Daleep Mukarji, Christian Aid Office, PO Box 100, London SE1 7RT (Tel: 020 7620 4444)

Accommodation in Israel
The Church of Scotland has two Christian Residential Centres in Israel which provide comfortable accommodation for pilgrims and visitors to the Holy Land. Further information is available from:
(a) St Andrew's Guest House, Jerusalem (PO Box 8619, Jerusalem)
    (Tel: 00 972 2 6732401; Fax: 00 972 2 6731711; E-mail: standjer@netvision.net.il)
(b) The Scots Hotel, St Andrew's, Galilee, Tiberias (PO Box 104, Tiberias)
    (Tel: 00 972 4 6710710; Fax: 00 972 4 6710711; E-mail: scottie@netvision.net.il)

A list of Overseas Appointments will be found in List K in Section 6.

A *World Mission Year Book* is available with more details of our partner churches and of people currently serving abroad, including those with ecumenical bodies and para-church bodies.

A list of Retired Missionaries will be found in List L in Section 6.

8. Assembly Arrangements Committee

Membership
Convener, Vice-Convener and ten members appointed by the General Assembly on the Report of the Nomination Committee; the Convener and Vice-Convener also to serve as Convener and Vice-Convener of the General Assembly's Business Committee.

The Clerks are non-voting members of the Assembly Arrangements Committee, and the Moderator and Moderator Designate are members of the Committee.

Convener: Rev. A. David K. Arnott MA BD
Vice-Convener: Rev. Janet S. Mathieson MA BD
Secretary: The Principal Clerk

Remit
The Committee's remit is:
- to make all necessary arrangements for the General Assembly;
- to advise the Moderator on his or her official duties if so required;
- to be responsible to the General Assembly for the care and maintenance of the Assembly Hall and the Moderator's flat;
- to be responsible to the General Assembly for all arrangements in connection with the letting of the General Assembly Hall;
- to conduct an annual review of progress made in discharging the remit and provide a written report to the Support and Services Council.

---

9. Central Services Committee

Membership
(13 members: nine appointed by the General Assembly, and four *ex officiis* and non-voting, namely the Principal Clerk, the Solicitor of the Church, the General Treasurer and the Human Resources Manager)

Convener: Rev. Anne R. Lithgow MA BD (2005)
Vice-Conveners: Mrs Pauline E.D. Weibye MA DPA MCIPD (2006)
                      Rev. Douglas S. Paterson MA BD (2006)

Staff
Administrative Secretary: Mrs Pauline Wilson BA
                             (E-mail: pwilson@cofscotland.org.uk)

Remit
- To be responsible for the proper maintenance and insurance of the Church Offices at 117–123 George Street and 21 Young Street, Edinburgh ('the Church Offices');
- To be responsible for matters relating to Health and Safety within the Church Offices;
- To be responsible for matters relating to Data Protection within the Church Offices and with respect to the General Assembly Councils based elsewhere;
- To be responsible for the allocation of accommodation within the Church Offices and the annual determination of rental charges to the Councils and other parties accommodated therein;
- To oversee the delivery of central services to departments within the Church Offices, to Councils of the General Assembly and, where appropriate, to the Statutory Corporations,

Presbyteries and Congregations, namely:
1. Those facilities directly managed by the Office Manager;
2. Information Technology (including the provision of support services to Presbytery Clerks);
3. Insurance;
4. Purchasing;
5. Human Resources;
6. Financial Services (as delivered by the General Treasurer's Department);
7. Legal Services (as delivered by the Law Department and subject to such oversight not infringing principles of 'client/solicitor' confidentiality);
8. Media Relations Services (as delivered by the Media Relations Unit);
9. Design Services (as delivered by the Design Services Unit);
10. Property Services.
- The Committee shall act as one of the employing agencies of the Church and shall, except in so far as specifically herein provided, assume and exercise the whole rights, functions and responsibilities of the former Personnel Committee;
- While the Committee shall *inter alia* have responsibility for determining the terms and conditions of the staff for whom it is the employing agency, any staff who are members of the Committee or who are appointed directly by the General Assembly shall not be present when matters solely relating to their own personal terms and conditions of employment/office are under consideration;
- To conduct an annual review of progress made in discharging this remit and provide a written report to the Support and Services Council.

10. Chaplains to HM Forces

Convener: Rev. James Gibson TD LTh LRAM
Vice-Convener: Rev. Neil N. Gardner MA BD
Secretary: Mr Douglas M. Hunter WS, HBJ Gateley Wareing LLP, Exchange Tower, 19 Canning Street, Edinburgh EH3 8EH

Recruitment
The Chaplains' Committee is entrusted with the task of recruitment of Chaplains for the Regular, Reserve and Auxiliary Forces. Vacancies occur periodically, and the Committee is happy to receive enquiries from all interested ministers.

Forces Registers
The Committee maintains a Register of all those who have been baptised and/or admitted to Communicant Membership by Service Chaplains.

At the present time, registers are being meticulously prepared and maintained. Parish Ministers are asked to take advantage of the facilities by applying for Certificates from the Secretary of the Committee.

Full information may be obtained from the Honorary Secretary, Mr Douglas M. Hunter, HBJ Gateley Wareing LLP, Exchange Tower, 19 Canning Street, Edinburgh EH3 8EH (Tel: 0131-228 2400).

A list of Chaplains will be found in List B in Section 6.

11. Church of Scotland Guild

National Office-bearers and Executive Staff

Convener:	Miss Esme F. Duncan MA Dip REd
Vice-Convener:	Mrs Elizabeth Dunn MBE
General Secretary:	Mrs Alison M. Twaddle MA
	(E-mail: atwaddle@cofscotland.org.uk)
Information Officer:	Mrs Fiona J. Punton MCIPR
	(E-mail: fpunton@cofscotland.org.uk)

The Church of Scotland Guild is a movement within the Church of Scotland whose aim is '**to invite and encourage both women and men to commit their lives to Jesus Christ and to enable them to express their faith in worship, prayer and action**'. Membership of the Guild is open to all who subscribe to that aim.

Groups at congregational level are free to organise themselves under the authority of the Kirk Session, as best suits their own local needs and circumstances. Large groups with frequent meetings and activities continue to operate with a committee or leadership team, while other, smaller groups simply share whatever tasks need to be done among the membership as a whole. Similarly, at Presbyterial Council level, frequency and style of meetings vary according to local needs, as do leadership patterns. Each Council may nominate one person to serve at national level, where five committees take forward the work of the Guild in accordance with the stated Aim.

These committees are:

- National Executive
- Finance and General Purposes
- Projects and Topics
- Programmes and Resources
- Marketing and Publicity

There has always been a close relationship between the Guild and other Departments of the Church, and members welcome the opportunity to contribute to the Church's wider mission through the Project Partnership Scheme and other joint ventures. The Guild is represented on both the Church and Society Council and the Mission and Discipleship Council.

The project scheme affords groups at congregational level the opportunity to select a project, or projects, from a range of up to six, selected from proposals submitted by a wide range of Church Departments and other Christian bodies. A project partner in each group seeks ways of promoting the project locally, increasing awareness of the issues raised by it, and encouraging support of a financial and practical nature. Support is available from the Project Co-ordinator at Council level and the Information Officer based at the Guild Office.

The Guild is very aware of the importance of good communication in any large organisation, and regularly sends mailings to its groups to pass on information and resources to the members. In addition, the Newsletter, sent to members three times per session, is a useful communication tool, as is the website www.cos-guild.org.uk. These are a means of sharing experiences and of communicating something of the wider interest and influence of the Guild, which participates in other national bodies such as the Network of Ecumenical Women in Scotland and the Scottish Women's Convention.

Each year, the Guild follows a Theme and produces a resources pack covering worship and study material. There is also a related Discussion Topic with supporting material and background information. The theme, topic and projects all relate to a common three-year strategy which, for 2006–9, is '**Let's Live: Body, Mind and Soul**'. Each of the six current projects reflects some aspect of fullness of life. The 2008–9 theme is **'He Restores my Soul'**, and Guilds are invited to explore the spiritual dimension of humanity and their personal faith journey. The related discussion topic is **'Let's Talk about the Search for Spirituality'**, which considers the current attraction of alternative spiritualities and the challenge they present to the Church.

Further information is available from the Guild Office (Tel: 0131-225 5722 ext. 317, or 0131-240 2217) or from the website (www.cos-guild.org.uk).

12. Church of Scotland Investors Trust

Membership
(Trustees are appointed by the General Assembly, on the nomination of the Investors Trust)
Chairman: Mrs I.J. Hunter MA
Vice-Chairman: Mr D.M. Simpson BA FFA
Treasurer: Mr I.W. Grimmond BAcc CA
Secretary: Mr F.E. Marsh MCIBS

Remit
The Church of Scotland Investors Trust was established by the Church of Scotland (Properties and Investments) Order Confirmation Act 1994 – Scottish Charity Number SC022884 – and offers investment services to the Church of Scotland and to bodies and trusts within or connected with the Church. It offers simple and economical facilities for investment in its three Funds, and investors receive the benefits of professional management, continuous portfolio supervision, spread of investment risk and economies of scale.

The three Funds are:

1. Deposit Fund
The Deposit Fund is intended for short-term investment and seeks to provide a competitive rate of interest while preserving nominal capital value. It is invested mainly in short-term loans to banks and building societies. Interest is calculated quarterly in arrears and paid gross on 15 May and 15 November. Withdrawals are on demand. The Fund is managed by Thomas Miller Investments Limited, Edinburgh and London.

2. Growth Fund
The Growth Fund is a unitised fund, largely equity-based, intended to provide a growing annual income sufficient to meet the Trustees' target distributions and to provide an increase in the value of capital long term. Units can be purchased or sold within the monthly dealing periods, and income is distributed gross on 15 May and 15 November. The Fund is managed by Newton Investment Management Limited, London.

3. Income Fund
The Income Fund is a unitised fund, invested predominantly in fixed-interest securities, intended to provide consistent high income and to protect the long-term value of capital. Units can be purchased or sold within the monthly dealing periods, and income is distributed gross on 15 March and 15 September. The Fund is managed by Baillie Gifford & Co., Edinburgh.

Further information and application forms for investment are available on the Church of Scotland website or by writing to the Secretary, The Church of Scotland Investors Trust, 121 George Street, Edinburgh EH2 4YN (E-mail: fmarsh@cofscotland.org.uk).

13. The Church of Scotland Pension Trustees

Chairman: Mr D.D. Fotheringham FFA
Vice-Chairman: Mr W.J. McCafferty ACII APFS TEP
Secretary: Mrs S. Dennison BA

Staff
Pensions Manager: Mrs S. Dennison BA
Assistant Pensions Administrators: Mrs M. Marshall
                                     Mr M. Hannam

Remit
The body acts as Trustees for the Church of Scotland's three Pension Schemes:
1.   The Church of Scotland Pension Scheme for Ministers and Overseas Missionaries
2.   The Church of Scotland Pension Scheme for Staff
3.   The Church of Scotland Pension Scheme for the Board of National Mission.
The Trustees have wide-ranging duties and powers detailed in the Trust Law, Pension Acts and other regulations, but in short the Trustees are responsible for the administration of the Pension Schemes and for the investment of the Scheme Funds. Six Trustees are appointed by the General Assembly, and members nominate up to three Trustees for each Scheme.
    The investment of the Funds is delegated to external Investment Managers under the guidelines and investment principles set by the Trustees: Baillie Gifford & Co., Newton Investment Management Ltd and Tilney Fund Management.
    The benefits provided by the three Pension Schemes differ in detail, but all provide a pension to the Scheme member and dependants on death of the member, and a lump-sum death benefit on death in service. Scheme members also have the option to improve their benefits by paying additional voluntary contributions (AVCs) to arrangements set up by the Trustees with leading Insurance Companies.
    Further information on any of the Church of Scotland Pension Schemes or on individual benefits can be obtained from the Pensions Manager, Church of Scotland Offices, 121 George Street, Edinburgh EH2 4YN (Tel: 0131-225 5722 ext. 206; Fax: 0131-240 2220; E-mail: pensions@cofscotland.org.uk).

14. Church of Scotland Trust

Membership
(Members are appointed by the General Assembly, on the nomination of the Trust)
Chairman: Mr Robert Brodie CB WS
Vice-Chairman: Mr Christopher N. Mackay WS

Treasurer:	Mr Iain W. Grimmond BAcc CA
Secretary and Clerk:	Mrs Jennifer M. Hamilton BA

Remit

The Church of Scotland Trust was established by Act of Parliament in 1932 and has Scottish Charity Number SC020269. The Trust's function since 1 January 1995 has been to hold properties outwith Scotland and to act as Trustee in a number of third-party trusts.

Further information can be obtained from the Secretary and Clerk of the Church of Scotland Trust, 121 George Street, Edinburgh EH2 4YN (Tel: 0131-240 2222; E-mail: jhamilton@ cofscotland.org.uk).

---

15. Committee on Church Art and Architecture

See entry in full under **The Mission and Discipleship Council** (number 4).

---

16. Committee Planning the Church Without Walls Celebration
(now renamed as Church Without Walls Group)

This group now sits within the Mission and Discipleship Council. Rev. Albert O. Bogle serves as Convener.

---

17. Design Services

Staff

Head of Design Services:	Peter Forrest
Senior Graphic Designer:	Claire Bewsey

The Design Services Section, which produces the Church of Scotland's *Life and Work* magazine, offers a comprehensive design service for all promotional materials, including magazines, leaflets, flyers, displays and exhibitions to both Councils and organisations of the wider Church. For further information, contact Peter Forrest (Tel: 0131-240 2224 or E-mail: pforrest@churchofscotland.co.uk).

18. Ecumenical Relations Committee

Remit
- to advise the General Assembly on matters of policy affecting ecumenical relations;
- to ensure that the members on the Committee serving on the other Councils are appropriately informed and resourced so as to be able to represent the ecumenical viewpoint on the Council on which they serve;
- to ensure appropriate support for the Ecumenical Officer's representative function in the event of his or her absence, whether through illness, holidays or other commitments;
- to nominate people from across the work of the Church of Scotland to represent the Church in Assemblies and Synods of other churches, ecumenical consultations and delegations to ecumenical assemblies and so on;
- to call for and receive reports from representatives of the Church of Scotland attending Assemblies and Synods of other churches and those ecumenical conferences and gatherings which are held from time to time;
- to ensure that appropriate parts of such reports are made available to relevant Councils;
- to ensure that information is channelled from and to ecumenical bodies of which the Church of Scotland is a member;
- to ensure that information is channelled from and to other churches in Scotland and beyond;
- to ensure the continued development of ecumenical relations by means of the Web and other publications;
- to ensure personal support for the Ecumenical Officer;
- to approve guidelines for the setting up and oversight of Local Ecumenical Partnerships;
- to conduct an annual review of progress made in discharging this remit and provide a written report to the Support and Services Council.

Membership
a)   Five members appointed by the General Assembly, each to serve as a member of one of the five Councils of the Church (excluding the Support and Services Council, on which the Convener of the Committee will sit).
b)   A Convener who is not a member of any of the other Councils and who will act as a personal support for the Ecumenical Officer, and a Vice-Convener, appointed by the General Assembly.
c)   A representative of the United Free Church of Scotland appointed by that Church.
d)   A representative of the Roman Catholic Church in Scotland appointed by the Bishops' Conference and one representative from each of three churches drawn from among the member churches of ACTS and the Baptist Union of Scotland, each to serve for a period of four years.
e)   The Committee may co-opt, as a full voting member, one of the four Church of Scotland representatives on the Scottish Churches' Forum.
f)   The Committee shall co-opt Church of Scotland members elected to the central bodies of Churches Together in Britain and Ireland (CTBI), the Conference of European Churches (CEC), the World Council of Churches (WCC), the World Alliance of Reformed Churches (WARC) and the Community of Protestant Churches in Europe (CPCE, formerly the Leuenberg Fellowship of Churches).
g)   The General Secretary of ACTS shall be invited to attend as a corresponding member.
h)   For the avoidance of doubt, while, for reasons of corporate governance, only Church of Scotland members of the Committee shall be entitled to vote, before any vote is taken the views of members representing other churches shall be ascertained.

Convener:	Rev. William D. Brown BD CQSW (2005)
Vice-Convener:	Rev. Lindsay Schluter ThE CertMin (2008)
Secretary and Ecumenical	
Officer:	Very Rev. Sheilagh M. Kesting BA BD DD
Administrative Officer:	Miss Rosalind Milne

INTER-CHURCH ORGANISATIONS

World Council of Churches

The Church of Scotland is a founder member of the World Council of Churches, formed in 1948. As its basis declares, it is 'a fellowship of Churches which confess the Lord Jesus Christ as God and Saviour according to the Scriptures, and therefore seek to fulfil their common calling to the glory of the one God, Father, Son and Holy Spirit'. Its member Churches, which number over 300, are drawn from all continents and include all the major traditions – Eastern and Oriental Orthodox, Reformed, Lutheran, Anglican, Baptist, Disciples, Methodist, Moravian, Friends, Pentecostalist and others. Although the Roman Catholic Church is not a member, there is very close co-operation with the departments in the Vatican.

The World Council holds its Assemblies every seven years. The last, held in Porto Alegre, Brazil, in February 2006, had the theme 'God, in your grace, transform the world'. At that Assembly, Mr Graham McGeoch was elected to the new Executive and to the Central Committee of the Council.

The World Council is taking forward the discussion among the churches on global economic justice. In June 2005, it hosted the Conference on World Mission and Evangelism in Athens. Currently, two documents are with the churches for study: 'The nature and mission of the church' and 'Called to be the One Church'.

The General Secretary is Rev. Dr Samuel Kobia, 150 route de Ferney, 1211 Geneva 2, Switzerland (Tel: 00 41 22 791 61 11; Fax: 00 41 22 791 03 61; E-mail: nan@wcc-coe.org; Website: www.wcc.oikumene.org).

World Alliance of Reformed Churches

The Church of Scotland is a founder member of the World Alliance of Reformed Churches, which began in 1875 as 'The Alliance of the Reformed Churches Throughout the World Holding the Presbyterian System' and which now includes also Churches of the Congregational tradition. Today it is composed of more than 200 Churches in nearly 100 countries, with an increasing number in Asia. It brings together, for mutual help and common action, large Churches which enjoy majority status and small minority Churches. It engages in theological dialogue with other Christian traditions – Orthodox, Roman Catholic, Lutheran, Methodist, Baptist and so on. It is organised in three main departments – Co-operation with Witness, Theology and Partnership. The twenty-fourth General Council was held in Accra, Ghana, from 30 July to 12 August 2004. The theme was 'That all may have life in fullness'. Rev. Alexander Horsburgh was elected to the Executive Committee. In 2010, it merges with the Reformed Ecumenical Council.

The General Secretary is Rev. Dr Setri Nyomi, 150 route de Ferney, 1211 Geneva 2, Switzerland (Tel: 00 41 22 791 62 38; Fax: 00 41 22 791 65 05; E-mail: sn@warc.ch; Website: www.warc.ch).

Conference of European Churches

The Church of Scotland is a founder member of the Conference of European Churches, formed in 1959 and until recently the only body which involved in common membership representatives of every European country (except Albania) from the Atlantic to the Urals. More than 100 Churches, Orthodox and Protestant, are members. Although the Roman Catholic Church is not a member, there is very close co-operation with the Council of European Catholic Bishops'

Conferences. With the removal of the long-standing political barriers in Europe, the Conference has now opportunities and responsibilities to assist the Church throughout the continent to offer united witness and service.

CEC will hold its thirteenth Assembly in Lyons, France from 15–21 July 2009 with the theme 'Called to One Hope in Christ'.

Its General Secretary is the Venerable Colin Williams, 150 route de Ferney, 1211 Geneva 2, Switzerland (Tel: 00 41 22 791 61 11; Fax: 00 41 22 791 03 61; E-mail: cec@cec-kek.org; Website: www.cec-kek.org).

Community of Protestant Churches in Europe
The Church of Scotland is a founder member of the Community of Protestant Churches in Europe (CPCE), which was formerly known as the Leuenberg Church Fellowship. The Fellowship came into being in 1973 on the basis of the Leuenberg Agreement between the Reformation churches in Europe; the name was changed to the CPCE in 2003. The Leuenberg Agreement stipulates that a common understanding of the Gospel based on the doctrine of Justification by Faith, and interpreted with reference to the proclamation of the Word of God, Baptism and the Lord's Supper, is sufficient to overcome the Lutheran–Reformed church division. The text entitled *The Church of Jesus Christ (1994)* may be regarded as the most significant document produced by the CPCE since its inception.

Over 100 Protestant churches in Europe, and a number of South American churches with European origin, have been signatories to the Leuenberg Agreement, including Lutheran, Reformed, United and Methodist Churches, as well as pre-Reformation Waldensian, Hussite and Czech Brethren, and they grant each other pulpit and table fellowship. Most of the CPCE member churches are minority churches, and this imparts a particular character to their life and witness. A General Assembly is held every six years – the sixth General Assembly was held in Budapest in 2006 – and a thirteen-member Council carries on the work of the CPCE in the intervening period.

The Director of the Office of the CPCE is Bishop Professor Dr Michael Bunker, Severin-Schreiber-Gasse 3, A-1180 Vienna (Tel: 00 43 1 4791523 900; Fax: 00 43 1 4791523 580; E-mail: office@leuenberg.eu; Website: www.leuenberg.eu).

CEC: Church and Society Commission
The Church of Scotland was a founder member of the European Ecumenical Commission for Church and Society (EECCS). The Commission owed its origins to the Christian concern and vision of a group of ministers and European civil servants about the future of Europe. It was established in 1973 by Churches recognising the importance of this venture. Membership included Churches and ecumenical bodies from the European Union. The process of integration with CEC was completed in 2000, and the name, Church and Society Commission (CSC), established. In Brussels, CSC monitors Community activity, maintains contact with MEPs and promotes dialogue between the Churches and the institutions. It plays an educational role and encourages the Churches' social and ethical responsibility in European affairs. It has a General Secretary, a study secretary and an executive secretary in Brussels and a small office in Strasbourg.

The Director is Rev. Rudiger Noll, Ecumenical Centre, 174 rue Joseph II, B-1000 Brussels, Belgium (Tel: 00 32 2 230 17 32; Fax: 00 32 2 231 14 13; E-mail: mo@cec-kek.be).

Churches Together in Britain and Ireland (CTBI)
In September 1990, Churches throughout Britain and Ireland solemnly committed themselves to one another, promising to one another to do everything possible together. To provide frameworks for this commitment to joint action, the Churches established CTBI for the United Kingdom and Ireland, and, for Scotland, ACTS, with sister organisations for Wales and for England.

In 2006, CTBI ceased being a separate ecumenical instrument and became an agency of the four national ecumenical bodies. It is governed by Trustees appointed by the national instruments, is managed by the General Secretaries and has a Forum of Senior Representatives which will incorporate its AGM. It retains two Commissions on Racial Justice and Interfaith Relations. It has three core portfolios – study, church and society, and interfaith – together with a communication officer.

The General Secretary of CTBI is Rev. Bob Fyffe, Third Floor, Bastille Court, 2 Paris Garden, London SE1 8ND (Tel: 020 7654 7254; Fax: 020 7654 7222). The General Secretariat can be contacted by telephoning 020 7654 7211 (E-mail: gensec@ctbi.org.uk; Website: www.ctbi.org.uk).

Action of Churches Together in Scotland (ACTS)
ACTS was restructured at the beginning of 2003. The new structure comprises the Scottish Churches' Forum (replacing the Central Council) composed of Church representatives from trustee member Churches. There are four Networks: Church Life, Faith Studies, Mission, and Church and Society. Contributing to the life of the Networks will be associated ecumenical groups. Such groups are expressions of the Churches' commitment to work together and to bring together key people in a defined field of interest or expertise. ACTS is an expression of the commitment of the Churches to one another.

ACTS is staffed by a General Secretary, an Assistant General Secretary and two Network Officers. Their offices are based in Alloa.

These structures facilitate regular consultation and intensive co-operation among those who frame the policies and deploy the resources of the Churches in Scotland and throughout Britain and Ireland. At the same time, they afford greater opportunity for a wide range of members of different Churches to meet in common prayer and study.

The General Secretary is Brother Stephen Smyth fms, 7 Forrester Lodge, Inglewood House, Alloa FK10 2HU (Tel: 01259 216980; Fax: 01259 215964; E-mail: ecumenical@acts-scotland.org; Website: www.acts-scotland.org).

Scottish Churches House
Scottish Churches House is a resource of the churches together in Scotland. It provides space for meetings, conferences and retreats, and offers its own programme of events throughout the year. Set in the attractive town of Dunblane, overlooking the Cathedral, it is a place of refreshment and reflection. The Warden is Alastair Hulbert. For information and bookings, contact the Bookings Secretary, Scottish Churches House, Dunblane FK15 0AJ (Tel: 01786 823588; Fax: 01786 825844; E-mail: reservations@scottishchurcheshouse.org; Website: www.scottishchurcheshouse. org).

19. Education and Nurture Task Group

See entry in full under **The Mission and Discipleship Council** (number 4).

20. Facilities Management Department

Staff
Facilities Manager: Carole Tait

The responsibilities of the Facilities Manager's Department include:
- management of a maintenance budget for the upkeep of the Church Offices at 121 George Street, Edinburgh;
- responsibility for all aspects of health and safety for staff, visitors and contractors working in the building;
- managing a team of staff providing the Offices with security, reception, mail room, print room, switchboard, day-to-day maintenance services and Committee room bookings;
- overseeing all sub-contracted services to include catering, cleaning, boiler-room maintenance, intruder alarm, fire alarms, lifts and water management;
- maintaining building records in accordance with the requirements of statutory legislation;
- overseeing all alterations to the building and ensuring, where applicable, that they meet DDR, Planning and Building Control regulations.

Design Services
Our designers offer a graphic-design service for full-colour promotional literature, display materials and exhibitions to both Councils and organisations of the wider Church. For further information, contact Peter Forrest (Tel: 0131-240 2224; E-mail: pforrest@churchofscotland.co.uk).

---

21. General Treasurer's Department

Staff

General Treasurer:		Mr Iain W. Grimmond BAcc CA
Deputy Treasurer:		Mrs Anne F. Macintosh BA CA
Assistant Treasurers:	Congregational Support	Mr Archie McDowall BA CA
	World Mission and Pensions	Post vacant
	General Trustees	Mr Robert A. Allan CIMA CIPFA
	Ministries	Miss Catherine E. Robertson BAcc CA
	Mission and Discipleship	Mrs Pauline E. Willder MA PgDipIS
Accountants:	Congregational Contributions	Mr Derek W.C. Cant
	Payroll and VAT	Mr Ross W. Donaldson
	Ministries	Mrs Kay C. Hastie BSc CA

Responsibilities of the General Treasurer's Department include:
- providing support, training and advice on financial and accounting matters to congregational treasurers;
- calculating and issuing to congregations their annual requirement for the Ministries and Mission Contribution, and processing payments;
- providing management and financial accounting support for the Councils, Committees and Statutory Corporations;
- providing banking arrangements and operating a central banking system for the Councils, Committees and Statutory Corporations;

- receiving and discharging legacies and bequests on behalf of the Councils, Committees and Statutory Corporations;
- making Gift Aid tax recoveries on behalf of the Councils, Committees and Statutory Corporations;
- making VAT returns and tax recoveries on behalf of the Councils, Committees and Statutory Corporations;
- payroll processing for the Ministries Council, the Support and Services Council and the Pension Schemes.

22. General Trustees

Membership
(New Trustees are appointed, as required, by the General Assembly, on the recommendation of the General Trustees)

Chairman:	Mr W. Findlay Turner CA (2007)
Vice-Chairman:	Rev. James A.P. Jack BSc BArch BD DMin RIBA ARIAS (2007)
Secretary and Clerk:	Mr David D. Robertson LLB NP
Depute Secretary and Clerk:	Mr T.R.W. Parker LLB

Committees:
Fabric Committee
Convener: Rev. James A.P. Jack BSc BArch BD DMin RIBA ARIAS
                                   (2004)

Chairman's Committee
Convener: Mr W. Findlay Turner CA (2007)

Glebes Committee
Convener: Rev. William Paterson BD (2003)

Finance Committee
Convener: Mr W. Findlay Turner CA (2004)

Audit Committee
Convener: Dr J. Kenneth Macaldowie LLD CA (2005)

Law Committee
Convener: Mr C. Noel Glen BL NP (2004)

Staff

Secretary and Clerk:	Mr. David D. Robertson LLB NP
Depute Secretary and Clerk:	Mr T.R.W. Parker LLB
Assistants:	Mr Keith J. Fairweather LLB (Glebes)
	Mr Keith S. Mason LLB NP (Ecclesiastical Buildings)
Treasurer:	Mr Iain W. Grimmond BAcc CA

| Deputy Treasurer: | Mrs Anne F. Macintosh BA CA |
| Assistant Treasurer: | Mr Robert A. Allan ACMA CPFA |

Remit

The General Trustees are a Property Corporation created and incorporated under the Church of Scotland (General Trustees) Order Confirmation Act 1921. They have Scottish Charity Number SC014574. Their duties, powers and responsibilities were greatly extended by the Church of Scotland (Property & Endowments) Acts and Orders 1925 to 1995, and they are also charged with the administration of the Central Fabric Fund (see below) and the Consolidated Fabric Fund and the Consolidated Stipend Fund in which monies held centrally for the benefit of individual congregations are lodged.

The scope of the work of the Trustees is broad, covering all facets of property administration, but particular reference is made to the following matters:

1.   **ECCLESIASTICAL BUILDINGS.** The Trustees' Fabric Committee considers proposals for work at buildings, regardless of how they are vested, and plans of new buildings. Details of all such projects should be submitted to the Committee before work is commenced. The Committee also deals with applications for the release of fabric monies held by the General Trustees for individual congregations, and considers applications for assistance from the Central Fabric Fund from which grants and/or loans may be given to assist congregations faced with expenditure on fabric. Application forms relating to consents for work and possible financial assistance from the Central Fabric Fund are available from the Secretary of the Trustees and require to be submitted through Presbytery with its approval. The Committee normally meets on the first or second Tuesday of each month, apart from July, when it meets on the second last Tuesday, and August, when there is no meeting.

2.   **SALE, PURCHASE AND LETTING OF PROPERTIES.** All sales or lets of properties vested in the General Trustees fall to be carried out by them in consultation with the Financial Board of the congregation concerned, and no steps should be taken towards any sale or let without prior consultation with the Secretary of the Trustees. Where property to be purchased is to be vested in the General Trustees, it is essential that contact be made at the earliest possible stage with the Solicitor to the Trustees, who is responsible for the lodging of offers for such properties and all subsequent legal procedure.

3.   **GLEBES.** The Trustees are responsible for the administration of Glebes vested in their ownership. All lets fall to be granted by them in consultation with the minister concerned. It should be noted that neither ministers nor Kirk Sessions may grant lets of Glebe land vested in the General Trustees. As part of their Glebe administration, the Trustees review regularly all Glebe rents.

4.   **INSURANCE.** Properties vested in the General Trustees must be insured with the Church of Scotland Insurance Co. Ltd, a company wholly owned by the Church of Scotland whose profits are applied for Church purposes. Insurance enquiries should be sent directly to the Company at 67 George Street, Edinburgh EH2 2JG (Tel: 0131-220 4119; Fax: 0131-220 4120; E-mail: enquiries@cosic.co.uk).

23. The Church of Scotland Housing and Loan Fund for Retired Ministers and Widows and Widowers of Ministers

Membership
The Trustees shall be a maximum of 11 in number, being:
1. four appointed by the General Assembly on the nomination of the Trustees, who, having served a term of three years, shall be eligible for reappointment;
2. three ministers and one member appointed by the Ministries Council;
3. three appointed by the Baird Trust.

Chairman: Mr J.G. Grahame Lees MA LLB NP
Deputy Chairman: Rev. Ian Taylor BD ThM
Secretary: Miss Lin J. Macmillan MA

Staff
Property Manager: Miss Hilary J. Hardy
Property Assistant: Mr John Lunn

Remit
The Fund, as established by the General Assembly, facilitates the provision of housing accommodation for retired ministers and widows, widowers and separated or divorced spouses of Church of Scotland ministers. When provided, help may take the form of either a house to rent or a house-purchase loan.

The Trustees may grant tenancy of one of their existing houses or they may agree to purchase for rental occupation an appropriate house of an applicant's choosing. Leases are normally on very advantageous terms as regards rental levels. Alternatively, the Trustees may grant a housing loan of up to 70 per cent of a house-purchase price but with an upper limit. Favourable rates of interest are charged.

The Trustees are also prepared to consider assisting those who have managed to house themselves but are seeking to move to more suitable accommodation. Those with a mortgaged home on retirement may be granted a loan to enable them to repay such a mortgage and thereafter to enjoy the favourable rates of interest charged by the Fund.

Ministers making application within five years of retirement, upon their application being approved, will be given a fairly firm commitment that, in due course, either a house will be made available for renting or a house-purchase loan will be offered. Only within nine months of a minister's intended retiral date will the Trustees initiate steps to find a suitable house; only within one year of that date will a loan be advanced. Applications submitted about ten years prior to retirement have the benefit of initial review and, if approved, a place on the preliminary applications list for appropriate decision in due time.

Donations and legacies over the years have been significant in building up this Fund, and the backbone has been provided by congregational contributions.

The Board of Trustees is a completely independent body answerable to the General Assembly, and enquiries and applications are dealt with in the strictest confidence.

Further information can be obtained from the Secretary, Miss Lin J. Macmillan MA, at the Church of Scotland Offices, 121 George Street, Edinburgh EH2 4YN (Tel: 0131-225 5722 ext. 310; Fax: 0131-240 2264; E-mail: lmacmillan@cofscotland.org.uk; Website: www.churchofscotland.org.uk).

24. Human Resources Department

Staff

Head of Human Resources and Information Technology:	Mr Mike O'Donnell Chartered FCIPD
Human Resources Manager:	Mrs Angela Ocak Chartered MCIPD
Senior Human Resources Adviser (Learning and Development):	Mrs Kelly Smith BA
Human Resources Adviser:	Sarah-Jayne McVeigh BA GraCIPD
Human Resources Assistant/ Personal Assistant:	Melanie Sherwood

Remit

The Human Resources Department has responsibility for Recruitment and Selection, Learning and Development, and producing and updating HR Policies and Procedures to ensure that the Central Services Committee, the Ministries Council and the World Mission Council, as employing agencies, are in line with current employment-law legislation. The Department produces contracts of employment and advises on any changes to an individual employee's terms and conditions of employment. It also provides professional Human Resources advice to the organisation on Employee Relations matters, Performance Management and Diversity and Equality.

Our main aim is to work closely with Councils within the organisation to influence strategy so that each Council is making best use of its people and its people opportunities. We take a consultancy role that facilitates and supports each Council's own initiatives and help each other share and work together in consultation with Amicus.

---

25. Information Technology Department

Staff

Information Technology Manager:	Vacant
Depute Information Technology Manager:	Veronica Hay

The Department provides computer facilities to Councils and Departments within 121 George Street and to Presbytery Clerks and other groups within the Councils. It is also responsible for the telephone service within 121 George Street and the provision of assistance and advice on this to other groups.

The facilities provided include:
- the provision and maintenance of data and voice networks
- the purchase and installation of hardware and software
- support for problems and guidance on the use of software
- development of in-house software
- maintenance of data within some central systems.

26. Law Department

Staff

Solicitor of the Church and of the General Trustees:	Mrs Janette S. Wilson LLB NP
Depute Solicitor:	Miss Mary E. Macleod LLB NP
Assistant Solicitors:	Mr Ian K. Johnstone MA LLB
	Mrs Jennifer M. Hamilton BA NP
	Mrs Elspeth Annan LLB NP
	Miss Susan Killean LLB NP
	Miss Mairead MacBeath LLB NP
	Mrs Anne Steele LLB NP

The Law Department of the Church was created in 1937/38. The Department acts in legal matters for the Church and all of its Courts, Councils, Committees, the Church of Scotland General Trustees, the Church of Scotland Trust and the Church of Scotland Investors Trust. It also acts for individual congregations and is available to give advice on any legal matter arising.

The Department is under the charge of the Solicitor of the Church, a post created at the same time as the formation of the Department and a post which is now customarily held along with the traditional posts of Law Agent of the General Assembly and the Custodier of former United Free Church titles (E-mail: lawdept@cofscotland.org.uk).

---

27. Legal Questions Committee

Membership

Convener, Vice-Convener and ten members appointed by the General Assembly on the Report of the Nomination Committee.

Convener:	Miss Carole Hope LLB WS
Vice-Convener:	Rev. Alan J. Hamilton LLB BD
Secretary:	The Depute Clerk

The Convener and Vice-Convener of the Assembly Arrangements Committee are also members of the Legal Questions Committee. The Assembly Clerks, Procurator and Solicitor of the Church are non-voting members of the Legal Questions Committee.

Remit

- to advise the General Assembly on questions of Church Law and of Constitutional Law affecting the relationship between Church and State;
- to advise and assist Agencies of the General Assembly in the preparation of proposed legislation and on questions of interpretation, including interpretation of and proposed changes to remits;
- to compile the statistics of the Church, except Youth and Finance; and to supervise on behalf of the General Assembly all arrangements for care of Church Records and for Presbytery visits;
- to conduct an annual review of progress made in discharging the remit and provide a written report to the Support and Services Council.

28. Media Relations and Communications Unit

Staff

Head of Media Relations and Communication:	Pat Holdgate
Senior Media Relations Officer:	Grant McLennan
Media Relations Officer:	Gordon Bell
Communications Adviser:	Jennie Rutte
Website Editor:	Shirley James

The Unit is the first point of contact between the Church and journalists from national and international media. The Unit issues regular press releases on matters of interest and maintains a large network of media contacts. Unit staffs provide advice and information on media matters to anyone within the Church and arrange media training for key personnel. Media Relations staff can be contacted on direct line 0131-240 2243. After 5pm, this number can be used to obtain details of out-of-hours arrangements for emergency media work.

The maintenance and development of the Church's communications strategy, and the promotion of that strategy within the central administration, presbyteries and congregations, are undertaken by the Communications Adviser. In conjunction with other Departments, the Communications Adviser also oversees the promotion of the Church at appropriate exhibitions/conferences.

Together with the Information Technology Department, the Unit has responsibility for the Church's website (www.churchofscotland.org.uk). The Website Editor also provides advice on Web-related matters to anyone within the Church.

---

29. Mission and Evangelism Task Group

See entry in full under **The Mission and Discipleship Council** (number 4).

---

30. Nomination Committee

Membership
(44 members)

Convener:	Rev. Colin A.M. Sinclair BA BD (2008)
Vice-Convener:	Rev. Ian W. Black MA BD (2008)
Secretary:	The Principal Clerk

Remit
To bring before the General Assembly names of persons to serve on the Boards and Standing Committees of the General Assembly.

31. Panel on Review and Reform

Membership
(10 members appointed by the General Assembly)
Convener: Rev. David S. Cameron BD (2006)
Vice-Convener: Rev. Marina D. Brown MA BD MTh (2007)
(The Ecumenical Officer attends but without the right to vote or make a motion.)

Staff
Administrative Secretary: Mrs Valerie A. Cox MA
                                     (Tel: 0131-225 5722 ext. 336;
                                     E-mail: vcox@cofscotland.org.uk

Remit
The remit of the Panel on Review and Reform, as determined by the General Assembly of 2004, is as follows:
• To listen to the voices of congregations, Presbyteries, Agencies and those beyond the Church of Scotland.
• To present a vision of what a Church in need of continual renewal might become and to offer paths by which congregations, Presbyteries and Agencies might travel towards that vision.
• To consider the changing needs, challenges and responsibilities of the Church.
• To make recommendations to the Council of Assembly, and, through the report of that Council, to report to the General Assembly.
• To have particular regard to the Gospel imperative of priority for the poor, needy and marginalised.

---

32. Parish Appraisal Committee

The Parish Appraisal Committee was discharged with effect from 31 May 2007. Planning and Deployment will remain an area of work for the Ministries Council. (See further under **The Ministries Council.**)

---

33. Parish Development Fund Committee

Membership
(11 members appointed by the General Assembly. In addition, the Committee has powers to co-opt up to six non-voting advisers with appropriate skills and knowledge.)
Convener: Rev. Dr Martin Fair (2006)
Vice-Convener: Ms Alexandra Bauer

Staff
Co-ordinator: Mr Graham Lumb

Administrator:	Ms Amy Norton
Development Workers:	Mrs Jessie Bruce
	Mrs Susan Smith
Contact details:	Tel: 0131-225 5722

Remit

The aim of the Parish Development Fund is to encourage local churches to work for the benefit of the whole community – and to take risks in living and sharing the Gospel in relevant ways.

The Committee considers applications which are in the spirit of the above aim and the following principles:

* making a positive difference in the lives of people in greatest need in the community
* encouraging partnership work
* helping local people develop their gifts
* encouraging imagination and creativity.

The Committee meets four times each year, with main grant applications considered in April and October. Applications should be submitted by the end of February or the end of August.

Further information on the types of projects supported by the Fund can be found in the Parish Development Fund section of the Church of Scotland website. Please contact the staff for informal discussion about grant-application enquiries and general advice on funding and project development.

---

34. Principal Clerk's Department

Staff

Principal Clerk:	Very Rev. Finlay A.J. Macdonald MA BD PhD DD
Depute Clerk:	Rev. Marjory A. MacLean LLB BD PhD
Personal Assistant to the	
Clerks of Assembly:	Mrs Linda Jamieson
Principal Administration Officer:	Mrs Alison Murray MA
(Assembly Arrangements and	
Moderatorial Support)	
Principal Administration Officer:	Mrs Pauline Wilson BA
(Council of Assembly, Central	
Services Committee and	
Nomination Committee)	

The Principal Clerk's Department has responsibility for the administration of the General Assembly and its Commissions, for supporting the Moderator in preparation for and during his or her year of office and for servicing the Council of Assembly, the Assembly Arrangements Committee, the Legal Questions Committee, the Committee to Nominate the Moderator, the Nomination Committee, the Committee on Overtures and Cases and the Committee on Classifying Returns to Overtures. The Clerks of Assembly are available for consultation on matters of Church law, practice and procedure.

Contact Details

Principal Clerk:	0131-240 2240
Depute Clerk:	0131-240 2232
Linda Jamieson:	0131-240 2240
Alison Murray:	0131-225 5722 (ext. 250)
Pauline Wilson:	0131-240 2229
Office fax number:	0131-240 2239
E-mail:	pcoffice@cofscotland.org.uk

35. Publishing Committee

See entry in full under **The Mission and Discipleship Council** (number 4).

36. Stewardship and Finance Committee

Remit

1. To teach, promote and encourage Christian Stewardship throughout the Church.
2. To provide programmes and training to assist congregations and their office-bearers in teaching, promoting and encouraging Christian Stewardship.
3. To be responsible with Presbyteries for allocating among congregations the expenditure contained in the Co-ordinated Budget approved by the Council of Assembly, and for seeking to ensure that congregations meet their obligations thereto, by transmitting regularly throughout the year to the General Treasurer of the Church contributions towards their allocations.
4. To report annually to the General Assembly on the attestation of Presbytery and Congregational Accounts, and provide advice or arrange training for Congregational Treasurers and others administering congregational finances.
5. To issue annually to each congregation a Schedule of Congregational Financial Statistics, to be completed and returned by a date determined by the Committee.
6. To set standards of financial management and accounting procedures and to provide financial and accounting services for all Councils and Committees of the General Assembly (except for the Social Care Council).
7. To maintain and update such statistical and financial information as is deemed necessary.
8. To approve and submit annually to the General Assembly the Report and Financial Statements of the Unincorporated Councils and Committees of the General Assembly. In order to enable the Committee to fulfil this part of its remit, the Social Care Council shall provide regular financial reports and such other information as may be required by the Committee.
9. To appoint Auditors for the Financial Statements of the Unincorporated Councils and Committees of the General Assembly.
10. To consider Reports received from the Auditors of the Financial Statements of the Unincorporated Councils and Committees of the General Assembly.
11. To ensure that all funds belonging to Councils and Committees of the General Assembly, which are not contained within the Financial Statements submitted to the General Assembly, are audited or independently examined annually.

12. To exercise custody over funds and to provide bank arrangements.
13. To operate a central banking system for all Councils (except for the Social Care Council), Committees and Statutory Corporations.
14. To consider taxation matters affecting Councils, Committees and Statutory Corporations and congregations of the Church.
15. To determine the types and rates of expenses that may be claimed by members serving Councils, Committees and Statutory Corporations.
16. To carry out such other duties as may be referred to the Committee from time to time by the General Assembly.
17. To conduct an annual review of progress made in discharging the remit and provide a written report for the Support and Services Council.

Membership
The Committee shall consist of a Convener, Vice-Convener and 16 members all appointed by the General Assembly. The General Treasurer and the Head of Stewardship shall be *ex officiis* members of the Committee and of all its Sub-Committees but shall not have voting rights.

Convener: Mrs Vivienne A. Dickson CA (2005)
Vice-Convener: Rev. Richard Baxter MA BD (2007)
General Treasurer: Mr Iain W. Grimmond BAcc CA
Head of Stewardship: Rev. Gordon D. Jamieson MA BD
Administrative Secretary: Mr Fred Marsh MCIBS

Promoting Christian Giving
Stewardship and Finance staff are responsible for promoting Christian giving through stewardship programmes, conferences for office-bearers or members, wider use of Gift Aid, and legacies. Contact the Church Offices to get in touch with the appropriate Stewardship Consultant or to obtain information about stewardship material produced by the Committee (Tel: 0131-225 5722 ext. 273; E-mail: stewardship@cofscotland.org.uk).

---

37. Worship and Doctrine Task Group

See entry in full under **The Mission and Discipleship Council** (number 4).

---

38. Safeguarding Office
Tel: 0131-240 2256; Fax: 0131-220 3113
E-mail: safeguarding@cofscotland.org.uk

(Reports through the Support and Services Council – see separate item, number 6)

Convener: Rev. John Christie (2005)
Vice-Convener: Anne Black (2005)

Staff

Head of Safeguarding | Fionna Miskelly
Assistant Head of Safeguarding: | Jennifer McCreanor
Training Officer: | Andrew Strachan

Remit

The Safeguarding Office, which developed from the Church's Child Protection Unit, plays a major part in the growing and ongoing work of child protection, in particular training and supporting all those who work with children in congregations. This service is shortly to be extended to include all vulnerable groups; the appropriate policies and procedures are currently being developed.

The Safeguarding Office exists to:

- continue the development of the Church of Scotland's Safeguarding Policies and Procedures;
- co-ordinate a national 'safe recruitment' system for all voluntary workers;
- recruit, train and support a team of voluntary trainers in Safeguarding matters across all the Presbyteries;
- facilitate, through the training network, training in Safeguarding matters for all voluntary workers and co-ordinators in congregations;
- develop resources relating to Safeguarding matters;
- provide support, advice and guidance to Presbyteries and congregations and liaise with other church denominations, para-church bodies and other voluntary organisations.

39. Scottish Churches Parliamentary Office
Tel: 0131-558 8137
E-mail: graham@actsparl.org

The Scottish Churches Parliamentary Officer is Rev. Graham K. Blount LLB BD PhD. The office is within the Scottish Storytelling Centre, 43–45 High Street, Edinburgh EH1 1SR.

The Church of Scotland and the Gaelic Language

Duilleagan Gàidhlig

Ro-ràdh

'S e seo a' cheud turas a tha duilleagan air leth againn ann an Gàidhlig anns an *Leabhar Bhliadhnail*, agus tha sinn fo fhiachan mòra don Fhear-dheasachaidh airson a bhith cho cuideachail agus cho deònach an ceum sònraichte seo a ghabhail. An deidh a bhith a' crìonadh fad ghrunn ghinealach, tha a' Ghàidhlig a-nis a' dèanamh adhartais. Tha e cudthromach gum biodh Eaglais na h-Alba a' toirt cùl-taic don leasachadh seo, agus gu dearbha tha i aig teis-meadhan a' ghluasaid seo. Ma bheir sinn sùil air eachdraidh, chì sinn nuair a bha a' Ghàidhlig a' fulang làmhachais-làidir anns na linntean a dh'fhalbh, gu robh an Eaglais glè shoirbheachail ann a bhith a' gabhail ceum-tòisich airson an cànan a dhìon.

Eachdraidh

Bha na thachair an dèidh Blàr Chùil Lodair 'na bhuille chruaidh don Ghàidhlig. Cha do chuidich Achd an Fhòghlaim ann an 1872 le cùisean, Achd nach tug fiù 's iomradh air a' Ghàidhlig. Mar thoradh air seo bha a' Ghàidhlig air a fuadach à sgoiltean na h-Alba. Ach bha a' Ghàidhlig air a cleachdadh anns an Eaglais agus bha sin na mheadhan air a cumail o bhith a' dol à sealladh mar chainnt làitheil.

Poileataics

Tha Pàrlamaid na h-Eòrpa a' toirt inbhe don Ghàidhlig mar aon de na mion-chànanan Eòrpach a tha i a' smaoineachadh a bu chòir a cuideachadh agus a h-altram. Beagan bhliadhnachan air ais chuir iad lagh an gnìomh a bha a' cur mar dhleasdanas air Pàrlamaid Bhreatainn àite a thoirt don Ghàidhlig. Ann an 2005, thug Pàrlamaid na h-Alba Achd Gàidhlig na h-Alba air adhart a' cur na Gàidhlig air stèidh mar chainnt nàiseanta, leis an aon spèis ris a' Bheurla.

Cultar

Tha An Comunn Gàidhealach agus buidhnean eile air obair ionmholta a dhèanamh bho chionn fada ann a bhith a' cur na Gàidhlig air adhart mar nì cudthromach nar cultar. Bho chionn ghoirid chuir An Comunn air bhonn co-chruinneachadh de riochdairean o na h-Eaglaisean airson dòighean a lorg air a bhith a' cleachdadh na Gàidhlig ann an adhradh follaiseach. Fad còrr is fichead bliadhna chaidh adhartas mòr a dhèanamh ann am fòghlam tro mheadhan na Gàidhlig, an toiseach tro chròileagain, bun-sgoiltean, agus a-nis ann an àrd-sgoiltean. Thàinig seo gu ìre nuair a stèidhicheadh Sabhal Mòr Ostaig ann am fòghlam àrd-ìre. Bidh an Sabhal Mòr mar phàirt chudthromach de dh'Oilthaigh ùr na Gàidhealtachd agus nan Eilean nuair a gheibh an Oilthaigh còraichean sgrìobhte. Tha Comann Albannach a' Bhìobaill glè dhealasach ann a bhith a' sìor thoirt taic don Ghàidhlig le bhith a' foillseachadh nan Sgriobtar anns a' chànan.

Eaglais na h-Alba

1.   Air feadh na dùthcha, tha adhradh air a chumail ann an Gàidhlig, air Ghàidhealtachd agus air Ghalldachd. (Mar eisimpleir, anns na bailtean mòra tha seirbheis Ghàidhlig air a cumail gach Sàbaid ann an Eaglais Ghàidhealach nam Manach Liatha ann an Dùn Eideann, agus ann an Eaglais Chaluim Chille agus Eaglais Sràid a' Ghàradair ann an Glaschu.) Tha còir gum biodh fios aig Clèireach na Clèire air eaglaisean far a bheil seirbheisean Gàidhlig air an cumail. Thug an t-Ard-sheanadh ann an 2008 misneachadh do Chlèirean coitheanalan freagarrach ainmeachadh far am bu chòir a' Ghàidhlig a bhith air a cleachdadh ann an adhradh nuair a bha iad a' cur phlànaichean-clèire air bhonn. A bharrachd air sin, tha goireasan ann a bheir cuideachadh don fheadhainn a tha airson Gàidhlig a chleachdadh ann an adhradh.

2.   Airson na ceud uaire, air a' bhliadhna seo chaidh Seirbheis Ghàidhlig an Ard-sheanaidh a chur air làraich-lìn. Chìthear seo air tasglann na h-Eaglais air www.churchofscotland. org.uk

3.   Cha mhòr bho stèidhicheadh *Life and Work* tha *Na Duilleagan Gàidhlig* air a bhith rim faotainn as-asgaidh do neach sam bith a tha gan iarraidh.

4.   Tha Eaglais na h-Alba, mar phàirt de dh'Iomairt Chonaltraidh na h-Eaglais, airson a bhith a' brosnadh cleachdadh na Gàidhlig. Tha duilleagan Gàidhlig air leth air an làraich-lìn.

5.   Bho chionn beagan bhliadhnachan tha an t-Ard-sheanadh air na nithean cudthromach seo a mholadh co-cheangailte ris a' Ghàidhlig.

  (i)   Tha an t-Ard-sheanadh a' cur mealadh-naidheachd air Pàrlamaid na h-Alba airson Achd a' Chànain Ghàidhlig (Alba) a stèidheachadh; tha e a' brosnachadh a' BhBC ach an toir iad cùl-taic do OFCOM a tha ag iarraidh craoladh na Gàidhlig a leudachadh; tha e duilich gu bheil chleachdadh na Gàidhlig a' dol an lughad anns an Eaglais, agus tha e a' toirt cuiridh do Chomhairlean na h-Eaglais, far a bheil sin freagarrach, rannsachadh a dhèanamh air dòighean a lorg a bheir don Ghàidhlig an t-àite sònraichte a chleachd a bhith aice ann am beatha spioradail na h-Alba.

(ii) Tha an t-Ard-sheanadh a' cur ìmpidh air Comhairle a' Mhisein agus na Deisciobalachd, ann an co-bhoinn ri Comhairle na Ministrealachd, rannsachadh a dhèanamh air inbhe na Gàidhlig ann an Eaglais na h-Alba ann an dùil ri aithisg a thoirt air beulaibh an Ard-sheanaidh ann an 2008 air mar a ghabhas leasachadh a dhèanamh air cleachdadh na Gàidhlig anns an Eaglais.

(iii) Tha an t-Ard-sheanadh a' gabhail beachd air àireamh nan sgìrean Gàidhlig, agus tha e a' cur ìmpidh Comhairle na Ministrealachd slatan-tomhais a thoirt chun an Ard-sheanaidh ann an 2008 airson gun tèid na sgìrean seo a chomharrachadh anns na bliadhnachan air thoiseach.

(iv) Tha an t-Ard-sheanadh a' cur ìmpidh air Comairle an Ard-sheanaidh cumail romhpa a bhith a' toirt cùl-taic don Ghàidhlig an taobh a-staigh na h-Eaglais, am measg rudan eile a bhith a' còmhradh ri buidhnean maoineachaidh freagarrach.

(v) Tha an t-Ard-sheanadh a' dèanamh toileachaidh ris an Aithisg air Leasachadh ann an Cleachdadh na Gàidhlig, agus tha e a' brosnachadh Comhairle a' Mhisein agus na Deisciobalachd na plànaichean a tha aca airson an ama air thoiseach a chur an gnìomh.

(vi) Tha an t-Ard-sheanadh a' dèanamh toileachaidh ris an naidheachd gu bheil Seanal Digiteach Gàidhlig ga chur air bhog, agus tha e a' cur ìmpidh air Comhaire na h-Eaglais agus na Coimhearsnachd, ann an co-bhoinn ri Comhairle an Ard-sheanaidh, a bhith a' còmhradh ri Comhairle nam Meadhanan Gàidhlig mun àite shònraichte a bu chòir a bhith aig prògraman spioradail anns na prògraman a bhios iad a' cur a-mach.

'S e àm air leth inntinneach a tha seo don Ghàidhlig, agus tha an Eaglais airson a bhith a' gabhail a h-àite anns an iomairt as leth ar cànain. 'S iad na duilleagan seo aon de na dòighean anns a bheil sinn a' dèanamh sin.

Introduction

This is the first year that the *Year Book* has featured dedicated pages in Gaelic, and appreciation is expressed to the Editor for his openness and willingness to bring about this historic development. After many generations of decline, Gaelic is once more moving forward. It is important that the Church of Scotland is seen to be encouraging this progress and indeed is part of it. History teaches that, in the past, when the Gaelic language has been under political oppression, the Church has stood successfully in the vanguard of the defence of the language.

History

The events of Culloden in 1746, as part of the Jacobite rebellion, dealt a cruel blow to the Gaelic language. This was compounded by the Education (Scotland) Act of 1872, which made no mention of the Gaelic language and, indeed, resulted in the outlawing of Gaelic in Scottish schools. The continued use of Gaelic in the Church proved to be the only formal antidote to the disappearance of Gaelic as a viable language.

Politics

The European Parliament recognises Gaelic as one of the minority European languages it sees as important to support and nurture. Some years ago, it passed appropriate legislation laying some responsibility on the United Kingdom Parliament. In 2005, the Scottish Parliament delivered the Gaelic (Scotland) Act, establishing Gaelic as a national language given the same respect as English.

Culture

Traditionally, An Comunn Gaidhealach has done an excellent job in promoting the cultural importance of Gaelic. It recently convened a gathering of representatives from Churches to research how they could help promote the use of Gaelic in public worship. For over twenty years now, there has been substantial growth in Gaelic-medium education, first of all through nurseries, then primary schools and now secondary schools. This has moved on to the establishing of Sabhal Mor Ostaig in the tertiary sector. The latter, all being well, will become a vital part of the new University of the Highlands and Islands when its charter is granted. The Scottish Bible Society is also eager to continue its support of Gaelic through the provision of Scriptures.

The Church of Scotland and its ongoing support for Gaelic

1. Across the nation, public worship continues to be conducted in Gaelic. The General Assembly of 2008 encouraged Presbyteries, as part of their planning, to identify appropriate congregations in which Gaelic must be used regularly in public worship. Furthermore, resources are available to encourage the use of Gaelic in worship in all congregations.
2. This year, for the first time, the annual General Assembly Gaelic Service was webcast as part of the wider General Assembly. This can be seen in the archives on www.churchofscotland.org.uk
3. Almost since its inception, *Na Duilleagan Gàidhlig*, as part of *Life and Work*, has been available free of charge to any who request it with their *Life and Work* subscription. This is still very much alive.
4. The Church of Scotland, as part of its Communication Strategy, is concerned to promote the use of Gaelic. There are dedicated Gaelic pages on the website.
5. Recent years have seen the General Assembly approve a number of important Deliverances relating to Gaelic. For example:
   (i) The General Assembly congratulate the Scottish Parliament on its passing of the Gaelic Language (Scotland) Bill, encourage the BBC to support OFCOM in its desire for the extension of Gaelic broadcasting, express regret at the substantial decrease in the use of Gaelic in the Church and invite Councils of the Church, where appropriate, to explore ways in which Gaelic can resume its distinctive place within the religious life of Scotland.
   (ii) The General Assembly instruct the Mission and Discipleship Council, in collaboration with the Ministries Council, to undertake an investigation into the present status of Gaelic in the Church of Scotland with a view to reporting to the 2008 General Assembly on the strategic development of the use of the language in the Kirk.
   (iii) The General Assembly note the statistics regarding Gaelic-speaking charges and instruct the Ministries Council to bring to the General Assembly of 2008 an agreed set of criteria for future determination of such designations.
   (iv) The General Assembly instruct the Council of Assembly to continue to support the development of Gaelic within the Church, including discussions with appropriate funding bodies.
   (v) The General Assembly welcome the Report on the Strategic Development of the Use of Gaelic and encourage the Mission and Discipleship Council to develop its future plans.
   (vi) The General Assembly welcome the launch of the Gaelic Digital Broadcasting channel and instruct the Church and Society Council, in co-operation with the Council of Assembly, to discuss with the Gaelic Media Council the significant place of religious programmes in its output.

These are exciting times for the Gaelic language, and the Church is responding to the challenge of our day.

SECTION 2

General Information

(1) OTHER CHURCHES IN THE UNITED KINGDOM

ASSOCIATED PRESBYTERIAN CHURCHES
Clerk of Presbytery: Rev. Archibald N. McPhail, APC Manse, Polvinister Road, Oban
PA34 5TN (Tel: 01631 567076; E-mail: archibaldmcphail@ntlworld.com).

THE REFORMED PRESBYTERIAN CHURCH OF SCOTLAND
Clerk of Presbytery: Rev. Andrew Quigley, Church Offices, 48 North Bridge Street, Airdrie
ML6 6NE (Tel: 01236 620107; E-mail: airdrierpcs@aol.com).

THE FREE CHURCH OF SCOTLAND
Principal Clerk: Rev. James MacIver, The Mound, Edinburgh EH1 2LS (Tel: 0131-226 5286;
E-mail: principal.clerk@freechurch.org).

THE FREE PRESBYTERIAN CHURCH OF SCOTLAND
Clerk of Synod: Rev. John Macleod, 133 Woodlands Road, Glasgow G3 6LE (Tel: 0141-332 9283;
E-mail: jmac1265@aol.com).

THE UNITED FREE CHURCH OF SCOTLAND
General Secretary: Rev. John Fulton BSc BD, United Free Church Offices, 11 Newton Place,
Glasgow G3 7PR (Tel: 0141-332 3435; E-mail: office@ufcos.org.uk).

THE PRESBYTERIAN CHURCH IN IRELAND
Clerk of the General Assembly and General Secretary: Rev. Dr Donald J. Watts,
Church House, Fisherwick Place, Belfast BT1 6DW (Tel: 02890 322284; E-mail:
clerk@presbyterianireland.org).

THE PRESBYTERIAN CHURCHES OF WALES
General Secretary: Rev. Ifan R.H. Roberts, Tabernacle Chapel, 81 Merthyr Road, Whitchurch,
Cardiff CF14 1DD (Tel: 02920 627465; Fax: 02920 616188; E-mail: swyddfa.office@
ebcpcw.org.uk).

THE UNITED REFORMED CHURCH
General Secretary: Rev. Roberta Rominger, 86 Tavistock Place, London WC1H 9RT (Tel: 020
7916 2020; Fax: 020 7916 2021; E-mail: roberta.rominger@urc.org.uk).

UNITED REFORMED CHURCH SYNOD OF SCOTLAND
Synod Clerk: Dr James Merrilees, Church House, 340 Cathedral Street, Glasgow G1 2BQ
(Tel: 0141-332 7667; E-mail: jmerrilees@urcscotland.org.uk).

BAPTIST UNION OF SCOTLAND
General Director: Rev. William G. Slack, 14 Aytoun Road, Glasgow G41 5RT (Tel: 0141-423
6169; E-mail: mary@scottishbaptist.org.uk).

CONGREGATIONAL FEDERATION IN SCOTLAND
Mrs Margaret Cowie, 23 Middleton Crescent, Bridge of Don, Aberdeen AB22 8HY (Tel: 01224
703248; E-mail: secretary@cfscotland.org.uk).

RELIGIOUS SOCIETY OF FRIENDS (QUAKERS)
Representative Friend: Pamala McDougall, Havana, 3 Teapot Lane, Inverkeilor, Arbroath DD1
5RP (Tel: 01241 830238; E-mail: pamjames@havana.wanadoo.co.uk).

ROMAN CATHOLIC CHURCH
Rev. Paul Conroy, General Secretariat, Bishops' Conference of Scotland, 64 Aitken Street, Airdrie ML6 6LT (Tel: 01236 764061; Fax: 01236 762489; E-mail: gensec@ bpsconfscot.com).

THE SALVATION ARMY
Scotland Secretary: Major Robert McIntyre, Scotland Secretariat, 12A Dryden Road, Loanhead EH20 9LZ (Tel: 0131-440 9101; E-mail: robert.mcintyre@salvationarmy.org.uk).

SCOTTISH EPISCOPAL CHURCH
General Secretary: Mr John F. Stuart, 21 Grosvenor Crescent, Edinburgh EH12 5EL (Tel: 0131-225 6357; E-mail: secgen@scotland.anglican.org).

THE SYNOD OF THE METHODIST CHURCH IN SCOTLAND
Secretary: Mrs Janet Murray, Methodist Church Office, Scottish Churches House, Kirk Street, Dunblane FK15 0AJ (Tel/Fax: 01786 820295; E-mail: meth@scottishchurcheshouse.org).

GENERAL SYNOD OF THE CHURCH OF ENGLAND
Secretary General: Mr William Fittall, Church House, Great Smith Street, London SW1P 3NZ (Tel: 020 7898 1000; E-mail: william.fittall@c-of-e.org.uk).

(2) OVERSEAS CHURCHES

PRESBYTERIAN CHURCH IN AMERICA
Stated Clerk: 1700 North Brown Road, Suite 105, Lawrenceville, GA 30043, USA (E-mail: ac@pcanet.org; Website: www.pcanet.org).

PRESBYTERIAN CHURCH IN CANADA
Clerk of Assembly: 50 Wynford Drive, Toronto, Ontario M3C 1J7, Canada (E-mail: pccadmin@presbycan.ca; Website: www.presbycan.ca).

UNITED CHURCH OF CANADA
General Secretary: Suite 300, 3250 Bloor Street West, Toronto, Ontario M8X 2Y4, Canada (E-mail: info@united-church.ca; Website: www.united-church.ca).

PRESBYTERIAN CHURCH (USA)
Stated Clerk: 100 Witherspoon Street, Louisville, KY 40202-1396, USA (E-mail: presbytel@pcusa.org; Website: www.pcusa.org).

REFORMED PRESBYTERIAN CHURCH OF NORTH AMERICA
Stated Clerk: 7408 Penn Avenue, Pittsburgh, PA 15208, USA (Website: www.reformedpresbyterian.org).

CUMBERLAND PRESBYTERIAN CHURCH
General Secretary: 1978 Union Avenue, Memphis, TN 38104, USA (E-mail: assembly@ cumberland.org; Website: www.cumberland.org).

REFORMED CHURCH IN AMERICA
General Secretary: 475 Riverside Drive, NY 10115, USA (E-mail: rcamail@rca.org; Website: www.rca.org).

UNITED CHURCH OF CHRIST
General Minister: 700 Prospect Avenue, Cleveland, OH 44115, USA
(Website: www.ucc.org).

UNITING CHURCH IN AUSTRALIA
General Secretary: PO Box A2266, Sydney South, New South Wales 1235, Australia (E-mail: enquiries@nat.uca.org.au; Website: www.uca.org.au).

PRESBYTERIAN CHURCH OF AUSTRALIA
Clerk of Assembly: PO Box 2196, Strawberry Hills, NSW 2012; 168 Chalmers Street, Surry Hills, NSW 2010, Australia (E-mail: general@pcnsw.org.au; Website: www.presbyterian.org.au).

PRESBYTERIAN CHURCH OF AOTEAROA, NEW ZEALAND
Executive Secretary: PO Box 9049, Wellington, New Zealand (E-mail: aes@presbyterian.org.nz; Website: www.presbyterian.org.nz).

EVANGELICAL PRESBYTERIAN CHURCH, GHANA
Synod Clerk: PO Box 18, Ho, Volta Region, Ghana.

PRESBYTERIAN CHURCH OF GHANA
Director of Ecumenical and Social Relations: PO Box 1800, Accra, Ghana.

PRESBYTERIAN CHURCH OF EAST AFRICA
Secretary General: PO Box 27573, 00506 Nairobi, Kenya.

CHURCH OF CENTRAL AFRICA PRESBYTERIAN
Secretary General, General Assembly: PO Box 30398, Lilongwe 3, Malawi.
General Secretary, Blantyre Synod: PO Box 413, Blantyre, Malawi.
General Secretary, Livingstonia Synod: PO Box 112, Mzuzu, Malawi.
General Secretary, Nkhoma Synod: PO Box 45, Nkhoma, Malawi.

IGREJA EVANGELICA DE CRISTO EM MOÇAMBIQUE (EVANGELICAL CHURCH OF CHRIST IN MOZAMBIQUE)
(Nampula) General Secretary: Cx. Postale 284, Nampula 70100, Mozambique.
(Zambezia) Superintendente: Cx. Postale 280, Zambezia, Quelimane, Mozambique.

PRESBYTERIAN CHURCH OF NIGERIA
Principal Clerk: 26–29 Ehere Road, Ogbor Hill, PO Box 2635, Aba, Abia State, Nigeria.

UNITING PRESBYTERIAN CHURCH IN SOUTHERN AFRICA (SOUTH AFRICA)
General Secretary: PO Box 96188, Brixton 2019, South Africa.

UNITING PRESBYTERIAN CHURCH IN SOUTHERN AFRICA (ZIMBABWE)
Presbytery Clerk: PO Box CY224, Causeway, Harare, Zimbabwe.

PRESBYTERIAN CHURCH OF SUDAN
Head Office: PO Box 40, Malakal, Sudan.

UNITED CHURCH OF ZAMBIA
General Secretary: Nationalist Road at Burma Road, PO Box 50122, 15101 Ridgeway, Lusaka, Zambia.

CHURCH OF BANGLADESH
Moderator: Synod Office, 54 Johnson Road, Dhaka 1100, Bangladesh.

CHURCH OF NORTH INDIA
General Secretary: Synod Office, 16 Pandit Pant Marg, New Delhi 110 001, India.

CHURCH OF SOUTH INDIA
General Secretary: Synod Office, 5 White's Road, Royapettah, Chennai 600 114, India.

PRESBYTERIAN CHURCH OF KOREA
General Secretary: CPO Box 1125, Seoul 110 611, Korea.

PRESBYTERIAN CHURCH IN THE REPUBLIC OF KOREA
General Secretary: 1501 The Korean Ecumenical Building, 136–156 Yunchi-Dong, Chongno-Ku, Seoul, Korea.

THE UNITED MISSION TO NEPAL
Executive Director: PO Box 126, Kathmandu, Nepal.

CHURCH OF PAKISTAN
General Secretary: c/o St John's Cathedral School, 1 Sir Syed Road, Peshawar 25000, NWFP, Pakistan.

PRESBYTERY OF LANKA
Moderator: 127/1 D S Senanayake Veedyan, Kandy, Sri Lanka.

PRESBYTERIAN CHURCH IN TAIWAN
General Secretary: 3 Lane 269 Roosevelt Road, Sec. 3, Taipei, Taiwan 10763, ROC.

CHURCH OF CHRIST IN THAILAND
General Secretary: 109 CCT (13th Floor), Surawong Road, Khet Bangrak, Bangkok 10500, Thailand.

PRESBYTERY OF GUYANA
Moderator: 169 Thomas Street, Kitty, Georgetown, Guyana.

NATIONAL PRESBYTERIAN CHURCH OF GUATEMALA
Executive Secretary: Av. Simeon Canas 7–13, Zona 2, Aptdo 655, Guatemala City, Guatemala (E-mail: ienpg@terra.com.gt).

UNITED CHURCH IN JAMAICA AND THE CAYMAN ISLANDS
General Secretary: 12 Carlton Crescent, PO Box 359, Kingston 10, Jamaica (E-mail: unitedchurch@colis.com).

PRESBYTERIAN CHURCH IN TRINIDAD AND TOBAGO
General Secretary: Box 92, Paradise Hill, San Fernando, Trinidad (E-mail: pctt@tstt.net.tt).

UNITED PROTESTANT CHURCH OF BELGIUM
Rue de Champ de Mars 5, B-1050 Bruxelles, Belgium (E-mail: epub@epub.be; Website: www.protestanet.be/eput/index.htm).

REFORMED CHRISTIAN CHURCH IN CROATIA
Bishop's Office: Vladimira Nazora 31, HR-32100 Vinkovci, Croatia (E-mail: reformed.church.rcc@vk.htnet.hr).

EVANGELICAL CHURCH OF THE CZECH BRETHREN
Moderator: Jungmannova 9, PO Box 466, CZ-11121 Praha 1, Czech Republic (E-mail: ekumena@srcce.cz; Website: www.srcce.cz).

EGLISE REFORMEE DE FRANCE
General Secretary: 47 rue de Clichy, F-75311 Paris, France (E-mail: erf@unacerf.org; Website: www.eglise-reformee-fr.org).

HUNGARIAN REFORMED CHURCH
General Secretary: PF Box 5, H-1440 Budapest, Hungary (E-mail: zsinat.kulugy@zsinatiiroda.hu; Website: www.reformatus.hu).

WALDENSIAN CHURCH
Moderator: Via Firenze 38, 00184 Rome, Italy (E-mail: moderatore@chiesavaldese.org; Website: www.chiesavaldese.org).

NETHERLANDS REFORMED CHURCH
Landelijk Dienstcentrum Samen op Weg-Kerken, Postbus 8504, NL-3503 RM Utrecht (E-mail: ccs@ngk.nl; Website: www.ngk.nl).

REFORMED CHURCH IN ROMANIA
Bishop's Office: Str. IC Bratianu No. 51, R-3400 Cluj-Napoca, Romania (E-mail: office@reformatus.ro).

REFORMED CHRISTIAN CHURCH IN YUGOSLAVIA
Bishop's Office: Bratstva 26, YU-24323 Feketic, Yugoslavia.

SYNOD OF THE NILE OF THE EVANGELICAL CHURCH
General Secretary: Synod of the Nile of the Evangelical Church, PO Box 1248, Cairo, Egypt (E-mail: epcegypt@yahoo.com).

DIOCESE OF THE EPISCOPAL CHURCH IN JERUSALEM AND THE MIDDLE EAST
Bishop's Office: PO Box 19122, Jerusalem 91191, via Israel (E-mail: ediocese-jer@j-diocese.com; Website: www.jerusalem.anglican.org).

NATIONAL EVANGELICAL SYNOD OF SYRIA AND LEBANON
General Secretary: PO Box 70890, Antelias, Lebanon (E-mail: nessl@minero.net).

[Full information on Churches overseas may be obtained from the World Mission Council.]

(3) SCOTTISH DIVINITY FACULTIES

[* denotes a Minister of the Church of Scotland]
[(R) Reader   (SL) Senior Lecturer   (L) Lecturer]

ABERDEEN

(School of Divinity, History and Philosophy)
King's College, Old Aberdeen AB24 3UB
(Tel: 01224 272380; Fax: 01224 273750;
E-mail: divinity@abdn.ac.uk)

Master of Christ's College:	Rev. J.H.A. Dick* MA MSc BD (E-mail: christs-college@abdn.ac.uk)
Head of School:	Professor Robert Frost MA PhD FRHistS
Professors:	Robert Segal BA MA PhD (Religious Studies) Joachim Schaper DipTheol PhD (Old Testament) Rev. John Swinton* BD PhD RNM RNMD (Practical Theology and Pastoral Care) John Webster MA PhD DD (Systematic Theology)
Readers:	Francesca Murphy BA MA PhD (Systematic Theology)
Senior Lecturers:	Andrew Clarke BA MA PhD (New Testament) Martin Mills MA PhD (Religious Studies)
Lecturers:	Kenneth Aitken BD PhD (Hebrew Bible) Thomas Bokedal ThD MTh (New Testament) Christopher Brittain BA MDiv PhD (Practical Theology) Brian Brock BS MA DipTheol DPhil (Moral and Practical Theology) Marie-Luise Ehrenschwendtner PhD (Church History) Jane Heath PhD (New Testament) Jutta Leonhardt-Balzer DipTheol PhD (New Testament) Gabriele Maranci BA MA PhD (Religious Studies) Nick Thompson BA MA MTh PhD (Church History) Lena-Sofia Tiemeyer BA MA MPhil (Old Testament/Hebrew Bible) Will Tuladhar-Douglas BA MA MPhil (Religious Studies) Donald Wood BA MA MPhil DPhil (Systematic Theology) Philip Ziegler BA MA MDiv ThD (Systematic Theology)

ST ANDREWS
(University College of St Mary)
St Mary's College, St Andrews, Fife KY16 9JU
(Tel: 01334 462850/1; Fax: 01334 462852)

Principal, Dean and Head of School: J.R. Davila BA MA PhD

Chairs: M.I. Aguilar BA MA STB PhD
(Religion and Politics)
David Brown MA PhD DPhil FBA
(Theology, Aesthetics and Culture and Wardlaw
Professor)
Kristin de Troyer STB MA STL PhD
P.F. Esler BA LLB LLM DPhil (Biblical Criticism)
T.A. Hart BA PhD (Divinity)
R.A. Piper BA BD PhD (Christian Origins)
A.J. Torrance* MA BD DrTheol
(Systematic Theology)

Readerships, Senior Lectureships, Lectureships:

I.C. Bradley* BA MA BD DPhil (R) (Practical Theology)
J.R. Davila BA MA PhD (Early Jewish Studies and Church History)
M. Elliott BA BD PhD (Church History)
S.R. Holmes BA MA MTh PGDip PhD (Theology)
G. Hopps BA MPhil PhD (Theology)
K. Iverson BS ThM PhD (New Testament)
B.W. Longenecker BD MRel PhD (New Testament)
G. Macaskill BSc DipTh PhD (New Testament)
N. MacDonald MA MPhil PhD (Old Testament and Hebrew)
E. Stoddart BD PhD (Practical Theology)

EDINBURGH
(School of Divinity and New College)
New College, Mound Place, Edinburgh EH1 2LX
(Tel: 0131-650 8900; Fax: 0131-650 7952; E-mail: divinity.faculty@ed.ac.uk)

Head of School: Rev. Professor David A.S. Fergusson* MA BD DPhil FRSE
Principal of New College: Rev. Professor A. Graeme Auld* MA BD PhD DLitt FSAScot
FRSE
Chairs: Rev. Professor A. Graeme Auld* MA BD PhD DLitt FSAScot
FRSE (Hebrew Bible)
Professor Hans Barstad DrTheol (Hebrew and Old Testament)
Professor Stewart J. Brown BA MA PhD FRHistS
(Ecclesiastical History)

Professor James L. Cox BA MDiv PhD (Religious Studies)
Rev. Professor David A.S. Fergusson* MA BD DPhil FRSE
(Divinity)
Professor Larry W. Hurtado BA MA PhD
(New Testament Language, Literature and Theology)
Professor Timothy Lim BA MPhil DPhil (Biblical Studies)
Rev. Professor Oliver O'Donovan MA DPhil (Christian Ethics)
Professor Marcella Althaus Reid BTh PhD
(Contextual Theology)

Readers, Senior Lecturers and Lecturers:

Biblical Studies:

David J. Reimer BTh BA MA MA (SL)
Graham Paul Foster PhD MSt BD
Helen K. Bond MTheol PhD (SL)

Theology and Ethics:

Jolyon Mitchell BA MA (SL)
Michael S. Northcott MA PhD (R)
Cecelia Clegg BD MSc PhD (L)
Rev. Ewan Kelly* MB ChB BD PhD (L) (part-time)
Nicholas S. Adams BA PhD (L)
John C. McDowell BD PhD (L)
Michael Purcell MA PhD PhL PhB (SL)
Sara Parvis BA PhD (L)

Ecclesiastical History:

Jane E.A. Dawson BA PhD DipEd (SL)
Jack Thompson BA PhD (SL)
Susan Hardman Moore MA PhD (L)

Religious Studies:

Jeanne Openshaw BA MA PhD (SL)
Elizabeth Kopping MA PhD DipSocSci MTh (L)
Steven Sutcliffe BA MPhil PhD
Hannah Holtschneider MPhil PhD (L)
Afeosemime U. Adogame BA MA PhD (L)
Christian Lange BA MA PhD (L)

Fulton Lecturer in Speech and Communication:
Richard Ellis BSc MEd LGSM

Hope Trust Post-Doctoral Fellow:
Rev. Alison Jack* MA BD PhD

GLASGOW
(Department of Theology and Religious Studies and Trinity College)
4 The Square, University of Glasgow, Glasgow G12 8QQ
(Tel: 0141-330 6526; Fax: 0141-330 4943; E-mail: divinity@arts.gla.ac.uk)

Head of Department: Professor W. Ian P. Hazlett
Principal of Trinity College: Professor W. Ian P. Hazlett

Chairs: W. Ian P. Hazlett BA BD Dr theol DLitt DD (Ecclesiastical History)
     Rev. David Jasper MA PhD BD DD TeolD FRSE (Literature and Theology)
     Werner Jeanrond Mag theol PhD (Divinity)
     Rev. George M. Newlands* MA BD PhD DLitt FRSA FRSE (Divinity)
     Perry Schmidt-Leukel Dipl theol MA Dr theol Dr theol habil
      (Systematic Theology and World Religions)
     Mona Siddiqui MA PhD DLitt FRSE (Public Understanding of Islam)

Honorary Professorships: Rev. Donald Macleod MA
     Rev. John K. Riches MA

Senior Lecturers and Lecturers:
 Biblical Studies: Ward W. Blanton BA MDiv PhD (L)
     Paul A. Holloway AB MA PhD (L)
     Rev. Alastair G. Hunter* MSc BD PhD (SL)
     Sarah Nicholson MTheol PhD (L)
     Yvonne M. Sherwood BA PhD DipJS (SL)

 Catholic Theology and Ethics:
     Julie P. Clague BSc PGCE PGDip MTh (L)

 Practical Theology: Douglas Gay MA BD PhD (L)
     Heather E. Walton BA MA(Econ) PhD (SL)

 Islamic Studies: Lloyd V.J. Ridgeon BA MA PhD (SL)

Honorary Lecturer in Church History:
     Rev. John R. McIntosh BA BD MLitt PhD

Honorary Lecturer in Inter-faith Studies:
     Sister Isabel Smyth MA

Centre for Advanced Studies in Christian Ministry:
Director: Dr Heather E. Walton

Centre for Literature, Theology and the Arts:
Co-Director: Dr Heather E. Walton

Centre for the Study of Islam:
Director: Professor Mona Siddiqui

Centre for Inter-faith Studies:
Director: Professor P. Schmidt-Leukel

Divinity Research School:
Director: Dr Paul Holloway

HIGHLAND THEOLOGICAL COLLEGE
High Street, Dingwall IV15 9HA
(Tel: 01349 780000; Fax: 01349 780201;
E-mail: htc@uhi.ac.uk)

Principal of HTC: Rev. Professor Andrew McGowan* BD STM PhD
Vice-Principal of HTC: Rev. Hector Morrison* BSc BD MTh ILTM

Lecturers: Hector Morrison* BSc BD MTh ILTM (Old Testament and Hebrew)
Jamie Grant PhD MA LLB (Biblical Studies)
Michael Bird BMin BA PhD (New Testament)
Innes Visagie MA BTh BA PhD (Pastoral Theology)
Nick Needham BD PhD (Church History)
Robert Shillaker BSc BA PhD (Systematic Theology)

(4) SOCIETIES AND ASSOCIATIONS

The undernoted list shows the name of the Association, along with the name and address of the Secretary.

INTER-CHURCH ASSOCIATIONS

THE FELLOWSHIP OF ST ANDREW: The fellowship promotes dialogue between Churches of the east and the west in Scotland. Further information available from the Secretary, Rev. Robert Pickles, The Manse, 3 Perth Road, Milnathort, Kinross KY13 9XU (Tel: 01577 863461; E-mail: robert.pickles1@btopenworld.com).

THE FELLOWSHIP OF ST THOMAS: An ecumenical association formed to promote informed interest in and learn from the experience of Churches in South Asia (India, Pakistan, Bangladesh, Nepal, Sri Lanka). Secretary: Dr R.L. Robinson, 43 Underwood Road, Burnside, Rutherglen, Glasgow G73 3TE (Tel: 0141-643 0612; E-mail: robinson.burnside@talktalk.net).

THE SCOTTISH ORDER OF CHRISTIAN UNITY: Secretary: Dr P.D. Theaker CChem FRSC, 5 Altamount Road, Blairgowrie PH10 6QL (Tel: 01250 871162; E-mail: socu@fish.co.uk; Website: www.socu.org).

CHURCH PASTORAL AID SOCIETY (CPAS): Ministry Adviser for Scotland: Rev. Richard W. Higginbottom, 2 Highfield Place, Bankfoot, Perth PH1 4AX (Tel: 01738 440877 or 787429; Mbl: 07963 625835; E-mail: rhigginbottom@cpas.org.uk). A UK home mission society working cross-denominationally in Scotland through consultancy, training and resources to encourage leadership development and, thereby, evangelism in the local church. Accredited officially to the Mission and Discipleship Council.

FRONTIER YOUTH TRUST: Encourages and resources those engaged in youth work, particularly with disadvantaged young people. Co-ordinator: Matt Hall, 8 Dalswinton Street, Glasgow G34 0PS (Tel: 0141-771 9151).

IONA COMMUNITY: Leader: Rev. Kathy Galloway, Fourth Floor, Savoy House, 140 Sauchiehall Street, Glasgow G2 3DH (Tel: 0141-332 6343; Fax: 0141-332 1090; E-mail: admin@iona.org.uk; Website: www.iona.org.uk); Warden: Malcolm King, Iona Abbey, Isle of Iona, Argyll PA76 6SN (Tel: 01681 700404).

SCOTTISH CHURCHES HOUSING ACTION: Unites the Scottish Churches in tackling homelessness; advises on using property for affordable housing. Chief Executive: Alastair Cameron, 28 Albany Street, Edinburgh EH1 3QH (Tel: 0131-477 4500; Fax: 0131-477 2710; E-mail: info@churches-housing.org; Website: www.churches-housing.org).

SCOTTISH CHURCHES WORLD EXCHANGE: SCWE provides training and support for church groups and others planning visits or exchanges between Scotland and church partners in the developing world. SCWE supports capacity-building within churches in the developing world by providing short-term Interns who have skills and experience which are relevant and useful in the work of partner churches. Recent SCWE Internships have included teachers, ministers, accountants, outdoor instructors, property specialists, bankers and lawyers. SCWE also provides training programmes for volunteers and Interns going with other organisations who wish to consult an ecumenical Christian organisation before going overseas (Tel: 0131-315 4444; Website: www.worldexchange.org.uk).

ST COLM'S INTERNATIONAL HOUSE: Available for ministers and church conferences: an excellent place to stay and an opportunity to support an important ecumenical project. English-language and Capacity-Building Courses for community leaders from the developing world. A place to meet in the heart of the Capital on the perimeter of the Royal Botanic Gardens (Tel: 0131-315 4444).

FRIENDS OF ST COLM'S: An association for all from any denomination who have trained, studied or been resident in St Colm's or have an interest in its work and life. There is an annual retreat, an annual lecture and some local associations for more regular meetings. It offers support to St Colm's International House. Secretary: c/o St Colm's International House, 23 Inverleith Terrace, Edinburgh EH3 5NS (Tel: 0131-315 4444).

SCOTTISH JOINT COMMITTEE ON RELIGIOUS AND MORAL EDUCATION: Mr Rob Whiteman, 121 George Street, Edinburgh EH2 4YN (Tel: 0131-225 5722), and Mr Lachlan Bradley, 6 Clairmont Gardens, Glasgow G3 7LW (Tel: 0141-353 3595).

YMCA SCOTLAND: National General Secretary: Mr Peter Crory, James Love House, 11 Rutland Street, Edinburgh EH1 2DQ (Tel: 0131-228 1464; E-mail: info@ymcascotland.org; Website: www.ymcascotland.org).

INTERSERVE SCOTLAND: We are part of Interserve, an international, evangelical and interdenominational organisation with over 150 years of Christian service. The purpose of Interserve is 'to make Jesus Christ known through holistic ministry in partnership with the global church, among the neediest peoples of Asia and the Arab world', and our vision is 'Lives and communities transformed through encounter with Jesus Christ'. Interserve supports over 700 people in cross-cultural ministry in a wide range of work including children and youth, the environment, evangelism, Bible training, engineering, agriculture, business development and health. We rely on supporters in Scotland and throughout the UK to join us. Director: Grace Penney, 4 Blairtummock Place, Panorama Business Village, Queenslie, Glasgow G33 4EN (Tel: 0141-781 1982; Fax: 0141-781 1576; E-mail: info@isscot.org; Website: www.interservescotland.org.uk).

SCRIPTURE UNION SCOTLAND: 70 Milton Street, Glasgow G4 0HR (Tel: 0141-332 1162; Fax: 0141-352 7600; E-mail: info@suscotland.org.uk; Website: www.suscotland.org.uk).

STUDENT CHRISTIAN MOVEMENT: Co-ordinator: Mr Martin Thompson, SCM Office, Unit 308F, The Big Peg, 120 Vyse Street, The Jewellery Quarter, Birmingham B18 6NF (Tel: 0121-200 3355; E-mail: scm@movement.org.uk; Website: www.movement.org.uk).

UNIVERSITIES AND COLLEGES CHRISTIAN FELLOWSHIP: Pod Bhogal, 38 De Montfort Street, Leicester LE1 7GP (Tel: 0116-255 1700; E-mail: pbhogal@uccf.org.uk).

WORLD DAY OF PRAYER: SCOTTISH COMMITTEE: Convener: Christian Williams, 61 McCallum Gardens, Strathview Estate, Bellshill ML4 2SR. Secretary: Morag Hannah, 8 Dovecote View, Kirkintilloch, Glasgow G66 3HY (Tel. 0141-776 2432; E mail: morag.hannah.wdp@virgin.net; Website: www.wdpscotland.org.uk).

CHURCH OF SCOTLAND SOCIETIES

AROS (Association of Returned Overseas Staff of the Church of Scotland World Mission Council): Hon. Secretary: Rev. Kenneth J. Pattison, 2 Castle Way, St Madoes, Glencarse, Perth PH2 7NY (Tel: 01738 860340).

FORUM OF GENERAL ASSEMBLY AND PRESBYTERY CLERKS: Rev. Rosemary Frew, 83 Milton Road, Kirkcaldy KY1 1TP (Tel: 01592 260315).

FORWARD TOGETHER: An organisation for evangelicals within the Church of Scotland. Secretary: Rev. Ian M. Watson LLB DipLP BD, The Manse, 2 Lanark Road, Kirkmuirhill, Lanark ML11 9RB (Tel: 01555 892409; Website: www.forwardtogether.org.uk).

FRIENDS OF ST COLM'S: Secretary: c/o St Colm's International House, 23 Inverleith Terrace, Edinburgh EH3 5NS (Tel: 0131-315 4444).

SCOTTISH CHURCH SOCIETY: Secretary: Rev. W. Gerald Jones MA BD MTh, The Manse, Kirkmichael, Maybole KA19 7PJ (Tel: 01655 750286).

SCOTTISH CHURCH THEOLOGY SOCIETY: Rev. Gordon R. Mackenzie BSc(Agr) BD, The Manse of Dyke, Brodie, Forres IV36 2TD (Tel: 01309 641239; E-mail: rev.g.mackenzie@btopenworld.com). The Society encourages theological exploration and discussion of the main issues confronting the Church in the twenty-first century.

SOCIETY OF FRIENDS OF ST ANDREW'S JERUSALEM: Hon. Secretary: Major J.M.K. Erskine MBE, World Mission Council, 121 George Street, Edinburgh EH2 4YN. Hon. Treasurer: Mrs Anne Macintosh BA CA, Assistant Treasurer, The Church of Scotland, 121 George Street, Edinburgh EH2 4YN (Tel: 0131-225 5722).

THE CHURCH OF SCOTLAND CHAPLAINS' ASSOCIATION: Hon. Secretary: Rev. Neil N. Gardner MA BD, The Manse of Canongate, Edinburgh EH8 8BN (Tel 0131-556 3515).

THE CHURCH OF SCOTLAND RETIRED MINISTERS' ASSOCIATION: Hon. Secretary: Rev. Elspeth G. Dougall MA BD, 60B Craigmillar Park, Edinburgh EH16 5PU (Tel: 0131-668 1342).

THE CHURCH SERVICE SOCIETY: Secretary: Rev. Neil N. Gardner MA BD, The Manse of Canongate, Edinburgh EH8 8BN (Tel: 0131-556 3515).

THE IRISH MINISTERS' FRATERNAL: Secretary: Rev. Eric G. McKimmon BA BD MTh, The Manse, St Andrews Road, Ceres, Cupar KY15 5NQ (Tel: 01334 829466).

THE NATIONAL CHURCH ASSOCIATION: Secretary: Miss Margaret P. Milne, 10 Balfron Crescent, Hamilton ML3 9UH.

BIBLE SOCIETIES

THE SCOTTISH BIBLE SOCIETY: Director of Programmes: Mr Colin S. Hay, 7 Hampton Terrace, Edinburgh EH12 5XU (Tel: 0131-347 9809).

WEST OF SCOTLAND BIBLE SOCIETY: Secretary: Rev. Finlay MacKenzie, 51 Rowallan Gardens, Glasgow G11 7LH (Tel: 0141-563 5276; E-mail: f.c.mack51@ntlworld.com).

GENERAL

THE BOYS' BRIGADE: Scottish Headquarters, Carronvale House, Carronvale Road, Larbert FK5 3LH (Tel: 01324 562008; Fax: 01324 552323; E-mail: carronvale@ boys-brigade.org.uk).

THE GIRLS' BRIGADE IN SCOTLAND: 11A Woodside Crescent, Glasgow G3 7UL (Tel: 0141-332 1765; E-mail: enquiries@girls-brigade-scotland.org.uk; Website: www.girls-brigade-scotland.org.uk).

GIRLGUIDING SCOTLAND: 16 Coates Crescent, Edinburgh EH3 7AH (Tel: 0131-226 4511; Fax: 0131-220 4828; E-mail: administrator@girlguiding-scot.org.uk).

THE SCOUT ASSOCIATION: Scottish Headquarters, Fordell Firs, Hillend, Dunfermline KY11 7HQ (Tel: 01383 419073; E-mail: shq@scouts-scotland.org.uk).

CLUBS FOR YOUNG PEOPLE (SCOTLAND): 88 Giles Street, Edinburgh EH6 6BZ (Tel: 0131-555 1729; E-mail: secretary@cypscotland.com).

YOUTH SCOTLAND: Balfour House, 19 Bonnington Grove, Edinburgh EH6 4BL (Tel: 0131-554 2561; Fax: 0131-454 3438; E-mail: office@youthscotland.org.uk).

CHRISTIAN AID SCOTLAND: Head of Christian Aid Scotland, The Pentagon Centre, 36 Washington Street, Glasgow G3 8AZ (Tel: 0141-221 7475; Fax: 0141-241 6145; E-mail: glasgow@christian-aid.org). Edinburgh Office: Tel: 0131-220 1254.

FEED THE MINDS: 36 Causton Street, London SW1P 4ST (Tel: 08451 212102).

LADIES' GAELIC SCHOOLS AND HIGHLAND BURSARY ASSOCIATION: Mr Donald J. Macdonald, 9 Hatton Place, Edinburgh EH9 1UD (Tel: 0131-667 1740).

RELATE SCOTLAND: Chief Executive: Mrs Hilary Campbell, 18 York Place, Edinburgh EH1 3EP (Tel: 0845 119 6088; Fax: 0845 119 6089; E-mail: enquiries@relatescotland.org.uk; Website: www.relatescotland.org.uk).

SCOTTISH CHURCH HISTORY SOCIETY: Hon. Secretary: Rev. William D. Graham MA BD, 48 Corbiehill Crescent, Edinburgh EH4 5BD (Tel: 0131-336 4071; E-mail: w.d.graham@btinternet.com).

SCOTTISH EVANGELICAL THEOLOGY SOCIETY: Secretary: Rev. David J.C. Easton MA BD, 'Rowanbank', Cormiston Road, Quothquan, Biggar ML12 6ND (Tel: 01899 308459; E-mail: deaston@btinternet.com; Website: www.setsonline.org.uk).

CHRISTIAN ENDEAVOUR IN SCOTLAND: Winning, Teaching and Training Youngsters for Christ and the Church: The Murray Library, 8 Shore Street, Anstruther KY10 3EA (Tel: 01333 310345 Monday, Wednesday and Friday mornings; E-mail: christine@ce-in-scotland.fsnet.co.uk; Website: www.cescotland.org.uk).

TEARFUND: 100 Church Road, Teddington TW11 8QE (Tel: 0845 355 8355). Manager: Peter Chirnside, Tearfund Scotland, Challenge House, 29 Canal Street, Glasgow G4 0AD (Tel: 0141-332 3621; E-mail: scotland@tearfund.org; Website: www.tearfund.org).

THE LEPROSY MISSION SCOTLAND: Suite 2, Earlsgate Lodge, Livilands Lane, Stirling FK8 2BG (Tel: 01786 449266; Fax: 01786 449766). National Director: Miss Linda Todd. Communications Manager (including Area Co-ordinator, Central and South): Mr Stuart McAra. Area Co-ordinator, North and Islands: Mr Jim Clark (Tel: 01343 843837; E-mail: contactus@tlmscotland.org.uk or meetings@tlmscotland.org.uk; Website: www.tlmscotland.org.uk).

DAYONE CHRISTIAN MINISTRIES (THE LORD'S DAY OBSERVANCE SOCIETY): Ryelands Road, Leominster, Herefordshire HR6 8NZ (Tel: 01568 613740).

THE SCOTTISH REFORMATION SOCIETY: Secretary: Rev. A. Sinclair Horne, The Magdalen Chapel, 41 Cowgate, Edinburgh EH1 1JR (Tel: 0131-220 1450; E-mail: ashbethany43@hotmail.co.uk; Website: www.magdalenchapel.org).

THE SOCIETY IN SCOTLAND FOR PROPAGATING CHRISTIAN KNOWLEDGE: J. Gordon Cunningham WS, Tods Murray LLP, Edinburgh Quay, 133 Fountainbridge, Edinburgh EH3 9AG (Tel: 0131-656 2000).

THE WALDENSIAN MISSIONS AID SOCIETY FOR WORK IN ITALY: David A. Lamb SSC, 36 Liberton Drive, Edinburgh EH16 6NN (Tel: 0131-664 3059; E-mail: david@dlamb.co.uk).

YWCA SCOTLAND: Chief Executive: Gill Martin, 7B Randolph Crescent, Edinburgh EH3 7TH (Tel: 0131-225 7592; E-mail: info@ywcascotland.org; Website: www.ywcascotland.org).

(5) TRUSTS AND FUNDS

THE SOCIETY FOR THE BENEFIT OF THE SONS AND DAUGHTERS OF THE CLERGY OF THE CHURCH OF SCOTLAND

Secretary and Treasurer: Mrs Fiona M.M. Watson CA
                                  17 Melville Street
                                  Edinburgh EH3 7PH (Tel: 0131-473 3500;
                                  E-mail: charity@scott-moncrieff.com)

Annual grants are made to assist in the education of the children (normally between the ages of 12 and 25 years) of ministers of the Church of Scotland. The Society also gives grants to aged and infirm daughters of ministers and ministers' unmarried daughters and sisters who are in need. Applications are to be lodged by 31 May in each year.

THE GLASGOW SOCIETY OF THE SONS AND DAUGHTERS OF MINISTERS OF THE CHURCH OF SCOTLAND

Secretary and Treasurer: Mrs Fiona M.M. Watson CA
                                  17 Melville Street
                                  Edinburgh EH3 7PH (Tel: 0131-473 3500;
                                  E-mail: charity@scott-moncrieff.com)

The Society's primary purpose is to grant financial assistance to children (no matter what age) of deceased ministers of the Church of Scotland. Applications are to be submitted by 1 February in each year. To the extent that funds are available, grants are also given for the children of ministers or retired ministers, although such grants are normally restricted to university and college students. These latter grants are considered in conjunction with the Edinburgh-based Society. Limited funds are also available for individual application for special needs or projects. Applications are to be submitted by 31 May in each year. Emergency applications can be dealt with at any time when need arises. Application forms may be obtained from the Secretary.

ESDAILE TRUST:
Clerk and Treasurer: Mrs Fiona M.M. Watson CA
                                  17 Melville Street
                                  Edinburgh EH3 7PH (Tel: 0131-473 3500;
                                  E-mail: charity@scott-moncrieff.com)

Assists education and advancement of daughters of ministers, missionaries and widowed deaconesses of the Church of Scotland between 12 and 25 years of age. Applications are to be lodged by 31 May in each year.

HOLIDAYS FOR MINISTERS

The undernoted hotels provide special terms for ministers and their families. Fuller information may be obtained from the establishments:

CRIEFF HYDRO Ltd and MURRAYPARK HOTEL: The William Meikle Trust Fund and Paton Fund make provision whereby active ministers and their spouses, members of the Diaconate and other full-time employees of the Church of Scotland may enjoy hotel and self-catering accommodation at certain times of the year. BIG Country provides supervised childcare for children aged 2 to 12 years. (Free supervised childcare is not available for guests staying at the Murraypark Hotel.) For all our guests, Crieff Hydro offers a wide range of leisure facilities such as the Leisure Pool, gym, in-house cinema, entertainment and many outdoor activities. To make a reservation, please contact Accommodation Sales on 01764 651670, quoting your employee reference number; they are available to take your call from 8am to 9pm daily. Alternatively, you can e-mail your enquiry to enquiries@crieffhydro.com or post it to Accommodation Sales Team, Crieff Hydro, Ferntower Road, Crieff PH7 3LQ.

THE CINTRA BEQUEST: The Trust provides financial assistance towards the cost of accommodation in Scotland for missionaries on leave, or for ministers on temporary holiday, or on rest. In addition, due to additional funds generously donated by the Tod Endowment Trust, grants can be given to defray the cost of obtaining rest and recuperation in Scotland. In appropriate cases, therefore, the cost of travel within Scotland may also be met. Applications should be made to Mrs J.S. Wilson, Solicitor, 121 George Street, Edinburgh EH2 4YN.

TOD ENDOWMENT TRUST: CINTRA BEQUEST: MINISTRY BENEVOLENT FUND: The Trustees of the Cintra Bequest and of the Church of Scotland Ministry Benevolent Fund can consider an application for a grant from the Tod Endowment funds from any ordained or commissioned minister or deacon in Scotland of at least two years' standing before the date of application, to assist with the cost of the beneficiary and his or her spouse or partner and dependants obtaining rest and recuperation in Scotland. The Trustees of the Church of Scotland Ministry Benevolent Fund can also consider an application from an ordained or commissioned minister or deacon who has retired. Application forms are available from Mrs J.S. Wilson, Solicitor (for the Cintra Bequest), and from Mrs C. Robertson, Assistant Treasurer (Ministries) (for the Ministry Benevolent Fund). The address in both cases is 121 George Street, Edinburgh EH2 4YN (Tel: 0131-225 5722). (Attention is drawn to separate individual entries for both the Cintra Bequest and the Church of Scotland Ministry Benevolent Fund.)

THE LYALL BEQUEST: Makes available the following benefits to ministers of the Church of Scotland:
1. A grant towards the cost of holiday accommodation in or close to the town of St Andrews may be paid to any minister and to his or her spouse at the rate of £100 per week each for a stay of one week or longer. Grants for a stay of less than one week may also be paid, at the rate of £14 per day each. Due to the number of applications which the Trustees now receive, an applicant will not be considered to be eligible if he or she has received a grant from the Bequest during the three years prior to the holiday for which the application is made. Applications prior to the holiday should be made to the Secretaries. Retired ministers are not eligible for grants.
2. Grants towards costs of sickness and convalescence so far as not covered by the National Health Service or otherwise may be available to applicants, who should apply to the Secretaries giving relevant details.
All communications should be addressed to Pagan Osborne, Solicitors, Secretaries to the Lyall Bequest, 106 South Street, St Andrews KY16 9QD (Tel: 01334 475001; E-mail: elcalderwood@pagan.co.uk).

MARGARET AND JOHN ROSS TRAVELLING FUND: Offers grants to ministers and their spouses for travelling and other expenses for trips to the Holy Land where the purpose is recuperation or relaxation. Applications should be made to the Secretary and Clerk, Church of Scotland Trust, 121 George Street, Edinburgh EH2 4YN (Tel: 0131-240 2222; E-mail: jhamilton@cofscotland.org.uk).

The undernoted represents a list of the more important trusts available for ministers, students and congregations. A brief indication is given of the trust purposes, but application should be made in each case to the person named for full particulars and forms of application.

THE ABERNETHY TRUST: Offers residential accommodation and outdoor activities for Youth Fellowships, Church family weekends, Bible Classes and so on at four outdoor centres in Scotland. Further details from the Executive Director, Abernethy Trust, Nethy Bridge PH25 3ED (Tel/Fax: 01479 821279; Website: www.abernethytrust.org.uk).

THE ARROL TRUST: The Arrol Trust gives small grants to young people between the ages of 16 and 25 for the purposes of travel which will provide education or work experience. Potential recipients would be young people with disabilities or who would for financial reasons be otherwise unable to undertake projects. It is expected that projects would be beneficial not only to applicants but also to the wider community. Application forms are available from Callum S. Kennedy WS, Lindsays WS, Caledonian Exchange, 19A Canning Street, Edinburgh EH3 8HE (Tel: 0131-229 1212).

THE BAIRD TRUST: Assists in the building and repair of churches and halls, endows Parishes and generally assists the work of the Church of Scotland. Apply to Ronald D. Oakes CA ACMA, 182 Bath Street, Glasgow G2 4HG (Tel: 0141-332 0476; Fax: 0141-331 0874; E-mail: baird.trust@btconnect.com).

THE REV. ALEXANDER BARCLAY BEQUEST: Assists mother, daughter, sister or niece of deceased minister of the Church of Scotland who at the time of his death was acting as his housekeeper and who is in needy circumstances. Apply to Robert Hugh Allan LLB DipLP NP, Pomphreys, 79 Quarry Street, Hamilton ML3 7AG (Tel: 01698 891616).

BELLAHOUSTON BEQUEST FUND: Gives grants to Protestant evangelical denominations in the City of Glasgow and certain areas within five miles of the city boundary for building and repairing churches and halls and the promotion of religion. Apply to Mr Donald B. Reid, Mitchells Roberton, 36 North Hanover Street, Glasgow G1 2AD.

BEQUEST FUND FOR MINISTERS: Assists ministers in outlying districts with manse furnishings, pastoral efficiency aids, educational or medical costs. Apply to A. Linda Parkhill CA, 60 Wellington Street, Glasgow G2 6HJ (Tel: 0141-226 4994).

CARNEGIE TRUST FOR THE UNIVERSITIES OF SCOTLAND: In cases of hardship, the Carnegie Trust is prepared to consider applications by students of Scottish birth or extraction (at least one parent born in Scotland), or who have had at least three years' education at a secondary school in Scotland, for financial assistance with the payment of their fees for a first degree at a Scottish university. For further details, students should apply to the Secretary, Carnegie Trust for the Universities of Scotland, Andrew Carnegie House, Pittencrieff Street, Dunfermline KY12 8AW (Tel: 01383 724990; Fax: 01383 749799; E-mail: jgray@carnegie-trust.org; Website: www.carnegie-trust.org).

CHURCH OF SCOTLAND INSURANCE CO. LTD: Undertakes insurance of Church property and pays surplus profits to Church schemes. It is authorised and regulated by the Financial Services Authority. The company can also arrange household insurance for members and adherents of the Church of Scotland. At 67 George Street, Edinburgh EH2 2JG (Tel: 0131-220 4119; Fax: 0131-220 4120; E-mail: enquiries@cosic.co.uk).

CHURCH OF SCOTLAND MINISTRY BENEVOLENT FUND: Makes grants to retired men and women who have been ordained or commissioned for the ministry of the Church of Scotland and to widows, widowers, orphans, spouses or children of such, who are in need. Apply to the Assistant Treasurer (Ministries), 121 George Street, Edinburgh EH2 4YN (Tel: 0131-225 5722).

CLARK BURSARY: Awarded to accepted candidate(s) for the ministry of the Church of Scotland whose studies for the ministry are pursued at the University of Aberdeen. Applications or recommendations for the Bursary to the Clerk to the Presbytery of Aberdeen, Mastrick Church, Greenfern Road, Aberdeen AB16 6TR by 16 October annually.

CRAIGCROOK MORTIFICATION:
Clerk and Factor: Mrs Fiona M.M. Watson CA
                                                          17 Melville Street
                                                          Edinburgh EH3 7PH (Tel: 0131-473 3500;
                                                          E-mail: charity@scott-moncrieff.com)

Pensions are paid to poor men and women over 60 years old, born in Scotland or who have resided in Scotland for not less than ten years. At present, pensions amount to £1,000–£1,500 p.a.
    Ministers are invited to notify the Clerk and Factor of deserving persons and should be prepared to act as a referee on the application form.

THE ALASTAIR CRERAR TRUST FOR SINGLE POOR: Provides churches, Christian organisations and individual Christians with grants to help single adults and groups of single people, who live on low incomes and have little capital, to improve their quality of life. Apply to the Secretary, James D. Crerar, 1 Beechwood Mains, Edinburgh EH12 6XN (Tel: 0131-337 3831; E-mail: jandvcrerar@yahoo.com).

CROMBIE SCHOLARSHIP: Provides grants annually on the nomination of the Deans of Faculty of Divinity of the Universities of St Andrews, Glasgow, Aberdeen and Edinburgh, who each nominate one matriculated student who has taken a University course in Greek (Classical or Hellenistic) and Hebrew. Award by recommendation only.

THE DRUMMOND TRUST: Makes grants towards the cost of publication of books of 'sound Christian doctrine and outreach'. The Trustees are also willing to receive grant requests towards the cost of audio-visual programme material, but not equipment. Requests for application forms should be made to the Secretaries, Hill and Robb, 3 Pitt Terrace, Stirling FK8 2EY (Tel: 01786 450985; E-mail: douglaswhyte@hillandrobb.co.uk). Manuscripts should *not* be sent.

THE DUNCAN TRUST: Makes grants annually to students for the ministry in the Faculties of Arts and Divinity. Preference is given to those born or educated within the bounds of the former Presbytery of Arbroath. Applications not later than 31 October to G.J.M. Dunlop, Brothockbank House, Arbroath DD11 1NE (Tel: 01241 872683).

FERGUSON BEQUEST FUND: For the maintenance and promotion of religious ordinances and education and missionary operations in the first instance in the Counties of Ayr, Kirkcudbright, Wigtown, Lanark, Renfrew and Dunbarton. Apply to Ronald D. Oakes CA ACMA, 182 Bath Street, Glasgow G2 4HG (Tel: 0141-332 0476; Fax: 0141-331 0874).

GEIKIE BEQUEST: Makes small grants to students for the ministry, including students studying for entry to the University, preference being given to those not eligible for SAAS awards. Apply to the Assistant Treasurer (Ministries), 121 George Street, Edinburgh EH2 4YN by September for distribution in November each year.

JAMES GILLAN'S BURSARY FUND: Bursaries are available for students for the ministry who were born or whose parents or parent have resided and had their home for not less than three years continually in the old counties (not Districts) of Moray or Nairn. Apply to R. and R. Urquhart, 117–121 High Street, Forres IV36 1AB.

HAMILTON BURSARY TRUST: Awarded, subject to the intention to serve overseas under the Church of Scotland World Mission Council or to serve with some other Overseas Mission Agency approved by the Council, to a student at the University of Aberdeen. Preference is given to a student born or residing in (1) Parish of Skene, (2) Parish of Echt, (3) the Presbytery of Aberdeen, Kincardine and Deeside, or Gordon; failing which to Accepted Candidate(s) for the Ministry of the Church of Scotland whose studies for the Ministry are pursued at Aberdeen University. Applications or recommendations for the Bursary to the Clerk to the Presbytery of Aberdeen by 16 October annually.

MARTIN HARCUS BEQUEST: Makes annual grants to candidates for the ministry resident within the City of Edinburgh. Applications to the Clerk to the Presbytery of Edinburgh, 10/1 Palmerston Place, Edinburgh EH12 5AA by 15 October (E-mail: edinburgh@cofscotland.org.uk).

THE HOPE TRUST: Gives some support to organisations involved in combating drink and drugs, and has as its main purpose the promotion of the Reformed Faith throughout the world. There is also a Scholarship programme for Postgraduate Theology Study in Scotland. Apply to Robert P. Miller SSC LLB, 31 Moray Place, Edinburgh EH3 6BY (Tel: 0131-226 5151).

KEAY THOM TRUST: The principal purposes of the Keay Thom Trust are:
1. To benefit the widows, daughters or other dependent female relatives of deceased ministers, or wives of ministers who are now divorced or separated, all of whom have supported the minister in the fulfilment of his duties and who, by reason of death, divorce or separation, have been required to leave the manse. The Trust can assist them in the purchase of a house or by providing financial or material assistance whether it be for the provision of accommodation or not.
2. To assist in the education or training of the above female relatives or any other children of deceased ministers.
Further information and application forms are available from Miller Hendry, Solicitors, 10 Blackfriars Street, Perth PH1 5NS (Tel: 01738 637311).

GILLIAN MACLAINE BURSARY FUND: Open to candidates for the ministry of the Church of Scotland of Scottish or Canadian nationality. Preference is given to Gaelic-speakers. Information and terms of award from Rev. George G. Cringles BD, Depute Clerk of the Presbytery of Argyll, St Oran's Manse, Connel, Oban PA37 1PJ.

THE E. McLAREN FUND: The persons intended to be benefited are widows and unmarried ladies, preference being given to ladies above 40 years of age in the following order:
(a) Widows and daughters of Officers in the Highland Regiment, and
(b) Widows and daughters of Scotsmen.
Further details from the Secretary, The E. McLaren Fund, 90 St Vincent Street, Glasgow G2 5UB (Tel: 0141-221 8004; Fax: 0141-221 8088; E-mail: rrs@bmkwilson.co.uk).

THE MISSES ANN AND MARGARET McMILLAN'S BEQUEST: Makes grants to ministers of the Free and United Free Churches, and of the Church of Scotland, in charges within the Synod of Argyll, with income not exceeding the minimum stipend of the Church of Scotland. Apply by 30 June in each year to Rev. Samuel McC. Harris, Trinity Manse, 12 Crichton Road, Rothesay, Isle of Bute PA20 9JR.

MORGAN BURSARY FUND: Makes grants to candidates for the Church of Scotland ministry studying at the University of Glasgow. Apply to Rev. Dr Angus Kerr, 260 Bath Street, Glasgow G2 4JP (Tel/Fax: 0141-332 6606).

NOVUM TRUST: Provides small short-term grants – typically between £200 and £2,500 – to initiate projects in Christian research and action which cannot readily be financed from other sources. Special consideration is given to proposals aimed at the welfare of young people, investment in training, new ways of communicating the faith, and work in association with overseas churches or on behalf of immigrants in Scotland. The Trust cannot support large building projects or individuals applying for maintenance during courses or training. Application forms and guidance notes from Rev. Alex. M. Millar, 121 George Street, Edinburgh EH2 4YN (E-mail: amillar@cofscotland.org.uk).

PARK MEMORIAL BURSARY FUND: Provides grants for the benefit of candidates for the ministry of the Church of Scotland from the Presbytery of Glasgow under full-time training. Apply to Rev. Dr Angus Kerr, Presbytery of Glasgow, 260 Bath Street, Glasgow G2 4JP (Tel: 0141-332 6606).

PATON TRUST: Assists ministers in ill health to have a recuperative holiday outwith, and free from the cares of, their parishes. Apply to Alan S. Cunningham CA, Alexander Sloan, Chartered Accountants, 144 West George Street, Glasgow G2 2HG (Tel: 0141-354 0354; Fax: 0141-354 0355; E-mail: alan.cunningham@alexandersloan.co.uk).

RENFIELD STREET TRUST: Assists in the building and repair of churches and halls. Apply to Ronald D. Oakes CA ACMA, 182 Bath Street, Glasgow G2 4HG (Tel: 0141-332 0476; Fax: 0141-331 0874; E-mail: renfieldsttrust@btconnect.com).

SCOTTISH CHURCHES ARCHITECTURAL HERITAGE TRUST: Assists congregations of any denomination in the preservation of the fabric of buildings in regular use for public worship. Apply to the Grants Administrator, Scottish Churches Architectural Heritage Trust, 15 North Bank Street, The Mound, Edinburgh EH1 2LP (Tel: 0131-225 8644; E-mail: info@scaht.org.uk).

MISS M.E. SWINTON PATERSON'S CHARITABLE TRUST: The Trust can give modest grants to support smaller congregations in urban or rural areas who require to fund essential maintenance or improvement works at their buildings. Apply to Mr Callum S. Kennedy WS, Messrs Lindsays WS, Caledonian Exchange, 19A Canning Street, Edinburgh EH3 8HE (Tel: 0131-229 1212).

SMIETON FUND: Makes small holiday grants to ministers. Administered at the discretion of the pastoral staff, who will give priority in cases of need. Applications to the Associate Secretary (Support and Development), Ministries Council, 121 George Street, Edinburgh EH2 4YN.

MARY DAVIDSON SMITH CLERICAL AND EDUCATIONAL FUND FOR ABERDEENSHIRE: Assists ministers who have been ordained for five years or over and are in full charge of a congregation in Aberdeen, Aberdeenshire and the north, to purchase books, or to travel for educational purposes, and assists their children with scholarships for further education or vocational training. Apply to Alan J. Innes MA LLB, 100 Union Street, Aberdeen AB10 1QR.

THE NAN STEVENSON CHARITABLE TRUST FOR RETIRED MINISTERS: Provides houses, or loans to purchase houses, for retired ministers or missionaries on similar terms to the Housing and Loan Fund, with preference given to those with a North Ayrshire connection. Secretary: Alan K. Saunderson, 17 Union Street, Largs KA30 8DG.

PRESBYTERY OF ARGYLL BURSARY FUND: Open to students who have been accepted as candidates for the ministry and the readership of the Church of Scotland. Preference is given to applicants who are natives of the bounds of the Presbytery, or are resident within the bounds of the Presbytery, or who have a strong connection with the bounds of the Presbytery. Information and terms of award from Rev. George G. Cringles BD, Depute Clerk of the Presbytery of Argyll, St Oran's Manse, Connel, Oban PA37 1PJ.

SYNOD OF GRAMPIAN CHILDREN OF THE CLERGY FUND: Makes annual grants to children of deceased ministers. Apply to Rev. Iain U. Thomson, Clerk and Treasurer, The Manse, Skene, Westhill AB32 6LX.

SYNOD OF GRAMPIAN WIDOWS FUND: Makes annual grants (currently £225 p.a.) to widows or widowers of deceased ministers who have served in a charge in the former Synod. Apply to Rev. Iain U. Thomson, Clerk and Treasurer, The Manse, Skene, Westhill AB32 6LX.

YOUNG MINISTERS' FURNISHING LOAN FUND: Makes loans (of £1,000) to ministers in their first charge to assist with furnishing the manse. Apply to the Assistant Treasurer (Ministries), 121 George Street, Edinburgh EH2 4YN.

---

(6) RECENT LORD HIGH COMMISSIONERS
TO THE GENERAL ASSEMBLY

1967/68	The Rt Hon. Lord Reith of Stonehaven GCVO GBE CB TD
1969	Her Majesty the Queen attended in person
1970	The Rt Hon. Margaret Herbison PC
1971/72	The Rt Hon. Lord Clydesmuir of Braidwood CB MBE TD
1973/74	The Rt Hon. Lord Ballantrae of Auchairne and the Bay of Islands GCMG GCVO DSO OBE
1975/76	Sir Hector MacLennan KT FRCPGLAS FRCOG
1977	Francis David Charteris, Earl of Wemyss and March KT LLD
1978/79	The Rt Hon. William Ross MBE LLD
1980/81	Andrew Douglas Alexander Thomas Bruce, Earl of Elgin and Kincardine KT DL JP
1982/83	Colonel Sir John Edward Gilmour BT DSO TD
1984/85	Charles Hector Fitzroy Maclean, Baron Maclean of Duart and Morvern KT GCVO KBE

1986/87	John Campbell Arbuthnott, Viscount of Arbuthnott KT CBE DSC FRSE FRSA
1988/89	Sir Iain Mark Tennant KT FRSA
1990/91	The Rt Hon. Donald MacArthur Ross FRSE
1992/93	The Rt Hon. Lord Macfarlane of Bearsden KT FRSE
1994/95	Lady Marion Fraser LT
1996	Her Royal Highness the Princess Royal LT LG GCVO
1997	The Rt Hon. Lord Macfarlane of Bearsden KT FRSE
1998/99	The Rt Hon. Lord Hogg of Cumbernauld
2000	His Royal Highness the Prince Charles, Duke of Rothesay KG KT GCB OM
2001/02	The Rt Hon. Viscount Younger of Leckie
	Her Majesty the Queen attended the opening of the General Assembly of 2002
2003/04	The Rt Hon. Lord Steel of Aikwood KT KBE
2005/06	The Rt Hon. Lord Mackay of Clashfern KT
2007	His Royal Highness the Prince Andrew, Duke of York KG KCVO
2008	The Rt Hon. George Reid MA

(7) RECENT MODERATORS
OF THE GENERAL ASSEMBLY

1967	W. Roy Sanderson DD, Stenton with Whittingehame
1968	J.B. Longmuir TD DD, Principal Clerk of Assembly
1969	T.M. Murchison MA DD, Glasgow: St Columba Summertown
1970	Hugh O. Douglas CBE DD LLD, Dundee: St Mary's
1971	Andrew Herron MA BD LLB LLD DD, Clerk to the Presbytery of Glasgow
1972	R.W.V. Selby Wright JP CVO TD DD FRSE, Edinburgh: Canongate
1973	George T.H. Reid MC MA BD DD, Aberdeen: Langstane
1974	David Steel MA BD DD, Linlithgow: St Michael's
1975	James G. Matheson MA BD DD, Portree
1976	Thomas F. Torrance MBE DLitt DD FRSE, University of Edinburgh
1977	John R. Gray VRD MA BD ThM DD, Dunblane: Cathedral
1978	Peter P. Brodie MA BD LLB DD, Alloa: St Mungo's
1979	Robert A.S. Barbour KCVO MC MA BD STM DD, University of Aberdeen
1980	William B. Johnston MA BD DD DLitt, Edinburgh: Colinton
1981	Andrew B. Doig BD STM DD, National Bible Society of Scotland
1982	John McIntyre CVO DD DLitt FRSE, University of Edinburgh
1983	J. Fraser McLuskey MC DD, London: St Columba's
1984	John M.K. Paterson MA ACII BD DD, Milngavie: St Paul's
1985	David M.B.A. Smith MA BD DUniv, Logie
1986	Robert Craig CBE DLitt LLD DD, Emeritus of Jerusalem
1987	Duncan Shaw *Bundesverdienstkreuz* Drhc PhD ThDr JP, Edinburgh: Craigentinny St Christopher's
1988	James A. Whyte MA LLD DUniv DD, University of St Andrews
1989	William J.G. McDonald MA BD DD, Edinburgh: Mayfield
1990	Robert Davidson MA BD DD FRSE, University of Glasgow
1991	William B.R. Macmillan MA BD LLD DD, Dundee: St Mary's
1992	Hugh R. Wyllie MA MCIBS DD FCIBS, Hamilton: Old Parish Church
1993	James L. Weatherhead CBE MA LLB DD, Principal Clerk of Assembly

1994	James A. Simpson BSc BD STM DD, Dornoch Cathedral
1995	James Harkness KCVO CB OBE MA DD, Chaplain General (Emeritus)
1996	John H. McIndoe MA BD STM DD, London: St Columba's linked with Newcastle: St Andrew's
1997	Alexander McDonald BA CMIWSc DUniv, General Secretary, Department of Ministry
1998	Alan Main TD MA BD STM PhD DD, Professor of Practical Theology at Christ's College, University of Aberdeen
1999	John B. Cairns LTh LLB LLD DD, Dumbarton: Riverside
2000	Andrew R.C. McLellan MA BD STM DD, Edinburgh: St Andrew's and St George's
2001	John D. Miller BA BD DD, Glasgow: Castlemilk East
2002	Finlay A.J. Macdonald MA BD PhD DD, Principal Clerk of Assembly
2003	Iain R. Torrance TD DPhil DD DTheol LHD CorrFRSE, University of Aberdeen
2004	Alison Elliot OBE MA MSc PhD LLD DD FRSE, Associate Director CTPI
2005	David W. Lacy BA BD DLitt, Kilmarnock: Henderson
2006	Alan D. McDonald LLB BD MTh DLitt DD, Cameron linked with St Andrews: St Leonard's
2007	Sheilagh M. Kesting BA BD DD, Secretary of Ecumenical Relations Committee
2008	David W. Lunan MA BD, Clerk to the Presbytery of Glasgow

---

MATTER OF PRECEDENCE

The Lord High Commissioner to the General Assembly of the Church of Scotland (while the Assembly is sitting) ranks next to the Sovereign and the Duke of Edinburgh and before the rest of the Royal Family.

The Moderator of the General Assembly of the Church of Scotland ranks next to the Lord Chancellor of Great Britain and before the Prime Minister and the Dukes.

---

(8) HER MAJESTY'S HOUSEHOLD IN SCOTLAND
ECCLESIASTICAL

Dean of the Chapel Royal: Very Rev. John B. Cairns LTh LLB LLD DD
Dean of the Order of the Thistle: Very Rev. Gilleasbuig Macmillan
CVO MA BD Drhc DD

Domestic Chaplains: Rev. Kenneth I. Mackenzie BD CPS
Rev. Neil N. Gardner MA BD

Chaplains in Ordinary: Very Rev. Gilleasbuig Macmillan
CVO MA BD Drhc DD
Rev. Charles Robertson MA JP
Rev. Norman W. Drummond MA BD

Rev. Alastair H. Symington MA BD
Very Rev. Prof. Iain R. Torrance
       TD DPhil DD DTheol LHD CorrFRSE
Very Rev. Finlay A.J. Macdonald
       MA BD PhD DD
Rev. James M. Gibson TD LTh LRAM
Rev. Angus Morrison MA BD PhD
Rev. E. Lorna Hood MA BD

Extra Chaplains:

Rev. Kenneth MacVicar MBE DFC TD MA
Very Rev. Prof. Robert A.S. Barbour
       KCVO MC BD STM DD
Rev. Alwyn Macfarlane MA
Rev. Mary I. Levison BA BD DD
Very Rev. William J. Morris KCVO PhD LLD DD JP
Rev. John MacLeod MA
Rev. A. Stewart Todd MA BD DD
Very Rev. James L. Weatherhead CBE MA LLB DD
Rev. Maxwell D. Craig MA BD ThM
Very Rev. James A. Simpson BSc BD STM DD
Very Rev. James Harkness
       KCVO CB OBE MA DD
Rev. John L. Paterson MA BD STM

(9) LONG SERVICE CERTIFICATES

Long Service Certificates, signed by the Moderator, are available for presentation to elders and others in respect of not less than thirty years of service. It should be noted that the period is years of *service*, not (for example) years of ordination in the case of an elder.

In the case of Sunday School teachers and Bible Class leaders, the qualifying period is twenty-one years of service.

Certificates are not issued posthumously, nor is it possible to make exceptions to the rules, for example by recognising quality of service in order to reduce the qualifying period, or by reducing the qualifying period on compassionate grounds, such as serious illness.

A Certificate will be issued only once to any particular individual.

Applications for Long Service Certificates should be made in writing to the Principal Clerk at 121 George Street, Edinburgh EH2 4YN by the parish minister, or by the session clerk on behalf of the Kirk Session. Certificates are not issued from this office to the individual recipients, nor should individuals make application themselves.

(10) LIBRARIES OF THE CHURCH

GENERAL ASSEMBLY LIBRARY AND RECORD ROOM
Most of the books contained in the General Assembly Library have been transferred to the New College Library. Records of the General Assembly, Synods, Presbyteries and Kirk Sessions are now in HM Register House, Edinburgh.

CHURCH MUSIC
The Library of New College contains a selection of works on Church music.

---

(11) RECORDS OF THE CHURCH OF SCOTLAND

Church records more than fifty years old, unless still in use, should be sent or delivered to the Principal Clerk for onward transmission to the Scottish Record Office. Where ministers or session clerks are approached by a local repository seeking a transfer of their records, they should inform the Principal Clerk, who will take the matter up with the National Archives of Scotland.

Where a temporary retransmission of records is sought, it is extremely helpful if notice can be given three months in advance so that appropriate procedures can be carried out satisfactorily.

SECTION 3

Church Procedure

(1) THE MINISTER AND BAPTISM

The administration of Baptism to infants is governed by Act V 2000 as amended by Act IX 2003. A Statement and Exposition of the Doctrine of Baptism may be found at page 13/8 in the published volume of Reports to the General Assembly of 2003.

The Act itself is as follows:

3.   Baptism signifies the action and love of God in Christ, through the Holy Spirit, and is a seal upon the gift of grace and the response of faith.
   (a)   Baptism shall be administered in the name of the Father and of the Son and of the Holy Spirit, with water, by sprinkling, pouring, or immersion.
   (b)   Baptism shall be administered to a person only once.
4.   Baptism may be administered to a person upon profession of faith.
   (a)   The minister and Kirk Session shall judge whether the person is of sufficient maturity to make personal profession of faith, where necessary in consultation with the parent(s) or legal guardian(s).
   (b)   Baptism may be administered only after the person has received such instruction in its meaning as the minister and Kirk Session consider necessary, according to such basis of instruction as may be authorised by the General Assembly.
   (c)   In cases of uncertainty as to whether a person has been baptised or validly baptised, baptism shall be administered conditionally.
5.   Baptism may be administered to a person with learning difficulties who makes an appropriate profession of faith, where the minister and Kirk Session are satisfied that the person shall be nurtured within the life and worship of the Church.
6.   Baptism may be administered to a child:
   (a)   where at least one parent, or other family member (with parental consent), having been baptised and being on the communion roll of the congregation, will undertake the Christian upbringing of the child;
   (b)   where at least one parent, or other family member (with parental consent), having been baptised but not on the communion roll of the congregation, satisfies the minister and Kirk Session that he or she is an adherent of the congregation and will undertake the Christian upbringing of the child;
   (c)   where at least one parent, or other family member (with parental consent), having been baptised, professes the Christian faith, undertakes to ensure that the child grows up in the life and worship of the Church and expresses the desire to seek admission to the communion roll of the congregation;
   (d)   where the child is under legal guardianship, and the minister and Kirk Session are satisfied that the child shall be nurtured within the life and worship of the congregation;
   and, in each of the above cases, only after the parent(s), or other family member, has received such instruction in its meaning as the minister and Kirk Session consider necessary, according to such basis of instruction as may be authorised by the General Assembly.
7.   Baptism shall normally be administered during the public worship of the congregation in which the person makes profession of faith, or of which the parent or other family member is on the communion roll, or is an adherent. In exceptional circumstances, baptism may be administered elsewhere (e.g. at home or in hospital). Further, a minister may administer baptism to a person resident outwith the minister's parish, and who is not otherwise

connected with the congregation, only with the consent of the minister of the parish in which the person would normally reside, or of the Presbytery.

8. In all cases, an entry shall be made in the Kirk Session's Baptismal Register and a Certificate of Baptism given by the minister. Where baptism is administered in a chaplaincy context, it shall be recorded in the Baptismal Register there, and, where possible, reported to the minister of the parish in which the person resides.

9. Baptism shall normally be administered by an ordained minister. In situations of emergency,

   (a) a minister may, exceptionally, notwithstanding the preceding provisions of the Act, respond to a request for baptism in accordance with his or her pastoral judgement, and

   (b) baptism may be validly administered by a person who is not ordained, always providing that it is administered in the name of the Father and of the Son and of the Holy Spirit, with water.

   In every occurrence of the latter case, of which a minister or chaplain becomes aware, an entry shall be made in the appropriate Baptismal Register and where possible reported to the Clerk of the Presbytery within which the baptism was administered.

10. Each Presbytery shall form, or designate, a committee to which reference may be made in cases where there is a dispute as to the interpretation of this Act. Without the consent of the Presbytery, no minister may administer baptism in a case where to his or her knowledge another minister has declined to do so.

11. The Church of Scotland, as part of the Universal Church, affirms the validity of the sacrament of baptism administered in the name of the Father and of the Son and of the Holy Spirit, with water, in accordance with the discipline of other members of the Universal Church.

---

(2) THE MINISTER AND MARRIAGE

1. BACKGROUND

Prior to 1939, every marriage in Scotland fell into one or other of two classes: regular or irregular. The former was marriage by a minister of religion after due notice of intention had been given; the latter could be effected in one of three ways: (1) declaration *de presenti*, (2) by promise *subsequente copula*, or (3) by co-habitation with habit and repute.

The Marriage (Scotland) Act of 1939 put an end to (1) and (2) and provided for a new classification of marriage as either religious or civil. Marriage by co-habitation with habit and repute was abolished by the Family Law (Scotland) Act 2006.

The law of marriage as it was thus established in 1939 had two important limitations to the celebration of marriage: (1) certain preliminaries had to be observed; and (2) in respect of religious marriage, the service had to be conducted according to the forms of either the Christian or the Jewish faith.

2. THE MARRIAGE (SCOTLAND) ACT 1977

These two conditions were radically altered by the Marriage (Scotland) Act 1977.

Since 1 January 1978, in conformity with the demands of a multi-racial society, the benefits of religious marriage have been extended to adherents of other faiths, the only requirements being the observance of monogamy and the satisfaction of the authorities with the forms of the vows imposed.

Since 1978, the calling of banns has also been discontinued. The couple themselves must each complete a Marriage Notice form and return this to the District Registrar for the area in which they are to be married, irrespective of where they live, at least fifteen days before the ceremony is due to take place. The form details the documents which require to be produced with it.

If everything is in order, the District Registrar will issue, not more than seven days before the date of the ceremony, a Marriage Schedule. This must be in the hands of the minister officiating at the marriage ceremony before the service begins. Under no circumstances must the minister deviate from this rule. To do so is an offence under the Act.

Ministers should note the advice given by the Procurator of the Church in 1962, that they should not officiate at any marriage until at least one day after the 16th birthday of the younger party.

3. THE MARRIAGE (SCOTLAND) ACT 2002

Although there have never been any limitations as to the place where a religious marriage can be celebrated, civil marriage originally could take place only in the Office of a Registrar. The Marriage (Scotland) Act 2002 permits the solemnisation of civil marriages at places approved by Local Authorities. Regulations have been made to specify the kinds of place which may be 'approved' with a view to ensuring that the places approved will not compromise the solemnity and dignity of civil marriage and will have no recent or continuing connection with any religion so as to undermine the distinction between religious and civil ceremonies.

4. PROCLAMATION OF BANNS

Proclamation of banns is no longer required in Scotland; but, in the Church of England, marriage is governed by the provisions of the Marriage Act 1949, which requires that the parties' intention to marry has to have been proclaimed and which provides that in the case of a party residing in Scotland a Certificate of Proclamation given according to the law or custom prevailing in Scotland shall be sufficient for the purpose. In the event that a minister is asked to call banns for a person resident within the registration district where his or her church is situated, the proclamation needs only to be made on one Sunday if the parties are known to the minister. If they are not, it should be made on two Sundays. In all cases, the Minister should, of course, have no reason to believe that there is any impediment to the marriage.

Proclamation should be made at the principal service of worship in this form:

There is a purpose of marriage between AB (Bachelor/Widower/Divorced), residing at .... in this Registration District, and CD (Spinster/Widow/Divorced), residing at .... in the Registration District of ...., of which proclamation is hereby made for the first and only (second and last) time.

Immediately after the second reading, or not less than forty-eight hours after the first and only reading, a Certificate of Proclamation signed by either the minister or the Session Clerk should be issued in the following terms:

At .... the ...... day of ...... 20 ....
It is hereby certified that AB, residing at ...., and CD, residing at ...., have been duly proclaimed in order to marriage in the Church of .... according to the custom of the Church of Scotland, and that no objections have been offered.
Signed .... minister or
Signed .... Session Clerk

5. MARRIAGE OF FOREIGNERS

Marriages in Scotland of foreigners, or of foreigners with British subjects, are, if they satisfy the requirements of Scots Law, valid within the United Kingdom and the various British overseas territories; but they will not necessarily be valid in the country to which the foreigner belongs. This will be so only if the requirements of the law of his or her country have also been complied with. It is therefore most important that, before the marriage, steps should be taken to obtain from the Consul, or other diplomatic representative of the country concerned, a satisfactory assurance that the marriage will be accepted as valid in the country concerned.

6. REMARRIAGE OF DIVORCED PERSONS

By virtue of Act XXVI 1959, a minister of the Church of Scotland may lawfully solemnise the marriage of a person whose former marriage has been dissolved by divorce and whose former spouse is still alive. The minister, however, must carefully adhere to the requirements of the Act which, as slightly altered in 1985, are briefly as follows:

1. The minister should not accede as a matter of routine to a request to solemnise such a marriage. To enable a decision to be made, he or she should take all reasonable steps to obtain relevant information, which should normally include the following:

    (a) Adequate information concerning the life and character of the parties. The Act enjoins the greatest caution in cases where no pastoral relationship exists between the minister and either or both of the parties concerned.

    (b) The grounds and circumstances of the divorce case.

    (c) Facts bearing upon the future well-being of any children concerned.

    (d) Whether any other minister has declined to solemnise the proposed marriage.

    (e) The denomination to which the parties belong. The Act enjoins that special care should be taken where one or more parties belong to a denomination whose discipline in this matter may differ from that of the Church of Scotland.

2. The minister should consider whether there is danger of scandal arising if he or she should solemnise the remarriage, at the same time taking into careful consideration before refusing to do so the moral and spiritual effect of a refusal on the parties concerned.

3. As a determinative factor, the minister should do all he or she can to be assured that there has been sincere repentance where guilt has existed on the part of any divorced person seeking remarriage. He or she should also give instruction, where needed, in the nature and requirements of a Christian marriage.

4. A minister is not required to solemnise a remarriage against his or her conscience. Every Presbytery is required to appoint certain individuals with one of whom ministers in doubt as to the correct course of action may consult if they so desire. The final decision, however, rests with the minister who has been asked to officiate.

---

(3) CONDUCT OF MARRIAGE SERVICES
(CODE OF GOOD PRACTICE)

The code which follows was submitted to the General Assembly in 1997. It appears, on page 1/10, in the Volume of Assembly Reports for that year within the Report of the Board of Practice and Procedure.

1. *Marriage in the Church of Scotland is solemnised by an ordained minister in a religious ceremony wherein, before God, and in the presence of the minister and at least two competent witnesses, the parties covenant together to take each other as husband and wife as long as they both shall live, and the minister declares the parties to be husband and wife. Before solemnising a marriage, a minister must be assured that the necessary legal requirements are being complied with and that the parties know of no legal impediment to their marriage, and he or she must afterwards ensure that the Marriage Schedule is duly completed.* (Act I 1977)

2. Any ordained minister of the Church of Scotland who is a member of Presbytery or who holds a current Ministerial Certificate may officiate at a marriage service (see Act II 1987).

3. While the marriage service should normally take place in church, a minister may, at his or her discretion, officiate at a marriage service outwith church premises. Wherever conducted, the ceremony will be such as to reflect appropriately both the joy and the solemnity of the occasion. In particular, a minister shall ensure that nothing is done which would bring the Church and its teaching into disrepute.

4. A minister agreeing to conduct a wedding should endeavour to establish a pastoral relationship with the couple within which adequate pre-marriage preparation and subsequent pastoral care may be given.

5. 'A minister should not refuse to perform ministerial functions for a person who is resident in his or her parish without sufficient reason' (Cox, *Practice and Procedure in the Church of Scotland*, sixth edition, page 55). Where either party to the proposed marriage has been divorced and the former spouse is still alive, the minister invited to officiate may solemnise such a marriage, having regard to the guidelines in the Act anent the Remarriage of Divorced Persons (Act XXVI 1959 as amended by Act II 1985).

6. A minister is acting as an agent of the National Church which is committed to bringing the ordinances of religion to the people of Scotland through a territorial ministry. As such, he or she shall not be entitled to charge a fee or allow a fee to be charged for conducting a marriage service. When a gift is spontaneously offered to a minister as a token of appreciation, the above consideration should not be taken to mean that he or she should not accept such an unsolicited gift. The Financial Board of a congregation is at liberty to set fees to cover such costs as heat and light, and in addition Organists and Church Officers are entitled to a fee in respect of their services at weddings.

7. A minister should not allow his or her name to be associated with any commercial enterprise that provides facilities for weddings.

8. A minister is not at liberty to enter the bounds of another minister's parish to perform ministerial functions without the previous consent of the minister of that parish. In terms of Act VIII 1933, a minister may 'officiate at a marriage or funeral by private invitation', but, for the avoidance of doubt, an invitation conveyed through a commercial enterprise shall not be regarded as a 'private invitation' within the meaning of that Act.

9. A minister invited to officiate at a Marriage Service where neither party is a member of his or her congregation or is resident within his or her own parish or has any connection with the parish within which the service is to take place should observe the following courtesies:
    (a) he or she should ascertain from the parties whether either of them has a Church of Scotland connection or has approached the appropriate parish minister(s);
    (b) if it transpires that a ministerial colleague has declined to officiate, then he or she (the invited minister) should ascertain the reasons therefor and shall take these and all other relevant factors into account in deciding whether or not to officiate.

(4) CONDUCT OF FUNERAL SERVICES: FEES

The General Assembly of 2007 received the Report of the Legal Questions Committee which included a statement regarding fees for funerals. That statement had been prepared in the light of approaches from two Presbyteries seeking guidance on the question of the charging of fees (on behalf of ministers) for the conduct of funerals. It had seemed to the Presbyteries that expectations and practice were unacceptably varied across the country, and that the question was complicated by the fact that, quite naturally and legitimately, ministers other than parish ministers occasionally conduct funeral services.

The full text of that statement was engrossed in the Minutes of the General Assembly, and it was felt that it would be helpful to include it also in the *Year Book*.

The statement
The (Legal Questions) Committee believes that the question is two-fold, relating firstly to parish ministers (including associate and assistant ministers, deacons and the like) within their regular ministry, and secondly to ministers and others taking an occasional funeral, for instance by private invitation or in the course of pastoral cover of another parish.

Ministers in receipt of a living
The Committee believes that the position of the minister of a parish, and of other paid staff on the ministry team of a parish, is clear. The Third Declaratory Article affirms the responsibility of the Church of Scotland to provide the ordinances of religion through its territorial ministry, while the stipend system (and, for other staff members, the salary) provides a living that enables that ministry to be exercised without charging fees for services conducted. The implication of this principle is that no family in Scotland should ever be charged for the services of a Church of Scotland minister at the time of bereavement. Clearly, therefore, no minister in receipt of a living should be charging separately (effectively being paid doubly) for any such service. The Committee is conscious that the position of congregations outside Scotland may be different, and is aware that the relevant Presbyteries will offer appropriate superintendence of these matters.

A related question is raised about the highly varied culture of gift-giving in different parts of the country. The Committee believes it would be unwise to seek to regulate this. In some places, an attempt to quash a universal and long-established practice would seem ungracious, while in other places there is no such practice, and encouragement in that direction would seem indelicate.

A second related question was raised about Funeral Directors charging for the services of the minister. The Committee believes that Presbyteries should make it clear to Funeral Directors that, in the case of Church of Scotland funerals, such a charge should not be made.

Ministers conducting occasional services
Turning to the position of ministers who do not receive a living that enables them to conduct funerals without charge, the Committee's starting point is the principle articulated above that no bereaved person should have to pay for the services of a minister. The territorial ministry and the parish system of this Church mean that a bereaved family should not find itself being contingently charged because the parish minister happens to be unavailable, or because the parish is vacant.

Where a funeral is being conducted as part of the ministry of the local parish, but where for any reason another minister is taking it and not otherwise being paid, it is the responsibility of the congregation (through its financial body) to ensure that appropriate fees and expenses are met.

Where that imposes a financial burden upon a congregation because of the weight of pastoral need, the need should be taken into account in calculating the resource-needs of that parish in the course of updating the Presbytery Plan.

It is beyond the remit of the Legal Questions Committee to make judgements about the appropriate level of payment. The Committee suggests that the Ministries Council should give the relevant advice on this aspect of the issue.

The Committee believes that these principles could be applied to the conduct of weddings and are perfectly compatible with the Guidelines on that subject which are reproduced in the *Year Book* at item 3 of section 3 dealing with Church Procedure.

(5) THE MINISTER AND WILLS

The Requirements of Writing (Scotland) Act 1995, which came into force on 1 August 1995, has removed the power of a minister to execute wills notarially. Further clarification, if required, may be obtained from the Solicitor of the Church.

(6) PROCEDURE IN A VACANCY

Procedure in a vacancy is regulated by Act VIII 2003 as amended by Acts IX and X 2004, II 2005, V 2006 and I and VI 2008. The text of the most immediately relevant sections is given here for general information. Schedules of Intimation referred to are also included. The full text of the Act and subsequent amendments can be obtained from the Principal Clerk.

1. Vacancy Procedure Committee

(1)   Each Presbytery shall appoint a number of its members to be available to serve on Vacancy Procedure Committees and shall provide information and training as required for those so appointed.

(2)   As soon as the Presbytery Clerk is aware that a vacancy has arisen or is anticipated, he or she shall consult the Moderator of the Presbytery and they shall appoint a Vacancy Procedure Committee of five persons from among those appointed in terms of subsection (1), which Committee shall (a) include at least one minister and at least one elder and (b) exclude any communicant member or former minister of the vacant charge or of any constituent congregation thereof. The Vacancy Procedure Committee shall include a Convener and Clerk, the latter of whom need not be a member of the Committee but may be the Presbytery Clerk. The same Vacancy Procedure Committee may serve for more than one vacancy at a time.

(3)   The Vacancy Procedure Committee shall have a quorum of three for its meetings.

(4)   The Convener of the Vacancy Procedure Committee may, where he or she reasonably believes a matter to be non-contentious, consult members individually, provided that reasonable efforts are made to consult all members of the Committee. A meeting shall be held at the request of any member of the Committee.

(5)   Every decision made by the Vacancy Procedure Committee shall be reported to the next meeting of Presbytery, but may not be recalled by Presbytery where the decision was subject to the provisions of section 2 below.

2. Request for Consideration by Presbytery

Where in this Act any decision by the Vacancy Procedure Committee is subject to the provisions of this section, the following rules shall apply:

(1)   The Presbytery Clerk shall intimate to all members of the Presbytery by mailing or at a Presbytery meeting the course of action or permission proposed, and shall arrange for one Sunday's pulpit intimation of the same to be made to the congregation or congregations concerned, in terms of Schedule A. The intimation having been made, it shall be displayed as prominently as possible at the church building for seven days.

(2)   Any four individuals, being communicant members of the congregation or full members of the Presbytery, may give written notice requesting that action be taken in terms of subsection (3) below, giving reasons for the request, within seven days after the pulpit intimation.

(3)   Upon receiving notice in terms of subsection (2), the Presbytery Clerk shall sist the process or permission referred to in subsection (1), which shall then require the approval of the Presbytery.

(4)   The Moderator of the Presbytery shall in such circumstances consider whether a meeting *pro re nata* of the Presbytery should be called in order to avoid prejudicial delay in the vacancy process.

(5)   The Presbytery Clerk shall cause to have served upon the congregation or congregations an edict in terms of Schedule B citing them to attend the meeting of Presbytery for their interest.

(6)   The consideration by Presbytery of any matter under this section shall not constitute an appeal or a Petition, and the decision of Presbytery shall be deemed to be a decision at first instance subject to the normal rights of appeal or dissent-and-complaint.

3. Causes of Vacancy

The causes of vacancy shall normally include:

(a)   the death of the minister of the charge;

(b)   the removal of status of the minister of the charge or the suspension of the minister in terms of section 20(2) of Act III 2001;

(c)   the dissolution of the pastoral tie in terms of Act I 1988 or Act XV 2002;

(d)   the demission of the charge and/or status of the minister of the charge;

(e)   the translation of the minister of the charge to another charge;

(f)   the termination of the tenure of the minister of the charge in terms of Act VI 1984.

4. Release of Departing Minister

The Presbytery Clerk shall be informed as soon as circumstances have occurred that cause a vacancy to arise or make it likely that a vacancy shall arise. Where the circumstances pertain to section 3(d) or (e) above, the Vacancy Procedure Committee shall

(1)   except in cases governed by subsection (2) below, decide whether to release the minister from his or her charge and, in any case involving translation to another charge or introduction to an appointment, instruct him or her to await the instructions of the Presbytery or another Presbytery;

(2)   in the case of a minister in the first five years of his or her first charge, decide whether there are exceptional circumstances to justify releasing him or her from his or her charge and proceeding in terms of subsection (1) above;

(3)   determine whether a vacancy has arisen or is anticipated and, as soon as possible, determine the date upon which the charge becomes actually vacant, and

(4)   inform the congregation or congregations by one Sunday's pulpit intimation as soon as convenient.

(5)   The provisions of section 2 above shall apply to the decisions of the Vacancy Procedure Committee in terms of subsections (1) and (2) above.

5. Demission of Charge

(1)   In the case where it is a condition of any basis of adjustment that a minister shall demit his or her charge to facilitate union or linking, and the minister has agreed in writing in terms of the appropriate regulations governing adjustments, formal application shall not be made to the Presbytery for permission to demit. The minister concerned shall be regarded as retiring in the interest of adjustment, and he or she shall retain a seat in Presbytery unless in terms of Act III 2000 (as amended) he or she elects to resign it.

(2)   A minister who demits his or her charge without retaining a seat in the Presbytery shall, if he or she retains status as a minister, be subject to the provisions of sections 5 to 15 of Act II 2000 (as amended).

6. Appointment of Interim Moderator

At the same time as the Vacancy Procedure Committee makes a decision in terms of section 4 above, or where circumstances pertain to section 3(a), (b), (c) or (f) above, the Vacancy Procedure Committee shall appoint an Interim Moderator for the charge and make intimation thereof to the congregation subject to the provisions of section 2 above. The Interim Moderator shall be either a ministerial member of the Presbytery in terms of Act III 2000 or Act V 2001 or a member of the Presbytery selected from a list of those who have received such preparation for the task as the Ministries Council shall from time to time recommend or provide, and he or she shall not be a member in the vacant charge nor a member of the Vacancy Procedure Committee. The name of the Interim Moderator shall be forwarded to the Ministries Council.

7. Duties of Interim Moderator

(1)   It shall be the duty of the Interim Moderator to preside at all meetings of the Kirk Session (or of the Kirk Sessions in the case of a linked charge) and to preside at all congregational meetings in connection with the vacancy, or at which the minister would have presided had the charge been full. In the case of a congregational meeting called by the Presbytery in connection with adjustment, the Interim Moderator, having constituted the meeting, shall relinquish the chair in favour of the representative of the Presbytery, but he or she shall be at liberty to speak at such a meeting. In consultation with the Kirk Session and the Financial Court, he or she shall make arrangements for the supply of the vacant pulpit.

(2)   The Interim Moderator appointed in a prospective vacancy may call and preside at meetings of the Kirk Session and of the congregation for the transaction of business relating to the said prospective vacancy. He or she shall be associated with the minister until the date of the actual vacancy; after that date, he or she shall take full charge.

(3)   The Interim Moderator shall act as an assessor to the Nominating Committee, being available to offer guidance and advice. If the Committee so desire, he or she may act as their Convener, but in no case shall he or she have a vote.

(4)   In the event of the absence of the Interim Moderator, the Vacancy Procedure Committee shall appoint a member of the Presbytery who is not a member of the vacant congregation to fulfil any of the rights and duties of the Interim Moderator in terms of this section.

(5) The Interim Moderator shall have the same duties and responsibilities towards all members of ministry teams referred to in section 16 of Act VII 2003 as if he or she were the parish minister, both in terms of this Act and in respect of the terms and conditions of such individuals.

8. Permission to Call

When the decision to release the minister from the charge has been made and the Interim Moderator appointed, the Vacancy Procedure Committee shall consider whether it may give permission to call a minister in terms of Act VII 2003, and may proceed subject to the provisions of section 2 above. The Vacancy Procedure Committee must refer the question of permission to call to the Presbytery if:

(a) shortfalls exist which in the opinion of the Committee require consideration in terms of section 9 hereunder;

(b) the Committee has reason to believe that the vacancy schedule referred to in section 10 below will not be approved;

(c) the Committee has reason to believe that the Presbytery will, in terms of section 11 below, instruct work to be carried out on the manse before a call can be sustained, and judges that the likely extent of such work warrants a delay in the granting of permission to call, or

(d) the Committee has reason to believe that the Presbytery may wish to delay or refuse the granting of permission for any reason.

Any decision by Presbytery to refuse permission to call shall be subject to appeal or dissent-and-complaint.

9. Shortfalls

(1) As soon as possible after intimation of a vacancy or anticipated vacancy reaches the Presbytery Clerk, the Presbytery shall ascertain whether the charge has current or accumulated shortfalls in contributions to central funds, and shall determine whether and to what extent any shortfalls that exist are justified.

(2) If the vacancy is in a charge in which the Presbytery has determined that shortfalls are to any extent unjustified, it shall not resolve to allow a call of any kind until:

(a) the shortfalls have been met to the extent to which the Presbytery determined that they were unjustified, or

(b) a scheme for the payment of the unjustified shortfall has been agreed between the congregation and the Presbytery and receives the concurrence of the Ministries Council and/or the Stewardship and Finance Committee for their respective interests, or

(c) a fresh appraisal of the charge in terms of Act VII 2003 has been carried out, regardless of the status of the charge in the current Presbytery plan:

(i) During such appraisal, no further steps may be taken in respect of filling the vacancy, and the Presbytery shall make final determination of what constitutes such steps.

(ii) Following such appraisal and any consequent adjustment or deferred adjustment, the shortfalls shall be met or declared justifiable or a scheme shall be agreed in terms of subsection (b) above; the Presbytery shall inform the Ministries Council and the Stewardship and Finance Committee of its decisions in terms of this section; and the Presbytery shall remove the suspension-of-vacancy process referred to in sub-paragraph (i).

10. Vacancy Schedule

(1)   When in terms of sections 4 and 6 above the decision to release the minister from the charge has been made and the Interim Moderator appointed, there shall be issued by the Ministries Council a Schedule or Schedules for completion by the responsible Financial Board(s) of the vacant congregation(s) in consultation with representatives of the Presbytery, setting forth the proposed arrangements for payment of ministerial expenses and for provision of a manse, showing the ministry requirements and details of any endowment income. The Schedule, along with an Extract Minute from each relevant Kirk Session containing a commitment fully and adequately to support the ministry, shall be forwarded to the Presbytery Clerk.

(2)   The Schedule shall be considered by the Vacancy Procedure Committee and, if approved, transmitted to the Ministries Council by the Presbytery Clerk. The Vacancy Procedure Committee or Presbytery must not sustain an appointment and call until the Schedule has been approved by them and by the Ministries Council, which shall intimate its decision within six weeks of receiving the schedule from the Presbytery.

(3)   The accuracy of the Vacancy Schedule shall be kept under review by the Vacancy Procedure Committee.

(4)   The provisions of section 2 above shall apply to the decisions of the Vacancy Procedure Committee.

11. Manse

As soon as possible after the manse becomes vacant, the Presbytery Property Committee shall inspect the manse and come to a view on what work, if any, must be carried out to render it suitable for a new incumbent. The views of the Property Committee should then be communicated to the Presbytery, which should, subject to any modifications which might be agreed by that Court, instruct the Financial Board of the congregation to have the work carried out. No induction date shall be fixed until the Presbytery Property Committee has again inspected the manse and confirmed that the work has been undertaken satisfactorily.

12. Advisory Committee

(1)   As soon as possible after intimation of a vacancy or anticipated vacancy reaches the Presbytery Clerk, the Vacancy Procedure Committee shall appoint an Advisory Committee of three, subject to the following conditions:

   (a)   at least one member shall be an elder and at least one shall be a minister;

   (b)   the Advisory Committee may comprise members of the Vacancy Procedure Committee and act as a support committee to congregations in a vacancy;

   (c)   the Advisory Committee may contain individuals who are not members of the Presbytery;

   (d)   the appointment shall be subject to section 2 above.

(2)   The Advisory Committee shall meet:

   (a)   before the election of the Nominating Committee, with the Kirk Session (or Kirk Sessions both separately and together) of the vacant charge, to consider together in the light of the whole circumstances of the parish or parishes (i) what kind of ministry would be best suited to their needs and (ii) which system of election of the Nominating Committee described in paragraph 14(2)(d) hereunder shall be used;

   (b)   with the Nominating Committee before it has taken any steps to fill the vacancy, to consider how it should proceed;

   (c)   with the Nominating Committee before it reports to the Kirk Session and Presbytery the identity of the nominee, to review the process followed and give any further advice it deems necessary;

(d)   with the Nominating Committee at any other time by request of either the Nominating Committee or the Advisory Committee.

In the case of charges which are in the opinion of the Presbytery remote, it will be adequate if the Interim Moderator (accompanied if possible by a member of the Nominating Committee) meets with the Advisory Committee for the purposes listed in paragraphs (a) to (c) above.

13. Electoral Register

(1)   It shall be the duty of the Kirk Session of a vacant congregation to proceed to make up the Electoral Register of the congregation. This shall contain (1) as communicants the names of those persons (a) whose names are on the communion roll of the congregation as at the date on which it is made up and who are not under Church discipline, (b) whose names have been added or restored to the communion roll on revision by the Kirk Session subsequently to the occurrence of the vacancy, and (c) who have given in valid Certificates of Transference by the date specified in terms of Schedule C hereto; and (2) as adherents the names of those persons who, being parishioners or regular worshippers in the congregation at the date when the vacancy occurred, and not being members of any other congregation, have claimed (in writing in the form prescribed in Schedule D and within the time specified in Schedule C) to be placed on the Electoral Register, the Kirk Session being satisfied that they desire to be permanently connected with the congregation and knowing of no adequate reasons why they should not be admitted as communicants should they so apply.

(2)   At a meeting to be held not later than fourteen days after intimation has been made in terms of Schedule C hereto, the Kirk Session shall decide on the claims of persons to be placed on the Electoral Register, such claims to be sent to the Session Clerk before the meeting. At this meeting, the Kirk Session may hear parties claiming to have an interest. The Kirk Session shall thereupon prepare the lists of names and addresses of communicants and of adherents which it is proposed shall be the Electoral Register of the congregation, the names being arranged in alphabetical order and numbered consecutively throughout. The decision of the Kirk Session in respect of any matter affecting the preparation of the Electoral Register shall be final.

(3)   The proposed Electoral Register having been prepared, the Interim Moderator shall cause intimation to be made on the first convenient Sunday in terms of Schedule E hereto that on that day an opportunity will be given for inspecting the Register after service, and that it will lie for inspection at such times and such places as the Kirk Session shall have determined; and further shall specify a day when the Kirk Session will meet to hear parties claiming an interest and will finally revise and adjust the Register. At this meeting, the list, having been revised, numbered and adjusted, shall on the authority of the court be attested by the Interim Moderator and the Clerk as the Electoral Register of the congregation.

(4)   This Register, along with a duplicate copy, shall without delay be transmitted to the Presbytery Clerk, who, in name of the Presbytery, shall attest and return the principal copy, retaining the duplicate copy in his or her own possession. For all purposes connected with this Act, the congregation shall be deemed to be those persons whose names are on the Electoral Register, and no other.

(5)   If after the attestation of the Register any communicant is given a Certificate of Transference, the Session Clerk shall delete that person's name from the Register and initial the deletion. Such a Certificate shall be granted only when application for it has been made in writing, and the said written application shall be retained until the vacancy is ended.

(6)   When a period of more than six months has elapsed between the Electoral Register being attested and the congregation being given permission to call, the Kirk Session shall have power, if it so desires, to revise and update the Electoral Register. Intimation of this intention shall be given in terms of Schedule F hereto. Additional names shall be added to the Register in the form of an Addendum which shall also contain authority for the deletions which have been made; two copies of this Addendum, duly attested, shall be lodged with the Presbytery Clerk, who, in name of the Presbytery, shall attest and return the principal copy, retaining the duplicate copy in his or her own possession.

14. Appointment of Nominating Committee

(1)   When permission to call has been given and the Electoral Register has been attested, intimation in terms of Schedule G shall be made that a meeting of the congregation is to be held to appoint a Committee of its own number for the purpose of nominating one person to the congregation with a view to the appointment of a minister.

(2)   (a)   The Interim Moderator shall preside at this meeting, and the Session Clerk, or in his or her absence a person appointed by the meeting, shall act as Clerk.

(b)   The Interim Moderator shall remind the congregation of the number of members it is required to appoint in terms of this section and shall call for Nominations. To constitute a valid Nomination, the name of a person on the Electoral Register has to be proposed and seconded, and assurance given by the proposer that the person is prepared to act on the Committee. The Clerk shall take a note of all Nominations in the order in which they are made.

(c)   When it appears to the Interim Moderator that the Nominations are complete, they shall be read to the congregation and an opportunity given for any withdrawals. If the number of persons nominated does not exceed the maximum fixed in terms of subsection (4) below, there is no need for a vote, and the Interim Moderator shall declare that these persons constitute a Nominating Committee.

(d)   If the number exceeds the maximum, the election shall proceed by one of the following means, chosen in advance by the Kirk Session, and being either (i) the submission of the names by the Interim Moderator, one by one as they appear on the list, to the vote of the congregation, each member having the right to vote for up to the maximum number fixed for the Committee, and voting being by standing up, or (ii) a system of written ballot devised by the Kirk Session to suit the size of the congregation and approved by the Vacancy Procedure Committee or the Presbytery. In either case, in the event of a tie for the last place, a further vote shall be taken between or among those tying.

(e)   The Interim Moderator shall, at the same meeting or as soon thereafter as the result of any ballot has been determined, announce the names of those thus elected to serve on the Nominating Committee, and intimate to them the time and place of their first meeting, which may be immediately after the congregational meeting provided that has been intimated along with the intimation of the congregational meeting.

(3)   Where there is an agreement between the Presbytery and the congregation or congregations that the minister to be inducted shall serve either in a team ministry involving another congregation or congregations, or in a designated post such as a chaplaincy, it shall be competent for the agreement to specify that the Presbytery shall appoint up to two representatives to serve on the Nominating Committee.

(4)   The Vacancy Procedure Committee shall, subject to the provisions of section 2 above,

determine the number who will act on the Nominating Committee, being an odd number up to a maximum of thirteen.

(5)   When the vacancy is in a linked charge, or when a union or linking of congregations has been agreed but not yet effected, or when there is agreement to a deferred union or a deferred linking, or where the appointment is to more than one post, the Vacancy Procedure Committee shall, subject to the provisions of section 2 above, determine how the number who will act on the Nominating Committee will be allocated among the congregations involved, unless provision for this has already been made in the Basis of Union or Basis of Linking as the case may be.

(6)   The Nominating Committee shall not have power to co-opt additional members, but the relevant Kirk Session shall have power when necessary to appoint a replacement for any of its appointees who ceases, by death or resignation, to be a member of the Nominating Committee, or who, by falling ill or by moving away from the area, is unable to serve as a member of it.

15. Constitution of the Nominating Committee

It shall be the duty of the Interim Moderator to summon and preside at the first meeting of the Nominating Committee, which may be held at the close of the congregational meeting at which it is appointed and at which the Committee shall appoint a Convener and a Clerk. The Clerk, who need not be a member of the Committee, shall keep regular minutes of all proceedings. The Convener shall have a deliberative vote (if he or she is not the Interim Moderator) but shall in no case have a casting vote. If the Clerk is not a member of the Committee, he or she shall have no vote. At all meetings of the Committee, only those present shall be entitled to vote.

16. Task of the Nominating Committee

(1)   The Nominating Committee shall have the duty of nominating one person to the congregation with a view to the election and appointment of a minister. It shall proceed by a process of announcement in a monthly vacancy list, application and interview, and may also advertise, receive recommendations and pursue enquiries in other ways.

(2)   The Committee shall give due weight to any guidelines which may from time to time be issued by the Ministries Council or the General Assembly.

(3)   The Committee shall make themselves aware of the roles of the other members of any ministry team as described in section 16 of Act VII 2003 and may meet with them for this purpose, but shall not acquire responsibility or authority for the negotiation or alteration of their terms and conditions.

17. Eligibility for Election

The following categories of persons, and no others, are eligible to be nominated, elected and called as ministers of parishes in the Church of Scotland, but always subject, where appropriate, to the provisions of Act IX 2002:

(1)   A minister of a parish of the Church, a minister holding some other appointment that entitles him or her to a seat in Presbytery or a minister holding a current Practising Certificate in terms of Section 5 of Act II 2000 (as amended).

(2)   A minister of the Church of Scotland who has retired from a parish or appointment as above, provided he or she has not reached his or her 65th birthday (or, subject to the provisions of Regulations II 2004, his or her 70th birthday).

(3)   (a)   A licentiate of the Church of Scotland who has satisfactorily completed, or has been granted exemption from, his or her period of probationary service.

(b)   A graduate candidate in terms of section 22 of Act X 2004.

(4)   A minister, licentiate or graduate candidate of the Church of Scotland who, with the approval of the World Mission Council, has entered the courts of an overseas Church as a full member, provided he or she has ceased to be such a member.

(5)   A minister, licentiate or graduate candidate of the Church of Scotland who has neither relinquished nor been judicially deprived of the status he or she possessed and who has served, or is serving, furth of Scotland in any Church which is a member of the World Alliance of Reformed Churches.

(6)   The holder of a Certificate of Eligibility in terms of Act IX 2002.

18. Ministers of a Team

Ministers occupying positions within a team ministry in the charge, or larger area including the charge, and former holders of such positions, shall be eligible to apply and shall not by virtue of office be deemed to have exercised undue influence in securing the call. A *locum tenens* in the vacant charge shall not by virtue of office be deemed to have exercised undue influence in securing the call. Any Interim Moderator in the current vacancy shall not be eligible to apply.

19. Ministers of Other Churches

(1)   Where a minister of a church furth of Scotland, who holds a certificate of eligibility in terms of Act IX 2002, is nominated, the nominee, Kirk Session and Presbytery may agree that he or she shall be inducted for a period of three years only and shall retain status as a minister of his or her denomination of origin.

(2)   Upon induction, such a minister shall be accountable to the Presbytery for the exercise of his or her ministry and to his or her own church for matters of life and doctrine. He or she shall be awarded corresponding membership of the Presbytery.

(3)   With the concurrence of the Presbytery and the Ministries Council, and at the request of the congregation, the period may be extended for one further period of not more than three years.

(4)   The provisions of this section shall apply in the case of an appointment as a member of a ministry team as defined in section 16(2)(a) of Act VII 2003 (as amended), provided that the appointment is one which the Presbytery deems must be held by a Ministry of Word and Sacrament.

20. Nomination

(1)   Before the candidate is asked to accept Nomination, the Interim Moderator shall ensure that the candidate is given an adequate opportunity to see the whole ecclesiastical buildings (including the manse) pertaining to the congregation, and to meet privately with all members of staff of the charge or of any wider ministry team, and shall be provided with a copy of the constitution of the congregation, a copy of the current Presbytery Plan and of any current Basis of Adjustment or Basis of Reviewable Tenure, and the most recent audited accounts and statement of funds, and the candidate shall acknowledge receipt in writing to the Interim Moderator.

(2)   Before any Nomination is intimated to the Kirk Session and Presbytery Clerk, the Clerk to the Nominating Committee shall secure the written consent thereto of the nominee.

(3)   Before reporting the Nomination to the Vacancy Procedure Committee, the Presbytery Clerk shall obtain from the nominee or Interim Moderator evidence of the eligibility of the nominee to be appointed to the charge.

(a)   In the case of a minister not being a member of any Presbytery of the Church of Scotland, this shall normally constitute an Exit Certificate in terms of Act X 2004, or evidence of status from the Ministries Council, or a current practising certificate, or certification from the Ministries Council of eligibility in terms of Act IX 2002.

(b)   In the case of a minister in the first five years of his or her first charge, this shall consist of an extract minute either from the Vacancy Procedure Committee of his or her current Presbytery, or from that Presbytery, exceptionally releasing the minister.

21. Preaching by Nominee

(1)   The Interim Moderator, on receiving notice of the Committee's Nomination, shall arrange that the nominee conduct public worship in the vacant church or churches, normally within four Sundays, and that the ballot take place immediately after each such service.

(2)   The Interim Moderator shall thereupon cause intimation to be made on two Sundays regarding the arrangements made in connection with the preaching by the nominee and the ballot thereafter, all in terms of Schedule H hereto.

22. Election of Minister

(1)   The Interim Moderator shall normally preside at all congregational meetings connected with the election, which shall be in all cases by ballot. The Interim Moderator shall be in charge of the ballot.

(2)   The Interim Moderator may invite one or more persons (not being persons whose names are on the Electoral Register of the vacant congregation) to assist him or her in the conduct of a ballot vote when he or she judges this desirable.

(3)   When a linking or a deferred union or deferred linking is involved, the Interim Moderator shall consult and reach agreement with the minister or Interim Moderator of the other congregation regarding the arrangements for the conduct of public worship in these congregations by the nominee as in section 21(1) above. The Interim Moderator shall in writing appoint a member of Presbytery to take full charge of the ballot vote for the other congregation. In the case of a deferred union or deferred linking, the minister already inducted shall not be so appointed, nor shall he or she be in any way involved in the conduct of the election.

23. Ballot Procedure

(1)   The Kirk Session shall arrange to have available at the time of election a sufficient supply of voting-papers printed in the form of Schedule I hereto, and these shall be put into the custody of the Interim Moderator who shall preside at the election, assisted as in section 22 above. He or she shall issue on request to any person whose name is on the Electoral Register a voting-paper, noting on the Register that this has been done. Facilities shall be provided whereby the voter may mark the paper in secrecy, and a ballot-box shall be available wherein the paper is to be deposited when marked. The Interim Moderator may assist any person who asks for help in respect of completing the voting-paper, but no other person whatever shall communicate with the voter at this stage. The Interim Moderator, or the deputy appointed by him or her, shall be responsible for the safe custody of ballot-box, papers and Electoral Register.

(2)   As soon as practicable, and at latest within twenty-four hours after the close of the voting, the Interim Moderator shall constitute the Kirk Session, or the joint Kirk Sessions when more than one congregation is involved, and in presence of the Kirk Session shall proceed with the counting of the votes, in which he or she may be assisted as provided in section 22 above. When more than one ballot-box has been used and when the votes of more than one congregation are involved, all ballot-boxes shall be emptied and the voting-papers shall be mixed together before counting begins so that the preponderance of votes in one area or in one congregation shall not be disclosed.

(3)   If the number voting For exceeds the number voting Against, the nominee shall be declared elected and the Nominating Committee shall be deemed to be discharged.

(4)   If the number voting For is equal to or less than the number voting Against, the Interim Moderator shall declare that there has been failure to elect and that the Nominating Committee is deemed to have been discharged. He or she shall proceed in terms of section 26(b) without further reference to the Presbytery.

(5)   After the counting has been completed, the Interim Moderator shall sign a declaration in one of the forms of Schedule J hereto, and this shall be recorded in the minute of the Kirk Session or of the Kirk Sessions. An extract shall be affixed to the notice-board of the church, or of each of the churches, concerned. In presence of the Kirk Session, the Interim Moderator shall then seal up the voting-papers along with the marked copy of the Electoral Register, and these shall be transmitted to the Presbytery Clerk in due course along with the other documents specified in section 27 below.

24. Withdrawal of Nominee

(1)   Should a nominee intimate withdrawal before he or she has preached as nominee, the Nominating Committee shall continue its task and seek to nominate another nominee.

(2)   Should a nominee intimate withdrawal after he or she has been elected, the Interim Moderator shall proceed in terms of sections 23(4) above and 26(b) below without further reference to the Presbytery.

25. The Call

(1)   The Interim Moderator shall, along with the intimation regarding the result of the voting, intimate the arrangements made for members of the congregation over a period of not less than eight days to subscribe the Call (Schedule K). Intimation shall be in the form of Schedule L hereto.

(2)   The Call may be subscribed on behalf of a member not present to sign in person, provided a mandate authorising such subscription is produced as in Schedule M. All such entries shall be initialled by the Interim Moderator or by the member of the Kirk Session appending them.

(3)   Those eligible to sign the call shall be all those whose names appear on the Electoral Register. A paper of concurrence in the Call may be signed by regular worshippers in the congregation and by adherents whose names have not been entered on the Electoral Register.

26. Failure to Nominate

The exercise by a congregation of its right to call a minister shall be subject to a time-limit of one year; this period shall be calculated from the date when intimation is given of the agreement to grant leave to call. If it appears that an appointment is not to be made within the allotted time (allowing one further calendar month for intimation to the Presbytery), the congregation may make application to the Presbytery for an extension, which will normally be for a further three months. In exceptional circumstances, and for clear cause shown, a further extension of three months may be granted. If no election has been made and intimated to the Presbytery by the expiry of that time, the permission to call shall be regarded as having lapsed. The Presbytery may thereupon look afresh at the question of adjustment. If the Presbytery is still satisfied that a minister should be appointed, it shall itself take steps to make such an appointment, proceeding in one of the following ways:

(a)   (i)   The Presbytery may discharge the Nominating Committee, strengthen the Advisory Committee which had been involved in the case by the appointment of an additional minister and elder, instruct that Committee to bring forward to a subsequent meeting the name of an eligible individual for appointment to the charge and intimate this instruction to the congregation. If satisfied with the recommendation brought by the Advisory Committee, the Presbytery shall thereupon make the appointment.

    (ii)   The Presbytery Clerk shall thereupon intimate to the person concerned the fact of his or her appointment, shall request him or her to forward a letter of acceptance along with appropriate Certificates if these are required in terms of section 27 below, and shall arrange with him or her to conduct public worship in the vacant church or churches on an early Sunday.

    (iii) The Presbytery Clerk shall cause intimation to be made in the form of Schedule N that the person appointed will conduct public worship on the day specified and that a Call in the usual form will lie with the Session Clerk or other suitable person for not less than eight free days to receive the signatures of the congregation. The conditions governing the signing of the Call shall be as in section 25 above.

    (iv) At the expiry of the time allowed, the Call shall be transmitted by the Session Clerk to the Presbytery Clerk who shall lay it, along with the documents referred to in sub-paragraph (ii) above, before the Presbytery at its first ordinary meeting or at a meeting *in hunc effectum*.

(b)   Otherwise, the Presbytery shall instruct that a fresh Nominating Committee be elected in terms of section 14 above. The process shall then be followed in terms of this Act from the point of the election of the Nominating Committee.

27. Transmission of Documents

(1)   After an election has been made, the Interim Moderator shall secure from the person appointed a letter of acceptance of the appointment.

(2)   The Interim Moderator shall then without delay transmit the relevant documents to the Presbytery Clerk. These are: the minute of Nomination by the Nominating Committee, all intimations made to the congregation thereafter, the declaration of the election and appointment, the voting-papers, the marked copy of the Register and the letter of acceptance. He or she shall also inform the Clerk of the steps taken in connection with the signing of the Call, and shall arrange that, at the expiry of the period allowed for subscription, the Call shall be transmitted by the Session Clerk to the Presbytery Clerk.

(3)   After the person elected has been inducted to the charge, the Presbytery Clerk shall:

    (a)   deliver to him or her the approved copy of the Vacancy Schedule referred to in section 10(2) above, and

    (b)   destroy the intimations and voting-papers lodged with him or her in terms of subsection (2) above and ensure that confidential documents and correspondence held locally are destroyed.

28. Sustaining the Call

(1)   All of the documents listed in section 27 above shall be laid before the Vacancy Procedure Committee, which may resolve to sustain the call and determine arrangements for the induction of the new minister, subject to (a) a request for the release, if appropriate, of the minister from his or her current charge in terms of this Act and (b) the provisions of section 2 above. The Moderator of the Presbytery shall, if no ordinary meeting of the Presbytery falls before the proposed induction date, call a meeting *pro re nata* for the induction.

(2)   In the event that the matter comes before the Presbytery in terms of section 2 above, the procedure shall be as follows:

    (a)   The Call and other relevant documents having been laid on the table, the Presbytery shall hear any person whom it considers to have an interest. In particular, the Advisory Committee shall be entitled to be heard if it so desires, or the Presbytery may ask for a report from it. The Presbytery shall then decide whether to sustain the appointment in terms of subsection (1) above, and in doing so shall give consideration to the number of signatures on the Call. It may delay reaching a decision and return the Call to the Kirk Session to give further opportunity for it to be subscribed.

(b)   If the Presbytery sustain an appointment and Call to a Graduate Candidate, and there be no appeal tendered in due form against its judgement, it shall appoint the day and hour and place at which the ordination and induction will take place.

(c)   If the Presbytery sustain an appointment and Call to a minister of the Church of Scotland not being a minister of a parish, or to a minister of another denomination, and there be no ecclesiastical impediment, the Presbytery shall appoint the day and hour and place at which the induction will take place.

(3)   In the event that the Call is not sustained, the Presbytery shall determine either (a) to give more time for it to be signed in terms of section 25 above or (b) to proceed in terms of subsection (a) or (b) of section 26 above.

29. Admission to a Charge

(1)   When the Presbytery has appointed a day for the ordination and induction of a Graduate Candidate, or for the induction of a minister already ordained, the Clerk shall arrange for an edict in the form of Schedule O to be read to the congregation on the two Sundays preceding the day appointed.

(2)   At the time and place named in the edict, the Presbytery having been constituted, the Moderator shall call for the return of the edict attested as having been duly served. If the minister is being translated from another Presbytery, the relevant minute of that Presbytery or of its Vacancy Procedure Committee agreeing to translation shall also be laid on the table. Any objection, to be valid at this stage, must have been intimated to the Presbytery Clerk at the objector's earliest opportunity, must be strictly directed to life or doctrine and must be substantiated immediately to the satisfaction of the Presbytery, in which case procedure shall be sisted and the Presbytery shall take appropriate steps to deal with the situation that has arisen. Otherwise, the Presbytery shall proceed with the ordination and induction, or with the induction, as hereunder.

(3)   The Presbytery shall proceed to the church where public worship shall be conducted by those appointed for the purpose. The Clerk shall read a brief narrative of the cause of the vacancy and of the steps taken for the settlement. The Moderator, having read the Preamble, shall, addressing him or her by name, put to the person to be inducted the questions prescribed (*see the Ordinal of the Church as authorised from time to time by the General Assembly*). Satisfactory answers having been given, the person to be inducted shall sign the Formula. If he or she has not already been ordained, the person to be inducted shall then kneel, and the Moderator by prayer and the imposition of hands, in which members of the Presbytery, appointed by the Presbytery for the purpose, and other ordained persons associated with it, if invited to share in such imposition of hands, shall join, shall ordain him or her to the office of the Holy Ministry. Prayer being ended, the Moderator shall say: 'I now declare you to have been ordained to the office of the Holy Ministry, and in name of the Lord Jesus Christ, the King and Head of the Church, and by authority of this Presbytery, I induct you to this charge, and in token thereof we give you the right hand of fellowship'. The Moderator with all other members of Presbytery present and those associated with it shall then give the right hand of fellowship. The Moderator shall then put the prescribed question to the members of the congregation. Suitable charges to the new minister and to the congregation shall then be given by the Moderator or by a minister appointed for the purpose.

(4)   When an ordained minister is being inducted to a charge, the act of ordination shall not be repeated, and the relevant words shall be omitted from the declaration. In other respects, the procedure shall be as in subsection (3) above.

(5)   When the appointment is for a limited or potentially limited period (including Reviewable Tenure, or an appointment in terms of section 19 above), the service shall proceed as in subsections (3) or (4) above, except that in the declaration the Moderator shall say: 'I induct you to this charge on the Basis of [specific Act and Section] and in terms of Minute of Presbytery of date . . .'.

(6)   After the service, the Presbytery shall resume its session, when the name of the new minister shall be added to the Roll of Presbytery, and the Clerk shall be instructed to send certified intimation of the induction to the Session Clerk to be engrossed in the minutes of the first meeting of Kirk Session thereafter, and, in the case of a translation from another Presbytery or where the minister was prior to the induction subject to the supervision of another Presbytery, to the Clerk of that Presbytery.

30. Service of Introduction

(1)   When a minister has been appointed to a linked charge, the Presbytery shall determine in which of the churches of the linking the induction is to take place. This shall be a service of induction to the charge, in consequence of which the person inducted shall become minister of each of the congregations embraced in the linking. The edict regarding the induction, which shall be in terms of Schedule O, shall be read in all of the churches concerned. There shall be no other service of induction; but, if the churches are far distant from one another, or for other good reason, the Presbytery may appoint a service of introduction to be held in the other church or churches. Intimation shall be given of such service, but not in edictal form.

(2)   In any case of deferred union or deferred linking, the minister elected and appointed shall be inducted 'to the vacant congregation of A in deferred union (or linking) with the congregation of B' and there shall be no need for any further act to establish his or her position as minister of the united congregation or of the linked congregation as the case may be. The Presbytery, however, shall in such a case arrange a service of introduction to the newly united congregation of AB or the newly linked congregation of B. Intimation shall be given of such service, but not in edictal form.

(3)   When an appointment has been made to an extra-parochial office wholly or mainly under control of the Church (community ministry, full-time chaplaincy in hospital, industry, prison or university, full-time clerkship and so on), the Presbytery may deem it appropriate to arrange a service of introduction to take place in a church or chapel suitable to the occasion.

(4)   When an appointment has been made to a parochial appointment other than that of an inducted minister, the Presbytery may arrange a service of introduction to take place within the parish. If ordination is involved, suitable arrangements shall be made and edictal intimation shall be given in terms of Schedule P.

(5)   A service of introduction not involving ordination shall follow the lines of an induction except that, instead of putting the normal questions to the minister, the Moderator shall ask him or her to affirm the vows taken at his or her ordination. Where the service, in terms of subsection (3) or (4) above, includes the ordination of the minister, the vows shall be put in full. In either case, in the declaration, the Moderator in place of 'I induct you to . . .' shall say: 'I welcome you as . . .'.

31. Demission of Status

If a minister seeks to demit his or her status as a minister of the Church of Scotland, any accompanying demission of a charge will be dealt with by the Vacancy Procedure Committee in terms of section 4 of this Act without further delay, but the question of demission of status shall be considered by the Presbytery itself. The Moderator of Presbytery, or a deputy appointed by him or her, shall first confer with the minister regarding his or her reasons and shall report to the Presbytery if there appears to be any reason not to grant permission to demit status. Any decision to grant permission to demit status shall be immediately reported to the Ministries Council.

32. Miscellaneous

For the purposes of this Act, intimations to congregations may be made (a) verbally during every act of worship or (b) in written intimations distributed to the whole congregation provided that the congregation's attention is specifically drawn to the presence of an intimation there in terms of this Act.

For the purposes of this Act, attestation of all intimations to congregations shall consist of certification thereof by the Session Clerk as follows:

(a)   Certification that all intimations received have been duly made on the correct number of Sundays shall be sent to the Presbytery Clerk before the service of induction or introduction.

(b)   Certification that any particular intimation received has been duly made on the correct number of Sundays shall be furnished on demand to the Vacancy Procedure Committee or the Presbytery Clerk.

(c)   Intimation shall be made immediately to the Presbytery Clerk in the event that intimation has not been duly made on the appropriate Sunday.

SCHEDULES

A INTIMATION OF ACTION OR DECISION OF VACANCY PROCEDURE COMMITTEE – Section 2(1)

To be read on one Sunday

The Vacancy Procedure Committee of the Presbytery of ……… proposes [here insert action or permission proposed]……. Any communicant member of the congregation(s) of A [and B] may submit to the Presbytery Clerk a request for this proposal to be considered at the next meeting of the Presbytery: where such requests are received from four individuals, being communicant members of the congregation(s) or full members of the Presbytery, the request shall be met. Such request should be submitted in writing to [name and postal address of Presbytery Clerk] by [date seven days after intimation].

A ………. B ……….   Presbytery Clerk

B EDICT CITING A CONGREGATION TO ATTEND – Section 2(5)

To be read on one Sunday

Intimation is hereby given that, in connection with the [anticipated] vacancy in this congregation, a valid request has been made for the matter of [here insert action or permission which had been proposed] to be considered by the Presbytery. [The proposed course of action] is in the meantime sisted.

Intimation is hereby further given that the Presbytery will meet to consider this matter at ....
on .... the .... day of .... at .... o'clock and that the congregation are hereby
cited to attend for their interests.

A .... B ....   Presbytery Clerk

C PREPARATION OF ELECTORAL REGISTER – Section 13(1) and (2)

To be read on two Sundays

Intimation is hereby given that in view of the [1]anticipated vacancy, the Kirk Session is about to
make up an Electoral Register of this congregation. Any communicant whose name is not already
on the Communion Roll as a member should hand in to the Session Clerk a Certificate of
Transference, and anyone wishing his or her name added to the Register as an adherent should
obtain from the Session Clerk, and complete and return to him or her, a Form of Adherent's
Claim. All such papers should be in the hands of the Session Clerk not later than .... The
Kirk Session will meet in .... on .... at .... to make up the Electoral Register,
when anyone wishing to support his or her claim in person should attend.

C .... D ....   Interim Moderator

[1] This word to be included where appropriate – otherwise to be deleted

D FORM OF ADHERENT'S CLAIM   Section 13(1)

I, [1] .... of [2] ...., being a parishioner or regular worshipper in the Church of .... and
not being a member of any other congregation in Scotland, claim to have my name put on the
Electoral Register of the parish of .... as an adherent.

Date ....   (Signed).......................

[1] Here enter full name in block capitals
[2] Here enter address in full

E INSPECTION OF ELECTORAL REGISTER – Section 13(3)

To be read on one Sunday

Intimation is hereby given that the proposed Electoral Register of this congregation has now
been prepared and that an opportunity of inspecting it will be given today in .... at the
close of this service, and that it will be open for inspection at .... on .... between the
hours of .... and .... each day. Any questions regarding entries in the Register should
be brought to the notice of the Kirk Session which is to meet in .... on .... at ....
o'clock, when it will finally make up the Electoral Register.

C .... D ....   Interim Moderator

F REVISION OF ELECTORAL REGISTER – Section 13(6)

To be read on two Sundays

Intimation is hereby given that, more than six months having elapsed since the Electoral Register of this congregation was finally made up, it is now proposed that it should be revised. An opportunity of inspecting the Register will be given in .... at the close of this service, and also at .... on .... between the hours of .... and .... each day. Anyone wishing his or her name added to the Electoral Register as a member should give in a Transference Certificate, or as an adherent should give in a Form of Adherent's Claim (copies of which may be had from the Session Clerk) not later than .... The Kirk Session will meet in .... on .... at .... o'clock, when it will finally make up the Revised Register.

C .... D ....   Interim Moderator

G INTIMATION OF ELECTION OF NOMINATING COMMITTEE – Section 14(1)

To be read on two Sundays

Intimation is hereby given that a meeting of this congregation will be held in the Church [or other arrangement may be given here] on Sunday .... at the close of morning worship for the purpose of appointing a Nominating Committee which will nominate one person to the congregation with a view to the appointment of a minister.

C .... D ....   Interim Moderator

H MINUTE OF NOMINATION BY NOMINATING COMMITTEE – Section 21

To be read on two Sundays

(1)   The Committee chosen by this congregation to nominate a person with a view to the election and appointment of a minister, at a meeting held at .... on ...., resolved to name and propose [1] ...., and they accordingly do name and propose the said ....

Date ....

E .... F ....   Convener of Committee

[1] The name and designation of the person should at this point be entered in full

(2)   Intimation is therefore hereby given that the Nominating Committee having, as by minute now read, named and proposed [Name], arrangements have been made whereby public worship will be conducted in this Church by him or her on Sunday the .... day of .... at .... o'clock; and that a vote will be taken by voting-papers immediately thereafter; and that electors may vote For or Against electing and appointing the said [Name] as minister of this vacant charge.

C .... D ....   Interim Moderator

I VOTING-PAPER – Section 23

FOR Electing [Name]
AGAINST Electing [Name]

Directions to Voters: If you are in favour of electing [Name], put a cross (x) on the upper space. If you are not in favour of electing [Name], put a cross (x) in the lower space. Do not put a tick or any other mark upon the paper; if you do, it will be regarded as spoilt and will not be counted.

Note: The Directions to Voters must be printed prominently on the face of the voting-paper

J DECLARATION OF ELECTION RESULT – Section 23(5)

First Form (Successful Election)

I hereby declare that the following are the results of the voting for the election and appointment of a minister to the vacant charge of [1] .... and that the said [Name] has accordingly been elected and appointed subject to the judgement of the courts of the Church.

Date ....   C .... D ....   Interim Moderator

[1] Here enter details

FOR Electing [Name]
AGAINST Electing [Name]

Second Form (Failure to Elect)

I hereby declare that the following are the results of the voting for the election and appointment of a minister to the vacant charge of [1] .... and that in consequence of this vote there has been a failure to elect, and the Nominating Committee is deemed to have been discharged. [Continue in terms of Schedule G if appropriate.]

Date ....   C .... D ....   Interim Moderator

[1] Here enter details

FOR Electing [Name]
AGAINST Electing [Name]

K THE CALL – Section 25(1)

Form of Call

We, members of the Church of Scotland and of the congregation known as ...., being without a minister, address this Call to be our minister to you, ..., of whose gifts and qualities we have been assured, and we warmly invite you to accept this Call, promising that we shall devote ourselves with you to worship, witness, mission and service in this parish, and also to the furtherance of these in the world, to the glory of God and for the advancement of His Kingdom.

Paper of Concurrence

We, regular worshippers in the congregation of the Church of Scotland known as ...., concur in the Call addressed by that congregation to .... to be their minister.

Note: The Call and Paper of Concurrence should be dated and attested by the Interim Moderator before they are transmitted to the Clerk of the Presbytery.

L SUBSCRIBING THE CALL – Section 25(1)

To be read on at least one Sunday

Intimation is hereby given that this congregation having elected [*Name*] to be their minister, a Call to the said [*Name*] has been prepared and will lie in ………. on ………. the ………. day of ………. between the hours of ………. and ………., when those whose names are on the Electoral Register of the congregation may sign in person or by means of mandates. Forms of mandate may be obtained from the Session Clerk.

A Paper of Concurrence will also be available for signature by persons who are connected with the congregation but whose names are not on the Electoral Register of the congregation.

C ………. D ……….   Interim Moderator

M MANDATE TO SIGN CALL – Section 25(2)

I, ………. of ………., being a person whose name is on the Electoral Register of the congregation, hereby authorise the Session Clerk, or other member of Session, to add my name to the Call addressed to [*Name*] to be our minister.

(Signed) ……............…….

N CITATION IN CASE OF NOMINATION BY PRESBYTERY – Section 26(a)(iii)

To be read on one Sunday

Intimation is hereby given that [*Name*], whom the Presbytery has appointed to be minister of this congregation, will conduct public worship in the Church on Sunday the ………. day of ………. at ………. o'clock.

Intimation is hereby further given that a Call addressed to the said [*Name*] will lie in ………. on ………. the ………. day of ………. between the hours of ………. and ………. during the day and between the hours of ………. and ………. in the evening, when members may sign in person or by means of mandates, forms of which may be had from the Session Clerk.

Intimation is hereby further given that the Presbytery will meet to deal with the appointment and Call at ………. on ………. the ………. day of ………. at ………. o'clock and that the congregation are hereby cited to attend for their interests.

A ………. B ……….   Presbytery Clerk

O EDICTAL INTIMATION OF ADMISSION – Section 29(1)

To be read on two Sundays

- Whereas the Presbytery of .... has received a Call from this congregation addressed to [*Name*] to be their minister, and the said Call has been sustained as a regular Call, and has been accepted by him/her[1];
- And whereas the said Presbytery, having judged the said [*Name*] qualified[2] for the ministry of the Gospel and for this charge, has resolved to proceed to his or her[3] ordination and induction on .... the .... day of .... at .... o'clock unless something occur which may reasonably impede it:

Notice is hereby given to all concerned that if they, or any of them, have anything to object to in the life or doctrine of the said [*Name*], they may appear at the Presbytery which is to meet at .... on .... the .... day of .... at .... o'clock; with certification that if no relevant objection be then made and immediately substantiated, the Presbytery will proceed without further delay.

By order of the Presbytery

A .... B .... Presbytery Clerk

[1] add, where appropriate, 'and his or her translation has been agreed to by the Presbytery of ....'
[2] omit 'for the ministry of the Gospel and' if the minister to be inducted has been ordained previously
[3] omit, where appropriate, 'ordination and'

P EDICTAL INTIMATION OF ORDINATION IN CASE OF INTRODUCTION – Section 30(1)

To be read on two Sundays

- Whereas [narrate circumstances requiring service of introduction]
- And whereas the Presbytery, having found the said [*Name*] to have been regularly appointed and to be qualified for the ministry of the Gospel and for the said appointment, has resolved to proceed to his or her ordination to the Holy Ministry and to his or her introduction as [specify appointment] on .... the .... day of .... at .... o'clock unless something occur which may reasonably impede it:

Notice is hereby given to all concerned that if they, or any of them, have anything to object to in the life or doctrine of the said [*Name*], they may appear at the Presbytery which is to meet at .... on .... the .... day of .... at .... o'clock; with certification that if no relevant objection be then made and immediately substantiated, the Presbytery will proceed without further delay.

By order of the Presbytery

A .... B ....   Presbytery Clerk

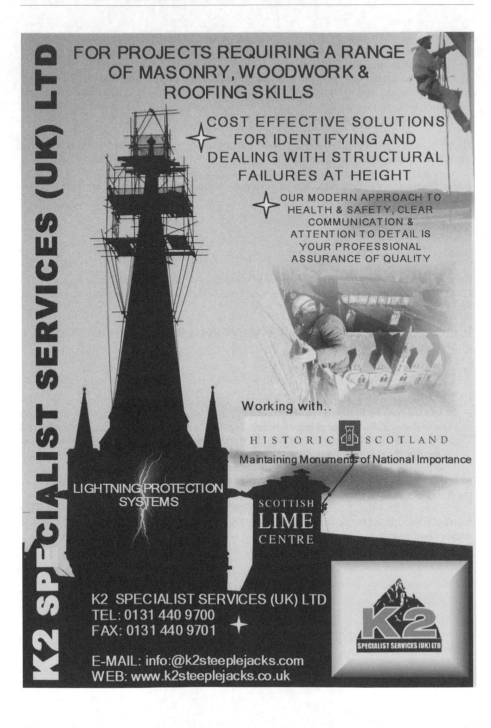

SECTION 4

The
General Assembly
of 2008

(1) THE GENERAL ASSEMBLY

The Lord High Commissioner:	The Rt Hon. George Reid MA
Moderator:	Right Rev. David W. Lunan MA BD
Chaplains to the Moderator:	Rev. Rolf H. Billes BD Rev. Iain A. Laing MA BD
Principal Clerk:	Very Rev. Finlay A.J. Macdonald MA BD PhD DD
Depute Clerk:	Rev. Marjory A. MacLean LLB BD PhD
Procurator:	Miss Laura Dunlop QC
Law Agent:	Mrs Janette S. Wilson LLB NP
Convener of the Business Committee:	Rev. William C. Hewitt BD DipPS
Vice-Convener of the Business Committee:	Rev. A. David K. Arnott MA BD
Precentor:	Rev. Douglas Galbraith MA BD BMus MPhil ARSCM
Assembly Officer:	Mr David McColl
Assistant Assembly Officer:	Mr Craig Marshall

(2) THE MODERATOR

The Right Reverend David W. Lunan MA BD

The roots of David's deep Christian faith are to be found in the home and family in which he grew up in Cambuslang, on the outskirts of Glasgow. While training for the ministry, he became involved in youth work in the Gorbals. The experience of working in the Gorbals was to prove formative in creating a lifelong commitment to the marginalised of society. On graduating, David spent a year at Princeton Seminary, New Jersey, and served at First Presbyterian Church, Philadelphia as a Peter Marshall Scholar. On returning to Scotland, David moved into the east end of Glasgow, where he became assistant leader of Calton Youth Club. He brought to that work his warm humanity, his respect for each individual and his gentle good humour, along with his overriding desire to be a servant of the Servant King. The years spent there have left a lasting impression on his life and ministry.

It is impossible to write about David without mentioning Maggie, his wife and soulmate. Maggie, who over the years has exercised her own distinctive ministry, shares David's deep beliefs and convictions. Together they have four adult sons – Andrew, Gordon, Iain and Malcolm

– who were all born in Lhanbryde, where David served as minister from 1975 to 1987. At St Andrew's-Lhanbryd, David enjoyed the friendship and respect of a diverse rural community. During his twelve-year ministry, the congregation developed ministries with children and new models for the eldership. David was instrumental in raising the profile of Christian Aid, an organisation that he and Maggie continue to support, and also helped open a hostel for homeless people in Elgin. Described as having the ability to recognise gifts in others and encourage them to use them, David saw six members of his congregation go to selection school for the ministry. He was Moderator of the Presbytery of Moray in 1985–6 and part-time hospital chaplain in Elgin. David was also Chaplain to Sir Iain Tennant, who was Lord High Commissioner to the General Assemblies of 1988 and 1989.

In 1987, David received a call back to Glasgow, to the city-centre charge of Renfield St Stephen's. He came at a time when the congregation was seeking to build bridges into the business and leisure communities that operated within the parish. Here, David and Maggie discovered a love for the vibrancy of city-centre living. During his time as minister, David introduced alternative styles of worship and oversaw the redevelopment of the Church Centre and the rebuilding of the church, after the collapse of the steeple, into a modern, flexible worship and meeting space. He was Moderator of the Presbytery of Glasgow in 2000–1.

When the post of Presbytery Clerk became vacant in Glasgow, the Presbytery Council was seeking someone who, in addition to processing business efficiently, could also develop a sense of fellowship among the presbyters. David was that person. Appointed in 2002, he applied to the task the same qualities which he had brought to the Calton Youth Club at the beginning of his ministry. David offered a listening ear to many colleagues in the ministry, initiated meetings with local MPs and MSPs and fostered links with Trades House, businesses, local charities and the police and fire services. Ecumenical links prospered under his guidance, and he was involved in quarterly church leaders' meetings and in the City Council-sponsored Forum of Faiths.

In the course of his ministry, David has undertaken a variety of work for the wider Church. He served on the first Assembly Council and on the Executive of the Board of Social Responsibility. He convened the Church's Committee on Health and Healing. David is frequently invited to speak at conferences on topics that include Ministries, Mission and Discipleship, World Mission and Review and Reform. Together with Maggie, he is Honorary Chaplain to the Church's Mission Partners and has co-led retreats and conferences. Study tours with Christian Aid to the Philippines, Malawi and South Africa have informed his continuing concern for world development and mission. He has a well-grounded understanding of the issues facing the wider Church.

To his year as Moderator, David Lunan will bring the qualities of humility, respect for each individual, gentle good humour and a close walk with God in his daily life, along with the lessons learned on his rich and varied faith journey. We look forward to supporting David during this coming year and following with interest where the road will lead him and Maggie on their many and varied duties.

Iain Laing and Rolf Billes, Chaplains

(3) DIGEST OF ASSEMBLY DECISIONS

Following the practice of recent years, this section of the *Year Book* contains the Editor's personal selection of the decisions of the most recent General Assembly which, in his view at the time of writing, seemed likely to be of most immediate or practical interest to those likely to read it.

It is readily recognised that such a selection will not satisfy everyone: as in former years, there will doubtless be some surprise that this decision rather than that decision has been highlighted. With the brief headline approach that the constraints of space inevitably dictate, full justice cannot be done to every important topic raised in every report. As always, however, those who wish to explore in more detail the editor's 'sins of omission' can obtain from the office of the Principal Clerk the full published volume of Assembly Reports. In due course, copies of that volume, including in addition the approved Deliverances on each Report, will be available from the same source.

REPORTS OF COUNCILS, COMMITTEES AND OTHER AGENCIES

Assembly Arrangements Committee
The General Assembly approved the Committee's proposal to consult the Church on further changes to the General Assembly; the Committee aims to report to the Assembly of 2009.

Chaplains to HM Forces Committee
The General Assembly commended to eligible ministers of the Church of Scotland consideration of offering to serve in the Royal Navy, Naval Reserve or Sea Cadets, Regular Army, Territorial Army or Army Cadet Force, Royal Air Force or Air Cadet Force Chaplaincy.

Church and Society Council
The General Assembly:
*   supported the development of a 'living wage' campaign and instructed the Church's employing agencies, local and national, to examine what implications this has for the Church's own pay policies;
*   urged all levels of government to fulfil their existing commitment to establishing a thoroughly integrated and affordable public-transport network;
*   affirmed, in light of the life, death and resurrection of the Lord Jesus Christ, that capital punishment is always and wholly unacceptable and does not provide an answer even to the most heinous of crimes; the Council was encouraged to work with other Churches and agencies around the world to advance this understanding, oppose death sentences and executions and promote the cause of the abolition of the death penalty worldwide;
*   welcomed the launch of the Gaelic Digital Broadcasting channel and instructed the Council, in co-operation with the Council of Assembly, to discuss with the Gaelic Media Council the significant place of religious programmes in its output;
*   called on the Scottish Government to ensure that a minimum level of 10,000 new affordable rented homes is added to the national stock each year;
*   deplored the construction of new casinos as tools of regeneration and urged Presbyteries to be pro-active in their opposition to any such development in their area.

Church of Scotland Guild
The General Assembly:
*   welcomed the Guild's continuing concern for those affected by domestic abuse and affirmed the Church's commitment to include this issue in its training programmes for its ministries;

• commended the Guild's efforts to address the issue of human trafficking through initiatives like the *Extra mile* and encouraged it to continue to press for meaningful debate on the connection between prostitution and the trafficking of people for the sex industry.

Church Without Walls Planning Group
The General Assembly instructed the Group to consult with the appropriate bodies to try to ensure that finance is in place in order that they may plan a Re-Energise 4 Conference as a follow-up to the National Gathering and a preparation for engaging with the Year of the Homecoming in 2009.

Committee on Ecumenical Relations
The General Assembly:
• encouraged the Committee to develop appropriate links with the Community of Protestant Churches in Europe;
• encouraged the Church to celebrate the legacy of John Calvin, born in 1509, in his quincentenary year of 2009 and to seek to share his gifts ecumenically.

Council of Assembly
The General Assembly:
• instructed the Council to continue to support the development of Gaelic within the Church, including discussions with appropriate funding bodies;
• recognising the concern reflected in a number of reports to the Assembly, instructed the Council to develop further a strategic approach to directing external communication, including the possibility of establishing a post for a director of Strategic Communication; the Council is to bring recommendations to the General Assembly of 2009.

General Trustees
The General Assembly:
• welcomed the proposals with regard to financial assistance for renewable-energy projects in ecclesiastical buildings;
• approved proposals with regard to the carrying out of a nationwide revaluation for insurance purposes on the ecclesiastical properties for which congregations are responsible, and instructed congregations and Presbyteries to implement them;
• invited the General Trustees, in consultation with the Legal Questions Committee, to produce accessible guidelines relating to the use and alienation of funds by congregations, especially in relation to heritable property, in light of current charity-law practice.

Iona Community Board
The General Assembly commended the Iona Community's commitment to the Christian Aid Climate Change Campaign and encouraged churches to associate with its aim of reducing energy consumption by 5 per cent each year.

Legal Questions Committee
The General Assembly:
• urged Presbyteries, wherever possible, to make the necessary determinations in relation to buildings during adjustment procedures, preferably before the induction of a new minister to the Charge, and to use arbitration only as a measure of genuine last resort;
• instructed Presbyteries and congregations to comply with the scheme for the naming of

congregations, as devised by the Law Department of the Church and the Office of the Scottish Charity Regulator and adopted by the Committee.

Ministries Council

The General Assembly:

*   gave thanks to God for forty years of the ordained ministry of women in the Church of Scotland and celebrated the unique contribution made by women to its life and work;
*   instructed the Council to work together with Presbyteries to ensure that women have full and equal opportunity to participate in the ministries of the Church and that all discrimination on the grounds of gender is eradicated;
*   instructed the Council, in partnership with the Legal Questions Committee, the Worship and Doctrine Task Group, the Ecumenical Relations Committee and such other Councils, Committees and Agencies of the Church as may be necessary, to prepare a detailed initial report on the options for ministerial tenure for presentation to the General Assembly of 2009;
*   instructed Presbyteries, Kirk Sessions and Financial Boards, as well as Councils, Committees, Agencies and Agents of the General Assembly, to study the Council's Report on congregational conflict; in the light of that report, they are to review with urgency their own practices to determine where these require immediate adjustment with a view both to avoiding destructive conflict and to dealing more effectively with, and resolving, conflict situations when and where these arise. Reports on any such adjustments are to be submitted to the Council by 31 March 2009;
*   affirmed the recommendation of the Council that the International Christian College in Glasgow be not approved at this time as a recognised provider for training for the full-time ministry of Word and Sacrament;
*   reaffirmed the Church's commitment to encouraging, equipping and training both men and women for the ordained ministry, and instructed the Council to continue research into the reasons why a disproportionately lower number of women than men present for training; the Council is to report to the General Assembly of 2009;
*   approved the decision of the Council to provide full funding for in-service training for all active Readers;
*   approved the setting-up of an Emerging Ministries Fund;
*   recognised that the ministry of Word and Sacrament can be exercised in a variety of ways ranging from full-time to part-time, stipendiary to non-stipendiary, and instructed the Council to work with ecumenical partners and the Mission and Discipleship Council, academic providers and other interested parties to bring forward to the General Assembly of 2011 a coherent and integrated model of selection and training which allows for flexible engagement in ministry.

Mission and Discipleship Council

The General Assembly:

*   encouraged all congregations to offer to their community a celebration of Christmas Day which includes worship;
*   welcomed the report on the Strategic Development of the Use of Gaelic and encouraged the Council to develop its future plans;
*   encouraged all Agencies of the central Church to consult in the first instance the Publishing Committee about their book-publishing requirements;
*   commended the advantages to congregations of early consultation with the Committee on Church Art and Architecture when considering proposed changes to buildings, in terms of saving both time and money;

- reminded Presbyteries of the importance of informing the Committee on Church Art and Architecture at an early stage of any prospective closure of a church building so that an accurate record of its design may be prepared and the furniture and fittings disposed of appropriately;
- affirmed the significance of the work done at 'The Well' Asian Information and Advice Centre in Glasgow, both as a local resource and as an indicator of the Church's commitment to building good relations with people of other faiths and cultures, acting honestly and with integrity and offering reliable and respected advice and support;
- encouraged congregations creatively to consider, in consultation with the General Trustees, the best use of glebe land in order to bring greater benefit to the environment, the congregation and the parish;
- urged every Presbytery to consider the appointment of one or more Presbytery Youth and Children's Trainers to assist in the ongoing development of children's and youth ministry in local churches;
- instructed the Council:
  1. to initiate a consultation with the Ministries Council and those employed by the Church to work with young people to start a process of the Church of Scotland discussing the fundamental theological and practical issues of Youth Ministry;
  2. to investigate possible ways of the Church supporting or providing relevant professional training for those employed by the Church to work with young people;
  3. to develop a code of good practice for churches employing someone in this area of ministry;
- celebrated the tenth anniversary of Youth Representatives at the General Assembly and instructed the Council to explore with the General Assembly Arrangements Committee the possibility of Youth Delegates being given an indicative vote at future General Assemblies.

Panel on Review and Reform
The General Assembly:
- encouraged the Church Without Walls Planning Group to plan and deliver national strategies which enable future regional networking opportunities for congregations, including ecumenical relationships;
- commended to congregations and Presbyteries the use of the Panel's Vacancy Process Flowchart in conjunction with the appropriate Acts anent Vacancy Procedure;
- instructed the Ministries Council to produce a vacancy-procedure manual of the entire vacancy process, together with an information leaflet for congregations which outlines what should be expected during a period of vacancy; a report is to be given to the General Assembly of 2009;
- urged the Ministries Council to produce a pro-forma for the compilation of a Parish Profile and to make it available on its webpage for use by congregations.

Safeguarding Committee
The General Assembly affirmed the Church's commitment, in partnership with social-service organisations, to ongoing pastoral care of survivors of sexual abuse and their families, and reasserted the commitment of the Church to create a safe environment for children and vulnerable adults in congregations.

Social Care Council
The General Assembly commended the Council for its continued ecumenical activity both at home

and overseas and congratulated the Secretary of the Council on his election as President of Eurodiaconia.

Special Commission on Structure and Change
The General Assembly:
- instructed the Panel on Review and Reform to bring to the General Assembly of 2010 proposals for an alternative Presbytery structure, including size, devolved powers, staffing and appropriate budgets, along with the resources necessary to facilitate and sustain such changes;
- instructed the Council of Assembly to consider new ways of promoting the representation of the views of Presbyteries on all Church Councils and to report to the General Assembly of 2009 with proposals;
- instructed the Council of Assembly to make the position of Secretary to the Council, upon the retiral of the present Principal Clerk, a separate role from that of the Principal Clerk and a full-time position;
- instructed the Council of Assembly to consider creative ways to encourage vocational development and fresh opportunity for new challenges in respect of senior appointments;
- resolved that the present system of congregational allocations based on income be revised to provide greater incentive to local congregations to raise funds through Stewardship and other means for local purposes, and instructed the Stewardship and Finance Committee to bring to the General Assembly of 2009 proposals for implementation in 2010 of the recommendations contained in sections 12.1 to 12.5 of the Report, without compromising the Church's often-repeated commitment to its poorest congregations;
- encouraged the Church to strive to create an environment and atmosphere of trust among all within the Church in order that actions are taken with the objective of furthering the Kingdom of God rather than the organisation;
- resolved to appoint a Special Commission of nine persons to consider a range of issues related to the Third Article Declaratory and to report to the General Assembly of 2010.

Stewardship and Finance Committee
The General Assembly:
- instructed the Committee, in consultation with the Council of Assembly, to explore the appointment of an External Funding Adviser;
- approved the change in terminology from 'Ministries and Mission Allocations' to 'Ministries and Mission Contributions';
- reminded all Presbyteries of the importance of the timeous attestation of congregational accounts as part of the governance processes of the Church of Scotland, so that congregations can be assured that the accounts which they lodge with the Scottish Charities Regulator are fully compliant with the Regulations anent Congregational Finance.

Trustees of the Church of Scotland Housing and Loan Fund
The General Assembly:
- regretted the imposition of a new taxation liability upon retired ministers and upon widow(er)s and ex-spouses of ministers given much-needed housing support from the Fund by way of a house-purchase loan;
- encouraged the Trustees to continue their efforts to persuade the government to bring in amending legislation under which loans or beneficial rates of interest to retired ministers and their families will be treated as excluded benefits for taxation purposes.

World Mission Council

The General Assembly:

- expressed solidarity with Churches that are in a minority situation and are faced with discrimination and violence, resolved to share common commitment and take decisive action collectively to assist such minority Churches that are caught in situations of violence and conflict, and instructed the Council:
  1. to find creative ways of including inter-religious dialogue as a vehicle to promote and protect the rights of minorities;
  2. to seek to bring about awareness of such situations in the global Christian community;
  3. to help and advise partner Churches in developing self-understanding and identification through capacity-building and theological education;
  4. to strengthen ecumenical groups and movements in minority Churches for the building of a tolerant society;
  5. to raise the issues facing minority Churches in international forums for redress and remedy;

  the Council is to report to the General Assembly of 2009.

- recognised that twinning provides a missionary opportunity whose time has come, encouraged congregations and Presbyteries to enter into twinning arrangements with overseas partner Churches, and instructed the World Mission Council to provide the necessary level of twinning support staff within the Department, working with the Budget Group of the Council of Assembly to seek any necessary additional finance;

- welcomed the preparations being made internationally and in Scotland for marking the centenary of the Edinburgh 1910 World Missionary Conference. Presbyteries and congregations were encouraged to be aware of the opportunities presented by the centenary as the year 2010 approaches.

SECTION 5

Presbytery Lists

SECTION 5 – PRESBYTERY LISTS

In each Presbytery list, the congregations are listed in alphabetical order. In a linked charge, the names appear under the first named congregation. Under the name of the congregation will be found the name of the minister and, where applicable, that of an associate minister, auxiliary minister and member of the Diaconate. The years indicated after a minister's name in the congregational section of each Presbytery list are the year of ordination (column 1) and the year of current appointment (column 2). Where only one date is given, it is both the year of ordination and the year of appointment.

In the second part of each Presbytery list, those named are listed alphabetically. The first date is the year of ordination, and the following date is the year of appointment or retirement. If the person concerned is retired, then the appointment last held will be shown in brackets.

KEY TO ABBREVIATIONS

(E)   Indicates a Church Extension charge. New Charge Developments are separately indicated.
(GD)   Indicates a charge where it is desirable that the minister should have a knowledge of Gaelic.
(GE)   Indicates a charge where public worship must be regularly conducted in Gaelic.
(H)   Indicates that a Hearing Aid Loop system has been installed. In Linked charges, the (H) is placed beside the appropriate building as far as possible.
(L)   Indicates that a Chair Lift has been installed.
(T)   Indicates that the minister has been appointed on the basis of Terminable Tenure.

PRESBYTERY NUMBERS

1	Edinburgh	18	Dumbarton
2	West Lothian	19	Argyll
3	Lothian	20	
4	Melrose and Peebles	21	
5	Duns	22	Falkirk
6	Jedburgh	23	Stirling
7	Annandale and Eskdale	24	Dunfermline
8	Dumfries and Kirkcudbright	25	Kirkcaldy
9	Wigtown and Stranraer	26	St Andrews
10	Ayr	27	Dunkeld and Meigle
11	Irvine and Kilmarnock	28	Perth
12	Ardrossan	29	Dundee
13	Lanark	30	Angus
14	Greenock and Paisley	31	Aberdeen
15		32	Kincardine and Deeside
16	Glasgow	33	Gordon
17	Hamilton	34	Buchan
		35	Moray
		36	Abernethy
		37	Inverness
		38	Lochaber
		39	Ross
		40	Sutherland
		41	Caithness
		42	Lochcarron – Skye
		43	Uist
		44	Lewis
		45	Orkney
		46	Shetland
		47	England
		48	Europe
		49	Jerusalem

(1) EDINBURGH

The Presbytery meets:
- at Palmerston Place Church, Edinburgh, on the first Tuesday of October, November, December, February, April and May and on the last Tuesday of June; when the first Tuesday of April falls in Holy Week, the meeting is on the second Tuesday;
- in the church of the Moderator on the second Tuesday of September;
- in a venue and on a date to be intimated in March.

Clerk:	REV. W. PETER GRAHAM MA BD		10/1 Palmerston Place, Edinburgh EH12 5AA [E-mail: edinburgh@cofscotland.org.uk]	0131-225 9137
1	**Edinburgh: Albany Deaf Church of Edinburgh (H)**			
	Alistair F. Kelly BL (Locum)	1961	19 Avon Place, Edinburgh EH4 6RE [E-mail: alistairkelly@tiscali.co.uk]	0131-317 9877
2	**Edinburgh: Balerno (H)**			
	Jared W. Hay BA MTh DipMin DMin	1987	2001	3 Johnsburn Road, Balerno EH14 7DN [E-mail: jared.hay@blueyonder.co.uk]	0131-449 3830
3	**Edinburgh: Barclay (0131-229 6810) (E-mail: admin@barclaychurch.org.uk)**			
	Samuel A.R. Torrens BD	1995	2005	113 Meadowspot, Edinburgh EH10 5UY [E-mail: samtorrens@blueyonder.co.uk]	0131-478 2376
4	**Edinburgh: Blackhall St Columba's (0131-332 4431) (E-mail: secretary@blackhallstcolumba.org.uk)**			
	Alexander B. Douglas BD	1979	1991	5 Blinkbonny Crescent, Edinburgh EH4 3NB [E-mail: alexandjill@douglas.net]	0131-343 3708
5	**Edinburgh: Bristo Memorial Craigmillar**			
	James Patterson BSc BD	2003	2006	72 Blackchapel Close, Edinburgh EH15 3SL [E-mail: patterson@jimandmegan.force9.co.uk]	0131-657 3266
	Agnes M. Rennie (Miss) DCS			3/1 Craigmillar Court, Edinburgh EH16 4AD	0131-661 8475
6	**Edinburgh: Broughton St Mary's (H) (0131-556 4786)**			
	Joanne C. Hood (Miss) MA BD	2003		103 East Claremont Street, Edinburgh EH7 4JA [E-mail: hood137@btinternet.com]	0131-556 7313
7	**Edinburgh: Canongate (H)**			
	Neil N. Gardner MA BD	1991	2006	The Manse of Canongate, Edinburgh EH8 8BN [E-mail: nng22@btinternet.com]	0131-556 3515

8   **Edinburgh: Carrick Knowe (H) (0131-334 1505) (E-mail: carrickknowechurch@btinternet.com)**
Fiona M. Mathieson (Mrs) BEd BD   1988   2001   21 Traquair Park West, Edinburgh EH12 7AN
[E-mail: fiona.mathieson@ukgateway.net]
0131-334 9774

9   **Edinburgh: Colinton (H) (0131-441 2232) (E-mail: church.office@colinton-parish.com)**
George J. Whyte BSc BD DMin   1981   1992   The Manse, Colinton, Edinburgh EH13 0JR
[E-mail: george.whyte@colinton-parish.com]
0131-441 2315

10 **Edinburgh: Colinton Mains (H)**
Ian A. McQuarrie BD   1993   17 Swanston Green, Edinburgh EH10 7EW
[E-mail: ian.mcquarrie1@btinternet.com]
0131-445 3451

11 **Edinburgh: Corstorphine Craigsbank (H) (0131-334 6365)**
Stewart M. McPherson BD CertMin   1991   2003   17 Craigs Bank, Edinburgh EH12 8HD
[E-mail: smcpherson@blueyonder.co.uk]
0131-467 6826
07814 901429 (Mbl)

12 **Edinburgh: Corstorphine Old (H) (0131-334 7864) (E-mail: corold@aol.com)**
Moira McDonald MA BD   1997   2005   23 Manse Road, Edinburgh EH12 7SW
[E-mail: moira.mc@tesco.net]
0131-476 5893

13 **Edinburgh: Corstorphine St Anne's (H) (0131-316 4740) (E-mail: stannesoffice@surefish.co.uk)**
MaryAnn R. Rennie (Mrs) BD MTh   1998   2002   23 Belgrave Road, Edinburgh EH12 6NG
[E-mail: maryann.rennie@blueyonder.co.uk]
0131-334 3188

14 **Edinburgh: Corstorphine St Ninian's (H) (0131-539 6204) (E-mail: office@st-ninians.co.uk)**
Alexander T. Stewart MA BD FSAScot   1975   1995   17 Templeland Road, Edinburgh EH12 8RZ
[E-mail: alextstewart@blueyonder.co.uk]
0131-334 2978

15 **Edinburgh: Craigentinny St Christopher's (0131-258 2759)**
Caroline R. Lockerbie PhD   2007   61 Milton Crescent, Edinburgh EH15 3PQ
[E-mail: carolinelockerbie@blueyonder.co.uk]
0131-258 2759

16 **Edinburgh: Craiglockhart (H) (E-mail: office@craiglockhartchurch.org.uk)**
Andrew Ritchie BD DipMin DMin   1984   1991   202 Colinton Road, Edinburgh EH14 1BP
[E-mail: andrewritchie@talk21.com]
0131-443 2020

17 **Edinburgh: Craigmillar Park (H) (0131-667 5862) (E-mail: cpkirk@btinternet.com)**
Sarah E.C. Nicol (Mrs) BSc BD   1985   1994   14 Hallhead Road, Edinburgh EH16 5QJ
0131-667 1623

18 Edinburgh: Cramond (H) (E-mail: cramond.kirk@blueyonder.co.uk)
G. Russell Barr BA BD MTh DMin   1979   1993   Manse of Cramond, Edinburgh EH4 6NS   0131-336 2036
[E-mail: rev.r.barr@blueyonder.co.uk]

19 Edinburgh: Currie (H) (0131-451 5141) (E-mail: currie_kirk@btconnect.com)
Lezley J. Kennedy BD ThM MTh   2000   2008   43 Lanark Road West, Currie EH14 5JX   0131-449 4719

20 Edinburgh: Dalmeny linked with Edinburgh: Queensferry
Vacant   1 Station Road, South Queensferry EH30 9HY   0131-331 1100
Sean Swindells BD MTh (Assoc)   1996   2007   112 Greenbank Crescent, Edinburgh EH10 5SZ   0131-447 4032
[E-mail: sswindells@blueyonder.co.uk]

21 Edinburgh: Davidson's Mains (H) (0131-312 6282) (E-mail: life@dmainschurch.plus.com)
Jeremy R.H. Middleton LLB BD   1981   1988   1 Hillpark Terrace, Edinburgh EH4 7SX   0131-336 3078
[E-mail: life@dmainschurch.plus.com]

22 Edinburgh: Dean (H)
Mark M. Foster BSc BD   1998   1 Ravelston Terrace, Edinburgh EH4 3EF   0131-332 5736
[E-mail: markmfoste-@mac.com]

23 Edinburgh: Drylaw (0131-343 6643)
Patricia Watson (Mrs) BD   2005   15 House o' Hill Gardens, Edinburgh EH4 2AR   0131-343 1441
[E-mail: patricia@patriciawatson.wanadoo.co.uk]   07969 942627 (Mbl)

24 Edinburgh: Duddingston (H) (E-mail: dodinskirk@aol.com)
James A.P. Jack   1989   2001   Manse of Duddingston, Old Church Lane, Edinburgh EH15 3PX
  BSc BArch BD DMin RIBA ARIAS   [E-mail: jamesapjack@aol.com]   0131-661 4240

25 Edinburgh: Fairmilehead (H) (0131-445 2374) (E-mail: fairmilehead.p.c@btconnect.com)
John R. Munro BD   1976   1992   6 Braid Crescent, Edinburgh EH10 6AU   0131-446 9363
[E-mail: revjohnmunro@hotmail.com]

26 Edinburgh: Gilmerton (New Charge Development)
Paul H. Beautyman MA BD   1993   2002   43 Ravenscroft Street, Edinburgh EH17 8QJ   0131-664 7538
[E-mail: ncdgilmerton@uk.uumail.com]

27 Edinburgh: Gorgie (H) (0131-337 7936)
Peter I. Barber MA BD   1984   1995   90 Myreside Road, Edinburgh EH10 5BZ   0131-337 2284
[E-mail: pibarber@toucansurf.com]

28 Edinburgh: Granton (H) (0131-552 3033)
Norman A. Smith MA BD   1997   2005   8 Wardie Crescent, Edinburgh EH5 1AG   0131-551 2159
[E-mail: norm@smith1971.fsnet.co.uk]
Marilynn Steele (Mrs) DCS   2 Northfield Gardens, Prestonpans EH32 9LQ   01875 811497
[E-mail: marilynnsteele@aol.com]

29 Edinburgh: Greenbank (H) (0131-447 9969) (E-mail: greenbankchurch@btconnect.com)
Alison J. Swindells (Mrs) LLB BD   1998   2007   112 Greenbank Crescent, Edinburgh EH10 5SZ   0131-447 4032
[E-mail: alisonswindells@blueyonder.co.uk]

30 Edinburgh: Greenside (H) (0131-556 5588)
Andrew F. Anderson MA BD   1981   80 Pilrig Street, Edinburgh EH6 5AS   0131-554 3277 (Tel/Fax)
[E-mail: andrew@pilrig.fsnet.co.uk]

31 Edinburgh: Greyfriars Tolbooth and Highland Kirk (GE) (H) (0131-225 1900) (E-mail: enquiries@greyfriarskirk.com)
Richard E. Frazer BA BD DMin   1986   2003   12 Tantallon Place, Edinburgh EH9 1NZ   0131-667 6610
[E-mail: tantallon@ukonline.co.uk]

32 Edinburgh: High (St Giles') (0131-225 4363) (E-mail: info@stgilescathedral.org.uk)
Gilleasbuig Macmillan   1969   1973   St Giles' Cathedral, Edinburgh EH1 1RE   0131-225 4363
  CVO MA BD DRhc DD   [E-mail: minister@stgilescathedral.org.uk]
Hilary W. Smith (Miss)   1999   2003   11 South Lauder Road, Edinburgh EH9 2NB   0131-667 6539
  BD DipMin MTh PhD (Assistant)   [E-mail: heloise.smith@virgin.net]

33 Edinburgh: Holyrood Abbey (H) (0131-661 6002)
Philip R. Hair BD   1980   1998   100 Willowbrae Avenue, Edinburgh EH8 7HU   0131-652 0640
[E-mail: phil@holyroodabbey.f2s.com]

34 Edinburgh: Holy Trinity (H) (0131-442 3304)
Kenneth S. Borthwick MA BD   1983   2005   16 Thorburn Road, Edinburgh EH13 0BQ   0131-441 1403
[E-mail: kennysamuel@aol.com]
Ian MacDonald (Assoc)   2005   12 Sighthill Crescent, Edinburgh EH11 4QE   0131-453 6279
Joyce Mitchell (Mrs) DCS   16/4 Murrayburn Place, Edinburgh EH14 2RR   0131-453 6548
Oliver M. Clegg BD (Youth Minister)   2003   256/5 Lanark Road, Edinburgh EH14 2LR   0131-443 0825

35 Edinburgh: Inverleith (H)
D. Hugh Davidson MA   1965   1975   43 Inverleith Gardens, Edinburgh EH3 5PR   0131-552 3874
[E-mail: hdavidson@freeuk.com]

36 Edinburgh: Juniper Green (H)
James S. Dewar MA BD   1983   2000   476 Lanark Road, Juniper Green, Edinburgh EH14 5BQ   0131-453 3494
[E-mail: jim.dewar@blueyonder.co.uk]

37 Edinburgh: Kaimes Lockhart Memorial
Iain D. Penman BD   1977   1995   76 Lasswade Road, Edinburgh EH16 6SF   0131-664 2287
[E-mail: iainpenmanklm@aol.com]

38 Edinburgh: Kirkliston
Vacant   43 Main Street, Kirkliston EH29 9AF   0131-333 3298

39 Edinburgh: Kirk o' Field (T) (H)
Ian D. Maxwell MA BD PhD   1977   1996   31 Hatton Place, Edirburgh EH9 1UA
[E-mail: i.d.maxwell@quista.net]   0131-667 7954

40 Edinburgh: Leith North (H) (0131-553 7378) (E-mail: nlpc-office@btinternet.com)
Kenneth S. Baird   1998   2003   6 Craighall Gardens, Edinburgh EH6 4RJ   0131-552 4411
MSc PhD BD CEng MIMarEST

41 Edinburgh: Leith St Andrew's (H)
Elizabeth J.B. Youngson BD   1996   2006   30 Lochend Road, Ecinburgh EH6 8BS
[E-mail: elizabeth.youngson@btinternet.com]   0131-554 7695

42 Edinburgh: Leith St Serf's (T) (H)
Sara R. Embleton (Mrs) BA BD MTh   1987   1999   20 Wilton Road, Edinburgh EH16 5NX
[E-mail: sara.embletcn@blueyonder.co.uk]   0131-478 1624

43 Edinburgh: Leith St Thomas' Junction Road (T)
George C. Shand MA BD   1981   2003   107 Easter Warriston Edinburgh EH7 4QZ
[E-mail: georgeshand@blueyonder.co.uk]   0131-467 7789

44 Edinburgh: Leith South (H) (0131-554 2578) (E-mail: slpc@dial.pipex.com)
Ian Y. Gilmour BD   1985   1995   37 Claremont Road, Edinburgh EH6 7NN
[E-mail: IanYG@blueyonder.co.uk]   0131-554 3062
Louise Duncan (Mrs) BD (Assoc)   2005   25 Elmwood Terrace, Edinburgh EH6 8DF   0131-538 0243

45 Edinburgh: Leith Wardie (H) (0131-551 3847) (E-mail: churchoffice@wardie.org.uk)
Brian C. Hilsley LLB BD   1990   35 Lomond Road, Edinburgh EH5 3JN
[E-mail: brianhilsley@btinternet.com]   0131-552 3328

46 Edinburgh: Liberton (H)
John N. Young MA BD PhD   1996   7 Kirk Park, Edinburgh EH16 6HZ
[E-mail: LLLjyoung@btinternet.com]   0131-664 3067

47 Edinburgh: Liberton Northfield (H) (0131-551 3847)
John M. McPake LTh   2000   9 Claverhouse Drive Edinburgh EH16 6BR
[E-mail: john_mcpake9@yahoo.co.uk]   0131-658 1754

48 Edinburgh: London Road (H) (0131-661 1149)
Sigrid Marten   1997   2006   26 Inchview Terrace. Edinburgh EH7 6TQ
[E-mail: minister.lrp-@phonecoop.coop]   0131-669 5311

49 Edinburgh: Marchmont St Giles' (H) (0131-447 4359)
Karen K. Watson BD MTh   1997   2002   19 Hope Terrace, Edinburgh EH9 2AP
[E-mail: karen@marchmontstgiles.org.uk]   0131-447 2834

50 **Edinburgh: Mayfield Salisbury (0131-667 1522)**
Scott S. McKenna BA BD MTh   1994   2000   26 Seton Place, Edinburgh EH9 2JT
[E-mail: scottsmckenna@aol.com]   0131-667 1286

51 **Edinburgh: Morningside (H) (0131-447 6745) (E-mail: office@morningsideparishchurch.org.uk)**
Derek Browning MA BD DMin   1987   2003   20 Braidburn Crescent, Edinburgh EH10 6EN
[E-mail: derek.browning@btinternet.com]   0131-447 1617 (Tel/Fax)
07050 133876 (Mbl)

52 **Edinburgh: Morningside United (H) (0131-447 3152)**
John R. Smith MA BD   1973   1998   1 Midmar Avenue, Edinburgh EH10 6BS
[E-mail: jrs@blueyonder.co.uk]   0131-447 8724

53 **Edinburgh: Muirhouse St Andrew's (E)**
R. Russell McLarty MA BD   1985   2006   9 Sanderson's Wynd, Tranent EH33 1DA   01875 614496
(Interim Minister)
Brenda Robson PhD (Auxiliary Minister)   Old School House, 2 Baird Road, Ratho, Newbridge EH28 8RA
[E-mail: brendarobson@tiscali.co.uk]   0131-333 2746

54 **Edinburgh: Murrayfield (H) (0131-337 1091) (E-mail: mpchurch@btconnect.com)**
William D. Brown BD CQSW   1987   2001   45 Murrayfield Gardens, Edinburgh EH12 6DH
[E-mail: wdb@fish.co.uk]   0131-337 5431

55 **Edinburgh: Newhaven (H)**
Peter Bluett   2007   158 Granton Road, Edinburgh EH5 3RF
[E-mail: pbo1128104@blueyonder.co.uk]   0131-476 5212

56 **Edinburgh: New Restalrig (H) (0131-661 5676)**
David L. Court BSc BD   1989   2000   19 Abercorn Road, Edinburgh EH8 7DP
[E-mail: david@dlc.org.uk]   0131-661 4045

57 **Edinburgh: Old Kirk (H) (0131-332 4354) (E-mail: minister.oldkirk@btinternet.com)**
Tony McLean-Foreman   1987   2007   24 Pennywell Road, Edinburgh EH4 4HD
[E-mail: tony@foreman.org.uk]   0131-332 4354

58 **Edinburgh: Palmerston Place (H) (0131-220 1690) (E-mail: admin@palmerstonplacechurch.com)**
Colin A.M. Sinclair BA BD   1981   1996   30B Cluny Gardens, Edinburgh EH10 6BJ
[E-mail: colins.ppc@virgin.net]   0131-447 9598
0131-225 3312 (Fax)

59 **Edinburgh: Pilrig St Paul's (0131-553 1876)**
John M. Tait BSc BD   1985   1999   78 Pilrig Street, Edinburgh EH6 5AS
[E-mail: john.m.tait@blueyonder.co.uk]   0131-554 1842

60 **Edinburgh: Polwarth (H) (0131-346 2711) (E-mail: polwarthchurch@tiscali.co.uk)**
Linda J. Dunbar BSc BA BD PhD FRHS   2000   2005   88 Craiglockhart Road, Edinburgh EH14 1EP
[E-mail: polwarthminister@ouvip.com]   0131-441 5335

61 **Edinburgh: Portobello Old (H)**
Andrew R.M. Patterson MA BD   1985   2006   6 Hamilton Terrace, Edinburgh EH15 1NB   0131-657 5545

62 **Edinburgh: Portobello St James' (H)**
Peter Webster BD   1977   2002   34 Brighton Place, Edinburgh EH15 1LT
[E-mail: peterwebster101@hotmail.com]   0131-669 1767

63 **Edinburgh: Portobello St Philip's Joppa (H) (0131-669 3641)**
Stewart G. Weaver BA BD PhD   2003   6 St Mary's Place, Edinburgh EH15 2QF
[E-mail: stewartweaver@btinternet.com]   0131-669 2410

64 **Edinburgh: Priestfield (H) (0131-667 5644)**
Thomas N. Johnston LTh   1972   1990   13 Lady Road, Edinturgh EH16 5PA
[E-mail: tomjohnstor_@blueyonder.co.uk]   0131-668 1620

65 **Edinburgh: Queensferry (H)** See Edinburgh: Dalmeny

66 **Edinburgh: Ratho**
Ian J. Wells BD   1999   2 Freelands Road, Ratho, Newbridge EH28 8NP
[E-mail: ianjwells@btinternet.com]   0131-333 1346

67 **Edinburgh: Reid Memorial (H) (0131-662 1203) (E-mail: reid.memorial@btinternet.com)**
Brian M. Embleton BD   1976   1985   20 Wilton Road, Edinburgh EH16 5NX
[E-mail: brianembleton@btinternet.com]   0131-667 3981

68 **Edinburgh: Richmond Craigmillar (H) (0131-661 6561)**
Elizabeth M. Henderson (Miss)   1985   1997   13 Wisp Green, Edirburgh EH15 3QX
MA BD MTh   [E-mail: lizhende@tscali.co.uk]   0131-669 1133
Stephen Manners MA BD   1989   2007   124 Fernieside Crescent, Edinburgh EH17 7DH
(Pastoral Assistant)   [E-mail: sk.manners@blueyonder.co.uk]   0131-620 0589

69 **Edinburgh: St Andrew's and St George's (H) (0131-225 3847) (E-mail: info@standrewsandstgeorges.org.uk)**
Vacant   25 Comely Bank, Edinburgh EH4 1AJ   0131-332 5324
Dorothy U. Anderson LLB DipLP BD   2006   5 West Castle Road, Edinburgh EH10 5AT   0131-229 5862
(Outreach Minister)

70 **Edinburgh: St Andrew's Clermiston**
Alistair H. Keil BD DipMin   1989   87 Drum Brae South, Edinburgh EH12 8TD
[E-mail: ahkeil@blueyonder.co.uk]   0131-339 4149

71 Edinburgh: St Catherine's Argyle (H) (0131-667 7220)
Vacant
5 Palmerston Road, Edinburgh EH9 1TL
0131-667 9344

72 Edinburgh: St Colm's (T) (H)
Douglas S. Paterson MA BD   1976   2005
6 Groathill Loan, Edinburgh EH4 2WL
[E-mail: dostpa@aol.com]
0131-315 4541

73 Edinburgh: St Cuthbert's (H) (0131-229 1142) (E-mail: office@stcuthberts.net)
David W. Denniston BD DipMin   1981   2008
34A Murrayfield Road, Edinburgh EH12 6ER
[E-mail: denniston.david@gmail.com]
0131-337 6637
07903 926727 (Mbl)

74 Edinburgh: St David's Broomhouse (H) (0131-443 9851)
Robert A. Mackenzie LLB BD   1993   2005
33 Traquair Park West, Edinburgh EH12 7AN
[E-mail: rob.anne@blueyonder.co.uk]
0131-334 1730

Liz Crocker (Mrs) DipComEd DCS
77C Craigcrook Road, Edinburgh EH4 3PH
0131-332 0227

75 Edinburgh: St George's West (H) (0131-225 7001) (E-mail: st-georges-west@btconnect.com)
Peter J. Macdonald BD DipMin   1986   1998
6 Wardie Avenue, Edinburgh EH5 2AB
[E-mail: peter@stgeorgeswest.com]
0131-552 4333

76 Edinburgh: St John's Oxgangs
Vacant
2 Caiystane Terrace, Edinburgh EH10 6SR
0131-445 1688

77 Edinburgh: St Margaret's (H) (0131-554 7400) (E-mail: stm.parish@virgin.net)
Carol H.M. Ford DSD RSAMD BD   2003
43 Moira Terrace, Edinburgh EH7 6TD
[E-mail: fordcar@fish.co.uk]
0131-669 7329

Pauline Rycroft-Sadi (Mrs) DCS   2006
6 Ashville Terrace, Edinburgh EH6 8DD
0131-554 6564

78 Edinburgh: St Martin's
Russel Moffat BD MTh PhD   1986   2008
5 Duddingston Crescent, Edinburgh EH15 3AS
[E-mail: rbmoffat@tiscali.co.uk]
0131-657 9894

79 Edinburgh: St Michael's (H) (E-mail: office@stmichaels-kirk.co.uk)
James D. Aitken BD   2002   2005
9 Merchiston Gardens, Edinburgh EH10 5DD
[E-mail: james.aitken2@btinternet.com]
0131-346 1970

80 Edinburgh: St Nicholas' Sighthill
Alan R. Cobain BD   2000   2008
122 Sighthill Loan, Edinburgh EH11 4NT
[E-mail: erinbro@hotmail.co.uk]
0131-442 2510

81	**Edinburgh: St Stephen's Comely Bank (0131-315 4616)**				
	Jonathan de Groot BD MTh CPS	2007		8 Blinkbonny Crescent, Edinburgh EH4 3NB	0131-332 3364
				[E-mail: minister@st-stephenschurch.org.uk]	
82	**Edinburgh: Slateford Longstone**				
	Michael W. Frew BSc BD	1978	2005	50 Kingsknowe Road South, Edinburgh EH14 2JW	0131-466 5308
				[E-mail: mwfrew@blueyonder.co.uk]	
83	**Edinburgh: Stenhouse St Aidan's**				
	Vacant			65 Balgreen Road, Edinburgh EH12 5UA	0131-337 7711
84	**Edinburgh: Stockbridge (H) (0131-332 0122) (E-mail: stockbridgechurch@btopenworld.com)**				
	Anne T. Logan (Mrs) MA BD MTh DMin	1981	1993	19 Eildon Street, Edinburgh EH3 5JU	0131-557 6052
				[E-mail: annetlogan@blueyonder.co.uk]	
85	**Edinburgh: Tron Moredun**				
	Vacant			467 Gilmerton Road, Edinburgh EH17 7JG	0131-666 2584
86	**Edinburgh: Viewforth (T) (H) (0131-229 1917)**				
	Anthony P. Thornthwaite MTh	1995		91 Morningside Drive, Edinburgh EH10 5NN	0131-447 6684
				[E-mail: tony.thornthwaite@blueyonder.co.uk]	

Name			Charge / Note	Address	Telephone
Aitken, Alexander R. MA	1965	1997	(Newhaven)	36 King's Meadow, Edinburgh EH16 5JW	0131-667 1404
Aitken, Ewan R. BA BD	1992	2002	Church and Society Council	159 Restalrig Avenue, Edinburgh EH7 6PJ	0131-467 1660
Anderson, Robert S. BD	1988	1997	Scottish Churches World Exchange	S Colm's International House, 23 Inverleith Terrace, Edinburgh EH3 5NS	0131-315 4444
Armitage, William L. BSc BD	1976	2006	(Edinburgh: London Road)	73 Toll House Grove, Tranent EH33 2QR	01875 612047
				[E-mail: bill@billarm.plus.com]	
Baigrie, R.A. MA	1945	1985	(Kirkurd with Newlands)	33 Inchcolm Terrace, South Queensferry EH30 9NA	0131-331 4311
Barrington, Charles W.H. MA BD	1997	2007	(Associate: Edinburgh: Balerno)	532 Lanark Road, Edinburgh EH14 5DH	0131-453 4826
Baxter, Richard F. OBE MA BD	1954	1990	(Assistant at St Andrew's and St George's)		
Beckett, David M. BA BD	1964	2002	(Greyfriars, Tolbooth and Highland Kirk)	138 Braid Road, Edinburgh EH10 6JB	0131-447 7735
				1=7, 31 Sciennes Road, Edinburgh EH9 1NT	0131-667 2672
				[E-mail: davidbeckett3@aol.com]	
Blakey, Ronald S. MA BD MTh	1962	2000	Editor: *The Year Book*	5 Moss Side Road, Biggar ML12 6GF	01899 229226
Booth, Jennifer (Mrs) BD	1996	2004	(Associate: Leith South)	39 Lilyhill Terrace, Edinburgh EH8 7DR	0131-661 3813
Boyd, Kenneth M. MA BD PhD FRCPE	1970	1996	University of Edinburgh: Medical Ethics	1 Doune Terrace, Edinburgh EH3 6DY	0131-225 6485
Brady, Ian D. BSc ARCST BD	1967	2001	(Edinburgh: Corstorphine Old)	28 Frankfield Crescent, Dalgety Bay, Dunfermline KY11 9LW	01383 825104
				[E-mail: pidb@dbay28.fsnet.co.uk]	
Brown, William D. MA	1963	1989	(Wishaw: Thornlie)	93 Craigend Park, Edinburgh EH16 5XY	0131-672 2936
				[E-mail: wdbrown@surefish.co.uk]	
Bruce, Lilian M. (Miss) BD MTh	1971	2001	(Daviot and Dunlichity with Moy, Dalarossie and Tomatin)	33 Falcon Court, Edinburgh EH10 4AF	

Name	Years	Role	Address	Tel.
Cameron, G. Gordon MA BD STM	1957 1997	(Juniper Green)	4 Ladywell Grove, Clackmannan FK10 4JQ	01259 723769
Cameron, John W.M. MA BD	1957 1996	(Liberton)	10 Plewlands Gardens, Edinburgh EH10 5JP	0131-447 1277
Chalmers, Murray MA	1965 2006	(Hospital Chaplain)	8 Easter Warriston, Edinburgh EH7 4QX	0131-552 4211
Clark, Christine M. (Mrs) BA BD MTh	2006 2008	Practising Certificate	32 Dreghorn Loan, Edinburgh EH13 0DE	0131-466 4353
Clinkenbeard, William W. BSc BD STM	1966 2000	(Edinburgh: Carrick Knowe)	4 Aline Court, Dalgety Bay, Dunfermline KY11 5GP [E-mail: bjclinks@compuserve.com]	01383 824011
Cook, John MA BD	1967 2005	(Edinburgh: Leith St Andrew's)	26 Silverknowes Court, Edinburgh EH4 5NR	0131-312 8447
Cook, John Weir MA BD	1962 2002	(Edinburgh: Portobello St Philip's Joppa)	74 Pinkie Road, Musselburgh EH21 7QT [E-mail: johnweircook.@hotmail.com]	0131-653 0992
Crichton, Thomas JP ChStJ MA	1965 2004	(Hospital Chaplain)	18 Carlton Terrace, Edinburgh EH7 5DD	0131-557 0009
Curran, Elizabeth M. (Miss) BD	1995 2008	(Aberlour)	27 Captain's Road, Edinburgh EH17 8HR [E-mail: ecurran8@aol.com]	0131-664 1358
Cuthell, Tom C. MA BD MTh	1965 2007	(Edinburgh: St Cuthbert's)	Flat 10, 2 Kingsburgh Crescent, Waterfront, Edinburgh EH5 1JS	0131-476 3864
Davidson, Ian M.P. MBE MA BD	1957 1994	(Stirling: Allan Park South with Church of the Holy Rude)	13/8 Craigend Park, Edinburgh EH16 5XX	0131-664 0074
Dawson, Michael S. BTech BD	1979 2005	(Associate: Edinburgh: Holy Trinity)	9 The Broich, Alva FK12 5NR [E-mail: mixpen.dawson@btinternet.com]	01259 769309
Denniston, Jane M. MA BD	2002	Ministries Council	34A Murrayfield Road, Edinburgh EH12 6ER	0131-337 6637
Dilbey, Mary D. (Miss) BD	1997 2002	(West Kirk of Calder)	41 Bonaly Rise, Edinburgh EH13 0QU	0131-441 9092
Dougall, Elspeth G. (Mrs) MA BD	1989 2001	(Edinburgh: Marchmont St Giles')	60B Craigmillar Park, Edinburgh EH16 5PU	0131-668 1342
Douglas, Colin R. MA BD STM	1969 2007	(Livingston Ecumenical Parish)	34 West Pilton Gardens, Edinburgh EH4 4EQ [E-mail: colinrdouglas@btinternet.com]	0131-551 3808
Doyle, Ian B. MA BD PhD	1946 1991	(Department of National Mission)	21 Lygon Road, Edinburgh EH16 5QD	0131-667 2697
Drummond, Rhoda (Miss) DCS	1983 1998	(Deaconess)	Flat K, 23 Grange Loan, Edinburgh EH9 2ER	0131-668 3631
Dunn, W. Iain C. DA LTh	1976 2004	(Pilrig and Dalmeny Street)	10 Fox Covert Avenue, Edinburgh EH12 6UQ	0131-334 1665
Elliott, Gavin J. MA BD	1998 2007	Ministries Council	c/o 121 George Street, Edinburgh EH2 4YN	0131-225 5722
Farquharson, Gordon MA BD DipEd	1968 2000	(Stonehaven: Dunnottar)	26 Learmonth Court, Edinburgh EH4 1PB [E-mail: gfarqu@talktalk.net]	0131-343 1047
Faulds, Norman L. MA BD FSAScot	1968 2000	(Aberlady with Gullane)	10 West Fenton Court, West Fenton, North Berwick EH39 5AE	01620 842331
Fergusson, David A.S. MA BD DPhil FRSE	1984 2000	University of Edinburgh	23 Riselaw Crescent, Edinburgh EH10 6HN	0131-447 4022
Forrester, Duncan B. MA BD DPhil DD FRSE	1962 1978	(University of Edinburgh)	25 Kingsburgh Road, Edinburgh EH12 6DZ [E-mail: dbforrester@dsl.pipex.com]	0131-337 5646
Forrester, Margaret R. (Mrs) MA BD	1974 2003	(Edinburgh: St Michael's)	25 Kingsburgh Road, Edinburgh EH12 6DZ [E-mail: margaretforrester@dsl.pipex.com]	0131-337 5646
Fraser, Shirley A. (Miss) MA BD	1992 2008	(Scottish Field Director: Friends International)	30 Parkhead Avenue, Edinburgh EH11 4SG	0131-443 7268
Galbraith, Douglas MA BD BMus MPhil ARSCM	1965 2005	(Office for Worship, Doctrine and Artistic Matters)	9 Bonnington Terrace, Edinburgh EH6 4BP	0131-555 0701
Gardner, John V.	1997 2003	(Glamis, Inverarity and Kinnettles)	75/1 Lockharton Avenue, Edinburgh EH14 1BD [E-mail: jvg66@hotmail.com]	0131-443 7126
Gibson, John C.L. MA BD DPhil	1959 1994	(University of Edinburgh)	Cairnbank, Morton Street South, Edinburgh EH15 2NB	0131-669 3635
Gordon, Margaret (Mrs) DCS		(Edinburgh: Corstorphine St Ninian's)	92 Lanark Road West, Currie EH14 5LA	0131-449 2554
Gordon, Tom MA BD	1974 1994	Chaplain: Marie Curie Hospice, Edinburgh	22 Gosford Road, Port Seton, Prestonpans EH32 0HF	01875 812262

Name	Years	Role	Address	Phone
Graham, W. Peter MA BD	1967 1993	Presbytery Clerk	23/6 East Comiston, Edinburgh EH10 6RZ [E-mail: edinburgh@cofscotland.org.uk]	0131-445 5763
Harkness, James CB OBE QHC MA DD	1961 1995	(Chaplain General: Army)	13 Saxe Coburg Place, Edinburgh EH3 5BR	0131-343 1297
Hill, J. William BA BD	1967 2001	(Corstorphine St Anne's)	33/9 Murrayfield Road, Edinburgh EH12 6EP	
Hutchison, Maureen (Mrs) DCS		(Deaconess)	23 Drylaw Crescent, Edinburgh EH4 2AU	0131-332 8020
Irving, William D. LTh	1985 2005	(Golspie)	122 Swanston Muir, Edinburgh EH10 7HY	0131-441 3384
Jamieson, Gordon D. MA BD	1974 2000	Head of Stewardship	44 Goldpark Place, Livingston EH54 6LW	01506 412020
Jeffrey, Eric W.S. JP MA	1954 1994	(Edinburgh Bristo Memorial)	13 Gillespie Crescent, Edinburgh EH10 4HT	0131-229 7815
Kant, Everard FVCM MTh	1953 1988	(Kinghorn)	1D/1 Maxwell Street, Edinburgh EH10 5GZ	0131-466 2607
Kelly, Ewan R. MB ChB BD PhD	1994 2006	Chaplain: St Columba's Hospice	15 Boswall Road, Edinburgh EH5 3RW	0131-551 7706
Laidlaw, Victor W.M. BD	1975 2008	(Edinburgh: St Catherine's Argyle)	9 Tern Road, Dunfermline KY11 8GA	01383 620134
Lawson, Kenneth C. MA BD	1963 1999	(Adviser in Adult Education)	56 Easter Drylaw View, Edinburgh EH4 2QP	0131-539 3311
Lyon, D.H.S. MA BD STM	1952 1986	(Board of World Mission and Unity)	30 Mansefield Road, Balerno EH14 7JZ	
McCaskill, George I.L. MA BD	1953 1990	(Religious Education)	19 Tyler's Acre Road, Edinburgh EH12 7HY	0131-334 7451
Macdonald, Finlay A.J. MA BD PhD DD	1971 1996	Principal Clerk	c/o 121 George Street, Edinburgh EH2 4YN	0131-225 5722
Macdonald, William J. BD	1976 2002	(Board of National Mission: New Charge Development)	1/13 North Werber Park, Edinburgh EH4 1SY	0131-332 0254
MacGregor, Margaret S. (Miss) MA BD DipEd	1985 1994	(Calcutta)	16 Learmonth Court, Edinburgh EH4 1PB	0131-332 1089
McGregor, Alistair G.C. QC BD	1987 2002	(Edinburgh: Leith North)	22 Primrose Bank Road, Edinburgh EH5 3JG	0131-551 2802
McGregor, T. Stewart MBE MA BD	1957 1998	(Chaplain: Edinburgh Royal Infirmary)	19 Lonsdale Terrace, Edinburgh EH3 9HL [E-mail: cetsm@dircon.uk]	0131-229 5332
Maclean, Ailsa G. (Mrs) BD DipCE	1979 1988	Chaplain: George Heriot's School	28 Swan Spring Avenue, Edinburgh EH10 6NJ	0131-445 1320
MacLean, Marjory A. (Miss) LLB BD PhD	1991 1998	Depute Clerk: General Assembly	c/o 121 George Street, Edinburgh EH2 4YN	0131-225 5722
McMahon, John K.S. MA BD	1998 2006	Lead Chaplain: NHS Lothian Primary Care and Mental Health	Department of Spiritual Care, Royal Edinburgh Hospital, Morningside Terrace, Edinburgh EH10 5HF [E-mail: john.mcmahon@1pct.scot.nhs.uk]	
MacMurchie, F. Lynne LLB BD	1998 2003	Health Care Chaplain	Edinburgh Community Mental Health Chaplaincy, 41 George IV Bridge, Edinburgh EH1 1EL	0131-220 5150
McPheat, Elspeth DCS		Deaconess: CrossReach	1/5 New Orchardfield, Edinburgh EH6 5ET	0131-554 4143
McPhee, Duncan C. MA BD	1953 1993	(Department of National Mission)	8 Belvedere Park, Edinburgh EH6 4LR	0131-552 6784
Macpherson, Allan S. MA	1967 1993	Merchiston Castle School	36 Craigmillar Castle Road, Edinburgh EH16 4AR	
Macpherson, Colin C.R. MA BD	1958 1996	(Dunfermline St Margaret's)	7 Eva Place, Edinburgh EH9 3ET	0131-667 1456
Mathieson, Angus R. MA BD	1988 1998	Ministries Council	21 Traquair Park West, Edinburgh EH12 7AN	0131-334 9774
Middleton, Paul BMus BD ThM PhD	2000 2005	University of Wales: Lampeter	Department of Theology and Religious Studies, University of Wales, Lampeter, Ceredigion SA48 7ED [E-mail: p.middleton@lamp.ac.uk]	01570 424801
Moir, Ian A. MA BD	1962 2000	(Adviser for Urban Priority Areas)	28/6 Comely Bank Avenue, Edinburgh EH4 1EL	0131-332 2748
Monteith, W. Graham BD PhD	1974 1994	(Flotta and Fara with Hoy and Walls)	20/3 Grandfield, Edinburgh EH6 4TL	0131-552 2564
Morrice, William G. MA BD STM PhD	1957 1991	(St John's College Durham)	Flat 37, The Cedars, 2 Manse Road, Edinburgh EH12 7SN [E-mail: w.g.morrice@btinternet.com]	0131-316 4845
Morrison, Mary B. (Mrs) MA BD DipEd	1978 2000	(Edinburgh: Stenhouse St Aidan's)	14 Eildon Terrace, Edinburgh EH3 5LU	0131-556 1962
Morton, Andrew R. MA BD DD	1956 1994	(Board of World Mission and Unity)	11 Oxford Terrace, Edinburgh EH4 1PX	0131-332 6592
Morton, R. Colin BA BD	1960 1998	(Jerusalem)	313 Lanark Road West, Currie EH14 5RS	0131-449 7359
Moyes, Sheila A. (Miss) DCS		(Deaconess)	158 Pilton Avenue, Edinburgh EH5 2JZ	0131-551 1731

Name			Position	Address	Tel.
Mulligan, Anne MA DCS	1968	2000	Deaconess: Hospital Chaplain	27A Craigour Avenue, Edinburgh EH17 1NH	0131-664 3426
Munro, George A.M.	1953	1996	(Edinburgh: Cluny)	108 Caiyside, Edinburgh EH10 7HR	0131-445 5829
Murrie, John BD	1966	2006	(Kirkliston)	31 Nicol Road, The Whins, Broxburn EH52 6JJ	01506 852464
Musgrave, Clarence W. BA BD ThM			(Jerusalem: St Andrew's)	4 Ravelston Heights, Edinburgh EH4 3LX [E-mail: cwm_edinburgh@btopenworld.com]	0131-332 6337
Nicol, Douglas A.O. MA BD	1974	1991	Mission and Discipleship Council	24 Corbiehill Avenue, Edinburgh EH4 5DR	0131-336 1965
Page, Ruth MA BD DPhil	1976	2000	(University of Edinburgh)	22/5 West Mill Bank, West Mill Road, Edinburgh EH13 0QT	0131-441 3740
Patterson, John M.	1976	1987	(Blackbraes and Shieldhill)	Flat 20, Murrayfield House, 66 Murrayfield Avenue, Edinburgh EH12 6AY	
Philip, James MA	1948	1997	(Holyrood Abbey)	3 Ferguson Gardens, Musselburgh EH21 6XF	0131-653 2310
Philp, Connie (Miss) BD	1980	1995	(Arbuthnott with Bervie)	Oaklands, 35 Canaan Lane, Edinburgh EH10 4SG	
Plate, Maria A.G. (Miss) LTh BA	1983	2000	(South Ronaldsay and Burray)	Flat 29, 77 Barnton Park View, Edinburgh EH4 6EL	0131-339 8539
Potts, Jean (Miss) DCS			(Deaconess)	28B East Claremont Street, Edinburgh EH7 4JP	0131-557 2144
Renton, Ian P.	1958	1990	(St Colm's)	98 Homeross House, Strathearn Road, Edinburgh EH9 2QY	0131-447 0601
Ridland, Alistair K. MA BD	1982	2000	Chaplain: Western General Hospital	13 Stewart Place, Kirkliston EH29 0BQ	0131-333 2711
Robertson, Charles LVO MA	1965	2005	(Edinburgh: Canongate)	3 Ross Gardens, Edinburgh EH9 3BS	0131-662 9025
Ronald, Norma A. (Miss) MBE DCS			(Deaconess)	2B Saughton Road North, Edinburgh EH12 7HG	0131-334 8736
Ross, Kenneth R. BA BD PhD	1982	1999	World Mission Council	c/o 121 George Street, Edinburgh EH2 4YN	0131-225 5722
Schofield, Melville F. MA	1960	2000	(Chaplain: Western General Hospitals)	25 Rowantree Grove, Currie EH14 5AT	0131-449 4745
Scott, Ian G. BSc BD STM	1965	2006	(Edinburgh: Greenbank)	50 Forthview Walk, Tranent EH33 1FE [E-mail: iandascott@tiscali.co.uk]	01875 612907
Scott, Martin DipMusEd RSAM BD PhD	1986	2000	Ministries Council	18 Covenanters Rise, Dunfermline KY11 8QS	01383 722328
Shewan, Frederick D. MA BD	1970	2005	(Edinburgh: Muirhouse St Andrew's)	38 Tremayne Place, Dunfermline KY12 9YH	01383 734354
Skinner, Donald M. MBE JP FIES	1962	2000	(Edinburgh: Gilmerton)	12 Straid-a-Cnoc, Clynder, Helensburgh G84 0QX	01436 831795
Slorach, Alexander CA BD	1970	2002	(Kirk of Lammermuir with Langton and Polwarth)	61 Inverleith Row, Edinburgh EH3 5PX	
Stephen, Donald M. TD MA BD ThM	1962	2001	(Edinburgh: Marchmont St Giles')	10 Hawkhead Crescent, Edinburgh EH16 6LR	0131-658 1216
Stevenson, John MA BD PhD	1963	2001	(Department of Education)	12 Swanston Gardens, Edinburgh EH10 7DL	0131-445 3960
Stirling, A. Douglas BSc	1956	1994	(Rhu and Shandon)	162 Avontoun Park, Linlithgow EH49 6QH	01506 845021
Stiven, Iain K. MA BD	1960	1997	(Strachur and Strathlachlan)	7 Gloucester Place, Edinburgh EH3 6EE	0131-225 8177
Taylor, Howard G. BSc BD MTh	1971	1998	(Chaplain: Heriot Watt University)	51 The Murrays, Edinburgh EH17 8UD [E-mail: HowardTaylor1944@live.co.uk]	0131-664 0751
Taylor, William R. MA BD	1983	2003	Chaplaincy Co-ordinator: Scottish Prison Service	33 Kingsknowe Drive, Edinburgh EH14 2JY	
Teague, Yvonne (Mrs) DCS			(Board of Ministry)	46 Craigcrook Avenue, Edinburgh EH4 3PX	0131-336 3113
Telfer, Iain J.M. BD DPS	1978	2001	Chaplain: Royal Infirmary	Royal Infirmary of Edinburgh, 51 Little France Crescent, Edinburgh EH16 4SA	0131-242 1997
Thom, Helen (Miss) DCS			(Deaconess)	84 Great King Street, Edinburgh EH3 6QU	0131-556 5687
Whyte, Iain A. BA BD STM PhD	1968	2001	Community Mental Health Chaplain	14 Carlingnose Point, North Queensferry, Inverkeithing KY11 1ER [E-mail: iainisabel@whytes28.fsnet.co.uk]	01383 410732
Wigglesworth, J. Christopher MBE BSc PhD BD	1968	1999	(St Andrew's College, Selly Oak)	12 Leven Terrace, Edinburgh EH3 9LW	0131-228 6335
Wilkie, James L. MA BD	1959	1998	(Board of World Mission)	7 Comely Bank Avenue, Edinburgh EH4 1EW [E-mail: jl.wilkie@btinternet.com]	0131-343 1552

Wilkinson, John BD MD FRCP DTM&H	1946	1975	(Kikuyu)	70 Craigleith Hill Gardens, Edinburgh EH4 2JH	0131-332 2994
Williams, Jenny M. (Miss) BSc CQSW BD	1996	1997	Christian Fellowship of Healing	16 Blantyre Terrace, Edinburgh EH10 5AE	0131-447 0050
Wilson, John M. MA	1964	1995	(Adviser in Religious Education)	27 Bellfield Street, Edinburgh EH15 2BR	0131-669 5257
Young, Alexander W. BD DipMin	1988	1999	Chaplain: Royal Infirmary	32 Lindsay Circus, The Hawthorns, Rosewell EH24 9EP	(Work) 0131-242 1997

EDINBURGH ADDRESSES

Albany — At Greenside
Balerno — Johnsburn Road, Balerno
Barclay — Barclay Place
Blackhall St Columba's — Queensferry Road
Bristo Memorial — Peffermill Road, Craigmillar
Broughton St Mary's — Bellevue Crescent
Canongate — Canongate
Carrick Knowe — North Saughton Road
Colinton — Dell Road
Colinton Mains — Oxgangs Road North
Corstorphine
 Craigsbank — Craig's Crescent
 Old — Kirk Loan
 St Anne's — Kaimes Road
 St Ninian's — St John's Road
Craigentinny St Christopher's — Craigentinny Road
Craiglockhart — Craiglockhart Avenue
Craigmillar Park — Craigmillar Park
Cramond — Cramond Glebe Road
Currie — Kirkgate, Currie
Davidson's Mains — Quality Street
Dean — Dean Path
Drylaw — Groathill Road North
Duddingston — Old Church Lane, Duddingston
Fairmilehead — Frogston Road West, Fairmilehead
Gilmerton — Ravenscroft Street
Gorgie — Gorgie Road
Granton — Boswall Parkway

Greenbank — Braidburn Terrace
Greenside — Royal Terrace
Greyfriars Tolbooth and Highland Kirk — Greyfriars Place
High (St Giles') — High Street
Holyrood Abbey — Dalziel Place x London Road
Holy Trinity — Hailesland Place, Wester Hailes
Inverleith — Inverleith Gardens
Juniper Green — Lanark Road, Juniper Green
Kaimes Lockhart Memorial — Gracemount Drive
Kirkliston — The Square, Kirkliston
Kirk o' Field — Pleasance
Leith
 North — Madeira Street off Ferry Road
 St Andrew's — Easter Road
 St Serf's — Ferry Road
 St Thomas' Junction Road — Great Junction Street
 South — Kirkgate, Leith
 Wardie — Primrosebank Road
Liberton — Kirkgate, Liberton
Northfield — Gilmerton Road, Liberton
London Road — London Road
Marchmont St Giles' — Kilgraston Road
Mayfield Salisbury — Mayfield Road x West Mayfield
Morningside — Cluny Gardens
Morningside United — Bruntsfield Place x Chamberlain Road
Muirhouse St Andrew's — Pennywell Gardens
Murrayfield — Abinger Gardens
Newhaven — Craighall Road
New Restalrig — Willowbrae Road

Old Kirk — Pennywell Road
Palmerston Place — Palmerston Place
Pilrig St Paul's — Pilrig Street
Polwarth — Polwarth Terrace x Harrison Road
Portobello
 Old — Bellfield Street
 St James' — Rosefield Place
 St Philip's Joppa — Abercorn Terrace
Priestfield — Dalkeith Road x Marchhall Place
Queensferry — The Loan, South Queensferry
Ratho — Baird Road, Ratho
Reid Memorial — West Savile Terrace
Richmond Craigmillar — Niddrie Mains Road
St Andrew's and St George's — George Street
St Andrew's Clermiston — Clermiston View
St Catherine's Argyle — Grange Road x Chalmers Crescent
St Colm's — Dalry Road x Cathcart Place
St Cuthbert's — Lothian Road
St David's Broomhouse — Broomhouse Crescent
St George's West — Shandwick Place
St John's Oxgangs — Oxgangs Road
St Margaret's — Restalrig Road South
St Martin's — Magdalene Drive
St Michael's — Slateford Road
St Nicholas' Sighthill — Calder Road
St Stephen's Comely Bank — Comely Bank
Slateford Longstone — Kingsknowe Road North
Stenhouse St Aidan's — Chesser Avenue
Stockbridge — Saxe Coburg Street
Tron Moredun — Craigour Gardens
Viewforth — Gilmore Place

(2) WEST LOTHIAN

Meets in the church of the incoming Moderator on the first Tuesday of September and in St John's Church Hall, Bathgate, on the first Tuesday of every other month, except December, when the meeting is on the second Tuesday, and January, July and August, when there is no meeting.

Clerk: REV. DUNCAN SHAW BD MTh   **St John's Manse, Mid Street, Bathgate EH48 1QD**   **01506 653146**
[E-mail: westlothian@cofscotland.org.uk]

Abercorn (H) linked with Pardovan, Kingscavil (H) and Winchburgh (H)
A. Scott Marshall DipComm BD   1984   1998   The Manse, Winchburgh, Broxburn EH52 6TT   01506 890919
[E-mail: pkwla@aol.com]

Armadale (H)
Vacant   70 Mount Pleasant, Armadale, Bathgate EH48 3HB   01501 730358

Avonbridge (H) linked with Torphichen (H)
Clifford R. Acklam BD MTh   1997   2000   Manse Road, Torphichen, Bathgate EH48 4LT   01506 652794
[E-mail: cliff@torphichen.org]

Bathgate: Boghall (H)
Dennis S. Rose LTh   1996   2004   1 Manse Place, Ash Grove, Bathgate EH48 1NJ   01506 652940
[E-mail: dsrosekirk@aol.com]

Bathgate: High (H)
Ronald G. Greig MA BD   1987   1998   19 Hunter Grove, Bathgate EH48 1NN   01506 652654
[E-mail: rongreig@tiscali.co.uk]

Bathgate: St John's (H)
Duncan Shaw BD MTh   1975   1978   St John's Manse, Mid Street, Bathgate EH48 1QD   01506 653146
[E-mail: westlothian@cofscotland.org.uk]

Blackburn and Seafield (H)
Robert A. Anderson MA BD DPhil   1980   1998   The Manse, 5 MacDonald Gardens, Blackburn, Bathgate EH47 7RE   01506 652825
[E-mail: robertanderson307@btinternet.com]

Blackridge (H) linked with Harthill: St Andrew's (H)
Robert B. Gehrke BSc BD CEng MIEE   1994   2006   East Main Street, Harthill, Shotts ML7 5QW   01501 751239
[E-mail: bob.gehrke@gmail.com]

Breich Valley
Thomas Preston BD   1978   2001   Stoneyburn, Bathgate EH47 8AU   01501 762018
[E-mail: t.preston980@btinternet.com]

Broxburn (H)

Terry Taylor BA MTh	2005		2 Church Street, Broxburn EH52 5EL [E-mail: revtaylor@iscali.co.uk]	01506 852825

Fauldhouse: St Andrew's (H)

Elizabeth Smith (Mrs) BD	1996	2000	7 Glebe Court, Fauldhouse, Bathgate EH47 9DX [E-mail: smithrevb@btinternet.com]	01501 771190

Harthill: St Andrew's See Blackridge

Kirknewton (H) and East Calder (H)

Vacant			8 Manse Court, East Calder, Livingston EH53 0HF	01506 880802

Kirk of Calder (H)

John M. Povey MA BD	1981		19 Maryfield Park, Mid Calder, Livingston EH53 0SB [E-mail: revjpovey@aol.com]	01506 882495
Phyllis Thomson (Miss) DCS		2003	63 Caroline Park, Mid Calder, Livingston EH53 0SJ	01506 883207

Linlithgow: St Michael's (H) (E-mail: info@stmichaels-parish.org.uk)

D. Stewart Gillan BSc MDiv PhD	1985	2004	St Michael's Manse, Kirkgate, Linlithgow EH49 7AL [E-mail: stewart@stmichaels-parish.org.uk]	01506 842195
John H. Paton BSc BD (Assoc)	1983	2008	Cross Flat, The Cross, Linlithgow EH49 7AL [E-mail: jonymar@globalnet.co.uk]	01506 842665
Thomas S. Riddell BSc (Aux)	1993	1994	4 The Maltings, Linlithgow EH49 6DS [E-mail: tsriddell@blueyonder.co.uk]	01506 843251

Linlithgow: St Ninian's Craigmailen (H)

W. Richard Houston BSc BD	1998	2004	29 Philip Avenue, Linlithgow EH49 7BH [E-mail: wrichardhouston@blueyonder.co.uk]	01506 202246

Livingston Ecumenical Parish
Incorporating the Worship Centres at:
Carmondean (H) and Knightsridge

Suzanna Bates BTh *(The Methodist Church)*			13 Eastcroft Court, Livingston EH54 7ET [E-mail: rev.suzanna@btinternet.com]	01506 464567

Craigshill (St Columba's) and Ladywell (St Paul's)

Appointment awaited			27 Heatherbank, Ladywell, Livingston EH54 6EE	01506 432326

Dedridge and Murieston

Eileen Thompson BD MTh *(Scottish Episcopal Church)*			53 Garry Walk, Craigshill, Livingston EH54 5AS [E-mail: eileenthompson@blueyonder.co.uk]	01506 433451

Livingston: Old (H)

Graham W. Smith BA BD FSAScot	1995		Manse of Livingston, Charlesfield Lane, Livingston EH54 7AJ [E-mail: info@gwsmith.abel.co.uk]	01506 420227

| Kay McIntosh (Mrs) DCS | 2008 | 4 Jacklin Green, Livingston EH54 8PZ
[E-mail: deaconess@backedge.co.uk] | 01506 495472 |

Pardovan, Kingscavil and Winchburgh See Abercorn

Polbeth Harwood linked with West Kirk of Calder (H)

| David A. Albon BA MCS | 1991 | 27 Learmonth Crescent, West Calder EH55 8AF
[E-mail: albon@onetel.com] | 01506 870460 |

Strathbrock (H)
Vacant

| | | 1 Manse Park, Uphall, Broxburn EH52 6NX | 01506 852550 |

Torphichen See Avonbridge

Uphall: South (H)

| Margaret Steele (Miss) BSc BD | 2000 | 8 Fernlea, Uphall, Broxburn EH52 6DF
[E-mail: mdsteele@tiscali.co.uk] | 01506 852788 |

West Kirk of Calder (H) See Polbeth Harwood

Whitburn: Brucefield (H)

| Richard J.G. Darroch BD MTh MA(CMS) | 1993 2003 | Brucefield Manse, Whitburn, Bathgate EH47 8NU
[E-mail: richdarr@aol.com] | 01501 740263 |

Whitburn: South (H)

| Christine Houghton (Mrs) BD | 1997 2004 | 5 Mansewood Crescent, Whitburn, Bathgate EH47 8HA
[E-mail: c.houghton1@btinternet.com] | 01501 740333 |

Black, David W. BSc BD	1968	2008	(Strathbrock)	66 Bridge Street, Newbridge EH28 8SH	0131-333 2609
Cameron, Ian MA BD	1953	1981	(Kilbrandon and Kilchattan)	Craigellen, West George Street, Blairgowrie PH10 6DZ	01250 872087
Dundas, Thomas B.S. LTh	1969	1996	(West Kirk of Calder)	35 Coolkill, Sandyford, Dublin 18, Republic of Ireland	00353 12953061
Mackay, Kenneth J. MA BD	1971	2007	(Edinburgh: St Nicholas' Sighthill)	46 Chuckethall Road, Livingston EH54 8FB [E-mail: knnth_mackay@yahoo.co.uk]	01506 410884
MacRae, Norman I. LTh	1966	2003	(Inverness: Trinity)	144 Hope Park Gardens, Bathgate EH48 2QX	01506 635254
Manson, Robert L. MA DPS	1956	1991	(Chaplain: Royal Edinburgh Hospital)	4 Murieston Drive, Livingston EH54 9AU [E-mail: roy@manson25.freeserve.co.uk]	01506 434746
Merrilees, Ann (Miss) DCS			(Deaconess)	23 Cuthill Brae, West Calder EH55 8QE [E-mail: ann@merrilees.freeserve.co.uk]	01501 762909
Moore, J.W. MA	1950	1983	(Daviot with Rayne)	31 Lennox Gardens, Linlithgow EH49 7PZ	01506 842534
Morrice, Charles S. MA BD PhD	1959	1997	(Kenya)	104 Baron's Hill Avenue, Linlithgow EH49 7JG [E-mail: cs.morrice@blueyonder.co.uk]	01506 847167

Morrison, Iain C. BA BD	1990	2003	(Linlithgow: St Ninian's Craigmailen)	Whaligoe, 53 Eastcroft Drive, Polmont, Falkirk FK2 0SU [E-mail: iain@kirkweb.org]	01324 713249
Murray, Ronald N.G. MA	1946	1986	(Pardovan and Kingscavil with Winchburgh)	Linlithgow Nursing Home, 45 St Ninian's Road, Linlithgow EH49 7BW	
Nelson, Georgina (Mrs) MA BD PhD DipEd	1990	1995	Hospital Chaplain	63 Hawthorn Bank, Seafield, Bathgate EH47 7EB	01506 670391
Nicol, Robert M.	1984	1996	(Jersey: St Columba's)	59 Kinloch View, Blackness Road, Linlithgow EH49 7HT	01506 652028
Smith, W. Ewing BSc	1962	1994	(Livingston: Old)	8 Hardy Gardens, Bathgate EH48 1NH [E-mail: wesmith@hardygdns.freeserve.co.uk]	
Trimble, Robert DCS			(Deacon)	5 Templar Rise, Dedridge, Livingston EH54 6PJ	01506 412504
Walker, Ian BD MEd DipMS	1973	2007	(Rutherglen: Wardlawhill)	92 Carseknowe, Linlithgow EH49 7LG [E-mail: walk102822@aol.com]	01506 844412
Whitson, William S. MA	1959	1999	(Cumbernauld: St Mungo's)	2 Chapman's Brae, Bathgate EH48 4LH [E-mail: william_whitson@tiscali.co.uk]	01506 650027

(3) LOTHIAN

Meets at Musselburgh: St Andrew's High Parish Church on the last Thursday of January and June and the first Thursday of March, April, May, September, October, November and December. (Alternative arrangements are made to avoid meeting on Maundy Thursday.)

Clerk:	MR JOHN D. McCULLOCH DL			Auchindinny House, Penicuik EH26 8PE [E-mail: lothian@cofscotland.org.uk]	01968 676300 (Tel/Fax)

Aberlady (H) linked with Gullane (H)

John B. Cairns LTh LLB LLD DD	1974	2001	The Manse, Hummel Road, Gullane EH31 2BG [E-mail: johncairns@mail.com]	01620 843192

Athelstaneford linked with Whitekirk and Tyninghame

Kenneth D.F. Walker MA BD PhD	1976		The Manse, Athelstaneford, North Berwick EH39 5BE [E-mail: kenver.wa.ker@btinternet.com]	01620 880378

Belhaven (H) linked with Spott

Laurence H. Twaddle MA BD MTh	1977	1978	The Manse, Belhaven Road, Dunbar EH42 1NH [E-mail: revtwaddle@aol.com]	01368 863098

Bilston linked with Glencorse (H) linked with Roslin (H)

John R. Wells BD DipMin	1991	2005	31A Manse Road, Roslin EH25 9LG [E-mail: wellsjr3@aol.com]	0131-440 2012

Bolton and Saltoun linked with Humbie linked with Yester (H)

Malcolm Lyon BD	2007		The Manse, Tweeddale Avenue, Gifford, Haddington EH41 4QN [E-mail: malcolmlyon2@hotmail.com]	01620 810515

Bonnyrigg (H)
John Mitchell LTh CMin   1991   9 Viewbank View, Bonnyrigg EH19 2HU   0131-663 8287 (Tel/Fax)
[E-mail: jmitchell241@tiscali.co.uk]

Borthwick (H) linked with Cranstoun, Crichton and Ford (H) linked with Fala and Soutra (H)
D. Graham Leitch MA BD   1974   2003   Cranstoun Cottage, Ford, Pathhead EH37 5RE   01875 320314
[E-mail: leitch@cranscott.fsnet.co.uk]
Andrew Don BD (Aux)   2006   5 Eskvale Court, Penicuik EH26 8HT   01968 675766
[E-mail: a.a.don@btinternet.com]

Cockenzie and Port Seton: Chalmers Memorial (H)
Robert L. Glover BMus BD MTh ARCO   1971   1997   Braemar Villa, 2 Links Road, Port Seton, Prestonpans EH32 0HA   01875 812481
[E-mail: rlglover@btinternet.com]

Cockenzie and Port Seton: Old (H)
Continued Vacancy   1 Links Road, Port Seton, Prestonpans EH32 0HA   01875 812310

Cockpen and Carrington (H) linked with Lasswade (H) and Rosewell (H)
Vacant   11 Pendreich Terrace, Bonnyrigg EH19 2DT   0131-663 6884
(Lasswade and Rosewell have united to form one charge)

Cranstoun, Crichton and Ford (H) See Borthwick

Dalkeith: St John's and King's Park (H)
Keith L. Mack BD MTh DPS   2002   13 Weir Crescent, Dalkeith EH22 3JN   0131-454 0206
[E-mail: kthmacker@aol.com]

Dalkeith: St Nicholas' Buccleuch (H)
Alexander G. Horsburgh MA BD   1995   2004   116 Bonnyrigg Road, Dalkeith EH22 3HZ   0131-663 3036
[E-mail: alexanderhorsburgh@googlemail.com]

Dirleton (H) linked with North Berwick: Abbey (H) (01620 890110) (E-mail: abbeychurch@hotmail.com)
David J. Graham BSc BD PhD   1982   1998   20 Westgate, North Berwick EH39 4AF   01620 892410
[E-mail: abbeychurch@btconnect.com]

Dunbar (H)
Eric W. Foggitt MA BSc BD   1991   2000   The Manse, Bayswell Road, Dunbar EH42 1AB   01368 863749 (Tel/Fax)
[E-mail: ericleric3@btopenworld.com]

Dunglass
Anne R. Lithgow (Mrs) MA BD   1992   1994   The Manse, Cockburnspath TD13 5XZ   01368 830713
[E-mail: anne.lithgow@btinternet.com]

Fala and Soutra See Borthwick

Garvald and Morham linked with Haddington: West (H)
Cameron Mackenzie BD 1997
15 West Road, Haddington EH41 3RD
[E-mail: mackenz550@aol.com]
01620 822213

Gladsmuir linked with Longniddry (H)
Robin E. Hill LLB BD PhD 2004
The Manse, Elcho Road, Longniddry EH32 0LB
[E-mail: robin.hill@homecall.co.uk]
01875 853195

Glencorse (H) See Bilston

Gorebridge (H)
Mark S. Nicholas MA BD 1999
100 Hunterfield Road, Gorebridge EH23 4TT
[E-mail: mark@nicholasfamily.wanadoo.co.uk]
01875 820387

Gullane See Aberlady

Haddington: St Mary's (H)
Jennifer Macrae (Mrs) MA BD 1998 2007
1 Nungate Gardens, Haddington EH41 4EE
[E-mail: minister@stmaryskirk.com]
01620 823109

Haddington: West See Garvald and Morham

Howgate (H) linked with Penicuik: South (H)
Ian A. Cathcart BSc BD 1994 2007
15 Stevenson Road, Penicuik EH26 0LU
[E-mail: iacjoc@tiscali.co.uk]
01968 674692

Humbie See Bolton and Saltoun
Lasswade and Rosewell See Cockpen and Carrington

Loanhead
Graham L. Duffin BSc BD DipEd 1989 2001
120 The Loan, Loanhead EH20 9AJ
[E-mail: gduffin@loanheadparishchurch.co.uk]
0131-448 2459

Longniddry See Gladsmuir

Musselburgh: Northesk (H)
Alison P. McDonald MA BD 1991 1998
16 New Street, Musselburgh EH21 6JP
[E-mail: alisonpmcdonald@btinternet.com]
0131-665 2128

Musselburgh: St Andrew's High (H) (0131-665 7239)
Yvonne E.S. Atkins (Mrs) BD 1997 2004
8 Ferguson Drive, Musselburgh EH21 6XA
[E-mail: yesatkins@yahoo.co.uk]
0131-665 1124

Musselburgh: St Clement's and St Ninian's
Muriel F. Willoughby (Mrs) MA BD — 2006 — The Manse, Wallyford Loan Road, Wallyford, Musselburgh EH21 8BU [E-mail: stcnmanse@btinternet.com] — 0131-653 6588

John Buchanan DCS — 2004 — 19 Gillespie Crescent, Edinburgh EH10 4HU — 0131-229 0794

Musselburgh: St Michael's Inveresk
Andrew B. Dick BD DipMin — 1986 1999 — 8 Hope Place, Musselburgh EH21 7QE [E-mail: dixbit@aol.com] — 0131-665 0545

Newbattle (H) (Website: http://freespace.virgin.net/newbattle.focus)
Monika R.W. Redman (Mrs) BA BD — 2003 — 70 Newbattle Abbey Crescent, Dalkeith EH22 3LW [E-mail: monika.walker@ukgateway.net] — 0131-663 3245

Gordon R. Steven BD DCS — 2004 — 51 Nantwich Drive, Edinburgh EH7 6RB [E-mail: grsteven@btinternet.com] — 0131-669 2054 / 07904 385256 (Mbl)

Newton
Vacant — The Manse, Newton, Dalkeith EH22 1SR — 0131-663 3845

North Berwick: Abbey See Dirleton

North Berwick: St Andrew Blackadder (H) (E-mail: admin@standrewblackadder.org.uk) (Website: www.standrewblackadder.org.uk)
Neil J. Dougall BD — 1991 2003 — 7 Marine Parade, North Berwick EH39 4LD [E-mail: neil@standrewblackadder.org.uk] — 01620 892132

Ormiston linked with Pencaitland
Vacant — The Manse, Pencaitland, Tranent EH34 5DL — 01875 340208

Pencaitland See Ormiston

Penicuik: North (H)
John W. Fraser MA BD — 1974 1982 — 93 John Street, Penicuik EH26 8AG [E-mail: revpnk@tiscali.co.uk] — 01968 672213

Penicuik: St Mungo's (H)
Vacant — 31A Kirkhill Road, Penicuik EH26 8JB — 01968 672916

Penicuik: South See Howgate

Prestonpans: Prestongrange
Robert R. Simpson BA BD — 1994 — The Manse, East Loan, Prestonpans EH32 9ED [E-mail: robert@pansmanse.co.uk] — 01875 810308

Roslin See Bilston
Spott See Belhaven

Tranent
Vacant — 244 Church Street, Tranent EH33 1BW — 01875 610210

Traprain
Howard J. Haslett BA BD — 1972 2000 — The Manse, Preston Road, East Linton EH40 3DS [E-mail: howard.haslett@btinternet.com] — 01620 860227 (Tel/Fax)

Whitekirk and Tyninghame See Athelstaneford
Yester See Bolton and Saltoun

Name			(Former charge)	Address	Telephone
Andrews, J. Edward MA BD DipCG FSAScot	1985	2005	(Armadale)	1A Meadowpark, Haddington EH41 4DS [E-mail: edward.andrews@btinternet.com]	(Tel/Fax) 01620 829804 (Mbl) 07808 720708
Bayne, Angus L. LTh BEd MTh	1969	2005	(Edinburgh: Bristo Memorial Craigmillar)	4 Myredale, Bonnyrigg EH19 3NW [E-mail: angus@nccookies.com]	0131-663 6871
Black, A. Graham MA	1964	2003	(Gladsmuir with Longniddry)	26 Hamilton Crescent, Gullane EH31 2HR [E-mail: grablack@aol.com]	01620 843899
Brown, Ronald H.	1974	1998	(Musselburgh: Northesk)	6 Monktonhall Farm Cottages, Musselburgh EH21 6RZ	0131-653 2531
Brown, William BD	1972	1997	(Edinburgh: Polwarth)	13 Thornyhall, Dalkeith EH22 2ND	0131-654 0929
Chalmers, William R. MA BD STM	1953	1992	(Dunbar)	18 Forest Road, Burghead, Elgin IV30 5XL	01343 835674
Forbes, Iain M. BSc BD	1964	2005	(Aberdeen: Beechgrove)	5 Auld Orchard, Lothian Street, Bonnyrigg EH19 3BR [E-mail: panama.forbes@tiscali.co.uk]	0131-454 0717
Fraser, John W. BEM MA BD PhD	1950	1983	(Farnell)	The Elms Nursing Home, 148 Whitehouse Loan, Edinburgh EH9 2EZ	
Gilfillan, James LTh	1968	1997	(East Kilbride: Old)	15 Long Cram, Haddington EH41 4NS	01620 824843
Hutchison, Alan E.W.			(Deacon)	132 Lochbridge Road, North Berwick EH39 4DR	01620 894077
Jones, Anne M. (Mrs) BD	1998	2002	Hospital Chaplain	7 North Elphinstone Farm, Tranent EH33 2ND [E-mail: revamjones@aol.com]	01875 614442
Levison, L. David MA BD	1943	1982	(Ormiston with Pencaitland)	Westdene Conservatory Flat, 506 Perth Road, Dundee DD2 1LS	01382 630460
Macdonell, Alasdair W. MA BD	1955	1992	(Haddington: St Mary's)	St Andrews Cottage, Duns Road, Gifford, Haddington EH41 4QW [E-mail: alasdair.macdonell@btinternet.com]	01620 810341
Macrae, Norman C. MA DipEd	1942	1985	(Loanhead)	49 Lixmount Avenue, Edinburgh EH5 3EW [E-mail: nandcmacrae@onetel.com]	0131-552 2428
Manson, James A. LTh	1981	2004	(Glencorse with Roslin)	31 Nursery Gardens, Kilmarnock KA1 3JA [E-mail: jamanson@supanet.com]	01563 535430
Pirie, Donald LTh	1975	2006	(Bolton and Saltoun with Humbie with Yester)	46 Caiystane Avenue, Edinburgh EH10 6SH	0131-445 2654
Ritchie, James McL. MA BD MPhil	1950	1985	(Coalsnaughton)	Flat 2/25, Croft-an-Righ, Edinburgh EH8 8EG [E-mail: jasritch_77@msn.com]	0131-557 1084
Robertson, James LTh	1970	2000	(Newton)	11 Southfield Square, Edinburgh EH15 1QS	0131-657 5661
Swan, Andrew F. BD	1983	2000	(Loanhead)	3 Mackenzie Gardens, Dolphinton, West Linton EH46 7HS	01968 682247
Thomson, William H.	1964	1999	(Edinburgh: Liberton Northfield)	3 Baird's Way, Bonnyrigg EH19 3NS [E-mail: wh.thomson@tiscali.co.uk]	0131-654 9799
Torrance, David W. MA BD	1955	1991	(Earlston)	38 Forth Street, North Berwick EH39 4JQ [E-mail: torrance103@btinternet.com]	(Tel/Fax) 01620 895109

Underwood, Florence A. (Mrs) BD	1992	2006	(Assistant: Gladsmuir with Longniddry)	The Shieling, Main Street, Stenton, Dunbar EH42 1TE [E-mail: geoffrey.underwood@homecall.co.uk]	01368 850629
Underwood, Geoffrey H. BD DipTh FPhS	1964	1992	(Cockenzie and Port Seton: Chalmers Memorial)	The Shieling, Main Street, Stenton, Dunbar EH42 1TE [E-mail: geoffrey.underwood@homecall.co.uk]	01368 850629
Whiteford, David H. CBE MA BD PhD	1943	1985	(Gullane)	3 Old Dean Road, Longniddry EH32 0QY	01875 852980

(4) MELROSE AND PEEBLES

Meets at Innerleithen on the first Tuesday of February, March, May, October, November and December, and on the fourth Tuesday of June, and in places to be appointed on the first Tuesday of September.

Clerk:	MR JACK STEWART	3 St Cuthbert's Drive, St Boswells, Melrose TD6 0DF [E-mail: melrosepeebles@cofscotland.org.uk]	01835 822600

Ashkirk linked with Selkirk (H)

James W. Campbell BD	1995		1 Loanside, Selkirk TD7 4DJ [E-mail: revjimashkirk@aol.com]	01750 22833

Bowden (H) and Melrose (H)

Alistair G. Bennett BSc BD	1978	1984	Tweedmount Road, Melrose TD6 9ST [E-mail: agbennettmelrose@aol.com]	01896 822217

Broughton, Glenholm and Kilbucho (H) linked with Skirling linked with Stobo and Drumelzier linked with Tweedsmuir (H)

Vacant	The Manse, Broughton, Biggar ML12 6HQ	01899 830331

Caddonfoot (H) linked with Galashiels: Trinity (H)

Morag A. Dawson BD	1999	2005	8 Mossilee Road, Galashiels TD1 1NF [E-mail: moragdawson@yahoo.co.uk]	01896 752420

Carlops linked with Kirkurd and Newlands (H) linked with West Linton: St Andrew's (H)

Thomas W. Burt BD	1982	1985	The Manse, West Linton EH46 7EN [E-mail: tomburt@westlinton.com]	01968 660221

Channelkirk and Lauder

Bruce K. Gardner MA BD PhD	1988	2008	Brownsmuir Park, Lauder TD2 6QD	01578 722320

Earlston

Michael D. Scouler MBE BSc BD	1988	1992	The Manse, High Street, Earlston TD4 6DE [E-mail: michaelscouler@hotmail.co.uk]	01896 849236

Eddleston (H) linked with Peebles: Old (H)
Malcolm M. Macdougall BD — 1981 — 2001 — The Old Manse, Innerleithen Road, Peebles EH45 8BD [E-mail: calum.macdougall@btopenworld.com] — 01721 720568

Ettrick and Yarrow
Samuel Siroky BA MTh — 2003 — Yarrow Manse, Yarrow, Selkirk TD7 5LA [E-mail: sesiroky@tiscali.co.uk] — 01750 82336

Galashiels: Old and St Paul's (H) (Website: www.oldparishandstpauls.org.uk)
Leslie M. Steele MA BD — 1973 — 1988 — Woodlea, Abbotsview Drive, Galashiels TD1 3SL [E-mail: leslie@oldparishandstpauls.org.uk] — 01896 752320

Galashiels: St John's (H)
Jane M. Howitt (Miss) MA BD — 1996 — 2006 — St John's Manse, Hawthorn Road, Galashiels TD1 2JZ [E-mail: jane@stjohrsgalashiels.co.uk] — 01896 752573

Galashiels: Trinity (H) See Caddonfoot

Innerleithen (H), Traquair and Walkerburn
Janice M. Faris (Mrs) BSc BD — 1991 — 2001 — The Manse, 1 Millwell Park, Innerleithen, Peebles EH44 6JF [E-mail: revjfaris@hotmail.com] — 01896 830309

Kirkurd and Newlands See Carlops

Lyne and Manor
Nancy M. Norman (Miss) BA MDiv MTh — 1988 — 1998 — 25 March Street, Peebles EH45 8EP [E-mail: nancy.norman1@btinternet.com] — 01721 721699

Maxton and Mertoun linked with Newtown linked with St Boswells
Sheila W. Moir (Ms) MTheol — 2008 — 7 Strae Brigs, St Boswells, Melrose TD6 0DH [E-mail: sheila377@btinternet.com] — 01835 822255

Newtown See Maxton and Mertoun
Peebles: Old See Eddleston

Peebles: St Andrew's Leckie (H) (01721 723121)
James H. Wallace MA BD — 1973 — 1983 — Mansefield, Innerleithen Road, Peebles EH45 8BE [E-mail: jimwallace@freeola.com] — 01721 721749 (Tel/Fax)

St Boswells See Maxton and Mertoun
Selkirk See Ashkirk
Skirling See Broughton, Glenholm and Kilbucho
Stobo and Drumelzier See Broughton, Glenholm and Kilbucho

Stow: St Mary of Wedale and Heriot
Catherine A. Buchan (Mrs) MA MDiv   2002   The Manse, 209 Galashiels Road, Stow, Galashiels TD1 2RE   01578 730237
[E-mail: c-abuchan@tiscali.co.uk]

Tweedsmuir See Broughton, Glenholm and Kilbucho
West Linton: St Andrew's See Carlops

Name	Years	Charge	Address	Telephone
Bowie, Adam McC.	1976 1996	(Cavers and Kirkton with Hobkirk and Southdean)	Glenfield, Redpath, Earlston TD4 6AD	01896 848173
Brown, Robert BSc	1962 1997	(Kilbrandon and Kilchattan)	11 Thornfield Terrace, Selkirk TD7 4DU [E-mail: ruwcb@tiscali.co.uk]	01750 20311
Cashman, P. Hamilton BSc	1985 1998	(Dirleton with North Berwick: Abbey)	38 Abbotsford Road, Galashiels TD1 3HR [E-mail: mcashman@tiscali.co.uk]	01896 752711
Deveny, Robert P.	2002	Borders Health Board	Blakeburn Cottage, Wester Housebyres, Melrose TD6 9BW	01896 822350
Dick, J. Ronald BD	1973 1996	Hospital Chaplain	5 Georgefield Farm Cottages, Earlston TD4 6BH	01896 848956
Dobie, Rachel J.W. (Mrs) LTh	1991 2008	(Broughton, Glenholm and Kilbucho with Skirling with Stobo and Drumelzier with Tweedsmuir)	20 Moss Side Crescent, Biggar ML12 6GE [E-mail: revracheldobie@aol.com]	01899 229244
Donald, Thomas W. LTh CA	1977 1987	(Bowden with Lilliesleaf)	The Quest, Huntly Road, Melrose TD6 9SB	01896 822345
Duncan, Charles A. MA	1956 1992	(Heriot with Stow: St Mary of Wedale)	10 Elm Grove, Galashiels TD1 3JA	01896 753261
Hardie, H. Warner BD	1979 2005	(Blackridge with Harthill: St Andrew's)	Keswick Cottage, Kingsmuir Drive, Peebles EH45 9AA [E-mail: hardies@bigfoot.com]	01721 724003
Hogg, Thomas M. BD	1986 2007	(Tranent)	22 Douglas Place, Galashiels TD1 3BT	01896 759381
Kellet, John M. MA	1962 1995	(Leith: South)	4 High Cottages, Walkerburn EH43 6AZ	01896 870351
Kennon, Stanley BA BD	1992 2000	Chaplain: Navy	The Chaplaincy, HMS Raleigh, Tor Point, Cornwall PL2 2PD	
Laing, William F. DSC VRD MA	1952 1986	(Selkirk: St Mary's West)	10 The Glebe, Selkirk TD7 5AB	01750 21210
MacFarlane, David C. MA	1957 1997	(Eddleston with Peebles: Old)	11 Station Bank, Peebles EH45 8EJ	01721 720639
Moore, W. Haisley MA	1966 1996	(Secretary: The Boys' Brigade)	26 Tweedbank Avenue, Tweedbank, Galashiels TD1 3SP	01896 668577
Munson, Winnie (Ms) BD	1996 2006	(Delting with Northmavine)	6 St Cuthbert's Drive, St Boswells, Melrose TD6 0DF	01835 823375
Rae, Andrew W.	1951 1987	(Annan: St Andrew's Greenknowe Erskine)	Roseneuk, Tweedside Road, Newtown St Boswells TD6 0PQ	01835 823783
Riddell, John A. MA BD	1967 2006	(Jedburgh: Trinity)	Orchid Cottage, Gingham Row, Earlston TD4 6ET	01896 848784
Taverner, Glyn R. MA BD	1957 1995	(Maxton and Mertoun with St Boswells)	Woodcot Cottage, Waverley Road, Innerleithen EH44 6QW	01896 830156
Thomson, George F.M. MA	1956 1988	(Dollar Associate)	6 Abbotsford Terrace, Darnick, Melrose TD6 9AD	01896 823112

(5) DUNS

Meets at Duns, in the Old Parish Church Hall, normally on the first Tuesday of February, March, April, May, October, November and December, on the last Tuesday in June, and in places to be appointed on the first Tuesday of September.

Clerk: MR PETER JOHNSON MBE MPhil   Todlaw, Duns TD11 3EJ   **01361 883724**
[E-mail: duns@cofscotland.org.uk]

Ayton (H) and Burnmouth linked with Foulden and Mordington linked with Grantshouse and Houndwood and Reston
Norman R. Whyte BD DipMin   1982   2006   The Manse, Beanburn, Ayton, Eyemouth TD14 5QY   01890 781333

Berwick-upon-Tweed: St Andrew's Wallace Green (H) and Lowick
Paul M.N. Sewell MA BD   1970   2003   3 Meadow Grange, Berwick-upon-Tweed TD15 1NW   01289 303304

Bonkyl and Preston linked with Chirnside (H) linked with Edrom: Allanton (H)
Duncan E. Murray BA BD   1970   2005   Parish Church Manse, The Glebe, Chirnside, Duns TD11 3XL   01890 819109
[E-mail: duncanemurray@tiscali.co.uk]

Chirnside   See Bonkyl and Preston

Coldingham and St Abb's linked with Eyemouth
Daniel G. Lindsay BD   1978   1979   Victoria Road, Eyemouth TD14 5JD   01890 750327

Coldstream (H) linked with Eccles
James B. Watson BSc   1968   2004   36 Bennecourt Drive, Coldstream TD12 1BY   01890 883149
[E-mail: jimwatson007@hotmail.com]

Duns (H)
Andrew A. Morrice MA BD   1999   The Manse, Duns TD11 3DG   01361 883755
[E-mail: andrew@morrice5.wanadoo.co.uk]

Eccles   See Coldstream
Edrom: Allanton   See Bonkyl and Preston
Eyemouth   See Coldingham and St Abb's

Fogo and Swinton linked with Ladykirk linked with Leitholm linked with Whitsome (H)
Alan C.D. Cartwright BSc BD   1976   Swinton, Duns TD11 3JJ

Foulden and Mordington   See Ayton and Burnmouth

Gordon: St Michael's linked with Greenlaw (H) linked with Legerwood linked with Westruther
Thomas S. Nicholson BD DPS   1982   1995   The Manse, Todholes, Greenlaw, Duns TD10 6XD   01361 810316

Grantshouse and Houndwood and Reston See Ayton and Burnmouth
Greenlaw See Gordon: St Michael's

Hutton and Fishwick and Paxton
Vacant

Ladykirk See Fogo and Swinton

Langton and Lammermuir Kirk
Ann Inglis (Mrs) LLB BD   1986   2003   The Manse, Cranshaws, Duns TD11 3SJ   01361 890289
(New name for Kirk of Lammermuir and Langton and Polwarth)

Legerwood See Gordon: St Michael's
Leitholm See Fogo and Swinton
Westruther See Gordon: St Michael's
Whitsome See Fogo and Swinton

Gaddes, Donald R.	1961	1994	(Kelso: North and Ednam)	35 Winterfield Gardens, Duns TD11 3EZ	01361 883172
				[E-mail: doruga@winterfield.fslife.co.uk]	
Gale, Ronald A.A. LTh	1982	1995	(Dunoon: Old and St Cuthbert's)	55 Lennel Mount, Coldstream TD12 4NS	01890 883699
Hay, Bruce J.L.	1957	1997	(Makerstoun and Smailholm with Stichill, Hume and Nenthorn)	Assynt, 1 East Ord Gardens, Berwick-upon-Tweed TD15 2LS	01289 303171
Higham, Robert D. BD	1985	2002	(Tiree)	36 Low Greens, Berwick-upon-Tweed TD15 1LZ	01289 302392
Hope, Geraldine H. (Mrs) MA BD	1986	2007	(Foulden and Mordington with Hutton and Fishwick and Paxton)	4 Well Court, Chirnside, Duns TD11 3UD	01890 818134
				[E-mail: geraldine.hope@virgin.net]	
Kerr, Andrew MA BLitt	1948	1991	(Kilbarchan: West)	Meikle Harelaw, Westruther, Gordon TD10 6XT	01578 740263
Landale, William S.	2004		Auxiliary Minister	Green Hope Guest House, Green Hope, Duns TD11 3SG	01361 890242
Ledgard, J. Christopher BA	1969	2004	(Ayton and Burnmouth with Grantshouse and Houndwood and Reston)	Streonshalh, 8 David Hume View, Chirnside, Duns TD11 3SX	01890 817105
Macleod, Allan M. MA	1945	1985	(Gordon: St Michael's with Legerwood with Westruther)	Silverlea, Machrihanish, Argyll PA28 6PZ	01890 771569
Neill, Bruce F. MA BD	1966	2007	(Maxton and Mertoun with St Boswells)	18 Brierydean, St Abbs, Eyemouth TD14 5PQ	01361 882727
Paterson, William BD	1977	2001	(Bonkyl and Preston with Chirnside with Edrom: Allanton)	Benachie, Gavinton, Duns TD11 3QT	

(6) JEDBURGH

Meets at Jedburgh on the first Wednesday of February, March, May, October, November and December and on the last Wednesday of June. Meets in the Moderator's church on the first Wednesday of September.

Clerk   REV. FRANK CAMPBELL   22 The Glebe, Ancrum, Jedburgh TD8 6UX   **01835   830318   (Tel)**
[E-mail: jedburgh@cofscotland.org.uk]   **01835   830262   (Fax)**

Ale and Teviot United (H)
Frank Campbell   1989   1991   22 The Glebe, Ancrum, Jedburgh TD8 6UX   01835   830318   (Tel)
[E-mail: jedburgh@cofscotland.org.uk]   01835   830262   (Fax)

Cavers and Kirkton linked with Hawick: Trinity
Vacant   Fenwick Park, Hawick TD9 9PA   01450   372705

Hawick: Burnfoot
Charles J. Finnie LTh DPS   1991   1997   29 Wilton Hill, Hawick TD9 8BA   01450   373181
[E-mail: charles.finnie@gmail.com]

Hawick: St Mary's and Old (H)
Marina D. Brown (Mrs) MA BD MTh   2000   2007   The Manse of St Mary's and Old, Braid Road, Hawick TD9 9LZ   01450   378163
[E-mail: smop07@btinternet.com]

Hawick: Teviot (H) and Roberton
Neil R. Combe BSc MSc BD   1984   Teviot Manse, Buccleuch Road, Hawick TD9 0EL   01450   372150
[E-mail: neil.combe@btinternet.com]

Hawick: Trinity (H) See Cavers and Kirkton

Hawick: Wilton linked with Teviothead
Lisa-Jane Rankin (Miss) BD CPS   2003   4 Wilton Hill Terrace, Hawick TD9 8BE   01450   370744   (Tel/Fax)
[E-mail: revlj@talktalk.net]

Hobkirk and Southdean linked with Ruberslaw
Vacant   The Manse, Denholm, Hawick TD9 8NB   01450   870268

Jedburgh: Old and Trinity (E-mail: www.jedburgh-parish.org.uk)
Graham D. Astles BD MSc   2007   The Manse, Honeyfield Drive, Jedburgh TD8 6LQ   01835   863417
[E-mail: minister@jedburgh-parish.org.uk]   07906   290568   (Mbl)

Kelso Country Churches
Jenny Earl MA BD — 2007 — The Manse, 1 The Meadow, Stichill, Kelso TD5 7TG — 01573 470607
[E-mail: jennyearl@btinternet.com]

Kelso: North (H) and Ednam (H) (01573 224154) (E-mail: office@kelsonorthandednam.org.uk) (Website: www.kelsonorthandednam.org.uk)
Tom McDonald BD — 1994 — 20 Forestfield, Kelso TD5 7BX — 01573 224677
[E-mail: revtom@20thepearlygates.co.uk]

Kelso: Old (H) and Sprouston
Marion E. Dodd (Miss) MA BD LRAM — 1988 1989 — Glebe Lane, Kelso TD5 7AU — 01573 226254
[E-mail: mariondodd@btinternet.com]

Linton, Morebattle, Hownam and Yetholm (H)
Robin D. McHaffie BD — 1979 1991 — The Manse, Main Street, Kirk Yetholm, Kelso TD5 8PF — 01573 420308
[E-mail: robinmchaffie@f2s.com]

Oxnam
Continued Vacancy

Ruberslaw See Hobkirk and Southdean
Teviothead See Hawick: Wilton

Auld, A. Graeme MA BD PhD DLitt FSAScot FRSE	1973	(University of Edinburgh)	Nether Swanshiel, Hobkirk, Bonchester Bridge, Hawick TD9 8JU	
Brown, Joseph MA	1954 1991	(Linton with Hownam and Morebattle with Yetholm)	The Orchard, Hermitage Lane, Shedden Park Road, Kelso TD5 7AN	01573 223481
Finlay, Quintin BA BD	1975 1996	(North Bute)	Ivy Cottage, Greenlees Farm, Kelso TD5 8BT	01573 223335
Fox, Dudley A.	1972 1988	(Kelso Old)	14 Pinnacle Hill Farm, Kelso TD5 8HD	
Hamilton, Robert MA BD	1938 1979	(Kelso Old)	Ridge Cottage, 391 Totnes Road, Collaton St Mary, Paignton TQ4 7PW	01803 526440
Longmuir, William LTh	1984 2001	(Bedrule with Denholm with Minto)	Viewfield, South Street, Gavinton, Duns TD11 3QT	01361 882728
McNicol, Bruce	1967 2006	(Jedburgh: Old and Edgerston)	42 Dounehill, Jedburgh TD8 6LJ [E-mail: mcnicol95@btinternet.com]	01835 862991
Ritchie, Garden W.M.	1961 1995	(Ardersier with Petty)	23 Croft Road, Kelso TD5 7EP	01573 224419
Shields, John M. MBE LTh	1972 2007	(Channelkirk and Lauder)	12 Eden Park, Ednam, Kelso TD5 7RG	01573 229015
Thompson, W.M.D. MA	1950 1997	(Crailing and Eckford with Oxnam with Roxburgh)		
Thomson, E.P. Lindsay MA	1964 2008	(Cavers and Kirkton with Hawick: Trinity)	Beech House, Eial, Cornhill-on-Tweed TD12 4TL [E-mail: eplindsayt@aol.com]	01890 820621

HAWICK ADDRESSES

Burnfoot	Fraser Avenue
St Mary's and Old	Kirk Wynd
Teviot	off Buccleuch Road
Trinity	Central Square
Wilton	Princes Street

(7) ANNANDALE AND ESKDALE

Meets on the first Tuesday of February, May, September and December, and the third Tuesday of March, June and October, in a venue to be determined by Presbytery.

Clerk: REV. C. BRYAN HASTON LTh — The Manse, Gretna Green, Gretna DG16 5DU
[E-mail: annandaleeskdale@cofscotland.org.uk]
[E-mail: cbhaston@nfs.demon.co.uk]
01461 338313 (Tel)
08701 640119 (Fax)

Annan: Old (H) linked with Dornock
Hugh D. Steele LTh DipMin   1994   2004 — 12 Plumdon Park Avenue, Annan DG12 6EY
[E-mail: hugdebra@aol.com]
01461 201405

Alexander J. Falconer   (Shared Pastoral Assistant) — 23 Summergate Road Annan DG12 6EX
[E-mail: falconer@falconer59.freeserve.co.uk]
01461 202943

Annan: St Andrew's (H) linked with Brydekirk
George K. Lind BD MCIBS   1998 — 1 Annerley Road, Annan DG12 6HE
[E-mail: gklind@one1.com]
01461 202626

Alexander J. Falconer   (Shared Pastoral Assistant) — 23 Summergate Road Annan DG12 6EX
[E-mail: falconer@falconer59.freeserve.co.uk]
01461 202943

Applegarth, Sibbaldbie (H) and Johnstone linked with Lochmaben (H)
Jack M. Brown BSc BD   1977   2002 — The Manse, Barrashead, Lochmaben, Lockerbie DG11 1QF
[E-mail: jackm.brown@tiscali.co.uk]
01387 810066

Brydekirk See Annan: St Andrew's

Canonbie United (H) linked with Liddesdale (H)
Alan D. Reid MA BD   1989 — 23 Langholm Street, Newcastleton TD9 0QX
[E-mail: canonbie.liddesdale@talktalk.net]
01387 375242

Dalton linked with Hightae linked with St Mungo
Vacant — The Manse, Hightae, Lockerbie DG11 1JL
01387 811499

Dornock See Annan: Old

Gretna: Old (H), Gretna: St Andrew's (H) and Half Morton and Kirkpatrick Fleming
C. Bryan Haston LTh   1975 — The Manse, Gretna Green, Gretna DG16 5DU
[E-mail: cbhaston@nfs.demon.co.uk]
01461 338313 (Tel)
08701 640119 (Fax)

Alexander J. Falconer   (Shared Pastoral Assistant) — 23 Summergate Road, Annan DG12 6EX
[E-mail: falconer@falconer59.freeserve.co.uk]
01461 202943

Hightae See Dalton

Hoddam linked with Kirtle-Eaglesfield linked with Middlebie linked with Waterbeck
Vacant

Kirkpatrick Juxta linked with Moffat: St Andrew's (H) linked with Wamphray
Adam Dillon BD ThM 2003 2008 The Manse, 1 Meadowbank, Moffat DG10 9LR 01683 220128
[E-mail: adamdillon@btinternet.com]

Kirtle-Eaglesfield See Hoddam

Langholm Eskdalemuir Ewes and Westerkirk
Robert B. Milne BTh 1999 1999 The Manse, Langholm DG13 0BL 01387 380252 (Tel)
01387 381399 (Fax)
[E-mail: rbmilne@aol.com]

Liddesdale (H) See Canonbie United
Lochmaben See Applegarth, Sibbaldbie and Johnstone

Lockerbie: Dryfesdale, Hutton and Corrie
Alexander C. Stoddart BD 2001 2008 The Manse, 5 Carlisle Road, Lockerbie DG11 2DW 01576 202361
[E-mail: sandystoddart@supanet.com]
(Charge formed by the union of Lockerbie: Dryfesdale with Hutton and Corrie)

Middlebie See Hoddam
Moffat: St Andrew's (H) See Kirkpatrick Juxta
St Mungo See Dalton

The Border Kirk (Church office: Chapel Street, Carlisle CA1 1JA; Tel: 01228 591757)
David Pitkeathly LLB BD 1996 2007 95 Pinecroft, Carlisle CA3 0DB 01228 593243 (Tel/Fax)
[E-mail: david.pitkeathly@virgin.net]

Tundergarth
Continued Vacancy

Wamphray See Kirkpatrick Juxta
Waterbeck See Hoddam

Annand, James M. MA BD	1955	1995	(Lockerbie: Dryfesdale)	48 Main Street, Newstead, Melrose TD6 9DX	0131-225 3393
Beveridge, S. Edwin P. BA	1959	2004	(Brydekirk with Hoddam)	19 Rothesay Terrace, Edinburgh EH3 7RY	
Byers, Alan J.	1959	1992	(Gamrie with King Edward)	Meadowbank, Plumdon Road, Annan DG12 6SJ	01461 206512
Byers, Mairi (Mrs) BTh CPS	1992	1998	(Jura)	Meadowbank, Plumdon Road, Annan DG12 6SJ	01461 206512
Fisher, D. Noel MA BD	1939	1979	(Glasgow: Sherbrooke St Gilbert's)	Sheraig Cottage, Killochries Fold, Kilmacolm PA13 4TE	
Gibb, James Daniel MacGhee BA LTh	1994	2006	(Aberfoyle with Port of Menteith)	21 Victoria Gardens, Eastriggs, Dumfries DG12 6TW	01461 40560

[E-mail: dannygibb@hotmail.co.uk]

Name	Dates	Charge	Address	Tel
MacMillan, William M. LTh	1980 1998	(Kilmory with Lamlash)	Balskia, 61 Queen Street, Lochmaben DG11 1PP	01387 811528
Macpherson, Duncan J. BSc BD	1993 2002	Chaplain: Army	Household Cavalry Regiment, Combermere Barracks, Windsor, Berkshire SL4 3DN	
Rennie, John D. MA	1962 1996	(Broughton, Glenholm and Kilbucho with Skirling with Stobo and Drumelzier with Tweedsmuir)	Dandoran, Ballplay Road, Moffat DG10 9JX [E-mail: tworennies@talktalk.net]	01683 220223
Ross Alan C. CA BD	1988 2007	(Eskdalemuir with Hutton and Corrie with Tundergarth)	Yarra, Ettrickbridge, Selkirk TD7 5JN [E-mail: alkaross@aol.com]	01750 52324
Seaman, Ronald S. MA	1967 2007	(Dornock)	1 Springfield Farm Court, Main Street, Springfield, Gretna DG16 5EH	01461 337228
Steenbergen, Pauline (Ms) MA BD	1996 2007	Congregational Facilitator	95 Pinecroft, Carlisle CA3 0DB [E-mail: pauline.steenbergen@virgin.net]	(Tel/Fax) 01228 593243 (Mbl) 07882 200215
Swinburne, Norman BA	1960 1993	(Sauchie)	Lamerosehay, Birch Hill Lane, Kirkbride, Wigton CA7 5HZ	01697 351497
Vivers, Katherine A.	2004	Auxiliary Minister	Flacket House, Eaglesfield, Lockerbie DG11 3AA [E-mail: katevivers@yahoo.co.uk]	01461 500412
Williams, Trevor C. LTh	1990 2007	(Hoddam with Kirtle-Eaglesfield with Middlebie with Waterbeck)	2 Trinity Way, Littlehampton, West Sussex BN17 5SS	

(8) DUMFRIES AND KIRKCUDBRIGHT

Meets at Dumfries on the first Wednesday of February, March, April, May, September, October, November and December, and the fourth Wednesday of June.

Clerk:	REV. GORDON M.A. SAVAGE MA BD		11 Laurieknowe, Dumfries DG2 7AH [E-mail: dumfrieskirkcudbright@cofscotland.org.uk]	01387 252929
Depute Clerk:	REV. WILLIAM T. HOGG MA BD		The Manse, Glasgow Road, Sanquhar DG4 6BZ [E-mail: wthogg@yahoo.com]	01659 50247

Auchencairn (H) and Rerrick linked with Buittle (H) and Kelton (H)
Alistair J. MacKichan MA BD   1984   2005   Auchencairn, Castle Douglas DG7 1QS   01556 640041
[E-mail: ali-mack5 @tiscali.co.uk]

Balmaclellan and Kells (H) linked with Carsphairn (H) linked with Dalry (H)
David S. Bartholomew BSc MSc PhD BD   1994   The Manse, Dalry, Castle Douglas DG7 3PJ   01644 430380
[E-mail: dhbart@care4free.net]

Balmaghie linked with Tarff and Twynholm (H)
Christopher Wallace BD DipMin   1988   Manse Road, Twynholm, Kirkcudbright DG6 4NY   01557 860381
[E-mail: cwallaceuc@hotmail.com]

Borgue linked with Gatehouse of Fleet
Valerie J. Ott (Mrs) BA BD   2002
The Manse, Planetree Park, Gatehouse of Fleet, Castle Douglas DG7 2EQ
[E-mail: dandvott@aol.com]
01557 814233

Buittle and Kelton See Auchencairn and Rerrick

Caerlaverock linked with Dumfries: St Mary's-Greyfriars
Jamie Milliken BD   2005
4 Georgetown Crescent, Dumfries DG1 4EQ
[E-mail: minister@stmarysgreyfriars.org.uk]
01387 257045

Carsphairn See Balmaclellan and Kells

Castle Douglas (H)
Robert J. Malloch BD   1987 2001
1 Castle View, Castle Douglas DG7 1BG
[E-mail: robert@scotnish.freeserve.co.uk]
01556 502171

Closeburn linked with Durisdeer
James W. Scott MA CDA   1952 1953
The Manse, Durisdeer, Thornhill DG3 5BJ
01848 500231

Colvend, Southwick and Kirkbean
James F. Gatherer BD   1984 2003
The Manse, Colvend, Dalbeattie DG5 4QN
[E-mail: james@gatherer.net]
01556 630255

Corsock and Kirkpatrick Durham linked with Crossmichael and Parton
Sally Marsh BTh MTh   2006
Knockdrocket, Clarebrand, Castle Douglas DG7 3AH
[E-mail: rev.sal@btinternet.com]
01556 503645

Crossmichael and Parton See Corsock and Kirkpatrick Durham

Cummertrees linked with Mouswald linked with Ruthwell (H)
James Williamson BA BD   1986 1991
The Manse, Ruthwell, Dumfries DG1 4NP
[E-mail: jimwill@rcmkirk.fsnet.co.uk]
01387 870217

Dalbeattie (H) linked with Urr (H)
Norman M. Hutcheson MA BD   1973 1988
36 Mill Street, Dalbeattie DG5 4HE
[E-mail: norman.hutcheson@virgin.net]
01556 610029

Dalry See Balmaclellan and Kells

Dumfries: Maxwelltown West (H)
Gordon M.A. Savage MA BD   1977 1984
Maxwelltown West Manse, 11 Laurieknowe, Dumfries DG2 7AH
[E-mail: gordon.savage@cdsmail.co.uk]
01387 252929

Dumfries: Northwest
Neil G. Campbell BA BD   1988   2006   27 St Anne's Road, Dumfries DG2 9HZ   01387 249964
[E-mail: mail@neilgcampbell.co.uk]
(Charge formed by the union of Dumfries: Lincluden and Holywood with Dumfries: Lochside)

Dumfries: St George's (H)
Donald Campbell BD   1997   9 Nunholm Park, Dumfries DG1 1JP   01387 252965
[E-mail: saint-georges@ukonline.co.uk]

Dumfries: St Mary's-Greyfriars (H) See Caerlaverock

Dumfries: St Michael's and South
Maurice S. Bond MTh BA DipEd PhD   1981   1999   39 Cardoness Stree, Dumfries DG1 3AL   01387 253849
[E-mail: maurice.bond3@tiscali.co.uk]

Dumfries: Troqueer (H)
William W. Kelly BSc BD   1994   Troqueer Manse, Troqueer Road, Dumfries DG2 7DF   01387 253043
[E-mail: wwkelly@yahoo.com]

Dunscore linked with Glencairn and Moniaive
Christine Sime (Miss) BSc BD   1994   Wallaceton, Auldgirth, Dumfries DG2 0TJ   01387 820245
[E-mail: revsime@aol.com]

Durisdeer See Closeburn
Gatehouse of Fleet See Borgue
Glencairn and Moniaive See Dunscore

Irongray, Lochrutton and Terregles
Vacant   Shawhead Road, Dumfries DG2 9SJ   01387 730287

Kirkconnel (H)
Vacant   The Manse, 31 Kingsway, Kirkconnel, Sanquhar DG4 6PN   01659 67241

Kirkcudbright (H)
Douglas R. Irving LLB BD WS   1984   1998   6 Bourtree Avenue, Kirkcudbright DG6 4AU   01557 330489
[E-mail: douglasirving05@tiscali.co.uk]

Kirkgunzeon
Continued Vacancy

Kirkmahoe
David M. Almond BD   1996   2008   The Manse, Kirkmahoe, Dumfries DG1 1ST   01387 710572
[E-mail: davidalmond1@btconnect.com]

Kirkmichael, Tinwald and Torthorwald
Louis C. Bezuidenhout BA MA BD DD	1978	2000	Manse of Tinwald, Tinwald, Dumfries DG1 3PL [E-mail: macbez@btinternet.com]	01387 710246
Elizabeth A. Mack (Miss) DipPEd (Aux)	1994	2006	24 Roberts Crescent, Dumfries DG2 7RS [E-mail: mackliz@btinternet.com]	01387 264847

Lochend and New Abbey
William Holland MA	1967	1971	The Manse, 28 Main Street, New Abbey, Dumfries DG2 8BY [E-mail: bilholland@aol.com]	01387 850232

Mouswald See Cummertrees

Penpont, Keir and Tynron linked with Thornhill (H)
Vacant		The Manse, Manse Park, Thornhill DG3 5ER	01848 331191

Ruthwell (H) See Cummertrees

Sanquhar: St Bride's (H)
William T. Hogg MA BD	1979	2000	St Bride's Manse, Glasgow Road, Sanquhar DG6 6BZ [E-mail: wthogg@yahoo.com]	01659 50247

Tarff and Twynholm See Balmaghie
Thornhill (H) See Penpont, Keir and Tynron
Urr See Dalbeattie

Bennett, David K.P. BA	1974	2000	(Kirkpatrick Irongray with Lochrutton with Terregles)	53 Anne Arundel Court, Heathhall, Dumfries DG1 3SL — 01387 257755
Duncan, Maureen M. (Mrs) BD	1996	2008	(Dunlop)	Dunedin, Whitepark, Castle Douglas DG7 1QA — 01556 502867 [E-mail: revmo@talktalk.net]
Geddes, Alexander J. MA BD	1960	1998	(Stewarton: St Columba's)	166 Georgetown Road, Dumfries DG1 4DT — 01387 252287 [E-mail: sandy.elizabeth@virgin.net]
Gillespie, Ann M. (Miss) DCS	1956	1996	(Deaconess)	Barlochan House, Palnackie, Castle Douglas DG7 1PF — 01556 600378
Greer, A. David C. LLB DMin DipAdultEd			(Barra)	10 Watling Street, Dumfries DG1 1HF — 01387 256113 [E-mail: kandadc@greer10.fsnet.co.uk]
Hamil, Robert BA	1956	1989	(Castle Douglas: St Ringan's)	11 St Andrew Drive, Castle Douglas DG7 1EW — 01556 502962
Hammond, Richard J. BA BD	1993	2007	(Kirkmahoe)	3 Marchfield Mount, Marchfield, Dumfries DG1 1SE — (Mbl) 07764 465783 [E-mail: libby.hammond@virgin.net]
Kirk, W. Logan MA BD MTh	1988	2000	(Dalton with Hightae with St Mungo)	2 Raecroft Avenue, Collin, Dumfries DG1 4LP — 01387 750489
Leishman, James S. LTh BD MA(Div)	1969	1999	(Kirkmichael with Tinwald with Torthorwald)	11 Hunter Avenue, Heathhall, Dumfries DG1 3UX — 01387 249241

Name	Charge	Years	Address	Phone
McKay, David M. MA BD	(Kirkpatrick Juxta with Moffat: St Andrew's with Wamphray)	1979 2007	20 Auld Brig View, Auldgirth, Dumfries DG2 0XE [E-mail: davidmckay20@tiscali.co.uk]	01387 740013
McKenzie, William M. DA	(Dumfries: Troqueer)	1958 1993	41 Kingholm Road, Dumfries DG1 4SR [E-mail: mckenzie.dumfries@virgin.net]	01387 253688
Miller, John G. BEd BD MTh	(Port Glasgow: St Martin's)	1983 2005	22 Lime Grove, Georgetown, Dumfries DG1 4SQ [E-mail: johnmiller22@hotmail.co.uk]	01387 252502
Miller, John R. MA BD	(Carsphairn with Dalry)	1958 1992	4 Fairgreen Court, Rhonehouse, Castle Douglas DG7 1SA	01556 680428
Morrison, James G. MBE MA	(Rotterdam)	1942 1980	1 Woodvale Lodge, Midsummer Meadows, Cambridge CB4 1HL	07812 148161
Owen, John J.C. LTh	(Applegarth and Sibbaldbie with Lochmaben)	1967 2001	5 Galla Avenue, Dalbeattie DG5 4JZ [E-mail: jj.owen@onetel.net]	01556 612125
Robertson, Ian W. MA BD	(Colvend, Southwick and Kirkbean)	1956 1995	10 Marjoriebanks, Lochmaben, Lockerbie DG11 1QH	01387 810541
Smith, Richmond OBE MA BD	(World Alliance of Reformed Churches)	1952 1983	Aignish, Merse Way, Kippford, Dalbeattie DG5 4LH	01556 620624
Strachan, Alexander E. MA BD	(Dumfries Health Care Chaplain)	1974 1999	2 Leafield Road, Dumfries DG1 2DS [E-mail: aestrachan@aol.com]	01387 279460
Sutherland, Colin A. LTh	(Blantyre: Livingstone Memorial)	1995 2007	71 Caulstran Road, Dumfries DG2 9FJ [E-mail: colin.csutherland@btinternet.com]	01387 279954
Vincent, C. Raymond MA FSAScot	(Stonehouse)	1952 1992	Rosebank, Newton Stewart Road, New Galloway, Castle Douglas DG7 3RT	01644 420451
Wilkie, James R. MA MTh	(Penpont, Keir and Tynron)	1957 1993	31 West Morton Street, Thornhill DG3 5NF	01848 331028
Wotherspoon, Robert C. LTh	(Corsock and Kirkpatrick Durham with Crossmichael and Parton)	1976 1998	7 Hillowton Drive, Castle Douglas DG7 1LL [E-mail: robert@wotherspoon11.wanadoo.co.uk]	01556 502267
Young, John MTh DipMin	(Airdrie: Broomknoll)	1963 1999	Craigview, North Street, Moniaive, Thornhill DG3 4HR	01848 200318

DUMFRIES ADDRESSES

Maxwelltown West	Laurieknowe		
Northwest	Lochside Road	St Michael's and South	St Michael's Street
St George's	George Street	Troqueer	Troqueer Road
St Mary's-Greyfriars	St Mary's Street		

(9) WIGTOWN AND STRANRAER

Meets at Glenluce, in the church hall, on the first Tuesday of March, October and December for ordinary business; on the first Tuesday of September for formal business followed by meetings of committees; on the first Tuesday of November, February and May for worship followed by meetings of committees; and at a church designated by the Moderator on the first Tuesday of June for Holy Communion followed by ordinary business.

Clerk:	**REV. DAVID W. DUTTON BA**	**79 Main Street, Sandhead, Stranraer DG9 9JF** [E-mail: wigtownstranraer@cofscotland.org.uk]	**01776 830497**

Ervie Kirkcolm linked with Leswalt

Michael J. Sheppard BD	1997	Ervie Manse, Stranraer DG9 0QZ [E-mail: mjs@uwclub.net]	01776 854225

Glasserton and Isle of Whithorn linked with Whithorn: St Ninian's Priory

Alexander I. Currie BD CPS	1990	The Manse, Whithorn, Newton Stewart DG8 8PT	01988 500267

Inch linked with Stranraer: Town Kirk (H)

John H. Burns BSc BD	1985 1988	Bayview Road, Stranraer DG9 8BE	01776 702383

Kirkcowan (H) linked with Wigtown (H)

Eric Boyle BA MTh	2006	Seaview Manse, Church Lane, Wigtown, Newton Stewart DG8 9HT [E-mail: ecthered@aol.com]	01988 402314

Kirkinner linked with Sorbie (H)

Jeffrey M. Mead BD	1978 1986	The Manse, Kirkinner, Newton Stewart DG8 9AL	01988 840643

Kirkmabreck linked with Monigaff (H)

Peter W.I. Aiken	1996 2005	Creebridge, Newton Stewart DG8 6NR [E-mail: aikenp@btinternet.com]	01671 403361

Kirkmaiden (H) linked with Stoneykirk

Vacant		Church Street, Sandhead, Stranraer DG9 9JJ	01776 830337
Mike Binks (Aux)	2007	Holly Bank, Corsbie Road, Newton Stewart DG8 6JD [E-mail: mike@hollybank.net]	01671 402201

Leswalt See Ervie Kirkcolm

Mochrum (H)

Vacant	Manse of Mochrum, Port William, Newton Stewart DG8 9QP 01988 700257

Monigaff (H) See Kirkmabreck

New Luce (H) linked with Old Luce (H)

Thomas M. McWhirter MA MSc BD	1992 1997	Glenluce, Newton Stewart DG8 0PU	01581 300319

Old Luce See New Luce

Penninghame (H)

Edward D. Lyons BD MTh	2007	The Manse, 1A Corvisel Road, Newton Stewart DG8 6LW [E-mail: edwardlyons@hotmail.com]	01671 404425

Portpatrick linked with Stranraer: St Ninian's (H)

Gordon Kennedy BSc BD MTh	1993 2000	2 Albert Terrace, London Road, Stranraer DG9 8AB [E-mail: gordon.k1@btinternet.com]	01776 702443

Sorbie See Kirkinner
Stoneykirk See Kirkmaiden

Stranraer: High Kirk (H)
Vacant

Stranraer: St Ninian's See Portpatrick
Stranraer: Town Kirk See Inch
Whithorn: St Ninian's Priory See Glasserton and Isle of Whithorn
Wigtown See Kirkcowan

Crawford, Joseph F. BA	1970	2006	(Bowden with Newtown)	21 South Street, Port William, Newton Stewart DG8 9SH	01988 700761
Dean, Roger A.F. LTh	1983	2004	(Mochrum)	Albion Cottage, 59 Main Street, Kirkinner, Newton Stewart DG8 9AN	01988 840621
				[E-mail: roger.dean4@btopenworld.com]	
Dutton, David W. BA	1973	2008	(Stranraer: High Kirk)	79 Main Street, Sandhead, Stranraer DG9 9JF	01776 830497
McGill, Thomas W.	1972	1990	(Portpatrick with Stranraer: St Ninian's)	Westfell Monreith, Newton Stewart DG8 9LT	01988 700449
Munro, Mary (Mrs) BA	1993	2004	(Auxiliary Minister)	14 Auchneil Crescent, Stranraer DG9 0JH	01776 702305
Munro, Sheila BD	1995	2003	Chaplain: RAF	15 Hamilton Rise, MPA, BFPO 655	
Ogilvy, Oliver M.	1959	1985	(Leswalt)	8 Dale Crescent, Stranraer DG9 0HG	01776 706285

(10) AYR

Meets on the first Tuesday of every month from September to May, excluding January, and on the fourth Tuesday of June. The June meeting will be held in the Moderator's church. One meeting will be held in a venue to be determined by the Business Committee. Other meetings will be held in Alloway Church Hall.

Clerk:	REV. JAMES CRICHTON MA BD MTh			30 Garden Street, Dalrymple KA6 6DG	01292 560263
				[E-mail: ayr@cofscotland.org.uk]	01292 560574 (Fax)
Presbytery Office:				St Leonard's Church, Ayr	01292 611117 (Tel/Fax)
				[E-mail: presbyter_office@btinternet.com]	

Alloway (H)

Neil A. McNaught BD MA	1987	1999	1A Parkview, Alloway, Ayr KA7 4QG	01292 441252
			[E-mail: neil@mcnaught3427.freeserve.co.uk]	

Annbank (H) linked with Tarbolton

Alexander Shuttleworth MA BD		2004	1 Kirkport, Tarbolton, Mauchline KA5 5QJ	01292 541236
			[E-mail: revshuttleworth@aol.com]	

Auchinleck (H) linked with Catrine

Stephen F. Clipston MA BD	1982	2006	28 Mauchline Road, Auchinleck KA18 2BN	01290 424776
			[E-mail: steveclipston@btinternet.com]	

Ayr: Auld Kirk of Ayr (St John the Baptist) (H)
David R. Gemmell MA BD — 1991 — 1999 — 58 Monument Road, Ayr KA7 2UB
[E-mail: drgemmell@hotmail.com] — 01292 262580 (Tel/Fax)

Ayr: Castlehill (H)
Elizabeth A. Crumlish (Mrs) BD — 1995 — 2008 — 3 Old Hillfoot Road, Ayr KA7 3LF
[E-mail: lizcrumlish@aol.com] — 01292 267332

Ayr: Newton on Ayr (H)
G. Stewart Birse CA BD BSc — 1980 — 1989 — 9 Nursery Grove, Ayr KA7 3PH
[E-mail: axhp44@dsl.pipex.com] — 01292 264251

Ayr: St Andrew's (H)
Harry B. Mealyea BArch BD — 1984 — 2000 — 31 Bellevue Crescent, Ayr KA7 2DP
[E-mail: mealyea@tiscali.co.uk] — 01292 261126

Ayr: St Columba (H)
Fraser R. Aitken MA BD — 1978 — 1991 — 2 Hazelwood Road, Ayr KA7 2PY
[E-mail: frasercolumba@msn.com] — 01292 284177

Ayr: St James' (H)
Robert McCrum BSc BD — 1982 — 2005 — 1 Prestwick Road, Ayr KA8 8LD
[E-mail: robert@stjamesayr.org.uk] — 01292 262420

Ayr: St Leonard's (H)
Robert Lynn MA BD — 1984 — 1989 — 7 Shawfield Avenue, Ayr KA7 4RE
[E-mail: robert@shawfield200.fsnet.co.uk] — 01292 442109

Ayr: St Quivox (H)
Vacant — 11 Springfield Avenue, Prestwick KA9 2HA — 01292 478306

Ayr: Wallacetown (H)
Mary C. McLauchlan (Mrs) LTh — 1997 — 2003 — 87 Forehill Road, Ayr KA7 3JR
[E-mail: mary@revmother.co.uk] — 01292 263878

Ballantrae (H) linked with St Colmon (Arnsheen Barrhill and Colmonell)
Vacant — Ballantrae, Girvan KA26 0NH — 01465 831252

Barr linked with Dailly linked with Girvan South
Ian K. McLachlan MA BD — 1999 — 30 Henrietta Street, Girvan KA26 9AL
[E-mail: iankmclachlan@yetiville.freeserve.co.uk] — 01465 713370

Catrine See Auchinleck

Coylton linked with Drongan: The Schaw Kirk 1998
David Whiteman BD — 4 Hamilton Place, Coylton, Ayr KA6 6JQ — 01292 571442
[E-mail: davesoo@sky.com]

Craigie linked with Symington 1996 2008
Glenda J. Keating (Mrs) MTh — 16 Kerrix Road, Symington, Kilmarnock KA1 5QD — 01563 830205
[E-mail: kirkglen@btinternet.com]

Crosshill (H) linked with Dalrymple (H) 1969
James Crichton MA BD MTh — 30 Garden Street, Dalrymple KA6 6DG — 01292 560263 (Tel) / 01292 560574 (Fax)
[E-mail: ayr@cofscotland.org.uk]

Dailly See Barr

Dalmellington linked with Patna: Waterside 1982 1999
Kenneth B. Yorke BD DipEd — 4 Carsphairn Road, Dalmellington, Ayr KA6 7RE — 01292 550353
[E-mail: k.yorke@200m.co.uk]
Muriel Wilson (Ms) DCS BD — 28 Bellevue Crescent, Ayr KA7 2DR — 01292 264939
[E-mail: muriel.wilson4@btinternet.com]

Dalrymple See Crosshill
Drongan: The Schaw Kirk See Coylton

Dundonald (H) 1982 1988
Robert Mayes BD — 64 Main Street, Dundonald, Kilmarnock KA2 9HG — 01563 850243
[E-mail: bobmayes@fsmail.net]

Fisherton (H) linked with Kirkoswald 2000 2003
Arrick D. Wilkinson BSc BD — The Manse, Kirkoswald, Maybole KA19 8HZ — 01655 760210
[E-mail: arrick@clergy.net]

Girvan: North (Old and St Andrew's) (H) 1999
Douglas G. McNab BA BD — 38 The Avenue, Girvan KA26 9DS — 01465 713203
[E-mail: dougmcnab@aol.com]

Girvan: South See Barr linked with Dailly

Kirkmichael linked with Straiton: St Cuthbert's 1984 1985
W. Gerald Jones MA BD MTh — Patna Road, Kirkmichael, Maybole KA19 7PJ — 01655 750286
[E-mail: revgerald@jonesg99.freeserve.co.uk]

Kirkoswald (H) See Fisherton

Lugar linked with Old Cumnock: Old (H)
John W. Paterson BSc BD DipEd
1994
33 Barrhill Road, Cumnock KA18 1PJ
[E-mail: ocochurchwow@hotmail.com]
01290 420769

Mauchline (H)
Alan B. Telfer BA BD
1983   1991
4 Westside Gardens, Mauchline KA5 5DJ
[E-mail: telferab@tiscali.co.uk]
01290 550386

Maybole
Vacant
Douglas T. Moore (Aux)
2003
9 Midton Avenue, Prestwick KA9 1PU
[E-mail: douglastmoore@hotmail.com]
01292 671352

Monkton and Prestwick: North (H)
Arthur A. Christie BD
1997   2000
40 Monkton Road, Prestwick KA9 1AR
[E-mail: revaac@btinternet.com]
01292 477499

Muirkirk (H) linked with Sorn
Vacant
2 Smallburn Road, Muirkirk, Cumnock KA18 3RF
01290 661157

New Cumnock (H)
Rona M. Young (Mrs) BD DipEd
1991   2001
37 Castle, New Cumnock, Cumnock KA18 4AG
[E-mail: revronyoung@hotmail.com]
01290 338296

Ochiltree linked with Stair
Vacant
10 Mauchline Road, Ochiltree, Cumnock KA18 2PZ
01290 700365

Old Cumnock: Old See Lugar

Old Cumnock: Trinity
Scott M. Rae MBE BD CPS
1976   2008
46 Ayr Road, Cumnock KA18 1DW
[E-mail: scottrae1@btopenworld.com]
01290 541609

Patna: Waterside See Dalmellington

Prestwick: Kingcase (H) (E-mail: office@kingcase.freeserve.co.uk)
T. David Watson BSc BD
1988   1997
15 Bellrock Avenue, Prestwick KA9 1SQ
[E-mail: tdavidwatson@btinternet.com]
01292 479571

Prestwick: St Nicholas' (H)
George R. Fiddes BD   1979 1985   3 Bellevue Road, Prestwick KA9 1NW   01292 477613
[E-mail: george@gfiddes.freeserve.co.uk]

Prestwick: South (H)
Kenneth C. Elliott BD BA CertMin   1989   68 St Quivox Road, Prestwick KA9 1JF   01292 478788
[E-mail: kcelliott@tiscali.co.uk]

St Colmon (Arnsheen Barrhill and Colmonell) See Ballantrae
Sorn See Muirkirk
Stair See Ochiltree
Straiton: St Cuthbert's See Kirkmichael
Symington See Craigie
Tarbolton See Annbank

Troon: Old (H)
Alastair H. Symington MA BD   1972 1998   85 Bentinck Drive, Troon KA10 6HZ   01292 313644
[E-mail: revahs@tiscali.co.uk]

Troon: Portland (H)
Ronald M.H. Boyd BD DipTh   1995 1999   89 South Beach, Troon KA10 6EQ   01292 313285
[E-mail: rmhboyd@wightcablenorth.net]

Troon: St Meddan's (H) (E-mail: st.meddan@virgin.net)
David L. Harper BSc BD   1972 1979   27 Bentinck Drive, Troon KA10 6HX   01292 311784
[E-mail: d.l.harper@btinternet.com]

Name			(Charge)	Address	Phone
Andrew, R.J.M. MA	1955	1994	(Uddingston: Old)	6A Ronaldshaw Park, Ayr KA7 2TS	01292 263430
Baker, Carolyn M. (Mrs) BD	1997	2008	(Ochiltree with Stair)	Clanary, 1 Maxwell Drive, Newton Stewart DG8 6EL [E-mail: cncbaker@btinternet.com]	
Blyth, James G.S. BSc BD	1963	1986	(Glenmuick)	40 Robsland Avenue, Ayr KA7 2RW	01292 261276
Bogle, Thomas C. BD	1983	2003	(Fisherton with Maybole: West)	38 McEwan Crescent, Mossblown, Ayr KA6 5DR	01292 521215
Campbell, Effie C. (Mrs) BD	1981	1991	(Old Cumnock: Crichton West with St Ninian's)		
Cranston, George BD	1976	2001	(Rutherglen: Wardlawhill)	7 Lansdowne Road, Ayr KA8 8LS	01292 264282
Dickie, Michael M. BSc	1955	1994	(Ayr: Castlehill)	20 Capperview, Prestwick KA9 1BH	01292 476627
Glencross, William M. LTh	1968	1999	(Bellshill: Macdonald Memorial)	8 Noltmire Road, Ayr KA8 9ES	01292 618512
Grant, J. Gordon MA BD PhD	1957	1997	(Edinburgh: Dean)	1 Lochay Place, Troon KA10 7HH	01292 317097
Guthrie, James A.	1969	2005	(Corsock and Kirkpatrick Durham with Crossmichael and Parton)	33 Fullarton Drive, Troon KA10 6LE	01292 311852
				2 Barrhill Road, Pinwherry, Girvan KA26 0QE [E-mail: p.h.m.guthrie@btinternet.com]	01465 841236
Hannah, William BD MCAM MIPR	1987	2001	(Muirkirk)	8 Dovecote View, Kirkintilloch, Glasgow G66 3HY	0141-776 1337
Helon, George G. BA BD	1984	2000	(Barr linked with Dailly)	9 Park Road, Maxwelltown, Dumfries DG2 7PW	01387 259255

Name	Ordained	Inducted	Charge/Role	Address	Tel
Johnston, Kenneth L. BA LTh	1969	2001	(Annbank)	2 Rylands, Prestwick KA9 2DX [E-mail: ken@kenston.co.uk]	01292 471980
Kent, Arthur F.S.	1966	1999	(Monkton and Prestwick: North)	17 St David's Drive, Evesham, Worcs WR11 6AS [E-mail: afskent@onetel.com]	01386 421562
King, Chris (Mrs) MA BD DCS	1991	2006	Deaconess	28 Kilnford Drive, Dundonald, Kilmarnock KA2 9ET	01563 851197
Lennox, Lawrie I. MA BD DipEd	1967	2008	(Cromar)	7 Carwinshoch View, Ayr KA7 4AY	01465 811262
Lochrie, John S. BSc BD MTh PhD	1965	1999	(St Colmon)	Cosyglen, Kilkerran, Maybole KA19 8LS	01292 288854
McCrorie, William			(Free Church Chaplain: Royal Brompton Hospital)	12 Shieling Park, Ayr KA7 2UR [E-mail: billewemcrorie@btinternet.com]	
Macdonald, Ian U.	1960	1997	(Tarbolton)	18 Belmont Road, Ayr KA7 2PF	01292 283085
McNidder, Roderick H. BD	1987	1997	Chaplain: NHS Ayrshire and Arran Trust	6 Hollow Park, Alloway, Ayr KA7 4SR	01292 442554
McPhail, Andrew M. BA	1968	2002	(Ayr: Wallacetown)	25 Maybole Road, Ayr KA7 2QA	01292 282108
Mitchell, Sheila M. (Miss) BD MTh	1995	2002	Chaplain: NHS Ayrshire and Arran Trust	Ailsa Hospital, Ayr KA6 6BQ	01292 610556
Ness, David T. LTh	1972	2008	(Ayr: St Quivox)	17 Winston Avenue, Prestwick KA9 2EZ [E-mail: dtness@tiscali.co.uk]	
Russell, Paul R. MA BD	1984	2006	Chaplain: NHS Ayrshire and Arran Trust	23 Nursery Wynd, Ayr KA7 3NZ	01292 618020
Sanderson, Alastair M. BA LTh	1971	2007	(Craigie with Symington)	26 Main Street, Monkton, Prestwick KA9 2QL [E-mail: alel@sanderson29.fsnet.co.uk]	01292 475819
Saunders, Campbell M. MA BD	1952	1989	(Ayr: St Leonard's)	42 Marle Park, Ayr KA7 4RN	01292 441673
Stirling, Ian R. BSc BD	1990	2002	Chaplain: The Ayrshire Hospice	Ayrshire Hospice, 35–37 Racecourse Road, Ayr KA7 2TG	01292 269200

AYR ADDRESSES

Ayr

Auld Kirk	Kirkport (116 High Street)
Castlehill	Castlehill Road x Hillfoot Road
Newton on Ayr	Main Street
St Andrew's	Park Circus
St Columba	Midton Road x Carrick Park
St James'	Prestwick Road x Falkland Park Road
St Leonard's	St Leonard's Road x Monument Road
Wallacetown	John Street x Church Street

Girvan

North	Montgomerie Street
South	Stair Park

Prestwick

Kingcase	Waterloo Road
Monkton and Prestwick North	Monkton Road
St Nicholas	Main Street
South	Main Street

Troon

Old	Ayr Street
Portland	St Meddan's Street
St Meddan's	St Meddan's Street

(11) IRVINE AND KILMARNOCK

The Presbytery meets ordinarily at 6:30pm in the Hall of Howard St Andrew's Church, Kilmarnock, on the first Tuesday of each month from September to May (except January and April), and on the fourth Tuesday in June. The September meeting begins with the celebration of Holy Communion.

Clerk:	REV. COLIN G.F. BROCKIE BSc(Eng) BD SOSc	36 Braehead Court, Kilmarnock KA3 7AB [E-mail: irvinekilmarnock@cofscotland.org.uk]	01563 526295
Depute Clerk:	I. STEUART DEY LLB NP	72 Dundonald Road, Kilmarnock KA1 1RZ [E-mail: steuart.dey@btinternet.com]	01563 521686
Treasurer:	JAMES McINTOSH BA CA	15 Dundonald Road, Kilmarnock KA1 1RU	01563 523552

The Presbytery office is manned each Tuesday, Wednesday and Thursday from 9am until 12:45pm. The office telephone number is 01563 526295.

Crosshouse T. Edward Marshall BD	1987	2007	27 Kilmarnock Road, Crosshouse, Kilmarnock KA2 0EZ [E-mail: marshall1862@btinternet.com]	01563 521035
Darvel (01560 722924) Charles M. Cameron BA BD PhD	1980	2001	46 West Main Street, Darvel KA17 0AQ	01560 322924
Dreghorn and Springside Gary E. Horsburgh BA	1976	1983	96A Townfoot, Dreghorn, Irvine KA11 4EZ	01294 217770
Dunlop Vacant			4 Dampark, Dunlop, Kilmarnock KA3 4BZ	01560 484083
Fenwick (H) Geoffrey Redmayne BSc BD MPhil	2000		2 Kirkton Place, Fenwick, Kilmarnock KA3 6DW [E-mail: gredmayne@btinternet.com]	01560 600217
Galston (H) (01563 820136) Graeme R. Wilson MCIBS BD ThM	2006		60 Brewland Street, Galston KA4 8DX [E-mail: graeme.wilson@gmail.com]	01563 820246
John H.B. Taylor MA BD DipEd FEIS (Assoc)	1952	1990	62 Woodlands Grove, Kilmarnock KA3 1TZ	01563 526698
Hurlford (H) James D. McCulloch BD MIOP MIP3	1996		12 Main Road, Crookedholm, Kilmarnock KA3 6JT	01563 535673
Irvine: Fullarton (H) (Website: www.fullartonchurch.co.uk) Neil Urquhart BD DipMin	1989		48 Waterside, Irvine KA12 8QJ [E-mail: neilurquhart@beeb.net]	01294 279909

Irvine: Girdle Toll (E) (H) (Website: www.girdletoll.fsbusiness.co.uk)
Clare B. Sutcliffe BSc BD | 2000 | 2 Littlestane Rise, Irvine KA11 2BJ [E-mail: revclare@tesco.net] | 01294 213565

Irvine: Mure (H)
Hugh M. Adamson BD | 1976 | West Road, Irvine KA12 8RE | 01294 279916

Irvine: Old (H) (01294 273503)
Robert Travers BA BD | 1993 1999 | 22 Kirk Vennel, Irvine KA12 0DQ [E-mail: robert.travers@tesco.net] | 01294 279265

Irvine: Relief Bourtreehill (H)
Andrew R. Black BD | 1987 2003 | 4 Kames Court, Irvine KA11 1RT [E-mail: andrewblack@tiscali.co.uk] | 01294 216939

Irvine: St Andrew's (H) (01294 276051)
Vacant | 206 Bank Street, Irvine KA12 0YD | 01294 211403

Kilmarnock: Grange (H) (07818 550606) (Website: www.grangechurch.org.uk)
Vacant | 51 Portland Road, Kilmarnock KA1 2EQ | 01563 525311

Kilmarnock: Henderson (H) (01563 541302) (Website: www.hendersonchurch.org.uk)
David W. Lacy BA BD DLitt | 1976 1989 | 52 London Road, Kilmarnock KA3 7AJ [E-mail: thelacys@tinyworld.co.uk] | 01563 523113 (Tel/Fax)

Kilmarnock: Laigh West High (H)
David S. Cameron BD | 2001 | 1 Holmes Farm Road, Kilmarnock KA1 1TP [E-mail: dvdcam5@msn.com] | 01563 525416

Kilmarnock: Old High Kirk (H)
William M. Hall BD | 1972 1979 | 107 Dundonald Road, Kilmarnock KA1 1UP [E-mail: revwillie@tiscali.co.uk] | 01563 525608

Kilmarnock: Riccarton (H)
Colin A. Strong BSc BD | 1989 2007 | 2 Jasmine Road, Kilmarnock KA1 2HD [E-mail: colinastrong@aol.com] | 01563 549490

Kilmarnock: St Andrew's and St Marnock's
James McNaughton BD DipMin | 1983 1989 | 35 South Gargieston Drive, Kilmarnock KA1 1TB [E-mail: jim@mcnaughtan.demon.co.uk] | 01563 521665

(Charge formed by the union of Kilmarnock: Howard St Andrew's and Kilmarnock: St Marnock's)

Kilmarnock: St John's Onthank (H)
Susan M. Anderson (Mrs)   1997   84 Wardneuk Drive, Kilmarnock KA3 2EX   01563 521815
[E-mail: stjohnthank@talktalk.net]

Kilmarnock: St Kentigern's (Website: www.stkentigern.org.uk)
S. Grant Barclay LLB BD   1995   1 Thirdpart Place, Kilmarnock KA1 1UL   01563 571280
[E-mail: grant.barclay@bigfoot.com]

Kilmarnock: St Ninian's Bellfield (01563 524705) linked with Kilmarnock: Shortlees
H. Taylor Brown BD CertMin   1997 2002   14 McLelland Drive, Kilmarnock KA1 1SF   01563 529920
[E-mail: htaylorbrown@hotmail.com]

Kilmarnock: Shortlees See Kilmarnock: St Ninian's Bellfield

Kilmaurs: St Maur's Glencairn (H) (Website: www.jimcorbett.freeserve.co.uk/page2.html)
John A. Urquhart BD   1993   9 Standalane, Kilmaurs, Kilmarnock KA3 2NB   01563 538289

Newmilns: Loudoun (H)
John Macleod MA BD   2000   Loudoun Manse, 116A Loudoun Road, Newmilns KA16 9HH   01560 320174

Stewarton: John Knox
Vacant   27 Avenue Street, Stewarton, Kilmarnock KA3 5AP   01560 482418

Stewarton: St Columba's (H)
Vacant   1 Kirk Glebe, Stewarton, Kilmarnock KA3 5BJ   01560 482453

Ayrshire Mission to the Deaf
Graeme R. Wilson MCIBS BD ThM   2006   60 Brewland Street, Galston KA4 8DX   01563 820246
(Chaplain)   [E-mail: graeme.wilson@gmail.com]

Banks, John MA BD	1968 2001	(Hospital Chaplain)	19 Victoria Drive, Troon KA10 6JF 01292 317758 [E-mail: johnbanksmabd@aol.com]
Brockie, Colin G.F. BSc(Eng) BD SOSc	1967 2007	(Presbytery Clerk)	36 Braehead Court, Kilmarnock KA3 7AB [E-mail: revcol@revcol.demon.co.uk]
Campbell, George H.	1957 1992	(Stewarton: John Knox)	20 Woodlands Grove, Kilmarnock KA3 1TZ 01563 536365 [E-mail: geen@ecampbell5.fsnet.co.uk]
Campbell, John A. JP FIEM	1984 1998	(Irvine: St Andrew's)	Flowerdale, Balmoral Lane, Blairgowrie PH10 7AF 01250 872795
Cant, Thomas M. MA BD	1964 2004	(Paisley: Laigh Kirk)	3 Meikle Cutstraw Farm, Stewarton, Kilmarnock KA3 5HU 01560 480566 [E-mail: revtmcant@aol.com]
Christie, Robert S MA BD ThM	1964 2001	(Kilmarnock: West High)	24 Homeroyal House, 2 Chalmers Crescent, Edinburgh EH9 1TP
Davidson, James BD DipAFH	1989 2002	(Wishaw: Old)	13 Redburn Place, Irvine KA12 9BQ 01294 312515

Davidson Kelly, Thomas A. MA BD FSAScot	1975	2002	(Glasgow: Govan Old)	2 Springhill Stables, Portland Road, Kilmarnock KA1 2EJ [E-mail: dks@springhillstables.freeserve.co.uk]	01563 573994
Gillon, C. Blair BD	1980	2007	(Glasgow: Ibrox)	East Muirshield Farmhouse, by Dunlop, Kilmarnock KA3 4EJ	01560 483778
Hare, Malcolm M.W. BA BD	1956	1994	(Kilmarnock: St Kentigern's)	21 Raith Road, Fenwick, Kilmarnock KA3 6DB	01560 600388
Hay, W.J.R. MA BD	1959	1995	(Buchanan with Drymen)	18 Jamieson Place, Stewarton, Kilmarnock KA3 3AY	01560 482799
Hosain-Lamarti, Samuel BD MTh PhD	1979	2006	(Stewarton: John Knox)	7 Dalwhinnie Crescent, Kilmarnock KA3 1QS [E-mail: samuel.h2@ukonline.co.uk]	01563 529632
Huggett, Judith A. (Miss) BA BD	1990	1998	Hospital Chaplain	4 Westmoor Crescent, Kilmarnock KA1 1TX	01563 526314
Jarvie, Thomas W. BD	1953	2005	(Kilmarnock: Riccarton)	3 Heston Place, Kilmarnock KA3 2JR	01563 572075
McAlpine, Richard H.M. BA FSAScot	1968	2000	(Lochgoilhead and Kilmorich)	7 Kingsford Place, Kilmarnock KA3 6FG	01563 525254
MacDonald, James M.	1964	1987	(Kilmarnock: St John's Onthank)	29 Carmel Place, Kilmaurs, Kilmarnock KA3 2QU	01292 266021
Morrison, Alistair H. BTh DipYCS	1985	2004	(Paisley: St Mark's Oldhall)	92 St Leonard's Road, Ayr KA7 2PU [E-mail: alistairmorrison@supanet.com]	
O'Leary, Thomas BD	1983	1998	(Lochwinnoch)	1 Carter's Place, Irvine KA12 0BU	01294 313274
Roy, James BA	1967	1982	(Irvine: Girdle Toll)	23 Bowes Rigg, Stewarton, Kilmarnock KA3 5EL [E-mail: jimroy@fountainmag.fsnet.co.uk]	01560 482185
Scott, Thomas T.	1968	1989	(Kilmarnock: St Marnock's)	6 North Hamilton Place, Kilmarnock KA1 2QN [E-mail: tomtscott@btinternet.com]	01563 531415
Shaw, Catherine A.M. MA	1998	2006	(Auxiliary Minister)	40 Merrygreen Place, Stewarton, Kilmarnock KA3 5EP [E-mail: catherine.shaw@tesco.net]	01560 483352
Urquhart, Barbara (Mrs) DCS			Deaconess and Presbytery S.S. Adviser	9 Standalane, Kilmaurs, Kilmarnock KA3 2NB	01563 538289
Welsh, Alex M. MA BD	1979	2007	Hospital Chaplain	8 Greenside Avenue, Prestwick KA9 2HB	01292 475341

IRVINE and KILMARNOCK ADDRESSES

Irvine

Dreghorn and Springside	Townfoot x Station Brae
Fullarton	Marress Road x Church Street
Girdle Toll	Bryce Knox Court
Mure	West Road
Old	Kirkgate
Relief Bourtreehill	Crofthead, Bourtreehill
St Andrew's	Caldon Road x Oaklands Ave

Kilmarnock

Ayrshire Mission to the Deaf	10 Clark Street	St Andrew's and St Marnock's	St Marnock Street
Grange	Woodstock Street	St John's Onthank	84 Wardneuk Street
Henderson	London Road	St Ninian's Bellfield	Whatriggs Road
Laigh	John Dickie Street	Shortlees	Central Avenue
Old High Kirk	Church Street x Soulis Street	West High	Portland Street
Riccarton	Old Street		

(12) ARDROSSAN

Meets at Saltcoats, New Trinity, on the first Tuesday of February, March, April, May, September, October, November and December; and on the second Tuesday of June.

Clerk:	REV. JOHNSTON R. McKAY MA BA PhD	15 Montgomerie Avenue, Fairlie, Largs KA29 0EE [E-mail: ardrossan@cofscotland.org.uk]	01475 568802 07885 876021 (Mbl)
Depute Clerk:	MR ALAN K. SAUNDERSON	17 Union Street, Largs KA30 8DG	01475 687217

Ardrossan: Barony St John's (H) (01294 465009)
Vacant — 10 Seafield Drive, Ardrossan KA22 8NU — 01294 463868

Ardrossan: Park (01294 463711)

William R. Johnston BD	1998	35 Ardneil Court, Ardrossan KA22 7NQ	01294 471808
Marion L.K. Howie (Mrs) MA ACRS (Aux)	1992	51 High Road, Stevenston KA20 3DY [E-mail: marion@howiefamily.net]	01294 466571

Beith: High (H) (01505 502686) linked with Beith: Trinity (H)

Roderick I.T. MacDonald BD CertMin	1992 2005	2 Glebe Court, Beith KA15 1ET [E-mail: rodannmac@btinternet.com]	01505 503858
Valerie G.C. Watson MA BD STM (Assoc)	1987 2007	14B Gladstone Road, Saltcoats KA21 5LD [E-mail: vgcwatson@tiscali.co.uk]	01294 470030

Beith: Trinity (H) See Beith: High

Brodick linked with Corrie linked with Lochranza and Pirnmill linked with Shiskine (H)
Angus Adamson BD — 2006 — 4 Manse Crescent, Brodick, Isle of Arran KA27 8AS [E-mail: s-adamson@corriecraviehome.fsnet.co.uk] — 01770 302334

Corrie See Brodick

Cumbrae
Vacant — Marine Parade, Millport, Isle of Cumbrae KA28 0ED — 01475 530416

Dalry: St Margaret's
Vacant — 33 Templand Crescent, Dalry KA24 5EZ

Dalry: Trinity (H)
Martin Thomson BSc DipEd BD — 1988 2004 — Trinity Manse, West Kilbride Road, Dalry KA24 5DX [E-mail: martin@thcmsonm40.freeserve.co.uk] — 01294 832363

Fairlie (H)
James Whyte BD — 1981 — 2006 — 14 Fairlieburne Gardens, Fairlie, Largs KA29 0ER [E-mail: jameswhyte89@btinternet.com] — 01475 568342

Fergushill
Vacant

Kilbirnie: Auld Kirk (H)
Ian W. Benzie BD — 1999 — 49 Holmhead, Kilbirnie KA25 6BS [E-mail: revian@btopenworld.com] — 01505 682348

Kilbirnie: St Columba's (H) (01505 685239)
Fiona C. Ross (Miss) BD DipMin — 1996 — 2004 — Manse of St Columba's, Dipple Road, Kilbirnie KA25 7JU [E-mail: fionaross@calvin78.freeserve.co.uk] — 01505 683342

Kilmory See Lamlash
Vacant

Kilwinning: Mansefield Trinity (E) (01294 550746)
Vacant — 27 Treesbank, Kilwinning KA13 6LY — 01294 558746

Kilwinning: Old
Alison Davidge MA BD — 1990 — 2006 — 54 Dalry Road, Kilwinning KA13 7HE — 01294 552606

Lamlash linked with Kilmory
Gillean P. Maclean (Mrs) BD — 1994 — 2008 — Lamlash, Isle of Arran KA27 8LE [E-mail: gmaclean@fish.co.uk] — 01770 600318

Largs: Clark Memorial (H) (01475 675186)
Stephen J. Smith BSc BD — 1993 — 1998 — 31 Douglas Street, Largs KA30 8PT [E-mail: stephenrevsteve@aol.com] — 01475 672370

Largs: St Columba's (01475 686212)
Roderick J. Grahame BD CPS — 1991 — 2002 — 17 Beachway, Largs KA30 8QH [E-mail: rjgrahame@supanet.com] — 01475 673107

Largs: St John's (H) (01475 674468)
Andrew F. McGurk BD — 1983 — 1993 — 1 Newhaven Grove, Largs KA30 8NS [E-mail: afmcg.largs@talk21.co.uk] — 01475 676123

Lochranza and Pirnmill See Brodick

Saltcoats: New Trinity (H) (01294 472001)				
Elaine W. McKinnon MA BD	1988	2006	1 Montgomerie Crescent, Saltcoats KA21 5BX [E-mail: elaine@newtrinity.co.uk]	01294 461143
Saltcoats: North (01294 464679)				
Alexander B. Noble MA BD ThM	1982	2003	25 Longfield Avenue, Saltcoats KA21 6DR	01294 604923
Saltcoats: St Cuthbert's (H)				
Brian H. Oxburgh BSc BD	1980	1988	10 Kennedy Road, Saltcoats KA21 5SF [E-mail: oxburgh9@aol.com]	01294 602674
Shiskine (H) See Brodick				
Stevenston: Ardeer linked with Stevenston: Livingstone (H)				
John M.M. Lafferty BD	1999		32 High Road, Stevenston KA20 3DR	01294 464180
Stevenston: High (H) (Website: www.highkirk.com)				
M. Scott Cameron MA BD	2002		Glencairn Street, Stevenston KA20 3DL [E-mail: revhighkirk@btinternet.com]	01294 463356
Stevenston: Livingstone (H) See Stevenston: Ardeer				
West Kilbride: Overton (H)				
James J. McNay MA BD	2008		Overton Manse, Gollenberry Avenue, West Kilbride KA23 9LJ [E-mail: j.mcnay@lycos.com]	01294 823186
West Kilbride: St Andrew's (H) (01294 829902)				
John C. Christie BSc BD	1968	2008	10 Cumberland Avenue, Helensburgh G84 8QG [E-mail: rev.jcc@btinternet.com]	01436 674078 / 07711 336392 (Mbl)
Whiting Bay and Kildonan				
Elizabeth R.L. Watson (Miss) BA BD	1981	1982	Whiting Bay, Brodick, Isle of Arran KA27 8RE [E-mail: revewatson@btinternet.com]	01770 700289

Name			Charge	Address	Tel
Bristow, Irene A. (Mrs) BD	1989	2005	(Lochgelly: Macainsh)	2D Montgomerie Road, Saltcoats KA21 5DP [E-mail: ibristow@btinternet.com]	01294 601537
Coogan, J. Melvyn LTh	1992	2004	(Carstairs with Carstairs Junction)	Flat E, 9 Silverdale Gardens, Largs KA30 9LT	01475 675955
Cruickshank, Norman BA BD	1983	2006	(West Kilbride: Overton)	24D Faulds Wynd, Seamill, West Kilbride KA23 9FA	01294 822239
Dailly, J.R. BD DipPS	1979	1979	Staff Chaplain: Army	DACG, HQ 42 (NW) Bde, Fulwood Barracks, Preston PR2 8AA	
Downie, Alexander S.	1975	1997	(Ardrossan: Park)	14 Korsankel Wynd, Saltcoats KA21 6HY	01294 464097
Drysdale, James H. LTh	1987	2006	(Blackbraes and Shieldhill)	10 John Clark Street, Largs KA30 9AH	01475 674870
Forsyth, D. Stuart MA	1948	1992	(Belhelvie)	39 Homemount House, Gogoside Road, Largs KA30 9LS	01475 673379
Gordon, David C.	1953	1988	(Gigha and Cara)	Quoys of Barnhouse, Stenness, Orkney KW16 3JY	

Name			Charge	Address	Tel
Harbison, David J.H.	1958	1998	(Beith: High with Beith: Trinity)	42 Mill Park, Dalry KA24 5BB [E-mail: djh@harbi.fsnet.co.uk]	01294 834092
Hebenton, David J. MA BD	1958	2002	(Ayton and Burnmouth linked with Grantshouse and Houndwood and Reston)	22B Faulds Wynd, Seamill, West Kilbride KA23 9FA	01294 829228
Leask, Rebecca M. (Mrs)	1977	1985	(Callander: St Bride's)	20 Strathclyde House, 31 Shore Road, Skelmorlie PA17 5AN [E-mail: rmleask@hotmail.com]	01475 520765
McCallum, Alexander D. BD	1987	2005	(Saltcoats: New Trinity)	33 Greeto Falls Avenue, Largs KA30 9HJ [E-mail: sandyandjose@madasafish.com]	01475 670133
McCance, Andrew M. BSc	1986	1995	(Coatbridge: Middle)	6A Douglas Place, Largs KA30 8PU	01475 673303
Mackay, Marjory H. (Mrs) BD DipEd CCE	1998	2008	(Cumbrae)	4 Golf Road, Millport, Isle of Cumbrae KA28 0HB [E-mail: mmackay@fish.co.uk]	01475 530388
McKay, Johnston R. MA BA PhD	1969	1987	(Religious Broadcasting: BBC)	15 Montgomerie Avenue, Fairlie, Largs KA29 0EE [E-mail: johnston.mckay@btopenworld.com]	01475 568802
MacLeod, Ian LTh BA MTh PhD	1969	2006	(Brodick with Corrie)	Cromla Cottage, Corrie, Isle of Arran KA27 8JB [E-mail: i.macleod829@btinternet.com]	01770 810237
Mitchell, D. Ross BA BD	1972	2007	(West Kilbride: St Andrew's)	11 Dunbar Gardens, Saltcoats KA21 6GJ [E-mail: ross.mitchell@virgin.net]	
Paterson, John H. BD	1977	2000	(Kirkintilloch: St David's Memorial Park)	Creag Bhan, Golf Course Road, Whiting Bay, Isle of Arran KA27 8QT	01770 700569
Roy, Iain M. MA BD	1960	1997	(Stevenston: Livingstone)	2 The Fieldings, Dunlop, Kilmarnock KA3 4AU	01560 483072
Selfridge, John BTh BREd	1969	1991	(Eddrachillis)	Strathclyde House, Apt 1, Shore Road, Skelmorlie PA17 5AN	01475 529514
Taylor, Andrew S. BTh FPhS	1959	1992	(Greenock Union)	9 Raillies Avenue, Largs KA30 8QY [E-mail: andrew@naylorlargs.fsnet.co.uk]	01475 674709
Thomson, Margaret (Mrs)	1988	1993	(Saltcoats: Erskine)	72 Knockrivoch Place, Ardrossan KA22 7PZ	01294 468685
Walker, David S. MA	1939	1978	(Makerstoun with Smailholm with Stichill, Hume and Nenthorn)	The Anchorage, Baycroft, Strachur, Argyll PA27 8BY	

(13) LANARK

Meets on the first Tuesday of February, March, April, May, September, October, November and December, and on the third Tuesday of June.

Clerk: REV. JAMES S.H. CUTLER BD CEng MIStructE   17 Mercat Loan, Biggar ML12 6DG   **01899   220625**
[E-mail: lanark@cofscotland.org.uk]

Biggar (H) (E-mail: j.francis@lanarkpresbytery.org)
James Francis BD PhD   2002   61 High Street, Biggar ML12 6DA [E-mail: revjim.francis@btinternet.com]   01899   220227

Black Mount linked with Culter linked with Libberton and Quothquan (E-mail: j.cutler@lanarkpresbytery.org)
James S.H. Cutler BD CEng MIStructE   1986   2004   17 Mercat Loan, Biggar ML12 6DG [E-mail: revjimcutler@btinternet.com]   01899   220625

Cairngryffe linked with Symington (E-mail: g.houston@lanarkpresbytery.org)
Graham R. Houston BSc BD MTh PhD   1978   2001   16 Abington Road, Symington, Biggar ML12 6JX
[E-mail: gandih@onetel.net]   01899 308838

Carluke: Kirkton (H) (01555 750778) (E-mail: iaindc@btinternet.com)
Iain D. Cunningham MA BD   1979   1987   9 Station Road, Carluke ML8 5AA
[E-mail: iaindc@btcnnect.com]   01555 771262

Carluke: St Andrew's (H) (E-mail: h.jamieson@lanarkpresbytery.org)
Helen E. Jamieson (Mrs) BD DipED   1989   120 Clyde Street, Carluke ML8 5BG
[E-mail: helen@hjarrieson.wanadoo.co.uk]   01555 771218

Carluke: St John's (H) (Website: www.carluke-stjohns.org.uk)
Roy J. Cowieson BD   1979   2007   18 Old Bridgend, Carluke ML8 4HN
[E-mail: roy.cowieson@btinternet.com]   01555 752519

Carnwath (H) (E-mail: b.gauld@lanarkpresbytery.org)
Beverly G.D.D. Gauld MA BD   1972   1978   The Manse, Carnwath, Lanark ML11 8JY
[E-mail: bevrev.gauld@southlanarkshire.gov.uk]   01555 840259

Carstairs and Carstairs Junction, The United Church of
Alan W. Gibson BA BD   2001   2008   11 Range View, Karres, Carstairs, Lanark ML11
[E-mail: awgibson82@hotmail.com]

Coalburn linked with Lesmahagow: Old (Church office: 01555 892425)
Aileen Robson BD   2003   9 Elm Bank, Lesmahagow, Lanark ML11 0EA
[E-mail: a.robson@lanarkpresbytery.org]   01555 895325

Crossford linked with Kirkfieldbank (E-mail: s.reid@lanarkpresbytery.org)
Steven Reid BAcc CA BD   1989   1997   74 Lanark Road, Crossford, Carluke ML8 5RE
[E-mail: steven.reid@sky.com]   01555 860415

Culter See Black Mount

Forth: St Paul's (H)
Sarah L. Ross (Mrs) BD MTh PGDip   2004   22 Lea Rig, Forth, Lanark ML11 8EA
[E-mail: rev_sross@btinternet.com]   01555 812832

Glencaple linked with Lowther
Margaret A. Muir (Miss) MA LLB BD   1989   2001   66 Carlisle Road, Crawford, Biggar ML12 6TW   01864 502625

Kirkfieldbank See Crossford

Kirkmuirhill (H) (E-mail: i.watson@lanarkpresbytery.org)
Ian M. Watson LLB DipLP BD   1998   2003
The Manse, 2 Lanark Road, Kirkmuirhill, Lanark ML11 9RB   01555 892409
[E-mail: ian.watson21@btopenworld.com]

Lanark: Greyfriars (Church office: 01555 661510) (E-mail: b.kerr@lanarkpresbytery.org) (Website: www.lanarkgreyfriars.com)
Bryan Kerr BA BD   2002   2007
Greyfriars Manse, 3 Bellefield Way, Lanark ML11 7NW   01555 663363 / 08700 518795 (Fax)
[E-mail: bryan@lanarkgreyfriars.com]

Lanark: St Nicholas' (E-mail: a.meikle@lanarkpresbytery.org)
Alison A. Meikle (Mrs) BD   1999   2002
2 Kaimhill Court, Lanark ML11 9HU   01555 662600
[E-mail: alison@lanarkstnichs.fsnet.co.uk]

Law
Vacant
The Manse, 53 Lawhill Road, Law, Carluke ML8 5EZ   01698 373180

Lesmahagow: Abbeygreen (E-mail: d.carmichael@lanarkpresbytery.org)
David S. Carmichael   1982
Abbeygreen Manse, Lesmahagow, Lanark ML11 0DB   01555 893384
[E-mail: david.carmichael@abbeygreen.org.uk]

Lesmahagow: Old (H)   See Coalburn
Libberton and Quothquan   See Black Mount
Lowther   See Glencaple
Symington   See Cairngryffe

The Douglas Valley Church (Church office: Tel/Fax: 01555 850000) (Website: www.douglasvalleychurch.org)
Vacant
The Manse, Douglas, Lanark ML11 0RB   01555 851213

Name			(Congregation)	Address	Phone
Cowell, Susan G. (Miss) BA BD	1986	1998	(Budapest)	3 Gavel Lane, Regency Gardens, Lanark ML11 9FB	01555 665509
Craig, William BA LTh	1974	1997	(Cambusbarron: The Bruce Memorial)	31 Heathfield Drive, Blackwood, Lanark ML11 9SR	01555 893710
Easton, David J.C. MA BD	1965	2005	(Glasgow: Burnside-Blairbeth)	Rowanbank, Corriston Road, Quothquan, Biggar ML12 6ND [E-mail: deaston@btinternet.com]	01899 308459
Findlay, Henry J.W. MA BD	1965	2005	(Wishaw: St Mark's)	2 Alva Gardens, Carluke ML8 5UY	01555 759995
Fox, George H.	1959	1977	(Coalsnaughton)	Braehead House, Crossford, Carluke ML8 5NQ	01555 860716
Jones, Philip H.	1968	1987	(Bishopbriggs: Kenmure)	39 Bankhouse, 62 Abbeygreen, Lesmahagow, Lanark ML11 0JS	
Pacitti, Stephen A. MA	1963	2003	(Black Mount with Culter with Libberton and Quothquan)	157 Nithsdale Road, Glasgow G41 5RD	0141-423 5792
Seath, Thomas J.G.	1980	1992	(Motherwell: Manse Road)	Flat 11, Wallace Court, South Vennel, Lanark ML11 7LL	01555 665399
Stewart, John M. MA BD	1964	2001	(Johnstone with Kirkpatrick Juxta)	5 Rathmor Road, Biggar ML12 6QG	01899 220398
Turnbull, John LTh	1994	2006	(Balfron with Fintry)	4 Rathmor Road, Biggar ML12 6QG	01899 221502
Young, David A.	1972	2003	(Kirkmuirhill)	15 Mannachie Rise, Forres IV36 2US [E-mail: youngdavid@aol.com]	01309 672849

(14) GREENOCK AND PAISLEY

Meets on the second Tuesday of September, October, November, December, February, March, April and May, and on the third Tuesday of June.

Clerk:	REV. ALAN H. WARD MA BD			
Presbytery Office:	The Presbytery Office as detailed below [E-mail: greenockpaisley@cofscotland.org.uk] 'Homelea', Faith Avenue, Quarrier's Village, Bridge of Weir PA11 3SX			01505 615033 (Tel) 01505 615088 (Fax)

Barrhead: Arthurlie (H) (0141-881 8442) James S.A. Cowan BD DipMin	1986	1998	10 Arthurlie Avenue, Barrhead, Glasgow G78 2BU [E-mail: jim_cowan@ntlworld.com]	0141-881 3457
Barrhead: Bourock (H) (0141-881 9813) Maureen Leitch (Mrs) BA BD	1995		14 Maxton Avenue, Barrhead, Glasgow G78 1DY [E-mail: maureen.leitch@ntlworld.com]	0141-881 1462
Barrhead: South and Levern (H) (0141-881 7825) Morris M. Dutch BD BA	1998	2002	3 Colinbar Circle, Barrhead, Glasgow G78 2BE [E-mail: mmdutch@yahoo.co.uk]	0141-571 4059
Bishopton (H) Gayle J.A. Taylor (Mrs) MA BD	1999		The Manse, Newton Road, Bishopton PA7 5JP [E-mail: gayletaylor@btinternet.com]	01505 862161
Bridge of Weir: Freeland (H) (01505 612610) Kenneth N. Gray BA BD	1988		15 Lawmarnock Crescent, Bridge of Weir PA11 3AS [E-mail: aandkgray@btinternet.com]	01505 690918
Bridge of Weir: St Machar's Ranfurly (01505 614364) Suzanne Dunleavy (Miss) BD DipEd	1990	1992	9 Glen Brae, Bridge of Weir PA11 3BH [E-mail: suzanne.durleavy@btinternet.com]	01505 612975
Caldwell John Campbell MA BA BSc	1973	2000	The Manse of Caldwell, Uplawmoor, Glasgow G78 4AL [E-mail: campbelljoh.n@talktalk.net]	01505 850215
Elderslie Kirk (H) (01505 323348) Robin N. Allison BD DipMin	1994	2005	282 Main Road, Elderslie, Johnstone PA5 9EF [E-mail: revrobin@sxy.com]	01505 321767

Erskine (0141-812 4620) Ian W. Bell LTh	1990	1998	The Manse, 7 Leven Place, Linburn, Erskine PA8 6AS [E-mail: rviwbepc@ntlworld.com]	0141-581 0955
Gourock: Old Gourock and Ashton (H) David T. Young BA BD	2007		331 Eldon Street, Gourock PA16 7QN [E-mail: davy_young@hotmail.com]	01475 635578
Gourock: St John's (H) Vacant			6 Barrhill Road, Gourock PA19 1JX	01475 632143
Greenock: Ardgowan Alan H. Ward MA BD	1978	2002	72 Forsyth Street, Greenock PA16 8SX [E-mail: alanhward@ntlworld.com]	01475 790849
Greenock: East End David J. McCarthy BSc BD	1985	2003	29 Denholm Street, Greenock PA16 8RH [E-mail: ncdgreenockeast@uk.uumail.com]	01475 722111
Eileen Manson (Mrs) DipCE (Aux)	1994	2005	1 Cambridge Avenue, Gourock PA19 1XT [E-mail: rev.eileen@ntlworld.com]	01475 632401
Greenock: Finnart St Paul's (H) David Mill KJSJ MA BD	1978	1979	105 Newark Street, Greenock PA16 7TW [E-mail: revandevmill@aol.com]	01475 639602
Greenock: Mount Kirk Francis E. Murphy BEng DipDSE BD	2006		76 Finnart Street, Greenock PA16 8HJ [E-mail: francis_e_murphy@hotmail.com]	01475 722338
Greenock: Old West Kirk C. Ian W. Johnson MA BD	1997		39 Fox Street, Greenock PA16 8PD [E-mail: ian.ciw.johnson@btinternet.com]	01475 888277
Greenock: St Margaret's (01475 781953) Isobel J.M. Kelly (Miss) MA BD DipEd	1974	1998	105 Finnart Street, Greenock PA16 8HN	01475 786590
Greenock: St Ninian's Allan G. McIntyre BD	1985		5 Auchmead Road, Greenock PA16 0PY [E-mail: agmcintyre@lineone.net]	01475 631878
Greenock: Wellpark Mid Kirk Alan K. Sorensen BD MTh DipMin FSAScot	1983	2000	101 Brisbane Street, Greenock PA16 8PA [E-mail: alan.sorensen@ntlworld.com]	01475 721741

Greenock: Westburn W. Douglas Hamilton BD	1975	1986	67 Forsyth Street, Greenock PA16 8SX [E-mail: revdwhamilton@hotmail.com]	01475 724003
William C. Hewitt BD DipPS	1977	1994	50 Ardgowan Street, Greenock PA16 8EP [E-mail: william.hewitt@ntlworld.com]	01475 721048
Houston and Killellan (H) Donald Campbell BD	1998	2007	The Manse of Houston, Main Street, Houston, Johnstone PA6 7EL [E-mail: houstonmanse@btinternet.com]	01505 612569
Howwood David Stewart MA DipEd BD MTh	1977	2001	The Manse, Beith Road, Howwood, Johnstone PA9 1AS [E-mail: revdavidst@aol.com]	01505 703678
Inchinnan (H) (0141-812 1263) Marilyn MacLaine (Mrs) LTh	1995		The Manse, Inchinnan, Renfrew PA4 9PH	0141-812 1688
Inverkip (H) Vacant			The Manse, Langhouse Road, Inverkip, Greenock PA16 0BJ	01475 521207
Johnstone: High (H) (01505 336303) Ann C. McCool (Mrs) BD DSD IPA ALCM	1989	2001	76 North Road, Johnstone PA5 8NF [E-mail: ann.mccool@ntlworld.com]	01505 320006
Johnstone: St Andrew's Trinity May Bell (Mrs) LTh	1998	2002	The Manse, 7 Leven Place, Linburn, Erskine PA8 6AS [E-mail: may.bell@ntlbusiness.com]	0141-581 7352
Johnstone: St Paul's (H) (01505 321632) Alistair N. Shaw MA BD	1982	2003	9 Stanley Drive, Brookfield, Johnstone PA5 8UF [E-mail: ans2006@talktalk.net]	01505 320060
Kilbarchan: East John Owain Jones MA BD FSAScot	1981	2002	East Manse, Church Street, Kilbarchan, Johnstone PA10 2JQ [E-mail: johnowainjones@ntlworld.com]	01505 702621
Kilbarchan: West Arthur Sherratt BD	1994		West Manse, Shuttle Street, Kilbarchan, Johnstone PA10 2JR [E-mail: arthur.sherratt@ntlworld.com]	01505 342930
Kilmacolm: Old (H) (01505 873911) Peter McEnhill BD PhD	1992	2007	The Old Kirk Manse, Glencairn Road, Kilmacolm PA13 4NJ [E-mail: petermcenhill@btinternet.com]	01505 873174

Kilmacolm: St Columba (H)
R. Douglas Cranston MA BD   1986   1992   6 Churchill Road, Kilmacolm PA13 4LH   01505 873271
[E-mail: robert.cranston@tiscali.co.uk]

Langbank (T)
William G. McKaig BD   1979   2007   The Manse, Main Road, Langbank, Port Glasgow PA14 6XP   01475 540252
[E-mail: bill.mckaig@virgin.net]

Linwood (H) (01505 328802)
Vacant   49 Napier Street, Linwood, Paisley PA3 3AJ   01505 325131

Lochwinnoch (T)
Christine Murdoch   1999   2007   1 Station Rise, Lochwinnoch PA12 4NA   01505 843484
[E-mail: rev.christine@btinternet.com]

Neilston (0141-881 9445)
Nan Low (Mrs) BD   2002   2008   The Manse, Neilston Road, Neilston, Glasgow G78 3NP   0141-881 1958
[E-mail: agnes.low846@btinternet.com]

Paisley: Abbey (H) (Tel: 0141-889 7654; Fax: 0141-887 3929)
Alan D. Birss MA BD   1979   1988   15 Main Road, Castlehead, Paisley PA2 6AJ   0141-889 3587
[E-mail: alan.birss@paisleyabbey.com]

Paisley: Castlehead
Esther J. Ninian (Miss) MA BD   1993   1998   28 Fulbar Crescent, Paisley PA2 9AS   01505 812304
[E-mail: esther.ninian@ntlworld.com]

Paisley: Glenburn (0141-884 2602)
Graham Nash MA BD   2006   10 Hawick Avenue, Paisley PA2 9LD   0141-884 4903
[E-mail: gpnash@btopenworld.com]

Paisley: Laigh Kirk (H) (0141-889 7700)
David J. Thom BD   2000   2005   25 John Neilson Avenue, Paisley PA1 2SX   0141-887 5434
[E-mail: david@thelaigh.co.uk]

Paisley: Lylesland (H) (0141-561 7139)
Vacant   36 Potterhill Avenue, Paisley PA2 8BA   0141-884 2882
Greta Gray (Miss) DCS   67 Crags Avenue, Paisley PA3 6SG   0141-884 6178

Paisley: Martyrs' (0141-889 6603)
Kenneth A.L. Mayne BA MSc CertEd   1976   2007   21 John Neilson Avenue, Paisley PA1 2SX   0141-889 2182

Paisley: Oakshaw Trinity (H) (Tel: 0141-889 4010; Fax: 0141-848 5139)
G. Hutton B. Steel MA BD   1982   2006   16 Golf Drive, Paisley PA1 3LA
[E-mail: hutton@oakshawtrinity.org.uk]   0141-887 0884

Paisley: St Columba Foxbar (H) (01505 812377)
Vacant   13 Corsebar Drive, Paisley PA2 9QD

Paisley: St James' (0141-889 2422)
Eleanor J. McMahon (Miss) BEd BD   1994   38 Woodland Avenue, Paisley PA2 8BH
[E-mail: eleanor.mcmahon@ntlworld.com]   0141-884 3246

Paisley: St Luke's (H)
D. Ritchie M. Gillon BD DipMin   1994   31 Southfield Avenue, Paisley PA2 8BX
[E-mail: revgillon@hotmail.com]   0141-884 6215

Paisley: St Mark's Oldhall (H) (0141-882 2755)
Robert G. McFarlane BD   2001   2005   36 Newtyle Road, Paisley PA1 3JX
[E-mail: robertmcf@hotmail.com]   0141-889 4279

Paisley: St Ninian's Ferguslie (E) (0141-887 9436) (New Charge Development)
William Wishart DCS   10 Stanely Drive, Paisley PA2 6HE
[E-mail: bill@saintninians.co.uk]   0141-884 4177

Paisley: Sandyford (Thread Street) (0141-889 5078)
David Kay BA BD MTh   1974   6 Southfield Avenue, Paisley PA2 8BY
[E-mail: davidkay@ntlworld.com]   0141-884 3600

Paisley: Sherwood Greenlaw (H) (0141-889 7060)
Alasdair F. Cameron BD CA   1986   1993   5 Greenlaw Drive, Paisley PA1 3RX
[E-mail: alcamron@fineone.net]   0141-889 3057

Paisley: Wallneuk North (0141-889 9265)
Vacant

Port Glasgow: Hamilton Bardrainney
James A. Munro BA BD DMS   1979   2002   80 Bardrainney Averue, Port Glasgow PA14 6HD
[E-mail: james@jmunro33.wanadoo.co.uk]   01475 701213

Port Glasgow: St Andrew's (H)
Andrew T. MacLean BA BD   1980   1993   St Andrew's Manse, Barr's Brae, Port Glasgow PA14 5QA
[E-mail: standrews.pg@mac.com]   01475 741486

Port Glasgow: St Martin's
Archibald Speirs BD — 1995 2006 — Clunebraehead, Clune Brae, Port Glasgow PA14 5SL [E-mail: archiespeirs1@aol.com] — 01475 704115

Renfrew: North (0141-885 2154)
E. Lorna Hood (Mrs) MA BD — 1978 1979 — 1 Alexandra Drive, Renfrew PA4 8UB [E-mail: lorna.hood@ntlworld.com] — 0141-886 2074

Renfrew: Old
Vacant — 31 Gibson Road, Renfrew PA4 0RH — 0141-886 2005

Renfrew: Trinity (H) (0141-885 2129)
Stuart C. Steell BD CertMin — 1992 — 25 Paisley Road, Renfrew PA4 8JH [E-mail: ssren@tiscali.co.uk] — 0141-886 2131

Skelmorlie and Wemyss Bay
Vacant — 3A Montgomerie Terrace, Skelmorlie PA17 5TD — 01475 520703

Name		Position	Address	Tel
Abeledo, Benjamin J.A. BTh DipTh PTh	1991 2000	Army Chaplain	40 Rawlinson Road, Catterick Garrison DL9 3AP [E-mail: benjamin.abeledo@btinternet.com]	01748 833816
Alexander, Douglas N. MA BD	1961 1999	(Bishopton)	West Morningside, Main Road, Langbank, Port Glasgow PA4 6XP	01475 540249
Armstrong, William R. BD	1979 2008	(Skelmorlie and Wemyss Bay)	3A Montgomerie Terrace, Skelmorlie PA17 5TD	01475 520703
Black, Janette M.K. (Mrs) BD	1993 2006	(Assistant: Paisley: Oakshaw Trinity)	5 Craigiehall Avenue, Erskine PA8 7DB	0141-812 0794
Cameron, Margaret (Miss) DCS		(Deaconess)	2 Rowans Gate, Paisley PA2 6RD	0141-840 2479
Chestnut, Alexander MBE BA	1948 1987	(Greenock: St Mark's Greenbank)	5 Douglas Street, Largs KA30 8PS	01475 674168
Copland, Agnes M. (Mrs) MBE DCS		(Deacon)	3 Craigmuschat Road, Gourock PA19 1SE	01475 631870
Cubie, John P. MA BD	1961 1999	(Caldwell)	36 Winram Place, St Andrews KY16 8XH	01334 474708
Forrest, Kenneth P. CBE BSc PhD	2006	Auxiliary Minister	5 Carruth Road, Bridge of Weir PA11 3HQ [E-mail: kenpforrest@hotmail.com]	01505 615033
Fraser, Ian C. BA BD	1983 2008	(Glasgow: St Luke's and St Andrew's)	62 Kingston Avenue, Neilston, Glasgow G78 3JG [E-mail: ianandlindafraser@gmail.com]	0141-563 6794
Gardner, Frank J. MA	1966 2007	(Gourock: Old Gourock and Ashton)	1 Levanne Place, Gourock PA16 1AX	(Tel/Fax) 01475 630187
Hetherington, Robert M. MA BD	1966 2002	(Barrhead South and Levern)	31 Brodie Park Crescent, Paisley PA2 6EU [E-mail: r-hetherington@sky.com]	0141-848 6560
Johnston, Mary (Miss) DCS		(Deaconess)	19 Lounsdale Drive, Paisley PA2 9ED	0141-849 1615
Lowe, Edwin MA BD	1950 1988	(Caldwell)	45 Duncarnock Crescent, Neilston, Glasgow G78 3HH [E-mail: edwin.lowe50@ntlworld.com]	0141-580 5726
McBain, Margaret (Miss) DCS	1966 2002	(Johnstone: St Andrew's Trinity)	33 Quarry Road, Paisley PA2 7RD	0141-884 2920
MacColl, James C. BSc BD	1989 2001	Teacher: Religious Education	Greenways, Winton, Kirkby Stephen, Cumbria CA17 4HL	01768 372290
MacColl, John BD DipMin			1 Birch Avenue, Johnstone PA5 0DD	01505 326506

Name			Designation	Address	Tel
McCully, M. Isobel (Miss) DCS	1966	2006	(Deacon)	10 Broadstone Avenue, Port Glasgow PA14 5BB [E-mail: mi.mccully@tesco.net]	01475 742240
Macdonald, Alexander MA BD			(Neilston)	35 Lochore Avenue, Paisley PA3 4BY [E-mail: alexmacdonald42@aol.com]	0141-889 0066
McDonald, Alexander BA CMIWSC DUniv	1968	1988	Department of Ministry	36 Alloway Grove, Paisley PA2 7DQ [E-mail: amcdonald1@ntlworld.com]	0141-560 1937
Macfarlane, Thomas G. BSc PhD BD	1956	1992	(Glasgow: South Shewlands)	12 Elphinstone Court, Lochwinnoch Road, Kilmacolm PA13 4DW	01505 874962
McLachlan, Fergus C. BD	1982	2002	Hospital Chaplain: Inverclyde Royal	46 Queen Square, Glasgow G41 2AZ [E-mail: fergus.mclachlan@irh.scot.nhs.uk]	(Home) 0141-423 3830 (Work) 01475 633777
Marshall, Fred J. BA	1946	1992	(Bermuda)	11 Myreton Avenue, Kilmacolm PA13 4LJ	0131-446 0205
Montgomery, Robert A. MA	1955	1992	(Quarrier's Village: Mount Zion)	93 Brisbane Street, Greenock PA16 8NY	01505 872028
Nicol, Joyce M. (Mrs) BA DCS			(Deacon)	[E-mail: joycenicol@hotmail.co.uk]	01475 723235
Page, John R. BD DipMin	1988	2003	(Gibraltar)	Flat 0/1 'Toward', The Lighthouses, Greenock Road, Wemyss Bay PA18 6DT	01475 520281
Palmer, S.W. BD	1980	1991	(Kilbarchan: East)	4 Bream Place, Houston PA6 7ZJ	01505 615280
Prentice, George BA BTh	1964	1997	(Paisley: Martyrs)	46 Victoria Gardens, Corsebar Road, Paisley PA2 9AQ [E-mail: g.prentice04@talktalk.net]	0141-842 1585
Scott, Ernest M. MA	1957	1992	(Port Glasgow: St Andrew's)	17 Brueacre Road, Wemyss Bay PA18 6ER [E-mail: ernie.scott@ernest70.fsnet.co.uk]	01475 522267
Simpson, James H. BD LLB	1964	2004	(Greenock: Mount Kirk)	82 Harbourside, Inverkip, Greenock PA16 0BF [E-mail: jameshsimpson@yahoo.co.uk]	01475 520582
Smillie, Andrew M. LTh	1990	2005	(Langbank)	7 Turnbull Avenue, West Freeland, Erskine PA8 7DL [E-mail: andrewsmillie@talktalk.net]	0141-812 7030
Stone, W. Vernon MA BD	1949	1985	(Langbank)	36 Woodrow Court, Port Glasgow Road, Kilmacolm KA13 4QA [E-mail: stone@kilmacolm.fsnet.co.uk]	01505 872644
Whyte, John H. MA	1946	1986	(Gourock: Ashton)	6 Castle Levan Manor, Cloch Road, Gourock PA19 1AY	01475 636788

GREENOCK ADDRESSES

Gourock
Old Gourock and Ashton — 41 Royal Street
St John's — Bath Street x St John's Road

Greenock
Ardgowan — 31 Union Street
Finnart St Paul's — Newark Street x Bentinck Street
Mount Kirk — Dempster Street at Murdieston Park
Old West Kirk — Esplanade x Campbell Street
St Margaret's — Finch Road x Kestrel Crescent
St Ninian's — Warwick Road, Larkfield
Wellpark Mid Kirk — Cathcart Square
Westburn — 9 Nelson Street

Port Glasgow
Hamilton Bardrainney — Bardrainney Avenue x Auchenbothie Road
St Andrew's — Princes Street
St Martin's — Mansion Avenue

PAISLEY ADDRESSES

Abbey	Town Centre
Castlehead	Canal Street
Glenburn	Nethercraigs Drive off Glenburn Road
Laigh Kirk	Causeyside Street

Lylesland	Rowan Street off Neilston Road
Martyrs'	Broomlands
Oakshaw Trinity	Churchill
St Columba Foxbar	Amochrie Road, Foxbar
St James'	Underwood Road
St Luke's	Neilston Road

St Mark's Oldhall	Glasgow Road, Ralston
St Ninian's Ferguslie	Blackstoun Road
Sandyford (Thread St)	Gallowhill
Sherwood Greenlaw	Glasgow Road
Wallneuk North	off Renfrew Road

(16) GLASGOW

Meets at Govan and Linthouse Parish Church, Govan Cross, Glasgow, on the second Tuesday of each month, except June when the meeting takes place on the second last Tuesday. In January, July and August, there is no meeting.

Clerk: REV. ANGUS KERR BD CertMin ThM DMin
260 Bath Street, Glasgow G2 4JP 0141-332 6606 (Tel/Fax)
[E-mail: glasgow@cofscotland.org.uk]
[E-mail: glasgowpresbytery@yahoo.co.uk]
[E-mail: glasgowpres@yahoo.co.uk]

Hon. Treasurer: DOUGLAS BLANEY

1 Banton linked with Twechar
Alexandra Farrington LTh 2003 Manse of Banton, Kilsyth, Glasgow G65 0QL 01236 826129
[E-mail: sandra.farrington@virgin.net]

2 Bishopbriggs: Kenmure
Iain A. Laing MA BD 1971 1992 5 Marchfield, Bishopbriggs, Glasgow G64 3PP 0141-772 1468
[E-mail: iandrlaing@yahoo.co.uk]

3 Bishopbriggs: Springfield
Ian Taylor BD ThM 1995 2006 64 Miller Drive, Bishopbriggs, Glasgow G64 1FB 0141-772 1540
[E-mail: taylorian@btinternet.com]

4 Broom (0141-639 3528)
James A.S. Boag BD CertMin 1992 2007 3 Laigh Road, Newton Mearns, Glasgow G77 5EX 0141-639 2916 (Tel)
[E-mail: office@churchofbroom.org.uk] 0141-639 3528 (Fax)
Margaret McLellan (Mrs) DCS 18 Broom Road East, Newton Mearns, Glasgow G77 5SD 0141-639 6853

5 Burnside Blairbeth (0141-634 4130)
William T.S. Wilson BSc BD 1999 2006 59 Blairbeth Road, Burnside, Glasgow G73 4JD 0141-583 6470
[E-mail: william.wilson@burnsideblairbethchurch.org.uk]
Colin Ogilvie DCS 32 Upper Bourtree Court, Glasgow G73 4HT 0141-442 1965
[E-mail: colin.ogilvie@burnsideblairbethchurch.org.uk]

6 **Busby (0141-644 2073)**
Jeremy C. Eve BSc BD   1998   17A Carmunnock Road, Busby, Glasgow G76 8SZ   0141-644 3670
                                                 [E-mail: j-eve@sky.com]

7 **Cadder (0141-772 7436)**
Graham S. Finch MA BD   1977   1999   6 Balmuildy Road, Bishopbriggs, Glasgow G64 3BS   0141-772 1363
                                                 [E-mail: gsf1957@ntlworld.com]

8 **Cambuslang: Flemington Hallside**
Neil Glover   2005   103 Overton Road, Cambuslang, Glasgow G72 7XA   0141-641 1049
                                                 [E-mail: neil@naglover.plus.com]   07779 280074 (Mbl)

9 **Cambuslang Parish Church**
Vacant

   (New charge formed by the union of Cambuslang: Old, Cambuslang: St Andrew's and Cambuslang; Trinity St Paul's)

10 **Campsie (01360 310939)**
David J. Torrance BD DipMin   1993   19 Redhills View, Lennoxtown, Glasgow G66 7BL   01360 312527
                                                 [E-mail: torrance@fish.co.uk]

11 **Chryston (H) (0141-779 4188)**
Mark Malcolm MA BD   1999   The Manse, 109 Main Street, Chryston, Glasgow G69 9LA   0141-779 1436
                                                 [E-mail: mark.minister@btinternet.com]   07731 737377 (Mbl)
David J. McAdam BSc BD (Assoc)   1990   12 Dunellan Crescent, Moodiesburn, Glasgow G69 0GA   01236 870472
                                                 [E-mail: dmca29@hotmail.co.uk]

12 **Eaglesham (01355 302047)**
Lynn M. McChlery BA BD   2005   The Manse, Cheapside Street, Eaglesham, Glasgow G76 0NS   01355 303495
                                                 [E-mail: lsmcchlery@btinternet.com]

13 **Fernhill and Cathkin**
Margaret McArthur BD DipMin   1995   82 Blairbeth Road, Rutherglen, Glasgow G73 4JA   0141-634 1508
                                                 [E-mail: maggiemac06@aol.com]

14 **Gartcosh (H) (01236 873770) linked with Glenboig**
Alexander M. Fraser BD DipMin   1985   26 Inchnock Avenue, Gartcosh, Glasgow G69 8EA   01236 872274
                                                 [E-mail: sandyfraser2@hotmail.com]

15 **Giffnock: Orchardhill (0141-638 3604)**
Chris Vermeulen DipLT BTh MA   1986   2005   23 Huntly Avenue, Giffnock, Glasgow G46 6LW   0141-620 3734
                                                 [E-mail: chris@orchardhill.org.uk]
Daniel Frank BA MDiv DMin (Assoc) 2003 2006   106 Ormonde Crescent, Glasgow G44 3SW   0141-586 0875
                                                 [E-mail: daniel@orchardhill.org.uk]

16	**Giffnock: South (0141-638 2599)** Edward V. Simpson BSc BD	1972	1983	5 Langtree Avenue, Whitecraigs, Glasgow G46 7LN [E-mail: eddie.simpson3@ntlworld.com]	0141-638 8767 (Tel) 0141-620 0605 (Fax)
17	**Giffnock: The Park** Calum D. Macdonald BD	1993	2001	41 Rouken Glen Road, Thornliebank, Glasgow G46 7JD [E-mail: parkhoose@msn.com]	0141-638 3023
18	**Glenboig** See Gartcosh				
19	**Greenbank (H) (0141-644 1841)** Jeanne Roddick BD	2003		Greenbank Manse, 38 Eaglesham Road, Clarkston, Glasgow G76 7DJ [E-mail: jeanne.roddick@ntlworld.com]	0141-644 1395
20	**Kilsyth: Anderson** Charles M. MacKinnon BD	1989	1999	Anderson Manse, Kingston Road, Kilsyth, Glasgow G65 0HR [E-mail: cm.ccmackinnon@tiscali.co.uk]	01236 822345
21	**Kilsyth: Burns and Old** Robert Sloan BD	1997	2005	The Grange, Glasgow Road, Kilsyth, Glasgow G65 9AE [E-mail: robertsloan@scotnet.co.uk]	01236 823116
22	**Kirkintilloch: Hillhead** Vacant			64 Waverley Park, Kensington Gate, Kirkintilloch, Glasgow G66 2BP	0141-776 6270
23	**Kirkintilloch: St Columba's (H)** David M. White BA BD	1988	1992	14 Crossdykes, Kirkintilloch, Glasgow G66 3EU [E-mail: write.to.me@ntlworld.com]	0141-578 4357
24	**Kirkintilloch: St David's Memorial Park (H)** Bryce Calder MA BD	1995	2001	2 Roman Road, Kirkintilloch, Glasgow G66 1EA [E-mail: ministry100@aol.com]	0141-776 1434
25	**Kirkintilloch: St Mary's** Mark E. Johnstone MA BD	1993	2001	St Mary's Manse, 60 Union Street, Kirkintilloch, Glasgow G66 1DH [E-mail: mark.johnstone2@ntlworld.com]	0141-776 1252
26	**Lenzie: Old (H)** Douglas W. Clark LTh	1993	2000	41 Kirkintilloch Road, Lenzie, Glasgow G66 4LB [E-mail: douglaswclark@hotmail.com]	0141-776 2184

27	**Lenzie: Union (H)** Daniel J.M. Carmichael MA BD	1994	2003	1 Larch Avenue, Lenzie, Glasgow G66 4HX [E-mail: minister@lupc.org]	0141-776 3831
28	**Maxwell Mearns Castle (Tel/Fax: 0141-639 5169)** David C. Cameron BD CertMin	1993		122 Broomfield Avenue, Newton Mearns, Glasgow G77 5JR [E-mail: maxwellmearns@hotmail.com]	0141-616 0642
29	**Mearns (H) (0141-639 6555)** Joseph A. Kavanagh BD DipPTh MTh	1992	1998	Manse of Mearns, Newton Mearns, Glasgow G77 5DE [E-mail: mearnskirk@hotmail.com]	0141-616 2410 (Tel/Fax)
30	**Milton of Campsie (H)** Julie H.C. Wilson BA BD PGCE	2006		Dunkeld, 33 Birdston Road, Milton of Campsie, Glasgow G66 8BX [E-mail: jhcwilson@msn.com]	01360 310548 07787 184800 (Mbl)
31	**Netherlee (H) (0141-637 2503)** Thomas Nelson BSc BD	1992	2002	25 Ormonde Avenue, Glasgow G44 3QY [E-mail: tomnelson@ntlworld.com]	0141-585 7502 (Tel/Fax)
32	**Newton Mearns (H) (0141-639 7373)** Vacant			28 Waterside Avenue, Newton Mearns, Glasgow G77 6TJ	0141-616 2079
33	**Rutherglen: Old (H)** Alexander Thomson BSc BD MPhil PhD	1973	1985	31 Highburgh Drive, Rutherglen, Glasgow G73 3RR [E-mail: alexander.thomson6@btopenworld.com]	0141-647 6178
34	**Rutherglen: Stonelaw (0141-647 5113)** Alistair S. May LLB BD PhD	2002		80 Blairbeth Road, Rutherglen, Glasgow G73 4JA [E-mail: alistair.may@ntlworld.com]	0141-583 0157
35	**Rutherglen: West and Wardlawhill** John W. Drummond MA BD	1971	1986	12 Albert Drive, Rutherglen, Glasgow G73 3RT	0141-569 8547
36	**Stamperland (0141-637 4999) (H)** George C. MacKay BD CertMin	1994	2004	109 Ormonde Avenue, Glasgow G44 3SN [E-mail: g.mackay3@btinternet.com]	0141-637 4976 (Tel/Fax)
37	**Stepps (H)** Neil Buchanan BD	1991	2005	2 Lenzie Road, Stepps, Glasgow G33 6DX [E-mail: neil.buchanan@talk21.com]	0141-779 5746
38	**Thornliebank (H)** Robert M. Silver BA BD	1995		19 Arthurlie Drive, Giffnock, Glasgow G46 6UR	0141-620 2133

No.	Name	Ord.	Ind.	Address	Tel.
39	**Torrance (T) (01360 620970)** Nigel L. Barge BSc BD	1991		1 Atholl Avenue, Torrance, Glasgow G64 4JA [E-mail: nigel@nbarge.freeserve.co.uk]	01360 622379
40	**Twechar** See Banton				
41	**Williamwood** Iain M.A. Reid MA BD	1990	2007	125 Greenwood Road, Clarkston, Glasgow G76 7LL	0141-571 7949
42	**Glasgow: Anderston Kelvingrove (0141-221 9408)** John A. Coutts BTh	1984	2004	16 Royal Terrace, Glasgow G3 7NY [E-mail: john@jmcoutts.org.uk]	0141-332 7704
43	**Glasgow: Baillieston Mure Memorial (0141-773 1216)** Vacant			28 Beech Avenue, Baillieston, Glasgow G69 6LF	0141-771 1217
44	**Glasgow: Baillieston St Andrew's (0141-771 6629)** Alisdair T. MacLeod-Mair MEd DipTheol	2001	2007	55 Station Park, Baillieston, Glasgow G69 7XY [E-mail: revalisdair@hotmail.com]	0141-771 1791
45	**Glasgow: Balshagray Victoria Park** Campbell Mackinnon BSc BD	1982	2001	20 St Kilda Drive, Glasgow G14 9JN [E-mail: cmackinnon@ntlworld.com]	0141-954 9780
46	**Glasgow: Barlanark Greyfriars** David I.W. Locke MA MSc BD	2000		4 Rhindmuir Grove, Glasgow G69 6NE [E-mail: revdavidlocke@ntlworld.com]	0141-771 1240
47	**Glasgow: Battlefield East (H) (0141-632 4206)** Alan C. Raeburn MA BD	1971	1977	110 Mount Annan Drive, Glasgow G44 4RZ [E-mail: acraeburn@hotmail.com]	0141-632 1514
48	**Glasgow: Blawarthill** Vacant			46 Earlbank Avenue, Glasgow G14 9HL	0141-579 6521
49	**Glasgow: Bridgeton St Francis in the East (H) (L) (Church House: Tel: 0141-554 8045)** Howard R. Hudson MA BD	1982	1984	10 Albany Drive, Rutherglen, Glasgow G73 3QN [E-mail: howard.hudson@ntlworld.com]	0141-587 8667
	Margaret S. Beaton (Miss) DCS			64 Gardenside Grove, Fernlee Meadows, Carmyle, Glasgow G32 8EZ [E-mail: margaret@churchhouse.plus.com]	0141-646 2297

No.	Congregation / Minister	Ordained	Inducted	Address	Tel
50	**Glasgow: Broomhill (0141-334 2540)**				
	William B. Ferguson BA BD	1971	1987	27 St Kilda Drive, Glasgow G14 9LN [E-mail: revferg@aol.com]	0141-959 3204
51	**Glasgow: Calton Parkhead (0141-554 3866)**				
	Vacant			98 Drumover Drive, Glasgow G31 5RP	0141-556 2520
52	**Glasgow: Cardonald (0141-882 6264)**				
	Calum MacLeod BA BD	1979	2007	133 Newtyle Road, Paisley PA1 3LB [E-mail: minister@cardonaldparish.co.uk]	0141-887 2726
53	**Glasgow: Carmunnock (0141-644 0655)**				
	G. Gray Fletcher BSc BD	1989	2001	The Manse, 161 Waterside Road, Carmunnock, Glasgow G76 9AJ [E-mail: gray.fletcher@virgin.net]	0141-644 1578 (Tel/Fax)
54	**Glasgow: Carmyle linked with Kenmuir Mount Vernon**				
	Murdo Maclean BD CertMin	1997	1999	3 Meryon Road, Glasgow G32 9NW [E-mail: murdo.maclean@ntlworld.com]	0141-778 2625
55	**Glasgow: Carnwadric (E)**				
	Graeme K. Bell BA BD	1983		62 Loganswell Road, Glasgow G46 8AX [E-mail: slbellmrs@yahoo.co.uk]	0141-638 5884
	Mary Gargrave (Mrs) DCS	1989		1B Spiers Grove, Glasgow G46 7RL	0141-638 1412
56	**Glasgow: Castlemilk East (H) (0141-634 2444)**				
	Vacant			4 Glasgow Road, Cambuslang, Glasgow G72 7BW	0141-641 1699
	Duncan Ross DCS	2006			
57	**Glasgow: Castlemilk West (H) (0141-634 1480)**				
	Vacant			156 Old Castle Road, Glasgow G44 5TW	0141-637 5451
58	**Glasgow: Cathcart Old (0141-637 4168)**				
	Neil W. Galbraith BD CertMin	1987	1996	21 Courthill Avenue, Cathcart, Glasgow G44 5AA [E-mail: revneilgalbraith@hotmail.com]	0141-633 5248 (Tel/Fax)
59	**Glasgow: Cathcart Trinity (H) (0141-637 6658)**				
	Ian Morrison BD	1991	2003	82 Merrylee Road, Glasgow G43 2QZ [E-mail: iain77@tiscali.co.uk]	0141-633 3744
	Wilma Pearson (Mrs) BD (Assoc)	2004		90 Newlands Road, Glasgow G43 2JR [E-mail: wilma.pearson@ntlworld.com]	0141-632 2491
60	**Glasgow: Cathedral (High or St Mungo's) (0141-552 6891)**				
	Laurence A.B. Whitley MA BD PhD	1975	2007	23 Laurel Park Close, Glasgow G13 1RD [E-mail: labwhitley@btinternet.com]	0141-954 0216

No.	Charge / Minister	Year(s)	Address	Telephone
61	**Glasgow: Colston Milton (0141-772 1922)** Christopher J. Rowe BA BD	2008	118 Birsay Road, Glasgow G22 7QP [E-mail: ministercolstonmilton@yahoo.co.uk]	0141-564 1138
62	**Glasgow: Colston Wellpark (H)** Vacant		16 Bishop's Gate Gardens, Colston, Glasgow G21 1XS	0141-589 8866
63	**Glasgow: Cranhill (H) (0141-774 3344)** Muriel B. Pearson (Ms) MA BD PCGE	2004	31 Lethamhill Crescent, Glasgow G33 2SH [E-mail: murielpearson@btinternet.com]	0141-770 6873 07951 888860 (Mbl)
64	**Glasgow: Croftfoot (H) (0141-637 3913)** John M. Lloyd BD CertMin	1984 1986	20 Victoria Road, Burnside, Rutherglen, Glasgow G73 3QG [E-mail: johnLloyd@croftfootparish.co.uk]	0141-647 5524
65	**Glasgow: Dennistoun New (H) (0141-550 2825)** Ian M.S. McInnes BD DipMin	1995 2008	31 Pencaitland Drive, Glasgow G32 8RL	0141-763 0000
66	**Glasgow: Drumchapel Drumry St Mary's (0141-944 1998)** Brian S. Sheret MA BD DPhil	1982 2002	8 Fruin Road, Glasgow G15 6SQ	0141-944 4493
67	**Glasgow: Drumchapel St Andrew's (0141-944 3758)** John S. Purves LLB BD	1983 1984	6 Firdon Crescent, Glasgow G15 6QQ [E-mail: john.s.purves@talk21.com]	0141-944 4566
68	**Glasgow: Drumchapel St Mark's** Audrey Jamieson BD MTh	2004 2007	146 Garscadden Road, Glasgow G15 6PR [E-mail: audrey.jamieson2@btinternet.com]	0141-944 5440
69	**Glasgow: Easterhouse St George's and St Peter's (E) (0141-771 8810)** Malcolm Cuthbertson BA BD	1984	3 Barony Gardens, Baillieston, Glasgow G69 6TS [E-mail: malcuth@aol.com]	0141-573 8200 (Tel) 0141-773 4878 (Fax)
70	**Glasgow: Eastwood** Vacant		54 Mansewood Road, Glasgow G43 1TL	0141-632 0724
71	**Glasgow: Gairbraid (H)** Vacant		1515 Maryhill Road, Glasgow G20 9AB	0141-946 1568
72	**Glasgow: Gardner Street (GE)** Vacant		148 Beechwood Drive, Glasgow G11 7DX	0141-563 2638

73 Glasgow: Garthamlock and Craigend East (E)
Valerie J. Duff (Miss) DMin   1993   1996   175 Tillycairn Drive, Garthamlock, Glasgow G33 5HS   0141-774 6364
[E-mail: valduff@tiscali.co.uk]
Marion Buchanan (Mrs) MA DCS   2 Lenzie Road, Stepps, Glasgow G33 6DX   0141-779 5746

74 Glasgow: Gorbals
Ian F. Galloway BA BD   1976   1996   44 Riverside Road, Glasgow G43 2EF   0141-649 5250
[E-mail: ianfgalloway@msn.com]

75 Glasgow: Govan and Linthouse
Moyna McGlynn (Mrs) BD PhD   1999   2008   19 Dumbreck Road, Glasgow G41 5LJ   0141-419 0308
[E-mail: moyna_mcglynn@hotmail.com]
(Charge formed by the union of Glasgow: Govan Old, Glasgow: Linthouse St Kenneth's and Glasgow: New Govan)

76 Glasgow: Govanhill Trinity
Lily F. McKinnon MA BD   1993   2006   12 Carleton Gate, Giffnock, Glasgow G46 6NU   0141-637 8399
[E-mail: lilygraeme@tiscali.co.uk]

77 Glasgow: High Carntyne (0141-778 4186)
Joan Ross (Miss) BSc BD PhD   1999   2005   163 Lethamhill Road, Glasgow G33 2SQ   0141-770 9247
[E-mail: joan@revdr.freeserve.co.uk]

78 Glasgow: Hillington Park (H)
John B. MacGregor BD   1999   2004   61 Ralston Avenue, Glasgow G52 3NB   0141-882 7000
[E-mail: johnmacgregor494@msn.com]

79 Glasgow: Householdwood St Christopher's
May M. Allison (Mrs) BD   1988   2001   12 Leverndale Court, Crookston, Glasgow G53 7SJ   0141-810 5953
[E-mail: revmayallison@hotmail.com]

80 Glasgow: Hyndland (H) (Website: www.hyndlandparishchurch.org)
Craig Lancaster MA BD   2004   24 Hughenden Gardens, Glasgow G12 9YH   0141-334 1002
[E-mail: craig@hyndlandparishchurch.org]

81 Glasgow: Ibrox (H) (0141-427 0896)
Elisabeth G.B. Spence (Miss) BD DipEd   1995   2008   59 Langhaul Road, Glasgow G53 7SE   0141-883 7744

82 Glasgow: John Ross Memorial Church for Deaf People
(Voice Text: 0141-420 1759; Text Only: 0141-429 6682; Fax: 0141-429 6860; ISDN Video Phone: 0141-418 0579)
Richard C. Durno DSW CQSW (Aux)   1989   1998   31 Springfield Road, Bishopbriggs, Glasgow G64 1PJ   (Voice/Text) 0141-772 1052
[E-mail: richard.durno@ntlworld.com]
[Website: www.deafconnections.co.uk]

83	**Glasgow: Jordanhill (Tel: 0141-959 2496)**				
	Colin C. Renwick BMus BD	1989	1996	96 Southbrae Drive, Glasgow G13 1TZ	0141-959 1310
				[E-mail: jordchurch@btconnect.com]	
84	**Glasgow: Kelvin Stevenson Memorial (0141-339 1750)**				
	Gordon Kirkwood BSc BD PGCE MTh	1987	2003	Flat 2/2, 94 Hyndland Road, Glasgow G12 9PZ	0141-334 5352
				[E-mail: gordonkirkwood@tiscali.co.uk]	
85	**Glasgow: Kelvinside Hillhead**				
	Vacant			39 Athole Gardens, Glasgow G12 9BQ	0141-339 2865
86	**Glasgow: Kenmuir Mount Vernon** See Carmyle				
87	**Glasgow: King's Park (H) (0141-632 1131)**				
	Sandra Boyd (Mrs) BEd BD	2007		1101 Aikenhead Road, Glasgow G44 5SL	0141-637 2803
				[E-mail: sandraboyd.bofa@btopenworld.com]	
88	**Glasgow: Kinning Park (0141-427 3063)**				
	Margaret H. Johnston BD	1988	2000	168 Arbroath Avenue, Cardonald, Glasgow G52 3HH	0141-810 3782
89	**Glasgow: Knightswood St Margaret's (H)**				
	Vacant			26 Airthrey Avenue, Glasgow G14 9LJ	0141-959 7075
90	**Glasgow: Langside (0141-632 7520)**				
	David N. McLachlan BD	1985	2004	36 Madison Avenue, Glasgow G44 5AQ	0141-637 0797
				[E-mail: dmclachlan77@hotmail.com]	
91	**Glasgow: Lansdowne**				
	Roy J.M. Henderson MA BD DipMin	1987	1992	18 Woodlands Drive, Glasgow G4 9EH	0141-339 2794
				[E-mail: roy.henderson7@ntlworld.com]	
92	**Glasgow: Lochwood (H) (0141-771 2649)**				
	Stuart M. Duff BA	1997		42 Rhindmuir Road, Swinton, Glasgow G69 6AZ	0141-773 2756
				[E-mail: stuart.duff@gmail.com]	
93	**Glasgow: Martyrs', The**				
	Ewen MacLean BA BD	1995		30 Louden Hill Road, Robroyston, Glasgow G33 1GA	0141-558 7451
				[E-mail: revewenmaclean@tiscali.co.uk]	
94	**Glasgow: Maryhill (H) (0141-946 3512)**				
	Anthony J.D. Craig BD	1987		111 Maxwell Avenue, Glasgow G61 1HT	0141-570 0642
				[E-mail: craig.glasgow@ntlworld.com]	
	Stuart C. Matthews BD MA (Assoc)	1987		6 Moss Head Road, Bearsden, Glasgow G61 3HN	0141-942 0804
	James Hamilton DCS	2006		6 Beckfield Gate, Robroyston, Glasgow G33 1SW	0141-558 3195

95 Glasgow: Merrylea (0141-637 2009) David P. Hood BD CertMin DipIOB(Scot)	1997	2001	4 Pilmuir Avenue, Glasgow G44 3HX [E-mail: dphood3@ntlworld.com]	0141-637 6700
96 Glasgow: Mosspark (H) (0141-882 2240) Alan H. MacKay BD	1974	2002	396 Kilmarnock Road, Glasgow G43 2DJ [E-mail: alanhmackay@aol.com]	0141-632 1247
97 Glasgow: Mount Florida (H) (0141-561 0307) Vacant			90 Mount Annan Drive, Glasgow G44 4RZ	0141-589 5381
98 Glasgow: Newlands South (H) (0141-632 3055) John D. Whiteford MA BD	1989	1997	24 Monreith Road, Glasgow G43 2NY [E-mail: jwhiteford@hotmail.com]	0141-632 2588
99 Glasgow: North Kelvinside William G. Alston	1961	1971	41 Mitre Road, Glasgow G14 9LE [E-mail: williamalstcn@hotmail.com]	0141-954 8250
100 Glasgow: Partick South (H) Alan L. Dunnett LLB BD	1994	1997	3 Branklyn Crescent Glasgow G13 1GJ [E-mail: dustydunnett@prtck2.freeserve.co.uk]	0141-959 3732
101 Glasgow: Partick Trinity (H) Stuart J. Smith BEng BD	1994		99 Balshagray Avenue, Glasgow G11 7EQ [E-mail: ssmith99@ntlworld.com]	0141-576 7149
102 Glasgow: Penilee St Andrew's (H) (0141-882 2691) Alastair J. Cherry BA BD FPLD	1982	2003	80 Tweedsmuir Road, Glasgow G52 2RX [E-mail: alastair.j.cherry@biopenworld.com]	0141-882 2460
103 Glasgow: Pollokshaws (0141-649 1879) Margaret Whyte (Mrs) BA BD	1988	2000	33 Mannering Road, Glasgow G41 3SW [E-mail: tdpwhyte@tiscali.co.uk]	0141-649 0458
104 Glasgow: Pollokshields (H) David R. Black MA BD	1986	1997	36 Glencairn Drive, Glasgow G41 4PW [E-mail: minister@pollokshieldschurch.org.uk]	0141-423 4000
105 Glasgow: Possilpark W.C. Campbell-Jack BD MTh PhD	1979	2003	108 Erradale Street, Lambhill, Glasgow G22 6PT [E-mail: c.c-j@homecall.co.uk]	0141-336 6909

106 Glasgow: Priesthill and Nitshill (0141-881 6541)
Douglas M. Nicol BD CA   1987   36 Springkell Drive, Glasgow G41 4EZ   0141-427 7877
                                                   [E-mail: dougiemnicol@aol.com]

107 Glasgow: Queen's Park (0141-423 3654)
T. Malcolm F. Duff MA BD   1985   2000   5 Alder Road, Glasgow G43 2UY   0141-637 5491
                                                   [E-mail: malcolm.duff@ntlworld.com]

108 Glasgow: Renfield St Stephen's (Tel: 0141-332 4293; Fax: 0141-332 8482)
Peter M. Gardner MA BD   1988   2002   101 Hill Street, Glasgow G3 6TY   0141-353 0349
                                                   [E-mail: pmg1@renfieldststephens.org]

109 Glasgow: Robroyston (New Charge Development) (0141-558 8414)
Vacant
Jean Porter (Ms) DCS   2006   2/2, 31 Castlefield Court, Glasgow G33 6NN   07729 316321 (Mbl)

110 Glasgow: Ruchazie (0141-774 2759)
William F. Hunter MA BD   1986   1999   18 Borthwick Street, Glasgow G33 3UU   0141-774 6860
                                                   [E-mail: billhunter@dsl.pipex.com]

111 Glasgow: Ruchill (0141-946 0466)
John C. Matthews MA BD OBE   1992   9 Kirklee Road, Glasgow G12 0RQ   0141-357 3249
                                                   [E-mail: jmatthews@kirklee9.fsnet.co.uk]

112 Glasgow: St Andrew's East (0141-554 1485)
Janette G. Reid (Miss) BD   1991   43 Broompark Drive, Glasgow G31 2JB   0141-554 3620
                                                   [E-mail: JANETTEGREID@aol.com]

113 Glasgow: St Columba (GE) (0141-221 3305)
Donald Michael MacInnes BD   2002   1 Reelick Avenue, Peterson Park, Glasgow G13 4NF   0141-952 0948
                                                   [E-mail: minister@highlandcathedral.org]

114 Glasgow: St David's Knightswood (0141-959 1024) (E-mail: dringlis@stdavidschurch.freeserve.co.uk)
Graham M. Thain LLB BD   1988   1999   60 Southbrae Drive, Glasgow G13 1QD   0141-959 2904
                                                   [E-mail: graham_thain@btopenworld.com]

115 Glasgow: St Enoch's Hogganfield (H) (Tel: 0141-770 5694; Fax: 0870 284 0084) (E-mail: church@st-enoch.org.uk) (Website: www.st-enoch.org.uk)
Vacant   43 Smithycroft Road, Glasgow G33 2RH   0141-770 7593
                                                                                                          0870 284 0085 (Fax)

116 Glasgow: St George's Tron (0141-221 2141)
William J.U. Philip MB ChB MRCP BD   2004   12 Dargarvel Avenue, Glasgow G41 5LU   0141-427 1402
[E-mail: wp@wphilip.com]

117 Glasgow: St James' (Pollok) (0141-882 4984)
John Mann BSc MDiv DMin   2004   30 Ralston Avenue, Glasgow G52 3NA   0141-883 7405
[E-mail: drjohnmann@hotmail.com]

118 Glasgow: St John's Renfield (0141-339 7021) (Website: www.stjohns-renfield.org.uk)
Vacant   26 Leicester Avenue, Glasgow G12 0LU   0141-339 4637

119 Glasgow: St Luke's and St Andrew's (0141-552 7241)
Vacant   10 Chalmers Street, Glasgow G40 2HA   0141-556 3883

120 Glasgow: St Margaret's Tollcross Park
George M. Murray LTh   1995   31 Kenmuir Avenue, Sandyhills, Glasgow G32 9LE   0141-778 5060
[E-mail: george.murray@ntlworld.com]

121 Glasgow: St Nicholas' Cardonald
Sandi McGill (Ms) BD   2002   2007   104 Lamington Road, Glasgow G52 2SE   0141-882 2065
[E-mail: smcgillbox-mail@yahoo.co.uk]

122 Glasgow: St Paul's (0141-770 8559)
Vacant   38 Lochview Drive, Glasgow G33 1QF   0141-770 9611

123 Glasgow: St Rollox
James K. Torrens MB ChB BD   2005   42 Melville Gardens, Bishopbriggs, Glasgow G64 3DE   0141-562 6296
[E-mail: james.torrens@ntlworld.com]

124 Glasgow: St Thomas' Gallowgate
Peter R. Davidge BD MTh   2003   8 Helenvale Court, Glasgow G31 4LB   07765 096599 (Mbl)
[E-mail: rev.davidge@virgin.net]

125 Glasgow: Sandyford Henderson Memorial (H) (L)
C. Peter White BVMS BD   1974   1997   66 Woodend Drive, Glasgow G13 1TG   0141-954 9013
[E-mail: revcpw@ntlworld.com]

126 Glasgow: Sandyhills (0141-778 3415)
Graham T. Atkinson MA BD   2006   60 Wester Road, Glasgow G32 9JJ   0141-778 2174
[E-mail: gtatkinson@o2.co.uk]

127 Glasgow: Scotstoun (T)
Richard Cameron BD DipMin — 2000
15 Northland Drive, Glasgow G14 9BE
[E-mail: rev.rickycam@virgin.net]
0141-959 4637

128 Glasgow: Shawlands (0141-649 1773)
Stephen A. Blakey BSc BD — 1977 2005
29 St Ronan's Drive, Glasgow G41 3SQ
[E-mail: shawlandskirk@aol.com]
0141-649 2034

129 Glasgow: Sherbrooke St Gilbert's (H) (0141-427 1968)
Thomas L. Pollock — 1982 2003
BA BD MTh FSAScot JP
114 Springkell Avenue, Glasgow G41 4EW
[E-mail: tompollock06@aol.com]
0141-427 2094

130 Glasgow: Shettleston New
Ronald A.S. Craig BAcc BD — 1983
Dot Getliffe (Mrs) DCS — 2008
211 Sandyhills Road, Glasgow G32 9NB
3 Woodview Terrace, Hamilton ML3 9DP
0141-778 1286
01698 423504

131 Glasgow: Shettleston Old (T) (H) (0141-778 2484)
Vacant
57 Mansionhouse Road, Mount Vernon, Glasgow G32 0RP
0141-778 8904

132 Glasgow: South Carntyne (H) (0141-778 1343)
Vacant
47 Broompark Drive, Glasgow G31 2JB
0141-554 3275

133 Glasgow: South Shawlands (T) (0141-649 4656)
Fiona Gardner (Mrs) BD MA MLitt — 1997
391 Kilmarnock Road, Glasgow G43 2NU
[E-mail: fionaandcolin@hotmail.com]
0141-632 0013

134 Glasgow: Springburn (H) (0141-557 2345)
Alan A. Ford BD AIBScot — 1977

Helen Hughes (Miss) DCS
3 Tofthill Avenue, Bishopbriggs, Glasgow G64 3PA
[E-mail: springburnchurch@dsl.pipex.com]
2/2 Burnbank Terrace, Glasgow G20 6UQ
0141-762 1844
07710 455737 (Mbl)
0141-333 9459

135 Glasgow: Temple Anniesland (0141-959 1814)
John Wilson BD — 1985
76 Victoria Park Drive North, Glasgow G14 9PJ
[E-mail: revjwilson@btinternet.com]
0141-959 5835

136 Glasgow: Toryglen (H)
Sandra Black (Mrs) BSc BD — 1988
36 Glencairn Drive, Glasgow G41 4PW
[E-mail: revsblack@btinternet.com]
0141-423 0867

137 Glasgow: Trinity Possil and Henry Drummond
Richard G. Buckley BD MTh — 1990
50 Highfield Drive, Glasgow G12 0HL
[E-mail: richardbuckley@hotmail.com]
0141-339 2870

138 Glasgow: Tron St Mary's

| P. Jill Clancy (Mrs) BD | 2000 | 2008 | Tron St Mary's Church, 128 Red Road, Balornock, Glasgow G21 4PJ | 0141-778 2413 |

[E-mail: jgibson@totalise.co.uk]

139 Glasgow: Victoria Tollcross

| Monica Michelin Salomon BD | 1999 | 2007 | 228 Hamilton Road, Glasgow G32 9QU | |

[E-mail: monica@michelin-salomon.freeserve.co.uk]

140 Glasgow: Wellington (H) (0141-339 0454)

| David I. Sinclair BSc BD PhD DipSW | 1990 | 2008 | 31 Hughenden Gardens, Glasgow G12 9YH | 0141-334 2343 |

141 Glasgow: Whiteinch (New Charge Development) (Website: www.whiteinchcofs.co.uk)

| Alan McWilliam BD | 1993 | 2000 | 65 Victoria Park Drive South, Glasgow G14 9NX | 0141-576 9020 |

[E-mail: alan@whiteinchchurch.org]

| Alex W. Smeed MA BD (Assoc) | | 2008 | 15 Victoria Park Street, Glasgow G14 9QA | 0141-954 0767 / 07709 756495 (Mbl) |

[E-mail: alex@whiteinchchurch.org]

142 Glasgow: Yoker (T)

| Karen E. Hendry BSc BD | | 2005 | 15 Coldingham Avenue, Glasgow G14 0PX | 0141-952 3620 |

[E-mail: karen@hendry-k.fsnet.co.uk]

Name			(Charge/Role)	Address	Phone
Alexander, Eric J. MA BD	1958	1997	(St George's Tron)	77 Norwood Park, Bearsden, Glasgow G61 2RZ	0141-942 4404
Allan, A.G.	1959	1989	(Candlish Polmadie)	30 Dalrymple Drive, East Mains, East Kilbride, Glasgow G74 4LF	01355 226190
Allen, Martin A.W. MA BD ThM	1977	2007	(Chryston)	Laelenge, High Barrwood Road, Kilsyth, Glasgow G65 0EE	01236 826616
Anderson, Colin M. BA BD STM MPhil	1968	2003	(Inverness: St Stephen's with The Old High)	83 Marlborough Avenue, Glasgow G11 7BT	0141-357 2838
Barr, Alexander C. MA BD	1950	1992	(St Nicholas' Cardonald)	25 Fisher Drive, Phoenix Park, Paisley PA1 2TP	0141-848 5941
Barr, John BSc PhD BD	1958	1979	(Kilmacolm: Old)	31 Kelvin Court, Glasgow G12 0AD	0141-357 4338
Bell, John L. MA BD FRSCM DUniv	1978	1988	(Iona Community)	Flat 2/1, 31 Lansdowne Crescent, Glasgow G20 6NH	0141-334 0688
Birch, James PgDip FRSA FIOC	2001	2007	(Auxiliary Minister)	1 Kirkhill Grove, Cambuslang, Glasgow G72 8EH	0141-583 1322
Bradley, Andrew W. BD	1975	2007	(Paisley: Lylesland)	Flat 1/1, 38 Cairnhill View, Bearsden, Glasgow G61 1RP	0141-931 5344
Brain, Ernest J.	1955	1985	(Liverpool: St Andrew's)	14 Chesterfield Court, 1240 Great Western Road, Glasgow G12 0BJ	0141-357 2249
Brain, Isobel J. (Mrs) MA	1987	1997	(Ballantrae)	14 Chesterfield Court, 1240 Great Western Road, Glasgow G12 0BJ	0141-357 2249
Brice, Dennis G. BSc BD	1981		(Taiwan)	13 Hermitage Avenue, Benfleet, Essex E57 1TQ	01702 555333
Brough, Robin BA	1968	2002	(Whitburn: Brucefield)	'Kildavanan', 10 Printers Lea, Lennoxtown, Glasgow G66 7GF	01360 310223
Bryden, William A. BD	1977	1984	(Yoker: Old with St Matthew's)	145 Bearsden Road, Glasgow G13 1BS	0141-959 5213
Bull, Alister W. BD DipMin	1994	2001	Head of Chaplaincy Service	Chaplaincy Centre Office, First Floor, Queen Mother's Hospital, Yorkhill Division, Dalnair Street, Glasgow G3 8SJ [E-mail: alister.bull@yorkhill.scot.nhs.uk]	0141-201 0000
Campbell, A. Iain MA DipEd	1961	1997	(Busby)	430 Clarkston Road, Glasgow G44 3QF [E-mail: bellmac@sagainternet.co.uk]	0141-637 7460
Cartledge, G.R.G. MA BD STM	1977	1993	Religious Education	5 Briar Grove, Newlands, Glasgow G43 2TG	0141-637 3228
Collard, John K. MA BD	1986	2003	Presbytery Congregational Facilitator	1 Nelson Terrace, East Kilbride, Glasgow G74 2EY	01355 520093
Coull, Morris C. BD	1974	2006	(Stirling: Allan Park South with the Church of the Holy Rude)	112 Greenock Road, Largs KA30 8PF	01475 686838

Name			Role	Address	Tel
Cunningham, Alexander MA BD	1961	2002	(Presbytery Clerk)	The Glen, 103 Glenmavis Road, Airdrie ML6 0PQ	01236 763012
Cunningham, James S.A. MA BD BLit PhD					
Currie, Robert MA	1992	2000	(Glasgow: Barlanark Greyfriars)	'Kirkland', 5 Inveresk Place, Coatbridge ML5 2DA	01236 421541
			(Community Minister)	Flat 3/2, 13 Redlands Road, Glasgow G12 0SJ	0141-334 5111
Dunnet, Linda (Mrs) DCS	1955	1990	Urban Mission Co-ordinator	International Christian College, 110 St James Road, Glasgow G4 0PS (Office)	
Easton, Lilly C. (Mrs)	1999	2007	(Airdrie: Clarkston)	3 Branklyn Crescent, Glasgow G13 1GJ (Home)	0141-959 3732
Ferguson, James B. LTh	1972	2002	(Lenzie: Union)	Flat 2, 90 Beith Street, Glasgow G11 6DQ	0141-586 7628
Finlay, William P. MA BD	1969	2000	(Glasgow: Townhead Blochairm)	3 Bridgeway Place, Kirkintilloch, Glasgow G66 3HW	0141-588 5868
Fisher, M. Leith MA BD	1967	2006	(Glasgow: Wellington)	High Corrie, Brodick, Isle of Arran KA27 8JB	01770 810689
				31 Millburn Avenue, Clydebank G81 1EP	0141-952 3023
				[E-mail: fleith@fish.co.uk]	
Fleming, Alexander F. MA BD	1966	1995	(Strathblane)	4 Horsburgh Avenue, Kilsyth, Glasgow G65 9BZ	01236 821461
Galloway, Kathy (Mrs) BD	1977	2002	Leader: Iona Community	20 Hamilton Park Avenue, Glasgow G12 8UU	0141-357 4079
Gibson, H. Marshall BD STM	1957	1996	(St Thomas' Gallowgate)	39 Burnthroom Drive, Glasgow G69 7XG	0141-771 0749
Gibson, Michael BD STM	1974	2001	(Giffnock: The Park)	12 Mile End Park, Pocklington, York YO42 2TH	
Grant, David I.M. MA BD	1969	2003	(Dalry: Trinity)	8 Mossbank Drive, Glasgow G33 1LS	0141-770 7186
Gray, Christine (Mrs)			(Deaconess)	11 Woodside Avenue, Thornliebank, Glasgow G46 7HR	0141-571 1008
Gregson, Elizabeth M. (Mrs) BD	1996	2001	(Drumchapel: St Andrew's)	17 Westfields, Bishopbriggs, Glasgow G64 3PL	0141-563 1918
Grimstone, A. Frank MA	1949	1986	(Calton Parkhead)	144C Howth Drive, Parkview Estate, Anniesland, Glasgow G13 1RL	0141-954 1009
Haley, Derek BD DPS	1960	1999	(Chaplain: Gartnavel Royal)	9 Kinnaird Crescent, Bearsden, Glasgow G61 2BN	0141-942 9281
Harper, Anne J.M. (Miss) BD STM MTh CertSocPsych	1979	1990	Hospital Chaplain	122 Greenock Road, Bishopton PA7 5AS	01505 862466
Harvey, W. John BA BD	1965	2002	(Edinburgh: Corstorphine Craigsbank)	501 Shields Road, Glasgow G41 2RF	0141-429 3774
Haughton, Frank MA BD	1942	2000	(Kirkintilloch: St Mary's)	64 Regent Street, Kirkintilloch, Glasgow G66 1JF	0141-777 6802
Hope, Evelyn P. (Miss) BA BD	1990	1998	(Wishaw: Thornlie)	Flat 0/1, 48 Moss-side Road, Glasgow G41 3UA	0141-649 1522
Houston, Thomas C.	1975	2004	(Glasgow: Priesthill and Nitshill)	110 Elder Crescent, Drumsagart, Glasgow G72 7GL	0141-641 1117
Hunter, Alastair G. MSc BD	1976	1980	University of Glasgow	487 Shields Road, Glasgow G41 2RG	0141-429 1687
Hutchison, Henry MA BEd BD MLitt PhD LLCM AMusLCM	1948	1993	(Carmunnock)	4A Briar Grove, Newlands, Glasgow G43 2TG	0141-637 2766
Irvine, Euphemia H.C. (Mrs) BD	1972	1988	(Milton of Campsie)	32 Baird Drive, Bargarran, Erskine PA8 6BB	0141-812 2777
Johnston, Robert W.M. MA BD STM	1964	1999	(Temple Anniesland)	13 Kilmardinny Crescent, Bearsden, Glasgow G61 3NP	0141-931 5862
Johnstone, H. Martin J. MA BD MTh PhD	1989	2000	Urban Priority Areas Adviser	3/1, 952 Pollokshaws Road, Glasgow G41 2ET	0141-636 5819
				[E-mail: priorityareas@uk.uumail.com]	
Keddie, David A. MA BD	1966	2005	(Glasgow: Linthouse St Kenneth's)	21 Ilay Road, Bearsden, Glasgow G61 1QG	0141-577 1408
				[E-mail: revked@hotmail.com]	
Kerr, Angus BD CertMin ThM DMin	1983	2008	Presbytery Clerk	27 Pelham Court, Thornton Grange, Jackton, East Kilbride, Glasgow G74 5PZ	
Lang, I. Pat (Miss) BSc	1996	2003	(Dunoon: The High Kirk)	37 Crawford Drive, Glasgow G15 6TW	0141-944 2240
Langlands, Cameron H. BD MTh ThM	1995	1999	Hospital Chaplain	G1/28 Plantation Park Gardens, Glasgow G51 1NW	(Mbl) 07890 752877
Levison, C.L. MA BD	1972	1998	Health Care Chaplaincy Training and Development Officer	5 Deaconsbank Avenue, Stewarton Road, Glasgow G46 7UN	0141-620 3492
Lewis, E.M.H. MA	1962	1993	(Drumchapel St Andrew's)	7 Cleveden Place, Glasgow G12 0HG	0141-334 5411

Name			Position	Address	Telephone
Lodge, Bernard P. BD	1967	2004	(Glasgow: Govanhill Trinity)	6 Darluith Park, Brookfield, Johnstone PA5 8DD	01505 320378
Lunan, David W. MA BD	1970	2002	(Presbytery Clerk)	142 Hill Street, Glasgow G3 6UA	0141-353 3687
Lyall, Ann (Miss) DCS			Chaplain: Lodging House Mission	117 Barlia Drive, Glasgow G45 0AY	0141-631 3643
McAreavey, William BA	1950	2001	(Kelvin Stevenson Memorial)	c/o Bisset, Heronbrook, Ladeside, Newmilns KA16 9BE	
Macaskill, Marjory (Mrs) LLB BD	1990	1998	Chaplain: University of Strathclyde	44 Forfar Avenue, Cardonald, Glasgow G52 3JQ	0141-883 5956
MacBain, Ian BD	1971	1993	(Coatbridge: Coatdyke)	24 Thornyburn Drive, Baillieston, Glasgow G69 7ER	0141-771 7030
MacDonald, Anne (Miss) BA DCS			Healthcare Chaplain Leverndale Hospital	c/o Leverndale Hospital, Glasgow G53 7TU	0141-840 1875
MacDonald, Kenneth MA BD	2001	2006	(Auxiliary Minister)	5 Henderland Road, Glasgow G61 1AH	0141-943 1103
McDougall, Hilary (Mrs) MA BD	2002	2008	Chaplain: Robin House (CHAS)	85 Stewarton Drive, Cambuslang, Glasgow G72 8DJ [E-mail: hilary.mcdougall@ntlworld.com]	0141-586 4301
MacFadyen, Anne M. (Mrs) BSc BD FSAScot	1995		(Auxiliary Minister)	295 Mearns Road, Glasgow G77 5LT	0141-639 3605
MacKenzie, Ian C. MA BD	1970	2005	Interim Minister	21 Wilson Street, Motherwell ML1 1NP [E-mail: iancmackenzie@ntlworld.com]	01698 301230
McLachlan, Eric BD MTh	1978	2005	(Cardonald)	268 Dyke Road, Knightswood, Glasgow G13 4QX [E-mail: eric.mclachlan@ntlworld.com]	0141-954 1574
McLaren, D. Muir MA BD MTh PhD	1971	2001	(Mosspark)	House 44, 145 Shawhill Road, Glasgow G43 1SX	0141-569 5503
McLay, Alastair D. BSc BD	1989	2004	(Glasgow: Shawlands)	183 King's Park Avenue, Glasgow G44 4HZ	0141-776 6235
Macleod, Donald BD LRAM DRSAM	1987	2008	(Blairgowrie)	9 Millersneuk Avenue, Lenzie G66 5HJ	0141-339 1294
Macnaughton, J.A. MA BD	1949	1989	(Hyndland)	62 Lauderdale Gardens, Glasgow G12 9QW	0141-616 6468
MacPherson, James B. DCS			(Deacon)	G/1, 104 Cartside Street, Glasgow G42 9TQ	0141-330 5419
MacQuarrie, Stuart BD BSc JP	1984	2001	Chaplain: Glasgow University	The Chaplaincy Centre, University of Glasgow, Glasgow G12 8QQ	0141-575 1137
MacQuien, Duncan DCS	1988		(Deacon)	55 Criffel Road, Mount Vernon, Glasgow G32 9JE	
Martindale, John P.F. BD	1994	2005	(Glasgow: Sandyhills)	50 Springfield Park Road, Burnside, Glasgow G73 3RG	
Miller, John D. BA BD DD	1971	2007	(Glasgow: Castlemilk East)	98 Kirkcaldy Road, Glasgow G41 4LD [E-mail: john@miller15.freeserve.co.uk]	
Moffat, Thomas BSc BD	1976	2008	(Culross and Torryburn)	Flat 8/1, 8 Cranston Street, Glasgow G3 8GG [E-mail: tom@gallus.org.uk]	0141-248 1886
Moore, William B.	1968	2002	Prison Chaplain: Low Moss	10 South Dumbreck Road, Kilsyth, Glasgow G65 9LX	01236 821918
Morrice, Alastair M. MA BD			(Rutherglen: Stonelaw)	5 Brechin Road, Kirriemuir DD8 4BX	
Morris, William J. KCVO PhD LLD DD JP	1951	2005	(Glasgow: Cathedral)	Whitehill Grove, Newton Mearns, Glasgow G77 5DH	0141-639 6327
Morrison, Roderick MA BD	1974	2008	(Glasgow: Gardner Street)	Flat 2/1, 73 Lumsden Street, Glasgow G3 6RH	0141-647 2682
Morton, Thomas MA BD LGSM	1945	1986	(Rutherglen: Stonelaw)	54 Greystone Avenue, Burnside, Rutherglen, Glasgow G73 3SW	0141-779 7204
Muir, Fred C. MA BD ThM ARCM	1961	1997	(Stepps)	20 Alexandra Avenue, Stepps, Glasgow G33 6BP	01476 574430
Myers, Frank BA	1952	1978	(Springburn)	18 Birmingham Close, Grantham NG31 8SD	
Newlands, George M. MA BD PhD DLitt FRSA FRSE	1970	1986	University of Glasgow (Sandyford Henderson Memorial)	12 Jamaica Street North Lane, Edinburgh EH3 6HQ	(Work) 0141-339 8855
Philip, George M. MA	1953	1996	(Sandyford Henderson Memorial)	44 Beech Avenue, Bearsden, Glasgow G61 3EX	0141-942 1327
Porter, Richard MA	1953	1988	(Govanhill)	47 Braemar Court, Hazelden Gardens, Glasgow G44 3HF	0141-629 2887
Ramsay, W.G.	1967	1999	(Springburn)	53 Kelvinvale, Kirkintilloch, Glasgow G66 1RD [E-mail: billram@btopenworld.com]	0141-776 2915
Robertson, Archibald MA BD	1957	1999	(Eastwood)	19 Canberra Court, Braidpark Drive, Glasgow G46 6NS	0141-637 7572
Robertson, Blair MA BD ThM	1990	1998	Chaplain: Southern General Hospital	c/o Chaplain's Office, Southern General Hospital, 1345 Govan Road, Glasgow G51 4TF	0141-201 2357

Ross, Donald M. MA	1953	1994	(Industrial Mission Organiser)	14 Cartsbridge Road, Busby, Glasgow G76 8DH — 0141-644 2220
Ross, Eileen M. (Mrs) BD MTh	2005	2008	(Cambuslang: Trinity St Paul's)	64 Stewart Crescent, Aberdeen AB16 8SR [E-mail: revemr@yahoo.co.uk]
Ross, James MA BD	1968	1998	(Kilsyth: Anderson)	53 Turnberry Gardens, Westerwood, Cumbernauld, Glasgow G68 0AY — 01236 730501
Saunders, Keith BD	1983	1999	Hospital Chaplain	Western Infirmary, Dumbarton Road, Glasgow G11 6NT — 0141-211 2000
Shackleton, William	1960	1996	(Greenock: Wellpark West)	3 Tynwald Avenue, Burnside, Glasgow G73 4RN — 0141-569 9407
Shanks, Norman J. MA BD DD	1983	2007	(Glasgow: Govan Old)	1 Marchmont Terrace, Glasgow G12 9LT — 0141-339 4421 [E-mail: mshnks@shanks1942.freeserve.co.uk]
Simpson, Neil A. BA BD PhD	1992	2001	(Glasgow: Yoker Old with Yoker St Matthew's)	c/o Glasgow Presbytery Office
Smith, G. Stewart MA BD STM	1966	2006	(Glasgow: King's Park)	33 Brent Road, Stewartfield, East Kilbride, Glasgow G74 4RA — (Tel/Fax) 01355 226718 [E-mail: stewart.smith@tinyworld.co.uk]
Smith, James S.A.	1956	1991	(Drongan: The Schaw Kirk)	146 Aros Drive, Glasgow G52 1TJ — 0141-883 9666
Spencer, John MA BD	1962	2001	(Dumfries: Lincluden with Holywood)	10 Kinkell Gardens, Kirkintilloch, Glasgow G66 2HJ — 0141-777 8935
Spiers, John M. LTh MTh	1972	2004	(Giffnock: Orchardhill)	58 Woodlands Road, Thornliebank, Glasgow G46 7JQ — (Tel/Fax) 0141-638 0632
Stewart, Diane E. BD	1988	2006	(Milton of Campsie)	4 Miller Gardens, Bishopbriggs, Glasgow G64 1FG — 0141-762 1358 [E-mail: destewar@fish.co.uk]
Stewart, Norma D. (Miss) MA MEd BD	1977	2000	(Glasgow: Strathbungo Queen's Park)	127 Nether Auldhouse Road, Glasgow G43 2YS — 0141-637 6956
Sutherland, Denis I.	1963	1995	(Hutchesontown)	56 Lime Crescent, Cumbernauld, Glasgow G67 3PQ — 01236 731723
Sutherland, Elizabeth W. (Miss) BD	1972	1996	(Balornock North with Barmulloch)	20 Kirkland Avenue, Blanefield, Glasgow G63 9BZ — 01360 770154 [E-mail: ewsutherland@aol.com]
Tait, Alexander	1967	1995	(St Enoch's Hogganfield)	129 Lochview Drive, Hogganfield, Glasgow G33 1LN — 0141-770 6027
Turner, Angus BD	1976	1998	(Industrial Chaplain)	46 Keir Street, Pollokshields, Glasgow G41 2LA — 0141-424 0493
Tuton, Robert M. MA	1957	1995	(Shettleston: Old)	6 Holmwood Gardens, Uddingston, Glasgow G71 7BH — 01698 321108
Walker, A.L.	1955	1988	(Trinity Possil and Henry Drummond)	11 Dundas Avenue, Torrance, Glasgow G64 4BD — 01360 622281
Walton, Ainslie MA MEd	1954	1995	(University of Aberdeen)	501 Shields Road, Glasgow G41 2RF — 0141-420 3327 [E-mail: revainslie@aol.com]
White, Elizabeth (Miss) DCS	1978	2004	(Deaconess)	Woodside House, Rodger Avenue, Rutherglen, Glasgow G73 3QZ
Younger, Adah (Mrs) BD			(Glasgow: Dennistoun Central)	Flat 0/1, 101 Greenhead Street, Glasgow G40 1HR — 0141-550 0878

GLASGOW ADDRESSES

Banton	Kelvinhead Road, Banton
Bishopbriggs	
Kenmure	Viewfield Road, Bishopbriggs
Springfield	Springfield Road
Broom	Mearns Road, Newton Mearns
Burnside Blairbeth	Church Avenue, Burnside
	Kirkriggs Avenue, Blairbeth
Busby	Church Road, Busby
Cadder	Cadder Road, Glasgow
Cambuslang	
Flemington Hallside	265 Hamilton Road
Parish	Cairns Road
Campsie	Main Street, Lennoxtown
Chryston	Main Street, Chryston
Eaglesham	Montgomery Street, Eaglesham
Fernhill and Cathkin	Neilvaig Drive
Gartcosh	113 Lochend Road, Gartcosh
Giffnock	
Orchardhill	Church Road
South	Eastwood Toll
The Park	Ravenscliffe Drive
Glenboig	138 Main Street, Glenboig
Greenbank	Eaglesham Road, Clarkston
Kilsyth	
Anderson	Kingston Road
Burns and Old	Church Street
Kirkintilloch	
Hillhead	Newdyke Road
St Columba's	Waterside Road nr Old Aisle Road
St David's Mem Pk	Alexander Street
St Mary's	Cowgate

Lenzie	
Old	Kirkintilloch Road x Garngaber Ave
Union	Moncrieff Ave x Kirkintilloch Road
Maxwell	
Mearns Castle	Waterfoot Road
Mearns	Mearns Road, Newton Mearns
Netherlee	Ormonde Drive x Ormonde Avenue
Newton Mearns	Ayr Road, Newton Mearns
Rutherglen	
Old	Main Street at Queen Street
Stonelaw	Stonelaw Road x Dryburgh Avenue
West and Wardlawhill	Glasgow Road nr Main Street
Stamperland	Stamperland Gardens, Clarkston
Stepps	Whitehill Avenue
Thornliebank	61 Spiersbridge Road
Torrance	School Road, Torrance
Twechar	Main Street, Twechar
Williamwood	Vardar Avenue x Seres Ave, Clarkston

Glasgow

Anderston Kelvingrove	Argyle Street x Elderslie Street
Baillieston	
Mure Memorial	Beech Avenue, Garrowhill
St Andrew's	Bredisholm Road
Balshagray Victoria Pk	Broomhill Cross
Barlanark Greyfriars	Edinburgh Road x Hallhill Road
Battlefield East	1216 Cathcart Road
Blawarthill	Millbrix Avenue
Bridgeton St Francis in the East	26 Queen Mary Street
Broomhill	Randolph Rd x Marlborough Ave
Calton Parkhead	122 Helenvale Street
Cardonald	2155 Paisley Road West
Carmunnock	Kirk Road, Carmunnock
Carmyle	South Carmyle Avenue
Carnwadric	556 Boydstone Road, Thornliebank
Castlemilk	
East	Barlia Terrace
West	Carmunnock Road
Cathcart	
Old	119 Carmunnock Road
Trinity	92 Clarkston Road
Cathedral	Cathedral Square
Colston Milton	Egilsay Crescent
Colston Wellpark	1378 Springburn Road
Cranhill	Bellrock Crescent x Bellrock Street
Croftfoot	Croftpark Ave x Crofthill Road
Dennistoun New	Whitehill Street and Armadale Street
Drumchapel	
Drumry St Mary's	Drumry Road East
St Andrew's	Garscadden Road
St Mark's	Kinfauns Drive
Easterhouse St George's and St Peter's	Boydnie Street
Eastwood	Mansewood Road
Gairbraid	1517 Maryhill Road
Gardner Street	Gardner Street x Muirpark Street
Garthamlock and Craigend East	Porchester Street x Balveny Street
Gorbals	Eglinton Street x Cumberland Street
Govan and Linthouse	Govan Cross
Govanhill Trinity	Daisy Street nr Allison Street
High Carntyne	358 Carntynehall Road
Hillington Park	24 Berryknowes Road
Househillwood St Christopher's	Meikle Road
Hyndland	Hyndland Road, opp Novar Drive
Ibrox	Carillon Road x Clifford Street
John Ross Memorial	100 Norfolk Street
Jordanhill	Woodend Drive x Munro Road
Kelvin Stevenson Mem	Belmont Street at Belmont Bridge
Kelvinside Hillhead	Huntly Gardens
Kenmuir Mount Vernon	London Road, Mount Vernon
King's Park	242 Castlemilk Road
Kinning Park	Eaglesham Place
Knightswood St Margaret's	Knightswood Cross
Langside	Ledard Road x Lochleven Road
Lansdowne	Gt Western Road at Kelvin Bridge
Lochwood	Liff Place
Martyrs', The	St Mungo Avenue
Maryhill	1990 Maryhill Road
Merrylea	78 Merrylee Road
Mosspark	149 Ashkirk Drive
Mount Florida	1123 Cathcart Road
Newlands South	Riverside Road x Langside Drive
North Kelvinside	153 Queen Margaret Drive
Partick	
South	Dumbarton Road
Trinity	20 Lawrence Street
Penilee St Andrew's	Bowfield Cres x Bowfield Avenue
Pollokshaws	223 Shawbridge Street
Pollokshields	Albert Drive x Shields Road
Possilpark	124 Saracen Street
Priesthill	Priesthill Road x Muirshiel Cresc
and Nitshill	Dove Street
Queen's Park	170 Queen's Drive
Renfield St Stephen's	260 Bath Street
Robroyston	34 Saughs Road
Ruchazie	Elibank Street x Milncroft Road
Ruchill	Shakespeare Street nr Maryhill Rd
St Andrew's East	681 Alexandra Parade
St Columba	300 St Vincent Street
St David's	
Knightswood	Boreland Drive nr Lincoln Avenue
St Enoch's Hogganfield	860 Cumbernauld Road
St George's Tron	163 Buchanan Street
St James' (Pollok)	Lyoncross Road x Byrebush Road
St John's Renfield	22 Beaconsfield Road
St Luke's and St Andrew's	Bain Square at Bain Street
St Margaret's	
Tollcross Pk	179 Braidfauld Street
St Nicholas' Cardonald	Hartlaw Crescent nr Gladsmuir Road
St Paul's	Langdale Street x Greenrig Street
St Rollox	Fountainwell Road
St Thomas' Gallowgate	Gallowgate opp Bluevale Street
Sandyford Henderson Memorial	Kelvinhaugh Street at Argyle Street
Sandyhills	28 Baillieston Rd nr Sandyhills Rd
Scotstoun	Earlbank Avenue x Ormiston Avenue
Shawlands	Shawlands Cross
Sherbrooke St Gilbert's	Nithsdale Rd x Sherbrooke Avenue
Shettleston New	679 Old Shettleston Road
Shettleston Old	99–111 Killin Street
South Carntyne	538 Carntyne Road
South Shawlands	Regwood Street x Deanston Drive

Springburn	Springburn Road x Atlas Street
Temple Anniesland	869 Crow Road
Toryglen	Glenmore Ave nr Prospecthill Road
Trinity Possil and Henry Drummond	Crowhill Street x Broadholm Street
Tron St Mary's	128 Red Road
Victoria Tollcross	1134 Tollcross Road
Wellington	University Ave x Southpark Avenue
Whiteinch	St Paul's R.C. Primary School, Primrose Street
Yoker	Dumbarton Road at Hawick Street

(17) HAMILTON

Meets at Motherwell: Dalziel St Andrew's Parish Church Halls, on the first Tuesday of February, March, May, September, October, November and December, and on the third Tuesday of June.

Presbytery Office: 353 Orbiston Street, Motherwell ML1 1QW   **01698 259135**
[E-mail: hamilton@cofscotland.org.uk]

Clerk: REV. SHAW J. PATERSON BSc BD MSc c/o The Presbytery Office
[E-mail: clerk@presbyteryofhamilton.co.uk]

Depute Clerk: REV. NORMAN B. McKEE BD c/o The Presbytery Office

Presbytery Treasurer: MR ROBERT A. ALLAN 7 Graham Place, Ashgill, Larkhall ML9 3BA   **01698 883246**
[E-mail: Fallan3246@aol.com]

1 **Airdrie: Broomknoll (H) (Tel: 01236 762101) (E-mail: airdrie-broomknoll@presbyteryofhamilton.co.uk)**
linked with **Calderbank (E-mail: calderbank@presbyteryofhamilton.co.uk)**
Vacant   38 Commonhead Street, Airdrie ML6 6NS   01236 602538

2 **Airdrie: Clarkston (E-mail: airdrie-clarkston@presbyteryofhamilton.co.uk)**
Vacant   Clarkston Manse, Forrest Street, Airdrie ML6 7BE   01236 769676

3 **Airdrie: Flowerhill (H) (E-mail: airdrie-flowerhill@presbyteryofhamilton.co.uk)**
Gary J. Caldwell BSc BD   2007   31 Victoria Place, Airdrie ML6 9BU   01236 754430
[E-mail: garyjcaldwell@btinternet.com]

4 **Airdrie: High (E-mail: airdrie-high@presbyteryofhamilton.co.uk)**
Ian R.W. McDonald BSc BD PhD   2007   17 Etive Drive, Airdrie ML6 9QL   01236 760023
[E-mail: ian@spingetastic.freeserve.co.uk]

5 **Airdrie: Jackson (Tel: 01236 733508) (E-mail: airdrie-jackson@presbyteryofhamilton.co.uk)**
Kay Gilchrist (Miss) BD   1996   2008   48 Dunrobin Road, Airdrie ML6 8LR   01236 763154

6 **Airdrie: New Monkland (H) (E-mail: airdrie-newmonkland@presbyteryofhamilton.co.uk) linked with Greengairs (E-mail: greengairs@presbyteryofhamilton.co.uk)**
William Jackson BD CertMin   1994 2008   3 Dykehead Crescent, Airdrie ML6 6PU   01236 763554

7 **Airdrie: St Columba's (E-mail: airdrie-stcolumbas@presbyteryofhamilton.co.uk)**
Margaret F. Currie BEd BD   1980 1987   52 Kennedy Drive, Airdrie ML6 9AW   01236 763173
[E-mail: margaretfcurrie@btinternet.com]

8 **Airdrie: The New Wellwynd (E-mail: airdrie-newwellwynd@presbyteryofhamilton.co.uk)**
Robert A. Hamilton BA BD   1995 2001   20 Arthur Avenue, Airdrie ML6 9EZ   01236 763022
[E-mail: revrob13@blueyonder.co.uk]

9 **Bargeddie (H) (E-mail: bargeddie@presbyteryofhamilton.co.uk)**
John Fairful BD   1994 2001   The Manse, Manse Road, Bargeddie, Baillieston, Glasgow G69 6UB   0141-771 1322

10 **Bellshill: Macdonald Memorial (E-mail: bellshill-macdonald@presbyteryofhamilton.co.uk) linked with Bellshill: Orbiston**
Alan McKenzie BSc BD   1988 2001   32 Adamson Street, Bellshill ML4 1DT   01698 849114
[E-mail: rev.a.mckenzie@btopenworld.com]

11 **Bellshill: Orbiston (E-mail: bellshill-orbiston@presbyteryofhamilton.co.uk)** See Bellshill: Macdonald Memorial

12 **Bellshill: West (H) (01698 747581) (E-mail: bellshill-west@presbyteryofhamilton.co.uk)**
Agnes A. Moore (Miss) BD   1987 2001   16 Croftpark Street, Bellshill ML4 1EY   01698 842877
[E-mail: revamoore@tiscali.co.uk]

13 **Blantyre: Livingstone Memorial (E-mail: blantyre-livingstone@presbyteryofhamilton.co.uk)**
Vacant   286 Glasgow Road, Blantyre, Glasgow G72 9DB   01698 823794

14 **Blantyre: Old (H) (E-mail: blantyre-old@presbyteryofhamilton.co.uk)**
Rosemary A. Smith (Ms) BD   1997   The Manse, Craigmuir Road, High Blantyre, Glasgow G72 9UA   01698 823130
[E-mail: revrosieanne@btopenworld.com]

15 **Blantyre: St Andrew's (E-mail: blantyre-standrews@presbyteryofhamilton.co.uk)**
J. Peter N. Johnston BSc BD   2001   332 Glasgow Road, Blantyre, Glasgow G72 9LQ   01698 828633
[E-mail: peter.johnston@standrewsblantyre.com]

16 **Bothwell (H) (E-mail: bothwell@presbyteryofhamilton.co.uk)**
James M. Gibson TD LTh LRAM   1978 1989   Manse Avenue, Bothwell, Glasgow G71 8PQ   01698 853189 (Tel)
[E-mail: jamesmgibson@msn.com]   01698 854903 (Fax)

17 **Calderbank** See Airdrie: Broomknoll

18 **Caldercruix and Longriggend (H) (E-mail: caldercruix@presbyteryofhamilton.co.uk)**
George M. Donaldson MA BD   1984   2005   Main Street, Caldercruix, Airdrie ML6 7RF
[E-mail: gmdonaldson@gmdonaldson.force9.co.uk]
01236 842279

19 **Carfin (E-mail: carfin@presbyteryofhamilton.co.uk) linked with Newarthill (E-mail: newarthill@presbyteryofhamilton.co.uk)**
Vacant   Church Street, Newarthill, Motherwell ML1 5HS
01698 860316

20 **Chapelhall (H) (E-mail: chapelhall@presbyteryofhamilton.co.uk)**
Vacant   Russell Street, Chapelhall, Airdrie ML6 8SG
01236 763439

21 **Chapelton (E-mail: chapelton@presbyteryofhamilton.co.uk)
linked with Strathaven: Rankin (H) (E-mail: strathaven-rankin@presbyteryofhamilton.co.uk)**
Shaw J. Paterson BSc BD MSc   1991   15 Lethame Road, Strathaven ML10 6AD
[E-mail: shaw@patersonsj.freeserve.co.uk]
Maxine Buck (Aux)   2007   Brownlee House, Mauldslie Road, Carluke ML8 5HW
01357 520019 (Tel)
01357 529316 (Fax)
01555 759063

22 **Cleland (H) (E-mail: cleland@presbyteryofhamilton.co.uk)**
John A. Jackson BD   1997   The Manse, Bellside Road, Cleland, Motherwell ML1 5NP
[E-mail: johnjackson@uk2.net]
01698 860260

23 **Coatbridge: Blairhill Dundyvan (H) (E-mail: coatbridge-blairhill@presbyteryofhamilton.co.uk)**
Patricia A. Carruth (Mrs) BD   1998   2004   18 Blairhill Street, Coatbridge ML5 1PG
01236 432304

24 **Coatbridge: Calder (H) (E-mail: coatbridge-calder@presbyteryofhamilton.co.uk)**
Amelia Davidson (Mrs) BD   2004   26 Bute Street, Coatbridge ML5 4HF
[E-mail: amelia@davidson1293.freeserve.co.uk]
01236 421516

25 **Coatbridge: Clifton (H) (E-mail: coatbridge-clifton@presbyteryofhamilton.co.uk)**
Vacant   132 Muiryhall Street, Coatbridge ML5 3NH
01236 421181

26 **Coatbridge: Middle (E-mail: coatbridge-middle@presbyteryofhamilton.co.uk)**
Vacant   47 Blair Road, Coatbridge ML5 1JQ
01236 432427

27 **Coatbridge: Old Monkland (E-mail: coatbridge-oldmonkland@presbyteryofhamilton.co.uk)**
Vacant   2 Brandon Way, Coatbridge ML5 5QT
01236 423788

28 **Coatbridge: St Andrew's (E-mail: coatbridge-standrews@presbyteryofhamilton.co.uk)**
Fiona Nicolson BA BD   1996   2005   77 Eglinton Street, Coatbridge ML5 3JF
01236 437271

29 **Coatbridge: Townhead (H) (E-mail: coatbridge-townhead@presbyteryofhamilton.co.uk)**
Ecilo Selemani LTh MTh   1993   2004   Crinan Crescent, Coatbridge ML5 2LH
[E-mail: eciloselemani@msn.com]
01236 702914

30 **Dalserf (E-mail: dalserf@presbyteryofhamilton.co.uk)**
    D. Cameron McPherson BSc BD DMin   1982   Manse Brae, Dalserf, Larkhall ML9 3BN   01698 882195
    [E-mail: dCameronMc@aol.com]

31 **East Kilbride: Claremont (H) (Tel: 01355 238088) (E-mail: ek-claremont@presbyteryofhamilton.co.uk)**
    Gordon R. Palmer MA BD STM   1986   2003   17 Deveron Road, East Kilbride, Glasgow G74 2HR   01355 248526
                                           [E-mail: gkrspalmer@blueyonder.co.uk]
    Paul Cathcart DCS   59 Glen Isla, St Lecnards, East Kilbride, Glasgow G74 3TG   0141-569 6865
                                                   [E-mail: paulcathcart@msn.com]

32 **East Kilbride: Greenhills (E) (Tel: 01355 221746) (E-mail: ek-greenhills@presbyteryofhamilton.co.uk)**
    John Brewster MA BD DipEd   1988   21 Turnberry Place, East Kilbride, Glasgow G75 8TB   01355 242564
                                          [E-mail: johnbrewster@blueyonder.co.uk]

33 **East Kilbride: Moncreiff (H) (Tel: 01355 223328) (E-mail: ek-moncreiff@presbyteryofhamilton.co.uk)**
    Alastair S. Lusk BD   1974   1983   16 Almond Drive, East Kilbride, Glasgow G74 2HX   01355 238639

34 **East Kilbride: Mossneuk (E) (Tel: 01355 260954) (E-mail: ek-mossneuk@presbyteryofhamilton.co.uk)**
    John L. McPake BA BD PhD   1987   2000   30 Eden Grove, Messneuk, East Kilbride, Glasgow G75 8XU   01355 234196

35 **East Kilbride: Old (H) (E-mail: ek-old@presbyteryofhamilton.co.uk)**
    Anne S. Paton BA BD   2001   40 Maxwell Drive, East Kilbride, Glasgow G74 4HJ   01355 220732
                                    [E-mail: annepaton@fsmail.net]

36 **East Kilbride: South (H) (E-mail: ek-south@presbyteryofhamilton.co.uk)**
    John C. Sharp BSc BD PhD   1980   7 Clamps Wood, East Kilbride, Glasgow G74 2HB   01355 247993

37 **East Kilbride: Stewartfield (New Charge Development)**
    Douglas W. Wallace MA BD   1981   2001   8 Thistle Place, Stewartfield, East Kilbride, Glasgow G74 4RH   01355 260879

38 **East Kilbride: West (H) (E-mail: ek-west@presbyteryofhamilton.co.uk)**
    Mahboob Masih BA MDiv MTh   1999   2008   4 East Milton Grove, East Kilbride, Glasgow G75 8FN   01355 224469
                                                 [E-mail: m_masih@sky.com]

39 **East Kilbride: Westwood (H) (Tel: 01355 245657) (E-mail: ek-westwood@presbyteryofhamilton.co.uk)**
    Kevin Mackenzie BD DPS   1989   1996   16 Inglewood Crescent, East Kilbride, Glasgow G75 8QD   01355 223992
                                               [E-mail: kevin@westwoodmanse.freeserve.co.uk]

40 **Glasford (E-mail: glassford@presbyteryofhamilton.co.uk) linked with Strathaven: East (E-mail: strathaven-east@presbyteryofhamilton.co.uk)**
    William T. Stewart BD   1980   68 Townhead Street, Strathaven ML10 6DJ   01357 521138

41 **Greengairs** See Airdrie: New Monkland

42 **Hamilton: Burnbank (E-mail: hamilton-burnbank@presbyteryofhamilton.co.uk)**
    linked with Hamilton: North (H) (E-mail: hamilton-north@presbyteryofhamilton.co.uk)
    Raymond D. McKenzie BD   1978   1987   9 South Park Road, Hamilton ML3 6PJ   01698 424609

43 **Hamilton: Cadzow (H) (Tel: 01698 428695) (E-mail: hamilton-cadzow@presbyteryofhamilton.co.uk)**
    Vacant   3 Carlisle Road, Hamilton ML3 7BZ   01698 421664

44 **Hamilton: Gilmour and Whitehill (H) (E-mail: hamilton-gilmourwhitehill@presbyteryofhamilton.co.uk)**
    Ronald J. Maxwell Stitt   1977   2000   86 Burnbank Centre, Burnbank, Hamilton ML3 0NA   01698 284201
    LTh BA ThM BREd DMin FSAScot

45 **Hamilton: Hillhouse (E-mail: hamilton-hillhouse@presbyteryofhamilton.co.uk)**
    David W.G. Burt BD DipMin   1989   1998   66 Wellhall Road, Hamilton ML3 9BY   01698 422300
                                                     [E-mail: dwgburt@blueyonder.co.uk]

46 **Hamilton: North** See Hamilton: Burnbank

47 **Hamilton: Old (H) (Tel: 01698 281905) (E-mail: hamilton-old@presbyteryofhamilton.co.uk)**
    John M.A. Thomson TD JP BD ThM 1978   2001   1 Chateau Grove, Hamilton ML3 7DS   01698 422511
                                                     [E-mail: jt@john1949.plus.com]

48 **Hamilton: St Andrew's (T) (E-mail: hamilton-standrews@presbyteryofhamilton.co.uk)**
    Norman MacLeod BTh   1999   2005   15 Bent Road, Hamilton ML3 6QB   01698 283264
                                                     [E-mail: normanmacleod@btopenworld.com]

49 **Hamilton: St John's (H) (Tel: 01698 283492) (E-mail: hamilton-stjohns@presbyteryofhamilton.co.uk)**
    Robert M. Kent MA BD   1973   1981   12 Castlehill Crescent, Hamilton ML3 7DG   01698 425002
                                                     [E-mail: robertmkent@btinternet.com]

50 **Hamilton: South (H) (Tel: 01698 281014) (E-mail: hamilton-south@presbyteryofhamilton.co.uk)**
    linked with Quarter (E-mail: quarter@presbyteryofhamilton.co.uk)
    George MacDonald BTh   2004   The Manse, Limekilnburn Road, Quarter, Hamilton ML3 7XA   01698 424511
                                                     [E-mail: george.macdonald1@btinternet.com]

51 **Hamilton: Trinity (Tel: 01698 284254) (E-mail: hamilton-trinity@presbyteryofhamilton.co.uk)**
    Karen E. Harbison (Mrs) MA BD   1991   69 Buchan Street, Hamilton ML3 8JY   01698 425326

52 **Hamilton: West (H) (Tel: 01698 284670) (E-mail: hamilton-west@presbyteryofhamilton.co.uk)**
    Elizabeth A. Waddell (Mrs) BD 1999   2005   43 Bothwell Road, Hamilton ML3 0BB   01698 458770

53 Holytown (E-mail: holytown@presbyteryofhamilton.co.uk) linked with New Stevenston: Wrangholm Kirk
Iain M. Goring BSc BD   1976   2006   The Manse, 260 Edinburgh Road, Holytown, Motherwell ML1 5RU   01698 832622
[E-mail: imgoring@tiscali.co.uk]

54 Kirk o' Shotts (H) (E-mail: kirk-o-shotts@presbyteryofhamilton.co.uk)
Sheila M. Spence (Mrs) MA BD   1979   The Manse, Kirk o Shotts, Salsburgh, Shotts ML7 4NS   01698 870208
[E-mail: sm_spence@hotmail.com]

55 Larkhall: Chalmers (H) (E-mail: larkhall-chalmers@presbyteryofhamilton.co.uk)
James S.G. Hastie CA BD   1990   Quarry Road, Larkhall ML9 1HH   01698 882238
[E-mail: jHastie@chalmers0.demon.co.uk]   08700 562133   (Fax)

56 Larkhall: St Machan's (H) (E-mail: larkhall-stmachans@presbyteryofhamilton.co.uk)
Alastair McKillop BD DipMin   1995   2004   2 Orchard Gate, Larkhall ML9 1HG   01698 321976

57 Larkhall: Trinity (E-mail: larkhall-trinity@presbyteryofhamilton.co.uk)
Lindsay Schluter (Miss) ThE CertMin   1995   13 Machan Avenue, Larkhall ML9 2HE   01698 881401

58 Motherwell: Crosshill (H) (E-mail: mwell-crosshill@presbyteryofhamilton.co.uk)
Gavin W.G. Black BD   2006   15 Orchard Street, Motherwell ML1 3JE   01698 263410
[E-mail: gavin.black12@blueyonder.co.uk]

59 Motherwell: Dalziel St Andrew's (H) (Tel: 01698 264097) (E-mail: mwell-dalziels:andrews@presbyteryofhamilton.co.uk)
Derek W. Hughes BSc BD DipEd   1990   1996   4 Pollock Street, Motherwell ML1 1LP   01698 263414
[E-mail: derekthecleric@btinternet.com]

60 Motherwell: North (E-mail: mwell-north@presbyteryofhamilton.co.uk)
Derek H.N. Pope BD   1987   1995   35 Birrens Road, Motherwell ML1 3NS   01698 266716
[E-mail: derekpopemotherwell@hotmail.com]

61 Motherwell: St Margaret's (E-mail: mwell-stmargarets@presbyteryofhamilton.co.uk)
Andrew M. Campbell BD   1984   70 Baron's Road, Motherwell ML1 2NB   01698 263803
[E-mail: drewdorca@hotmail.com]

62 Motherwell: St Mary's (H) (E-mail: mwell-stmarys@presbyteryofhamilton.co.uk)
David W. Doyle MA BD   1977   1987   19 Orchard Street, Motherwell ML1 3JE   01698 263472

63 Motherwell: South (H)
Vacant

64 Newarthill See Carfin

65	**Newmains: Bonkle (H) (E-mail: bonkle@presbyteryofhamilton.co.uk)** **linked with Newmains: Coltness Memorial (H) (E-mail: coltness@presbyteryofhamilton.co.uk)** Graham Raeburn MTh 2004 5 Kirkgate, Newmains, Wishaw ML2 9BT [E-mail: grahamraeburn@tiscali.co.uk]		01698 383858
66	**Newmains: Coltness Memorial** See Newmains: Bonkle		
67	**New Stevenston: Wrangholm Kirk (E-mail: wrangholm@presbyteryofhamilton.co.uk)** See Holytown		
68	**Overtown (E-mail: overtown@presbyteryofhamilton.co.uk)** Vacant The Manse, Main Street, Overtown, Wishaw ML2 0QP		01698 372330
69	**Quarter** See Hamilton: South		
70	**Shotts: Calderhead Erskine (E-mail: calderhead-erskine@presbyteryofhamilton.co.uk)** Vacant The Manse, 9 Kirk Road, Shotts ML7 5ET		01501 820042
71	**Stonehouse: St Ninian's (H) (E-mail: stonehouse@presbyteryofhamilton.co.uk)** Paul G.R. Grant BD MTh 2003 4 Hamilton Way, Stonehouse, Larkhall ML9 3PU [E-mail: agpg@surefish.co.uk]		01698 792947
72	**Strathaven: Avendale Old and Drumclog (H) (Tel: 01357 529748) (E-mail: strathaven-avendaleold@presbyteryofhamilton.co.uk and** **E-mail: drumclog@presbyteryofhamilton.co.uk)** Vacant Kirk Street, Strathaven ML10 6BA		01357 520077
73	**Strathaven: East** See Glasford		
74	**Strathaven: Rankin** See Chapelton		
75	**Strathaven: West (E-mail: strathaven-west@presbyteryofhamilton.co.uk)** Una B. Stewart (Ms) BD DipEd 1995 2002 6 Avenel Crescent, Strathaven ML10 6JF [E-mail: rev.ubs@virgin.net]		01357 529086
76	**Uddingston: Burnhead (H) (E-mail: uddingston-burnhead@presbyteryofhamilton.co.uk)** Vacant 90 Laburnum Road, Uddingston, Glasgow G71 5DB Karen Hamilton (Mrs) DCS 6 Beckfield Gate, Glasgow G33 1SW		01698 813716 0141-558 3195
77	**Uddingston: Old (H) (Tel: 01698 814015) (E-mail: uddingston-old@presbyteryofhamilton.co.uk)** Norman B. McKee BD 1987 1994 1 Belmont Avenue, Uddingston, Glasgow G71 7AX [E-mail: n.mckee1@btinternet.com]		01698 814757
78	**Uddingston: Viewpark (H) (E-mail: uddingston-viewpark@presbyteryofhamilton.co.uk)** Michael G. Lyall BD 1993 2001 14 Holmbrae Road, Uddingston, Glasgow G71 6AP [E-mail: michaellyall@blueyonder.co.uk]		01698 813113

79 Wishaw: Cambusnethan North (H) (E-mail: wishaw-cambusnethannorth@presbyteryofhamilton.co.uk)
Mhorag Macdonald (Ms) MA BD   1989   350 Kirk Road, Wishaw ML2 8LH   01698 381305
[E-mail: mhorag@mhorag.force9.co.uk]

80 Wishaw: Cambusnethan Old (E-mail: wishaw-cambusnethanold@presbyteryofhamilton.co.uk)
and Morningside (E-mail: wishaw-morningside@presbyteryofhamilton.co.uk)
Iain C. Murdoch MA LLB DipEd BD   1995   22 Coronation Street, Wishaw ML2 8LF   01698 384235
[E-mail: iaincmurdoch@btopenworld.com]

81 Wishaw: Craigneuk and Belhaven (H) (E-mail: wishaw-craigneukbelhaven@presbyteryofhamilton.co.uk) linked with Wishaw: Old
Vacant   100 Glen Road, Wishaw ML2 7NP   01698 372495

82 Wishaw: Old (H) (Tel: 01698 376080) (E-mail: wishaw-old@presbyteryofhamilton.co.uk) See Wishaw: Craigneuk and Belhaven

83 Wishaw: St Mark's (E-mail: wishaw-stmarks@presbyteryofhamilton.co.uk)
Graham Austin BD   1997   2008   The Manse, 32 Coltness Road, Wishaw ML2 7EX   01698 384596

84 Wishaw: South Wishaw (H)
Klaus O.F. Buwert LLB BD   1984   1999   Wishaw South Manse, 16 West Thornlie Street, Wishaw ML2 7AR   01698 372356
[E-mail: k.buwert@btinternet.com]

Name			Charge	Address	Phone
Anderson, Catherine B. (Mrs) DCS	1973	2007	(Deaconess)	3 Mosshill Road, Bellshill ML4 1NQ	01698 745907
Barrie, Arthur P. LTh	1951	1986	(Hamilton: Cadzow)	30 Airbles Crescent, Motherwell ML1 3AR	
Beattie, William G. BD BSc	1995	2003	(Hamilton: St Andrew's)	33 Dungavel Gardens, Hamilton ML3 7PE	01698 423804
Brown, Allan B. BD MTh			(Chaplain: Shotts Prison)	HMP Shotts, Scott Drive, Shotts ML7 4LE	01501 824071
				[E-mail: alan.brown3@sps.gov.uk]	
Colvin, Sharon E.F. (Mrs) BD LRAM LTCL	1985	2007	(Airdrie: Jackson)	25 Balblair Road, Airdrie ML6 6GQ	01698 299600
Cook, J. Stanley BD Dip PSS	1974	2001	(Hamilton: West)	Mansend, 137A Old Manse Road, Netherton, Wishaw ML2 0EW	
				[E-mail: stancook@blueyonder.co.uk]	
Cullen, William T. BA LTh	1984	1996	(Kilmarnock: St John's Onthank)	5 Laurel Wynd, Cambuslang, Glasgow G72 7BA	0141-641 4337
Currie, David E.P. BSc BD	1983	2000	(Congregational Development Consultant)	21 Rosa Burn Avenue, Lindsayfield, East Kilbride, Glasgow G75 9DE	01355 248510
Currie, R. David BSc BD	1984	2004	(Cambuslang: Flemington Hallside)	59 Kethers Street, Motherwell ML1 3HN	01698 323424
Dunn, W. Stuart LTh	1970	2006	(Motherwell: Crosshill)	10 Macrostie Gardens, Crieff PH7 4LP	01764 655178
Fraser, James P.	1951	1988	(Strathaven: Avendale Old and Drumclog)	26 Hamilton Road, Strathaven ML10 6JA	01357 522758
Grier, James BD	1991	2005	(Coatbridge: Middle)	14 Love Drive, Bellshill ML4 1BY	01698 742545
Handley, John	1954	1993	(Motherwell: Clason Memorial)	12 Airbles Crescent, Motherwell ML1 3AR	01698 262733
Hunter, James E. LTh	1974	1997	(Blantyre: Livingstone Memorial)	57 Dalwhinnie Avenue, Blantyre, Glasgow G72 9NQ	01698 826177
King, Crawford S. MA	1958	1984	(Glenboig)	Rawyards House, Motherwell Street, Airdrie ML6 7HP	
McAlpine, John BSc	1998	2004	(Auxiliary Minister)	201 Bonkle Road, Newmains, Wishaw ML2 9AA	01698 384610
McCabe, George	1963	1996	(Airdrie: High)	Flat 8, Park Court, 2 Craighouse Park, Edinburgh EH10 5LD	0131-447 9522
McDonald, John A. MA BD	1978	1997	(Cumbernauld: Condorrat)	17 Thomson Drive, Bellshill ML4 3ND	
Mackenzie, James G. BA BD	1980	2005	(Jersey: St Columba's)	10 Sandpiper Crescent, Carnbroe, Coatbridge ML5 4UW	

Martin, James MA BD DD   1946 1987   (Glasgow: High Carntyne)   9 Magnolia Street, Wishaw ML2 7EQ   01698 385825
Melrose, J.H. Loudon MA BD MEd   1955 1996   (Gourock: Old Gourock and Ashton [Assoc])   1 Laverock Avenue, Hamilton ML3 7DD   01698 427958
Munton, James G. BA   1969 2002   (Coatbridge: Old Monkland)   2 Moorcroft Drive, Airdrie ML6 8ES   01236 754848
                                                                                               [E-mail: jacjim@supanet.com]

Price, Peter O. CBE QHC BA FPhS   1960 1996   (Blantyre: Old)   22 Old Bothwell Road, Bothwell, Glasgow G71 8AW   01698 854032
                                                                                               [E-mail: peteroprice@aol.com]

Rogerson, Stuart D. BSc BD   1980 2001   (Strathaven: West)   17 Westfield Park, Strathaven ML10 6XH   01357 523321
                                                                                               [E-mail: srogerson@cnetwork.co.uk]

Ross, Keith W.   1984 2007   Congregational Development Officer   Easter Bavlaw Farm, Balerno EH14   (Mbl) 07855 163449
                                                                for the Presbytery of Hamilton

Salmond, James S. BA BD MTh ThD   1979 2003   (Holytown)   165 Torbothie Road, Shotts ML7 5NE
Stevenson, John LTh   1998 2006   (Cambuslang: St Andrew's)   20 Knowehead Gardens, Uddingston, Glasgow G71 7PY   01698 817582
                                                                                               [E-mail: therev20@sky.com]

Thorne, Leslie W. BA LTh   1987 2001   (Coatbridge: Clifton)   'Hatherleigh', 9 Chatton Walk, Coatbridge ML5 4FH   01236 432241
                                                                                               [E-mail: lesthorne@tiscali.co.uk]   (Mbl) 07963 199921

Wilson, James H. LTh   1970 1996   (Cleland)   21 Austine Drive, Hamilton ML3 7YE   01698 457042
                                                                                               [E-mail: wilsonjh@blueyonder.co.uk]

Wyllie, Hugh R. MA DD FCIBS   1962 2000   (Hamilton: Old)   18 Chantinghall Road, Hamilton ML3 3NP   01698 420002
Zambonini, James LIADip   1997   Auxiliary Minister   100 Old Manse Road, Wishaw ML2 0EP   01698 350887

HAMILTON ADDRESSES

Airdrie
Broomknoll — Broomknoll Street
Clarkston — Forrest Street
Flowerhill — 89 Graham Street
High — North Bridge Street
Jackson — Glen Road
New Monkland — Glenmavis
St Columba's — Thrashbush Road
The New Wellwynd — Wellwynd

Coatbridge
Blairhill Dundyvan — Blairhill Street
Calder — Calder Street
Clifton — Muiryhall Street x Jackson Street
Middle — Bank Street
Old Monkland — Woodside Street
St Andrew's — Church Street
Townhead — Crinan Crescent

East Kilbride
Claremont — High Common Road, St Leonard's

Greenhills — Greenhills Centre
Moncreiff — Calderwood Road
Mossneuk — Eden Drive
Old — Montgomery Street
South — Baird Hill, Murray
West — Kittoch Street
Westwood — Belmont Drive, Westwood

Hamilton
Burnbank — High Blantyre Road
Cadzow — Woodside Walk
Gilmour and Whitehill — Glasgow Road, Burnbank
   — Abbotsford Road, Whitehill
Hillhouse — Clerkwell Road
North — Windmill Road
Old — Leechlee Road
St Andrew's — Avon Street
St John's — Duke Street
South — Strathaven Road
Trinity — Neilsland Square off North Road
West — Burnbank Road

Motherwell
Crosshill — Windmillhill Street x Airbles Street
Dalziel St Andrew's — Merry Street and Muir Street
North — Chesters Crescent
St Margaret's — Shields Road
St Mary's — Avon Street
South — Gavin Street

Uddingston
Burnhead — Laburnum Road
Old — Old Glasgow Road
Viewpark — Old Edinburgh Road

Wishaw
Cambusnethan North — Kirk Road
Cambusnethan Old — Kirk Road
Craigneuk and Belhaven — Craigneuk Street
Old — Main Street
St Mark's — Coltness Road
Thornlie — West Thornlie Street

(18) DUMBARTON

Meets at Dumbarton, in Riverside Church Halls, on the first Tuesday of February, March, April, May, October, November and December, on the second Tuesday of June and September (and April when the first Tuesday falls in Holy Week), and at the incoming Moderator's church on the first Tuesday of June for the installation of the Moderator.

Clerk:	REV. J. COLIN CASKIE BA BD			11 Ardenconnel Way, Rhu, Helensburgh G84 8LX [E-mail: dumbarton@cofscotland.org.uk]	01436 820213

Alexandria

Elizabeth W. Houston (Miss) MA BD DipEd	1985	1995	32 Ledrish Avenue, Balloch, Alexandria G83 8JB	01389 751933

Arrochar linked with Luss

H. Dane Sherrard BD DMin	1971	1998	The Manse, Luss, Alexandria G83 8NZ [E-mail: dane@cadder.demon.co.uk]	01436 860240 07801 939138 (Mbl)

Baldernock (H)

Andrew P. Lees BD	1984	2002	The Manse, Bardowie, Milngavie, Glasgow G62 6ES [E-mail: thereverenc@alees.fsnet.co.uk]	01360 620471

Bearsden: Baljaffray (H)

Ian McEwan BSc PhD BD FRSE	2008		5 Fintry Gardens, Bearsden, Glasgow G61 4RJ [E-mail: mcewan7@btinternet.com]	0141-942 0366

Bearsden: Cross (H)

John W.F. Harris MA	1967	2006	61 Drymen Road, Bearsden, Glasgow G61 2SU [E-mail: jwfh@bearsdencross.org]	0141-942 0507 07711 573877 (Mbl)

Bearsden: Killermont (H)

Alan J. Hamilton LLB BD	2003		8 Clathic Avenue, Bearsden, Glasgow G61 2HF [E-mail: alanj@hamilton63.freeserve.co.uk]	0141-942 0021

Bearsden: New Kilpatrick (H) (0141-942 8827) (E-mail: mail@nkchurch.org.uk)

David D. Scott BSc BD	1981	1999	51 Manse Road, Bearsden, Glasgow G61 3PN [E-mail: mail@nkchurch.org.uk]	0141-942 0035

Bearsden: Westerton Fairlie Memorial (H) (0141-942 6960)

Christine M. Goldie (Miss) LLB BD MTh	1984	2008	3 Camniesburn Road, Bearsden, Glasgow G61 1PW [E-mail: christine.goldie@ntlworld.com]	0141-942 2672

Bonhill (H) (01389 756516)
Ian H. Miller BA BD — 1975 — 1 Glebe Gardens, Bonhill, Alexandria G83 9NZ [E-mail: ianmiller@bonhillchurch.freeserve.co.uk] — 01389 753039

Cardross (H) (01389 841322)
Andrew J. Scobie MA BD — 1963 1965 — The Manse, Main Road, Cardross, Dumbarton G82 5LB [E-mail: ascobie55@cardross.dunbartonshire.co.uk] — 01389 841289 / 07889 670252 (Mbl)

Clydebank: Abbotsford (E-mail: abbotsford@lineone.net) (Website: www.abbotsford.org.uk)
Roderick G. Hamilton MA BD — 1992 1996 — 35 Montrose Street, Clydebank G81 2PA [E-mail: rghamilton@ntlworld.com] — 0141-952 5151

Clydebank: Faifley
Gregor McIntyre BSc BD — 1991 — Kirklea, Cochno Road, Hardgate, Clydebank G81 6PT [E-mail: mail@gregormcintyre.com] — 01389 876836

Clydebank: Kilbowie St Andrew's
Peggy Roberts (Mrs) BA BD — 2003 — 5 Melfort Avenue, Clydebank G81 2HX [E-mail: peggy.r@ntlworld.com] — 0141-951 2455

Clydebank: Radnor Park (H)
Margaret J.B. Yule (Mrs) BD — 1992 — 11 Tiree Gardens, Old Kilpatrick, Glasgow G60 5AT [E-mail: mjbyule@yahoo.co.uk] — 01389 875599

Clydebank: St Cuthbert's (T) linked with Duntocher (H)
David Donaldson MA BD DMin — 1969 2002 — The Manse, Roman Road, Duntocher, Clydebank G81 6BT [E-mail: david.donaldson3@btopenworld.com] — 01389 873471

Craigrownie linked with Rosneath: St Modan's (H)
Vacant — Edenkiln, Argyll Road, Kilcreggan, Helensburgh G84 0JW — 01436 842274

Dalmuir: Barclay (0141-941 3988)
Fiona E. Maxwell BA BD — 2004 — 16 Parkhall Road, Dalmuir, Clydebank G81 3RJ [E-mail: fionamaxi@btinternet.com] — 0141-941 3317

Dumbarton: Riverside (H) (01389 742551)
Robert J. Watt BD — 1994 2002 — 5 Kirkton Road, Dumbarton G82 4AS [E-mail: robertjwatt@blueyonder.co.uk] — 01389 762512

Dumbarton: St Andrew's (H)
Vacant — 17 Mansewood Drive, Dumbarton G82 3EU — 01389 604259

Dumbarton: West Kirk (H) Vacant			3 Havoc Road, Dumbarton G82 4JW	01389 604840
Duntocher (H) See Clydebank: St Cuthbert's				
Garelochhead (01436 810589) Alastair S. Duncan MA BD	1989		Old School Road, Garelochhead, Helensburgh G84 0AT [E-mail: gpc@churchuk.fsnet.co.uk]	01436 810022
Helensburgh: Park (H) (01436 674825) Gavin McFadyen BEng BD	2006		Park Manse, 35 East Argyle Street, Helensburgh G84 7EL [E-mail: parkchurchminister@tiscali.co.uk]	01436 679970
Helensburgh: St Columba (H) George Vidits BD MTh	2000	2006	46 Suffolk Street, Helensburgh G84 9QZ [E-mail: george.vidits@btinternet.com]	01436 672054
Helensburgh: The West Kirk (H) (01436 676880) David W. Clark MA BD	1975	1986	37 Campbell Street, Helensburgh G84 9NH [E-mail: clarkdw@lineone.net]	01436 674063
Jamestown (H) Norma Moore (Ms) MA BD	1995	2004	26 Kessog's Gardens, Balloch, Alexandria G83 8QJ [E-mail: norma.moore5@btinternet.com]	01389 756447
Kilmaronock Gartocharn Janet P.H. MacMahon (Mrs) MSc BD	1992	2006	Kilmaronock Manse, Alexandria G83 8SB [E-mail: janetmacmhon@yahoo.co.uk]	01360 660295
Luss See Arrochar				
Milngavie: Cairns (H) (0141-956 4868) Andrew Frater BA BD MTh	1987	1994	4 Cairns Drive, Milngavie, Glasgow G62 8AJ [E-mail: office@cairnschurch.org.uk]	0141-956 1717
Milngavie: St Luke's (0141-956 4226) Ramsay B. Shields BA BD	1990	1997	70 Hunter Road, Milngavie, Glasgow G62 7BY [E-mail: rbs@minister.com]	0141-577 9171 (Tel) 0141-577 9181 (Fax)
Milngavie: St Paul's (H) (0141-956 4405) Fergus C. Buchanan MA BD MTh	1982	1988	8 Buchanan Street, Milngavie, Glasgow G62 8DD [E-mail: f.c.buchanan@ntlworld.com]	0141-956 1043

Old Kilpatrick Bowling
Jeanette Whitecross (Mrs) BD   2002   The Manse, 175 Dumbarton Road, Old Kilpatrick, Glasgow G60 5JQ
[E-mail: jwx@hotmail.co.uk]   01389 873130

Renton: Trinity (H)
Vacant   38 Main Street, Renton, Dumbarton G82 4PU   01389 752017

Rhu and Shandon (H)
J. Colin Caskie BA BD   1977 2002   11 Ardenconnel Way, Rhu, Helensburgh G84 8LX
[E-mail: colin@jcaskie.eclipse.co.uk]   01436 820213

Rosneath: St Modan's See Craigrownie

Name			Position	Address	Telephone
Booth, Frederick M. LTh	1970	2005	(Helensburgh: St Columba)	Achnashie Coach House, Clynder, Helensburgh G84 0QD	01436 831522
Britchfield, Alison E.P (Mrs) MA BD	1987	1992	Chaplain: Royal Navy	HMNB, Faslane, Helensburgh G84 8HL	
Crombie, William D. MA BD	1947	1987	(Calton New with St Andrew's)	32 Westbourne Drive, Bearsden, Glasgow G61 4BH	0141-943 0235
Davidson, Professor Robert MA BD DD FRSE	1956	1991	(University of Glasgow)	30 Dungoyne Drive, Bearsden, Glasgow G61 3AP	0141-942 1810
Donaghy, Leslie G. BD DipMin PGCE FSAScot	1990	2004	(Dumbarton: St Andrew's)	130 Dumbuck Road, Dumbarton G82 3LZ	01389 604251
Easton, I.A.G. MA FIPM	1945	1988	Lecturer	6 Edgehill Road, Bearsden, Glasgow G61 3AD	0141-942 4214
Ferguson, Archibald M. MSc PhD CEng FRINA	1989	2004	Auxiliary Minister	The Whins, Barrowfield, Cardross, Dumbarton G82 5NL [E-mail: archieferguson@supanet.com]	01389 841517
Hamilton, David G. MA BD	1971	2004	(Braes of Rannoch with Foss and Rannoch)	79 Finlay Rise, Milngavie, Glasgow G62 6QL [E-mail: davidhamilton@onetel.com]	0141-956 4202
Houston, Peter M. FPhS	1952	1997	(Renfrew: Old)	25 Honeysuckle Lane, Jamestown, Alexandria G83 8PL	01389 721165 (Mbl) 07770 390936
Hudson, Eric V. LTh	1971	2007	(Bearsden: Westerton Fairlie Memorial)	2 Murrayfield Drive, Bearsden, Glasgow G61 1JE	0141-942 6110
Jack, Robert MA BD	1950	1996	(Bearsden: Killermont)	142 Turnhill Drive, Erskine PA8 7AH	0141-812 8370
Kemp, Tina MA		2005	Auxiliary Minister	12 Oaktree Gardens, Dumbarton G82 1EU	01389 730477
Lawson, Alexander H. ThM ThD FPhS	1950	1988	(Clydebank: Kilbowie)	Erskine Park Nursing Home, Bishopton PA7	
McIntyre, J. Ainslie MA BD	1963	1984	(University of Glasgow)	60 Bonnaughton Road, Bearsden, Glasgow G61 4DB [E-mail: jamcintyre@hotmail.com]	0141-942 5143 (Mbl) 07050 295103
Munro, David P. MA BD STM	1953	1996	(Bearsden: North)	14 Birch Road, Killearn, Glasgow G63 9SQ	01360 550098
O'Donnell, Barbara		2007	Auxiliary Minister	Ashbank, 258 Main Street, Alexandria G83 0NU	01389 752356
Ramage, Alistair E. BA ADB CertEd	1996	2004	Auxiliary Minister	6 Claremont Gardens, Milngavie, Glasgow G62 6PG [E-mail: ara3@waitrose.com]	0141-956 2897
Shackleton, Scott J.S. BA BD PhD	1993	1993	Chaplain: Royal Navy	HMS Neptune, HMNB Clyde, Faslane, Helensburgh G84 8HL	
Spence, C.K.O. MC TD MA BD	1949	1983	(Craigrownie)	8B Cairndhu Gardens, Helensburgh G84 8PG	01436 678838

Steven, Harold A.M. LTh FSA Scot   1970 2001   (Baldernock)   9 Cairnhill Road, Bearsden, Glasgow G61 1AT   0141-942 1598
Wright, Malcolm LTh   1970 2003   (Craigrownie with Rosneath: St Modan's)   30 Clairinsh, Drumkinnon Gate, Balloch, Alexandria G83 8SE   01389 720338

DUMBARTON ADDRESSES

Clydebank
Abbotsford   Town Centre
Faifley   Faifley Road
Kilbowie St Andrew's   Kilbowie Road
Radnor Park   Radnor Street
St Cuthbert's   Linnvale

Dumbarton
Riverside   High Street
St Andrew's   Aitkenbar Circle
West Kirk   West Bridgend

Helensburgh
Park   Charlotte Street
St Columba   Sinclair Street
The West Kirk   Colquhoun Square

(19) ARGYLL

Meets at various locations in Argyll on the first Tuesday or Wednesday of March, June, September and December. For details, contact the Presbytery Clerk.

Clerk: MR IAN MACLAGAN LLB FSAScot   Carmonadh, Eastlands Road, Rothesay, Isle of Bute PA20 9JZ   01700 503015
[E-mail: argyll@cofscotland.org.uk]

Depute Clerk: REV. GEORGE G. CRINGLES BD   St Oran's Manse, Connel, Oban PA37 1PJ   01631 710242
[E-mail: george.cringles@btinternet.com]

Treasurer: MRS PAMELA A. GIBSON   Allt Ban, Portsonachan, Dalmally PA33 1BJ   01866 833344
[E-mail: justpam1@tesco.net]

Appin linked with Lismore
Roderick D.M. Campbell TD BD FSAScot   1975   2008   The Manse, Appin PA38 4DD   01631 730206
[E-mail: rdmcampbell@aol.com]

Ardchattan (H)
Jeffrey A. McCormick BD   1984   Ardchattan Manse, North Connel, Oban PA37 1RG   01631 710364
[E-mail: jeff.mcc@virgin.net]

Ardrishaig (H) linked with South Knapdale
David Carruthers BD   1998   The Manse, Park Road, Ardrishaig, Lochgilphead PA30 8HE   01546 603269

Campbeltown: Highland (H)
Michael J. Lind LLB BD   1984   1997   Highland Church Manse, Kirk Street, Campbeltown PA28 6BN   01586 551146
[E-mail: myknan@tescali.co.uk]

Campbeltown: Lorne and Lowland (H)
Philip D. Burroughs BSc BTh DTS   1998   2004   Lorne and Lowland Manse, Castlehill, Campbeltown PA28 6AN   01586 552468
[E-mail: burroughs@btinternet.com]

Kirsty-Ann Burroughs (Mrs)   2007   Lorne and Lowland Manse, Castlehill, Campbeltown PA28 6AN   01586 552468
BA BD CertTheol DRM PhD (Aux)   [E-mail: burroughs@btinternet.com]

Coll linked with Connel
George G. Cringles BD   1981   2002   St Oran's Manse, Connel, Oban PA37 1PJ   (Connel) 01631 710242
[E-mail: george.cringles@btinternet.com]   (Coll) 01879 230366

Colonsay and Oronsay (Website: www.islandchurches.org.uk)
Vacant

Connel See Coll

Craignish linked with Kilbrandon and Kilchattan linked with Kilninver and Kilmelford
T. Alastair McLachlan BSc   1972   2004   The Manse, Kilmelford, Oban PA34 4XA   01852 200565
[E-mail: talastair@btinternet.com]

Cumlodden, Lochfyneside and Lochgair
Roderick MacLeod   1966   1985   Cumlodden Manse, Furnace, Inveraray PA32 8XU   01499 500288
MA BD PhD(Edin) PhD(Open)   [E-mail: revroddy@yahoo.co.uk]

Dunoon: St John's linked with Sandbank (H)
Joseph Stewart LTh   1979   1989   23 Bullwood Road, Dunoon PA23 7QJ   01369 702128
Glenda M. Wilson (Mrs) DCS   1990   2006   108 Sandhaven, Sandbank, Dunoon PA23 8QW   01369 700848
[E-mail: GlendaMWilson@aol.com]

Dunoon: The High Kirk (H) linked with Innellan linked with Toward
Anthony M. Jones   1994   2007   7A Mathieson Lane, Innellan, Dunoon PA23 7SH   01369 830276
BD DPS DipTheol CertMin FRSA   [E-mail: revanthonymjones@amserve.com]
Ruth I. Griffiths (Mrs) (Aux)   2004   Kirkwood, Mathieson Lane, Innellan, Dunoon PA23 7TA   01369 830145
[E-mail: ruthigriffiths@googlemail.com]

Gigha and Cara (H) (GD)
Anne McIvor (Miss) SRD BD   1996   2008   The Manse, Isle of Gigha PA41 7AA   01583 505245
[E-mail: annemcivor@btinternet.com]

Glassary, Kilmartin and Ford linked with North Knapdale
Richard B. West   1994   2005   The Manse, Kilmichael Glassary, Lochgilphead PA31 8QA   01546 606926
[E-mail: richard.west999@btinternet.com]

Glenaray and Inveraray
Vacant — The Manse, Inveraray PA32 8XT — 01499 302060

Glenorchy and Innishael linked with Strathfillan
Elizabeth Gibson (Mrs) MA MLitt BD   2003   2008 — The Manse, Dalmally PA33 1AA [E-mail: lizgibson@phonecoop.coop] — 01838 200386

Innellan (H) See Dunoon: The High Kirk

Iona linked with Kilfinichen and Kilvickeon and the Ross of Mull
Sydney S. Graham BD DipYL MPhil   1987   2004 — The Manse, Bunessan, Isle of Mull PA67 6DW [E-mail: syd@sydgraham.force9.co.uk] — 01681 700227

Jura (GD)
Vacant — Church of Scotland Manse, Craighouse, Isle of Jura PA60 7XG — 01496 820384

Kilarrow (H) linked with Kildalton and Oa (GD) (H)
Vacant — The Manse, Bowmore, Isle of Islay PA43 7LH — 01496 810271

Kilberry linked with Tarbert (H)
Vacant — The Manse, Tarbert, Argyll PA29

Kilbrandon and Kilchattan See Craignish

Kilcalmonell linked with Killean and Kilchenzie (H)
Vacant — The Manse, Muasdale, Tarbert, Argyll PA29 6XD — 01583 421249

Kilchoman (GD) linked with Kilmeny linked with Portnahaven (GD)
Stephen Fulcher BA MA   1993   2003 — The Manse, Port Charlotte, Isle of Islay PA48 7TW [E-mail: scr@fish.co.uk] — 01496 850241

Kilchrenan and Dalavich linked with Muckairn
Vacant — Muckairn Manse, Taynuilt PA35 1HW — 01866 822204

Kildalton and Oa (GD) (H) See Kilarrow

Kilfinan linked with Kilmodan and Colintraive linked with Kyles (H)
David Mitchell BD DipPTheol MSc   1988   2006 — West Cowal Manse, Kames, Tighnabruaich PA21 2AD [E-mail: revdmitchell@yahoo.co.uk] — 01700 811045

Kilfinichen and Kilvickeon and the Ross of Mull See Iona
Killean and Kilchenzie (H) See Kilcalmonell
Kilmeny See Kilchoman
Kilmodan and Colintraive See Kilfinan

Kilmore (GD) and Oban (E-mail: obancofs@btinternet.com) (Website: www.obanchurch.com)
Dugald J.R. Cameron BD DipMin MTh   1990 2007   Kilmore and Oban Manse, Ganavan Road, Oban PA34 5TU   01631 566253

Kilmun (St Munn's) (H) linked with Strone (H) and Ardentinny
Franklin G. Wyatt MA MDiv DMin   1974 2004   The Manse, Blairmore, Dunoon PA23 8TE
[E-mail: shorechurches@btinternet.com]   01369 840313

Kilninver and Kilmelford See Craignish

Kirn (H)
Vacant   Kirn Manse, 13 Dhailling Park, Hunter Street, Kirn, Dunoon PA23 8FK   01369 702256
Glenda M. Wilson (Mrs) DCS   1990 2006   108 Sandhaven, Sandbank, Dunoon PA23 8QW
[E-mail: GlendaMWilson@aol.com]   01369 700848

Kyles See Kilfinan
Lismore See Appin

Lochgilphead
Hilda C. Smith (Miss) MA BD MSc   1992 2005   Parish Church Manse, Manse Brae, Lochgilphead PA31 8QZ
[E-mail: hilda.smith2@btinternet.com]   01546 602238

Lochgoilhead (H) and Kilmorich
James Macfarlane PhD   1991 2000   The Manse, Lochgoilhead, Cairndow PA24 8AA
[E-mail: jmacfarlane@stmac.demon.co.uk]   01301 703059

Muckairn See Kilchrenan

Mull, Isle of, Kilninian and Kilmore linked with Salen (H) and Ulva linked with Tobermory (GD) (H) linked with Torosay (H) and Kinlochspelvie
Robert C. Nelson BA BD   1980 2003   The Manse, Gruline Road, Salen, Aros, Isle of Mull PA72 6JF
[E-mail: robertnelson@onetel.net]   01680 300001

North Knapdale See Glassary, Kilmartin and Ford
Portnahaven See Kilchoman

Rothesay: Trinity (H)
Samuel McC. Harris BA BD   1974 2004   12 Crichton Road, Rothesay, Isle of Bute PA20 9JR   01700 503010

Saddell and Carradale (H) linked with Skipness
John Vischer   1993 2006   The Manse, Carradale, Campbeltown PA28 6QG
[E-mail: j_vischer@yahoo.co.uk]   01583 431253

Salen and Ulva See Mull
Sandbank See Dunoon: St John's
Skipness See Saddell and Carradale
South Knapdale See Ardrishaig

Southend (H)
Martin R. Forrest BA MA BD   1988   2001   St Blaans Manse, Southend, Campbeltown PA28 6RQ   01586 830274
[E-mail: jmr.forrest@btopenworld.com]

Strachur and Strathlachlan
Robert K. Mackenzie MA BD PhD   1976   1998   The Manse, Strachur, Cairndow PA27 8DG   01369 860246
[E-mail: rkmackenzie@strachurmanse.fsnet.co.uk]

Strathfillan See Glenorchy
Strone (H) and Ardentinny See Kilmun
Tarbert See Kilberry

The United Church of Bute
Ian S. Currie MBE BD   1975   2005   10 Bishop Terrace, Rothesay, Isle of Bute PA20 9HF   01700 504502
[E-mail: ianscurrie@tiscali.co.uk]
Raymond Deans DCS   1994   2003   60 Ardmory Road, Rothesay, Isle of Bute PA20 0PG   01700 504893
[E-mail: deans@fisl.co.uk]

Tiree (GD)
Vacant   The Manse, Scarinish, Isle of Tiree PA77 6TN   01879 220377

Tobermory See Mull
Torosay and Kinlochspelvie See Mull
Toward (H) See Dunoon: The High Kirk

Name			Role	Address	Phone
Anderson, David P.	2002	2007	Chaplain: Army	3 Bn The Royal Regiment of Scotland (Black Watch), BFPO 806	
Bell, Douglas W. MA LLB BD	1975	1993	(Alexandria: North)	3 Cairnbaan Lea, Cairnbaan, Lochgilphead PA31 8BA	01546 606815
Bristow, W.H.G. BEd HDipRE DipSpecEd	1951	2002	(Chaplain: Army)	Laith Cottage, Southend, Campbeltown PA28 6RU	01586 830667
Dunlop, Alistair J. MA FSAScot	1965	2004	(Saddell and Carradale)	8 Pipers Road, Cairnbaan, Lochgilphead PA31 8UF [E-mail: dunrevn@btinternet.com]	01546 600316
Erskine, Austin U.	1986	2001	(Anwoth and Girthon with Borgue)	'Anwoth', 8 Dunloskin View, Kirn, Dunoon PA23 8HW	01369 701295
Fenemore, John H.C.	1980	1993	(Edinburgh: Colinton Mains)	Seaford Cottage, 74E Shore Road, Innellan, Dunoon PA23 7TR	01369 830678
Forrest, Alan B. MA	1956	1993	(Uphall: South)	126 Shore Road, Innellan, Dunoon PA23 7SX	01369 830424
Forrest, Janice (Mrs) DCS			Part-time Hospital Chaplain: Campbeltown	St Blaans Manse, Southend, Campbeltown PA28 6RQ	01586 830274
Gibson, Frank S. BL BD STM DSWA DD	1963	1995	(Kilarrow with Kilmeny)	163 Gilbertstoun, Edinburgh EH15 2RG	0131-657 5208
Goss, Alister J. BD	1975	2007	Industrial Chaplain	79 Weymouth Crescent, Gourock PA19 1HR [E-mail: scimwest@hotmail.com]	01475 638944

Name			Charge	Address	Tel.
Grainger, Ian G.	1985	1991	(Maxton with Newtown)	Seaview, Ardtun, Bunessan, Isle of Mull PA67 6DH	01681 700457
Gray, William LTh	1971	2006	(Kilberry with Tarbert)	Lochnagar, Longsdale Road, Oban PA34 5DZ [E-mail: gray98@hotmail.com]	01631 567471
Henderson, Charles M.	1952	1989	(Campbeltown: Highland)	Springbank House, Askomill Walk, Campbeltown PA28 6EP	01586 552759
Henderson, Grahame M. BD	1974	2008	(Kirn)	[E-mail: ghende5884@aol.com]	
Hood, Catriona A.	2006		Auxiliary Minister	2 Bellmhor Court, Campbeltown PA28 6AN	01586 552065
Hood, H. Stanley C. MA BD	1966	2000	(London: Crown Court)	10 Dalriada Place, Kilmichael Glassary, Lochgilphead PA31 8QA	01546 606168
Inglis, Donald B.C. MA MEd BD	1975	2000	(Turriff: St Andrew's)	'Lindores', 11 Bullwood Road, Dunoon PA23 7QJ	01369 701334
Lamont, Archibald	1952	1994	(Kilcalmonell with Skipness)	8 Achlonan, Taynuilt PA35 1JJ	01866 822385
Marshall, Freda (Mrs) BD FCII	1993	2005	(Colonsay and Oronsay with Kilbrandon and Kilchattan)	All Mhaluidh, Glenview, Dalmally PA33 1BE [E-mail: mail@freda.org.uk]	01838 200693
Millar, Margaret R.M. (Miss) BTh	1977	2008	(Kilchrenan and Dalavich with Muckairn)	Fearnoch Cottage, Fearnoch, Taynuilt PA35 1JB [E-mail: macoje@aol.com]	01866 822416
Miller, Harry Galbraith MA BD	1941	1985	(Iona and Ross of Mull)	16 Lobnitz Avenue, Renfrew PA4 0TG	0141-886 2147
Morrison, Angus W. MA BD	1959	1999	(Kildalton and Oa)	1 Livingstone Way, Port Ellen, Isle of Islay PA42 7EP	01496 300043
Pollock, William MA BD PhD	1987	2002	(Isle of Mull Parishes)	Correay, Salen, Aros, Isle of Mull PA72 6JF	01680 300507
Ritchie, Walter M.	1973	1999	(Uphall: South)	Hazel Cottage, Barr Mor View, Kilmartin, Lochgilphead PA31 8UN	01546 510343
Stewart, Jean E. (Mrs)	1983	1989	(Kildalton and Oa)	Tigh-na-Truain, Port Ellen, Isle of Islay PA42 7AH	01496 302068
Taylor, Alan T. BD	1980	2005	(Isle of Mull Parishes)	Erray Road, Tobermory, Isle of Mull PA75 6PS	01688 302496
Troup, Harold J.G. MA	1951	1980	(Garelochhead)	Tighshee, Isle of Iona PA76 6SP	01681 700309
Watson, James LTh	1968	1994	(Bowden with Lilliesleaf)	7 Lochan Avenue, Kirn, Dunoon PA23 8HT	01369 702851
Wilkinson, W. Brian MA BD	1968	2007	(Glenaray and Inveraray)	3 Achlonan, Taynuilt PA35 1JJ [E-mail: brianwilkinson@f2s.com]	01866 822036

Communion Sundays

Church	Sundays	Church	Sundays
Ardrishaig	4th Apr, 1st Nov	Kilarrow	1st Mar, Jun, Sep, Dec
Campbeltown		Kilberry with Tarbert	1st May, Oct
Highland	1st May, Nov	Kilcalmonell	1st Jul, 3rd Nov
Lorne and Lowland	1st May, Nov	Kilchoman	1st Jul, 2nd Dec, Easter
Craignish	1st Jun, Nov	Kildalton	Last Jan, Jun, Oct, Easter
Cumlodden, Lochfyneside and Lochgair	1st May, 3rd Nov	Kilfinan	Last Apr, Oct
Dunoon		Killean and Kilchenzie	1st Mar, Jul, Oct
St John's	1st Mar, Jun, Nov	Kilmeny	2nd May, 3rd Nov
The High Kirk	1st Feb, Jun, Oct	Kilmodan and Colintraive	1st Apr, Sep
Gigha and Cara	1st May, Nov	Kilmun	Last Jun, Nov
Glassary, Kilmartin and Ford	1st Apr, Sep	Kilninver and Kilmelford	Last Feb, Jun, Oct
Glenaray and Inveraray	1st Apr, Jul, Oct, Dec	Kirn	2nd Jun, Oct
Innellan	1st Mar, Jun, Sep, Dec	Kyles	1st May, Nov
Invertussa and Bellanoch	2nd May, Nov	Lochgair	Last Apr, Oct
Jura	Passion Sun, 2nd Jul, 3rd Nov	Lochgilphead	2nd Oct (Gaelic), 1st Apr, Nov

Church	Sundays
Lochgoilhead and Kilmorich	2nd Mar, Jun, Sep, Nov
North Knapdale	1st Aug, Easter
Portnahaven	3rd Oct, 2nd May
Rothesay Trinity	3rd Jul
Saddell and Carradale	1st Feb, Jun, Nov
Sandbank	2nd May, 1st Nov
Skipness	1st Jan, May, Nov
Southend	2nd May, Nov
South Knapdale	1st Jun, Dec
Strachur and Strathlachlan	4th Apr, 1st Nov
Strone and Ardentinny	1st Mar, Apr, 1st Nov
Tayvallich	Last Feb, Jun, Oct
The United Church of Bute	2nd May, Nov
Toward	1st Feb, Jun, Nov
	Last Feb, May, Aug, Nov

(22) FALKIRK

Meets at Larbert Old Parish Church, Falkirk, on the first Tuesday of September, October, November, December, March and May, on the fourth Tuesday of January and on the third Tuesday of June.

Clerk:	REV. JEROME O'BRIEN BA LLB BTh	3 Orchard Grove, Polmont, Falkirk FK2 0XE [E-mail: falkirk@cofscotland.org.uk]	01324 718677 01324 471656 (Presby)
Treasurer:	MR IAN MACDONALD	1 Jones Avenue, Larbert FK5 3ER [E-mail: ian_macdonald1938@hotmail.com]	01324 553603

Airth (H)
Vacant
The Manse, Airth, Falkirk FK2 8LS — 01324 831474

Blackbraes and Shieldhill linked with Muiravonside
Louise J.E. McClements BD — 2008
81 Stevenson Avenue, Polmont, Falkirk FK2 0GU
[E-mail: louise.mcclements@virgin.net] — 01324 717757

Bo'ness: Old (H)
David S. Randall BA BD — 2003
10 Dundas Street, Bo'ness EH51 0DG
[E-mail: dsrandall@blueyonder.co.uk] — 01506 822206

Bo'ness: St Andrew's (Website: www.standonline.org.uk) (01506 825803)
Albert O. Bogle BD MTh — 1981
St Andrew's Manse, 11 Erngath Road, Bo'ness EH51 9DP
[E-mail: albertbogle@mac.com] — 01506 822195

Bonnybridge: St Helen's (H) (01324 815756)
Vacant
133 Falkirk Road, Bonnybridge FK4 1BA — 01324 812621 (Tel/Fax)

Bothkennar and Carronshore
Andrew J. Moore BSc BD — 2007
11 Hunter Place, Greenmount Park, Carronshore, Falkirk FK2 8QS
[E-mail: theminister@themoores.me.uk] — 01324 570525

Brightons (H)
Murdo M. Campbell BD DipMin — 1997 2007
The Manse, Maddiston Road, Brightons, Falkirk FK2 0JP
[E-mail: murdocampbell@hotmail.com] — 01324 712062

Carriden (H)
R. Gordon Reid BSc BD MIEE — 1993
The Spires, Foredale Terrace, Carriden, Bo'ness EH51 9LW — 01506 822141

Cumbernauld: Abronhill (H)
Joyce A. Keyes (Mrs) BD — 1996
26 Ash Road, Cumbernauld, Glasgow G67 3ED — 01236 723833
Linda Black (Miss) BSc DCS — 2003
148 Rowan Road, Cumbernauld, Glasgow G67 3DA — 01236 786265

Cumbernauld: Condorrat (H)
Vacant
11 Rosehill Drive, Cumbernauld, Glasgow G67 4EQ ... 01236 721464

Cumbernauld: Kildrum (H)
Elinor J. Gordon (Miss) BD   1988   2004
64 Southfield Road, Balloch, Cumbernauld, Glasgow G68 9DZ ... 01236 723204
[E-mail: elinorgordon@aol.com]

David Nicholson DCS
2D Doon Side, Kildrum, Cumbernauld, Glasgow G67 2HX ... 01236 732260
[E-mail: deacdave@btopenworld.com]

Cumbernauld: Old (H) (Website: cumbernauldold.org.uk)
Catriona Ogilvie (Mrs) MA BD   1999
The Manse, 23 Baronhill, Cumbernauld, Glasgow G67 2SD ... 01236 721912
Valerie Cuthbertson (Miss) DCS
105 Bellshill Road, Motherwell ML1 3SJ ... 01698 259001

Cumbernauld: St Mungo's
Neil MacKinnon BD   1990   1999
18 Fergusson Road, Cumbernauld, Glasgow G67 1LS ... 01236 721513
[E-mail: neil.mackinnon@homecall.co.uk]
Ronald M. Mackinnon DCS
71 Cromarty Road, Cairnhill, Airdrie ML6 9RL ... 01236 762024

Denny: Dunipace (H)
Jean W. Gallacher (Miss)   1989
BD CMin CTheol DMin
Dunipace Manse, Denny FK6 6QJ ... 01324 824540

Denny: Old
John Murning BD   1988   2002
31 Duke Street, Denny FK6 6NR ... 01324 824508
[E-mail: bridgebuilder@supanet.com]

Denny: Westpark (H) (Website: www.westparkchurch.org.uk)
Andrew Barrie BSc BD   1984   2000
13 Baxter Crescent, Denny FK6 5EZ ... 01324 876224
[E-mail: andrew.barrie@blueyonder.co.uk]
David Wandrum (Aux)   1993   2005
5 Cawder View, Carrickstone Meadows, Cumbernauld,
Glasgow G68 0BN ... 01236 723288

Falkirk: Bainsford
Michael R. Philip BD   1978   2001
1 Valleyview Place, Newcarron Village, Falkirk FK2 7JB ... 01324 621087
[E-mail: mrphilip@btinternet.com]

Falkirk: Camelon (Church office: 01324 870011)
Stuart Sharp MTheol DipPA   2001
30 Cotland Drive, Falkirk FK2 7GE ... 01324 623631
Margaret Corrie (Miss) DCS
44 Sunnyside Street, Falkirk FK1 4BH ... 01324 670656

Falkirk: Erskine (H) Glen D. Macaulay BD	1999	Burnbrae Road, Falkirk FK1 5SD [E-mail: gd.macaulay@blueyonder.co.uk]	01324 623701
Falkirk: Grahamston United (H) Ian Wilkie BD PGCE	2001 2007	16 Cromwell Road, Falkirk FK1 1SF [E-mail: yanbluejeans@aol.com]	01324 624461 07877 803280 (Mbl)
Falkirk: Laurieston linked with Redding and Westquarter Vacant		11 Polmont Road, Laurieston, Falkirk FK2 9QQ	01324 621196
Falkirk: Old and St Modan's (H) Robert S.T. Allan LLB DipLP BD	1991 2003	9 Major's Loan, Falkirk FK1 5QF	01324 625124
Falkirk: St Andrew's West (H) Alastair M. Horne BSc BD	1989 1997	1 Maggiewood's Loan, Falkirk FK1 5SJ	01324 623308
Falkirk: St James' Ronald W. Smith BA BEd BD	1979 2007	13 Wallace Place, Falkirk FK2 7EN	01324 632501
Grangemouth: Abbotsgrange Vacant		8 Naismith Court, Grangemouth FK3 9BQ	01324 482109
Grangemouth: Kirk of the Holy Rood David J. Smith BD DipMin	1992 2003	The Manse, Bowhouse Road, Grangemouth FK3 0EX [E-mail: davidkhrocd@tiscali.co.uk]	01324 471595
Grangemouth: Zetland (H) Ian W. Black MA BD	1976 1991	Ronaldshay Crescent, Grangemouth FK3 9JH	01324 472868
Haggs (H) Helen F. Christie (Mrs) BD	1998	5 Watson Place, Dennyloanhead, Bonnybridge FK4 2BG	01324 813786
Larbert: East Melville D. Crosthwaite BD DipEd DipMin Lorna A. MacDougall (Miss) MA (Aux)	1984 2003	1 Cortachy Avenue, Carron, Falkirk FK2 8DH 34 Millar Place, Carron, Falkirk FK2 8QB	01324 562402 01324 552739
Larbert: Old (H) Clifford A.J. Rennie MA BD	1973	The Manse, 38 South Broomage Avenue, Larbert FK5 3ED	01324 562868
Larbert: West (H) Gavin Boswell BTheol	1993 1999	11 Carronvale Road, Larbert FK5 3LZ	01324 562878

Muiravonside See Blackbraes and Shieldhill

Polmont: Old
Jerome O'Brien BA LLB BTh   2001   2005   3 Orchard Grove, Polmont, Falkirk FK2 0XE   01324 718677

Redding and Westquarter See Falkirk: Laurieston

Slamannan
Raymond Thomson BD DipMin   1992   Slamannan, Falkirk FK1 3EN   01324 851307

Stenhouse and Carron (H)
William Thomson BD   2001   2007   The Manse, 21 Tipperary Place, Stenhousemuir, Larbert FK5 4SX   01324 416628

Name			Charge	Address	Phone
Barclay, Neil W. BSc BEd BD	1986	2006	(Falkirk: Grahamston United)	4 Gibsongray Street, Falkirk FK2 7LN	01324 874681
Blair, Douglas B. LTh	1969	2004	(Grangemouth: Dundas)	Flat 6, Hanover Grange, Forth Street, Grangemouth FK3 8LF	01324 484414
Brown, James BA BD DipHSW DipPsychol	1973	2001	(Abercorn with Dalmeny)	Fern Cottage, 3 Philpingstone Lane, Bo'ness EH51 9JP	01506 822454
Chalmers, George A. MA BD MLitt	1962	2002	(Catrine with Sorn)	3 Cricket Place, Brightons, Falkirk FK2 0HZ	01324 712030
Goodman, Richard A.	1976	1986	(Isle of Mull Associate)	Carrowdale Nursing Home, Beaufort Drive, Falkirk FK2 8SN	01324 551788
Gunn, F. Derek BD	1986	1997	(Falkirk: Bainsford)	6 Yardley Place, Falkirk FK2 7FH	01324 624938
Hardie, Robert K. MA BD	1968	2005	(Stenhouse and Carron)	33 Palace Street, Berwick-upon-Tweed TD15 1HN	01324 711352
Heriot, Charles R. JP BA	1962	1996	(Brightons)	20 Eastcroft Drive, Polmont, Falkirk FK2 0SU	01324 634483
Hill, Stanley LTh	1967	1998	(Muiravonside)	28 Creteil Court, Falkirk FK1 1UL	01324 880109
Holland, John C.	1976	1985	(Strone and Ardentinny)	7 Polmont Park, Polmont, Falkirk FK2 0XT	01324 671489
Kesting, Sheilagh M. (Miss) BA BD	1980	1993	Ecumenical Relations	12 Glenview Drive, Falkirk FK1 5JU	001 242 373 2568
Kirkland, Scott R.McL. BD MAR	1996	2005	Lucaya Presbyterian Kirk, Bahamas	PO Box F-40777, Freeport, Bahamas	001 242 373 4961 (Fax)
McCallum, John	1962	1998	(Falkirk: Irving Camelon)	11 Burnbrae Gardens, Falkirk FK1 5SB	01324 619766
McDonald, William G. MA BD	1959	1975	(Falkirk: Grahamston United)	38 St Mary Street, St Andrews KY16 8AZ	01334 470481
McDowall, Ronald J. BD	1980	2001	(Falkirk: Laurieston with Redding and Westquarter)	'Kailas', Windsor Road, Falkirk FK1 5EJ	01324 871947
McMullin, J. Andrew MA	1960	1996	(Blackbraes and Shieldhill)	33 Eastcroft Drive, Polmont, Falkirk FK2 0SU	01324 624938
Martin, Neil DCS			(Deacon)	3 Strathmiglo Place, Stenhousemuir, Larbert FK5 4UQ	01324 551362
Mathers, Daniel L. BD	1982	2001	(Grangemouth: Charing Cross and West)	10 Ercall Road, Brightons, Falkirk FK2 0RS	01324 872253
Maxton, Ronald M. MA	1955	1995	(Dollar: Associate)	5 Rulley View, Denny FK6 6QQ	01324 825441
Miller, Elsie M. (Miss) DCS			(Deaconess)	30 Swinton Avenue, Rowansbank, Baillieston, Glasgow G69 6JR	0141-771 0857
Munroe, Henry BA LTh LTI	1971	1988	(Denny: Dunipace North with Old)	Viewforth, High Road, Maddiston, Falkirk FK2 0BL	01324 712446
Paul, Iain BSc PhD BD PhD	1976	1991	(Wishaw: Craigneuk and Belhaven)	11 Hope Park Terrace, Larbert Road, Bonnybridge FK4 1DY	
Ross, Evan J. LTh	1986	1998	(Cowdenbeath: West with Mossgreen and Crossgates)	5 Arneil Place, Brightons, Falkirk FK2 0NJ	01324 719936
Scott, Donald H. BA BD	1987	2002	Prison Chaplain	Polmont Young Offenders' Institution, Newlands Road, Brightons, Falkirk FK2 0DE	01324 722241

Smith, Richard BD	1976 2002	(Denny: Old)	Easter Wayside, 46 Kennedy Way, Airth, Falkirk FK2 8GB	01324 831386
			[E-mail: richards@uklinux.net]	
Talman, Hugh MA	1943 1987	(Polmont: Old)	Niagara, 70 Lawers Crescent, Polmont, Falkirk FK2 0QU	01324 711240
Whiteford, Robert S. MA	1945 1986	(Shapinsay)	= Wellside Court, Wellside Place, Falkirk FK1 5RG	01324 610562
Wilson, Phyllis M. (Mrs) DipCom DipRE	1985 2006	(Motherwell: South Dalziel)	'Landemer', 17 Sneddon Place, Airth, Falkirk FK2 8GH	01324 832257
			[E-mail: thomas.wilson38@btinternet.com]	

FALKIRK ADDRESSES

Blackbraes and Shieldhill	Main Street x Anderson Crescent	Haggs	Glasgow Road
Bo'ness: Old	Panbrae Road	Larbert: East	Kirk Avenue
St Andrew's	Grahamsdyke Avenue	Old	Denny Road x Stirling Road
Carriden	Carriden Brae	West	Main Street
Cumbernauld: Abronhill	Larch Road	Muiravonside	off Vellore Road
Condorrat	Main Road	Polmont: Old	Kirk Entry/Bo'ness Road
Kildrum	Clouden Road	Redding and Westquarter	Main Street
Old	Baronhill	Slamannan	Manse Place
St Mungo's	St Mungo's Road	Stenhouse and Carron	Church Street
Denny: Dunipace	Stirling Street		
Old	Denny Cross		
Westpark	Duke Street		
Falkirk: Bainsford	Hendry Street, Bainsford		
Camelon	Dorrator Road		
Erskine	Cockburn Street x Hodge Street		
Grahamston	Bute Street		
Laurieston	Main Falkirk Road		
Old and St Modan's	Kirk Wynd		
St Andrew's West	Newmarket Street		
St James'	Thornhill Road x Firs Street		
Grangemouth: Abbotsgrange	Abbot's Road		
Kirk of the Holy Rood	Bowhouse Road		
Zetland	Ronadshay Crescent		

(23) STIRLING

Meets at the Moderator's church on the second Thursday of September; and at Stirling: Allan Park South Church on the second Thursday of every other month except January, July and August, when there is no meeting.

Clerk:	MISS DOROTHY KINLOCH DL OBE	3 Julia Cottages, Bridgend, Callander FK17 8AE	01877 330238
		Presbytery Office, St Columba's Church, Park Terrace,	01786 449522
		Stirling FK8 2NA	(Mon–Fri: 9:30am–12 noon)
		[E-mail: stirling@eofscotland.org.uk]	
Treasurer:	MR GILMOUR CUTHBERTSON	'Denovan', 1 Doune Road, Dunblane FK15 9AR	01786 823487

Aberfoyle (H) linked with Port of Menteith (H)

Linda Stewart (Mrs) BD	2001	2008	The Manse, Loch Ard Road, Aberfoyle, Stirling FK8 3SZ	01877 382391
			[E-mail: lindacstewart@tiscali.co.uk]	

Alloa: North (H) linked with Alloa: West Elizabeth Clelland (Mrs) BD	2002		30 Claremont, Alloa FK10 2DF [E-mail: liz_clelland@yahoo.co.uk]	01259 210403
Alloa: St Mungo's (H) Alan F.M. Downie MA BD	1977	1996	37A Claremont, Alloa FK10 2DG [E-mail: alan@stmungos.fsnet.co.uk]	01259 213872
Alloa: West See Alloa: North				
Alva James N.R. McNeil BSc BD	1990	1997	The Manse, 34 Ochil Road, Alva FK12 5JT	01259 760262
Balfron linked with Fintry (H) Willem J. Bezuidenhout BA BD MHEd MEd	2007		7 Station Road, Balfron, Glasgow G63 0SX [E-mail: willembezuidenhout@btinternet.com]	01360 440285
Balquhidder linked with Killin and Ardeonaig (H) John Lincoln MPhil BD	1986		The Manse, Killin FK21 8TN [E-mail: coin22@gmail.com]	01567 820247
Bannockburn: Allan (H) (Website: www.allanchurch.org.uk) Jim Landels BD CertMin	1990		The Manse, Bogend Road, Bannockburn, Stirling FK7 8NP [E-mail: revjimlandels@btinternet.com]	01786 814692
Bannockburn: Ladywell (H) Elizabeth M.D. Robertson (Miss) BD CertMin	1997		57 The Firs, Bannockburn FK7 0EG [E-mail: lizrob@talktalk.net]	01786 812467
Bridge of Allan (H) (01786 834155) Gillian Weighton (Mrs) BD STM	1992	2004	29 Keir Street, Bridge of Allan, Stirling FK9 4QJ [E-mail: gillweighton@aol.com]	01786 832753
Buchanan linked with Drymen Alexander J. MacPherson BD	1986	1997	Buchanan Manse, Drymen, Glasgow G63 0AQ [E-mail: revalex@gmail.com]	01360 870212
Buchlyvie (H) linked with Gartmore (H) Elaine H. MacRae (Mrs) BD	1985	2004	The Manse, Kippen, Stirling FK8 3DN [E-mail: ge.macrae@btopenworld.com]	01786 871170

Callander (H) (Tel/Fax: 01877 331409)

Stanley A. Brook BD MTh	1977	2004	3 Aveland Park Road, Callander FK17 8FD [E-mail: stan_brook@hotmail.com]	01877 330097

Cambusbarron: The Bruce Memorial (H)

Brian G. Webster BSc BD	1998	14 Woodside Court, Cambusbarron, Stirling FK7 9PH [E-mail: Revwebby@aol.com]	01786 450579

Clackmannan (H)

Scott Raby LTh	1991	2007	The Manse, Port Street, Clackmannan FK10 4JH [E-mail: minister@clackmannankirk.org]	01259 211255

Cowie (H) and Plean linked with Fallin

Vacant	The Manse, Plean, Stirling FK7 8BX	01786 813287

Dollar (H) linked with Glendevon linked with Muckhart (Website: www.dollarparishchurch.org.uk)

Suzanne G. Fletcher (Mrs) BA MDiv MA	2001	2004	2 Manse Road, Dollar FK14 7AJ [E-mail: revfletcher@btinternet.com]	01259 743432
J. Mary Henderson (Miss) MA BD DipEd PhD (Assoc)	1990	2005	Glebe House, Muckhart, Dollar FK14 7JN [E-mail: jmary.henderson@tiscali.co.uk]	01259 781655

Drymen See Buchanan

Dunblane: Cathedral (H)

Colin G. McIntosh BSc BD	1976	1988	Cathedral Manse, The Cross, Dunblane FK15 0AQ [E-mail: revcolcath@netscape.net]	01786 822205
Sally Foster-Fulton (Mrs) BA BD (Assoc)	1999	2007	21 Craiglea, Causewayhead, Stirling FK9 5EE	01786 463060

Dunblane: St Blane's (H)

Alexander B. Mitchell BD	1981	2003	49 Roman Way, Dunblane FK15 9DJ [E-mail: alex.mitchell@btopenworld.com]	01786 822268

Fallin See Cowie and Plean
Fintry See Balfron

Gargunnock linked with Kilmadock linked with Kincardine-in-Menteith

Richard S. Campbell LTh	1993	2001	The Manse, Gargunnock, Stirling FK8 3BQ [E-mail: revrichards@btinternet.com]	01786 860678

Gartmore See Buchlyvie
Glendevon See Dollar

Killearn (H)

Philip R.M. Malloch LLB BD	1970	1993	2 The Oaks, Killearn, Glasgow G63 9SF [E-mail: pmalloch@mac.com]	01360 550045

Killin and Ardeonaig (H) See Balquhidder
Kilmadock See Gargunnock
Kincardine-in-Menteith See Gargunnock

Kippen (H) linked with Norrieston
Gordon MacRae BD MTh   1985   1998   The Manse, Kippen, Stirling FK8 3DN   01786 870229
[E-mail: ge.macrae@btopenworld.com]

Lecropt (H)
William M. Gilmour MA BD   1969   1983   5 Henderson Street, Bridge of Allan, Stirling FK9 4NA   01786 832382
[E-mail: heleng_fk9@firefly.uk.net]

Logie (H)
R. Stuart M. Fulton BA BD   1991   2006   21 Craiglea, Causewayhead, Stirling FK9 5EE   01786 463060
[E-mail: stuart.fulton@btinternet.com]

Menstrie (H)
Mairi F. Lovett BSc BA DipPS MTh   2005   The Manse, 7 Long Row, Menstrie FK11 7BA   01259 761461
[E-mail: mairi@kanyo.co.uk]

Muckhart See Dollar
Norrieston See Kippen
Port of Menteith See Aberfoyle

Sauchie and Coalsnaughton
Alan T. McKean BD CertMin   1982   2003   19 Graygoran, Sauchie, Alloa FK10 3ET   01259 212037
[E-mail: almack2@freeuk.com]

Stirling: Allan Park South (H) linked with Church of the Holy Rude (H)
Stuart Davidson BD   2008   22 Laurelhill Place, Stirling FK8 2JH   01786 473999
[E-mail: stu2art@msn.com]

Stirling: Church of the Holy Rude (H) See Stirling: Allan Park South

Stirling: North (H) (01786 463376) (Website: www.northparishchurch.com)
Calum Jack BSc BD   2004   18 Shirra's Brae Road, Stirling FK7 0BA   01786 475378
[E-mail: info@northparishchurch.com]

Stirling: St Columba's (H) (01786 449516)
Kenneth G. Russell BD CCE   1986   2001   5 Clifford Road, Stirling FK8 2AQ   01786 475802
[E-mail: kenrussell1000@hotmail.com]

Stirling: St Mark's
Stuart Davidson BD — 2008 — 176 Drip Road, Stirling FK8 1RR [E-mail: stu2art@msn.com] — 01786 473716

Stirling: St Ninians Old (H)
Gary J. McIntyre BD DipMin — 1993 1998 — 7 Randolph Road, Stirling FK8 2AJ [E-mail: garymcintyr-@btopenworld.com] — 01786 474421

Stirling: Viewfield (T) (H)
Vacant — 7 Windsor Place, Stirling FK8 2HY — 01786 474534

Strathblane (H)
Alex H. Green MA BD — 1986 1995 — The Manse, Strathblane, Glasgow G63 9AB — 01360 770226

Tillicoultry (H)
James Cochrane LTh — 1994 2000 — The Manse, Dollar Road, Tillicoultry FK13 6PD [E-mail: jcochrane1@tiscali.co.uk] — 01259 750340 / 01259 752951 (Fax)

Tullibody: St Serf's (H)
Donald M. Thomson BD — 1975 2007 — 16 Menstrie Road, Tullibody, Alloa FK10 2RG [E-mail: donniethomson@tiscali.co.uk] — 01259 729804

Name			Charge	Address / E-mail	Phone
Aitken, E. Douglas MA	1961	1998	(Clackmannan)	1 Dolan Grove, Saline, Dunfermline KY12 9UP [E-mail: douglasaitken14@btinternet.com]	01383 852730
Benson, James W. BA BD DipEd	1975	1996	(Balquhidder)	1 Sunnyside, Dunblane FK15 9HA	01786 822624
Blackley, Jean R.M. (Mrs) BD	1989	2001	(Banton with Twechar)	8 Rodders Grove, Alva FK12 5RR	01259 760198
Brown, James H. BD	1977	2005	(Helensburgh: Park)	1- Gullipen View, Callander FK17 8HN [E-mail: reyjimbrown@yahoo.co.uk]	01877 339425
Brown, T. John MA BD	1995	2006	(Tullibody: St Serf's)	1 Callendar Park Walk, Callendar Grange, Falkirk FK1 1TA [E-mail: johnbrown1cpw@talktalk.net]	01324 617352
Cloggie, June (Mrs)	1997	2006	(Auxiliary Minister: Callander)	1 A Tulipan Crescent, Callander FK17 8AR	01877 331021
Craig, Maxwell D. BD ThM	1966	2000	(Jerusalem: St Andrew's: Locum)	3 Queen's Road, Stirling FK8 2QY [E-mail: maxwellcraig@hotmail.com]	01786 472319
Cruickshank, Alistair A.B. MA	1991	2004	(Auxiliary Minister)	Tistle Cottage, 2A Chapel Place, Dollar FK14 7DW	01259 742549
Doherty, Arthur James DipTh	1957	1993	(Fintry)	1 Murdiston Avenue, Callander FK17 8AY	
Gillespie, Irene C. (Mrs) BD	1991	2007	(Tiree)	3- King O'Muirs Drive, Tullibody, Alloa FK10 3AY [E-mail: revicg@btinternet.com]	01259 723937
Izett, William A.F.	1968	2000	(Law)	1 Duke Street, Clackmannan FK10 4EF	01259 724203
MacCormick, Moira G. BA LTh	1986	2003	(Buchlyvie with Gartmore)	1- Rankine Wynd, Tullibody, Alloa FK10 2UW [E-mail: mmaccormick@compuserve.com]	01259 724619
McCreadie, David W.	1961	1995	(Kirkmabreck)	23 Willoughby Place, Callander PH17 8DG	01877 330785
McIntosh, Hamish N.M. MA	1949	1987	(Fintry)	1 Forth Crescent, Stirling FK8 1LE	01786 470453
Murray, Douglas R. MA BD	1994	2004	(Lausanne)	3- Forth Park, Bridge of Allan, Stirling FK9 5NT [E-mail: d-smurray@supanet.com]	01786 831081
Nicol, John C. MA BD	1965	2002	(Bridge of Allan: Holy Trinity)	3- King O'Muirs Drive, Tullibody, Alloa FK10 3AY [E-mail: jchalmersnicol@aol.com]	01259 212305

Name			Parish	Address	Tel
Ovens, Samuel B. BD	1982	1993	(Slamannan)	21 Bevan Drive, Alva FK12 5PD	01259 222723
Paterson, John L. MA BD STM	1964	2003	(Linlithgow: St Michael's)	'Kirkmichael', 22 Waterfront Way, Stirling FK9 5GH [E-mail: lornandian.paterson@virgin.net]	01786 447165
Pryce, Stuart F.A.	1963	1997	(Dumfries: St George's)	36 Forth Park, Bridge of Allan, Stirling FK9 5NT	01786 831026
Rennie, James B. MA	1959	1992	(Leochel Cushnie and Lynturk with Tough)	17 Oliphant Court, Riverside, Stirling FK8 1US	
Robertson, Alex	1974	1993	(Baldernock)	4 Moray Park, Moray Street, Doune FK16 6DJ	01786 841894
Sangster, Ernest G. BD ThM	1958	1997	(Alva)	6 Law Hill Road, Dollar FK14 7BG	01877 330565
Scott, James F.	1957	1997	(Dyce)	5 Gullipen View, Callander FK17 8HN	01786 825976
Scoular, J. Marshall	1954	1996	(Kippen)	2H Buccleuch Court, Dunblane FK15 0AH	01259 220665
Sherry, George T. LTh	1977	2004	(Menstrie)	37 Moubray Gardens, Silver Meadows, Cambus, Alloa FK10 2NQ [E-mail: georgetaylorsherry@tiscali.co.uk]	
Silcox, John R. BD DipPhilEd CPP CF TD	1976	1984	School Chaplain	Queen Victoria School, Dunblane FK15 0JY	01786 824944
Sinclair, James H. MA BD	1966	2004	(Auchencairn and Kerrick with Buittle and Kelton)	16 Delaney Court, Alloa FK10 1RB	01259 729001
Stewart, Angus T. MA BD PhD	1962	1999	(Glasgow: Greenbank)	Mansefield, Station Road, Buchlyvie, Stirling FK8 3NE	01360 850117
Todd, A. Stewart MA BD DD	1952	1993	(Aberdeen: St Machar's Cathedral)	Ferntoun House, 11 Bedford Place, Alloa FK10 1LJ	01259 212737
Watson, Jean S. (Miss) MA	1993	2004	(Auxiliary Minister)	29 Strachan Crescent, Dollar FK14 7HL	01259 742872
Watt, Robert MA BD	1943	1982	(Aberdeen: Woodside South)	1 Coldstream Avenue, Dunblane FK15 9JN	01786 823632
Wright, John P. BD	1977	2000	(Glasgow: New Govan)	Plane Castle, Airth, Falkirk FK2 8SF	01786 480840

STIRLING ADDRESSES

Allan Park South	Dumbarton Road	St Columba's	Park Terrace
Holy Rude	St John Street	St Mark's	Drip Road
North	Springfield Road	St Ninians Old	Kirk Wynd, St Ninians

Viewfield

Barnton Street

(24) DUNFERMLINE

Meets at Dunfermline in the Abbey Church Hall, Abbey Park Place, on the first Thursday of each month, except January, July and August when there is no meeting, and June when it meets on the last Thursday.

Clerk: REV. ELIZABETH S.S. KENNY BD RGN SCM   The Manse, Carnock, Dunfermline KY12 9JG   01383 850327
[E-mail: dunfermline@cofscotland.org.uk]

Aberdour: St Fillan's (H) (Website: www.stfillans.presbytery.org)

Peter S. Gerbrandy-Baird   2004   St Fillan's Manse, 36 Bellhouse Road, Aberdour, Fife KY3 0TL   01383 861522
MA BD MSc FRSA FRGS

Beath and Cowdenbeath: North (H)
David W. Redmayne BSc BD — 2001 — 10 Stuart Place, Cowdenbeath KY4 9BN — [E-mail: david@redmayne.freeserve.co.uk] — 01383 511033

Cairneyhill (H) (01383 882352) linked with Limekilns (H) (01383 873337)
Norman M. Grant BD — 1990 — The Manse, 10 Church Street, Limekilns, Dunfermline KY11 3HT — [E-mail: norman.grant@which.net] — 01383 872341

Carnock and Oakley (H)
Elizabeth S.S. Kenny BD RGN SCM — 1989 — The Manse, Carnock, Dunfermline KY12 9JG — [E-mail: esskenny@ecosse.net] — 01383 850327

Cowdenbeath: Trinity (H)
David G. Adams BD — 1991 1999 — 66 Barclay Street, Cowdenbeath KY4 9LD — [E-mail: trinity@fsmail.net] — 01383 515089
John Wyllie (Pastoral Assistant) — 51 Seafar Street, Kelty KY4 0JX — 01383 839200

Culross and Torryburn (H)
Vacant — Culross, Dunfermline KY12 8JD — 01383 880231

Dalgety (H) (01383 824092) (E-mail: office@dalgety-church.co.uk) (Website: www.dalgety-church.co.uk)
Donald G.B. McCorkindale BD DipMin — 1992 2000 — 9 St Colme Drive, Dalgety Bay, Dunfermline KY11 9LQ — [E-mail: donald@da.gety-church.co.uk] — 01383 822316 (Tel/Fax)

Dunfermline: Abbey (H) (Website: www.dunfabbey.freeserve.co.uk)
Alistair L. Jessamine MA BD — 1979 1991 — 12 Garvock Hill, Dunfermline KY12 7UU — [E-mail: alistairjessamine@dunfermlineabbey.wanadoo.co.uk] — 01383 721022

Dunfermline: Gillespie Memorial (H) (01383 621253) (E-mail: gillespie.church@btopenworld.com)
Vacant — 4 Killin Court, Dunfermline KY12 7XF — 01383 723329

Dunfermline: North
Ian G. Thom BSc PhD BD — 1990 2007 — 13 Barbour Grove, Dunfermline KY12 9YB — [E-mail: the.thoms@btinternet.com] — 01383 733471
Andrew E. Paterson (Aux) — 6 The Willows, Kelty KY4 0FQ — 01383 830998

Dunfermline: St Andrew's Erskine (01383 841660)
Ann Allison BSc PhD BD — 2000 — 71A Townhill Road, Dunfermline KY12 0BN — [E-mail: revann@sky.com] — 01383 734657

Dunfermline: St Leonard's (01383 620106) (E-mail: stleonards_dunf@lineone.net) (Website: www.stleonardsparishchurch.org.uk)
Andrew J. Philip BSc BD — 1996 2004 — 12 Torvean Place, Dunfermline KY11 4YY — [E-mail: andrewphilip@minister.com] — 01383 721054 (Tel) / 0871 242 5222 (Fax)

Dunfermline: St Margaret's
Iain M. Greenshields
BD DipRS ACMA MSc MTh — 1985 2007 — 38 Garvock Hill, Dunfermline KY12 7UU — 01383 723955
[E-mail: rev_imaclg@hotmail.com]

Dunfermline: St Ninian's
Elizabeth A. Fisk (Mrs) BD — 1996 — 51 St John's Drive, Dunfermline KY12 7TL — 01383 722256
Jacqueline Thomson (Mrs) MTh DCS — 2004 — 1 Barron Terrace, Leven KY8 4DL — 01333 301115

Dunfermline: St Paul's East (New Charge Development)
Vacant — 9 Dover Drive, Dunfermline KY11 8HQ — 01383 620704

Dunfermline: Townhill and Kingseat (H)
Vacant — 161 Main Street, Townhill, Dunfermline KY12 0EZ — 01383 727275

Inverkeithing linked with North Queensferry (T)
Christopher D. Park BSc BD — 1977 2005 — 1 Dover Way, Dunfermline KY11 8HR — 01383 432158
[E-mail: chrispark8649@hotmail.com]

Kelty (Website: www.keltykirk.org.uk)
Lee Messeder BD PgDipMin — 2003 2007 — 15 Arlick Road, Kelty KY4 0BH — 01383 830291
[E-mail: messeder.74@tiscali.co.uk]

Limekilns See Cairneyhill

Lochgelly and Benarty: St Serf's
Elisabeth M. Stenhouse (Ms) BD — 2006 — 82 Main Street, Lochgelly KY5 9AA — 01592 780435
[E-mail: elisabeth@stenhouse.freeserve.co.uk]
Patricia Munro (Miss) BSc DCS — 1986 2007

North Queensferry See Inverkeithing

Rosyth
Violet C.C. McKay (Mrs) BD — 1988 2002 — 42 Woodside Avenue, Rosyth KY11 2LA — 01383 412776
[E-mail: v.mckay@btinternet.com]
Morag Crawford (Miss) MSc DCS — 118 Wester Drylaw Place, Edinburgh EH4 2TG — 0131-332 2253
[E-mail: morag.crawford@virgin.net]

Saline and Blairingone
Robert P. Boyle LTh — 1990 2003 — 8 The Glebe, Saline, Dunfermline KY12 9UT — 01383 853062
[E-mail: boab.boyle@btinternet.com]

Tulliallan and Kincardine

Jock Stein MA BD	1973	2002	(Holm)	62 Toll Road, Kincardine, Alloa FK10 4QZ [E-mail: handsel@dial.pipex.com] 01259 730538
Margaret E. Stein (Mrs) DA BD DipRE	1984	2002	(Holm) Ministries Council	62 Toll Road, Kincardine, Alloa FK10 4QZ [E-mail: handsel@dial.pipex.com] 01259 730538

Name			Charge / Role	Address	Phone
Brown, Peter MA BD FRAScot	1953	1987		2= Inchmickery Avenue, Dalgety Bay, Dunfermline KY11 5NF	01383 822456
Chalmers, John P. BD	1979	1995	Ministries Council	10 Liggars Place, Dunfermline KY12 7XZ	01383 739130
Evans, Mark DCS		2006	Chaplain: Queen Margaret Hospital, Dunfermline	1= Easter Drylaw Drive, Edinburgh EH4 2QA	(Home) 0131-343 3089 (Office) 01383 674136
Farquhar, William E. BA BD	1987	2006	(Dunfermline: Townhill and Kingseat)	29 Queens Drive, Middlewich, Cheshire CW10 0DG	01606 835097
Gisbey, John E. MA BD MSc DipEd	1964	2002	(Thornhill)	Whitemyre House, 28 St Andrews Road, Largoward, Leven KY9 1HZ	01334 840540
Jenkins, Gordon F.C. MA BD PhD	1968	2006	(Dunfermline: North)	5= Porterfield, Comrie, Dunfermline KY12 9XQ	01383 851078
McLellan, Andrew R.C. MA BD STM DD	1970	2002	HM Inspector of Prisons	4 Liggars Place, Dunfermline KY12 7XZ	01383 725959
Macpherson, Stewart M. MA	1953	1990	(Dunfermline: Abbey)	1=6 Halbeath Road, Dunfermline KY11 4LB	01383 722851
Melville, David D. BD	1989	2008	(Kirkconnel)	2= Porterfield, Comrie, Dunfermline KY12 9HJ	01383 850075
Orr, J. McMichael MA BD PhD	1949	1986	(Aberfoyle with Port of Menteith)	9 Overhaven, Limekilns, Dunfermline KY11 3JH	01383 872245
Oswald, John BSc PhD BD	1997	2008	Interim Minister	1 Woodlands Meadow, Rosemount, Blairgowrie PH10 6GZ [E-mail: revdocoz@bigfoot.com]	01250 872598
Reid, A. Gordon BSc BD	1982	2008	(Dunfermline: Gillespie Memorial)	7 Arkleston Crescent, Paisley PA3 4TG [E-mail: reid501@fsmail.net]	(Mbl) 07773 300989
Reid, David MSc LTh FSAScot	1961	1992	(St Monans with Largoward)	North Lethans, Saline, Dunfermline KY12 9TE	01383 733144
Scott, Jayne E. (Mrs) BA MEd		2003	(Principal: SCOC)	13 Covenanters Rise, Dunfermline KY11 8QS	01383 722328
Scott, John LTh	1969	1996	(Aberdour: St Fillan's)	32 White's Quay, St David's Harbour, Dalgety Bay, Dunfermline	01383 820896
Shewan, Frederick D.F. MA BD	1970	2005	(Edinburgh: Muirhouse St Andrew's)	33 Tremayne Place, Dunfermline KY12 9YH	01383 734354
Stuart, Anne (Miss) DCS			(Deaconess)	19 St Colme Crescent, Aberdour, Burntisland KY3 0ST	01383 860049
Taylor, David J. MA BD	1982	2007	(Irongray, Lochrutton and Terregles)	32 Croft an Righ, Inverkeithing KY11 1PF	01383 413227
Vint, Allan S. BSc BD MTh	1989	2008	Mission Development Officer	St Ninian's Church, Allan Crescent, Dunfermline KY11 4HE [E-mail: allan@vint.co.uk]	(Mbl) 07795 483070
Whyte, Isabel H. (Mrs) BD		1993	Chaplain: Queen Margaret Hospital, Dunfermline	14 Carlingnose Point, North Queensferry, Inverkeithing KY11 1ER [E-mail: iainisabel@whytes28.fsnet.co.uk]	01383 410732

(25) KIRKCALDY

Meets at Kirkcaldy, in St Brycedale Hall, on the first Tuesday of February, March, April, May, November and December, on the second Tuesday of September, and on the fourth Tuesday of June.

Clerk:	REV. ROSEMARY FREW (Mrs) MA BD	83 Milton Road, Kirkcaldy KY1 1TP [E-mail: kirkcaldy@cofscotland.org.uk]	01592 260315
Depute Clerk:	MR DOUGLAS G. HAMILL BEM	41 Abbots Mill, Kirkcaldy KY2 5PE [E-mail: hamilldg@tiscali.co.uk]	01592 267500

Auchterderran: St Fothad's linked with Kinglassie

Vacant	7 Woodend Road, Cardenden, Lochgelly KY5 0NE	01592 720213

Auchtertool linked with Kirkcaldy: Linktown (H) (01592 641080)
Catriona M. Morrison (Mrs) MA BD — 1995 2000 — 16 Raith Crescent, Kirkcaldy KY2 5NN [E-mail: cm-morrison@beeb.net] — 01592 265536

Buckhaven (01592 715577) and Wemyss
Wilma Cairns (Miss) BD — 1999 2004 — 181 Wellesley Road, Buckhaven, Leven KY8 1JA [E-mail: wilcairns@aol.com] — 01592 712870

Burntisland (H)
Alan Sharp BSc BD — 1980 2001 — 21 Ramsay Crescent, Burntisland KY3 9JL [E-mail: alansharp03@aol.com] — 01592 874303

Dysart (H)
Tilly Wilson (Miss) MTh — 1990 1998 — 1 School Brae, Dysart, Kirkcaldy KY1 2XB [E-mail: tillywilson@blueyonder.co.uk] — 01592 655887

Glenrothes: Christ's Kirk (H)
Vacant — 12 The Limekilns, Glenrothes KY6 3QJ — 01592 620536

Glenrothes: St Columba's (01592 752539)
Diane L. Hobson (Mrs) BA BD — 2002 2005 — 40 Liberton Drive, Glenrothes KY6 3PB [E-mail: dianehobson.rev@btinternet.com] — 01592 741215
Sarah McDowall (Mrs) DCS — 116 Scott Road, Glenrothes KY6 1AE [E-mail: sarah.e.m@blueyonder.co.uk] — 01592 562386

Glenrothes: St Margaret's (H) (01592 610310)
John P. McLean BSc BPhil BD — 1994 — 8 Alburne Park, Glenrothes KY7 5RB [E-mail: john@mcleanmail.me.uk] — 01592 752241

Glenrothes: St Ninian's (H) (01592 610560) (E-mail: st-ninians@tiscali.co.uk)
Allistair Roy BD DipSW PGDip — 2007 — 1 Cawdor Drive, Glenrothes KY6 2HN [E-mail: alli@stninians.co.uk] — 01592 611963

Innerleven: East (H)
James L. Templeton BSc BD — 1975 — 77 McDonald Street, Methil, Leven KY8 3AJ [E-mail: jamestempleton@btinternet.com] — 01333 426310

Kennoway, Windygates and Balgonie: St Kenneth's (01333 351372) (E-mail: administration@st-kenneths.freeserve.co.uk)
Richard Baxter MA BD — 1997 — 2 Fernhill Gardens, Windygates, Leven KY8 5DZ [E-mail: richard-baxter@msn.com] — 01333 352329
Maureen Paterson (Mrs) BSc (Aux) — 1992 1994 — 91 Dalmahoy Crescent, Kirkcaldy KY2 6TA [E-mail: m.e.paterson@blueyonder.co.uk] — 01592 262300

Kinghorn
James Reid BD — 1985 1997 — 17 Myre Crescent, Kinghorn, Burntisland KY3 9UB [E-mail: jim17reid@aol.com] — 01592 890269

Kinglassie See Auchterderran: St Fothad's

Kirkcaldy: Abbotshall (H)
Rosemary Frew (Mrs) MA BD — 1988 2005 — 83 Milton Road, Kirkcaldy KY1 1TP [E-mail: rosiefrew@blueyonder.co.uk] — 01592 260315

Kirkcaldy: Linktown (01592 641080) See Auchtertool

Kirkcaldy: Pathhead (H) (Tel/Fax: 01592 204635) (E-mail: pathhead@btinternet.com) (Website: www.pathheadparishchurch.co.uk)
Andrew C. Donald BD DPS — 1992 2005 — 73 Loughborough Road, Kirkcaldy KY1 3DD [E-mail: andrewcdonald@blueyonder.co.uk] — 01592 652215

Kirkcaldy: St Andrew's (H)
Vacant — — — 15 Harcourt Road, Kirkcaldy KY2 5HQ — 01592 260816

Kirkcaldy: St Bryce Kirk (H) (01592 640016) (E-mail: office@stbrycekirk.org.uk)
Ken Froude MA BD — 1979 — 6 East Fergus Place, Kirkcaldy KY1 1XT [E-mail: kenfroude@blueyonder.co.uk] — 01592 264480

Kirkcaldy: St John's
Nicola Frail BLE MBA MDiv — 2000 2004 — 25 Bennochy Avenue, Kirkcaldy KY2 5QE [E-mail: nrfscot@hotmail.com] — 01592 263821

Kirkcaldy: Templehall (H)
Anthony J.R. Fowler BSc BD — 1982 2004 — 35 Appin Crescent, Kirkcaldy KY2 6EJ [E-mail: ajrf@btinternet.com] — 01592 260156

Kirkcaldy: Torbain
Ian Elston BD MTh — 1999 — 91 Sauchenbush Road, Kirkcaldy KY2 5RN [E-mail: elston667@btinternet.com] — 01592 263015

Kirkcaldy: Viewforth (H) linked with Thornton
Anne J. Job — 2000 — 66 Viewforth Street, Kirkcaldy KY1 3DJ [E-mail: aj@ajjob.co.uk] — 01592 652502

Leslie: Trinity
Melvyn J. Griffiths BTh DipTheol — 1978 2006 — 4 Valley Drive, Leslie, Glenrothes KY6 3BQ [E-mail: mel@thehavyn.wanadoo.co.uk] — 01592 741008

Leven

| Gilbert C. Nisbet CA BD | 1993 | 2007 | 5 Forman Road, Leven KY8 4HH [E-mail: gcn-leven@blueyonder.co.uk] | 01333 303339 |

Markinch

| Alexander R. Forsyth TD BA MTh | 1973 | 2002 | 7 Guthrie Crescent, Markinch, Glenrothes KY7 6AY [E-mail: forsythar@aol.com] | 01592 758264 |

Methil (H)

| Vacant | | | Alma House, 2 School Brae, Methilhill, Leven KY8 2BT | 01592 713708 |

Methilhill and Denbeath

| Elisabeth F. Cranfield (Miss) MA BD | 1988 | | 9 Chemiss Road, Methilhill, Leven KY8 2BS [E-mail: ecranfield@btinternet.com] | 01592 713142 |

Thornton See Kirkcaldy: Viewforth

Collins, Mitchell BD CPS	1996	2005	(Creich, Flisk and Kilmany with Monimail)	6 Netherby Park, Glenrothes KY6 3PL [E-mail: collinsmit@aol.com]	01592 205622
Connolly, Daniel BD DipTheol DipMin	1983		Army Chaplain	2 CS Reg, RLC, BFPO 47	
Cooper, M.W. MA	1944	1979	(Kirkcaldy: Abbotshall)	Applegarth, Sunny Park, Kinross KY13 7BX	01577 263204
Dick, James S. MA BTh	1988	1997	(Glasgow: Ruchazie)	20 Church Street, Kirkcaldy KY1 2AD [E-mail: jim.s.dick@googlemail.com]	01592 260289
Donald, Kenneth W. BA BD	1982	2008	(Wemyss)	[E-mail: kenneth@kdonald.freeserve.co.uk]	
Duncan, John C. BD MPhil	1987	2001	Army Chaplain	4 Bn The Royal Regiment of Scotland (The Highlanders), St Barbara's Barracks, BFPO 38	
Elston, Peter K.	1963	2000	(Dalgety)	6 Cairngorm Crescent, Kirkcaldy KY2 5RF [E-mail: peterkelston@btinternet.com]	01337 831406
Ferguson, David J.	1966	2001	(Bellie with Speymouth)	4 Russell Gardens, Ladybank, Cupar KY15 7LT	
Forrester, Ian L. MA	1964	1996	(Friockheim, Kinnell with Inverkeilor and Lunan)	8 Bennochy Avenue, Kirkcaldy KY2 5QE	01592 260251
Gatt, David W.	1981	1995	(Thornton)	15 Beech Avenue, Thornton, Kirkcaldy KY1 4AT	01592 774328
Gibson, Ivor MA	1957	1993	(Abercorn with Dalmeny)	15 McInnes Road, Glenrothes KY7 6BA	01592 759982
Gordon, Ian D. LTh	1972	2001	(Markinch)	2 Somerville Way, Glenrothes KY7 5GE	01592 742487
McAlpine, Robin J. BDS BD	1988	1997	Regional Development Officer	10 Seton Place, Kirkcaldy KY2 6UX [E-mail: mcalpine@cofscotland.org.uk]	01592 643518
McDonald, Ian J.M. MA BD	1984	1996	Chaplain, Kirkcaldy Acute Hospitals	11 James Grove, Kirkcaldy KY1 1TN [E-mail: ian.mcdonald@faht.scot.nhs.uk]	01592 203775
McLeod, Alistair G.	1988	2005	(Glenrothes: St Columba's)	13 Greenmantle Way, Glenrothes KY6 3QG [E-mail: aagm@talktalk.net]	01592 744558

MacLeod, Norman	1960	1988	(Orwell with Portmoak)	224 Muirfield Drive, Glenrothes KY6 2PZ	01592 610281
McNaught, Samuel M. MA BD MTh	1968	2002	(Kirkcaldy: St John's)	6 Munro Court, Glenrothes KY7 5GD	01592 742352
				[E-mail: sjmcnaught@btinternet.com]	
Munro, Andrew MA BD PhD	1972	2000	(Glencaple with Lowther)	7 Dunvegan Avenue, Kirkcaldy KY2 5SG	01592 566129
				[E-mail: am.smm@blueyonder.co.uk]	
Sutherland, William	1964	1993	(Bo'ness Old)	88 Dunrobin Road, Kirkcaldy KY2 5YT	01592 205510
Thomson, John D. BD	1985	2005	(Kirkcaldy: Pathhead)	5 Tottenham Court, Hill Street, Dysart, Kirkcaldy KY1 2XY	01592 655313
				[E-mail: j.thomson10@sky.com]	
Tomlinson, Bryan L. TD	1969	2003	(Kirkcaldy: Abbotshall)	2 Duddingston Drive, Kirkcaldy KY2 6JP	01592 564843
				[E-mail: abbkirk@blueyonder.co.uk]	
Webster, Elspeth H. (Miss) DCS			(Deaconess)	82 Broomhill Avenue, Burntisland KY3 0BP	01592 873616

KIRKCALDY ADDRESSES

Abbotshall	Abbotshall Road	Pathhead	Harriet Street x Church Street	Templehall	Beauly Place
Linktown	Nicol Street x High Street	St Andrew's	Victoria Road x Victoria Gdns	Torbain	Lindores Drive
		St Bryce Kirk	St Brycedale Avenue x Kirk Wynd	Viewforth	Viewforth Street x Viewforth Terrace
		St John's	Elgin Street		

(26) ST ANDREWS

Meets at Cupar, in St John's Church Hall, on the second Wednesday of February, March, April, May, September, October, November and December; and on the last Wednesday of June.

Clerk:	REV. JAMES G. REDPATH BD DipPTh			The Manse, Kirk Wynd, Strathmiglo, Cupar KY14 7QS	01337 860256
				[E-mail: standrews@cofscotland.org.uk]	

Abdie and Dunbog (H) linked with Newburgh (H)

Lynn Brady (Miss) BD DipMin	1996	2002	2 Guthrie Court, Capar Road, Newburgh, Cupar KY14 6HA	01337 842228
			[E-mail: lynn@revbrady.freeserve.co.uk]	

Anstruther

Vacant			The James Melville Manse, Anstruther KY10 3EX	01333 311808

Auchtermuchty (H) linked with Edenshead and Strathmiglo

James G. Redpath BD DipPTh	1988	2006	The Manse, Kirk Wynd, Strathmiglo, Cupar KY14 7QS	01337 860256
			[E-mail: james.redpath2@btinternet.com]	

Balmerino (H) linked with Wormit (H)

James Connolly DipTh CertMin MA(Theol)	1982	2004	5 Westwater Place, Newport-on-Tay DD6 8NS	01382 542626
			[E-mail: jim@conrollyuk.wanadoo.co.uk]	

Boarhills and Dunino linked with St Andrews: Martyrs'
Vacant
49 Irvine Crescent, St Andrews KY16 8LG — 01334 472948

Cameron linked with St Andrews: St Leonard's (01334 478702) (E-mail: stlencam@btconnect.com)
Alan D. McDonald LLB BD MTh DLitt DD 1979 1998
1 Cairnhill Gardens, St Andrews KY16 8QY — 01334 472793
[E-mail: alan.d.mcdonald@talk21.com]

Carnbee linked with Pittenweem
Margaret E.S. Rose BD 2007
29 Milton Road, Pittenweem, Anstruther KY10 2LN — 01333 312838
[E-mail: mgt.r@btopenworld.com]

Cellardyke (H) linked with Kilrenny
Vacant
Toll Road, Cellardyke, Anstruther KY10 3BH — 01333 310810

Ceres, Kemback and Springfield
Eric G. McKimmon BA BD MTh 1983 2005
The Manse, St Andrews Road, Ceres, Cupar KY15 5NQ — 01334 829466
[E-mail: McKimmonCeres@aol.com]

Crail linked with Kingsbarns (H)
Michael J. Erskine MA BD 1985 2002
Church Manse, St Andrews Road, Crail, Anstruther KY10 3UH — 01333 450358

Creich, Flisk and Kilmany linked with Monimail
Neil McLay BA BD 2006
Creich Manse, Brunton, Cupar KY15 4PA — 01337 870332
[E-mail: neilmclay@gmail.com]

Cupar: Old (H) and St Michael of Tarvit
Kenneth S. Jeffrey BA BD PhD 2002
76 Hogarth Drive, Cupar KY15 5YH — 01334 653196
[E-mail: ksjeffrey@btopenworld.com]

Cupar: St John's linked with Dairsie
A. Sheila Blount (Mrs) BD BA 1978 2002
23 Hogarth Drive, Cupar KY15 5YH — 01334 656408
[E-mail: asblount@fish.co.uk]

Dairsie See Cupar: St John's
Edenshead and Strathmiglo See Auchtermuchty

Elie (H) linked with Kilconquhar and Colinsburgh (H)
Brian McDowell BA BD 1999 2007
30 Bank Street, Elie, Leven KY9 1BW — 01333 330685

Falkland (01337 858442) linked with Freuchie (H)
George G. Nicol BD DPhil 1982 2006
1 Newton Road, Falkland, Cupar KY15 7AQ — 01337 858557
[E-mail: ggnicol@totalise.co.uk]

Freuchie (H) See Falkland

Howe of Fife				
Gordon A. McCracken BD CertMin DMin	1988	2008	83 Church Street, Ladybank, Cupar KY15 7ND [E-mail: gordonangus@btopenworld.com]	01337 830513
Cameron Harrison (Aux)		2006	Woodfield House, Pitor Muir, St Andrews KY16 8LP	01334 478067

Kilconquhar and Colinsburgh See Elie
Kilrenny See Cellardyke
Kingsbarns See Crail

Largo and Newburn (H) linked with Largo: St David's				
John A.H. Murdoch BA BD DPSS	1979	2006	The Manse, Church Place, Upper Largo, Leven KY8 6EH [E-mail: jm.largo@tiinternet.com]	01333 360286

Largo: St David's See Largo and Newburn

Largoward (H) linked with St Monans (H)				
Donald G. MacEwan MA BD PhD		2001	The Manse, St Monans, Anstruther KY10 2DD [E-mail: maiadona@fish.co.uk]	01333 730258

Leuchars: St Athernase				
Caroline Taylor (Mrs) MA BD	1995	2003	7 David Wilson Park, Balmullo, St Andrews KY16 0NP [E-mail: caro234@tiinternet.com]	01334 870038

Monimail See Creich, Flisk and Kilmany
Newburgh See Abdie and Dunbog

Newport-on-Tay (H)				
W. Kenneth Pryde DA BD		1994	57 Cupar Road, Newport-on-Tay DD6 8DF [E-mail: wkpryde@hotmail.com]	01382 543165 (Tel/Fax)

Pittenweem See Carnbee

St Andrews: Holy Trinity				
Rory MacLeod BA MBA BD	1994	2004	19 Priory Gardens, St Andrews KY16 8XX [E-mail: annicerory@hotmail.com]	01334 461098

St Andrews: Hope Park (H) linked with Strathkinness				
A. David K. Arnott MA BD	1971	1996	20 Priory Gardens, St Andrews KY16 8XX [E-mail: adka@arnetts.wanadoo.co.uk]	01334 472912 (Tel/Fax)

St Andrews: Martyrs' (H) See Boarhills and Dunino
St Andrews: St Leonard's (H) See Cameron
St Monans See Largoward
Strathkinness See St Andrews: Hope Park

Tayport
Colin J. Dempster BD CertMin   1990   27 Bell Street, Tayport DD6 9AP   01382 552861
[E-mail: demps@tayportc.fsnet.co.uk]

Wormit See Balmerino

Name			Charge	Address	Telephone
Alexander, James S. MA BD BA PhD	1966	1973	University of St Andrews	5 Strathkinness High Road, St Andrews KY16 9RP	01334 472680
Bennett, G. Alestair A. TD MA	1938	1976	(Strathkinness)	7 Bonfield Park, Strathkinness, St Andrews KY16 9SY	01334 850249
Bews, James MA	1942	1981	(Dundee: Craigiebank)	21 Baltrymonth Court, St Andrews KY16 8XT	01334 476087
Blount, Graham K. LLB BD PhD	1976	1998	Parliamentary Officer	23 Hogarth Drive, Cupar KY15 5YH	01334 656408
Bradley, Ian MA BD DPhil	1990	1990	University of St Andrews	4 Donaldson Gardens, St Andrews KY16 9DN	01334 475389
Brown, Lawson R. MA	1960	1997	(Cameron with St Andrew's: St Leonard's)	10 Park Street, St Andrews KY16 8AQ	01334 473413
Cameron, James K. MA BD PhD FRHistS	1953	1989	(University of St Andrews)	Priorscroft, 71 Hepburn Gardens, St Andrews KY16 9LS	01334 473996
Cameron, John U. BA BSc PhD BD ThD	1974	2008	(Dundee: Broughty Ferry St Stephen's and West)	10 Howard Place, St Andrews KY16 9HL	01334 474474
Casebow, Brian C. MA BD	1959	1993	(Edinburgh: Salisbury)	'The Rowans', 67 St Michael's Drive, Cupar KY15 5BP	01334 656385
Douglas, Peter C. JP	1966	1993	(Boarhills linked with Dunino)	The Old Schoolhouse, Flisk, Newburgh, Cupar KY14 6HN	01337 870218
Earnshaw, Philip BA BSc BD	1986	1996	(Glasgow: Pollokshields)	22 Castle Street, St Monans, Anstruther KY10 2AP	01333 730640
Edington, George L.	1952	1989	(Tayport)	64B Burghmuir Road, Perth PH1 1LH	
Fairlie, George BD BVMS MRCVS	1971	2002	(Crail with Kingsbarns)	41 Warrack Street, St Andrews KY16 8DR	01334 475868
Fraser, Ann G. BD CertMin	1990	2007	(Auchtermuchty)	24 Irvine Crescent, St Andrews KY16 8LG	01334 461329 (Tel/Fax)
				[E-mail: anngilfraser@btinternet.com]	
Galloway, Robert W.C. LTh	1970	1998	(Cromarty)	22 Haughgate, Leven KY8 4SG	01333 426223
Gibson, Henry M. MA BD PhD	1960	1999	(Dundee: The High Kirk)	4 Comerton Place, Drumoig, Leuchars, St Andrews KY16 0NQ	01382 542199
Gordon, Peter M. MA BD	1958	1995	(Airdrie: West)	3 Cupar Road, Cuparmuir, Cupar KY15 5RH	01334 652341
				[E-mail: machrie@madasafish.com]	
Hegarty, John D. LTh ABSC	1988	2004	(Buckie: South and West with Enzie)	26 Montgomery Way, Kinross KY13 8FD	01577 863829
				[E-mail: john.hegarty@tesco.net]	
Henney, William MA DD	1957	1996	(St Andrews: Hope Park)	30 Doocot Road, St Andrews KY16 9LP	01334 472560
Hill, Roy MA	1962	1997	(Lisbon)	Forgan Cottage, Kinnessburn Road, St Andrews KY16 8AD	01334 472121
Learmonth, Walter LTh	1968	1997	(Ceres with Springfield)	14 Marionfield Place, Cupar KY15 5JN	01334 656290
Lithgow, Thomas MA	1945	1982	(Banchory Devenick with Maryculter)	c/o Milne, Bairds (Lawyers), 7 St Catherine Street, Cupar KY15 4LS	
McCartney, Alexander C. BTh	1973	1995	(Caputh and Clunie with Kinclaven)	10 The Glebe, Crail, Anstruther KY10 3UT	01333 451194
McGregor, Duncan J. MIFM	1982	1996	(Channelkirk with Lauder: Old)	14 Mount Melville, St Andrews KY16 8NG	01334 478314
Macintyre, William J. MA BD DD	1951	1989	(Crail with Kingsbarns)	Tigh a' Ghobhainn, Lochton, Crail, Anstruther KY10 3XE	01333 450327
Mackenzie, A. Cameron MA	1955	1995	(Biggar)	Hedgerow, 5 Shiels Avenue, Freuchie, Cupar KY15 7JD	01337 857763
MacNab, Hamish S.D. MA	1948	1987	(Kilrenny)	Fairhill, Northmuir, Kirriemuir DD8 4PF	01575 572564
Meager, Peter MA BD CertMgmt(Open)	1971	1998	(Elie with Kilconquhar and Colinsburgh)	7 Lorraine Drive, Cupar KY15 5DY	01334 656991
Neilson, Peter MA BD MTh	1975	2006	Mission Consultant	Linne Bheag, 2 School Green, Anstruther KY10 3HF	01333 310477
				[E-mail: neilson.peter@btinternet.com]	07818 418608 (Mbl)
Paton, Iain F. BD FCIS	1980	2006	(Elie with Kilconquhar and Colinsburgh)	Lindisfarne, 19 Links Road, Lundin Links, Leven KY8 6AS	01333 320765

Name			Position	Address	Tel
Porteous, James K. DD	1944	1997	(Cupar: St John's)	16 Market Street, St Andrews KY16 9NS	01334 828509
Reid, Alan A.S. MA BD STM	1962	1995	(Bridge of Allan: Chalmers)	Wayside Cottage, Bridgend, Ceres, Cupar KY15 5LS	0131-225 5722
Robb, Nigel J. FCP MA BD ThM MTh	1981	1998	Associate Secretary: Worship and Doctrine: Mission and Discipleship Council	c/o 121 George Street, Edinburgh EH2 4YN [E-mail: nrobb@cofscotland.org.uk]	
Robertson, Norma P. (Miss) BD DMin MTh	1993	2002	(Kincardine O'Neil with Lumphanan)	82 Hogarth Drive, Cupar KY15 5YU [E-mail: normapr@fish.co.uk]	01334 650595
Roy, Alan J. BSc BD	1960	1999	(Aberuthven with Dunning)	14 Comerton Place, Drumoig, Leuchars, St Andrews KY16 0NQ [E-mail: roma.roy@btopenworld.com]	01382 542225
Salters, Robert B. MA BD PhD	1966	1971	(University of St Andrews)	Vine Cottage, 119 South Street, St Andrews KY16 9UH	01334 473198
Stevenson, A.L. LLB MLitt DPA FPEA	1984	1993	(Balmerino linked with Wormit)	41 Main Street, Dairsie, Cupar KY15 4SR	01334 870582
Strong, Clifford LTh	1983	1995	(Creich, Flisk and Kilmany with Monimail)	60 Maryknowe, Gauldry, Newport-on-Tay DD6 8SL	01382 330445
Taylor, Ian BSc MA LTh DipEd	1983	1997	(Abdie and Dunbog with Newburgh)	Lundie Cottage, Arncroach, Anstruther KY10 2RN	01333 720222
Thomson, P.G. MA BD MTh ThD	1947	1989	(Irvine: Fullarton)	Fullarton, 2 Beech Walk, Crail, Anstruther KY10 3UN	01333 450423
Thrower, Charles G. BSc	1965	2002	(Carnbee with Pittenweem)	Grange House, Wester Grangemuir, Pittenweem, Anstruther KY10 2RB [E-mail: c-thrower@pittenweem2.freeserve.co.uk]	01333 312631
Torrance, Alan J. MA BD DrTheol	1984	1999	University of St Andrews	Kincaple House, Kincaple, St Andrews KY16 9SH	(Home) 01334 850755 (Office) 01334 462843
Turnbull, James J. MA	1940	1981	(Arbirlot with Colliston)	Woodlands, Beech Avenue, Ladybank, Cupar KY15 7NG	01337 830279
Tyre, Robert	1960	1998	(Aberdeen: St Ninian's with Stockethill)	44 Doocot Road, St Andrews KY16 8QP [E-mail: robert@roberttyre.wanadoo.co.uk]	01334 473093
Walker, James B. MA BD DPhil	1975	1993	Chaplain: University of St Andrews	1 Gillespie Terrace, The Scores, St Andrews KY16 9AT [E-mail: james.walker@st-andrews.ac.uk]	(Tel) 01334 462866 (Fax) 01334 462868
Wilson, Robert McL. MA BD PhD DD FBA	1946	1983	(University of St Andrews)	10 Murrayfield Road, St Andrews KY16 9NB	01334 474331
Wotherspoon, Ian G. BA LTh	1967	2004	(Coatbridge: St Andrew's)	11 Bowiehill, Auchtermuchty, Cupar KY14 7AQ [E-mail: wotherspoonrig@aol.com]	01337 827561
Wright, Lynda (Miss) BEd DCS			Deacon: Retreat Leader, Key House	6 Key Cottage, High Street, Falkland, Cupar KY15 7BD	01337 857705
Young, Evelyn M. (Mrs) BSc BD	1984	2003	(Kilmun (St Munn's) with Strone and Ardentinny)	2 Priestden Place, St Andrews KY16 8DP	01334 479662

(27) DUNKELD AND MEIGLE

Meets at Pitlochry on the first Tuesday of September and December, on the third Tuesday of February, April and October, and at the Moderator's church on the third Tuesday of June.

Clerk:	**REV. JOHN RUSSELL MA**	**Kilblaan, Gladstone Terrace, Birnam, Dunkeld PH8 0DP**		**01350 728896**
		[E-mail: dunkeldmeigle@cofscotland.org.uk]		

Aberfeldy (H) linked with Amulree (H) and Strathbraan linked with Dull and Weem (H)
Mark Drane BD   2007   The Manse, Taybridge Terrace, Aberfeldy PH15 2BS   01887 820656
[E-mail: mark_drare@hotmail.co.uk]

Alyth (H)
Sheila M. Kirk BA LLB BD   2007   The Manse, Cambridge Street, Alyth, Blairgowrie PH11 8AW   01828 632104
[E-mail: sheilamkirk@tiscali.co.uk]

Amulree and Strathbraan See Aberfeldy

Ardler, Kettins and Meigle
Vacant   The Manse, Dundee Road, Meigle, Blairgowrie PH12 8SB   01828 640278

Bendochy linked with Coupar Angus: Abbey
Bruce Dempsey BD   1997   Caddam Road, Coupar Angus, Blairgowrie PH13 9EF   01828 627331
[E-mail: revbruce.dempsey@btopenworld.com]
Grace Saunders (Ms) (Aux)   2007   40 Perth Street, Blairgowrie PH10 6DQ   01250 873981

Blair Atholl and Struan linked with Tenandry
Brian Ian Murray BD   2002   Blair Atholl, Pitlochry PH18 5SX   01796 481213
[E-mail: athollkirks@yahoo.co.uk]

Blairgowrie
Harry Mowbray   2003   2008   The Manse, Upper David Street, Blairgowrie PH10 6HB   01250 872146

Braes of Rannoch linked with Foss and Rannoch (H)
Christine A.Y. Ritchie (Mrs) BD DipMin   2002   2005   The Manse, Kinloch Rannoch, Pitlochry PH16 5QA   01882 632381
[E-mail: critchie@fish.co.uk]

Caputh and Clunie (H) linked with Kinclaven (H)
William Ewart BSc BD   1972   2004   Caputh Manse, Caputh, Perth PH1 4JH   01738 710520
[E-mail: ewe@surefish.co.uk]

Coupar Angus: Abbey See Bendochy
Dull and Weem See Aberfeldy

Dunkeld (H)
R. Fraser Penny BA BD   1984   2001   Cathedral Manse, Dunkeld PH8 0AW   01350 727249
[E-mail: fraserpenn@aol.com]   01350 727102 (Fax)

Fortingall and Glenlyon linked with Kenmore and Lawers
Anne J. Brennan BSc BD MTh   1999   The Manse, Balnaskeag, Kenmore, Aberfeldy PH15 2HB   01887 830218
[E-mail: annebrennan@yahoo.co.uk]

Foss and Rannoch See Braes of Rannoch

Grantully, Logierait and Strathtay
Rosemary Legge (Mrs) BSc BD MTh — 1992 2006 — The Manse, Strathtay Pitlochry PH9 0PG [E-mail: GLScofs@a3l.com] — 01887 840251

Kenmore and Lawers (H) See Fortingall and Glenlyon
Kinclaven See Caputh and Clunie

Kirkmichael, Straloch and Glenshee linked with Rattray (H)
Malcolm H. MacRae MA PhD — 1971 2005 — The Manse, Alyth Road, Rattray, Blairgowrie PH10 7HF [E-mail: malcolm.macrae1@btopenworld.com] — 01250 872462

Pitlochry (H) (01796 472160)
Malcolm Ramsay BA LLB DipMin — 1986 1998 — Manse Road, Moulin Pitlochry PH16 5EP [E-mail: malcolmramsay@gracias.eclipse.co.uk] — 01796 472774

Rattray See Kirkmichael, Straloch and Glenshee
Tenandry See Blair Atholl and Struan

Name			Position	Address	Phone
Cassells, Alexander K. MA BD	1961	1997	(Leuchars: St Athernase and Guardbridge)	Balloch Cottage, Keltneyburn, Aberfeldy PH15 2LS	01887 830758
Creegan, Christine M. (Mrs) MTh	1993	2005	(Grantully, Logierait and Strathtay)	Lonaig, 28 Lettoch Terrace, Pitlochry PH16 5BA [E-mail: christine@creegans.co.uk]	01796 472422
Dick, Tom MA	1951	1990	(Dunkeld)	Ivo Dhachaidh, Callybrae, Dunkeld PH8 0EP	01350 727338
Duncan, James BTh FSAScot	1980	1995	(Blair Atholl and Struan)	25 Knockard Avenue, Pitlochry PH16 5JE	01796 474096
Henderson, John D. MA BD	1953	1992	(Cluny with Monymusk)	Aldersyde, George Street, Blairgowrie PH10 6HP	01250 875181
Knox, John W. MTheol	1992	1997	(Lochgelly: Macainsh)	Heatherlea, Main Street, Ardler, Blairgowrie PH12 8SR	01828 640731
McAlister, D.J.B. MA BD PhD	1951	1989	(North Berwick: Blackadder)	2 Duff Avenue, Moulin, Pitlochry PH16 5EN	01796 473591
MacVicar, Kenneth MBE DFC TD MA	1950	1990	(Kenmore with Lawers with Fortingall and Glenlyon)	Ileray, Kenmore, Aberfeldy PH15 2HE	01887 830514
Ormiston, Hugh C. BSc BD MPhil PhD	1969	2004	(Kirkmichael, Straloch and Glenshee with Rattray)	Cedar Lea, Main Road, Woodside, Blairgowrie PH13 9NP	01828 670539
Robertson, Iain M. MA	1967	1992	(Carriden)	St Colme's, Perth Road, Birnam, Dunkeld PH8 0BH	01350 727455
Robertson, Matthew LTh	1968	2002	(Cawdor with Croy and Dalcross)	Inver, Strathtay, Pitlochry PH9 0PG	01887 840780
Russell, John MA	1959	2000	(Tillicoultry)	Kilblaan, Gladstone Terrace, Birnam, Dunkeld PH8 0DP	01350 728896
Shannon, W.G. MA BD	1955	1998	(Pitlochry)	19 Knockard Road, Pitlochry PH16 5HJ	01796 473533
Tait, Thomas W. BD	1972	1997	(Rattray)	20 Cedar Avenue, Blairgowrie PH10 6TT	01250 874833
White, Brock A. LTh	1971	2001	(Kirkcaldy: Templehall)	1 Littlewood Gardens, Blairgowrie PH10 6XZ	01250 870399
Whyte, William B. BD	1973	2003	(Nairn: St Ninian's)	The Old Inn, Park Hill Road, Rattray, Blairgowrie PH10 7DS	01250 874401
Wilson, John M. MA BD	1965	2004	(Altnaharra and Farr)	Eerbice, The Terrace, Blair Atholl, Pitlochry PH18 5SZ	01796 481619
Wilson, Mary D. (Mrs) RGN SCM DTM	1990	2004	(Auxiliary Minister)	Eerbice, The Terrace, Blair Atholl, Pitlochry PH18 5SZ	01796 481619
Young, G. Stuart	1961	1996	(Blairgowrie: St Andrew's)	7 James Place, Stanley, Perth PH1 4PD	01738 828473

(28) PERTH

Meets at Scone: Old, at 7:00pm, in the Elizabeth Ashton Hall, on the second Tuesday of February, March, June, September, November and December in each year.

Clerk: REV. DOUGLAS M. MAIN BD

Presbytery Office: 209 High Street, Perth PH1 5PB   01738 451177
                      [E-mail: perth@cofscotland.org.uk]

Abernethy and Dron and Arngask
Alexander C. Wark MA BD STM   1982   2008   3 Manse Road, Abernethy, Perth PH2 9JP   01738 850607
                                                    [E-mail: alecwark@yahoo.co.uk]

Almondbank Tibbermore linked with Methven and Logiealmond
Philip W. Patterson BMus BD   1999   2008   The Manse, Pitcairngreen, Perth PH1 3EA   01738 583217
                                                    [E-mail: philip.patterson@btinternet.com]

Ardoch (H) linked with Blackford (H)
Stuart D.B. Picken MA BD PhD   1966   2005   3 Millhill Crescent, Greenloaning, Dunblane FK15 0LH   01786 880217
                                                    [E-mail: picken@eikoku.demon.co.uk]

Auchterarder (H)
Michael R.R. Shewan MA BD CPS   1985   1998   24 High Street, Auchterarder, Perth PH3 1DF   01764 662210
                                                    [E-mail: michaelshewan@onetel.net]

Auchtergaven and Moneydie
Iain McFadzean MA BD   1989   2005   Bankfoot, Perth PH1 4BS   01738 787235
                                                    [E-mail: iainmcfadzean@hotmail.com]

Blackford See Ardoch

Cargill Burrelton linked with Collace
Jose R. Carvalho BD   2002   Manse Road, Woodside, Blairgowrie PH13 9NQ   01828 670352
                                                    [E-mail: joecarvalho@btinternet.com]

Cleish (H) linked with Fossoway: St Serf's and Devonside
Joanne G. Finlay (Mrs)   1996   2005   The Manse, Cleish, Kinross KY13 7LR   01577 850231
DipTMus BD AdvDipCouns   [E-mail: joanne.finlay196@btinternet.com]

Collace See Cargill and Burrelton

Comrie (H) linked with Dundurn (H)
Graham McWilliams BSc BD — 2005 — The Manse, Strowan Road, Comrie, Crieff PH6 2ES [E-mail: Themansefamily@aol.com] — 01764 671045 (Tel/Fax)

Crieff (H)
James W. MacDonald BD — 1976 2002 — 8 Strathearn Terrace, Crieff PH7 3AQ [E-mail: rev_up@btinternet.com] — 01764 653907

Dunbarney (H) and Forgandenny
Allan J. Wilson BSc MEd BD — 2007 — Dunbarney Manse, Manse Road, Bridge of Earn, Perth PH2 9DY [E-mail: allanjwilson@dfpchurch.org.uk] — 01738 812211

Dundurn See Comrie

Errol (H) linked with Kilspindie and Rait
Douglas M. Main BD — 1986 2005 — South Bank, Errol, Perth PH2 7PZ [E-mail: revdmain@aol.com] — 01821 642279

Fossoway: St Serf's and Devonside See Cleish

Fowlis Wester, Madderty and Monzie linked with Gask
Eleanor D. Muir (Miss) MTheol DipPTheol — 1986 2008 — Beechview, Abercairney, Crieff PH7 3NF — 01764 652116

Gask (H) See Fowlis Wester, Madderty and Monzie
Kilspindie and Rait See Errol

Kinross (H)
Vacant — 15 Station Road, Kinross KY13 8TG — 01577 862952

Methven and Logiealmond See Almondbank Tibbermore

Muthill (H) linked with Trinity Gask and Kinkell
Vacant — Muthill, Crieff PH5 2AR — 01764 681205

Orwell (H) and Portmoak (H)
Robert G.D.W. Pickles BD MPhil — 2003 — 41 Auld Mart Road, Milnathort, Kinross KY13 9FR [E-mail: robert.pickles1@btopenworld.com] — 01577 863461

Perth: Craigie (H)
Vacant — 46 Abbot Street, Perth PH2 0EE — 01738 623748

Perth: Kinnoull (H)
David I. Souter BD — 1996 2001 — 1 Mount Tabor Avenue, Perth PH2 7BT [E-mail: d.souter@blueyonder.co.uk] — 01738 626046

Perth: Letham St Mark's (H)
James C. Stewart BD DipMin — 1997 — 35 Rose Crescent, Perth PH1 1NT [E-mail: jimstewartrev@lineone.net] — 01738 624167

Kenneth McKay DCS — 11F Balgowan Road, Perth PH1 2JG [E-mail: kennydandcs@hotmail.com] — 01738 621169

Perth: Moncreiffe (T)
Isobel Birrell (Mrs) BD — 1994 1999 — Hiddlehame, 5 Hewat Place, Perth PH1 2UD [E-mail: isobel.birrell@peacenik.co.uk] — 01738 625694

Perth: North (01738 622298)
Vacant — 127 Glasgow Road, Perth PH2 0LU — 01738 625728

Perth: Riverside (New Charge Development)
Grant MacLaughlan BA BD — 1998 2007 — 44 Hay Street, Perth PH1 5HS [E-mail: revgrm@btconnect.com] — 01738 631148

Perth: St John the Baptist's (H) (01738 626159)
Vacant — 15 Comely Bank, Perth PH2 7HU — 01738 621755

Perth: St Leonard's-in-the-Fields and Trinity (H) (01738 632238)
Vacant — 5 Strathearn Terrace, Perth PH2 0LS — 01738 621709

Perth: St Matthew's (Office: 01738 6367757; Vestry: 01738 630725)
Scott Burton BD DipMin — 1999 2007 — 23 Kincarrathie Crescent, Perth PH2 7HH [E-mail: sburton@supanet.com] — 01738 626828

Redgorton and Stanley
Derek G. Lawson LLB BD — 1998 — 22 King Street, Stanley, Perth PH1 4ND [E-mail: dglawson@talktalk.net] — 01738 828247

St Madoes and Kinfauns
Marc F. Bircham BD MTh — 2000 — Glencarse, Perth PH2 7NF [E-mail: mark.bircham@btinternet.com] — 01738 860837

St Martin's linked with Scone: New (H) (01738 553900)
James Gemmell BD MTh — 1999 2007 — 24 Victoria Road, Scone, Perth PH2 6JW [E-mail: james.gemmell3@btinternet.com] — 01738 551467

Scone: New See St Martin's

Scone: Old (H)

J. Bruce Thomson JP MA BD   1972   1983   Burnside, Scone, Perth PH2 6LP   01738 552030
[E-mail: RevBruceThomson@aol.com]

The Stewartry of Strathearn (H) (01738 621674) (E-mail: office@stewartryofstrathearn.org.uk)

Vacant   Manse of Aberdalgie, Aberdalgie, Perth PH2 0QD   01738 625854

Trinity Gask and Kinkell See Muthill

Ballentine, Ann M. (Miss) MA BD	1981	2007	(Kirknewton and East Calder)	17 Nellfield Road, Crieff PH7 3DU [E-mail: ann.ballentine@hotmail.com]	01764 652567
Barr, George K. ARIBA BD PhD	1967	1993	(Uddingston: Viewpark)	7 Tay Avenue, Comrie, Crieff PH6 2PE [E-mail: gbarr2@compuserve.com]	01764 670454
Barr, T. Leslie LTh	1969	1997	(Kinross)	8 Fairfield Road, Kelty KY4 0BY	01383 839330
Bertram, Thomas A.	1972	1995	(Patna: Waterside)	3 Scrimgeours Corner, 29 West High Street, Crieff PH7 4AP	01764 652066
Birrell, John M. MA LLB BD	1974	1996	Hospital Chaplain: Perth Royal Infirmary	'Hiddlehame', 5 Hewat Place, Perth PH1 2UD [E-mail: john.birrell@nhs.net]	01738 625694
Brown, Elizabeth (Mrs)	1996	2007	(Perth: St John the Baptist's)	8 Viewlands Place, Perth PH1 1BS [E-mail: liz.brown@blueyonder.co.uk]	01738 552391
Buchan, William DipTheol BD	1987	2001	(Kilwinning: Abbey)	34 Bridgewater Avenue, Auchterarder PH3 1DQ [E-mail: wbuchan3@aol.com]	01764 660306
Cairns, Evelyn BD	2004		Chaplain: Rachel House	15 Tala Park, Kinross KY13 8AB [E-mail: revelyn@chas.org.uk]	01577 863990
Campbell, Andrew B. BD DPS MTh	1979	2006	Mission and Discipleship Council	'L.ndisfarne', 4 Nellfield Road, Crieff PH7 3DN [E-mail: acampbell@cofscotland.org.uk]	01764 653299
Carr, W. Stanley MA	1951	1991	(Largs: St Columba's)	16 Gannochy Walk, Perth PH2 7LW	01738 627422
Coleman, Sidney H. BA BD MTh	1961	2001	(Glasgow: Merrylea)	'Blaven', 11 Clyde Place, Perth PH2 0EZ [E-mail: sidney.coleman@blueyonder.co.uk]	01738 565072
Craig, Joan H. (Miss) MTheol	1986	2005	(Orkney: East Mainland)	7 Jedburgh Place, Perth PH1 1SJ [E-mail: joanhcraig@bigfoot.com]	01738 580180
Donaldson, Robert B. BSocSc	1953	1997	(Kilchoman with Portnahaven)	11 Strathearn Court, Crieff PH7 3DS	01764 654976
Drummond, Alfred G. BD DMin	1991	2006	Scottish General Secretary: Evangelical Alliance	10 Errochty Court, Perth PH1 2SU	
Fleming, Hamish K. MA	1966	2001	(Banchory Ternan: East)	36 Earnmuir Road, Comrie, Crieff PH6 2EY	01764 679178
Galbraith, W. James L. BSc BD MICE	1973	1996	(Kilchrenan and Dalavich with Muckairn)	1 Mayfield Gardens, Milnathort, Kinross KY13 9GD	01577 863887
Gaston, A. Ray C. MA BD	1969	2002	(Leuchars: St Athernase)	'Hamewith', 13 Manse Road, Dollar FK14 7AL	01259 743202
Gregory, J.C. LTh	1968	1992	(Blantyre: St Andrew's)	2 Southlands Road, Auchterarder PH3 1BA	01764 664594
Grimson, John A. MA	1950	1986	(Glasgow: Wellington: Associate)	29 Highland Road, Turret Park, Crieff PH7 4LE	01764 653063
Gunn, Alexander M. MA BD	1967	2006	(Aberfeldy with Amulree and Strathbraan with Dull and Weem)	'Navarone', 12 Cornhill Road, Perth PH1 1LR [E-mail: sandygunn@btinternet.com]	01738 443216
Halliday, Archibald R. BD MTh	1964	1999	(Duffus, Spynie and Hopeman)	2 Pittenzie Place, Crieff PH7 3JL	01764 656464
Henry, Malcolm N. MA BD	1951	1987	(Perth: Craigie)	Kelton, Castle Douglas DG7 1RU	01556 504144
Houston, Alexander McR.	1939	1977	(Tibbermore)	120 Glasgow Road, Perth PH2 0LU	01738 628056
Hughes, Clifford E. MA BD	1993	2001	(Haddington: St Mary's)	Pavilion Cottage, Briglands, Rumbling Bridge, Kinross KY13 0PS	01577 840506

Name			Charge	Address	Tel
Kelly, T. Clifford	1973	1995	(Ferintosh)	20 Whinfield Drive, Kinross KY13 8UB	01577 864946
Lawson, James B. MA BD	1961	2002	(South Uist)	4 Cowden Way, Comrie, Crieff PH6 2NW [E-mail: james.lawson7@btopenworld.com]	01764 679180
Lawson, Ronald G. MA BD	1964	1999	(Greenock: Wellpark Mid Kirk)	6 East Brougham Street, Stanley, Perth PH1 4NJ	01738 828871
Low, J.E. Stewart MA	1957	1997	(Tarbat)	15 Stormont Place, Scone, Perth PH2 6SR	01738 552023
McCormick, Alastair F.	1962	1998	(Creich with Rosehall)	14 Balmanno Park, Bridge of Earn, Perth PH2 9RJ	01738 813588
McGregor, William LTh	1987	2003	(Auchtergaven and Moneydie)	'Ard Choille', 7 Taypark Road, Luncarty, Perth PH1 3FE [E-mail: bill.mcgregor@dsl.pipex.com]	01738 827866
MacKenzie, Donald W. MA	1941	1983	(Auchterarder: The Barony)	81 Kingswell Terrace, Perth PH1 2DA	01738 633716
MacLean, Nigel R. MA BD	1940	1986	(Perth: St Paul's)	9 Hay Street, Perth PH1 5HS	01738 626728
MacMillan, Riada M. (Mrs) BD	1991	1998	(Perth: Craigend Moncreiffe with Rhynd)	73 Muirend Gardens, Perth PH1 1JR	01738 628867
McNaughton, David J.H. BA CA	1976	1995	(Killin and Ardeonaig)	30 Hollybush Road, Crieff PH7 3HB	01764 653028
McQuilken, John E. MA BD	1969	1992	(Glenaray and Inveraray)	18 Clark Terrace, Crieff PH7 3QE	01764 655764
Millar, Alexander M. MA BD MBA	1980	2001	Associate Secretary: Mission and Discipleship Council	c/o 121 George Street, Edinburgh EH2 4YN [E-mail: amillar@cofscotland.org.uk]	0131-225 5722
Millar, Archibald E. DipTh	1965	1991	(Perth: St Stephen's)	7 Maple Place, Perth PH1 1RT	01738 621813
Millar, Jennifer M. (Mrs) BD DipMin	1986	1995	Teacher: Religious and Moral Education	17 Mapledene Road, Scone, Perth PH2 6NX	01738 550270
Munro, Gillian (Miss) BSc BD	1989	2003	Head of Department of Spiritual Care, NHS Tayside	Royal Dundee Liff Hospital, Liff, Dundee DD2 5ND	01382 423116
Pattison, Kenneth J. MA BD STM	1967	2004	(Kilmuir and Logie Easter)	2 Castle Way, St Madoes, Glencarse, Perth PH2 7NY [E-mail: k_pattison@btinternet.com]	01738 860340
Reid, David T. BA BD	1954	1993	(Cleish with Fossoway: St Serf's and Devonside)	Benarty, Wester Balgedie, Kinross KY13 9HE	01592 840214
Robertson, Thomas G.M. LTh	1971	2004	(Edenshead and Strathmiglo)	23 Muirend Avenue, Perth PH1 1JL	01738 624432
Shirra, James MA	1945	1987	(St Martin's with Scone: New)	17 Dunbarney Avenue, Bridge of Earn, Perth PH2 9BP	01738 812610
Simpson, James A. BSc BD STM DD	1960	2000	(Dornoch Cathedral)	'Dornoch', Perth Road, Bankfoot, Perth PH1 4ED [E-mail: dr.j.simpson@btinternet.com]	01738 787710
Sloan, Robert P. MA BD	1968	2007	(Braemar and Crathie)	1 Broomhill Avenue, Perth PH1 1EN [E-mail: sloans1@btinternet.com]	01738 443904
Stenhouse, W. Duncan MA BD	1989	2006	(Dunbarney and Forgandenny)	32 Sandport Gait, Kinross KY13 8FB [E-mail: duncan.stenhouse@btinternet.com]	01577 866992
Stewart, Anne E. (Mrs) BD CertMin	1998		Prison Chaplain	35 Rose Crescent, Perth PH1 1NT [E-mail: jahare06@tiscali.co.uk]	01738 624167
Stewart, Gordon G. MA	1961	2000	(Perth: St Leonard's-in-the-Fields and Trinity)	'Balnoe', South Street, Rattray, Blairgowrie PH10 7BZ	01250 870626
Stewart, Robin J. MA BD STM	1959	1995	(Orwell with Portmoak)	'Oakbrae', Perth Road, Murthly, Perth PH1 4HF	01738 710220
Tait, Henry A.G. MA BD	1966	1997	(Crieff: South and Monzievaird)	14 Shieling Hill Place, Crieff PH7 4ER	01764 652325
Taylor, A.H.S. MA BD	1957	1992	(Brydekirk with Hoddam)	41 Anderson Drive, Perth PH1 1LF	01738 626579
Thomson, Peter D. MA BD	1968	2004	(Comrie with Dundurn)	34 Queen Street, Perth PH2 0EJ [E-mail: rev.pdt@blueyonder.co.uk]	01738 622418
Williamson, Colin R. LLB BD	1972	2008	(The Stewartry of Strathearn)	McCavitt's Loaning, Shanrod Road, Balloolymore, Katesbridge, Co. Down BT32 5PG	

PERTH ADDRESSES

Craigie	Abbot Street	Letham St Mark's	Rannoch Road	St John's	St John's Street
Kinnoull	Dundee Rd near Queen's Bridge	Moncreiffe	Glenbruar Crescent	St Leonard's-in-the-Fields and Trinity	Marshall Place
		North	Mill Street near Kinnoull Street	St Matthew's	Tay Street
		Riverside	Bute Drive		

(29) DUNDEE

Meets at Dundee, Meadowside St Paul's Church Halls, Nethergate, on the second Wednesday of February, March, May, September, November and December, and on the fourth Wednesday of June.

Clerk: REV. JAMES L. WILSON BD CPS   [E-mail: dundee@cofscotland.org.uk]   **01382 459249** (Home)
[E-mail: r3vjw@aol.com]   07885 618659 (Mobile)

Presbytery Office: Whitfield Parish Church, Haddington Crescent, Dundee DD4 0NA   **01382 503012**

Abernyte linked with Inchture and Kinnaird linked with Longforgan (H)
Ian McIlroy BSS BD   1996   2006   The Manse, Longforgan, Dundee DD2 5EU   01382 360238
[E-mail: ian.mcilroy@dundeepresbytery.org.uk]

Auchterhouse (H) linked with Murroes and Tealing (T)
David A. Collins BSc BD   1993   2006   New Kirk Manse, 25 Ballinard Gardens, Broughty Ferry,   01382 778874
Dundee DD5 1BZ
[E-mail: david.collins@dundeepresbytery.org.uk]

Dundee: Balgay (H)
George K. Robson LTh DPS BA   1983   1987   150 City Road, Dundee DD2 2PW   01382 668806
[E-mail: george.robson@dundeepresbytery.org.uk]

Dundee: Barnhill St Margaret's (H) (01382 737294) (E-mail: church.office@btconnect.com)
Vacant   The Manse, Invermark Terrace, Broughty Ferry, Dundee DD5 2QU   01382 779278

Dundee: Broughty Ferry New Kirk (H)
Catherine E.E. Collins (Mrs) MA BD   1993   2006   New Kirk Manse, 25 Ballinard Gardens, Broughty Ferry,   01382 778874
Dundee DD5 1BZ
[E-mail: catherine.col ins@dundeepresbytery.org.uk]

Dundee: Broughty Ferry St James' (H)
Alberto A. de Paula BD MTh   1991   2005   2 Ferry Road, Monifieth, Dundee DD5 4NT   01382 534468
[E-mail: alberto.depaula@dundeepresbytery.org.uk]

Dundee: Broughty Ferry St Luke's and Queen Street (01382 770329)
C. Graham Taylor BSc BD FIAB   2001   22 Albert Road, Broughty Ferry, Dundee DD5 1AZ   01382 779212
[E-mail: graham.taylor@dundeepresbytery.org.uk]

Dundee: Broughty Ferry St Stephen's and West (H)
Vacant — 33 Camperdown Street, Broughty Ferry, Dundee DD5 3AA — 01382 477403

Dundee: Camperdown (H) (01382 623958)
Vacant — Camperdown Manse, Myrekirk Road, Dundee DD2 4SF — 01382 621383

Dundee: Chalmers Ardler (H)
Kenneth D. Stott MA BD — 1989 1997 — The Manse, Turnberry Avenue, Dundee DD2 3TP [E-mail: arkstotts@aol.com] — 01382 827439
Jane Martin (Miss) DCS — 16 Wentworth Road, Ardler, Dundee DD2 8SD — 01382 813786

Dundee: Clepington and Fairmuir
Vacant — 9 Abercorn Street, Dundee DD4 7HY — 01382 458314

Dundee: Craigiebank (H) (01382 731173) linked with Dundee: Douglas and Mid Craigie
Vacant — 16 Silverbutton Yard, Dundee DD4 9RL
Edith F. McMillan (Mrs) MA BD (Assoc) — 1981 — 19 Americanmuir Road, Dundee DD3 9AA — 01382 812423
Jeannie Allan (Mrs) DCS — 2005 — 12C Hindmarsh Avenue, Dundee DD3 7LW — 01382 827299

Dundee: Douglas and Mid Craigie See Dundee: Craigiebank

Dundee: Downfield South (H) (01382 810624)
Vacant — 15 Elgin Street, Dundee DD3 8NL — 01382 889498

Dundee: Dundee (St Mary's) (H) (01382 226271)
Keith F. Hall MA BD — 1980 1994 — 33 Strathern Road, West Ferry, Dundee DD5 1PP — 01382 778808

Dundee: Fintry Parish Church (01382 508191)
Colin M. Brough BSc BD — 1998 2002 — 4 Clive Street, Dundee DD4 7AW [E-mail: colin.brough@dundeepresbytery.org.uk] — 01382 458629

Dundee: Lochee (H)
Hazel Wilson (Ms) MA BD DipEd DMS — 1991 2006 — 32 Clayhills Drive, Dundee DD2 1SX [E-mail: hazel.wilson@dundeepresbytery.org.uk] — 01382 561989

Dundee: Logie and St John's Cross (H) (01382 668514)
David S. Scott MA BD — 1987 1999 — 7 Hyndford Street, Dundee DD2 1HQ [E-mail: david.scott@dundeepresbytery.org.uk] — 01382 641572

Dundee: Mains (H) (01382 812166)
John M. Pickering BSc BD DipEd — 1997 2004 — 9 Elgin Street, Dundee DD3 8NL — 01382 827207

Dundee: Meadowside St Paul's (H) (01382 202255)

Maudeen I. MacDougall (Miss) BA BD	1978		36 Blackness Avenue, Dundee DD2 1HH	01382 668828

Dundee: Menzieshill

Harry J. Brown LTh	1991	1996	The Manse, Charleston Drive, Dundee DD2 4ED [E-mail: harrybrown@aol.com]	01382 667446
David Sutherland (Aux)			6 Cromarty Drive, Dundee DD2 2UQ [E-mail: dave.sutherland@dundeepresbytery.org.uk]	01382 621473

Dundee: St Andrew's (H) (01382 224860)

Ian D. Petrie MA BD	1970	1986	77 Blackness Avenue, Dundee DD2 1JN [E-mail: ian.petrie@dundeepresbytery.org.uk]	01382 641695

Dundee: St David's High Kirk (H)

Marion J. Paton (Miss) BMus BD	1991	2007	6 Adelaide Place, Dundee DD3 6LF [E-mail: marion.paton@dundeepresbytery.org.uk]	01382 203788

Dundee: Steeple (H) (01382 223880)

David M. Clark MA BD	1989	2000	128 Arbroath Road, Dundee DD4 7HR [E-mail: david.clark@dundeepresbytery.org.uk]	01382 455411

Dundee: Stobswell (H) (01382 461397)

William McLaren MA BD	1990	2007	23 Shamrock Street, Dundee DD4 7AH [E-mail: william.mclaren@dundeepresbytery.org.uk]	01382 459119

Dundee: Strathmartine (H) (01382 825817)

Stewart McMillan BD	1983	1990	19 Americanmuir Road, Dundee DD3 9AA	01382 812423

Dundee: Trinity (H) (01382 459997)

David J.H. Laing BD DPS	1976	2008	5 Castlewood Avenue, Emmock Woods, The Barns of Claverhouse, Dundee DD4 9FP [E-mail: edlaing@tiscali.co.uk]	01382 506151

Dundee: West

Andrew T. Greaves BD	1985	2000	Manse of Dundee West Church, Wards of Keithock, by Brechin DD9 7PZ [E-mail: andrew.greaves@dundeepresbytery.org.uk]	01356 624479

Dundee: Whitfield (E) (H) (01382 503012) (New Charge Development)

James L. Wilson BD CPS	1986	2001	53 Old Craigie Road, Dundee DD4 7JD [E-mail: r3vjw@aol.com]	01382 459249

Fowlis and Liff linked with Lundie and Muirhead of Liff (H)

Donna M. Hays (Mrs) MTheol DipEd DipTMHA	2004		149 Coupar Angus Road, Muirhead of Liff, Dundee DD2 5QN [E-mail: dmhays32@aol.com]	01382 580210

Inchture and Kinnaird See Abernyte

Invergowrie (H)
Robert J. Ramsay LLB NP BD   1986   1997   2 Boniface Place, Invergowrie, Dundee DD2 5DW   01382 561118
[E-mail: robert.ramsay@dundeepresbytery.org.uk]

Longforgan See Abernyte
Lundie and Muirhead of Liff See Fowlis and Liff

Monifieth (H)
Vacant   St Rule's Manse, Church Street, Monifieth, Dundee DD5 4JP   01382 532607
Donald W. Fraser MA   1958   1959   Queen Street, Monifieth, Dundee DD5 4HG   01382 532646
[E-mail: donald.fraser@dundeepresbytery.org.uk]
David B. Jamieson MA BD STM   1974   8A Albert Street, Monifieth, Dundee DD5 4JS   01382 532772
(New charge formed by the union of Monifieth: Panmure, Monifieth: St Rule's and Monifieth: South)

Monikie and Newbigging
Vacant   59B Broomwell Gardens, Monikie, Dundee DD5 3QP   01382 370200

Murroes and Tealing See Auchterhouse

Barrett, Leslie M. BD FRICS	1991	2001	Chaplain: University of Abertay, Dundee	Dunelm Cottage, Logie, Cupar KY15 4SJ [E-mail: l.barrett@abertay.ac.uk]	01334 870396
Campbell, Gordon MA BD CDipAF DipHSM MCMI MIHM AFRIN FRSGS FRGS FSAScot				2 Falkland Place, Kingoodie, Invergowrie, Dundee DD2 5DY [E-mail: gordon.campbell@dundeepresbytery.org.uk]	01382 561383
Clarkson, Robert G.	1950	1989	Auxiliary Minister: Chaplain: University of Dundee (Dundee: Strathmartine)	320 Strathmartine Road, Dundee DD3 8QG [E-mail: rob.gov@virgin.net]	01382 825380
Craik, Sheila (Mrs) BD	1989	2001	(Dundee: Camperdown)	35 Haldane Terrace, Dundee DD3 0HT	01382 802078
Cramb, Erik M. LTh	1973	1989	(Industrial Mission Organiser)	Flat 35, Braehead, Methven Walk, Dundee DD2 3FJ [E-mail: erikcramb@aol.com]	01382 526196
Donald, Robert M. LTh BA	1969	2005	(Kilmodan and Colintraive)	2 Blacklaw Drive, Birkhill, Dundee DD2 5RJ [E-mail: robbie.donald@dundeepresbytery.org.uk]	01382 581337
Douglas, Fiona C. (Miss) MA BD PhD	1989	1997	Chaplain: University of Dundee	10 Springfield, Dundee DD1 4JE	01382 344157
Ferguson, John F. MA BD	1987	2001	(Perth: Kinnoull)	10 Glamis Crescent, Inchture, Perth PH14 9QU	01828 687881
Foggie, Janet P. MA BD PhD	2003		Chaplain: Royal Victoria Hospital	39 Tullideph Road, Dundee DD2 2JD	01382 660152
Gammack, George BD	1985	1999	(Dundee: Whitfield)	13A Hill Street, Broughty Ferry, Dundee DD5 2JP	01382 778636
Hawdon, John E. BA MTh AICS	1961	1995	(Dundee: Clepington)	53 Hillside Road, Dundee DD2 1QT [E-mail: john.hawdon@dundeepresbytery.org.uk]	01382 646212
Hudson, J. Harrison DipTh MA BD	1961	1999	(Dundee: St Peter's McCheyne)	22 Hamilton Avenue, Tayport DD6 9BW	01382 552052
Ingram, J.R.	1954	1978	(Chaplain: RAF)	48 Marlee Road, Broughty Ferry, Dundee DD5 3EX	01382 736400
Kay, Elizabeth (Miss) DipYCS	1993	2007	(Auxiliary Minister)	1 Kintail Walk, Inchture, Perth PH14 9RY [E-mail: liz.kay@dundeepresbytery.org.uk]	01828 686029

Name			Role	Address	Phone
Laidlaw, John J. MA	1964	1973	(Adviser in Religious Education)	14 Dalhousie Road, Barnhill, Dundee DD5 2SQ	01382 477458
McLeod, David C. BSc MEng BD	1969	2001	(Dundee: Fairmuir)	6 Carseview Gardens, Dundee DD2 1NE	01382 641371
McMillan, Charles D. LTh	1979	2004	(Elgin: High)	11 Troon Terrace, The Orchard, Ardler, Dundee DD2 3FX	01382 831358
Mair, Michael V.A. MA BD	1967	2007	(Craigiebank with Dundee: Douglas and Mid Craigie)	6 Emmockwoods Drive, Dundee DD4 9FD [E-mail: mike.mair@dundeepresbytery.org.uk]	01382 502114
Malvenan, Dorothy DCS	1964	1990	(The Deaf Association, Dundee)	Flat 19, 6 Craigie Street, Dundee DD4 6PF	01382 462495
Miller, Charles W. MA	1953	1994	(Fowlis and Liff)	'Palm Springs', Parkside, Auchterhouse, Dundee DD3 0RF	01382 320407
Milroy, Tom	1960	1992	(Monifieth: St Rule's)	9 Long Row, Westhaven, Carnoustie DD7 6BE	01241 856654
Mitchell, Jack MA BD CTh	1987	1996	(Dundee: Menzieshill)	10 Invergowrie Drive, Dundee DD2 1RF	01382 642301
Mowat, Gilbert M. MA	1948	1986	(Dundee: Albany-Butterburn)	7 Dunmore Gardens, Dundee DD2 1PP	01382 566013
Powrie, James E. LTh	1969	1995	(Dundee: Chalmers Ardler)	3 Kirktonhill Road, Kirriemuir DD8 4HU	01575 572503
Quigley, Barbara D. (Mrs) MTheol ThM DPS	1979		Religious Education Teacher	7 Albany Terrace, Dundee DD3 6HQ	01382 223059
Rae, Robert LTh	1968	1983	(Chaplain: Dundee Acute Hospitals)	14 Neddertoun View, Liff, Dundee DD3 5RU	01382 581790
Robertson, Thomas P.	1963	2001	(Dundee: Broughty Ferry St James')	'The Shire', 10 Durie Vale, Windygates, Leven KY8 5EF [E-mail: tom.robertson@dundeepresbytery.org.uk]	01333 351812
Rogers, James M. BA DB DCult	1955	1996	(Gibraltar)	24 Mansion Drive, Dalclaverhouse, Dundee DD4 9DD	01382 506162
Roy, James A. MA BD	1965	2006	(Dundee: Lochee West)	'Beechwood', 7 Northview Terrace, Wormit, Newport-on-Tay DD6 8PP [E-mail: jim.roy@dundeepresbytery.org.uk]	01382 543578
Scroggie, John C.	1951	1985	(Mains)	23 Cliffburn Gardens, Broughty Ferry, Dundee DD5 3NB	01382 739354
Scoular, Stanley	1963	2000	(Rosyth)	31 Duns Crescent, Dundee DD4 0RY	01382 501653
Simpson, James H. BSc	1996	2005	(Auxiliary Minister)	11 Claypotts Place, Broughty Ferry, Dundee DD5 1LG	01382 776520
Smith, Lilian MA DCS			(Deaconess)	6 Fintry Mains, Dundee DD4 9HF	01382 500052
Strickland, Alexander LTh	1971	2005	Dairsie with Kemback with Strathkinness) Workplace Chaplain: Tayside and North Fife	12 Ballumbie Braes, Dundee DD5 0UN	01382 505551
Webster, Allan F. MA BD	1978	2008		65 Clepington Road, Dundee DD4 7BQ [E-mail: allanfwebster@aol.com]	01382 458764

DUNDEE ADDRESSES

Balgay	200 Lochee Road
Barnhill St Margaret's	10 Invermark Terrace
Broughty Ferry	
New Kirk	370 Queen Street
St James'	5 Fort Street
St Luke's and Queen Street	5 West Queen Street
St Stephen's and West	96 Dundee Road
Camperdown	22 Brownhill Road
Chalmers Ardler	Turnberry Avenue
Clepington and Fairmuir	Isla Street x Main Street/ 329 Clepington Road
Craigiebank	Craigie Avenue at Greendykes Road
Douglas and Mid Craigie	Balbeggie Place/ Longtown Terrace
Downfield South	Haldane Street off Strathmartine Road
Dundee (St Mary's)	Nethergate
Fintry	Fintry Road x Fintry Drive
Lochee	191 High Street, Lochee
Logie and St John's (Cross)	Shaftesbury Rd x Blackness Ave
Mains	Foot of Old Glamis Road
Meadowside St Paul's	114 Nethergate
Menzieshill	Charleston Drive, Menzieshill
St Andrew's	2 King Street
St David's High Kirk	119A Kinghorne Road and 273 Strathmore Avenue
Steeple	Nethergate
Stobswell	170 Albert Street
Strathmartine	513 Strathmartine Road
Trinity	73 Crescent Street
West	130 Perth Road
Whitfield	Haddington Crescent

(30) ANGUS

Meets at Forfar in St Margaret's Church Hall, on the first Tuesday of each month, except June when it meets on the last Tuesday, and January, July and August when there is no meeting.

Clerk:	**REV. MATTHEW S. BICKET BD**	
Depute Clerk:	**REV. MICHAEL S. GOSS BD DPS**	
Presbytery Office:	**St Margaret's Church, West High Street, Forfar DD8 1BJ**	**01307 464224**
	[E-mail: angus@cofscotland.org.uk]	

Aberlemno (H) linked with Guthrie and Rescobie
Brian Ramsay BD DPS MLitt 1980 1984 The Manse, Guthrie, Forfar DD8 2TP 01241 828243

Arbirlot linked with Carmyllie
Ian O. Coltart CA BD 1988 2004 The Manse, Arbirlot, Arbroath DD11 2NX 01241 434479

Arbroath: Knox's (H) linked with Arbroath: St Vigeans (H)
Ian G. Gough MA BD MTh DMin 1974 1990 The Manse, St Vigeans, Arbroath DD11 4RD 01241 873206
[E-mail: iangough@btinternet.com]

Arbroath: Old and Abbey (H) (Church office: 01241 877068)
Valerie L. Allen (Ms) BMus MDiv 1990 1996 51 Cliffburn Road, Arbroath DD11 5BA 01241 872196 (Tel/Fax)
[E-mail: VL2allen@aol.com]

Arbroath: St Andrew's (H) (E-mail: st_andrews_arbroath@lineone.net)
W. Martin Fair BA BD DMin 1992 92 Grampian Gardens, Arbroath DD11 4AQ 01241 873238 (Tel/Fax)
[E-mail: martinfair@aol.com]

Arbroath: St Vigeans See Arbroath: Knox's

Arbroath: West Kirk (H)
Alasdair G. Graham BD DipMin 1981 1986 1 Charles Avenue, Arbroath DD11 2EY 01241 872244
[E-mail: alasdair.graham@lineone.net]

Barry linked with Carnoustie
Michael S. Goss BD DPS 1991 2003 44 Terrace Road, Carnoustie DD7 7AR 01241 410194 (Tel/Fax)
[E-mail: michaelgoss@blueyonder.co.uk] 07787 141567 (Mbl)

Brechin: Cathedral (H) (Cathedral office: 01356 629360) (E-mail: scott.rennie@tiscali.co.uk) (Website: www.brechincathedral.org.uk)
Scott Rennie MA BD STM   1999   Chanonry Wynd, Brechin DD9 6JS   01356 622783
[E-mail: scott@smrennie.orangehome.co.uk]

Brechin: Gardner Memorial (H) linked with Farnell
Vacant   15 Caldhame Gardens, Brechin DD9 7JJ   01356 622789

Carmyllie See Arbirlot
Carnoustie See Barry

Carnoustie: Panbride (H)
Matthew S. Bicket BD   1989   8 Arbroath Road, Carnoustie DD7 6BL   01241 854478 (Tel)
[E-mail: matthew@bicket.freeserve.co.uk]   01241 855088 (Fax)

Colliston linked with Friockheim Kinnell linked with Inverkeilor and Lunan (H)
Peter A. Phillips BA   1995 2004   The Manse, Inverkeilor, Arbroath DD11 5SA   01241 830464
[E-mail: peter@peterphillips6.orangehome.co.uk]

Dun and Hillside
Linda J. Broadley (Mrs) LTh DipEd   1996 2004   4 Manse Road, Hillside, Montrose DD10 9FB   01674 830288
[E-mail: lindabroadley@btinternet.com]

Dunnichen, Letham and Kirkden
Vacant   7 Braehead Road, Letham, Forfar DD8 2PG   01307 818916

Eassie and Nevay linked with Newtyle
Carleen Robertson (Miss) BD   1992   2 Kirkton Road, Newtyle, Blairgowrie PH12 8TS   01828 650461
[E-mail: carleen.robertson@tesco.net]

Edzell Lethnot Glenesk (H) linked with Fern Careston Menmuir
Alan G.N. Watt MTh DipCommEd CQSW   1996 2003   Glenesk Cottage, Dunlappie Road, Edzell, Brechin DD9 7UB   01356 648455
[E-mail: alangnwatt@aol.com]

Farnell See Brechin: Gardner Memorial
Fern Careston Menmuir See Edzell Lethnot Glenesk

Forfar: East and Old (H)
Vacant   The Manse, Lour Road, Forfar DD8 2BB   01674 672060
    01307 464303

Forfar: Lowson Memorial (H)
Karen Fenwick PhD MPhil BSc BD   2006   1 Jamieson Street, Forfar DD8 2HY   01307 468585
[E-mail: kmfenwick@talktalk.net]

Forfar: St Margaret's (H) (Church office: 01307 464224)
Vacant — 15 Potters Park Crescent, Forfar DD8 1HH — 01307 466390

Friockheim Kinnell See Colliston

Glamis (H), Inverarity and Kinnettles
John F. Davidson BSc DipEdTech 1970 2005 — 12 Turfbeg Road, Forfar DD8 3LT [E-mail: davidson900@btinternet.com] — 01307 466038

Guthrie and Rescobie See Aberlemno

Inchbrayock linked with Montrose: Melville South
David S. Dixon MA BD 1976 1994 — The Manse, Ferryden, Montrose DD10 9SD [E-mail: david@inchbrayock.wanadoo.co.uk] — 01674 672108

Inverkeilor and Lunan See Colliston

Kirriemuir: St Andrew's (H) linked with Oathlaw Tannadice
David J. Taverner MCIBS ACIS BD 1996 2002 — 26 Quarry Park, Kirriemuir DD8 4DR [E-mail: rahereuk@hotmail.com] — 01575 575561

Montrose: Melville South See Inchbrayock

Montrose: Old and St Andrew's
Ian A. McLean BSc BD DMin 1981 2008 — 2 Rosehill Road, Montrose DD10 8ST [E-mail: iamclean@lineone.net] — 01674 575561

Newtyle See Eassie and Nevay
Oathlaw Tannadice See Kirriemuir: St Andrew's

The Glens and Kirriemuir: Old (H) (Church office: 01575 572819) (Website: www.gkopc.co.uk)
Malcolm I.G. Rooney DPE BEd BD 1993 1999 — 20 Strathmore Avenue, Kirriemuir DD8 4DJ [E-mail: malcolm@gkopc.co.uk] — 01575 573724 / 07909 993233 (Mbl)
Linda Stevens (Mrs) BSc BD PgDip 2006 — 17 North Latch Road, Brechin DD9 6LE [E-mail: linda@gkopc.co.uk] — 01356 623415 / 07701 052552 (Mbl)
(Team Minister)

The Isla Parishes
Ben Pieterse BA BTh LTh 2001 — Balduff House, Kilry, Blairgowrie PH11 8HS [E-mail: benhp1@gmail.com] — 01575 560260

Name			(Charge)	Address	Phone
Anderson, James W. BSc MTh	1986	1997	(Kincardine O'Neil with Lumphanan)	47 Glebe Road, Arbroath DD11 4HJ	01674 672029
Anderson, John F. MA BD FSAScot	1966	2006	(Aberdeen: Mannofeld)	8 Eider Close, Montrose DD10 9NE [E-mail: jfa941@aol.com]	
Brodie, James BEM MA BD STM	1955	1974	(Hurlford)	25A Keptie Road, Arbroath DD11 3ED	01241 873298
Butters, David	1964	1998	(Turriff: St Ninian's and Forglen)	6A Millgate, Friockheim, Arbroath DD11 4TN	01241 828030
Douglas, Iain M. MA BD MPhil DipEd	1960	2002	(Farnell with Montrose: St Andrew's)	Old School House, Kinnell, Friockheim, Arbroath DD11 4UL	01241 828717
Drysdale James P.R.	1967	1999	(Brechin: Gardner Memorial)	51 Airlie Street, Brechin DD9 6JX	01356 625201
Duncan, Robert F. MTheol	1986	2001	(Lochgelly: St Andrew's)	25 Rowan Avenue, Kirriemuir DD8 4TB	01575 573973
Herkes, Moira BD	1985	2007	(Brechin: Gardner Memorial)	38 King O'Muirs Drive, Tullibody, Alloa FK10 3AY [E-mail: mossherkes@btinternet.com]	01259 725533
Hodge, William N.T.	1966	1995	(Longside)	'Tullochgorum', 61 South Street, Forfar DD8 2BS	01307 461944
Milton, Eric G. RD	1963	1994	(Blairdaff)	16 Bruce Court, Links Parade, Carnoustie DD7 7JE	01241 854928
Norrie, Graham MA BD	1967	2007	(Forfar: East and Old)	'Novar', 14A Wyllie Street, Forfar DD8 3DN	01307 468152
Perry, Joseph B.	1955	1989	(Farnell)	19 Guthrie Street, Letham, Forfar DD8 2PS	01307 818741
Reid, Albert B. BD BSc	1996	2001	(Ardler, Kettins and Meigle)	1 Dundee Street, Letham, Forfar DD8 2PQ	01307 818416
Robertson, George R. LTh	1985	2004	(Udny and Pitmedden)	3 Slateford Gardens, Edzell, Brechin DD9 7SX [E-mail: george.robertson@tesco.net]	01356 647322
Searle, David C. MA DipTh	1965	2003	(Warden: Rutherford House)	12 Cairnie Road, Arbroath DD11 3DY	01241 872794
Smith, Hamish G.	1965	1993	(Auchterless with Rothienorman)	11A Guthrie Street, Letham, Forfar DD8 2PS	01307 818973
Thomas, Martyn R.H. CEng MIStructE	1987	2002	(Fowlis and Liff with Lundie and Muirhead of Liff)		
Thomas, Shirley (Mrs) (Aux)	2000	2006	(Auxiliary Minister)	14 Kirkgait, Letham, Forfar DD8 2XQ	01307 818084
Warnock, Denis MA	1952	1990	(Kirkcaldy: Torbain)	14 Kirkgait, Letham, Forfar DD8 2XQ	01307 818084
Williamson, Tom MA BD	1941	1982	(Dyke with Edinkillie)	19 Keptie Road, Arbroath DD11 3ED	01241 872740
Youngson, Peter	1961	1996	(Kirriemuir: St Andrew's)	Storyville Residential Home, Beechwood Place, Kirriemuir DD8 5DZ 'Coreen', Woodside, Northmuir, Kirriemuir DD8 4PG	01575 572832

ANGUS ADDRESSES

Arbroath
Knox's — Howard Street
Old and Abbey — West Abbey Street
St Andrew's — Hamilton Green
West Kirk — Keptie Street

Brechin
Cathedral — Bishops Close
Gardner Memorial — South Esk Street

Carnoustie — Dundee Street
Panbride — Arbroath Road

Forfar
East and Old — East High Street
Lowson Memorial — Jamieson Street
St Margaret's — West High Street

Kirriemuir
Old — High Street
St Andrew's — Glamis Road

Montrose
Melville South — Castle Street
Old and St Andrew's — High Street

(31) ABERDEEN

Meets at Queen's Cross Church, Albyn Place, Aberdeen AB10 1UN, on the first Tuesday of February, March, April, May, September, October, November and December, and on the fourth Tuesday of June.

Joint Clerks:	REV. GEORGE S. COWIE BSc BD REV. JOHN A. FERGUSON BD DipMin DMin	
Deputy Clerk and Administrative Secretary	MRS MOYRA CAMERON	
Presbytery Office:	Mastrick Church, Greenfern Road, Aberdeen AB16 6TR [E-mail: aberdeen@cofscotland.org.uk]	01224 690494
Hon. Treasurer:	MR A. SHARP	27 Hutchison Terrace, Aberdeen AB10 7NN	01224 315702

Aberdeen: Bridge of Don Oldmachar (01224 709299) (Website: www.oldmacharchurch.org)
Vacant   60 Newburgh Circle, Aberdeen AB22 8QZ   01224 708137

Aberdeen: Cove (E)
David Swan BVMS BD   2005   4 Charleston Way, Cove, Aberdeen AB12 3FA   01224 899933
                                        [E-mail: david@covechurch.org.uk]
Mark Johnston BSc BD DipMin (Assoc) 1998 2003 5 Bruce Walk, Redmoss, Aberdeen AB12 3LX   01224 874269
                                        [E-mail: mark@covechurch.org.uk]

Aberdeen: Craigiebuckler (H) (01224 315649)
Kenneth L. Petrie MA BD   1984 1999 185 Springfield Road, Aberdeen AB15 8AA   01224 315125
                                        [E-mail: patandkenneth@aol.com]

Aberdeen: Ferryhill (H) (01224 213093)
John H.A. Dick MA MSc BD   1982   54 Polmuir Road, Aberdeen AB11 7RT   01224 586933
                                        [E-mail: jhadick01@talktalk.net]

Aberdeen: Garthdee (H) linked with Aberdeen: Ruthrieston West (H)
Vacant

Aberdeen: Gilcomston South (H) (01224 647144)
D. Dominic Smart BSc BD MTh 1988   37 Richmondhill Road, Aberdeen AB15 5EQ   01224 314326
                                        [E-mail: smartdd@btconnect.com]

Aberdeen: High Hilton (H) (01224 494717)
A. Peter Dickson BSc BD   1996   24 Rosehill Drive, Aberdeen AB24 4JJ   01224 484155
                                                                 [E-mail: peter@highhilton.com]

Aberdeen: Holburn West (H) (01224 571120)
Duncan C. Eddie MA BD   1992   1999   31 Cranford Road, Aberdeen AB10 7NJ   01224 325873
                                                                 [E-mail: nacnud@ceddie.freeserve.co.uk]

Aberdeen: Mannofield (H) (01224 310087) (E-mail: mannofieldchurch@xalt.co.uk)
Keith T. Blackwood BD DipMin   1997   2007   21 Forest Avenue, Aberdeen AB15 4TU   01224 315748
                                                                 [E-mail: k2blackwood@btinternet.com]

Aberdeen: Mastrick (H) (01224 694121)
Lesley P. Risby (Mrs) BD   1994   2005   8 Corse Wynd, Kingswells, Aberdeen AB15 8TP   01224 749346
                                                                 [E-mail: mrsrisby@hotmail.com]
Benjamin D.W. Byun BA MDiv MTh PhD   2 Eastside Gardens, Bucksburn, Aberdeen AB21 9SN   01224 710274
  (Parish Assistant)   [E-mail: benjamin@byun1.fsnet.co.uk]

Aberdeen: Middlefield (H)
This charge is to be served by two ministers, each of whom will serve on the basis of a 50 per cent time commitment. One appointment has been made; a second is awaited.
Elspeth Harley BA MTh   1991   2007   8 Donmouth Road, Aberdeen AB23 8DT   01224 703017
                                                                 [E-mail: eharley@hotmail.co.uk]
Vacant
Michael Phillippo
  MTh BSc BVetMed MRCVS (Aux)   25 Deeside Crescent, Aberdeen AB15 7PT   01224 318317

Aberdeen: Midstocket
Marian Cowie MA BD MTh   1990   2006   54 Woodstock Road Aberdeen AB15 5JF   01224 208001
                                                                 [E-mail: mcowieou@aol.com]

Aberdeen: New Stockethill (New Charge Development)
Ian M. Aitken MA BD   1999   52 Ashgrove Road West, Aberdeen AB16 5EE   01224 686929
                                                                 [E-mail: ncdstockethill@uk.uumail.com]

Aberdeen: Northfield
Scott C. Guy BD   1989   1999   28 Byron Crescent, Aberdeen AB16 7EX   01224 692332

Aberdeen: Queen Street
Graham D.S. Deans MA BD MTh DMin   1978   2008   51 Osborne Place, Aberdeen AB25 2BX   01224 646429

Aberdeen: Queen's Cross (H) (01224 644742)
Vacant   1 St Swithin Street, Aberdeen AB10 6XH   01224 322549

Aberdeen: Rubislaw (H) (01224 645477) 1977 1987 45 Rubislaw Den South, Aberdeen AB15 4BD 01224 314878
Andrew G.N. Wilson MA BD DMin [E-mail: agn.wilson@virgin.net]

Aberdeen: Ruthrieston West (H) See Aberdeen: Garthdee

Aberdeen: St Columba's Bridge of Don (H) (01224 825653) 1991 151 Jesmond Avenue, Aberdeen AB22 8UG 01224 705337
Louis Kinsey BD DipMin [E-mail: louis@stcolumbaschurch.org.uk]

Aberdeen: St George's Tillydrone (H) (01224 482204) 1991 2003 127 Clifton Road, Aberdeen AB24 4RH 01224 483976
James Weir BD [E-mail: rjimw@sky.com]

Aberdeen: St John's Church for Deaf People (H) (01224 494566) 1979 1991 15 Deeside Crescent, Aberdeen AB15 7PT (Voice/Text) 01224 315595
John R. Osbeck BD

Aberdeen: St Machar's Cathedral (H) (01224 485988) 18 The Chanonry, Old Aberdeen AB24 1RQ 01224 483688
Alan D. Falconer MA BD DLitt [E-mail: minister@stmachar.com]

Aberdeen: St Mark's (H) (01224 640672) 1989 65 Mile-end Avenue, Aberdeen AB15 5PU 01224 622470
John M. Watson LTh [E-mail: drjohn@johnmutchwatson.wanadoo.co.uk]

Aberdeen: St Mary's (H) (01224 487227) 2003 456 King Street, Aberdeen AB24 3DE 01224 633778
Elsie J. Fortune (Mrs) BSc BD

Aberdeen: St Nicholas Kincorth, South of 1989 2002 The Manse, Kincorth Circle, Aberdeen AB12 5NX 01224 872820
Edward C. McKenna BD DPS

Aberdeen: St Nicholas Uniting, Kirk of (H) (01224 643494) 1984 2005 12 Louisville Avenue, Aberdeen AB15 4TX 01224 314318
B. Stephen C. Taylor BA BBS MA MDiv [E-mail: minister@kirk-of-st-nicholas.org.uk] 01224 649242 (Fax)

Aberdeen: St Stephen's (H) (01224 624443) 1982 1989 6 Belvidere Street, Aberdeen AB25 2QS 01224 635694
James M. Davies BSc BD [E-mail: daviesjim@btinternet.com]

Aberdeen: South Holburn (H) (01224 211730) 1991 2006 54 Woodstock Road, Aberdeen AB15 5JF 01224 315042
George S. Cowie BSc BD [E-mail: gscowie@aol.com]

Aberdeen: Summerhill (H) (Website: www.summerhillchurch.org.uk)
Vacant
36 Stronsay Drive, Aberdeen AB15 6JL
01224 324669

Aberdeen: Torry St Fittick's (H) (01224 899183)
Iain C. Barclay   1976   1999
MBE TD MA BD MTh MPhil PhD
11 Devanha Gardens East, Aberdeen AB11 7UH
[E-mail: i.c.barclay@virgin.net]
01224 588245
07968 131930 (Mbl)
07625 383830 (Pager)

Aberdeen: Woodside (H) (01224 277249)
Markus Auffermann DipTheol   1999   2006
322 Clifton Road, Aberdeen AB24 4HQ
[E-mail: mauffermann@yahoo.com]
01224 484562

Bucksburn Stoneywood (H) (01224 712411)
Nigel Parker BD MTh DMin   1994
25 Gilbert Road, Bucksburn, Aberdeen AB21 9AN
[E-mail: nigel@revparker.fsnet.co.uk]
01224 712635

Cults (H)
Ewen J. Gilchrist BD DipMin DipComm   1982   2005
1 Cairnlee Terrace, Bieldside, Aberdeen AB15 9AE
[E-mail: hobgoblins@kincarrathie.fsnet.co.uk]
01224 861692

Dyce (H) (01224 771295)
Vacant
144 Victoria Street, Dyce, Aberdeen AB21 7BE
01224 722380

Kingswells
Dolly Purnell BD   2003   2004
Kingswells Manse, Lang Stracht, Aberdeen AB15 8PL
[E-mail: neilanddolly.purnell@btinternet.com]
01224 740229

Newhills (H) (Tel/Fax: 01224 716161)
Hugh M. Wallace MA BD   1980   2007
Newhills Manse, Bucksburn, Aberdeen AB21 9SS
[E-mail: revhugh@hotmail.com]
01224 712655

Peterculter (H) (01224 735845)
John A. Ferguson BD DipMin DMin   1988   1999
7 Howie Lane, Peterculter AB14 0LJ
[E-mail: jc.ferguson@virgin.net]
01224 735041

Aitchison, James W. BD   1993
Chaplain: Army
2 Bn Prince of Wales Royal Regiment, Clive Barracks,
Tern Hill, Shropshire TF9 3QE

Alexander, William M. BD   1971   1998
(Berriedale and Dunbeath with Latheron)
110 Fairview Circle, Danestone, Aberdeen AB22 8YR
01224 703752

Beattie, Walter G. MA BD   1956   1995
(Arbroath: Old and Abbey)
126 Seafield Road, Aberdeen AB15 7YQ
01224 329259

Black, W. Graham MA BD   1983   1999
Urban Prayer Ministry
72 Linksview, Linksfield Road, Aberdeen AB24 5RG
[E-mail: graham.black@virgin.net]
01224 492491

Name			Charge	Address	Tel.
Brown, Robert F. MA BD ThM	1971	2008	(Aberdeen: Queen's Cross)	55 Hilton Drive, Aberdeen AB24 4NJ [E-mail: Bjacob546@aol.com]	01224 491451
Bryden, Agnes Y. (Mrs) DCS	1970	2003	(Deaconess)	Angusfield House, 226 Queen's Road, Aberdeen AB15 8DN	
Campbell, W.M.M. BD CPS	1973	1989	(Hospital Chaplain)	43 Murray Terrace, Aberdeen AB11 7SA	07761 235815
Coutts, Fred MA BD	1966	2002	Hospital Chaplain	Ladebank, 1 Manse Place, Hatton, Peterhead AB42 0QU	01779 841320
Crawford, Michael S.M. LTh	1950	1987	(Aberdeen: St Mary's)	9 Craigton Avenue, Aberdeen AB15 7RP	01224 208341
Dickson, John C. MA	1957	1995	(Aberdeen: St Fittick's)	36 Queen Victoria Park, Inchmarlo, Banchory AB31 4AL	01330 826236
Douglas, Andrew M. MA	1982	1991	(High Hilton)	219 Countesswells Road, Aberdeen AB15 7RD	01224 311932
Falconer, James B. BD	1953	1995	Hospital Chaplain	3 Brimmond Walk, Westhill AB32 6XH	01224 744621
Finlayson, Ena (Miss) DCS	1960	1995	(Deaconess)	16E Denwood, Aberdeen AB15 6JF	01224 321147
Goldie, George D. ALCM	1971	2005	(Greyfriars)	27 Broomhill Avenue, Aberdeen AB10 6JL	01224 322503
Gordon, Laurie Y.	1975	2004	(John Knox)	1 Alder Drive, Portlethen, Aberdeen AB12 4WA	01224 782703
Graham, A. David M. BA BD	1963	1999	(Aberdeen: Rosemount)	Elmhill House, 27 Shaw Crescent, Aberdeen AB25 3BT	01224 648041
Grainger, Harvey L. LTh	1991	2003	(Kingswells)	13 St Ronan's Crescent, Peterculter, Aberdeen AB14 0RL [E-mail: harveygrainger@tiscali.co.uk]	01224 739824 (Mbl) 07768 333216
Haddow, Angus BSc	1957	1991	(Methlick)	25 Lerwick Road, Aberdeen AB16 6RF	01224 696362
Hamilton, Helen (Miss) BD	1988	1988	(Glasgow: St James' Pollok)	The Cottage, West Tilbouries, Maryculter, Aberdeen AB12 5GD	01224 739632
Hutchison, A. Scott MA BD DD	1991	1999	(Hospital Chaplain)	Ashfield, Drumoak, Banchory AB31 5AG	01330 811309
Hutchison, Alison M. (Mrs) BD DipMin	1984	1999	Hospital Chaplain	Ashfield, Drumoak, Banchory AB31 5AG [E-mail: amhutch62@aol.com]	01330 811309
Hutchison, David S. BSc BD ThM	1963	2001	(Aberdeen: Torry St Fittick's)	51 Don Street, Aberdeen AB24 1UH	01224 276122
Jack, David LTh	1983	2006	(West Mearns)	7 Cromwell Road, Aberdeen AB15 4UH [E-mail: david@cromwell7.fsnet.co.uk]	01224 325355
Johnstone, William MA BD	1968	2006	(University of Aberdeen)	9/5 Mount Alvernia, Edinburgh EH16 6AW	0131-664 3140
Jolly, Andrew J. BD CertMin			Chaplain to the Oil Industry	Chaplain's Office, Total E and P (UK) PLC, Crawpeel Road, Altens, Aberdeen AB12 3FG [E-mail: andrew.jolly@uloilandgaschaplaincy.com]	01224 297532/3
Kerr, Hugh F. MA BD			(Aberdeen: Ruthrieston South)	134C Great Western Road, Aberdeen AB10 6QE	01224 580091
Lundie, Ann V. DCS			(Deaconess)	20 Langdykes Drive, Cove, Aberdeen AB12 3HW [E-mail: ann.lundie@btopenworld.com]	01224 898416
McCallum, Moyra (Miss) MA BD DCS			(Deaconess)	176 Hilton Drive, Aberdeen AB24 4LT [E-mail: moymac@aol.com]	01224 486240
Maciver, Norman MA BD DMin	1976	2006	(Newhills)	4 Mundi Crescent, Newmachar, Aberdeen AB21 0LY [E-mail: norirene@aol.com]	01651 869442
Main, Alan TD MA BD STM PhD DD	1963	2001	(University of Aberdeen)	Kirkfield, Barthol Chapel, Inverurie AB51 8TD [E-mail: amain@talktalk.net]	01651 806773
Montgomerie, Jean B. (Miss) MA BD	1973	2005	(Forfar: St Margaret's)	12 St Ronan's Place, Peterculter, Aberdeen AB14 0QX [E-mail: revjeanb@tiscali.co.uk]	01224 732350
Richardson, Thomas C. LTh ThB	1971	2004	(Cults: West)	19 Kinkell Road, Aberdeen AB15 8HR [E-mail: thomas.richardson7@btinternet.com]	01224 315328
Rodgers, D. Mark BA BD MTh	1987	2003	Hospital Chaplain	152D Gray Street, Aberdeen AB10 6JW	01224 210810
Sefton, Henry R. MA BD STM PhD	1957	1992	(University of Aberdeen)	25 Albury Place, Aberdeen AB11 6TQ	01224 572305

Smith, Angus MA LTh	1965	2006	(Industrial Chaplain)	3/7 West Powburn, West Savile Gait, Edinburgh EH9 3EW	0131-667 1761
Stewart, James C. MA BD STM	1960	2000	(Aberdeen: Kirk of St Nicholas)	54 Murray Terrace, Aberdeen AB11 7SB	01224 587071
Strachan, Ian M. MA BD	1959	1994	(Ashkirk with Selkirk)	'Cardenwell', Glen Drive, Dyce, Aberdeen AB21 7EN	01224 772028
Swinton, John BD PhD	1999		University of Aberdeen	51 Newburgh Circle, Bridge of Don, Aberdeen AB22 8XA	01224 825637
				[E-mail: j.swinton@abdn.ac.uk]	
Torrance, Iain R. TD DPhil DD DTheol LHD CorrFRSE	1982	2005	President: Princeton Theological Seminary	54 Mercer Street, PO Box 552, Princeton, NJ 08542-0803, USA	001 609 497 7800
Wilkie, William E. LTh	1978	2001	(Aberdeen: St Nicholas Kincorth, South of)	32 Broomfield Park, Portlethen, Aberdeen AB12 4XT	01224 782052
Wilson, Thomas F. BD	1984	1996	Education	55 Allison Close, Cove, Aberdeen AB12 3WG	01224 873501
Wood, James L.K.	1967	1995	(Ruthrieston West)	1 Glen Drive, Dyce, Aberdeen AB21 7EN	01224 722543

ABERDEEN ADDRESSES

Bridge of Don Oldmachar	Ashwood Park	Kingswells	Old Skene Road, Kingswells
Cove	Loirston Primary School, Loirston Avenue	Mannofield	Great Western Road x Craigton Road
Craigiebuckler	Springfield Road	Mastrick	Greenfern Road
Cults	Quarry Road, Cults	Middlefield	Manor Avenue
Dyce	Victoria Street, Dyce	Midstocket	Mid Stocket Road
Ferryhill	Fonthill Road x Polmuir Road	New Stockethill	
Garthdee	Ramsay Gardens	Northfield	Byron Crescent
Gilcomston South	Union Street x Summer Street	Peterculter	Craigton Crescent
High Hilton	Hilton Drive	Queen Street	Queen Street
Holburn West	Great Western Road	Queen's Cross	Albyn Place
		Rubislaw	Queen's Gardens
		Ruthrieston West	Broomhill Road
		St Columba's	Braehead Way, Bridge of Don
		St George's	Hayton Road, Tillydrone
		St John's for the Deaf	Smithfield Road

St Machar's	The Chanonry
St Mark's	Rosemount Viaduct
St Mary's	King Street
St Nicholas Kincorth, South of	Kincorth Circle
St Nicholas Uniting, Kirk of	Union Street
St Stephen's	Powis Place
South Holburn	Holburn Street
Summerhill	Stronsay Drive
Torry St Fittick's	Walker Road
Woodside	Church Street, Woodside

(32) KINCARDINE AND DEESIDE

Meets in Birse and Feughside Church, Finzean, Banchory on the first Tuesday of September, October, November, December, March and May, and on the last Tuesday of June at 7pm.

Clerk: REV. HUGH CONKEY BSc BD   39 St Ternans Road, Newtonhill, Stonehaven AB39 3PF   01569 739297
[E-mail: kincardinedeeside@cofscotland.org.uk]

Aberluthnott linked with Laurencekirk (H)
Ronald Gall BSc BD   1985   2001   Aberdeen Road, Laurencekirk AB30 1AJ   01561 378838
[E-mail: ronniegall@tiscali.co.uk]

Aboyne and Dinnet (H) (01339 886989) linked with Cromar (E-mail: aboynedinnet.cos@virgin.net)
Douglas I. Campbell BD DPS   2004   49 Charlton Crescent, Aboyne AB34 5GN   01339 886447
[E-mail: douglas.campbell@btinternet.com]

Arbuthnott, Bervie and Kinneff
Georgina M. Baxendale (Mrs) BD   1981   2006   10 Kirkburn, Inverbervie, Montrose DD10 0RT   01561 362633
[E-mail: georgiebaxendale6@tiscali.co.uk]
(Charge formed by the union of Arbuthnott and Bervie with Kinneff)

Banchory-Devenick and Maryculter/Cookney
Vacant   The Manse, Kirkton of Maryculter, Aberdeen AB12 5FS   01224 735776

Banchory-Ternan: East (H) (Tel: 01330 820380) (E-mail: eastchurch@banchory.fsbusiness.co.uk)
Mary M. Haddow (Mrs) BD   2001   East Manse, Station Road, Banchory AB31 5YP   01330 822481
[E-mail: mary_haddow@btconnect.com]
Anthony Stephen MA BD (Assistant Minister   2001   72 Grant Road, Banchory AB31 5UU   01330 825038
and Youth Leader)   [E-mail: tonys@edgerock.org]

Banchory-Ternan: West (H)
Donald K. Walker BD   1979   1995   2 Wilson Road, Banchory AB31 5UY   01330 822811
[E-mail: btw@uk2.net]
Anthony Stephen MA BD (Assistant Minister   2001   72 Grant Road, Banchory AB31 5UU   01330 825038
and Youth Leader)   [E-mail: tonys@edgerock.org]

Birse and Feughside
Jack Holt BSc BD   1985   1994   The Manse, Finzean, Banchory AB31 6PB   01330 850237
[E-mail: jholt@finzeanmanse.wanadoo.co.uk]

Braemar and Crathie
Kenneth I. Mackenzie BD CPS   1990   2005   Manse, Crathie, Ballater AB35 5UL   01339 742208
[E-mail: crathiemanse@tiscali.co.uk]

Cromar See Aboyne and Dinnet

Drumoak (H)-Durris (H)
James Scott MA BD   1973   1992   Manse, Durris, Banchory AB31 6BU   01330 844557
[E-mail: jimscott73@yahoo.co.uk]

Glenmuick (Ballater) (H)
Anthony Watts BD DipTechEd JP   1999   The Manse, Craigendarroch Walk, Ballater AB35 5ZB   01339 754014
[E-mail: tony.watts6@btinternet.com]

Laurencekirk See Aberluthnott

Parish / Minister	Ord.	Ind.	Address	Tel
Mearns Coastal George I. Hastie MA BD	1971	1998	The Manse, Kirkton, St Cyrus, Montrose DD10 0BW	01674 850880 (Tel/Fax)
Mid Deeside Norman Nicoll BD	2003		The Manse, Torphins, Banchory AB31 4GQ [E-mail: middeesidemanse1@btinternet.com]	01339 882276
Newtonhill Hugh Conkey BSc BD	1987	2001	39 St Ternans Road Newtonhill, Stonehaven AB39 3PF [E-mail: hugh@conkey.plus.com]	01569 730143
Portlethen (H) (01224 782883) Flora J. Munro (Mrs) BD DMin	1993	2004	18 Rowanbank Road, Portlethen, Aberdeen AB12 4NX [E-mail: floramunro@aol.co.uk]	01224 780211
Stonehaven: Dunnottar (H) Rosslyn P. Duncan	2007		Dunnottar Manse, Stonehaven AB39 3XL [E-mail: rpduncan@btinternet.com]	01569 762876
Stonehaven: Fetteresso (H) (Tel: 01569 767689) (E-mail: office@fetteressokirk.org.uk) Vacant			11 South Lodge Drive, Stonehaven AB39 2PN	01569 762876
Stonehaven: South (H) David J. Stewart BD MTh DipMin	2000		South Church Manse, Cameron Street, Stonehaven AB39 2HE [E-mail: brigodon@clara.co.uk]	01569 762576
West Mearns Catherine A. Hepburn (Miss) BA BD	1982	2000	West Mearns Parish Church Manse, Fettercairn, Laurencekirk AE30 1UE [E-mail: chepburn@fish.co.uk]	01561 340203

Name			(former charge)	Address	Tel
Brown, J.W.S. BTh	1960	1995	(Cromar)		
Christie, Andrew C. LTh	1975	2000	(Banchory-Devenick and Maryculter/Cookney)	0 Forestside Road, Banchory AB31 5ZH	01330 824353
Forbes, John W.A. BD	1973	1999	(Edzell Lethnot with Fern, Careston and Menmuir with Glenesk)	7 Broadstraik Close, Elrick, Aberdeen AB32 6JP	01224 746888
Gray, Robert MA BD	1942	1982	(Stonehaven: Fetteresso)	Mid Clune, Finzean, Banchory AB31 6PL	01330 850283
Kinninburgh, Elizabeth B.F. (Miss) MA BD	1970	1986	(Birse with Finzean with Strachan)	Park Drive, Stonehaven AB39 2NW	01569 767027
Lamb, A. Douglas MA	1964	2002	(Dalry: St Margaret's)	30 Denstrath Road, Edzell Woods, Brechin DD9 7XF [E-mail: lamb.edzell@talk21.com]	01339 886757
Massie, Robert W. LTh	1989	2007	(Monifieth: St Rule's)	23 Boswell Road, Portlethen, Aberdeen AB12 4BA [E-mail: r_massie@sky.com]	01356 648139

Nicholson, William	1949	1986	(Banchory-Ternan: East with Durris)	10 Pantoch Gardens, Banchory AB31 5ZD	01330 823875
Smith, Albert E. BD	1983	2006	(Methlick)	42 Haulkerton Crescent, Laurencekirk AB30 1FB	01561 376111
				[E-mail: aesmethlick@aol.com]	
Taylor, Peter R. JP BD	1977	2001	(Torphins)	42 Beltie Road, Torphins, Banchory AB31 4JT	01339 882780
Tierney, John P. MA	1945	1985	(Peterhead West Associate)	3 Queenshill Drive, Aboyne AB34 5DG	01339 886741
Wallace, William F. BDS BD	1968	2008	(Wick: Pulteneytown and Thrumster)	Lachan Cottage, 29 Station Road, Banchory AB31 5XX	01330 822259
				[E-mail: williamwallace39@btopenworld.com]	
Watt, William D. LTh	1978	1996	(Aboyne – Dinnet)	2 West Toll Crescent, Aboyne AB34 5GB	01339 886943

(33) GORDON

Meets at various locations on the first Tuesday of February, March, April, May, September, October, November and December, and on the fourth Tuesday of June.

Clerk: MR GERALD MOORE
7 Allathan Park, Pitmedden, Ellon AB41 7PX   01651 842526
[E-mail: gordon@cofscotland.org.uk]

Barthol Chapel linked with Tarves
Isabel C. Buchan (Mrs) BSc BD RE(PgCE)   1975   2006
8 Murray Avenue, Tarves, Ellon AB41 7LZ   01651 851250
[E-mail: buchan.123@btinternet.com]

Belhelvie (H)
Paul McKeown BSc PhD BD   2000   2005
Belhelvie Manse, Balmedie, Aberdeen AB23 8YR   01358 742227
[E-mail: prmckeown@tiscali.co.uk]

Blairdaff and Chapel of Garioch
Vacant
John C. Mack JP (Aux)   1985   2004
The Manse, Chapel of Garioch, Inverurie AB51 5HE   01467 681619
The Willows, Auchleven, Insch AB52 6QB   01464 820387

Cluny (H) linked with Monymusk (H)
G. Euan D. Glen BSc BD   1992
The Manse, 26 St Ninian's, Monymusk, Inverurie AB51 7HF   01467 651470
[E-mail: euanglen@aol.com]

Culsalmond and Rayne linked with Daviot (H)
Mary M. Cranfield (Miss) MA BD DMin   1989
The Manse, Daviot, Inverurie AB51 0HY   01467 671241
[E-mail: marymc@ukgateway.net]

Cushnie and Tough (T) (H)
Margaret J. Garden (Miss) BD   1993   2000
The Manse, Muir of Fowlis, Alford AB33 8JU   01975 581239
[E-mail: mj-garden@btinternet.com]

Daviot See Culsalmond and Rayne

Echt linked with Midmar (T) Alan Murray BSc BD PhD	2003		The Manse, Echt, Westhill AB32 7AB [E-mail: ladecottage@btinternet.com]	01330 860004
Ellon Stephen Emery BD DPS	2006		The Manse, 12 Union Street, Ellon AB41 9BA [E-mail: stephen.emery2@btinternet.com]	01358 720476
Fintray Kinellar Keithhall Ellen Larson Davidson BA MDiv		2007	20 Kinmohr Rise, Blackburn, Aberdeen AB21 0LJ [E-mail: larsondavidson@gmail.com]	01224 791350
Foveran Vacant			The Manse, Foveran, Ellon AB41 6AP	01358 789288
Howe Trinity John A. Cook MA BD	1986	2000	The Manse, 110 Main Street, Alford AB33 8AD [E-mail: john.cook2@homecall.co.uk]	01975 562282
Huntly Cairnie Glass Thomas R. Calder LLB BD WS	1994		The Manse, Queen Street, Huntly AB54 8EB [E-mail: cairniechurch@aol.com]	01466 792630
Insch-Leslie-Premnay-Oyne (H) Jane C. Taylor (Miss) BD DipMin	1990	2001	22 Western Road, Insch AB52 6JR [E-mail: jane.c.taylor@btinternet.com]	01464 820914
Inverurie: St Andrew's T. Graeme Longmuir KJSJ MA BEd FASC	1976	2001	St Andrew's Manse, 1 Ury Dale, Inverurie AB51 3XW [E-mail: standrew@ukonline.co.uk]	01467 620468
Inverurie: West Ian B. Groves BD CPS	1989		West Manse, 1 Westburn Place, Inverurie AB51 5QS [E-mail: i.groves@inveruriewestchurch.org]	01467 620285
Kemnay John P. Renton BA LTh	1976	1990	Kemnay, Inverurie AB51 9ND [E-mail: johnrenton@btinternet.com]	01467 642219 (Tel/Fax)
Kintore (H) Alan Greig BSc BD	1977	1992	28 Oakhill Road, Kintore, Inverurie AB51 0FH [E-mail: greig@kincarr.free-online.co.uk]	01467 632219 (Tel/Fax)

Meldrum and Bourtie

Minister	Ordained	Inducted	Address	Tel
Hugh O'Brien CSS MTheol	2001		The Manse, Urquhart Road, Oldmeldrum, Inverurie AB51 0EX [E-mail: minister@meldrum-bourtiechurch.org]	01651 872250

Methlick

Matthew Christopher Canlis BA MDiv MLitt	2007		The Manse, Manse Road, Methlick, Ellon AB41 7DG	01651 806215

Midmar See Echt

Monymusk See Cluny

New Machar

Manson C. Merchant BD CPS	1992	2001	The Manse, Newmachar, Aberdeen AB21 0RD [E-mail: mc.merchant@btinternet.com]	01651 862278

Noth

Vacant			Manse of Noth, Kennethmont, Huntly AB54 4NP	01464 831244

Skene (H)

Iain U. Thomson MA BD	1970	1972	The Manse, Kirkton of Skene, Skene AB32 6LX [E-mail: iainuthomson@googlemail.com]	01224 743277
Marion G. Stewart (Miss) DCS			Kirk Cottage, Kirkton of Skene, Skene AB32 6XE	01224 743407

Strathbogie Drumblade

Neil I.M. MacGregor BD	1995		49 Deveron Park, Huntly AB54 8UZ	01466 792702

(Charge formed by the union of Drumblade and Huntly Strathbogie)

Tarves See Barthol Chapel

Udny and Pitmedden

Regine U. Cheyne (Mrs) MA BSc BD	1988	2005	Manse Road, Udny Green, Udny, Ellon AB41 7RS	01651 842052

Upper Donside (H)

Brian Dingwall BTh CQSW	1999	2006	The Manse, Lumsden, Huntly AB54 4GQ [E-mail: briandingwall@tiscali.co.uk]	01464 861757

Andrew, John MA BD DipRE DipEd	1961	1995	(Teacher: Religious Education)	Cartar's Croft, Midmar, Inverurie AB51 7NJ	01330 833208
Bowie, Alfred LTh	1974	1998	(Alford with Keig with Tullynessle Forbes)	17 Stewart Road, Alford AB33 8UA	01975 563824
Buchan, Alexander MA BD PGCE	1975	1992	(North Ronaldsay with Sanday)	8 Murray Avenue, Tarves, Ellon AB41 7LZ [E-mail: revabuchan@bluebucket.org]	01651 851250
Collie, Joyce P. (Miss) MA PhD	1966	1994	(Corgarff Strathdon and Glenbuchat Towie)	Muir of Fowlis Nursing Home, Muir of Fowlis, Alford AB33	01358 723055
Craggs, Sheila (Mrs)	2001	2008	(Ellon: Auxiliary Minister)	7 Morar Court, Ellon AB41 9GG	01224 722820
Dryden, Ian MA DipEd	1988	2001	(New Machar)	16 Glenhome Gardens, Dyce, Aberdeen AB21 7FG	01358 723981
Hawthorn, Daniel MA BD DMin	1965	2004	(Belhelvie)	7 Crimond Drive, Ellon AB41 8BT [E-mail: donhawthorn@compuserve.com]	

Name		Year	Year	Address	Tel
Jones, Robert A. LTh CA	(Marnoch)	1966	1997	13 Gordon Terrace, Inverurie AB51 4GT	01467 622691
Lister, Douglas	(Largo and Newburn)	1945	1986	Gowanbank, Port Elphinstone, Inverurie AB51 3UN	01467 621262
				[E-mail: pastillister@surf.scotland.uk]	
Lyon, Andrew LTh	(Fraserburgh West with Rathen West)	1971	2007	Barmekyn, Keig, Alford AB33 8BH	01975 562768
				[E-mail: andrew@lyon60.orangehome.co.uk]	
Macalister, Eleanor	(Ellon)	1994	2006	2 Crimond Drive, Ellon AB41 8BT	01358 722711
				[E-mail: macal1ster@aol.com]	
Macallan, Gerald B.	(Kintore)	1954	1992	33 Thorngrove House, 500 Great Western Road, Aberdeen AB10 6PF	01224 316125
McLean, John MA BD	(Bathgate: Boghall)	1967	2003	15 Eastside Drive, Westhill AB32 6QN	01224 747701
McLeish, Robert S.	(Insch-Leslie-Premnay-Oyne)	1970	2000	19 Western Road, Insch AB52 6JR	01464 820749
Rodger, Matthew A. BD	(Ellon)	1978	1999	15 Meadowlands Drive, Westhill AB32 6EJ	01224 743184
Scott, Allan D. BD	(Culsalmond with Daviot with Rayne)	1977	1989	23 Barclay Road, Inverurie AB51 3QP	01467 625161
Stewart, George C. MA	(Drumblade with Huntly Strathbogie)	1952	1995	104 Scott Drive, Huntly AB54 8PF	01466 792503
Stoddart, A. Grainger	(Meldrum and Bourtie)	1975	2001	6 Mayfield Gardens, Insch AB52 6XL	01464 821124
Wallace, R.J. Stuart MA	(Foveran)	1947	1986	Manse View, Manse Road, Methlick, Ellon AB41 7DW	01651 806843

(34) BUCHAN

Meets at St Kane's Centre, New Deer, Turriff on the first Tuesday of February, March, May, September, October, November and December, and on the third Tuesday of June.

Clerk: MR GEORGE W. BERSTAN   Faithlie, Victoria Terrace, Turriff AB53 4EE   **01888 562392**
[E-mail: buchan@cofscotland.org.uk]

Aberdour linked with Pitsligo linked with Sandhaven
Vacant   The Manse, 49 Pitslgo Street, Rosehearty, Fraserburgh AB43 7JL   01346 571237

Auchaber United linked with Auchterless
Alison Jaffrey (Mrs) MA BD FSAScot   1990   1999   The Manse, Auchterless, Turriff AB53 8BA   01888 511217
[E-mail: alison.jaffrey@bigfoot.com]

Auchterless See Auchaber United

Banff linked with King Edward (E-mail: banffkirk@bigfoot.com)
Alan Macgregor BA BD   1992   1998   7 Colleonard Road, Banff AB45 1DZ   01261 812107

Crimond linked with Lonmay
Vacant   The Manse, Crimond, Fraserburgh AB43 8QJ   01346 532431

Cruden (H)
Rodger Neilson JP BSc BD   1972   1974   Hatton, Peterhead AB42 0QQ   01779 841229
[E-mail: rodger.neilson@virgin.net]

Charge / Minister	Years	Address	Telephone
Deer (H) James Wishart BD	1986	The Manse, Old Deer, Peterhead AB42 5JB [E-mail: jWishart06@aol.com]	01771 623582
Fordyce Iain A. Sutherland BSc BD	1996 2000	Seafield Terrace, Portsoy, Banff AB45 2QB [E-mail: RevISutherland@aol.com]	01261 842272
Fraserburgh: Old Peter B. Park BD MCIBS	1997 2007	4 Robbies Road, Fraserburgh AB43 7AF [E-mail: peterpark9@btinternet.com]	01346 515332
Fraserburgh: South (H) linked with Inverallochy and Rathen: East Ronald F. Yule	1982	15 Victoria Street, Fraserburgh AB43 9PJ	01346 518244 (Tel) 0870 055 4665 (Fax)
Fraserburgh: West (H) linked with Rathen: West Vacant		23 Strichen Road, Fraserburgh AB43 9SA	01346 513303
Fyvie linked with Rothienorman Robert J. Thorburn BD	1978 2004	The Manse, Fyvie, Turriff AB53 8RD [E-mail: rjthorburn@aol.com]	01651 891230
Gardenstown Donald N. Martin BD	1996	The Manse, Fernie Brae, Gardenstown, Banff AB45 3YL [E-mail: ferniebrae@googlemail.com]	01261 851256
Inverallochy and Rathen: East See Fraserburgh: South **King Edward** See Banff			
Longside Robert A. Fowlie BD	2007	9 Anderson Drive, Longside, Peterhead AB42 4XG [E-mail: bobfowlie@tiscali.co.uk]	01779 821224
Lommay See Crimond			
Macduff David J. Randall MA BD ThM	1971	The Manse, Macduff AB45 3QL [E-mail: djrandall479@btinternet.com]	01261 832316
Marnoch Paul van Sittert BA BD	1997 2007	Marnoch Manse, 53 South Street, Aberchirder, Huntly AB54 7TS [E-mail: vansittert@btinternet.com]	01466 781143

Maud and Savoch linked with New Deer: St Kane's
Alistair P. Donald MA PhD BD   1999   The Manse, New Deer, Turriff AB53 6TD   01771 644216
[E-mail: ap.donald@googlemail.com]

Monquhitter and New Byth linked with Turriff: St Andrew's
James Cook MA MDiv   1999   2002   Balmellie Road, Turriff AB53 4SP   01888 560304
[E-mail: jmscook9@aol.com]

New Deer: St Kane's See Maud and Savoch

New Pitsligo linked with Strichen and Tyrie
Iain Macnee LTh BD MA PhD   1975   2004   Kingsville, Strichen, Fraserburgh AB43 6SQ   01771 637365
[E-mail: strichen_tyrie@talktalk.net]

Ordiquhill and Cornhill (H) linked with Whitehills
Brian Hendrie BD   1992   2005   6 Craigneen Place, Whitehills, Banff AB45 2NE   01261 861671
[E-mail: brianandyvonne@98duncansby.freeserve.co.uk]

Peterhead: Old
Pauline Thomson MA BD   2006   1 Hawthorn Road, Peterhead AB42 2DW   01779 472618

Peterhead: St Andrew's (H)
Vacant   1 Landale Road, Peterhead AB42 1QN   01779 472141

Peterhead: Trinity
L. Paul McClenaghan BA   1973   1996   18 Landale Road, Peterhead AB42 1QP   01779 472405
[E-mail: paul.mcclenaghan@gmail.com]

Pitsligo See Aberdour
Rathen: West See Fraserburgh: West
Rothienorman See Fyvie

St Fergus
Vacant

Sandhaven See Aberdour
Strichen and Tyrie See New Pitsligo
Turriff: St Andrew's See Monquhitter and New Byth

Turriff: St Ninian's and Forglen
Murdo C. Macdonald MA BD   2002   4 Deveronside Drive, Turriff AB53 4SP   01888 563850

Whitehills See Ordiquhill and Cornhill

Blaikie, James BD	1972	1997	(Berwick-on-Tweed: St Andrew's Wallace Green and Lowick)	57 Glenugie View, Peterhead AB42 2BW	01779 490625
Fawkes, G.M. Allan BA BSc JP	1979	2000	(Lonmay with Rathen: West)	3 Northfield Gardens, Hatton, Peterhead AB42 0SW	01779 841814
Hendrie, Yvonne (Mrs) MA BD	1995		Hospital Chaplain	6 Craigneen Place, Whitehills, Banff AB45 2NE	01261 861671
McKay, Margaret (Mrs) MA BD MTh	1991	2003	(Auchaber United with Auchterless)	The Smithy, Knowes of Elrick, Aberchirder, Huntly AB54 7PP [E-mail: mgt_mckay@yahoo.com.uk]	(Tel) 01466 780208 (Fax) 01466 780015
Mackenzie, Seoras L. BD	1996	1998	Chaplain: Army	1 Logistic Support Regiment, BFPO 47	
McMillan, William J. CA LTh BD	1969	2004	(Sandsting and Aithsting with Walls and Sandness)	7 Ardinn Drive, Turriff AB53 4PR [E-mail: revbillymcmillan@aol.com]	01888 560727
Noble, George S. DipTh	1972	2000	(Carfin with Newarthill)	Craigowan, 3 Main Street, Inverallochy, Fraserburgh AB43 8XX	01346 582749
Ross, David S. MSc PhD BD	1978	2003	Prison Chaplain Service	3–5 Abbey Street, Old Deer, Peterhead AB42 5LN [E-mail: padsross@btinternet.com]	01771 623994
Taylor, William MA MEd	1984	1996	(Buckie: North)	23 York Street, Peterhead AB42 1SN [E-mail: william.taylor@globalnet.co.uk]	01779 481798

(35) MORAY

Meets at St Andrew's-Lhanbryd and Urquhart on the first Tuesday of February, March, May, September, October, November and December, and at the Moderator's church on the fourth Tuesday of June.

| Clerk: | REV. HUGH M.C. SMITH LTh | | | Mortlach Manse, Dufftown, Keith AB55 4AR [E-mail: moray@cofscotland.org.uk] [E-mail: clerk@moraypresbytery.plus.com] | 01340 820538 |
| Depute Clerk: | REV. GRAHAM W. CRAWFORD BSc BD STM | | | The Manse, Prospect Terrace, Lossiemouth IV31 6JS | 01343 810676 |

Aberlour (H)

| Vacant | | | Mary Avenue, Aberlour AB38 9QN | 01340 871027 |

Alves and Burghead linked with Kinloss and Findhorn

| Duncan Shaw LTh CPS | 1984 | 2006 | The Manse, 4 Manse Road, Kinloss, Forres IV36 3GH | 01309 690931 |

Bellie linked with Speymouth

| Alison C. Mehigan BD DPS | 2003 | 11 The Square, Fochabers IV32 7DG [E-mail: alisonc@mehigan-ug.fsnet.co.uk] | 01343 820256 |
| Margaret King MA DCS | 2007 | 56 Murrayfield, Fochabers IV32 7EZ | 01343 820937 |

Birnie and Pluscarden linked with Elgin High

| Julie M. Woods (Mrs) BTh | 2005 | Daisy Bank, 5 Forteath Avenue, Elgin IV30 1TQ [E-mail: missjulie@btinternet.com] | 01343 542449 |

Douglas F. Stevenson BD DipMin (Assoc)	1991	2008	The Manse of Birnie and Pluscarden, Birnie, Elgin IV30 8SU [E-mail: dfstevenson@aol.com]	01343 549487
Buckie: North (H) J. Gordon Mathew MA BD	1973	2006	14 St Peter's Road, Buckie AB56 1DL [E-mail: jgmathew@lineone.net]	01542 831328
Buckie: South and West (H) linked with Enzie Vacant			41 East Church Street, Buckie AB56 1ES	01542 832103
Cullen and Deskford Wilma A. Johnston MTheol MTh	2006		3 Seafield Place, Cullen, Buckie AB56 4UU [E-mail: revwilmaj@btinternet.com]	01542 841851
Dallas linked with Forres: St Leonard's (H) linked with Rafford Vacant			St Leonard's Manse, Nelson Road, Forres IV36 1DR	01309 672380
Duffus, Spynie and Hopeman (H) Bruce B. Lawrie BD	1974	2001	The Manse, Duffus, Elgin IV30 5QP [E-mail: blawrie@zetnet.co.uk]	01343 830276
Dyke linked with Edinkillie Gordon R. Mackenzie BScAgr BD	1977	2003	Manse of Dyke, Brodie, Forres IV36 2TD [E-mail: rev.g.mackenzie@btopenworld.com]	01309 641239
Edinkillie See Dyke				
Elgin: High See Birnie and Pluscarden				
Elgin: St Giles' (H) and St Columba's South (01343 551501) George B. Rollo BD	1974	1986	(Office and Church Halls: Greyfriars Street, Elgin IV30 1LF) 18 Reidhaven Street, Elgin IV30 1QH [E-mail: gbrstgiles@hotmail.com]	01343 547208
James M. Cowie BD (Assoc)	1977	2007	2 Hay Place, Elgin IV30 1LZ [E-mail: jim911@btinternet.com]	01343 544957
Anne Attenburrow BSc MBChB (Aux)	2006	2008	4 Jock Inksons Brae, Elgin IV30 1QE	01343 552330
Enzie See Buckie South and West				
Findochty linked with Portknockie linked with Rathven Vacant			20 Netherton Terrace, Findochty, Buckie AB56 4QD	01542 833484
Forres: St Laurence (H) Barry J. Boyd LTh DPS	1993		12 Mackenzie Drive, Forres IV36 2JP [E-mail: barryj.boydstlaurence@btinternet.com]	01309 672260 07778 731018 (Mbl)

Forres: St Leonard's See Dallas

Keith: North, Newmill, Boharm and Rothiemay (H) (01542 886390)
T. Douglas McRoberts BD CPS FRSA	1975	2002	North Manse, Church Road, Keith AB55 5BR
			[E-mail: doug_mcroberts@btinternet.com]
Ian Cunningham DCS			The Manse, Rothiemay, Huntly AB54 7NE
			[E-mail: icunninghamdcs@btinternet.com]

01542 882559

01466 711334

Keith: St Rufus, Botriphnie and Grange (H)
Ranald S.R. Gauld MA LLB BD	1991	1995	Church Road, Keith AB55 5BR
Kay Gauld (Mrs) BD STM PhD (Assoc)	1999		Church Road, Keith AB55 5BR
			[E-mail: kay_gauld@strufus.fsnet.co.uk]

01542 882799
01542 882799

Kinloss and Findhorn See Alves and Burghead

Knockando, Elchies and Archiestown (H) linked with Rothes
Robert J.M. Anderson BD	1993	2000	Manse Brae, Rothes, Aberlour AB38 7AF
			[E-mail: robert@carmanse.freeserve.co.uk]

01340 831381 (Tel/Fax)

Lossiemouth: St Gerardine's High (H)
Thomas M. Bryson BD	1997	2002	The Manse, St Gerardine's Road, Lossiemouth IV31 6RA
			[E-mail: thomas@bryson547.fsworld.co.uk]

01343 813146

Lossiemouth: St James'
Graham W. Crawford BSc BD STM	1991	2003	The Manse, Prospect Terrace, Lossiemouth IV31 6JS
			[E-mail: pictishreiver@aol.com]

01343 810676

Mortlach and Cabrach (H)
Hugh M.C. Smith LTh	1973	1982	Mortlach Manse, Dufftown, Keith AB55 4AR
			[E-mail: clerk@moraypresbytery.plus.com]

01340 820380

Pluscarden See Birnie
Portknockie See Findochty
Rafford See Dallas
Rathven See Findochty
Rothes See Knockando, Elchies and Archiestown

St Andrew's-Lhanbryd (H) and Urquhart
Rolf H. Billes BD	1996	2001	39 St Andrews Road, Lhanbryde, Elgin IV30 8PU
			[E-mail: rolf.billes@lineone.net]

01343 843995

Speymouth See Bellie

Name			Charge	Address	Tel
Bain, Brian LTh	1980	2007	(Gask with Methven and Logiealmond)	Bayview, 13 Stewart Street, Portgordon, Buckie AB56 5QT	01542 831215
Davidson, A.A.B. MA BD	1960	1997	(Grange with Rothiemay)	11 Sutors Rise, Nairn IV12 5BU	
Douglas, Christina A. (Mrs)	1987	1993	(Inveraven and Glenlivet)	White Cottage, St Fillans, Crieff PH6 2ND	
Evans, John W. MA BD	1945	1984	(Elgin High)	15 Weaver Place, Elgin IV30 1HB	01343 543607
Gow, Neil BSc MEd BD	1996	2008	(Foveran)	Hillhead Lodge, Portknockie, Buckie AB56 4PB	01542 840625
				[E-mail: ngow@beeb.net]	
Henig, Gordon BSc BD	1997	2003	(Bellie with Speymouth)	59 Woodside Drive, Forres IV36 2UF	01309 672558
King, Margaret R. (Miss) MA DCS	2002			56 Murrayfield, Fochabers IV32 7EZ	01343 820937
				[E-mail: margaretrking@aol.com]	
Macaulay, Alick Hugh MA	1943	1981		5 Duke Street, Fochabers IV32 7DN	01343 820726
Miller, William B.	1950	1987	(Cawdor with Croy and Dalcross)	10 Kirkhill Drive, Lhanbryde, Elgin IV30 8QA	01343 842368
Morton, Alasdair J. MA BD DipEd FEIS	1960	2000	(Bowden with Newtown)	16 St Leonard's Road, Forres IV36 1DW	01309 671719
				[E-mail: alasgilmor@compuserve.com]	
Morton, Gillian M. (Mrs) MA BD PGCE	1983	1996	(Hospital Chaplain)	16 St Leonard's Road, Forres IV36 1DW	01309 671719
				[E-mail: alasgilmor@compuserve.com]	
Poole, Ann McColl (Mrs) DipEd ACE LTh	1983	2003	(Dyke with Edinkillie)	Kirkside Cottage, Dyke, Forres IV36 2TF	01309 641046
Scotland, Ronald J. BD	1993	2003	(Birnie with Pluscarden)	7A Rose Avenue, Elgin IV30 1NX	01343 543086
Spence, Alexander	1944	1989	(Elgin: St Giles': Associate)	6 Inglis Court, Edzell, Brechin DD9 7SR	01356 648502
Wright, David L. MA BD	1957	1998	(Stornoway: St Columba)	34 Wyvis Drive, Nairn IV12 4TP	01667 451613
Thomson, James M. BA	1952	2000	(Elgin: St Giles' and St Columba's South: Associate)	48 Mayne Road, Elgin IV30 1PD	01343 547664

(36) ABERNETHY

Meets at Boat of Garten on the first Tuesday of February, March, April, June, September, October, November and December.

Clerk: REV. JAMES A.I. MACEWAN MA BD   **The Manse, Nethy Bridge PH25 3DG   01479 821280**
[E-mail: abernethy@cofscotland.org.uk]

Abernethy (H) linked with Cromdale (H) and Advie
James A.I. MacEwan MA BD   1973   1980   The Manse, Nethy Bridge PH25 3DG   01479 821280
[E-mail: manse@nethybridge.freeserve.co.uk]

Alvie and Insh (T) (H) linked with Rothiemurchus and Aviemore (H)
Ron C. Whyte BD CPS   1990   2007   The Manse, 8 Dalfaber Park, Aviemore PH22 1QF   01479 810280
[E-mail: ron4xst@aol.com]

Boat of Garten (H) and Kincardine linked with Duthil (H) 1993 1999
David W. Whyte LTh — Deshar Road, Boat of Garten PH24 3BN — 01479 831252
[E-mail: djwhyte@fish.co.uk]

Cromdale and Advie See Abernethy

Dulnain Bridge (H) linked with Grantown-on-Spey (H) 1988
Morris Smith BD — The Manse, Golf Course Road, Grantown-on-Spey PH26 3HY — 01479 872084
[E-mail: mosmith.themanse@btinternet.com]

Duthil See Boat of Garten and Kincardine
Grantown-on-Spey See Dulnain Bridge

Kingussie (H) 1974 2003
Helen Cook (Mrs) BD — The Manse, 18 Hillside Avenue, Kingussie PH21 1PA — 01540 661311
[E-mail: revhcook@tiscali.co.uk]

Laggan linked with Newtonmore (H)
Vacant — The Manse, Fort William Road, Newtonmore PH20 1DG — 01540 673238

Newtonmore See Laggan
Rothiemurchus and Aviemore (H) See Alvie and Insh

Tomintoul (H), Glenlivet and Inveraven 1975 1992
Sven S. Bjarnason CandTheol — The Manse, Tomintoul, Ballindalloch AB37 9HA — 01807 580254
[E-mail: sven@bjarnason.org.uk]

Bardgett, Frank D. MA BD PhD 1987 2001 (Board of National Mission) Tigh an Iasgair, Street of Kincardine, Boat of Garten PH24 3BY — 01479 831751
[E-mail: tigh@bardgett.plus.com]

(37) INVERNESS

Meets at Inverness, in the Dr Black Memorial Hall, on the first Tuesday of February, March, April, May, September, October, November and December, and at the Moderator's church on the fourth Tuesday of June.

Clerk: REV. ALASTAIR S. YOUNGER BScEcon ASCC   3 Elm Park, Inverness IV2 4WN   01463 232462 (Tel/Fax)
[E-mail: inverness@cofscotland.org.uk]

Ardersier (H) linked with Petty

Alexander Whiteford LTh	1996	Ardersier, Inverness IV2 7SX [E-mail: a.whiteford@ukonline.co.uk]	01667 462224

Auldearn and Dalmore linked with Nairn: St Ninian's

Richard Reid BSc BD MTh	1991 2005	The Manse, Auldearn, Nairn IV12 5SX	01667 451675

Cawdor (H) linked with Croy and Dalcross (H)

Janet S. Mathieson MA BD	2003	The Manse, Croy, Inverness IV2 5PH [E-mail: jan@mathieson99.fsnet.co.uk]	01667 493217

Croy and Dalcross See Cawdor

Culloden: The Barn (H)

James H. Robertson BSc BD	1975 1994	45 Oakdene Court, Culloden IV2 7XL [E-mail: revjimrculloden@aol.com]	01463 790504

Daviot and Dunlichity linked with Moy, Dalarossie and Tomatin

Reginald F. Campbell BD DipChEd	1979 2003	The Manse, Daviot, Inverness IV2 5XL	01463 772242

Dores and Boleskine
Vacant

Inverness: Crown (H) (01463 238929)

Peter H. Donald MA PhD BD	1991 1998	39 Southside Road, Inverness IV2 4XA [E-mail: pdonald7@aol.com]	01463 230537

Inverness: Dalneigh and Bona (GD) (H)

Fergus A. Robertson MA BD	1971 1999	9 St Mungo Road, Inverness IV3 5AS	01463 232339

Inverness: East (H)

Vacant		2 Victoria Drive, Inverness IV2 3QD	01463 231269

Inverness: Hilton

Duncan MacPherson LLB BD	1994	66 Culduthel Mains Crescent, Inverness IV2 6RG [E-mail: duncan@hiltonchurch.freeserve.uk]	01463 231417

Inverness: Inshes (H)

Alistair Malcolm BD DPS	1976 1992	48 Redwood Crescent, Milton of Leys, Inverness IV2 6HB [E-mail: alimalcolm@7inverness.freeserve.co.uk]	01463 772402

Inverness: Kinmylies (E) (H)

Peter M. Humphris BSc BD	1976 2001	2 Balnafettack Place, Inverness IV3 8TQ [E-mail: peter@humphris.co.uk]	01463 709893

Inverness: Ness Bank (T) (H) S. John Chambers OBE BSc	1972	1998	15 Ballifeary Road, Inverness IV3 5PJ [E-mail: chambers@ballifeary.freeserve.co.uk]	01463 234653
Inverness: Old High St Stephen's Peter W. Nimmo BD ThM	1996	2004	24 Damfield Road, Inverness IV2 3HU [E-mail: peternimmo@minister.com]	01463 250802
Inverness: St Columba High (H) Alastair S. Younger BScEcon ASCC	1969	1976	3 Elm Park, Inverness IV2 4WN [E-mail: asyounger@aol.com]	01463 232462 (Tel/Fax)
Inverness: Trinity (H) Alistair Murray BD	1984	2004	60 Kenneth Street, Inverness IV3 5PZ [E-mail: a.murray111@btinternet.com]	01463 234756
Kilmorack and Erchless Edgar J. Ogston BSc BD	1976	2007	'Roselynn', Croyard Road, Beauly IV4 7DJ [E-mail: edgar.ogston@macfish.com]	01463 782260
Kiltarlity linked with Kirkhill Vacant			Wardlaw Manse, Wardlaw Road, Kirkhill, Inverness IV5 7NZ	01463 831662
Kirkhill See Kiltarlity				
Moy, Dalarossie and Tomatin See Daviot and Dunlichity				
Nairn: Old (H) Ian W.F. Hamilton BD LTh ALCM AVCM	1978	1986	3 Manse Road, Nairn IV12 4RN [E-mail: reviwfh@btinternet.com]	01667 452203
Nairn: St Ninian's (H) See Auldearn and Dalmore				
Petty See Ardersier				
Urquhart and Glenmoriston (H) Hugh F. Watt BD DPS	1986	1996	Blairbeg, Drumnadrochit, Inverness IV3 6UG [E-mail: hw@tinyworld.co.uk]	01456 450231

Black, Archibald T. BSc	1964	1997	(Inverness: Ness Bank)	16 Elm Park, Inverness IV2 4WN	01463 230588
Brown, Derek G. BD DipMin DMin	1989	1994	Chaplain: NHS Highland	Cathedral Manse, Cnoc-an-Lobht, Dornoch IV25 3HN [E-mail: revsbrown@aol.com]	01862 810296

Name			(Parish)	Address	Phone
Buell, F. Bart BA MDiv	1980	1995	(Urquhart and Glenmoriston)	6 Towerhill Place, Cradlehall, Inverness IV2 5FN [E-mail: bart@tower22.freeserve.co.uk]	01463 794634
Charlton, George W.	1952	1992	(Fort Augustus with Glengarry)	1 Drumfield Road, Inverness IV2 4XL	01463 242802
Chisholm, Archibald F. MA	1957	1997	(Braes of Rannoch with Foss and Rannoch)	22 Seabank Road, Nairn IV12 4EU	01667 452001
Christie, James LTh	1993	2003	(Dores and Boleskine)	20 Wester Inshes Crescent, Inverness IV2 5HL	01463 710534
Clyne, Douglas R. BD	1973	2004	(Fraserburgh: Old)	27 River Park, Nairn IV12 5SP [E-mail: manse1@supanet.com]	01667 456372
Donn, Thomas M. MA	1932	1969	(Duthil)	Kingsmills Nursing Home, Inverness	
Frizzell, R. Stewart BD	1961	2000	(Wick: Old)	58 Boswell Road, Inverness IV2 3EW	01463 231907
Jeffrey, Stewart D. BSc BD	1962	1997	(Banff with King Edward)	10 Grigor Drive, Inverness IV2 4LP [E-mail: stewart.jeffrey@talktalk.net]	01463 230085
Lacey, Eric R. BD	1971	1992	(Creich with Rosehall)	38 Laggan Road, Inverness IV2 4EW	01463 235006
Livesley, Anthony LTh	1979	1997	(Kiltearn)	87 Beech Avenue, Nairn IV12 5SX [E-mail: a.livesley@tesco.net]	01667 455126
Logan, Robert J.V. MA BD	1962	2001	(Abdie and Dunbog with Newburgh)	Lindores, 1 Murray Place, Smithton, Inverness IV2 7PX [E-mail: rjvlogan@btinternet.com]	01463 790226
Macdonald, Aonghas I. MA BD	1967	2007	(Inverness: East)	41 Castlehill Park, Inverness IV2 5GJ [E-mail: aonghas@ukonline.co.uk]	01463 792275
Macritchie, Iain A.M. BSc BD STM PhD	1987	1998	Chaplain: Inverness Hospitals	7 Merlin Crescent, Inverness IV2 3TE	01463 235204
Morrison, Hector BSc BD MTh	1981	1994	Lecturer: Highland Theological College	24 Oak Avenue, Inverness IV2 4NX	01463 238561
Rettie, James A. BTh	1981	1999	(Melness and Eriboll with Tongue)	2 Trantham Drive, Westhill, Inverness IV2 5QT	01463 798896
Robb, Rodney P.T.	1995	2004	(Stirling: St Mark's)	2A Mayfield Road, Inverness IV2 4AE	
Stirling, G. Alan S. MA	1960	1999	(Leochel Cushnie and Lynturk with Tough)	57 Lochlann Road, Culloden, Inverness IV2 7HJ	01463 798313
Turner, Fraser K. LTh	1994	2007	(Kiltarlity with Kirkhill)	[E-mail: fraseratq@yahoo.co.uk]	
Waugh, John L. LTh	1973	2002	(Ardclach with Auldearn and Dalmore)	58 Wyvis Drive, Nairn IV12 4TP (Tel/Fax) [E-mail: jswaugh@care4free.net]	01667 456397
Wilson, Ian M.	1988	1993	(Cawdor with Croy and Dalcross)	17 Spires Crescent, Nairn IV12 5PZ	01667 452977

INVERNESS ADDRESSES

Inverness			
Crown	Kingsmills Road x Midmills Road	Inshes	Inshes Retail Park
Dalneigh and Bona	St Mary's Avenue	Kinmylies	Kinmylies Way
East	Academy Street x Margaret Street	Ness Bank	Ness Bank x Castle Road
Hilton	Druid Road x Tomatin Road	St Columba High	Bank Street x Fraser Street
		St Stephen's	Old Edinburgh Road x Southside Road
The Old High	Church Street x Church Lane		
Trinity	Huntly Place x Upper Kessock Street		

Nairn	
Old	Academy Street x Seabank Road
St Ninian's	High Street x Queen Street

(38) LOCHABER

Meets at Caol, Fort William, in Kilmallie Church Hall at 6pm, on the first Tuesday of September and December, on the last Tuesday of October and on the fourth Tuesday of March. The June meeting is held at 6pm on the first Tuesday in the church of the incoming Moderator.

Clerk:	**MRS ELLA GILL**	**5 Camus Inas, Acharacle PH36 4JQ** [E-mail: lochaber@cofscotland.org.uk]	**01967 431834**
Treasurer:	**MRS PAT WALKER**	**Tigh a' Chlann, Inverroy, Roy Bridge PH31 4AQ** [E-mail: pw-15@tiscali.co.uk]	**01397 712028**

Acharacle (H) linked with Ardnamurchan
Vacant
The Manse, Acharacle, Argyll PH36 4JU
01967 431561

Ardgour linked with Strontian
Vacant
The Manse, Ardgour, Fort William PH33 7AH
01855 841230

Ardnamurchan See Acharacle

Duror (H) linked with Glencoe: St Munda's (H) (T)
Alison H. Burnside (Mrs) MA BD   1991   2002
The Manse, Ballachulish PH49 4JG
[E-mail: alisonskyona@aol.com]
01855 811998

Fort Augustus linked with Glengarry
Adrian P.J. Varwell BA BD PhD   1983   2001
The Manse, Fort Augustus PH32 4BH
[E-mail: a-varwell@ecosse.net]
01320 366210

Fort William: Duncansburgh MacIntosh (H) linked with Kilmonivaig
Donald A. MacQuarrie BSc BD   1979   1990
The Manse of Duncansburgh, The Parade, Fort William PH33 6BA
[E-mail: pdmacq@ukgateway.net]
01397 702297

Glencoe: St Munda's See Duror
Glengarry See Fort Augustus

Kilmallie
Richard T. Corbett BSc MSc PhD BD   1992   2005
Kilmallie Manse, Corpach, Fort William PH33 7JS
[E-mail: revcorbett@pgen.net]
01397 772736

Kilmonivaig See Fort William: Duncansburgh MacIntosh

Kinlochleven (H) linked with Nether Lochaber (H)
Vacant
Lochaber Road, Kinlochleven, Argyll PA40 4QW   01855 831227

Morvern
Vacant
The Manse, Lochaline, Morvern, Oban PA34 5UU   01967 421267

Nether Lochaber See Kinlochleven

North West Lochaber
Vacant
Janet Anderson (Miss) DCS   4 Clanranald Place, Arisaig PH39 4NN   01687 450398
(Parish Assistant and Deacon)   [E-mail: jaskye@tiscali.co.uk]
(Charge formed by the union of Arisaig and the Small Isles with Mallaig; St Columba and Knoydart)

Strontian See Ardgour

Anderson, David M. MSc FCOptom	1984		Auxiliary Minister	'Mirlo-', 1 Dumfries Place, Fort William PH33 6UQ	01397 703203
Beaton, Jamesina (Miss) DCS			(Deaconess)	Farhill, Fort Augustus PH32 4DS	01320 366252
Burnside, William A.M. MA BD PGCE	1990		Teacher: Religious Education	The Manse, Ballachulish PH49 4JG	01855 811998
Carmichael, James A. LTh	1976	2006	(Ardgour with Strontian)	Linnhe View, 5 Clovulin, Ardgour, Fort William PH33 7AB	01855 841351
Lamb, Alan H.W. BA MTh	1959	2005	(Associate Minister)	Smiddy House, Arisaig PH39 4NH	01687 450227
				[E-mail: handalamb@talktalk.net]	
Olsen, Heather C. (Miss) BD	1978	2003	(Creich with Rosehall)	4 Riverside Park, Lochyside, Coull, Fort William PH33 7RA	01397 700023
Rae, Peter C. BSc BD	1968	2000	(Beath and Cowdenbeath North)	Rodan, Badabrie, Banavie, Fort William PH33 7LX	01397 772603
Winning, A. Ann MA DipEd BD	1984	2006	(Morvern)	'Westerne', 13C Carnoch, Glencoe, Ballachulish PH49 4HQ	01855 811929
				[E-mail: annw@morvern13.fslife.co.uk]	

LOCHABER Communion Sundays

Acharacle	1st Mar, Jun, Sep, Dec
Ardgour	1st Jun, Sep, Dec, Easter
Ardnamurchan	1st Apr, Aug, Dec
Arisaig and Moidart	1st May, Nov
Duror	2nd Jun, 3rd Nov
Fort Augustus	1st Jan, Apr, Jul, Oct
Fort William Duncansburgh MacIntosh	1st Apr, Jun, Oct
Glencoe	1st Apr, Oct
Glengarry	1st Jan, Apr, Jul, Oct
Kilmallie	3rd Mar, May, Sep, 1st Dec
Kilmonivaig	1st May, Nov
Kinlochleven	1st Feb, Apr, Jun, Oct, Dec
Mallaig	4th May, 3rd Nov
Morvern	Easter, 1st Jul, 4th Sep, 1st Dec
Nether Lochaber	1st Apr, Oct
Strontian	1st Jun, Sep, Dec

(39) ROSS

Meets in Dingwall on the first Tuesday of each month, except January, May, July and August.

Clerk: REV. THOMAS M. McWILLIAM MA BD — Guidhadden, 7 Woodholme Crescent, Culbokie, Dingwall IV7 8JH [E-mail: ross@cofscotland.org.uk] — 01349 877014

Alness Ronald Morrison BD	1996		27 Darroch Brae, Alness IV17 0SD [E-mail: ranald@morrison89.freeserve.co.uk]	01349 882238
Avoch linked with Fortrose and Rosemarkie Alison J. Grainger BD	1995	2006	5 Nessway, Fortrose IV10 8SS [E-mail: revajgrainger@btinternet.com]	01381 620068
Contin Gordon McLean LTh	1972	2005	The Manse, Contin, Strathpeffer IV14 9ES [E-mail: gmaclean@hotmail.co.uk]	01997 421380
Cromarty John Tallach MA MLitt	1970	1999	Denny Road, Cromarty IV11 8YT [E-mail: j.tallach@tiscali.co.uk]	01381 600802
Dingwall: Castle Street (H) Bruce Ritchie BSc BD PhD	1977	2006	16 Achany Road, Dingwall IV15 9JB	01349 863167
Dingwall: St Clement's (H) Russel Smith BD	1994		8 Castlehill Road, Dingwall IV15 9PB [E-mail: russel@stclementschurch.fsnet.co.uk]	01349 861011
Fearn Abbey and Nigg linked with Tarbat David V. Scott BTh	1994	2006	Church of Scotland Manse, Fearn, Tain IV20 1TN	01862 832626 (Tel/Fax)
Ferintosh Andrew F. Graham BTh DPS	2001	2006	Ferintosh Manse, Leanaig Road, Conon Bridge, Dingwall IV7 8BE [E-mail: andy@afg1960.wanadoo.co.uk]	01349 861275

Fodderty and Strathpeffer Ivan C. Warwick MA BD TD	1980	1999	The Manse, Strathpeffer IV14 9DL [E-mail: L70rev@btinternet.com]	01997 421398 07775 530709 (Mbl)
Fortrose and Rosemarkie See Avoch				
Invergordon Kenneth Donald Macleod BD CPS	1989	2000	The Manse, Cromlet Drive, Invergordon IV18 0BA [E-mail: kd-macleod@tiscali.co.uk]	01349 852273
Killearnan linked with Knockbain Iain Ramsden BTh	1999		The Church of Scotland Manse, Coldwell Road, Artafallie, North Kessock, Inverness IV1 3ZE [E-mail: s4rev@cqm.co.uk]	01463 731333
Kilmuir and Logie Easter Thomas J.R. Mackinnon LTh DipMin	1996	2005	Delny, Invergordon IV18 0NW [E-mail: tmackinnor@aol.com]	01862 842280
Kiltearn (H) Donald A. MacSween BD	1991	1998	The Manse, Swordale Road, Evanton, Dingwall IV16 9UZ [E-mail: donaldmacsween@hotmail.com]	01349 830472
Knockbain See Killearnan				
Lochbroom and Ullapool (GD) Vacant			The Manse, Garve Road, Ullapool IV26 2SX	01854 612050
Resolis and Urquhart (T) C.J. Grant Bell	1983	2002	The Manse, Culbokie, Dingwall IV7 8JN	01349 877452
Rosskeen Robert Jones BSc BD	1990		Rosskeen Manse, Perrins Road, Alness IV17 0SX [E-mail: rob-jones@freeuk.com]	01349 882265
Tain Douglas A. Horne BD	1977		14 Kingsway Avenue, Tain IV19 1NJ [E-mail: douglas.horne@virgin.net]	01862 894140
Tarbat (T) See Fearn Abbey and Nigg				

Urray and Kilchrist

J. Alastair Gordon BSc BD			The Manse, Corrie Road, Muir of Ord IV6 7TL [E-mail: jagordon_muir@tiscali.co.uk]	2000	01463 870259

Buchan, John BD MTh	1968	1993	(Fodderty and Strathpeffer)	'Faithlie', 45 Swanston Avenue, Inverness IV3 6QW	01463 713114
Dupar, Kenneth W. BA BD PhD	1965	1993	(Christ's College, Aberdeen)	The Old Manse, The Causeway, Cromarty IV11 8XJ	01381 600428
Forsyth, James LTh	1970	2000	(Fearn Abbey with Nigg Chapelhill)	Rhives Lodge, Golspie, Sutherland KW10 6DD	
Glass, Alexander OBE MA	1998		Auxiliary Minister: Attached to Presbytery Clerk	Craigton, Tulloch Avenue, Dingwall IV15 9TU	01349 863258
Holroyd, Gordon BTh FPhS FSAScot	1959	1993	(Dingwall: St Clement's)	22 Stuarthill Drive, Maryburgh, Dingwall IV15 9HU	01349 863379
Liddell, Margaret (Miss) BD DipTh	1987	1997	(Contin)	20 Wyvis Crescent, Conon Bridge, Dingwall IV7 8BZ [E-mail: margaretliddell@alktalk.net]	01349 865997
McGowan, Prof. Andrew T.B. BD STM PhD	1979	1994	Highland Theological College	4 Kintail Place, Dingwall IV15 9RL [E-mail: andrew.mcgowan@htc.uhi.ac.uk]	(Home) 01349 867639 (Work) 01349 780208 (Fax) 01349 780001
Macgregor, John BD	2001	2006	Chaplain: Army	2 Bn The Royal Regiment of Scotland (Highland Fusiliers), Glencorse Barracks, Penicuik EH26	
Mackinnon, R.M. LTh	1968	1995	(Kilmuir and Logie Easter)	27 Riverford Crescent, Conon Bridge, Dingwall IV7 8HL	01349 866293
MacLennan, Alasdair J. BD DCE	1978	2001	(Resolis and Urquhart)	Airdale, Seaforth Road, Muir of Ord IV6 7TA	01463 870704
Macleod, John MA	1959	1993	(Resolis and Urquhart)	'Benview', 19 Balvaird, Muir of Ord IV6 7RG [E-mail: sheilaandjohn@yahoo.co.uk]	01463 871286
McWilliam, Thomas M. MA BD	1964	2003	(Contin)	Guidhadden, 7 Woodholme Crescent, Culbokie, Dingwall IV7 8JH	01349 877014
Niven, William W. BTh	1982	1995	(Alness)	4 Obsdale Park, Alness IV17 0TP	01349 882427
Rutherford, Ellen B. (Miss) MBE DCS			(Deaconess)	41 Duncanston, Conon Bridge, Dingwall IV7 8JB	01349 877439

(40) SUTHERLAND

Meets at Lairg on the first Tuesday of March, May, September, November and December, and on the first Tuesday of June at the Moderator's church.

Clerk:	REV. J.L. GOSKIRK LTh	The Manse, Lairg, Sutherland IV27 4EH [E-mail: sutherland@cofscotland.org.uk]	01549 402373

Altnaharra and Farr

Vacant	The Manse, Bettyhill, Thurso KW14 7SZ	01641 521208

Assynt and Stoer

Continued Vacancy	Canisp Road, Lochinver, Lairg IV27 4LH	01571 844342

Clyne (H) linked with Kildonan and Loth Helmsdale (H)
Ian W. McCree BD   1971   1987   Golf Road, Brora KW9 6QS   01408 621239
[E-mail: ian@mccree.f9.co.uk]

Creich linked with Rosehall
Vacant   Church of Scotland Manse, Dornoch Road, Bonar Bridge, Ardgay IV24 3EB   01863 766256

Dornoch Cathedral (H)
Susan M. Brown (Mrs) BD DipMin   1985   1998   Cnoc-an-Lobht, Dornoch IV25 3HN   01862 810296
[E-mail: revsbrown@aol.com]

Durness and Kinlochbervie
John T. Mann BSc BD   1990   1998   Manse Road, Kinlochbervie, Lairg IV27 4RG   01971 521287
[E-mail: jtmklb@aol.com]

Eddrachillis
John MacPherson BSc BD   1993   Church of Scotland Manse, Scourie, Lairg IV27 4TQ   01971 502431

Golspie
John B. Sterrett BA BD PhD   2007   The Manse, Fountain Road, Golspie KW10 6TH   01408 633295 (Tel/Fax)
[E-mail: johnbsterrett@yahoo.co.uk]

Kildonan and Loth Helmsdale (H) See Clyne

Kincardine Croick and Edderton
Graeme W.M. Muckart MTh MSc FSAScot   1983   2004   The Manse, Ardgay IV24 3BG   01863 766285
[E-mail: avqt18@dsl.pipex.com]

Lairg (H) linked with Rogart (H)
J.L. Goskirk LTh   1968   The Manse, Lairg IV27 4EH   01549 402373

Melness and Tongue (H)
John F. Mackie BD   1979   2000   New Manse, Glebelands, Tongue, Lairg IV27 4XL   01847 611230
[E-mail: john.mackie1@virgin.net]

Rogart See Lairg
Rosehall See Creich

Archer, Nicholas D.C.   BA BD   1971 1992   Fillview, Edderton, Tain IV19 4AJ   01862 821494
Macdonald, Michael   2004   (Dores and Boleskire)   73 Firhill, Alness IV17 0RT   01349 884268
                        Auxiliary Minister   [E-mail: michaeljmac2@btinternet.com]

(41) CAITHNESS

Meets alternately at Wick and Thurso on the first Tuesday of February, March, May, September, November and December, and the third Tuesday of June.

Clerk: MR JAMES R.H. HOUSTON MBA MA Lyndene House, Weydale, Thurso KW14 8YN 01847 893955
[E-mail: caithness@cofscotland.org.uk]

Bower linked with Watten
Alastair H. Gray MA BD 1978 2005 Station Road, Watten, Wick KW1 5YN 01955 621220
[E-mail: alastair.h.gray@btinternet.com]

Canisbay linked with Dunnet linked with Keiss
Vacant The Manse, Canisbay, Wick KW1 4YH 01955 611309

Dunnet See Canisbay

Halkirk and Westerdale
Kenneth Warner BD DA DipTD 1981 Abbey Manse, Halkirk KW12 6UU 01847 831227
[E-mail: wrnrkenn@aol.com]

Keiss See Canisbay

Olrig linked with Thurso: St Peter's and St Andrew's (H)
Vacant The Manse, 40 Rose Street, Thurso KW14 8RF 01847 895186

The North Coast Parish
Paul R. Read BSc MA 2000 2006 Church of Scotland Manse, Reay, Thurso KW14 7RE 01847 811441
[E-mail: PRead747@aol.com]

The Parish of Latheron
Vacant Central Manse, Lybster KW3 6BN 01593 721231
John Craw DCS Craiglockhart, Latheronwheel, Latheron KW5 6DW 01593 741779

Thurso: St Peter's and St Andrew's See Olrig

Thurso: West (H)
Ronald Johnstone BD 1977 1984 Thorkel Road, Thurso KW14 7LW 01847 892663
[E-mail: ronaldjohnstone@tiscali.co.uk]

Watten See Bower

Wick: Bridge Street linked with Wick: Old (H) (L)
Vacant

Wick: Old See Wick: Bridge Street

Wick: Pulteneytown (H) and Thrumster
Vacant

Mappin, Michael G. BA   1961 1998   (Bower with Watten)   Mansfield, Miller Avenue, Wick KW1 4DF   01955 602167

The Manse, Coronation Street, Wick KW1 5LS   01955 603166

Mundays, Banks Road, Watten, Wick KW1 5YL   01955 621720

CAITHNESS Communion Sundays

Bower	1st Jul, Dec	North Coast	Mar, Easter, Jun, Sep, Dec	Watten	1st Jul, Dec
Canisbay	1st Jun, Nov	Olrig	last May, Nov	Wick	
Dunnet	last May, Nov	Thurso		Bridge Street	1st Apr, Oct
Halkirk and Westerdale	Apr, Jul, Oct	St Peter's and		Old	4th Apr, Sep
Keiss	1st May, 3rd Nov	St Andrew's	Mar, Jun, Sep, Dec	Pulteneytown and	
Latheron	Apr, Jul, Sep, Nov	West	4th Mar, Jun, Nov	Thrumster	1st Mar, Jun, Sep, Dec

(42) LOCHCARRON – SKYE

Meets in Kyle on the first Tuesday of each month, except January, May, July and August.

Clerk: REV. ALLAN J. MACARTHUR BD   High Barn, Croft Road, Lochcarron, Strathcarron IV54 8YA   **01520 722278 (Tel)**
01520 722674 (Fax)
[E-mail: lochcarronskye@cofscotland.org.uk]
[E-mail: a.macarthur@btinternet.com]

Applecross, Lochcarron and Torridon (GD)
David Macleod   2008   The Manse, Colonel's Road, Lochcarron, Strathcarron IV54 8YG   01520 722829
[E-mail: david.macleod@hotmail.co.uk]

Bracadale and Duirinish (GD)
Vacant   Kinloch Manse, Durvegan, Isle of Skye IV55 8WQ   01470 521457

Gairloch and Dundonnell
Derek Morrison   1995 2000   Church of Scotland Manse, The Glebe, Gairloch IV21 2BT   01445 712053 (Tel/Fax)
[E-mail: derekmorrison1@aol.com]

Glenelg and Kintail Roderick N. MacRae BTh	2001	2004	Church of Scotland Manse, Inverinate, Kyle IV40 8HE [E-mail: barvalous@msn.com]	01599 511245
Kilmuir and Stenscholl (GD) Ivor MacDonald BSc MSc BD	1993	2000	Staffin, Portree, Isle of Skye IV51 9JX [E-mail: ivormacdonald@btinternet.com]	01470 562759 (Tel/Fax)
Lochalsh John M. Macdonald	2002		The Church of Scotland Manse, Main Street, Kyle IV40 8DA [E-mail: john.macdonald53@btinternet.com]	01599 534294
Portree (GD) Sandor Fazakas BD MTh	1976	2007	Viewfield Road, Portree, Isle of Skye IV51 9ES [E-mail: fazakass52@yahoo.com]	01478 611868
Snizort (H) (GD) Vacant			The Manse, Kensaleyre, Snizort, Portree, Isle of Skye IV51 9XE	01470 532260
Strath and Sleat (GD) Ben Johnstone MA BD DMin	1973	2003	The Manse, 6 Upper Breakish, Isle of Skye IV42 8PY [E-mail: benonskye@onetel.com]	01471 820063
John D. Urquhart BA BD	1998	2003	The Manse, The Glebe, Kilmore, Teangue, Isle of Skye IV44 8RG [E-mail: ministear@hotmail.co.uk]	01471 844469

Name			Role	Address	Telephone
Beaton, Donald MA BD MTh	1961	2002	(Glenelg and Kintail)	Kilmaluag Croft, North Duntulm, Isle of Skye IV51 9UF	01470 552296
Ferguson, John LTh BD DD	1973	2002	(Portree)	9 Braeview Park, Beauly, Inverness IV4 7ED [E-mail: effieferguson@tiscali.co.uk]	01463 783900
Kellas, David J. MA BD	1966	2004	(Kilfinan with Kyles)	Babhunn, Glenelg, Kyle IV40 8LA [E-mail: davidkellas@beeb.net]	01599 522257
Macarthur, Allan J. BD	1973	1998	(Applecross, Lochcarron and Torridon)	High Barn, Croft Road, Lochcarron, Strathcarron IV54 8YA [E-mail: a.macarthur@btinternet.com]	(Tel) 01520 722278 (Fax) 01520 722674
McCulloch, Alen J.R. MA BD	1990	1995	Chaplain: Royal Navy	The Chaplaincy, HMS Drake, HMNB Devonport, Plymouth PL2 2BG [E-mail: avijoen90@hotmail.com]	
Macleod, Donald LTh	1988	2000	(Snizort)	Burnside, Upper Galder, Glenelg, Kyle IV40 8JZ [E-mail: donaldpmacleod_7@btinternet.com]	01599 522265
Martin, George M. MA BD	1987	2005	(Applecross, Lochcarron and Torridon)	8(1) Buckingham Terrace, Edinburgh EH4 3AA	0131-343 3937
Murray, John W.		2003	Auxiliary Minister	Totescore, Kilmuir, Portree, Isle of Skye IV51 9YN [E-mail: jwm7@hotmail.co.uk]	01470 542297

LOCHCARRON – SKYE Communion Sundays

Applecross	4th Jun	Glenshiel	1st Jul	Plockton and Kyle	2nd May, 1st Oct
Arnisort	1st Sep	Kilmuir	1st Mar, Sep	Portree	Easter, Pentecost, Christmas, 2nd Mar, Aug, 1st Nov
Bracadale	3rd Mar, Sep	Kintail	3rd Apr, Jul	Sleat	Last May
Broadford	Last Feb	Kyleakin	Last Sep	Snizort	1st Jan, 4th Mar
Duirinish	3rd Jan, Easter, 3rd Sep	Lochalsh and Stromeferry	4th Jan, Jun, Sep, Christmas, Easter	Stenscholl	1st Jun, Dec
Dundonnell	4th Jun	Lochcarron and Shieldaig	Easter; communion held on a revolving basis when there is a fifth Sunday in the month	Strath	4th Jan
Elgol	1st Aug			Torridon and Kinlochewe	2nd May
Gairloch	3rd Jun, Nov				
Glenelg	2nd Jun, Nov				

In the Parish of Strath and Sleat, Easter communion is held on a revolving basis.

(43) UIST

Meets on the first Tuesday of February, March, September and November in Bernera, and on the third Tuesday of June in Leverburgh.

Clerk: REV. MURDO SMITH MA BD   Scarista, Isle of Harris HS3 3HX   **01859 550200**
[E-mail: uist@cofscotland.org.uk]

Barra (GD)
Vacant   Cuithir, Castlebay, Isle of Barra HS9 5XD   01871 810230

Benbecula (GD) (H)
Andrew A. Downie BD BSc DipEd DipMin ThB 1994 2006 Church of Scotland Manse, Griminish, Isle of Benbecula HS7 5QA 01870 602180
[E-mail: andownie@yahoo.co.uk]

Berneray and Lochmaddy (GD) (H)
Donald Campbell MA BD DipTh 1997 2004 Church of Scotland Manse, Lochmaddy, Isle of North Uist HS6 5AA 01876 500414
[E-mail: dc@hebrides.net]

Carinish (GD) (H)
Iain Maciver BD   2007   Church of Scotland Manse, Clachan, Lochport, Lochmaddy, Isle of North Uist HS6 5HD   01876 580219
[E-mail: iain.maciver@hebrides.net]

Kilmuir and Paible (GE)
Vacant   Paible, Isle of North Uist HS6 5ED   01876 510310

Manish-Scarista (GD) (H)
Murdo Smith MA BD 1988 Scarista, Isle of Harris HS3 3HX 01859 550200
[E-mail: uist@cofscotland.org.uk]

South Uist (GD)
Jackie G. Petrie ... 1989 2004 ... Daliburgh, Lochboisdale, Isle of South Uist HS8 5SS ... 01878 700265
[E-mail: jackiegpetrie@yahoo.com]

Tarbert (GE) (H)
Norman MacIver BD ... 1976 1988 ... The Manse, Manse Road, Tarbert, Isle of Harris HS3 3DF ... 01859 502231
[E-mail: norman@n-cmaciver.freeserve.co.uk]

Name	Ord	Ind	Charge	Address	Tel
MacDonald, Angus J. BSc BD	1995	2001	(Lochmaddy and Trumisgarry)	7 Memorial Avenue, Stornoway, Isle of Lewis HS1 2QR	01851 706634
MacInnes, David MA BD	1966	1999	(Kilmuir and Paible)	9 Golf View Road, Kinmylies, Inverness IV3 8SZ	01463 717377
Macpherson, Kenneth J. BD	1988	2002	(Benbecula)	70 Baile na Cille, Balivanich, Isle of Benbecula HS7 5ND	01870 602751
Morrison, Donald John	2001		Auxiliary Minister	22 Kyles, Tarbert, Isle of Harris HS3 3BS	01859 502341
Muir, Alexander MA BD	1982	1996	(Carinish)	14 West Mackenzie Park, Inverness IV2 3ST	01463 712096
Smith, John M.	1956	1992	(Lochmaddy)	Hamersay, Clachan, Locheport, Lochmaddy, Isle of North Uist HS6 5HD	01876 580332

UIST Communion Sundays

Charge	Date	Charge	Date	Charge	Date
Barra	2nd Mar, June, Sep, Easter, Advent	Carinish	4th Mar, Aug	South Uist	1st Jun
Benbecula	2nd Mar, Sep	Kilmuir and Paible	1st Jun, 3rd Nov	Howmore	1st Sep
Berneray and Lochmaddy	4th Jun, last Oct	Manish-Scarista	3rd Apr, 1st Oct	Daliburgh	
				Tarbert	2nd Mar, 3rd Sep

(44) LEWIS

Meets at Stornoway, in St Columba's Church Hall, on the first Tuesday of February, March, June, September and November. It also meets if required in April and December on dates to be decided.

Clerk: REV. THOMAS S. SINCLAIR MA LTh BD   An Caladh, East Tarbert,
Tarbert, Isle of Harris HS3 3DB   01859 502849
[E-mail: lewis@cofscotland.org.uk]   07816 455820 (Mbl)
[E-mail: thomas@sinclair.com]

Barvas (GD) (H)
Paul Amed LTh DPS ... 1992 2008 ... Barvas, Isle of Lewis HS2 0QY ... 01851 840218
[E-mail: paulamed@hebrides.net]

Carloway (GD) (H)
Vacant

Knock, Carloway, Isle of Lewis HS2 9AU

01851 643255

Cross Ness (GE) (H)
Ian Murdo M. Macdonald DPA BD   2001

Cross Manse, Swainbost, Ness, Isle of Lewis HS2 0TB
[E-mail: ianmurdo@crosschurch.fsnet.co.uk]

01851 810375

Kinloch (GE) (H)
Iain M. Campbell BD   2004   2008

Laxay, Lochs, Isle of Lewis HS2 9LA
[E-mail: ianmstudy@aol.com]

01851 830218

Knock (GE) (H)
Fergus J. MacBain BD DipMin   1999   2002

Knock Manse, Garrabost, Point, Isle of Lewis HS2 0PW
[E-mail: fergusjohn@macbain.freeserve.co.uk]

01851 870362

Lochs-Crossbost (GD) (H)
Andrew W.F. Coghill BD DPS   1993

Leurbost, Lochs, Isle of Lewis HS2 9NS
[E-mail: andcoghill@aol.com]

01851 860243 (Tel/Fax)
07776 480748 (Mbl)

Lochs-in-Bernera (GD) (H) linked with Uig (GE) (H)
Hugh Maurice Stewart DPA BD   2008

4 Seaview, Knock, Point, Isle of Lewis HS2 0PD
(Temporary Manse)
[E-mail: h4hughie@hotmail.com]

01851 870691
07786 651796 (Mbl)

Stornoway: High (GD) (H)
William B. Black MA BD   1972   1998

1 Goathill Road, Stornoway, Isle of Lewis HS1 2NJ
[E-mail: willieblack@lineone.net]

01851 703106

Stornoway: Martin's Memorial (H) (Church office: 01851 700820)
Thomas MacNeil MA BD   2002   2006

Matheson Road, Stornoway, Isle of Lewis HS1 2LR
[E-mail: tommymacneil@hotmail.com]

01851 704238

Stornoway: St Columba (GD) (H) (Church office: 01851 701546)
Angus Morrison MA BD PhD   1979   2000

Lewis Street, Stornoway, Isle of Lewis HS1 2JF
[E-mail: morrisonangus@btconnect.com]

01851 703350

Uig (GE) (H) See Lochs-in-Bernera

Macdonald, James LTh CPS   1984 2001   (Knock)

Elim, 8A Lower Bayble, Point, Isle of Lewis HS2 0QA
[E-mail: elim8a@hotmail.co.uk]

01851 870173

Maclean, Donald A. DCS   (Deacon)

8 Upper Barvas, Isle of Lewis HS2 0QX

01851 840454

MacLennan, Donald Angus   1975 2006   (Kinloch)

4 Kestrel Place, Inverness IV2 3YH
[E-mail: maclennankinloch@btinternet.com]

01463 243750
(Mbl) 07799 668270

Macleod, William   1957 2006   (Uig)   54 Lower Barvas, Isle of Lewis HS2 0QY   01851 840217
Sinclair, Thomas Suter MA LTh BD   1966 2004   (Stornoway: Martin's Memorial)   An Caladh, East Tarbert, Tarbert, Isle of Harris HS3 3DB   01859 502849
                                                                                                    [E-mail: lewis@cofscotland.org.uk]   (Mbl) 07816 455820
                                                                                                    [E-mail: thomas@sinclair.com]

LEWIS Communion Sundays

Barvas	3rd Mar, Sep	Lochs-Crossbost	4th Mar, Sep
Carloway	1st Mar, last Sep	Lochs-in-Bernera	1st Apr, 2nd Sep
Cross Ness	2nd Mar, Oct	Stornoway	
Kinloch	3rd Mar, 2nd Jun, 2nd Sep	High	3rd Feb, last Aug
Knock	3rd Apr, 1st Nov	Martin's Memorial	3rd Feb, last Aug, 1st Dec, Easter
		Stornoway St Columba	3rd Feb, last Aug
		Uig	3rd Jun, 1st Sep

(45) ORKNEY

Normally meets at Kirkwall, in the East Church King Street Halls, on the second Tuesday of September, February and May, and on the last Tuesday of November.

Clerk: REV. TREVOR G. HUNT BA BD   The Manse, Finstown, Orkney KW17 2EG   01856 761328 (Tel/Fax)
                                              [E-mail: orkney@cofscotland.org.uk]   07753 423333 (Mbl)
                                              [E-mail (personal): trevorghunt@yahoo.co.uk]

Birsay, Harray and Sandwick
Andrea E. Price (Mrs)   1997   2001   The Manse, North Biggings Road, Dounby, Orkney KW17 2HZ   01856 771803
                                               [E-mail: andreaneil@andreaneil.plus.com]

East Mainland
Miriam Gross   West Manse, Holm, Orkney KW17 2SB   01856 781422 (Tel/Fax)
                                               [E-mail: rev.m.gross@googlemail.com]

Eday linked with Stronsay: Moncur Memorial (H)
Jennifer D. George (Ms) BA MDiv PhD   2000   2005   Manse, Stronsay, Orkney KW17 2AF   01857 616311
                                                      [E-mail: jennifergeorge@btinternet.com]

Evie (H) linked with Firth (H) linked with Rendall
Trevor G. Hunt BA BD   1986   Manse, Finstown, Orkney KW17 2EG   01856 761328 (Tel/Fax)
                                               [E-mail: trevorghunt@yahoo.co.uk]   07753 423333 (Mbl)

Firth (H) (01856 761117) See Evie

Flotta linked with Hoy and Walls
Vacant — South Isles Manse, Longhope, Stromness, Orkney KW16 3PG — 01856 701325

Hoy and Walls See Flotta

Kirkwall: East (H)
Allan McCafferty BSc BD — 1993 — East Church Manse, Thoms Street, Kirkwall, Orkney KW15 1PF [E-mail: amcc@grad.com] — 01856 875469

Kirkwall: St Magnus Cathedral (H)
G. Fraser H. Macnaughton MA BD — 1982 2002 — Berstane Road, Kirkwall, Orkney KW15 1NA [E-mail: fmacnaug@fish.co.uk] — 01856 873312

North Ronaldsay linked with Sanday (H)
John L. McNab MA BD — 1997 2002 — The Manse, Sanday, Orkney KW17 2BW — 01857 600429

Orphir (H) linked with Stenness (H)
Vacant — Stenness Manse, Stenness, Stromness, Orkney KW16 3HH — 01856 761331

Papa Westray linked with Westray
Iain D. MacDonald BD — 1993 — The Manse, Hilldavale, Westray, Orkney KW17 2DW [E-mail: idmacdonald@btinternet.com] — 01857 677357 (Tel/Fax) 07710 443780 (Mbl)

Rendall See Evie

Rousay (Church centre: 01856 821271)
Continuing Vacancy

Sanday See North Ronaldsay

Shapinsay (50 per cent part-time)
Vacant

South Ronaldsay and Burray
Vacant — St Margaret's Manse, Church Road, St Margaret's Hope, Orkney KW17 2SR — 01856 831288

Stenness See Orphir

Stromness (H)
Fiona L. Lillie (Mrs) BA BD MLitt — 1995 1999 — 5 Manse Lane, Stromness, Orkney KW16 3AP [E-mail: fionalillie@btinternet.com] — 01856 850203

Stronsay: Moncur Memorial See Eday
Westray See Papa Westray

Brown, R. Graeme BA BD	1961 1998	(Birsay with Rousay)	Bring Deeps, Orphir, Orkney KW17 2LX [E-mail: graeme_sibyl@btinternet.com]	(Tel/Fax) 01856 811707
Clark, Thomas L. BD	1985 2008	(Orphir with Stenness)	Stenness Manse, Stenness, Orkney KW16 3HH [E-mail: toml.clark@btopenworld.com]	01856 761331

(46) SHETLAND

Meets at Lerwick on the first Tuesday of March, April, June, September, October, November and December.

Clerk: REV. CHARLES H.M. GREIG MA BD	The Manse, Sandwick, Shetland ZE2 9HW [E-mail: shetland@cofscotland.org.uk]	01950 431244

Burra Isle linked with Tingwall

Vacant	The Manse, 25 Hoga Lee, East Voe, Scalloway, Shetland ZE1 0UU	

Delting linked with Northmavine

Vacant		The Manse, Grindwell, Brae, Shetland ZE2 9QJ	01806 522219
Robert M. MacGregor (Aux) CMIOSH DipOSH RSP	2004	Olna Cottage, Brae, Shetland ZE2 9QS [E-mail: shetlandsafety@aol.com]	01806 522773

Dunrossness and St Ninian's inc. Fair Isle linked with Sandwick, Cunningsburgh and Quarff

Charles H.M. Greig MA BD	1976 1997	The Manse, Sandwick, Shetland ZE2 9HW [E-mail: chm.greig@btopenworld.com]	01950 431244

Fetlar linked with Unst linked with Yell

David Cooper BA MPhil (David Cooper is a minister of the Methodist Church)	1975 2008	Southerhouse, Gutcher, Yell, Shetland ZE2 9DF	01957 744258

Lerwick and Bressay

Gordon Oliver BD	1979 2002	The Manse, 82 St Olaf Street, Lerwick, Shetland ZE1 0ES [E-mail: stolaf@tiscali.co.uk]	01595 692125

Nesting and Lunnasting linked with Whalsay and Skerries

Irene A. Charlton (Mrs) BTh	1994 1997	The Manse, Marrister, Symbister, Whalsay, Shetland ZE2 9AE [E-mail: irene.charlton@virgin.net]	01806 566767
Richard M. Charlton (Aux)	2001	The Manse, Marrister, Symbister, Whalsay, Shetland ZE2 9AE [E-mail: richardm.charlton@virgin.net]	01806 566767

Northmavine See Delting

Sandsting and Aithsting linked with Walls and Sandness
Thomas Macintyre MA BD   1972   2006   The Manse, Happyhansel, Walls, Shetland ZE2 9PB   01595 809709
[E-mail: the2macs.macintyre@btinternet.com]

Sandwick, Cunningsburgh and Quarff See Dunrossness and St N.nian's
Tingwall See Burra Isle
Unst See Fetlar
Walls and Sandness See Sandsting and Aithsting
Whalsay and Skerries See Nesting and Lunnasting
Yell See Fetlar

Blair, James N.	1962 1986	(Sandsting and Aithsting with Walls)	2 Swinister, Sandwick, Shetland ZE2 9HH	01950 431472
Douglas, Marilyn (Miss) DCS	1988 2004	Presbytery Assistant	Heimda, Quarff, Shetland ZE2 9EZ	01950 477584
Kirkpatrick, Alice H. (Miss) MA BD FSAScot	1987 2000	(Northmavine)	4 Stendaal, Skellister, South Nesting, Shetland ZE2 9XA	
Knox, R. Alan MA LTh AInstAM	1965 2005	(Fetlar with Unst with Yell)	27 Killyvalley Road, Garvagh, Co. Londonderry, Northern Ireland BT51 5LX	02829 558925
Smith, Catherine (Mrs) DCS	1964 2003	(Presbytery Assistant)	21 Lingaro, Bixter, Shetland ZE2 9NN	01595 810207
Williamson, Magnus J.C.	1982 1999	(Fetlar with Yell)	Creekhaven, Houll Road, Scalloway, Shetland ZE1 0XA	01595 880023
Wilson, W. Stewart DA	1980 1997	(Kirkcudbright)	Aesterheull, Fair Isle, Shetland ZE2 9JU	01595 760273

(47) ENGLAND

Meets at London, in Crown Court Church, on the second Tuesday of March and December, and at St Columba's, Pont Street, on the second Tuesday of June and October.

Clerk: REV. SCOTT J. BROWN QHC BD RN   35 Stag Way, Funtley, Fareham, Hants PO15 6TW   01329 236895 (Home)
[E-mail: england@cofscotland.org.uk]   02392 625552 (Work)
07769 847876 (Mbl)

Corby: St Andrew's (H)
Vacant   6 Honiton Gardens, Corby, Northants NN18 8BW   01536 203175

Corby: St Ninian's (H) (01536 265245)
Alexander T. McAspurren BD MTh   2002   2008   The Manse, 46 Glyndebourne Gardens, Corby, Northants NN18 0PZ   01536 352430
[E-mail: alexander.mcaspurren@ntlworld.com]

Guernsey: St Andrew's in the Grange (H)
Graeme W. Beebee BD 1993 2003 The Manse, Le Villocq, Castel, Guernsey GY5 7SB 01481 257345
[E-mail: beehive@cwgsy.net]

Jersey: St Columba's (H)
Randolph Scott MA BD 1991 2006 18 Claremont Avenue, St Saviour, Jersey JE2 7SF 01534 730659
[E-mail: rev.rs@tinyworld.co.uk]

Liverpool: St Andrew's
Continued Vacancy
Session Clerk: Mr Robert Cottle 0151-524 1915

London: Crown Court (H) (020 7836 5643)
P.L. Majcher BD 1982 2007 53 Sidmouth Street, London WC1H 8JB 020 7278 5022
[E-mail: minister@crowncourtchurch.org.uk]
Timothy Fletcher BA FCMA (Aux) 1998 37 Harestone Valley Road, Caterham, Surrey CR3 6HN 01883 340826

London: St Columba's (H) (020 7584 2321) linked with Newcastle: St Andrew's (H)
Barry W. Dunsmore MA BD 1982 2000 29 Hollywood Road, Chelsea, London SW10 9HT 020 7376 5230
[E-mail: office@stcolumbas.org.uk]
Dorothy Lunn (Aux) 2001 2002 14 Bellerby Drive, Ouston, Co. Durham DH2 1TW 0191-492 0647
[E-mail: dorothylunn@hotmail.com]

Newcastle: St Andrews See London: St Columba's

Bowie, A. Glen CBE BA BSc 1954 1984 (Principal Chaplain: RAF) 16 Weir Road, Hemingford Grey, Huntingdon PE18 9EH 01480 381425
Brown, Scott J. QHC BD RN 1993 Principal Chaplain: Royal Navy Principal Church of Scotland and Free Churches Chaplain (Naval), 02392 625552
and Director Naval Chaplaincy Service (Capability), (Mbl) 07769 847876
Directorate General Naval Chaplaincy Service, MP 1.2,
Leach Building, Whale Island, Portsmouth PO2 8BY
[E-mail: clerk@presbyteryofengland.org.uk]
Cairns, W. Alexander BD 1978 2006 (Corby: St Andrew's) Kirkton House, Kirkton of Craig, Montrose DD10 9TB (Mbl) 07808 588045
[E-mail: sandy.cairns@btinternet.com]
Cameron, R. Neil 1975 1981 Chaplain: Community The Church Centre, Rhine Area Support Unit, BFPO 40 0049 2161 472770
Coulter, David G. 1989 1994 Chaplain: Army 8 Ashdown Terrace, Tidworth, Wilts SP9 7SQ 01980 842175
BA BD MDA PhD CF
[E-mail: padredgcoulter@aol.com]
Craig, Gordon T. BD 1988 Chaplain: RAF 40 Aiden Road, Quarrington, Sleaford, Lincs NG34 8UU 01529 300264
Cross, Brian F. MA 1961 1998 (Coalburn) 1474 High Road, Whetstone, London N20 9QD 020 8492 9313

Name	Position	Years	Address	Tel
Dalton, Mark BD DipMin	Chaplain: RN	2002	The Chaplaincy, HMS *Seahawk*, RNAS Culdrose, Helston TR12 7RH [E-mail: mark.dalton242@mod.uk]	
Devenney, David J. BD	Chaplain: RN	1997 2003	8 Hinton Close, Lympstone, Exmouth, Devon EX8 5JG [E-mail: davidjdevenney@freeuk.com]	01395 266570
Dowswell, James A.M.	(Lerwick and Bressay)	1991 2001	Mill House, High Street, Staplehurst, Tonbridge, Kent TN12 0AV	01580 891271
Drummond, J.S. MA	(Corby: St Ninian's)	1949 1978	77 Low Road, Hellesdon, Norwich NR6 5AG	01603 417736
Duncan, Denis M. BD PhD	(Editor: *The British Weekly*)	1944 1986	80A Woodland Rise, London N10 3UJ	(Tel) 020 8883 1831 (Fax) 020 8374 4708
Fields, James MA BD STM	School Chaplain	1988 1997	The Bungalow, The Ridgeway, Mill Hill, London NW7 1QX	020 8201 1397
Hood, Adam J.J. MA BD DPhil	Lecturer	1989	67A Farquhar Road, Edgbaston, Birmingham B15 2QP [E-mail: adamhood1@hotmail.com]	0121-452 2606
Kingston, David V.F. BD DipPTh	Chaplain: Army	1993	CSFC Chaplain, RAF Akrotiri, Cyprus, BFPO 57	
Lugton, George L. MA BD	(Guernsey: St Andrew's in the Grange)	1955 1997	6 Cbs de Beauvoir, Rue Cohu, Guernsey GY5 7TE	(Tel/Fax) 01481 254285
Macfarlane, Peter T. BA LTh	(Chaplain: Army)	1970 1994	4 rue de Rives, 37160 Abilly, France	
McIndoe, John H. MA BD STM DD	(London: St Columba's with Newcastle: St Andrew's	1966 2000	5 Dunlin, Westerlands Park, Glasgow G12 0FE	0141-579 1366
MacLeod, C. Angus MA BD	Chaplain: Army	1996	1 Mechanised Brigade, Delhi Barracks, Tidworth, Wilts SP9 7DX [E-mail: padreangusmac@hotmail.com]	(Work) 01980 602326 (Home) 01980 842380
MacLeod, Rory N. MA BD	Chaplain: Army	1986 1992	25 Redford Gardens, Edinburgh EH13 0AP	0131-441 6522
Martin, Anthony M. BA BD	Chaplain: Army	1989		01189 763409
Milloy, A. Miller DPE LTh DipTrMan	General Secretary: United Bible Societies	1979 1998	3 Lea Wood Road, Fleet, Hants GU51 5AL	01252 628455
Mills, Peter W. BD CPS	Chaplain-in-Chief, Royal Air Force	1984		
Norwood, David W. BA	(Lisbon)	1948 1980	6 Kempton Close, Thundersley, Benfleet, Essex SS7 3SG	01268 747219
Prentice, Donald K. BSc BD	Chaplain: Army	1989 1992	3 Rifles, Redford Barracks, Colinton Road, Edinburgh EH13 0PP	
Rennie, Alistair M. MA BD	(Kincardine Croick and Edderton)	1939 1986	Noble's Yard, St Mary's Gate, Wirksworth, Derbyshire DE4 4DQ [E-mail: alistairrennie@lineone.net]	01629 820289
Stewart, Charles E. BSc BD PhD	School Chaplain	1976 2000	The Royal Hospital School, Holbrook, Ipswich IP9 2RX	01473 326200
Thomson, Steven BSc BD	Chaplain: Royal Navy	2001 2004	The Chaplaincy, HMS *Sultan*, Military Road, Gosport PO12 3BY	
Trevorrow, James A. LTh	(Glasgow: Cranhill)	1971 2003	12 Test Green, Corby, Northants NN17 2HA [E-mail: jimtrevorrow@compuserve.com]	01536 264018
Walker, R. Forbes BSc BD ThM	School Chaplain	1987 2000	2 Helmleigh, Priory Road, Ascot, Berks SL5 8EA	01344 883272
Wallace, Donald S.	(Chaplain: RAF)	1950 1980	7 Delfield Close, Watford, Herts WD1 3BL	01923 223289
Ward, Michael J. BSc BD PhD MA	Chaplain: College	1983 2004	19 Devonshire Avenue, Grimsby, Lincs DN32 0BW [E-mail: revmw@btopenworld.com]	01472 877079
Whitton, John P.	(Deputy Chaplain General)	1977 1999	115 Sycamore Road, Farnborough, Hants GU14 6RE [E-mail: john_whittonuk@yahoo.co.uk]	01252 674488

ENGLAND – Church Addresses

		Liverpool	**London**
Corby	Occupation Road		Crown Court WC2
St Andrew's			St Columba's Pont Street SW1
St Ninian's	Beanfield Avenue	The Western Rooms,	
		Anglican Cathedral	**Newcastle**
			Sandyford Road

Crown Court

(48) EUROPE

Clerk: REV. JOHN A. COWIE BSc BD   Jan Willem Brouwersstraat 9, NL-1071 LH Amsterdam   **Tel: 0031 20 672 2288**
[E-mail: europe@cofscotland.org.uk]   **Fax: 0031 842 221513**
[E-mail: j.cowie@chello.nl]

Amsterdam
John A. Cowie BSc BD   1983   Jan Willem Brouwersstraat 9, NL-1071 LH Amsterdam,   0031 20 672 2288
The Netherlands   Fax: 0031 842 221513
[E-mail: j.cowie@chello.nl]

Brussels (E-mail: secretary@churchofscotland.be)
Andrew Gardner BSc BD PhD   1997   23 Square des Nations, B-1000 Brussels, Belgium   0032 2 672 40 56
[E-mail: minister@churchofscotland.be]

Budapest (Church telephone: +36 13730725)
Aaron Stevens   2006   H-1145 Budapest, Uzsoki u. 34b, Hungary   0036 (1) 2516896
[E-mail: revastevens@yahoo.co.uk]   (Mbl) 0036 203179592
Otto Pecsuk (Assoc)   2006   1119 Budapest, Allende Park 9. III/II, Hungary   0036 (7) 2947635
[E-mail: opecsuk@yahoo.com]

Colombo, Sri Lanka: St Andrew's Scots Kirk
John P.S. Purves BSc BD   1978   73 Galle Road, Colpetty, Colombo 3, Sri Lanka   0094 (11) 2386774
[E-mail: reverend@sltnet.lk]

Costa del Sol
Vacant   Lux Mundi Centro Ecumenico, Calle Nueva 3, Fuengirola,   0034 951 260 982
E-29460 Malaga, Spain
[E-mail: info@kirkojocks.eu]

Geneva
Ian A. Manson BA BD   1989   2001   20 Ancienne Route, 1218 Grand Saconnex, Geneva, Switzerland   0041 22 798 29 09
(Office) 0041 22 788 08 31
[E-mail: cofsg@pingnet.ch]

Gibraltar
Vacant

St Andrew's Manse, 29 Scud Hill, Gibraltar
[E-mail: scotskirk@gibraltar.gi]

00350 200 77040

Lausanne
G. Melvyn Wood MA BD   1982   2004

26 Avenue de Rumire, CH-1005 Lausanne, Switzerland   (Tel/Fax) 0041 21 323 98 28
[E-mail: scotskirklausanne@bluewin.ch]

Lisbon
William B. Ross LTh CPS   1988   2006

Av. Eng. Adelino Amaro da Costa, 2086, 2750 Cascais, Portugal
[E-mail: cofslx@netcabo.pt]

00351 21 483 7885

Malta
Vacant

La Romagnola, 13 Triq is-Seiqia, Mosra Kola, Attard   (Tel/Fax) 00356 214 15465
BZN 05, Malta
Church address: 210 Old Baker Street, Valletta, Malta
[E-mail: minister@saintandrewsmalta.com]

Paris
Alan Miller BA MA BD   2000   2006

10 Rue Thimmonier, F-75009 Paris, France
[E-mail: scotskirk@wanadoo.fr]
[E-mail: afmiller@orange.fr]

0033 1 48 78 47 94

Regensburg (University)
Rhona Dunphy (Mrs)   2005

Hirtensteig 1, 93155 Hemau-Laufenthal, Germany
[E-mail: rhona@dunphy.de]

0049 (949) 1903666

Rome: St Andrew's
William B. McCulloch BD   1997   2002

Via XX Settembre 7, 00187 Rome, Italy   (Tel) 0039 06 482 7627
[E-mail: revwbmcculloch@hotmail.com]   (Fax) 0039 06 487 4370

Rotterdam
Robert A. Calvert BSc BD DMin   1983   1995

Meeuwenstraat 4A, NL-3071 PE Rotterdam, The Netherlands
[E-mail: scotsintchurch@cs.com]

0031 10 220 4199

Turin
Alexander B. Cairns MA   1957   2007

Via S. Pio V, 10125 Turin, Italy
[E-mail: dorothycairns@aol.com]
Church address: Via Sant Anselmo 6, 10125 Turin, Italy

0039 011 650 5770
0039 011 650 9467

Warwick, Bermuda: Christ Church
Vacant

Mailing address: PO Box PG88, Paget PG BX, Bermuda   Office: 001 441 236 1882
Church address: Christ Church, Middle Road, Warwick, Bermuda
[E-mail: christchurch@logic.bm; Website: www.christchurch.bm]
Manse address: The Manse, 6 Manse Road, Paget PG 01, Bermuda

Conference of European Churches

Matthew Z. Ross LLB BD MTh FSAScot	1998	2003	Church and Society Commission, Ecumenical Centre, Rue Joseph II 174, B-1000 Brussels, Belgium [E-mail: mzr@cec-kek.be]	(Tel) 0032 2 230 1732 (Fax) 0032 2 231 1413 (Mbl) 0044 7711 706950
James M. Brown MA BD	1982		Neustrasse 15, D-4630 Bochum, Germany [E-mail: j.brown@web.de]	0049 234 133 65
Joanne Evans-Boiten BD	2004	2008	Oude Veerdam 2, NL-3212 MA Simonshaven, The Netherlands	0031 181 454229
T. Alan W. Garrity BSc BD MTh	1969	1987	17 Solomon's View, Dunlop, Kilmarnock KA3 4ES	
Professor A.I.C. Heron BD DTheol	1975		University of Erlangen, Kochstrasse 6, D-91054 Erlangen, Germany [E-mail: arheron@theologie.uni-erlangen.de]	0049 9131 852202
Stewart J. Lamont BSc BD	1972	2008		
James Sharp (Auxiliary Minister: training and education)	2005		102 Rue des Eaux-Vivres, CH-1207 Geneva, Switzerland [E-mail: jimsharp@bluewin.ch]	0041 22 786 4847
John Shedden CBE BD DipPSS	1971	2008	Dunster, Horsecombe Grove, Combe Down, Bath BA2 7QP	
Bertalan Tamas			St Columba's Scottish Mission, Vorosmarty utca 51, H-1064 Budapest, Hungary [E-mail: rch@mail.elender.hu]	0036 1 343 8479
Derek Yarwood			Chaplain's Department, Garrison HQ, Princess Royal Barracks, BFPO 47, Germany	0044 5241 77924
(Rome) David F. Huie MA BD	1962	(2001)	15 Rosebank Gardens, Largs KA30 8TD [E-mail: david.huie@btopenworld.com]	01475 670733
(Brussels) Charles C. McNeill OBE BD	1962	(1991)	17 All Saints Way, Beachamwell, Swaffham, Norfolk PE37 8BU	
(Gibraltar) D. Stuart Philip MA	1952	(1990)	6 St Bernard's Crescent, Edinburgh EH4 1NP	0131-332 7499
(Brussels) Thomas C. Pitkeathly MA CA BD	1984	2004	1 Lammermuir Court, Gullane EH31 2HU	01620 843373
(Rotterdam) Joost Pot BSc (Aux)	1992	2004	[E-mail: j.pot@wanadoo.nl]	

(49) JERUSALEM

Jerusalem: St Andrew's
Vacant

PO Box 8619, Jerusalem 91086, Israel   (Tel) 00972 2 673 2401

Tiberias: St Andrew's
Jennifer C. Zielinski (Mrs) (Reader)

PO Box 104, Tiberias 14100, Israel   (Tel) 00972 4 671 0710
[E-mail: scottie2@netvision.net.il]   (Fax) 00972 4 671 0711

SECTION 6

Additional Lists
of Personnel

LIST A – AUXILIARY MINISTERS

NAME	ORD	ADDRESS	TEL	PR
Anderson, David M. MSc FCOptom	1984	1 Dumfries Place, Fort William PH33 6UQ	01397 703203	38
Attenburrow, Anne BSc MBChB	2006	4 Jock Inksons Brae, Elgin IV30 1QE	01343 552330	35
Binks, Mike	2007	Holly Bank, Corsbie Road, Newton Stewart DG8 6JD	01671 402201	9
Brown, Elizabeth (Mrs) JP RGN	1996	25 Highfield Road, Scone, Perth PH2 6RN	01738 552391	28
Buck, Maxine	2007	Brownlee House, Mauldslie Road, Carluke ML8 5HW	01555 759063	18
Burroughs, Kirsty-Ann (Mrs) BA BD CertTheol DRM PhD	2007	Lorne and Lowland Manse, Castlehill, Campbeltown PA28 6AN	01586 552468	19
Cameron, Ann	2005	30 Wilson Road, Banchory AB31 5UY	01330 825953	32
Campbell, Gordon MA BD CDipAF DipHSM MCMI MIHM AFRIN FRSGS FRGS FSAScot	2001	2 Falkland Place, Kingoodie, Invergowrie, Dundee DD2 5DY	01382 561383	29
Charlton, Richard	2001	The Manse, Symbister, Whalsay, Shetland ZE2 9AE	01806 566767	46
Don, Andrew	2006	5 Eskdale Court, Penicuik EH26 8HT	01968 675766	3
Durno, Richard C. DSW CQSW (Community Minister)	1989	Durnada House, 31 Springfield Road, Bishopbriggs, Glasgow G64 1PJ	0141-772 1052	16
Ferguson, Archibald M. MSc PhD CEng FRINA	1989	The Whins, 2 Barrowfield, Station Road, Cardross, Dumbarton G82 5NL	01389 841517	18
Fletcher, Timothy E.G. BA FCMA	1998	37 Hareston Valley Road, Caterham, Surrey CR3 6HN	01883 340826	47
Forrest, Kenneth P. CBE BSc PhD	2006	5 Carruth Road, Bridge of Weir PA11 3HQ	01505 615033	14
Glass, Alexander OBE MA	1998	Craigton, Tulloch Avenue, Dingwall IV15 9TU	01349 863258	39
Griffiths, Ruth I. (Mrs)	2004	Kirkwood, Mathieson Lane, Innellan, Dunoon PA23 7TA	01369 830145	19
Harrison, Cameron	2006	Woodfield House, Priormuir, St Andrews KY16 8LP	01334 478067	26
Hood, Catriona A.	2006	2 Bellmhor Court, Campbeltown PA28 6AN	01586 552065	19
Howie, Marion L.K. (Mrs) MA ARCS	1992	51 High Road, Stevenston KA20 3DY	01294 466571	12
Kay, Elizabeth (Miss) DipYCS	1993	1 Kintail Walk, Inchture, Perth PH14 9RY	01828 686029	29
Kemp, Tina MA	2005	12 Oaktree Gardens, Dumbarton G82 1EU	01389 730477	18
Landale, William S.	2005	Green Hope Guest House, Green Hope, Duns TD11 3SG	01361 890242	5
Lunn, Dorothy	2002	14 Bellerby Drive, Ouston, Co. Durham DH2 1TN	0191-492 0647	47
Macdonald, Michael	2004	73 Firhill, Alness IV17 0RT	01349 884268	40
MacDougall, Lorna A. (Miss) MA	2003	34 Millar Place, Carron, Falkirk FK2 8QB	01324 552739	22
MacGregor, Robert M. MIOSH DipOSH RSP	2004	Olna Cottage, Brae, Shetland ZE2 9QS	01806 522604	46
Mack, John C. JP	1985	The Willows, Auchleven, Insch AB52 6QB	01464 820387	33
Manson, Eileen (Mrs) DCE	1994	1 Cambridge Avenue, Gourock PA19 1XT	01475 632401	14
Moore, Douglas T.	2003	9 Midton Avenue, Prestwick KA9 1PU	01292 671352	10
Morrison, Donald John	2001	22 Kyles, Tarbert, Isle of Harris HS3 3BS	01859 502341	43
Murray, John W.	2003	1 Totescore, Kilmuir, Portree, Isle of Skye IV51 9YN	01470 542297	42
O'Donnell, Barbara	2007	Ashbank, 258 Main Street, Alexandria G83 0NU	01389 752356	18
Paterson, Andrew E. JP	1994	6 The Willows, Kelty KY4 0FQ	01383 830998	24
Paterson, Maureen (Mrs) BSc	1992	91 Dalmahoy Crescent, Kirkcaldy KY2 6TA	01592 262300	25
Phillippo, Michael MTh BSc BVetMed MRCVS	2003	25 Deeside Crescent, Aberdeen AB15 7PT	01224 318317	31

NAME	ORD	ADDRESS	TEL	PR
Ramage, Alistair E. MA BA ADB CertEd	1996	16 Claremont Gardens, Milngavie, Glasgow G62 6PG	0141-956 2897	18
Riddell, Thomas S. BSc CEng FIChemE	1993	4 The Maltings, Linlithgow EH49 6DS	01506 843251	2
Robson, Brenda (Dr)	2005	Old School House, 2 Baird Road, Ratho, Newbridge EH28 8RA	0131-333 2746	1
Saunders, Grace	2007	40 Perth Street, Blairgowrie PH10 6DQ	01250 873981	27
Sharp, James	2005	102 Rue des Eaux-Vivres, CH-1207 Geneva, Switzerland	0041 22 786 4847	48
Sutherland, David	2001	6 Cromarty Drive, Dundee DD2 2UQ	01382 621473	29
Vivers, Katherine (Mrs)	2004	Blacket House, Eaglesfield, Lockerbie DG11 3AA	01461 500412	7
Wandrum, David	1993	5 Cawder View, Carrickstone Meadows, Cumbernauld, Glasgow G68 0BN	01236 723288	22
Zambonini, James LIADip	1997	100 Old Manse Road, Netherton, Wishaw ML2 0EP	01698 350889	17

AUXILIARY MINISTERS: RETIRED

NAME	ORD	ADDRESS	TEL	PR
Birch, Jim PGDip FRSA FIOC	2001	1 Kirkhill Grove, Cambuslang, Glasgow G72 8EH	0141-583 1722	16
Cloggie, June (Mrs)	1997	11A Tulipan Crescent, Callander FK17 8AR	01877 331021	23
Craggs, Sheila (Mrs)	2001	7 Morar Court, Ellon AB41 9GG	01358 723055	33
Cruikshank, Alistair A.B. MA	1991	Thistle Cottage, 2A Chapel Place, Dollar FK14 7DW	01259 742549	23
Jenkinson, John J. JP LTCL ALCM DipEd DipSen	1991	8 Rosehall Terrace, Falkirk FK1 1PY	01324 625498	22
McAlpine, John BSc	1988	Braeside, 201 Bonkle Road, Newmains, Wishaw ML2 9AA	01698 384610	17
MacDonald, Kenneth MA BA	2001	5 Henderland Road, Bearsden, Glasgow G61 1AH	0141-943 1103	16
MacFadyen, Anne M. (Mrs) BSc BD FSAScot	1995	295 Mearns Road, Glasgow G77 5LT	0141-639 3605	16
Mack, Elizabeth A. (Miss) DipPEd	1994	24 Roberts Crescent, Dumfries DG2 7RS	01387 264847	8
Mailer, Colin	2000	Innis Chonain, Back Row, Polmont, Falkirk FK2 0RD	01324 712401	22
Munro, Mary (Mrs) BA	1993	14 Auchneel Crescent, Stranraer DG9 0JH	01776 870250	9
Pot, Joost BSc	1992	Rijksstraatweg 12, NL-2988 BJ Ridderkerk, The Netherlands	0031 18 042 0894	48
Shaw, Catherine A.M. MA	1998	40 Merrygreen Place, Stewarton, Kilmarnock KA3 5EP	01560 483352	11
Simpson, James H. BSc	1996	11 Claypotts Place, Broughty Ferry, Dundee DD5 1LG	01382 776520	29
Thomas, Shirley A. (Mrs) DipSocSci AMIA	1988	14 Kirkgait, Letham, Forfar DD8 2XQ	01307 818084	30
Watson, Jean S. (Miss) MA	1993	29 Strachan Crescent, Dollar FK14 9HL	01259 742872	23
Wilson, Mary D. (Mrs) RGN SCM DTM	1990	'Berbice', The Terrace, Bridge of Tilt, Blair Atholl, Pitlochry PH18 5SZ	01796 481619	27

LIST B – CHAPLAINS TO HM FORCES

NAME	ORD	COM	BCH	ADDRESS
Abeledo, Benjamin J.A. BTh DipTh PTh	1991	1999	A	2 Bn 1TB, Helles Barracks, Catterick Garrison, North Yorks DL9 4HH
Aitchison, James W. BD	1993		A	2PWRR, SEME Bordon, Hants GU35 0NE

Name	Branch	Year	Unit / Address
Almond, David M. BD	TA	2002	West Lowland Bn
Anderson, David P. BSc BD	A	2007	3 Scots, Fort George, Ardersier, Inverness IV1 2TD
Andrews, J. Edward MA BD DipCG FSAScot	TA		Glasgow and Lanark Bn
Barclay, Iain C. MBE TD MA BD MTh MPhil PhD	TA		306 Field Hospital (V)
Barclay, Iain C. MBE TD MA BD MTh MPhil PhD	TA		Black Watch Bn
Barclay, Iain C. MBE TD MA BD MTh MPhil PhD	TA		Aberdeen Universities Officer Training Corps
Blakey, Stephen A. BSc BD	TA	1987	6 Bn The Royal Regiment of Scotland
Britchfield, Alison E.P. (Mrs) MA BD	RN	1993	The Chaplaincy, HMS Neptune, Helensburgh G84 8HL
Brown, Scott J. QHC BD RN	RN		Staff Chaplain DGNCS, MP 1.2, Leach Building, Whale Island, Portsmouth, Hants PO2 8BY
Bryson, Thomas M. BD	TA		2 Bn The Highlanders
Campbell, Roderick D.M. TD BD FSAScot	TA		Argyll and Sutherland Highlanders Bn
Connolly, Daniel BD DipTheol DipMin	A	1983	27 Regt RLC, Travers Barracks, Aldershot GU11 2BX
Coulter, David G. BA BD MDA PhD CF	A	1989	MOD Chaps (A), Trenchard Lines, Upavon, Pewsey, Wilts SN9 6BE
Craig, Gordon T. BD DipMin	RAF	1988	Chaplaincy Services (RAF), HQ Air Command, RAF High Wycombe, Bucks HP14 4UE
Dalton, Mark BD DipMin	RN	2002	The Chaplaincy, HMS Seahawk, RNAS Culdrose, Helston TR12 7RH
Davidson Kelly, Thomas A. MA BD FSAScot	TA		Army Personnel Centre, Glasgow
Devenney, David J. BD	RN	1997	The Chaplaincy, CTCRM, Lympstone, Exmouth, Devon EX8 5AR
Duncan, John C. BD MPhil	A	1987	Chaplain, 4 Scots and 2 Bn REME, St Barbara Barracks, Fallingbostel, BFPO 38
Forsyth, Alexander R. TD BA MTh	TA		25 (Highland) Field Ambulance (V)
Frail, Nicola BLE MBA MDiv	TA		205 (Scottish) Field Hospital
Francis, James BD PhD	TA		Queen's Own Yeomanry (V)
Kennon, Stan MA BD	RN	1992	The Chaplaincy, HMS Raleigh, Tor Point, Cornwall PL2
Kingston, David V.F. BD DipPTh	A	1993	CSFC Chaplain, RAF Akrotiri, Cyprus, BFPO 57
Kinsey, Louis BD DipMin	TA		205 (Scottish) Field Hospital (V)
McCulloch, Alen J.R. MA BD	RN	1990	Tri-Service Team of Chaplains, UK Contingency Operating Base, Basra, Iraq
McDonald, Ross J. BA BD ThM	RNR	1995	HMS Dalriada
Macgregor, John BD	A	2001	2 Scots, Glencorse Barracks, Milton Bridge, Penicuik EH26 0NP
Mackenzie, Seoras L. BD	A	1996	Chaplain, 1LSR, Princess Royal Barracks, BFPO 47
MacLean, Marjory A. LLB BD PhD	RNR		HMS Scotia
MacLeod, C. Angus MA BD	A	1996	HQ 1 Mech. Bde and Sig. Sqn, Delhi Barracks, Tidworth SP9 7DX
MacLeod, Rory N. MA BD	A	1986	1 Scots, Dreghorn Barracks, Edinburgh EH13 9QW
MacPherson, Duncan J. BSc BD	A	1993	HCR, Combermere Barracks, Windsor, Berkshire SL4 3DN
Mathieson, Angus R. MA BD	TA		Resident Battalion, Dreghorn and Glencorse Barracks
Mills, Peter W. BD CPS	RAF	1984	Chaplaincy Services (RAF), HQ Air Command, RAF High Wycombe, Bucks HP14 4UE
Munro, Sheila BD	RAF	1995	15 Hamilton Rise, MPA, BFPO 655
Prentice, Donald K. BSc BD	A	1989	3 Rifles, Redford Barracks, Colinton Road, Edinburgh EH13 0PP
Shackleton, Scott J.S. BA BD	RN	1993	The Chaplaincy, HMS Drake, HMNB Devonport, Plymouth PL2 2BG

Sutherland, Iain A. BSc BD			TA	2 Bn The Highlanders
Thom, David J. BD			TA	105 Regiment Royal Artillery (V)
Thom, David J. BD			TA	Cumbria ACF
Thomson, Steven BSc BD	2001	2004	RN	The Chaplaincy, HMS *Sultan*, Military Road, Gosport, Hants PO12 3BY
Thornthwaite, Anthony P. MTh			TA	Resident Battalion, Redford Barracks and The Castle
Walker, James B. MA BD DPhil			TA	Tayforth Universities Officer Training Corps
Warwick, Ivan C. MA BD TD			TA	1 Bn The Highlanders
Whiteford, Alexander LTh			TA	Resident Battalion, Fort George

LIST C – HOSPITAL CHAPLAINS ('Full-time' Chaplains are listed first in each area)

LOTHIAN

EDINBURGH – LOTHIAN UNIVERSITY HOSPITALS
ROYAL INFIRMARY

Rev. Alexander Young	32 Alnwickhill Park, Edinburgh EH16 6UH	0131-242 1991
Rev. Iain Telfer	27A Craigour Avenue, Edinburgh EH17 7NH	0131-242 1996
Anne Mulligan		
WESTERN GENERAL HOSPITAL [0131-537 1000]		
Rev. Alistair K. Ridland	13 Stewart Place, Kirkliston EH29 2BQ	0131-537 1400
LOTHIAN PRIMARY CARE		
ROYAL EDINBURGH HOSPITAL [0131-537 6734]		
Rev. John McMahon		
Rev. Lynne MacMurchie		
Rev. Patricia Allen	1 Westgate, Dunbar EH42 1JL	
ROYAL HOSPITAL FOR SICK CHILDREN [0131-536 0000]		
Rev. Caroline Upton	10 (3FL) Montagu Terrace, Edinburgh EH3 5QX	0131-536 0144
EDINBURGH COMMUNITY MENTAL HEALTH		
Rev. Lynne MacMurchie	41 George IV Bridge, Edinburgh EH1 1EL	0131-220 5150
LIVINGSTON – ST JOHN'S HOSPITAL [01506 419666]		
Rev. Dr Georgina Nelson	Chaplain's Office, St John's Hospital, Livingston	01506 522188

HOSPICES

MARIE CURIE HOSPICE, EDINBURGH	Rev. Tom Gordon	Frogston Road West, Edinburgh EH10 7DR	(Tel) 0131-470 2201
			(Fax) 0131-470 2200
ST COLUMBA'S HOSPICE	Rev. Ewan Kelly	15 Boswall Road, Edinburgh EH5 3RW	0131-551 1381

HOSPITALS

CORSTORPHINE	Rev. J. William Hill	33/9 Murrayfield Road, Edinburgh EH12 6EP	0131-554 1842
EASTERN GENERAL	Rev. John Tait	52 Pilrig Street, Edinburgh EH6 5AS	
LINLITHGOW ST MICHAEL'S	Rev. Dr Georgina Nelson	Chaplain's Office, St John's Hospital, Livingston	01506 522188
BELHAVEN	Rev. Laurence H. Twaddle	The Manse, Belhaven Road, Dunbar EH42 1NH	01368 863098
EDENHALL	Rev. Anne M. Jones	7 North Elphinstone Farm, Tranent EH33 2ND	01875 614442
HERDMANFLAT	Rev. Anne M. Jones	7 North Elphinstone Farm, Tranent EH33 2ND	01875 614442
LOANHEAD	Mrs Susan Duncan	35 Kilmaurs Road, Edinburgh EH16 5DB	0131-667 2995
ROODLANDS	Rev. Kenneth D.F. Walker	The Manse, Athelstaneford, North Berwick EH39 5BE	01620 880378
ROSSLYNLEE	Rev. John W. Fraser	North Manse, Penicuik EH26 8AG	01968 672213

BORDERS

MELROSE – BORDERS GENERAL HOSPITAL [01896 754333]	Rev. J. Ronald Dick	Chaplaincy Centre, Borders General Hospital, Melrose TD6 9BS	
DINGLETON	Rev. John Riddell	Orchid Cottage, Gingham Row, Earlston TD4 6ET	01721 721749
HAY LODGE, PEEBLES	Rev. James H. Wallace	Innerleithen Road, Peebles EH45 8BD	01361 883755
KNOLL	Rev. Andrew Morrice	The Manse, Castle Street, Duns TD11 3DG	01573 420308
INCH	Rev. Robin McHaffie	Kirk Yetholm, Kelso TD5 8RD	

DUMFRIES AND GALLOWAY

DUMFRIES AND GALLOWAY ROYAL INFIRMARY [01387 241625]	Rev. Alexander E. Strachan		
THOMAS HOPE, LANGHOLM	Rev. Robert B. Milne	The Manse, Langholm DG13 0BL	01896 668577
LOCHMABEN			
MOFFAT			
NEW ANNAN	Rev. Mairi C. Byers	Meadowbank, Plumdon Road, Annan DG12 6SJ	01461 206512
CASTLE DOUGLAS	Rev. Robert Malloch	1 Castle View, Castle Douglas DG7 1BG	01556 502171
DUMFRIES AND GALLOWAY ROYAL INFIRMARY			
KIRKCUDBRIGHT	Rev. Douglas R. Irving	6 Bourtree Avenue, Kirkcudbright DG6 4AU	01557 330489
THORNHILL			
NEWTON STEWART			

AYRSHIRE AND ARRAN

AYRSHIRE AND ARRAN PRIMARY CARE
[01292 513023]
AILSA HOSPITAL, AYR
AYR HOSPITAL
AYRSHIRE AND ARRAN ACUTE HOSPITALS
[01563 521133]

	Rev. Sheila Mitchell	Chaplaincy Centre, Dalmellington Road, Ayr KA6 6AB	01292 475341
	Rev. Paul Russell		
CROSSHOUSE HOSPITAL KILMARNOCK	Rev. Alex Welsh	8 Greenside Avenue, Prestwick KA9 2HB	
AYR/BIGGART HOSPITALS [01292 610555]	Rev. Judith Huggett	4 Westmoor Crescent, Kilmarnock KA1 1TX	01292 442554
EAST AYRSHIRE COMMUNITY	Rev. Roderick H. McNidder	6 Hollow Park, Alloway, Ayr KA7 4SR	01290 420769
	Rev. John Paterson	33 Barrhill Road, Cumnock KA18 1PJ	
WAR MEMORIAL, ARRAN	Rev. Elizabeth Watson	The Manse, Whiting Bay, Isle of Arran KA27 8RE	01770 700289
LADY MARGARET, MILLPORT	Rev. Marjory H. Mackay	The Manse, Millport, Isle of Cumbrae KA28 0ED	01475 530416

LANARKSHIRE

LOCKHART	Rev. Alison Meikle	2 Kaimhill Court, Lanark ML11 9HU	01555 662600
CLELAND	Rev. John Jackson	The Manse, Bellside Road, Cleland, Motherwell ML1 5NP	01698 860260
KELLO	Rev. James Francis	61 High Street, Biggar ML12 6DA	01899 220227
ROADMEETINGS	Rev. Helen E. Jamieson	120 Clyde Street, Carluke ML8 5BG	01555 771218
WISHAW GENERAL	Rev. James S.G. Hastie	Chalmers Manse, Quarry Road, Larkhall ML9 1HH	01698 882238
	Rev. J. Allardyce	6 Kelso Crescent, Wishaw ML2 7HD	01698 372657
	Rev. Sharon Colvin	48 Dunrobin Road, Airdrie ML6 8LR	01236 763154
	Rev. Mhorag MacDonald	350 Kirk Road, Wishaw ML2 8LH	01698 381305
STRATHCLYDE	Rev. David W. Doyle	19 Orchard Street, Motherwell ML1 3JE	01698 263472
HAIRMYRES	Rev. John Brewster	21 Turnberry Place, East Kilbride, Glasgow G75 8TB	01355 242564
	Rev. Dr John McPake	30 Eden Grove, East Kilbride, Glasgow G75 8XY	01355 234196
	Rev. James S.G. Hastie	Chalmers Manse, Quarry Road, Larkhall ML9 1HH	01698 882238
KIRKLANDS			
STONEHOUSE			
UDSTON	Rev. J. Stanley Cook	137A Old Manse Road, Netherton, Wishaw ML2 0EW	01698 299600
COATHILL			
MONKLANDS GENERAL	Rev. James Munton	2 Moorcroft Drive, Airdrie ML6 8ES	01236 754848
	Rev. James Grier	14 Love Drive, Bellshill ML4 1BY	01698 742545
	Rev. Kay Gilchrist	45 Hawthorn Drive, Craigneuk, Airdrie ML6 8AP	
WESTER MOFFAT	Rev. James Munton	2 Moorcroft Drive, Airdrie ML6 8ES	01263 754848
HARTWOODHILL	Rev. Derek Pope	35 Birrens Road, Motherwell ML1 3NS	01698 266716
HATTONLEA	Rev. Agnes Moore	16 Croftpark Street, Bellshill ML4 1EY	01698 842877
MOTHERWELL PSYCHIATRIC			
COMMUNITY MENTAL HEALTH CARE	Rev. J. Stanley Cook	137A Old Manse Road, Netherton, Wishaw ML2 0EW	01698 299600
	Rev. Sharon Colvin	48 Dunrobin Road, Airdrie ML6 8LR	01236 763154

GREATER GLASGOW AND CLYDE

NORTH GLASGOW UNIVERSITY HOSPITALS

GLASGOW ROYAL INFIRMARY [0141-211 4000/4661]

Institution	Chaplain	Address	Phone
WESTERN INFIRMARY [0141-211 2000]	Rev. Anne J.M. Harper	122 Greenock Road, Bishopton PA7 5AS	0141-211 2000/2812
GARTNAVEL GENERAL [0141-211 3000]	Rev. Keith Saunders	1 Beckfield Drive, Robroyston, Glasgow G33 1SR	0141-211 3000/3026
GLASGOW HOMEOPATHIC [0141-211 1600]	Rev. Keith Saunders	1 Beckfield Drive, Robroyston, Glasgow G33 1SR	0141-211 1600
	Rev. Keith Saunders	1 Beckfield Drive, Robroyston, Glasgow G33 1SR	

GREATER GLASGOW PRIMARY CARE — Rev. Cameron H. Langlands: Co-ordinator

Institution	Chaplain	Address	Phone
GARTNAVEL ROYAL HOSPITAL [0141-211 3686]	Rev. Gordon B. Armstrong: North/East Sector	Chaplain's Office, Old College of Nursing, Stobhill Hospital, 133 Balornock Road, Glasgow G21 3UW	0141-232 0609
	Ms Anne MacDonald: South Sector	Chaplain's Office, Leverndale Hospital, 510 Crookston Road, Glasgow G53 7TU	0141-211 6695

SOUTH GLASGOW UNIVERSITY HOSPITALS

SOUTHERN GENERAL HOSPITAL [0141-201 2156] — Rev. Ann Purdie; Rev. Blair Robertson: Co-ordinator

VICTORIA INFIRMARY

Institution	Chaplain	Address	Phone
YORKHILL NHS TRUST [0141-201 0595]	Rev. Alistair Bull	Royal Hospital for Sick Children, Glasgow G3 8SG	01360 312527

GREATER GLASGOW PRIMARY CARE

Institution	Chaplain	Address	Phone
ROYAL INFIRMARY	Rev. David Torrance	19 Redhills View, Lennoxtown, Glasgow G65 7BL	0141-883 5618
STOBHILL	Rev. Alastair MacDonald	42 Roman Way, Dunblane FK15 9DJ	0141-632 1514
LEVERNDALE	Mrs Sandra Bell	62 Loganswell Road, Thornliebank, Glasgow G46 8AX	0141-959 7158
VICTORIA INFIRMARY/MEARNSKIRK	Rev. John Beaton	33 North Birbiston Road, Lennoxtown, Glasgow G65 7LZ	0141-569 8547
KNIGHTSWOOD/DRUMCHAPEL	Miss Anne MacDonald	62 Berwick Drive, Glasgow G52 3JA	0141-647 6178
RUTHERGLEN TAKARE	Rev. Alan Raeburn	110 Mount Annan Drive, Glasgow G44 4RZ	0141-429 5599
	Rev. Andrew McMillan	1 Swallow Gardens, Glasgow G13 4QD	0141-762 1844
	Rev. J.W. Drummond	12 Albert Drive, Rutherglen, Glasgow G73 3RT	0141-531 1346
	Rev. Alexander Thomson	31 Highburgh Drive, Rutherglen, Glasgow G73 3RR	
PRINCE AND PRINCESS OF WALES HOSPICE	Rev. Stuart Webster	71 Carlton Place, Glasgow G5 9TD	
FOURHILLS NURSING HOME	Rev. W.G. Ramsay	3 Tofthill Avenue, Bishopbriggs, Glasgow G64 3PN	
HUNTERS HILL MARIE CURIE CENTRE	Miss Dawn Allan	1 Belmont Road, Glasgow G21 3AY	
INVERCLYDE ROYAL HOSPITAL (Whole-time) GREENOCK [01475 633777]	Rev. Fergus McLachlan	Chaplain's Office, Inverclyde Royal Hospital, Larkfield Road, Greenock PA16 0XN	01475 723235
(Part-time)	Mrs Joyce Nicol	93 Brisbane Street, Greenock PA16 8NY	

Institution	Chaplain	Address	Phone
DYKEBAR MERCHISTON HOUSE	Rev. Thomas Cant	18 Oldhall Road, Paisley PA1 3HL	0141-882 2277
JOHNSTONE	Rev. Thomas Cant	18 Oldhall Road, Paisley PA1 3HL	0141-882 2277

	Chaplain	Address	Telephone
ROYAL ALEXANDRA	Rev. Arthur Sherratt	West Manse, Kilbarchan, Johnstone PA10 2JR	01805 702669
	Rev. Douglas Ralph	24 Kinpurnie Road, Paisley PA1 3HH	0141-883 3505
	Rev. Ritchie Gillon	31 Southfield Avenue, Paisley PA2 8BX	0141-884 6215
	Rev. David Kay	6 Southfield Avenue, Paisley PA2 8BY	0141-884 3600
	Rev. E. Lorna Hood (Mrs)	North Manse, 1 Alexandra Drive, Renfrew PA4 8UB	0141-886 2074
	Rev. Robin Allison	282 Main Road, Elderslie, Johnstone PA5 9EF	01505 321767
RAVENSCRAIG	Rev. Christine Murdoch	1 Station Rise, Lochwinnoch PA12 4NA	01505 843484
	Rev. David Mill	105 Newark Street, Greenock PA16 7TW	01475 639602
	Rev. Douglas Cranston	6 Churchill Road, Kilmacolm PA13 4LH	01505 873271
DUMBARTON JOINT	Rev. Daniel Cheyne	217 Glasgow Road, Dumbarton G82 1EE	01389 763075
VALE OF LEVEN GENERAL	Rev. Ian Miller	1 Glebe Gardens, Bonhill, Alexandria G83 9HB	01389 753039
VALE OF LEVEN GERIATRIC	Rev. Frederick Booth	Achnashie Coach House, Clynder, Helensburgh G84 0QD	01436 831858

FORTH VALLEY

	Chaplain	Address	Telephone
PRIMARY CARE	Rev. Robert MacLeod	13 Cannons Way, Falkirk FK2 7QG	01324 631008
BO'NESS	Mr Frank Hartley	49 Argyll Place, Kilsyth, Glasgow G65 0PY	01236 824135
FALKIRK ROYAL INFIRMARY	Rev. Helen Christie	5 Watson Place, Dennyloanhead, Bonnybridge FK4 2BG	01324 813786
	Rev. Margery Collin	2 Saughtonhall Crescent, Edinburgh EH12 5RF	0131-337 7153
BANNOCKBURN	Rev. James Landels	Allan Manse, Bogend Road, Bannockburn, Stirling FK7 8NP	01786 814692
CLACKMANNAN COUNTY	Rev. Eleanor Forgan	18 Alexandra Drive, Alloa FK10 2DQ	01259 212836
KILDEAN	Rev. Eleanor Forgan	18 Alexandra Drive, Alloa FK10 2DQ	01259 212836
SAUCHIE	Rev. Eleanor Forgan	18 Alexandra Drive, Alloa FK10 2DQ	01259 212836
STIRLING ROYAL INFIRMARY	Rev. Gary McIntyre	7 Randolph Road, Stirling FK8 2AJ	01786 474421
	Rev. Kenneth Russell	5 Clifford Road, Stirling FK8 2QU	01786 475802

FIFE

	Chaplain	Address	Telephone
QUEEN MARGARET HOSPITAL, DUNFERMLINE [01383 674136]	Mr Mark Evans DCS	Queen Margaret Hospital, Whitefield Road, Dunfermline KY12 0SU	01383 674136
VICTORIA HOSPITAL, KIRKCALDY [01592 643355]	Rev. Ian J.M. McDonald	11 James Grove, Kirkcaldy KY1 1TN	01592 203775
LYNEBANK	Rev. Elizabeth Fisk	51 St John's Drive, Dunfermline KY12 7TL	01383 720256
CAMERON	Rev. James L. Templeton	Innerleven Manse, McDonald Street, Methil, Leven KY8 3AJ	01333 426310
	Rev. Kenneth Donald	33 Main Road, East Wemyss, Kirkcaldy KY1 4RE	01592 713260
GLENROTHES	Rev. Ian D. Gordon	2 Somerville Way, Forester's Grove, Glenrothes KY7 5GE	01592 742487
RANDOLPH WEMYSS	Rev. Elizabeth Cranfield	9 Chemiss Road, Methilhill, Leven KY8 2BS	01592 713142
ADAMSON, CUPAR	Rev. Lynn Brady	2 Guthrie Court, Cupar Road, Newburgh, Cupar KY14 6HA	01337 842228
NETHERLEA, NEWPORT	Rev. James Connolly	5 Westwater Place, Newport-on-Tay DD6 8NS	01382 542626
STRATHEDEN, CUPAR	Mr Allan Grant	6 Normandy Place, Rosyth, Dunfermline KY11 2HJ	01383 428760
ST ANDREWS MEMORIAL	Rev. David Arnott	20 Priory Gardens, St Andrews KY16 8XX	01334 472912

TAYSIDE

Head of Spiritual Care

Head of Spiritual Care	Rev. Gillian Munro	Royal Dundee Liff Hospital, Dundee DD2 5NF	01382 423116
DUNDEE NINEWELLS HOSPITAL [01382 660111]	Rev. David J. Gordon		
PERTH ROYAL INFIRMARY [01738 473896]	Rev. John M. Birrell		
ABERFELDY	Rev. Anne Brennan	The Manse, Balnaskeag, Kenmore, Aberfeldy PH15 2HB	01887 830218
BLAIRGOWRIE RATTRAY	Rev. Ian Knox	Heatherlea, Main Street, Ardler, Blairgowrie PH12 8SR	01828 640731
IRVINE MEMORIAL	Rev. Ian Murray	The Manse, Blair Atholl, Pitlochry PH18 5SX	01796 481213
CRIEFF COTTAGE	Rev. James W. MacDonald	8 Strathearn Terrace, Crieff PH7 3AQ	01764 653907
MACMILLAN HOSPICE	Rev. John M. Birrell		
MURRAY ROYAL	Rev. Peter Meager		
ST MARGARET'S COTTAGE	Rev. John M. Birrell		
ROYAL VICTORIA	Rev. David J. Gordon	7 Lorraine Drive, Cupar KY15 5DY	01334 656991
ASHLUDIE	Rev. Roy Massie	St Rule's Manse, 8 Church Street, Monifieth DD5 4JP	01382 532607
DUNDEE, ROYAL LIFF	Rev. David Jamieson	Panmure Manse, 8A Albert Street, Monifieth DD5 4JS	01382 532772
STRATHMARTINE	Rev. James Milne	St Margaret's Rectory, Ancrum Road, Dundee DD2 2IL	01382 667227
	Rev. James Milne	St Margaret's Rectory, Ancrum Road, Dundee DD2 2IL	01382 667227
ARBROATH INFIRMARY	Rev. Alasdair G. Graham	1 Charles Avenue, Arbroath DD11 2EZ	01241 872244
BRECHIN INFIRMARY	Mr Gordon Anderson	33 Grampian View, Montrose DD10 9SU	01674 674915
CARSEVIEW MEDICAL CENTRE	Rev. Janet P. Foggie	39 Tullideph Road, Dundee DD2 2JD	01382 660152
LITTLE CAIRNIE	Rev. Ian G. Gough	St Vigeans Manse, Arbroath DD11 4RD	01241 873206
MONTROSE ROYAL	Rev. Iain Coltart	The Manse, Arbirlot, Arbroath DD11 2NX	01241 434479
STRACATHRO	Mr Gordon Anderson	33 Grampian View, Montrose DD10 9SU	01674 674915
SUNNYSIDE ROYAL	Mr Gordon Anderson	33 Grampian View, Montrose DD10 9SU	01674 674915
WHITEHILLS HEALTH AND COMMUNITY CARE CENTRE	Rev. Rona Phillips	The Manse, Inverkeilor, Arbroath DD11 5SA	01241 830464

GRAMPIAN

Head of Spiritual Care:
Rev. Fred Coutts, Chaplains' Office, Aberdeen Royal Infirmary, Foresterhill, Aberdeen AB25 2ZN

1. ACUTE SECTOR
ABERDEEN ROYAL INFIRMARY, ABERDEEN MATERNITY HOSPITAL
Chaplains' Office, Aberdeen Royal Infirmary, Foresterhill, Aberdeen AB25 2ZN   01224 553166
Rev. Fred Coutts
Rev. Sylvia Spencer (Chaplain's Assistant)   01224 553316

ROYAL ABERDEEN CHILDREN'S HOSPITAL
Chaplain's Office, Royal Aberdeen Children's Hospital, Westburn Drive, Aberdeen AB25 2ZG
Rev. James Falconer — 01224 554905

ROXBURGHE HOUSE
Chaplain's Office, Roxburghe House, Ashgrove Road, Aberdeen AB25 2ZH
Rev. Alison Hutchison — 01224 557077

WOODEND HOSPITAL
Chaplain's Office, Woodend Hospital, Eday Road, Aberdeen AB15 6XS
Rev. Mark Rodgers — 01224 556788

DR GRAY'S HOSPITAL, ELGIN
Rev. George Rollo, 18 Reidhaven Street, Elgin IV30 1QH — 01343 547208
Rev. Andrew Willis, Deanshaugh Croft, Mulben, Keith AB55 6YJ — 01542 860240
Rev. Norma Milne, 26 Green Road, Huntly AB54 8BE — 01466 793841

THE OAKS, ELGIN
Rev. Stuart Macdonald, 55 Forsyth Street, Hopeman, Elgin IV30 2SY — 01343 831175

2. MENTAL HEALTH
ROYAL CORNHILL HOSPITAL, WOODLANDS
Chaplain's Office, Royal Cornhill Hospital, Cornhill Road, Aberdeen AB25 2ZH.
Rev. Muriel Knox — 01224 557293
Miss Pamela Adam (Chaplain's Assistant)
Mr Donald Meston (Chaplain's Assistant)

3. COMMUNITY HOSPITALS

ABOYNE	Rev. Douglas Campbell	49 Charlton Crescent, Aboyne AB24 5GN	01339 886447
GLEN O'DEE, BANCHORY	Rev. Donald Walker	2 Wilson Road, Banchory AB31 3UY	01330 822811
CAMPBELL, PORTSOY	Rev. Iain Suther and	The Manse, Portsoy, Banff AB45 2QB	01261 842272
CHALMERS, BANFF	Rev. David J. Randall	The Manse, Macduff AB45 3QL	01261 832316
FLEMING, ABERLOUR	Rev. Andrew Willis	Deanshaugh Croft, Mulben, Keith AB55 6YJ	01542 860240
FRASERBURGH	Rev. James Newell	39 Grattan Place, Fraserburgh AB43 9SD	01346 514905
INVERURIE	Rev. Ian B. Groves	1 Westburn Place, Inverurie AB51 5QS	01467 620285
INSCH			
JUBILEE, HUNTLY	Rev. Thomas Calder	The Manse, Queen Street, Huntly AB54 5EB	01466 792630
KINCARDINE COMMUNITY,	Rev. David Stewart	South Manse, Cameron Street, Stonehaven AB39 2HE	01569 762576
STONEHAVEN	Rev. Rosslyn Duncan	Dunnottar Manse, Stonehaven AB39 3XL	01569 762876
LEANCHOIL, FORRES	Rev. David Young	15 Mannachie Rise, Forres IV36 2US	01309 672284
MAUD	Rev. Alastair Donald	New Deer Manse, Turriff AB53 6TG	01771 644216
MUIRTON	Rev. Andrew Willis		
PETERHEAD COMMUNITY	Rev. David S. Ross	3–5 Abbey Street, Deer, Peterhead AB42 5LN	01771 623994
SEAFIELD, BUCKIE	Rev. Andrew Willis	Deanshaugh Croft, Mulben, Keith AB55 6YJ	01542 860240
STEPHEN, DUFFTOWN	Rev. Hugh M.C. Smith	The Manse, Church Street, Dufftown, Keith AB55 4AR	01340 820380

TURNER, KEITH	Rev. Kay Gauld	The Manse, Church Road, Keith AB55 5BR	01542 882799
TURRIFF	Rev. Yvonne Hendrie	6 Craigneen Place, Whitehills, Banff AB45 2NE	01261 861671
UGIE, PETERHEAD	Mrs Sena Allen	Berea Cottage, Kirk Street, Peterhead AB42 1RY	01779 477327

HIGHLAND

THE RAIGMORE HOSPITAL [01463 704000]	Rev. Iain MacRitchie	7 Merlin Crescent, Inverness IV2 3TE	01479 872084
	Rev. Derek Brown	Cathedral Manse, Dornoch IV25 3HV	01340 661311
IAN CHARLES	Rev. Morris Smith	Golf Course Road, Grantown-on-Spey PH26 3HY	01463 704000
ST VINCENT	Rev. Helen Cook	The Manse, West Terrace, Kingussie PH21 1HA	
NEW CRAIGS	Rev. Michael Hickford	Chaplain's Office, New Craigs Hospital, Leachkin Road, Inverness IV3 8NP	
NAIRN TOWN AND COUNTY	Rev. Ian Hamilton	3 Manse Road, Nairn IV12 4RN	01667 452203
BELFORD AND BELHAVEN	Rev. Donald A. MacQuarrie	Manse of Duncansburgh, Fort William PH33 6BA	01397 702297
GLENCOE	Rev. Alison Burnside	The Manse, Ballachulish PH49 4JG	01855 811998
ROSS MEMORIAL, DINGWALL	Rev. Russel Smith	8 Castlehill Road, Dingwall IV15 9PB	01349 861011
INVERGORDON COUNTY	Rev. Kenneth D. Macleod	The Manse, Cromlet Drive, Invergordon IV18 0BA	01349 852273
LAWSON MEMORIAL	Rev. Eric Paterson	Free Church Manse, Golspie KW10 6TT	01408 633529
MIGDALE	Rev. Kenneth Hunter	Free Church Manse, Gower Street, Brora KW9 6PU	01408 621271
CAITHNESS GENERAL	Mr John Craw	'Craiglockhart', Latheronwheel, Latheron KW5 6DW	01593 741779
DUNBAR	Rev. Alastair H. Gray	The Manse, Station Road, Watten, Wick KW1 5YN	01955 621220
BROADFORD MACKINNON MEMORIAL	Rev. Dr Ben Johnstone	The Shiants, 5 Upper Breakish, Breakish, Isle of Skye IV42 8PY	01471 822538
PORTREE	Rev. Donald G. MacDonald	Free Church Manse, 3 Sluggans, Portree, Isle of Skye IV51 9LY	01478 613256
CAMPBELTOWN	Mrs Margaret Sinclair	2 Quarry Park, Furnace, Inveraray PA32 8XW	01499 500633
LOCHGILPHEAD			
ISLAY	Rev. Stephen Fulcher	The Manse, Main Street, Port Charlotte, Isle of Islay PA48 7TW	01496 850241
DUNOON	Rev. Ruth Griffiths	Kirkwood, Mathieson Lane, Innellan, Dunoon PA23 7TA	01369 830145
ROTHESAY	Mr Raymond Deans	60 Ardmory Road, Rothesay PA20 0PG	01700 504893
LORN AND THE ISLANDS DISTRICT GENERAL	Rev. Elizabeth Gibson	Rudha-na-Cloiche, The Esplanade, Oban PA34 5AQ	01631 562759

WESTERN ISLES HEALTH BOARD

UIST AND BARRA HOSPITAL WESTERN ISLES, STORNOWAY	Rev. T.K. Shadakshari	69 Plasterfield, Stornoway, Isle of Lewis HS1 2UR	01851 701727

ORKNEY HEALTH BOARD

BALFOUR AND EASTBANK	Mrs Marion Dicken	6 Claymore Brae, Kirkwall KW15 1UQ	01856 879509

LIST D – FULL-TIME INDUSTRIAL CHAPLAINS

EDINBURGH (Edinburgh City Mission Appointment)	Mr John Hopper	26 Mulberry Drive, Dunfermline KY11 5BZ	01383 737189
EDINBURGH (Methodist Appointment)	Rev. Linda Bandelier	5 Dudley Terrace, Edinburgh EH6 4QQ	0131-554 1636
GREATER GLASGOW AND LANARKSHIRE	Post vacant		
WEST OF SCOTLAND	Rev. Alister Goss	79 Weymouth Crescent, Gourock PA19 1HR	01475 638944
OFFSHORE OIL INDUSTRY	Rev. Andrew Jolly	Total E and P UK PLC, Crawpeel Road, Aberdeen AB12 3FG	(Office) 01224 297532
ABERDEEN CITY CENTRE (part-time)	Mrs Cate Adams	The Citadel, 28 Castle Street, Aberdeen AB11 5BG	01224 597373
NORTH OF SCOTLAND and NATIONAL CO-ORDINATOR	Mr Lewis Rose DCS	16 Gean Drive, Blackburn, Aberdeen AB21 0YN	01224 790145
TAYSIDE AND NORTH FIFE	Rev. Allan F. Webster	65 Clepington Road, Dundee DD4 7BQ	01382 458764

LIST E – PRISON CHAPLAINS

ADVISER TO SCOTTISH PRISON SERVICE (NATIONAL)	Rev. William Taylor	HM Prison, Edinburgh EH11 3LN	0131-444 3082
ABERDEEN CRAIGINCHES	Rev. Dr David Ross	HM Prison, Aberdeen AB11 8FN	01224 238300
	Rev. Louis Kinsey	HM Prison, Aberdeen AB11 8FN	01224 238300
	Rev. Iain Barclay	HM Prison, Aberdeen AB11 8FN	01224 238300
CORNTON VALE	Rev. Colin Shreenan	HM Prison, Cornton Vale, Stirling FK9 5NU	01786 832591
DUMFRIES	Rev. Neil Campbell	HM Prison, Dumfries DG2 9AX	01387 261218

EDINBURGH: SAUGHTON	Rev. Colin Reed	Chaplaincy Centre, HMP Edinburgh EH11 3LN	0131-444 3115
	Rev. William Taylor	HM Prison, Edinburgh EH11 3LN	0131-444 3082
	Rev. Robert Akroyd	HM Prison, Edinburgh EH11 3LN	0131-444 3115
GLASGOW: BARLINNIE	Rev. Edward V. Simpson	5 Langtree Avenue, Glasgow G46 7LN	0141-638 8767
	Rev. Ian McInnes	46 Earlbank Avenue, Glasgow G14 9HL	0141-954 0328
	Rev. Douglas Clark	41 Kirkintilloch Road, Lenzie, Glasgow G66 4LB	0141-770 2184
	Rev. Alexander Wilson	HM Prison, Barlinnie, Glasgow G33 2QX	0141-770 2059
	Rev. Dr William D. Moore	Chaplaincy Centre, HM Prison, Barlinnie, Glasgow G33 2QX	0141-770 2059
GLENOCHIL	Rev. Alan F.M. Downie	37A Claremont, Alloa FK10 2DG	01259 213872
GREENOCK	Rev. James Munro	80 Bardrainney Avenue, Port Glasgow PA14 6UD	01475 701213
INVERNESS	Rev. Alexander Shaw	HM Prison, Inverness IV2 3HN	01463 229000
	Rev. Christopher Smart	HM Prison, Inverness IV2 3HN	01463 229000
KILMARNOCK	Rev. Andrew Black	HMP Bowhouse, Mauchline Road, Kilmarnock KA1 5AA	01563 548928
	Rev. Morag Dawson	206 Bank Street, Irvine KA12 0YB	01294 211403
OPEN ESTATE: CASTLE HUNTLY AND NORANSIDE	Rev. Anne E. Stewart	Open Estate Chaplaincy, HMP Castle Huntly, Longforgan, Dundee DD2 5HL	01382 319388
PERTH INCLUDING FRIARTON	Rev. Graham Matthews	Chaplaincy Centre, HMP Perth PH2 8AT	01738 622293
	Mrs Deirdre Yellowlees	Ringmill House, Gannochy Farm, Perth PH2 7JH	01738 633773
PETERHEAD	Rev. Dr David Ross	HM Prison, Peterhead AB42 6YY	01779 479101
POLMONT	Rev. Donald H. Scott	Chaplaincy Centre, HMYOI Polmont, Falkirk FK2 0AB	01324 711558
	Mr Craig Bryan	Chaplaincy Centre, HMYOI Polmont, Falkirk FK2 0AB	01324 711558
SHOTTS	Rev. Allan Brown	Chaplaincy Centre, HMP Shotts ML7 4LE	01501 824071

LIST F – UNIVERSITY CHAPLAINS

ABERDEEN	Easter Smart MDiv	01224 484271
ABERTAY, DUNDEE	Leslie M. Barrett BD FRICS	01382 308447
CALEDONIAN	Ewen MacLean BA BD (Honorary)	0141-558 7451
CAMBRIDGE	Vacant	

DUNDEE	Fiona C. Douglas BD PhD	01382 344157
EDINBURGH	Diane Williams	0131-650 2595
GLASGOW	Stuart D. MacQuarrie JP BD BSc	0141-330 5419
HERIOT-WATT	Vacant	
NAPIER	John Smith (Honorary)	0131-447 8724
OXFORD	Carla Grosch-Miller (U.R.C. and C. of S.)	01865 554358
PAISLEY	Morris M. Dutch BD BA	0141-571 4059
ROBERT GORDON	Daniel French	01224 262000 (ext 3506)
ST ANDREWS	James B. Walker MA BD DPhil	01334 462866
STIRLING	Gillian Weightor BD STM (Honorary)	01786 832753
STRATHCLYDE	Marjory Macask II LLB BD	0141-553 4144

LIST G – THE DIACONATE

NAME	COM	APP	ADDRESS	TEL	PRES
Allan, Jean (Mrs) DCS	1989	2005	12C Hindmarsh Avenue, Dundee DD3 7LW	01382 827299	29
Anderson, Janet (Miss) DCS	1979	2006	4 Clanranald Place, Arisaig PH39 4NN	01687 450398	38
			[E-mail: jaskye@tiscali.co.uk]		
Beaton, Margaret (Miss) DCS	1989	1988	64 Gardenside Grove, Carmyle, Glasgow G32 8EZ	0141-646 2297	16
Bell, Sandra (Mrs)	2001	2004	62 Loganswell Road, Thornliebank, Glasgow G46 8AX	0141-638 5884	16
Black, Linda (Miss) BSc DCS	1993	2004	148 Rowan Road, Abronhill, Cumbernauld, Glasgow G67 3DA	01236 786265	22
			[E-mail: lnan@blueyonder.co.uk]		
Buchanan, John (Mr) DCS	1988	2004	19 Gillespie Crescent, Edinburgh EH10 4HJ	0131-229 0794	3
Buchanan, Marion (Miss) MA DCS	1983	2006	2 Lenzie Road, Stepps, Glasgow G33 6DX	0141-779 5746	16
Burns, Marjory (Mrs) DCS	1997	1998	22 Kirklee Road, Mossend, Bellshill ML4 2QN	01698 292685	17
			[E-mail: bellburns@blueyonder.co.uk]	07972 075272 (Mbl)	
Carson, Christine (Miss) MA DCS	2006		36 Upper Wellhead, Limekilns, Dunfermline KY11 3JQ	01383 873131	24
				07919 137294 (Mbl)	
Cathcart, John Paul (Mr) DCS	2000		54 Denholm Crescent, Murray, East Kilbride, Glasgow G75 0BU	01355 521906	17
			[E-mail: paulcathcart@msn.com]	07708 396074 (Mbl)	
Corrie, Margaret (Miss) DCS	1989	1998	44 Sunnyside Street, Camelon, Falkirk FK1 4BH	01324 670656	22
Craw, John (Mr) DCS	1998	2002	'Craiglockhart', Latheronwheel, Latheron KW5 6DW	01593 741779	41
Crawford, Morag (Miss) MSc DCS	1977	1998	118 Wester Drylaw Place, Edinburgh EH4 2TG	0131-332 2253 (Tel/Fax)	24
			[E-mail: morag.crawford.dcs@blueyonder.co.uk]	07970 982563 (Mbl)	
Crocker, Elizabeth (Mrs) DCS DipComEd	1985	2003	77C Craigcrook Road, Edinburgh EH4 3PH	0131-332 0227	1
Cunningham, Ian (Mr) DCS	1994	2002	The Manse, Rothiemay, Huntly AB54 7NE	01466 711334	35
Cuthbertson, Valerie DipTMus DCS	2003		105 Bellshill Road, Motherwell ML1 3SJ	01698 259001	22
			[E-mail: vcuthbertson@tiscali.co.uk]		

Deans, Raymond (Mr) DCS	1994	2003	60 Ardmory Road, Rothesay, Isle of Bute PA20 0PG [E-mail: r.deans93@btinternet.com]	01700 504893	19
Douglas, Marilyn (Miss) DCS	1988	2004	Heimdal, Quarff, Shetland ZE2 9EY	01950 477584	46
Dunnett, Linda (Mrs)	1976	2000	3 Branklyn Crescent, Glasgow G13 1GJ	0141-959 3732	[16]
Evans, Mark (Mr) BSc RGN DCS	1988	2006	13 Easter Drylaw Drive, Edinburgh EH4 2QA [E-mail: markevans@faht.scot.nhs.uk]	0131-343 3089 / 01383 674136 (Office)	24
Forrest, Janice (Mrs)	1990		The Manse, Southend, Campbeltown PA28 6RQ	01586 830274	19
Gargrave, Mary (Mrs) DCS	1989	2002	1B Spiers Grove, Glasgow G46 7RL	0141-638 1412	16
Getliffe, Dorothy (Mrs) DCS BA BD	2006		3 Woodview Terrace, Hamilton ML3 9DP [E-mail: DGetliffe@aol.com]	01698 423304	17
Gordon, Margaret (Mrs) DCS	1998	2001	92 Lanark Road West, Currie EH14 5LA	0131-449 2554	1
Gray, Greta (Miss) DCS	1992	1998	67 Crags Avenue, Paisley PA2 6SG	0141-884 6178	14
Hamilton, James (Mr) DCS	1997	2002	6 Beckfield Gate, Glasgow G33 1SW [E-mail: j.hamilton111@btinternet.com]	0141-558 3195	16
Hamilton, Karen (Mrs) DCS	1995	2004	6 Beckfield Gate, Glasgow G33 1SW [E-mail: k.hamilton6@btinternet.com]	0141-558 3195	17
Hughes, Helen (Miss) DCS	1977	2002	2/2, 43 Burnbank Terrace, Glasgow G20 6UQ [E-mail: helenhughes@fish.co.uk]	0141-333 9459	16
King, Chris (Mrs) DCS	2002	2005	28 Kilnford, Dundonald, Kilmarnock KA2 9ET [E-mail: chrisking99@tiscali.co.uk]	01563 851197	10
King, Margaret (Miss) DCS	2002		56 Murrayfield, Fochabers IV32 7EZ	01343 820937	35
Love, Joanna (Ms) BSc DCS	2006		92 Everard Drive, Glasgow G21 1XQ	0141-563 5859	16
Lyall, Ann (Miss) DCS	1980	2003	117 Barlia Drive, Glasgow G45 0AY [E-mail: ann.lyall@btinternet.com]	0141-631 3643	16
MacDonald, Anne (Miss) BA	1980	2002	502 Castle Gait, Paisley PA1 2PA	0141-840 1875	16
McDowall, Sarah (Mrs) DCS	1991	2003	116 Scott Road, Glenrothes KY6 1AE	01592 562386	25
McIntosh, Kay (Mrs) DCS	1990		4 Jacklin Green, Livingston EH54 8PZ	01506 495472	2
McKay, Kenneth (Mr) DCS	1996	1998	11F Balgowan Road, Letham, Perth PH1 2JG [E-mail: kennydandcs@hotmail.com]	01738 621169 / 07952 076331 (Mbl)	28
MacKinnon, Ronald (Mr) DCS	1996	2004	12 Mossywood Court, McGregor Avenue, Airdrie ML6 7DY	01236 763389	22
McLellan, Margaret (Mrs)	1986	2000	18 Broom Road East, Newton Mearns, Glasgow G77 5SD	0141-639 6853	16
McPheat, Elspeth (Miss)	1985	2001	11/5 New Orchardfield, Edinburgh EH6 5ET	0131-554 4143	1
Martin, Jane (Miss) DCS	1979	1979	16 Wentworth Road, Dundee DD2 3SD [E-mail: janimar@aol.com]	01382 813786	29
Mitchell, Joyce (Mrs) DCS	1994	1993	16/4 Murrayburn Place, Edinburgh EH14 2RR [E-mail: joyce@mitchell71.freeserve.co.uk]	0131-453 6548	1
Mulligan, Anne MA DCS	1974	1986	27A Craigour Avenue, Edinburgh EH17 7NH [E-mail: mulliganne@aol.com]	0131-664 3426 / 0131-242 1996 (Office)	1
Munro, Patricia (Miss) BSc DCS	1986	2002	82 Balbedie Avenue, Lochore, Lochgelly KY5 8HP [E-mail: pat_munro@btinternet.com]	01592 869240	24
Nicholson, David (Mr) DCS	1994	1993	2D Doonside, Kildrum, Cumbernauld, Glasgow G67 2HX	01236 732260 / 07703 332270 (Mbl)	22

NAME	COM		ADDRESS	TEL	PRES
Nicol, Joyce (Mrs) BA DCS	1974	1998	93 Brisbane Street, Greenock PA16 8NY	01475 723235 (Mbl) 07957 642709	14
Ogilvie, Colin (Mr) DCS	1998	2003	32 Upper Bourtree Court, Glasgow G73 4HT	0141-569 2750	16
Porter, Jean (Mrs) DCS	2006		Flat 2/2, 31 Castlefield Court, Millerston, Glasgow G33 6NN	07729 316321	16
Rennie, Agnes M. (Miss) DCS	1974	1979	3/1 Craigmillar Court, Edinburgh EH16 4AD	0131-661 8475	1
Rose, Lewis (Mr) DCS	1993	2005	16 Gean Drive, Blackburn, Aberdeen AB21 0YN [E-mail: scimnorth@uk.uumail.com]	01224 790145 (Mbl) 07899 790466	31
Ross, Duncan (Mr) DCS	1996	2006	4 Glasgow Road, Cambuslang, Glasgow G72 7BW	0141-641 1699	16
Rycroft-Sadi, Pauline (Mrs) DCS	2003	2006	6 Ashville Terrace, Edinburgh EH6 8DD [E-mail: ssornacnud@hotmail.com]	0131-554 6564 (Mbl) 07759 436303	1
Steele, Marilynn J. (Mrs) BD DCS	1999	1999	2 Northfield Gardens, Prestonpans EH32 9LQ	01875 811497	1
Steven, Gordon BD DCS	1997	2004	51 Nantwich Drive, Edinburgh EH7 6RB	0131-669 2054	3
Stewart, Marion (Miss) DCS	1991	1994	Kirk Cottage, Kirkton of Skene, Westhill, Skene AB32 6XE	(Mbl) 07904 385256 01224 743407	33
Thomson, Jacqueline (Mrs) MTh DCS	2004	2004	1 Barron Terrace, Leven KY8 4DL [E-mail: jacquelinethomson@blueycnder.co.uk]	01333 301115	24
Thomson, Phyllis (Miss) DCS	2003	2003	63 Caroline Park, Mid Calder, Livingston EH53 0SJ	01506 883207	2
Urquhart, Barbara (Mrs) DCS	1986	2006	9 Standalane, Kilmaurs, Kilmarnock KA3 2NB	01563 538289	11
Wilson, Glenda (Mrs) DCS	1990	2006	108 Sandhaven, Sandbank, Dunoon PA23 8QW	01369 700848	19
Wilson, Muriel (Miss) MA BD DCS	1997	2001	28 Bellevue Crescent, Ayr KA7 2DR [E-mail: muriel.wilson4@btinternet.com]	01292 264939	10
Wishart, William (Mr) DCS	1994	2004	10 Stanley Drive, Paisley PA2 6HE	0141-884 4177 (Mbl) 07846 555654	14
Wright, Lynda (Miss) BEd DCS	1979	1992	Key Cottage, High Street, Falkland, Cupar KY15 7BU	01337 857705	26

THE DIACONATE (Retired List)

NAME	COM	ADDRESS	TEL	PRES
Anderson, Catherine B. (Mrs) DCS	1975	13 Mosshill Road, Bellshill, Motherwell ML4 1NQ	01698 745907	17
Anderson, Mary (Miss) DCS	1955	33 Ryehill Terrace, Edinburgh EH6 8EN	0131-553 2818	1
Bayes, Muriel C. (Mrs) DCS	1963	Flat 6, Carleton Court, 10 Fenwick Road, Glasgow G46 4AN	0141-633 0865	16
Beaton, Jamesina (Miss) DCS	1953	Farhills, Fort Augustus PH32 4DS	01320 366252	38
Cameron, Margaret (Miss) DCS	1961	2 Rowans Gate, Paisley PA2 6RD	0141-840 2479	14
Copland, Agnes M. (Mrs) MBE DCS	1950	3 Craigmuschat Road, Gourock PA19 1SE	01475 635870	14
Cunningham, Alison W. (Miss) DCS	1961	23 Strathblane Road, Milngavie, Glasgow G62 8DL	0141-563 9232	18

Name	Year	Address	Phone	
Drummond, Rhoda (Miss) DCS	1960	Flat K, 23 Grange Loan, Edinburgh EH9 2ER	0131-668 3631	1
Erskine, Morag (Miss) DCS	1979	111 Mains Drive, Park Mains, Erskine PA8 7JU	0141-812 6096	14
Finlayson, Ellena B. (Miss) DCS	1963	16E Denwood, Summerhill, Aberdeen AB15 6JF	01224 321147	31
Flockhart, Andrew (Mr) DCS	1988	Flat 0/1, 8 Hardie Avenue, Rutherglen, Glasgow G73 3AS	0141-569 0716	16
Gillon, Phyllis (Miss) DCS	1957	The Hermitage Home, 15 Hermitage Drive, Edinburgh EH10 6BX	0131-447 0664	1
Gordon, Fiona S. (Mrs) MA DCS	1958	Machrie, 3 Cupar Road, Cuparmuir, Cupar KY15 5RH [E-mail: machrie@madasafish.com]	01334 652341	26
Gray, Catherine (Miss) DCS	1969	10C Eastern View, Gourock PA19 1RJ	01475 637479	14
Gray, Christine (Mrs) DCS	1969	11 Woodside Avenue, Thornliebank, Glasgow G46 7HR	0141-571 1008	16
Howden, Margaret (Miss) DCS	1954	38 Munro Street, Kirkcaldy KY1 1PY	01592 205913	25
Hutchison, Alan E.W. (Mr) DCS	1988	132 Lochbridge Road, North Berwick EH39 4DR	01620 894077	3
Hutchison, Maureen (Mrs) DCS	1961	23 Drylaw Crescent, Edinburgh EH4 2AU	0131-332 8020	1
Johnston, Mary (Miss) DCS	1988	19 Lounsdale Drive, Paisley PA2 9ED	0141-849 1615	14
Lundie, Ann V. (Miss) DCS	1972	20 Langdykes Drive, Cove, Aberdeen AB12 3HW	01224 898416	31
McBain, Margaret (Miss) DCS	1974	33 Quarry Road, Paisley PA2 7RD	0141-884 2920	14
McCallum, Moyra (Miss) MA BD DCS	1965	176 Hilton Drive, Aberdeen AB24 4LT [E-mail: moymac@aol.com]	01224 486240	31
McCully, M. Isobel (Miss) DCS	1974	10 Broadstone Avenue, Port Glasgow PA14 5BB	01475 742240	14
MacLean, Donald A. (Mr) DCS	1988	8 Upper Barvas, Isle of Lewis HS2 0QX	01851 840454	44
McNaughton, Janette (Miss) DCS	1982	4 Dunellan Avenue, Moodiesburn, Glasgow G69 0GB	01236 870180	22
MacPherson, James B. (Mr) DCS	1988	104 Cartside Street, Glasgow G42 9TQ	0141-616 6468	16
MacQuien, Duncan (Mr) DCS	1988	35 Criffel Road, Mount Vernon, Glasgow G32 9JE	0141-575 1137	14
Malvenan, Dorothy (Miss) DCS	1937	Flat 19, 6 Craigie Street, Dundee DD4 6PF	01382 462495	29
Martin, Neil (Mr) DCS	1988	3 Strathmiglo Place, Stenhousemuir, Larbert FK5 4UQ	01324 551362	22
Merrilees, Ann (Miss) DCS	1994	23 Cuthill Brae, Willow Wood Residential Park, West Calder EH55 8QE [E-mail: ann@merrilees.freeserve.co.uk]	01501 762909	2
Miller, Elsie M. (Miss) DCS	1974	30 Swinton Avenue, Rowanbank, Baillieston, Glasgow G69 6JR	0141-771 0857	22
Morrison, Jean (Dr) DCS	1964	45 Corslet Road, Currie EH14 5LZ [E-mail: jean.morrison@blueyonder.co.uk]	0131-449 6859	1
Mortimer, Aileen (Miss) BSc DCS	1976	38 Sinclair Way, Knightsridge, Livingston EH54 8HW	01506 430504	2
Moyes, Sheila (Miss) DCS	1957	158 Pilton Avenue, Edinburgh EH5 2JZ	0131-551 1731	1
Palmer, Christine (Ms) DCS	2003	39 Fortingall Place, Perth PH1 2NF [E-mail: chrisjpalmer@blueyonder.co.uk]	01738 587488	28
Potts, Jean M. (Miss) DCS	1973	28B East Claremont Street, Edinburgh EH7 4JP	0131-557 2144	1
Ramsay, Katherine (Miss) MA DCS	1958	25 Homeroyal House, 2 Chalmers Crescent, Edinburgh EH9 1TP	0131-667 4791	1
Ronald, Norma A. (Miss) MBE DCS	1961	2B Saughton Road North, Edinburgh EH12 7HG	0131-334 8736	1
Rutherford, Ellen B. (Miss) MBE DCS	1962	41 Duncanston, Conon Bridge, Dingwall IV7 8JB	01349 877439	39
Smith, Catherine (Mrs) DCS	1964	21 Lingaro, Bixter, Shetland ZE2 9NN	01595 810207	46
Smith, Lillian (Miss) MA DCS	1977	6 Fintry Mains, Dundee DD4 9HF	01382 500052	29
Stuart, Anne (Miss) DCS	1966	1 Murrell Terrace, Burntisland KY3 0XH	01383 860049	24
Tait, Agnes (Mrs) DCS	1995	10 Carnoustie Crescent, Greenhills, East Kilbride, Glasgow G75 8TE		

NAME	ORD	ADDRESS	TEL	PRES
Teague, Yvonne (Mrs) DCS	1965	46 Craigcrook Avenue, Edinburgh EH4 3PX	0131-336 3113	1
Thom, Helen (Miss) BA DipEd MA DCS	1959	84 Great King Street, Edinburgh EH3 6QU	0131-556 5687	1
Trimble, Robert DCS	1988	5 Templar Rise, Livingston EH54 6PJ	01506 412504	2
Webster, Elspeth H. (Miss) DCS	1950	82 Broomhill Avenue, Burntisland KY3 0BP	01592 873616	25
Weir, Minnie Mullo (Miss) MA DCS	1934	37 Stratheam Court, Stratheam Terrace, Crieff PH7 3DS	01764 654189	28
White, Elizabeth (Miss) DCS	1950	Rodger Park Nursing Home, 10 Rodger Drive, Rutherglen, Glasgow G73 3QZ		16

THE DIACONATE (Supplementary List)

NAME	ORD	ADDRESS	TEL
Gilroy, Lorraine (Mrs)	1988	5 Bluebell Drive, Cheverel Court, Bedward CO12 0GE	02476 366031
Guthrie, Jennifer M. (Miss) DCS	1993	14 Eskview Terrace, Ferryden, Montrose DD10 9RD	01674 674413
Harris, Judith (Mrs)	1988	243 Western Avenue, Sandfields, Port Talbot, West Glamorgan SA12 7NF	01639 884855
Hood, Katrina (Mrs)	1982	67C Farquhar Road, Edgbaston, Birmingham B18 2QP	
Hudson, Sandra (Mrs)	1969	10 Albany Drive, Rutherglen, Glasgow G73 3QN	
Muir, Alison M. (Mrs)	1978	77 Arthur Street, Dunfermline KY12 0JJ	
Ramsden, Christine (Miss)	1970	2 Wykeham Close, Bassett, Southampton SO16 7LZ	
Walker, Wikje (Mrs)		24 Brodie's Yard, Queen Street, Coupar Angus PH13 9RA	01828 628251
Wallace, Catherine (Mrs)		4 Thornwood Court, Setauket, NY 11733, USA	

LIST H – MINISTERS HAVING RESIGNED MEMBERSHIP OF PRESBYTERY (in Terms of Act III 1992)

(Resignation of Presbytery membership does not imply the lack of a practising certificate.)

NAME	ORD	ADDRESS	TEL	PRES
Anderson, Kenneth G. MA BD	1967	8 School Road, Arbroath DD11 2LT	01241 874825	30
Bailey, W. Grahame MA BD	1939	148 Craiglea Drive, Edinburgh EH10 5PU	0131-447 1663	1
Barbour, Robin A.S. KCVO MC BD STM DD	1954	Old Fincastle, Pitlochry PH16 5RJ	01796 473209	27
Bartholomew, Julia (Mrs) BSc BD	2002	Kippenhill, Dunning, Perth PH2 0RA	01764 684929	28
Beck, John C. BD	1975	43A Balvenie Street, Dufftown, Keith AB55 4AS		35
Bonar, Sandy LTh	1988	7 Westbank Court, Westbank Terrace, Macmerry, Tranent EH33 1QS [E-mail: sandy.bonar@btinternet.com]	01875 615165	3
Brown, Alastair BD	1986	52 Henderson Drive, Kintore, Inverurie AB51 0FB	01467 632787	32

Name	Year	Address	Tel	No.
Caie, Albert LTh	1983	34 Ringwell Gardens, Stonehouse, Larkhall ML9 3QW	01698 792187	32
Campbell, J. Ewan R. MA BD	1967	93 The Moorings, Dalgety Bay, Dunfermline KY11 9GP	01383 820765	25
Cooper, George MA BD	1943	8 Leighton Square, Alyth, Blairgowrie PH11 8AQ	01828 633746	27
Craig, Eric MA BD BA	1959	5 West Relugas Road, Edinburgh EH9 2PW	0131-667 8210	1
Craig, Gordon W. MBE MA BD	1972	1 Beley Bridge, Dunino, St Andrews KY16 8LT	01334 880285	26
Crawford, S.G. Victor	1980	Crofton, 65 Main Road, East Wemyss, Kirkcaldy KY1 4RL	01592 712325	25
Cumming, David P.L. MA	1957	Shillong, Tarbat Ness Road, Portmahomack, Tain IV20 1YA	01862 871794	19
Donaldson, Colin V.	1982	3A Playfair Terrace, St Andrews KY16 9HX	01334 472889	3
Douglas, Ian P. LTh	1974	'Stonecroft', 1 Tortorston Drive, Tortorston, Blackhills, Peterhead AB42 3LY	01779 474728	34
Drake, Wendy F. (Mrs) BD	1978	21 William Black Place, South Queensferry EH30 9QR [E-mail: revwdrake@hotmail.co.uk]	0131-331 1520	1
Drummond, R. Hugh	1953	19 Winton Park, Edinburgh EH10 7EX [E-mail: hughdrummond1@activemail.co.uk]	0131-445 3634	1
Ferguson, Ronald MA BD ThM	1972	Vinbreck, Orphir, Orkney KW17 2RE [E-mail: ronbluebrazil@aol.com]	01856 811378	45
Finlayson, Duncan MA	1943	Flat 3, Nicholson Court, Kinnettas Road, Strathpeffer IV14 9BG	01997 420014	39
Gordon, Alasdair B. BD LLB EdD	1970	31 Binghill Park, Milltimber, Aberdeen AB13 0EE [E-mail: alasdairbgordon@hotmail.com]	01224 732464	31
Greig, James C.G. MA BD STM	1955	Block 2, Flat 2, Station Lofts, Strathblane, Glasgow G63 9BD [E-mail: jgreig@netcomuk.co.uk]	01360 771915	16
Grubb, George D.W. BA BD BPhil DMin	1962	10 Wellhead Close, South Queensferry EH30 9WA	0131-331 2072	1
Hamilton, David S.M. MA BD STM	1958	49 Paddocks Lane, Cheltenham GL50 4NU	01242 254917	47
Hosie, James MA BD MTh	1959	Hilbre, Baycrofts, Strachur, Cairndow, Argyll PA27 8BY	01369 860634	19
Howie, William MA BD STM	1964	26 Morgan Road, Aberdeen, AB16 5JY	01224 483669	31
Hurst, Frederick R. MA	1965	Flat 6, 21 Bulldale Place, Glasgow G14 0NE	0141-959 2604	40
Lambie, Andrew E. BD	1957	1 Mercat Loan, Biggar ML12 6DG	01899 221352	13
Levison, Mary I. (Mrs) BA BD DD	1978	Chamberlain Nursing Home, 7–9 Chamberlain Road, Edinburgh EH10 4DJ		1
Lindsay, W. Douglas BD CPS	1978	3 Drummond Place, Calderwood, East Kilbride, Glasgow G74 3AD	01355 234169	16
Lynn, Joyce (Mrs) MIPM BD	1995	Simbister, Sanday, Orkney KW17 2BA	01857 600289	1
McDonald, William J.G. DD	1953	7 Blacket Place, Edinburgh EH9 1RN	0131-667 2100	1
Macfarlane, Alwyn J.C. MA	1957	Flat 12, Homeburn House, 177 Fenwick Road, Giffnock, Glasgow G46 6JD	0141-620 3235	1
Macfarlane, Donald MA	1940	8 Muirfield Gardens, Inverness IV2 4HF	01463 231977	37
Macfarlane, Kenneth	1963	9 Bonnington Road, Peebles EH45 9HF	01721 723609	4
McGillivray, A. Gordon MA BD STM	1951	Greenfield Crescent, Balerno EH14 7HD	0131-449 4747	1
Mackenzie, J.A.R. MA	1947	West Lodge, Inverness Road, Nairn IV12 4SD	01667 452827	26
McKenzie, Mary O. (Miss)	1976	4 Dunellan Avenue, Moodiesburn, Glasgow G69 0GB	01236 870180	16
Mackie, Steven G. MA BD	1956	38 Grange Loan, Edinburgh EH9 2NR	0131-667 9532	6
Mair, John BSc	1965	21 Kenilworth Avenue, Helensburgh G84 7JR	01436 671744	18
Marshall, James S. MA PhD	1939	25 St Mary's Street, St Andrews KY16 8AZ	01334 476136	26
Millar, John L. MA BD	1981	17 Whittingehame Court, 1350 Great Western Road, Glasgow G12 0BH	0141-339 4098	38
Miller, Irene B. (Mrs) MA BD	1984	5 Braeside Park, Aberfeldy PH15 2DT	01887 829396	27
Morton, Andrew Q. MA BSc BD FRSE	1949	Sunnyside, 4A Manse Street, Aberdour, Burntisland KY3 0TY		18

NAME	ORD	ADDRESS	TEL	PRES
Munro, John P.L. MA BD PhD	1977	5 Marchmont Crescent, Edinburgh EH9 1HN [E-mail: jplr.munro@yahoo.co.uk]	0131-445 5829	1
Murison, William G.	1951	21 Hailes Gardens, Edinburgh EH13 0JL	0131-441 2460	1
Ogston, David D. MA BD	1970	13 Alder Grove, Scone, Perth PH2 6TA		28
Paterson, John M.K. MA ACII BD DD	1964	58 Orchard Drive, Edinburgh EH4 2DZ	0131-332 5876	1
Ramsay, Alan MA	1967	12 Riverside Grove, Lochyside, Fort William PH33 7NY		38
Reid, William M. MA BD	1966	10 Rue Rossini, F-75009 Paris, France		48
Ritchie, Malcolm A.	1955	Roadside Cottage, Tayvallich, Lochgilphead PA31 8PN	01546 870616	19
Scott, J. Miller MA BD FSAScot DD	1949	St Martins, Trinity Place, St Andrews KY16 8SG	01334 479518	26
Shaw of Chapelverna, Duncan Bundesverdienstkreuz Drhc PhD ThDr JP	1951	4 Sydney Terrace, Edinburgh EH7 6SL	0131-337 2130	19
Shaw, D.W.D. BA BD LLB WS DD	1960	4/13 Succoth Court, Edinburgh EH12 6BZ		26
Simpson, Gordon M. MA BD	1959	37 Spottiswoode Gardens, St Andrews KY16 8SA	01334 473406	25
Smith, J.A. Wemyss MA	1947	Rapplaroan, 42 Beltie Road, Torphins, Banchory AB31 4JT	01339 882780	32
Smith, Ralph C.P. MA STM	1960	2A Waverley Road, Eskbank, Dalkeith EH22 3DJ [E-mail: rcpsmith@waitrose.com]	0131-663 1234	1
Speed, David K. LTh	1969	153 West Princes Street, Helensburgh G84 8EZ	01436 674493	16
Spowart, Mary G. (Mrs) BD	1978	Aldersyde, St Abbs Road, Coldingham, Eyemouth TD14 5NR	01890 771697	26
Thomson, Andrew BA	1976	3 Laurel Wynd, Drumfargard Village, Cambuslang, Glasgow G72 7BH [E-mail: andrewthomson@hotmail.com]	0141-641 2936	16
Thomson, Gilbert L. BA	1965	3 Fortharfield, Freuchie, Cupar KY15 7JJ	01337 857431	25
Todd, James F. BD CPS	1984	21 Harrow Terrace, Wick KW1 5AX	01955 605320	41
Urie, D.M.L. MA BD PhD	1940	7 Glebe Park, Kincardine O'Neil, Aboyne AB34 5ED	01339 884204	32
Weatherhead, James L. CBE MA LLB DD	1960	59 Brechin Road, Kirriemuir DD8 4DE	01575 572237	30
Webster, John G. BSc	1964	Plane Tree, King's Cross, Brodick, Isle of Arran KA27 8RG	01770 700747	16
Westmarland, Colin A.	1971	PO Box 5, Cospicua, CSPOI, Malta	00356 216 923552	48
Wilkie, George D. OBE BL	1948	2/37 Barnton Avenue West, Edinburgh EH4 6EB	0131-339 3973	1
Wylie, W. Andrew	1953	Well Rose Cottage, Peat Inn, Cupar KY15 5LH	01334 840600	26

LIST I – MINISTERS HOLDING PRACTISING CERTIFICATES (under Act II, as amended by Act VIII 2000)

Not all Presbyteries have stated whether or not some of those listed have taken a seat in Presbytery. There is still some variation in practice.

NAME	ORD	ADDRESS	TEL	PRES
Alexander, Helen J.R.	1981	3/18 Fisher Street, Fullarton 5063, Australia	0061 8837 97536	1
Alexander, Ian W. BA BD STM	1990	5 Comiston Gardens, Edinburgh EH10 5QH	0131-447 4519	1

Name	Year	Address	Tel	No.
Anderson, David MA BD	1975	Rowan Cottage, Aberlour Gardens, Aberlour AB38 9LD	01340 871906	35
Anderson, Kenneth G. MA BD	1967	8 School Road, Arbroath DD11 2LT	01241 874825	30
Arbuthnott, Joan E. (Mrs) MA BD	1993	139/1 New Street, Musselburgh EH21 6DH	0131-665 6736	3
Barbour, Robin A.S. KCVO MC BD STM DD	1954	Old Fincastle, Pitlochry PH16 5RJ	01796 473209	27
Barron, Jane L. (Mrs) BA DipEd BD	1999	Riverdog Cottage, 37 Queen Street, Newport-on-Tay DD6 8BD		26
Bartholomew, Julia (Mrs) BSc BD	2002	Kippenhill, Dunning, Perth PH2 0RA	01764 684929	28
Beattie, Warren BSc BD	1991	Director for Mission Outreach, OMF International, 2 Cluny Road, Singapore 259570	0065 6319 4550	1
Black, James S. BD DPS	1976	7 Breck Terrace, Penicuik EH26 0RJ [E-mail: jsb.black@btopenworld.com]	01968 677559	3
Blane, Quintin A. BSc BD MSc	1979	18D Kirkhill Road, Penicuik EH26 8HZ [E-mail: quintin@qab.org.uk]	01968 670017	3
Bonar, Sandy LTh	1988	7 Westbank Court, Westbank Terrace, Macmerry, Tranent EH33 1QS [E-mail: sandy.bonar@btinternet.com]	01875 615165	3
Bowman, Norman M. MA BD	1940	Abbotsford Nursing Home, 98 Eglinton Road, Ardrossan KA22 8NN		12
Boyd, Ian R. MA BD PhD	1989	33 Castleton Drive, Newton Mearns, Glasgow G77 3LE		32
Caie, Albert LTh	1983	34 Ringwell Gardens, Stonehouse, Larkhall ML9 3QW	01698 792187	14
Campbell, Thomas R. MA BD	1986	Craigleith, Bowfield Road, Howwood, Johnstone PA9 1BS	01505 702461	2
Currie, Gordon C.M. MA BD	1975	43 Deanburn Park, Linlithgow EH49 6HA	01506 842759	33
Davidson, Mark R. MA BD STM	2005	20 Kinmohr Rise, Blackburn, Aberdeen AB21 0LJ	01224 791350	24
Davies, Gareth W. BA BD	1979	Pitadro House, Fordell Gardens, Dunfermline KY11 7EY	01383 417634	1
Dickson, Graham T. MA BD	1985	19/4 Stead's Place, Edinburgh EH6 5DY [E-mail: gtd22@blueyonder.co.uk]	0131-476 0187	3
Donaldson, Colin V.	1982	3A Playfair Terrace, St Andrews KY16 9HX	01334 472889	1
Drake, Wendy F. (Mrs) BD	1978	21 William Black Place, South Queensferry EH30 9QR [E-mail: revwdrake@hotmail.co.uk]	0131-331 1520	
Drummond, Norman W. MA BD	1976	c/o Columba 1400 Ltd, Staffin, Isle of Skye IV51 9JY	01478 611400	42
Ellis, David W. GIMechE GIProdE	1962	4 Wester Tarsappie, Rhynd Road, Perth PH2 8PT	01738 449618	16
Ferguson, Ronald MA BD ThM	1972	Vinbreck, Orphir, Orkney KW17 2RE [E-mail: ronbluebrazil@aol.com]	01856 811378	45
Fleming, Thomas G.	1961	Longwood, Humbie EH36 5PN [E-mail: rossflock@ednet.co.uk]	01875 833208	22
Flockhart, D. Ross OBE BA BD DUniv	1955			3
Fowler, Richard C.A. BSc MSc BD	1978	4 Gardentown, Whalsay, Shetland ZE2 9AB	01806 566538	46
Fraser, Ian M. MA BD PhD	1946	Ferndale, Gargunnock, Stirling FK8 3BW	01786 860612	23
Frew, John M. MA BD	1946	17 The Furrows, Walton-on-Thames KT12 3JQ		16
Fyall, Robert S. MA BD PhD	1986	7 Queen's Gate, Clarkston, Glasgow G76 7HE		16
Gillies, Jan E. (Mrs) BD	1998	18 McIntyre Lane, Macmerry, Tranent EH33 1QL [E-mail: jgillies@fish.co.uk]		3
Gilmour, Robert M. MA BD	1942	'Bellevue', Station Road, Watten, Wick KW1 5YN	01955 621317	37

Name & Qualifications	Year	Address	Tel.	No.
Grubb, George D.W. BA BD BPhil DMin	1962	10 Wellhead Close, South Queensferry EH30 9WA	0131-331 2072	1
Hamilton, David S.M. MA BD STM	1958	49 Paddocks Lane, Cheltenham GL50 4NU	01242 254917	47
Henderson, Frances M. BA BD	2006	Stoneyburn Farm, Crawford, Biggar ML12 6RH [E-mail: frances.henderson@tiscali.co.uk]	01864 502387	3
Hibbert, Frederick W. BD	1986	4 Cemydd Terrace, Senghemydd, Caerphilly, Mid Glamorgan CF83 4HL	02920 831653	1
Higgins, G.K.	1957	150 Broughty Ferry Road, Dundee DD4 6JJ	01382 461288	29
Hosie, James MA BD MTh	1959	Hilbre, Baycrofts, Strachur, Cairndow PA27 8BY	01369 860634	19
Ireland, Andrew BA BTh DipRD	1963	48 Jubilee Court, St Margaret's Street, Dunfermline KY12 7PE	01383 732223	24
Jack, Alison M. (Mrs) MA BD PhD	1998	Glenallan, Doune Road, Dunblane FK15 9AT	01786 823241	23
Jamieson, Esther M.M. (Mrs) BD	1984	1 Redburn, Bayview, Stornoway HS1 2UV [E-mail: iandejamieson@btinternet.com]	01851 704789	44
Jenkinson, John J. JP LTCL ALCM DipEd DipSen	1991	8 Rosehall Terrace, Falkirk FK1 1PY	01324 625498	22
Johnstone, Donald B.	1969	22 Glenhove Road, Cumbernauld, Glasgow G67 2JZ	01236 612479	22
Lawrie, Robert M. MTheol	1973	59 Cliffburn Road, Arbroath DD11 5BA	01241 439292	30
Liddiard, F.G.B. MA BD MSc DipMin LLCM(TD)	1994	18/1 John's Place, Edinburgh EH6 7EN	0131-554 9765	1
Logan, Thomas M. LTh	1957	34 Trinity Fields Crescent, Brechin DD9 6YF	01356 622966	30
Lyall, David BSc BD STM PhD	1971	3 Duncan Court, Kilmarnock KA3 7TF	01563 524398	11
Macaskill, Donald MA BD PhD	1965	16 Brian Crescent, Tunbridge Wells, Kent TN4 0AP	01892 670323	47
McDonald, Ross J. BA BD ThM	1994	44 Forfar Avenue, Glasgow G52 3Q	0141-883 5956	16
Macfarlane, Kenneth	1998	HMS Dalriada, Navy Buildings, Eldon Street, Greenock PA16 7SL	07952 558767 (Mbl)	
McGillivray, A. Gordon MA BD STM	1963	9 Bonnington Road, Peebles EH45 9HF	01721 723609	4
McKean, Martin J. BD DipMin	1951	7 Greenfield Crescent, Balerno EH14 7HD	0131-449 4747	1
Mackie, Steven G. MA BD	1984	56 Greenknowe Drive, Edinburgh EH14 2JX	0131-466 1157	1
MacPherson, Gordon C.	1956	38 Grange Loan, Edinburgh EH9 2NR	0131-667 9532	1
McPherson, William BD DipEd	1963	203 Capelrig Road, Patterton, Newton Mearns, Glasgow G77 6ND	0141-616 2107	16
Mailer, Colin (Aux)	1993	83 Laburnum Avenue, Port Seton, Prestonpans EH32 0UD	01875 812252	22
Main, Arthur W.A. BD	1996	Innis Chonain, Back Row, Polmont, Falkirk FK2 0RD	01324 712401	16
Marr, Ian MA BD	1954	13/3 Eildon Terrace, Edinburgh EH3 5NL	0131-556 1344	28
Masson, John D. MA BD PhD BSc	1984	116 Jeanfield Road, Perth PH1 1LF / 2 Beechgrove, Craw Hall, Brampton CA8 1TS [E-mail: john.masson@btinternet.com]	01738 632530 / ex-directory	7
Matheson, Iain G. BD BMus	1985	16 New Street, Musselburgh EH21 6JP [E-mail: igmatheson@tiscali.co.uk]	0131-665 2128	1
Millar, Peter W. MA BD PhD	1971	35/6 Mid Steil, Edinburgh EH10 5XB [E-mail: ionacottage@hotmail.com]	0131-447 6186	1
Miller, Irene B. (Mrs) MA BD	1984	2 Braeside Park, Aberfeldy PH15 2DT	01887 829396	27
Mills, Archibald MA PhD	1953	32 High Street, South Queensferry EH30 9PP	0131-331 3906	1
Moodie, Alastair R. MA BD	1978	5 Buckingham Terrace, Glasgow G12 8EB		16
Morton, Andrew Q. MA BSc BD FRSE	1949	Sunnyside, 4A Manse Street, Aberdour, Burntisland KY3 0TY		18

Name	Year	Address	Tel	No.
Munro, Alexander W. MA BD	1978	Columba House, 12 Alexandra Road, Southport PR9 0NB [E-mail: awmunro@tiscali.co.uk]	01704 543044	47
Munro, John P.L. MA BD PhD	1977	5 Marchmont Crescent, Edinburgh EH9 1HN [E-mail: jplmunro@yahoo.co.uk]	0131-445 5829	1
Newell, Alison M. (Mrs) BD	1986	1A Inverleith Terrace, Edinburgh EH3 5NS [E-mail: alinewell@aol.com]	0131-556 3505	1
Newell, J. Philip MA BD PhD	1982	1A Inverleith Terrace, Edinburgh EH3 5NS	0131-556 3505	1
Notman, John R. BSc BD	1990	5 Dovecote Road, Bromsgrove, Worcs B61 7BN		32
Ogston, David D. MA BD	1970	13 Alder Grove, Scone, Perth PH2 6TA		28
Ostler, John H. MA LTh	1975	5 Osborne Terrace, Port Seton, Prestonpans EH32 0BZ	01875 814358	3
Owen, Catherine W. MTh	1984	10 Waverley Park, Kirkintilloch, Glasgow G66 2BP	0141-776 0407	16
Provan, Iain W. MA BA PhD	1991	Regent College, 5800 University Boulevard, Vancouver BC V6T 2E4, Canada	001 604 224 3245	1
Reamonn, Paraic BA BD	1982			
Ritchie, James BD MTh	2000	68 Hammerman Drive, The Campus, Hilton, Aberdeen AB24 4SH [E-mail: jim.ritchie1@btopenworld.com]	01224 484332	31
Rodwell, Anna J. (Mrs) BD DipMin	1998	The Old Mill House, Hownam Howgate, Kelso TD5 8AJ [E-mail: anna.rodwell@googlemail.com]	01573 440761	6
Roy, Alistair A. MA BD	1955	1 Broaddykes Close, Kingswells, Aberdeen AB15 8UF	01224 743310	31
Sawers, Hugh BA	1968	2 Rosemount Meadows, Castlepark, Bothwell, Glasgow G71 8EL	01698 853960	17
Scott, J. Miller MA BD FSAScot DD	1949	St Martins, Trinity Place, St Andrews KY16 8SG	01334 479518	26
Scouller, Hugh BSc BD	1985	The Mercat Hotel, High Street, Haddington EH41 3EP [E-mail: h.scouller@btinternet.com]		3
Shaw, D.W.D. BA BD LLB WS DD	1960	4/13 Succoth Court, Edinburgh EH12 6BZ	0131-337 2130	26
Stewart, Fraser M.C. BSc BD	1980	12A Crowlista, Uig, Isle of Lewis HS2 9JF	01851 672413	44
Stewart, Margaret L. (Mrs) BSc MB ChB BD	1985	28 Inch Crescent, Bathgate EH48 1EU	01506 653428	2
Storrar, William F. MA BD PhD	1984	Director, Centre of Theological Enquiry, 50 Stockton Street, Princeton, NJ 08540, USA		1
Strachan, David G. BD DPS	1978	1 Deeside Park, Aberdeen AB15 7PQ	01224 324101	31
Strachan, Gordon MA BD PhD	1963	59 Merchiston Crescent, Edinburgh EH10 5AH	0131-229 3654	1
Thomas, W. Colville BTh BPhil DPS DSc	1964	11 Muirfield Crescent, Gullane EH31 2HN	01620 842415	3
Todd, James F. BD CPS	1984	21 Harrow Terrace, Wick KW1 5AX	01955 605320	41
Tollick, Frank BSc DipEd	1958	3 Bellhouse Road, Aberdour, Burntisland KY3 0TL	01383 860559	24
Turnbull, Julian S. BSc BD MSc CEng MBCS	1980	25 Hamilton Road, Gullane EH31 2HP [E-mail: jules-turnbull@zetnet.co.uk]	01620 842958	3
Weatherhead, James L. CBE MA LLB DD	1960	59 Brechin Road, Kirriemuir DD8 4DE	01575 572237	30
Weir, Mary K. (Mrs) BD PhD	1968	1249 Millar Road RR1, SITEH-46, BC V0N 1G0, Canada	001 604 947 0636	1
Williamson, Colin R. LLB BD	1972	McCavit's Loaning, Shamrod Road, Balloolymore, Katesbridge, Co. Down BT32 5PG		28
Wood, Peter J. MA BD	1993	97 Broad Street, Cambourne, Cambridgeshire CB3 6DH	01954 205216	47

LIST J – PRESBYTERY/PARISH WORKERS (PPWs)

Associate Ministers and Deacons employed by the Ministries Council and placed in charges appear under the name of the charge.

NAME	APP	ADDRESS	APPOINTMENT	TEL	PRES
Baker, Paula (Mrs)	2007	Kernow, 18 Main Street, Buckpool, Buckie AB56 1XQ [E-mail: mikepaulabaker@aol.com]	Presbytery of Moray: Children's Ministry Training and Development	01542 832662	35
Bauer, Alex (Ms)	2001	Linwood Parish Church, Clippens Road, Linwood, Paisley PA3 3PY	Paisley: Linwood: Youth Worker	07903 120226 (Mbl)	14
Benzie, Andria (Mrs)	2008	293 Lee Crescent North, Bridge of Don, Aberdeen AB22 8GF	Aberdeen: St George's Tillydrone: Parish Assistant	01224 824670	31
Black, Colm	2001	Hilton Church of Scotland, 4 Tomatin Road, Inverness IV2 4UA [E-mail: families@hiltonchurch.org.uk]	Inverness: Hilton: Parish Assistant	01463 233310	37
Byun, Benjamin (Rev.) PhD	2007	Mastrick Parish Church, Greenfern Road, Aberdeen AB16 6TR [E-mail: benjamin@byun1.fsnet.co.uk]	Aberdeen: Mastrick: Parish Assistant	01224 710274	31
Campbell, Alasdair	2000	3 Gellatly Road, Dunfermline KY11 4BH	Dunfermline: Dalgety/Forth Churches Group: Parish Assistant	01383 726238	24
Carrigan, Patrick	2008	43 Linburn Grove, Dunfermline KY11 4LQ	Dunfermline: Gillespie Memorial Town Centre Worker:	01383 733165	24
Clipston, David	2002/2008	Barlanark Greyfriars Church, Edinburgh Road, Glasgow	Glasgow: Barlanark Greyfriars Youth Worker		16
Close, David	2001	12–14 Wallace Street, Paisley PA3 2BU	The Star Project: Paisley North	0141-889 5850	14
Collard, John (Rev.)	2003	1 Nelson Terrace, East Kilbride, Glasgow G74 2EY [E-mail: jkcollard@blueyonder.co.uk]	Glasgow Presbytery Congregational Facilitator	01355 520093	16
Cowie, Marjorie (Miss)	2002	35 Balbirnie Avenue, Markinch, Glenrothes KY7 6BS	Glenrothes: St Margaret's: Parish Assistant	01592 758402	25
Crumlin, Melodie (Mrs)	2000	St Luke's and St Andrew's Church, 17 Bain Street, Glasgow G40 2JZ [E-mail: melodiegccp@aol.com]	PEEK (Possibilities for East End Kids): Project Development Manager	0141-552 5757	16
Dale-Pimentil, Sheila (Mrs)	1999/2007	3 Golf Road, Lundin Links, Leven KY8 6BB	Kennoway, Windygates and Balgonie St Kenneth's: Parish Assistant	01333 329618	25
Finch, John	2002	71 Maxwell Avenue, Westerton, Bearsden, Glasgow G61 1NZ [E-mail: johnfinch10@ntlworld.com]		0141-587 7390 07715 119263 (Mbl)	
Finegan, Sarah (Mrs) BA	2007	261 Main Street, East Calder, Livingston EH53 0ED	Kirknewton and East Calder: Youth Worker (P/T)	01506 882628	2

Name		Address [E-mail]	Position	Telephone	No.
Forbes, Farquhar	2006/2008	Invararnie House, Invararnie, Inverness IV2 6XA [E-mail: ff@insheschurch.org]	Inverness: Inshes: Youth Worker	07749 539981 (Mbl)	37
Haringman, Paul BA	2003	19 Dewarton, Gorebridge EH23 4NX [E-mail: haringman@onetel.com]	Newbattle: Youth Worker	01875 320687	3
Harvey, Ruth (Ms)	2007	Croslands, Beacon Street, Penrith, Cumbria CA11 7TZ [E-mail: ruthharvey@phonecoop.coop]	Congregational Facilitator (p/t): Presbytery of Annandale and Eskdale	01768 840749 / 07882 259631 (Mbl)	7
Hunter, Jean (Mrs)	2006	The Manse, Shiskine, Isle of Arran KA27 8EP [E-mail: jane@hunter4277.fsnet.co.uk]	Brodick with Corrie with Lochranza: Parish Assistant	01770 860380	12
Hutchison, John BA	2001	30/4 West Pilton Gardens, Edinburgh EH4 4EG	Edinburgh: The Old Kirk: Parish Assistant	0131-538 1622	1
Johnston, Mark (Rev.)	2003	5 Bruce Walk, Redmoss, Nigg, Aberdeen AB12 3LX	Aberdeen: Cove New Charge Development Associate Minister	01224 874269	31
Jones, Helen (Miss)	2007	36 Sydney Place, Lockerbie DG11 2JB [E-mail: aandeyouth@gmail.com]	Presbytery of Annandale and Eskdale (Youth Worker)	01576 202863 / 07789 631822 (Mbl)	7
Manners, Stephen (Rev.)	2007	124 Fernieside Crescent, Edinburgh EH17 7DH [E-mail: sk.manners@blueyonder.co.uk]	Edinburgh: Richmond Craigmillar: Parish Assistant	0131-620 0589	1
Morrison, Richard	2007	Idlewylde, Canonbie DG14 0RE	Presbytery of Annandale and Eskdale (Youth Worker)	01387 371381 / 07988 671445 (Mbl)	7
Reford, Susan (Miss)	2001	32 Jedburgh Street, Blantyre, Glasgow G72 0SU [E-mail: susan.reford@biopenworld.com]	Congregational Development Officer: Hamilton Presbytery	01698 820122	17
Robertson, Stefanie	2005/2008	Barn Church, Culloden, Inverness IV2 7WB [E-mail: stef.robertson@yahoo.co.uk]	Culloden: The Barn: Community Project Worker	01463 798946	37
Ross, Keith (Rev.) MA BD	2007	Easter Bavelaw House, Pentland Hills Regional Park EH14 5JS		07855 163449 (Mbl)	
Smith, David	2003	66 Hendry Road, Kirkcaldy KY2 5DB [E-mail: dave@tibal.org.uk]	Lochgelly and Benarty Children's and Young People's Development Worker	01592 641823 / 07882 200215 (Mbl)	24
Steenbergen, Pauline (Rev.)	2007	95 Pinecroft, Carlisle CA3 0DB [E-mail: pauline.steenbergen@virgin.net]	Congregational Facilitator (p/t): Presbytery of Annandale and Eskdale	01228 593243	7
Thomson, John D. (Rev.) BD	2007	3 Tottenham Court, Hill Street, Dysart, Kirkcaldy KY1 2XY [E-mail: j.thomson10@sky.com]	Kennoway, Windygates and Balgonie St Kenneth's: Parish Assistant	01592 655213	25
Vint, Allan S. (Rev.) BSc BD MTh	2008	St Ninian's Church, Allan Crescent, Dunfermline KY11 4HE [E-mail: allan@vint.co.uk]	Mission Development Officer: Dunfermline Presbytery	07795 483070 (Mbl)	24
Wilson, Peter BA	2005/2008	45 Meadowbank Road, Kirknewton EH27 8BH	Kirknewton and East Calder: Youth Worker (p/t)	01506 883779	2
Wyllie, John	2007	51 Seafar Drive, Kelty KY4 0JX	Cowdenbeath: Trinity: Pastoral Assistant	01383 839200	24

Young, Neil James   2001   Holmlea, Main Street, Banton, Kilsyth, Glasgow G65 0QY   Glasgow: St Paul's Youth Worker   0141-770 8559   16
[E-mail: neil.young@bigfoot.com]   07748 808488 (Mbl)

LIST K – OVERSEAS LOCATIONS

EUROPE

AMSTERDAM   The English Reformed Church, The Begijnhof (off the Spui). Service each Sunday at 10:30am.

BRUSSELS   St Andrew's Church, Chaussée de Vleurgat 181 (off Ave. Louise). Service each Sunday at 11:00am.
[E-mail: st-andrews@welcome.to]

BUDAPEST   St Columba's Scottish Mission, Vorosmarty utca 51, H-1054 Budapest, Hungary.   (Church Tel) 0036 1 343 8479
Service in English and Sunday School each Sunday at 11:00am.
The General Synod of the Reformed Church in Hungary, 440 Budapest, PF5, Hungary.
[E-mail: zsinat.kulugy@zsinatiiroda.hu]   (Tel/Fax) 0036 1 460 0708

COSTA DEL SOL   Services at Lux Mundi Ecumenical Centre, Calle Nueva 7, Fuengirola. Service each Sunday at 10:30am.

GENEVA   [E-mail: cofsg@pingnet.ch; Website: www.churchofscotlandgeneva.com]
The Calvin Auditoire, Place de la Taconnerie (beside Cathedral of St Pierre). Service each Sunday at 11:00am.

GIBRALTAR   St Andrew's Church, Governor's Parade. Service each Sunday at 10:30am.

LAUSANNE   26 Avenue de Rumine, CH-1005 Lausanne, Switzerland. Service each Sunday at 10:30am.
[E-mail: scotskirklausanne@bluewin.ch]

LISBON   St Andrew's Church, Rua da Arriaga 13–15, Lisbon, Portugal. Service each Sunday at 11:00am.

MALTA   St Andrew's Church, 210 Old Bakery Street, Valletta. Service each Sunday at 10:30am.

PARIS   [E-mail: scotskirk@wanadoo.fr; Website: www.scotskirkparis.com]
The Scots Kirk, 17 Rue Bayard, F-75008 Paris (Metro: Roosevelt)
Service each Sunday at 10:30am.

ROME   Via XX Settembre 7, 00187 Rome, Italy. Service each Sunday at 11:00am.   (Fax) 0039 06 487 4370

ROTTERDAM
[E-mail: scotsintchurch@cs.com; Website: www.scotsintchurch.com]
The Scots Kirk, Schiedamsevest 121, Rotterdam. Service each Sunday at 10:30am.
Informal service at 9:15am.
(Tel/Fax) 0031 10 220 4199
(Tel) 0031 10 412 4779

AFRICA

MALAWI
Church of Central Africa Presbyterian
Synod of Blantyre

Synod of Livingstonia
Dr Andrew and Mrs Felicity Gaston (1997)
Miss Helen Scott (2000, held previous appointment)
LISAP, PO Box 279, Ekwendeni, Malawi
CCAP Girls' Secondary School, PO Box 2, Ekwendeni, Malawi

ZAMBIA
United Church of Zambia
Rev. Colin D. Johnston (1994) (Ecum)
PO Box 21225, Kitwe, Zambia
[E-mail: revcdj@zamnet.zm]
United Church of Zambia Synod Office, Lusaka, Zambia
[E-mail: uczsynod@zamnet.zm]
(Tel) 00260 1 250 641
(Fax) 00260 1 252 198

THE CARIBBEAN, CENTRAL AND SOUTH AMERICA

BAHAMAS
Vacant
St Andrew's Manse, PO Box N1099, Nassau

Rev. Scott R.McL. Kirkland (2006)
Lucaya Presbyterian Kirk, PO Box F-40777, Freeport, Bahamas
(Tel) 001 242 322 5475
(Fax) 001 242 323 1960
(Tel) 001 242 373 2568
(Fax) 001 242 373 4961

BERMUDA
Mailing address: PO Box PG88, Paget PG BX, Bermuda
Church address: Christ Church, Middle Road, Warwick, Bermuda
[Church website: www.christchurch.bm]
(Tel) 001 441 236 1882
(Fax) 001 441 232 0552

This charge now operates within the Presbytery of Europe.

TRINIDAD
Rev. Garwell Bacchas
Church of Scotland Greyfriars St Ann's,
50 Frederick Street, Port of Spain, Trinidad
[E-mail: greyfriars@tstt.net.tt]
(Tel) 001 868 627 9312

ASIA

BANGLADESH

Church of Bangladesh

Mr James Pender (2004) (Ecum)   c/o St Thomas' Church, 54 Johnston Road, Dhaka 1100, Bangladesh   (Tel: 0121-472 4744)
[E-mal: ohenepender@yahoo.co.uk]

Mr David Hall and Mrs Sarah Hall (2005) (Ecum)   c/o St Thomas' Church, 54 Johnston Road, Dhaka 1100, Bangladesh

Dr Helen Brannam (2006) (Ecum)   c/o St Thomas' Church, 54 Johnston Road, Dhaka 1100, Bangladesh

Ecumenical Appointments

CHINA

Together with Scottish Churches China Group

Ian Groves   York University; returning to China in autumn 2008 as a Long Term Amity Teacher

Anne and Mick Kavanagh (1997)   Hezuo Teachers' College for Minority Nationalities, Hezuo, Gansu Province, 747000, P. R. of China

Kate Jarman (2006)   Hechi Teachers' College, Yizhou, Guangxi Province, 546300, P. R. of China
Angela Evans (2006)   Dingxi Teachers' College, Dingxi, Gansu Province, 743000, P. R. of China
Christine Green (2006)   Wuwei Occupational College, 21 Xian Jian Road, Wuwei, Gansu Province, 743000, P. R. of China

David Clements (2006)   Northwest Normal University, 803 East Anning Road, Lanzhou, Gansu Province, 730070, P. R. of China

Placements are not yet confirmed for Kath Saltwell and Gordon Paterson (2007).

SRI LANKA   St Andrew's Scots Kirk, Colombo
[E-mail: reverend@sltnet.lk]

This charge now operates within the Presbytery of Europe.

MIDDLE EAST AND NORTH AFRICA

ISRAEL   [NOTE: Church Services are held in St Andrew's Scots Memorial Church, Jerusalem, each Sunday at 10am, and at St Andrew's, Galilee (contact minister for worship time)]

Jerusalem
Vacant   St Andrew's, Jerusalem, PO Box 8619, Jerusalem 91086, Israel
(Tel: 00972 2 6732401; Fax: 00972 2 673 1711)
[Website: www.scothotels.co.il]

Tiberias
Vacant   St Andrew's, Galilee, PO Box 104, Tiberias, Israel
(Tel: 00972 6 6721165; Fax: 00972 6 6790145)
[Website: www.scothotels.co.il]

LIST L – OVERSEAS RESIGNED AND RETIRED MISSION PARTNERS (ten or more years' service)

Jaffa — Tabeetha School, PO Box 8170, 21 Yefet Street, Jaffa, Israel (Tel: 00972 3 6821581; Fax: 00972 3 6819357) [E-mail: costab@zahav.net.il; Website: www.tabeetha.htmlplant.com]

NAME	APP	RET	AREA	ADDRESS
Aitken, Faith (Mrs)	1957	1968	Nigeria	High West, Urlar Road, Aberfeldy PH15 2ET
	1987	1990	Zambia	
Anderson, Karen (Mrs)	1992	2006	Israel	23 Allanpark Street, Largs KA30 9AG
Anderson, Kathleen (Mrs)	1955	1968	Pakistan	1A Elms Avenue, Great Shelford, Cambridge CB2 5LN
Archibald, Mary L. (Miss)	1964	1982	Nigeria/Ghana	490 Low Main Street, Wishaw ML2 7PL
Barbour, Edith R. (Miss)	1952	1983	North India	13/11 Pratik Nagar, Yerwada, Pune 411006, Maharashta, India
Baxter, Rev. Richard and Mrs Ray	1954	1969	Malawi	138 Braid Road, Edinburgh EH10 6JB
Berkeley, Dr John and Dr Muriel	1967	1977	Bhutan	Drumbeg, Coylumbridge, Aviemore PH22 1QU
Boyle, Lexa (Miss)	1995	1998	Yemen	7 Maxwell Grove, Glasgow G41 5JP
Bone, Mr David and Mrs Isobel	1959	1992	Aden/Yemen/Sudan	315 Blackness Road, Dundee DD2 1SH
Bone, Elizabeth (Mrs)	1977	1988	Malawi	2A Elm Street, Dundee DD2 2AY
Brodie, Rev. Jim	1950	1964	Malawi	25A Keptie Road, Arbroath DD11 3ED
	1980	1984	North India	
Brown, Janet H. (Miss)	1955	1974	Nepal	6 Baxter Park Terrace, Dundee DD4 6NL
Burnett, Dr Fiona	1996	1998	Pakistan	The Glenholm Centre, Broughton, Biggar ML12 6JF
Burnett, Dr Robin and Mrs Storm	1967	1980	Zambia	79 Bank Street, Irvine KA12 0LL
Burt, M.R.C. (Miss)	1988	1998	Nigeria	22 The Loaning, Chirnside, Duns TD11 3YE
	1964	1967	South Africa	
Byers, Rev. Alan and Rev. Mairi	1968	1977	Kenya	Meadowbank, Plumdon Road, Annan DG12 6SJ
	1940	1975	Ghana	
Campbell, George H.	1960	1971	Livingstonia	20 Woodlands Grove, Kilmarnock KA3 1TZ
Coltart, Rev. Ian O.	1957	1971	North India	The Manse, Arbirlot, Arbroath DD11 2NX
Conacher, Marion (Miss)	1967	1985	India	41 Magdalene Drive, Edinburgh EH15 3BG
Cooper, Rev. George	1963	1993	Kenya	8 Leighton Square, Alyth, Blairgowrie PH11 8AQ
Crosbie, Ann R. (Miss)	1966	1986	Nigeria	21 Fieldhead Square, Glasgow G43 IHL
	1955	1967	Malawi	
Dawson, Miss Anne	1976	2000	Malawi	5 Cattle Market, Clackmannan FK10 4EH

Dick, Dr James and Mrs Anne	1954	1957	North India	1 Tummel Place, Comrie, Crieff PH6 2PG
Dodman, Rev. Roy and Mrs Jane	1957	1968	Nepal	
Dougall, Ian C.	1983	2006	Jamaica	PO Box 64, Stony Hill, Kingston 9, Jamaica
Drever, Dr Bryan	1960	1990	Kenya	60B Craigmillar Park, Edinburgh EH16 5PU
Duncan, Mr David and Mrs Allison	1962	1982	Aden/Yemen/Pakistan	188 Addison Road, King's Head, Birmingham
Duncan, Rev. Graham and Mrs Sandra	1952	1969	Nigeria	7 Newhailes Avenue, Musselburgh EH21 6DW
Dunlop, Mr Walter T. and Mrs Jennifer	1977	1987	South Africa	56 Daphne Road, Maroelana, 0081 Pretoria, South Africa
Fauchelle, Mrs Margaret	1998	2006	Malawi/Israel	50 Oxgangs Road, Edinburgh EH13 9DR
Ferguson, Mr John K.P.	1979	1994	Zambia, Malawi, Zimbabwe	Flat 3, 22 North Avenue, Devonport, Auckland 1309, New Zealand
Finlay, Carol (Ms)	1991	1999	Pakistan	15 Ashgrove, Craigshill, Livingston EH54 5JQ
Fischbacher, Dr Colin M. and Mrs Sally	1977	1989	Malawi	96 Eroomfield Crescent, Edinburgh EH12 7LX
Foster, Joyce (Miss) BSc	1990	2001	Malawi	11 Earclay Square, Gosforth, Newcastle-upon-Tyne NE3 2JB
Fowler, Rev. Margaret	1986	1998	Kenya	99 Sixth Street, Newtongrange EH22 4LA
Fucella, Rev. Mike and Mrs Jane	1968	1972	Malawi	
	1972	1981	Jamaica	PO Box 3097, Negril, Westmorland, Jamaica
	1988	2007	Thailand	95/5 Sathorn SOI 9, Pikul, Sathorn Road, Yamnawa, Sathorn, Bangkok 10120, Thailand
Gall, E.G. (Miss)	1990	2006	Blantyre	151 Raeburn Heights, Glenrothes KY16 1BW
Hutchison, C.M. (Mr)	1940	1962	Calabar	75 Crampian Road, Torry, Aberdeen AB11 8ED
Irvine, Mr Clive and Mrs Su	1951	1972	Nepal	McGregor Flat, 92 Blackford Avenue, Edinburgh EH9 3ES
Irvine, Elsabe (Mrs)	1984	1999	Malawi	60 Thirlestane Road, Edinburgh EH9 1AR
Irvine, Dr Geoffrey C. and Mrs Dorothy	1951	1987	Kenya	Lakeside, PO Box 1356 Naivasha, Kenya
Karam, Ishbel (Mrs)	1952	1989	Pakistan	Hillgarth, Baltasound, Unst, Shetland ZE2 9DY
King, Mrs Betty	1968	1985	North India	23 Main Street, Newstead, Melrose TD6 9DX
Knowles, Dr John K. and Mrs Heather	1955	1971	Malawi	Trollopes Hill, Monton Combe, Bath BA2 7HX
	1976	1992	Malawi	
Laidlay, Dr Rorie and Mrs Una	1961	1968	Yemen	Isles View, 5 Bell's Road, Lerwick, Shetland ZE1 0QB
	1968	1971	Pakistan	
	1971	1978	Yemen	
Liddell, Margaret (Miss)	1964	1980	Zambia	20 Wyvis Crescent, Conon Bridge, Dingwall IV7 8BZ
Logie, Robina (Mrs)	1950	1960	North India	23 Stonefield Drive, Inverurie AB51 9DZ
Lyon, Rev. D.H.S.	1952	1972	Nagpur	30 Mansfield Road, Balerno EH14 7IZ
McArthur, G. (Mr)	1956	1972	South Africa	3 Craigcrook Road, Edinburgh EH4 3NQ
McCulloch, Lesley (Mrs)	1982	1992	Malawi/Pakistan	316 North Jones Street, Port Angeles, WA 98362-4218, USA
McCutcheon, Agnes W.F. (Miss)	1957	1989	India	10A Hugh Murray Grove, Cambuslang, Glasgow G72 7NG
MacDonald, Dr Alistair and Mrs Freda	1949	1962	Nigeria	10 Millside, Morpeth, Northumberland NE61 1PN
McDougall, Rev. John N.	1935	1960	West Pakistan	Everll Orr Home, Allendale Road, Mount Albert, Auckland 3, New Zealand

Name	From	To	Country	Address
McGoff, A.W. (Miss)	1954	1974	Kolhapur	6 Mossvale Walk, Craigend, Glasgow G33 5PF
MacGregor, Rev. Margaret	1959	1994	India	Gordon Flat, 16 Learmonth Court, Edinburgh EH4 1PB
McKenzie, Rev. Robert P.	1936	1951	India	23 Foulis Crescent, Edinburgh EH14 5BN
McKenzie, Rev. W.M.	1958	1974	Zambia	Troqueer Road, Dumfries DG2 7DF
MacKinnon, E.L. (Miss)	1952	1972	Nigeria	
McMahon, Rev. Robert and Mrs Jessie	1959	1976	North India	7 Ridgepark Drive, Lanark ML11 7PG
McMillan, Helen (Miss)	1981	2003	Pakistan	17/1 New Orchardfield, Edinburgh EH6 5ET
Macrae, Rev. Norman	1943	1960	Nigeria	49 Lixmount Avenue, Edinburgh EH5 3EW
Malley, Beryl Stevenson (Miss)	1982	1992	Malawi	272/2 Craigcrook Road, Edinburgh EH4 7TF
Marshall, Rev. Fred J.	1946	1992	Bermuda	Flat 3, 31 Oswald Road, Edinburgh EH9 2HT
Millar, Rev. Margaret R.M.	1967	1996	Malawi/Zambia	The Manse, Taynuilt, Argyll PA35 1HW
Millar, Rev. Peter	1976	1989	South India	
Moir, Rev. Ian and Mrs Elsie	1962	1973	South Africa	28/6 Comely Bank Avenue, Edinburgh EH4 1EL
Moore, Rev. J. Wilfred and Mrs Lillian	1943	1957	Ghana	31 Lennox Gardens, Linlithgow EH49 7PZ
Morrice, Rev. Dr Charles and Mrs Margaret	1971	1998	Buenos Aires/Kenya	104 Baron's Hill Avenue, Linlithgow EH49 7JG
Morton, Rev. Alasdair J.	1960	1973	Zambia	St Leonard's, 16 St Leonard's Road, Forres IV36 1DW
Morton, Rev. Colin	1988	1998	Israel	313 Lanark Road West, Currie EH14 5RS
Munro, Harriet (Miss)	1959	1969	Malawi	26 The Forge, Braidpark Drive, Glasgow G46 6LB
Murison, Rev. W.G.	1951	1971	Santalia	21 Hailes Gardens, Edinburgh EH13 0JL
Murray, Rev. Douglas and Mrs Sheila	1994	2004	Switzerland	Flat 9, 4 Bonnington Gait, Edinburgh EH6 5NZ
Murray, Mr Ian and Mrs Isabel	1962	2000	Pakistan	17 Piershill Terrace, Edinburgh EH8 7EY
Musgrave, Rev. Clarence W. and Mrs Joan	1966	1980	Zambia	4 Ravelston Heights, Edinburgh EH4 3LX
Musk, Mrs Lily	2000	2006	Jerusalem	1 Tulloch Place, St Andrews KY16 8XJ
	1959	1959	Malawi	
	1959	1974	Zambia	
Nelson, Rev. John and Mrs Anne	1947	1952	North India	7 Manse Road, Roslin EH25 9LF
	1952	1959	North India	
	1970	1973		
Nicholson, Rev. Thomas S.	1981	1995	Taiwan	Todholes, Greenlaw, Duns TD10 6XD
Nicol, Catherine (Miss)	1960	2000	Pakistan	St Columba Christian Girls' RTC, Barah Patthar, Sialkot 2, Pakistan
Nutter, Margaret (Miss)	1966	1979	Pakistan	Kilmorich, 14 Balloch Road, Balloch, Alexandria G83 8SR
Pacitti, Rev. Stephen A.	1977	1996	Taiwan	157 Nithsdale Road, Pollokshields, Glasgow G41 5RD
Pattison, Rev. Kenneth and Mrs Susan	1966	1977	Malawi	2 Castle Way, St Madoes, Glencarse, Perth PH2 7NY
Philip, Rev. David Stuart	1978	1991	Gibraltar	6 St Bernard's Crescent, Edinburgh EH4 1NP
Philip, Mrs Margaret	1951	1968	Nigeria	Penlan, Holm Farm Road, Catrine, Mauchline KA5 6TA
Philpot, Rev. David	1981	1995	WCC Geneva	2/27 Pentland Drive, Edinburgh EH10 6PX
Reid, Dr Ann	1988	1996	Ghana	19 Cloughwood Crescent, Shevington, Lancs WN6 8EP
Reid, Margaret I. (Miss)	1964	1982	Malawi	26A Angle Park Terrace, Edinburgh EH11 2JT

Rennie, Rev. Alistair M.	1939	1976	Malawi	Notle's Yard, St Mary's Gate, Wirksworth, Derbyshire DE4 4DQ
Ritchie, Isbhel M. (Miss)	1955	1996	Eastern Himalaya	8 Ross Street, Dunfermline KY12 0AN
Ritchie, Rev. J.M.	1974	1977	Yemen	46 St James' Gardens, Penicuik EH26 9DU
Ritchie, Margaret (Miss)	1968	1978	Zambia	1 Afton Bridgend, New Cumnock KA18 4AX
Ritchie, Mary Scott (Miss)	1968	1991	Malawi/Zambia/Israel	Afton Villa, 1 Afton Bridgend, New Cumnock KA18 4AX
Ross, Rev. Prof. Kenneth and Mrs Hester	1988	1998	Malawi	35 Madeira Street, Edinburgh EH6 4AJ
Rough, Mary E. (Miss)	1966	1987	Blantyre	9 Glebe Street, Dumfries DG1 2LF
Roy, Rev. Alan J.	1960	1972	Zambia	14 Comerton Place, Drumoig, St Andrews KY16 0NQ
Russell, M.M. (Miss)	1946	1969	Nigeria	14 Hozier Street, Carluke ML8 5DW
Samuel, Lynda (Mrs)	1974	1990	Madras	28 Eraehead, Methven Walk, Dundee DD2 3FJ [E-mail: rasam42@onetel.com]
Shepherd, Dr Clyne	1956	1968	Nigeria	10 Kingsknowe Road South, Edinburgh EH14 2JE
Smith, Mr Harry and Mrs Margaret	1959	1967	Nigeria	31 Woodville Crescent, Sunderland SR4 8RE
Smith, M.L. (Miss)	1968	1970	Malawi	6 Fintry Mains, Dundee DD4 9HF
Smith, Rev. W. Ewing	1956	1973	Madras	8 Hardy Gardens, Bathgate EH48 1NH
Sneddon, Mr Sandy and Mrs Marie	1962	1978	Delhi	84 Creenend Gardens, Edinburgh EH17 7QH
Steedman, Marcha (Mrs) (née Hamilton)	1986	2003	Pakistan	
Stewart, Marion G. (Miss)	1955	1966	North India	Muir of Blebo, Blebo Craigs, Cupar KY15 5TZ
Stiven, Rev. Iain	1976	1989	Malawi/Israel	Kirk Cottage, Kirkton of Skene, Westhill, Skene AB32 6XX
Stone, W. Vernon MA BD	1959	1969	Pakistan	7 Gloucester Place, Edinburgh EH3 6EE
Taylor, Rev. A.T.H.	1949	1966	Zambia	36 Woodrow Court, Port Glasgow Road, Kilmacolm PA13 4QA
Tennant, Frances (Miss)	1938	1972	Nigeria/Jamaica	4 The Pleasance, Strathkinness, St Andrews KY16 9SD
Wallace, A. Dorothy (Miss)	1965	1977	Pakistan	101 St John's Road, Edinburgh EH12 6NN
Walker, Rev. Donald and Mrs Judith	1953	1991	North India	7 Bynack Place, Nethy Bridge PH25 3DU
Westmarland, Rev. Colin	1981	1994	Zambia	2 Wilson Road, Banchory AB31 3UY
Wilkie, Rev. James L.	1975	2001	Malta	PO Box 5, Cospicua, CSPOl, Malta
Wilkinson, Dr Alison	1959	1976	Zambia	7 Comely Bank Avenue, Edinburgh EH4 1EW
Wilkinson, Rev. John	1992	2007	Kenya	5 Birch Avenue, Stirling FK8 2PL
Wilson, Irene (Ms)	1946	1975	Kenya	70 Craigleith Hill Gardens, Edinburgh EH4 2JH
Wilson, M.H. (Miss)	1993	2004	Israel	7 Lady's Well, Moat Road, Annan DG12 5AD
Wilson, Rev. Mark	1946	1977	Nasik	37 Kings Avenue, Longniddry EH32 0QN
	1953	1978	Nagpur	

LIST M – PARISH ASSISTANTS AND PROJECT WORKERS

Those who in previous years would have been named here are now included in List J – Presbytery/Parish Workers.

LIST N – READERS

1. EDINBURGH

Name	Address	Telephone
Christie, Gillian L. (Mrs)	45 Allan Park Drive, Edinburgh EH16 1LW	0131-443 4472
Davies, Ruth (Mrs) (attached to Liberton)	4 Hawkhead Grove, Edinburgh EH16 6LS	0131-664 3608
Farrant, Yvonne (Mrs)	Flat 7, 14 Duddingston Mills, Edinburgh EH8 7NF [E-mail: yfarrant@charis.org.uk]	0131-661 0672
Farrell, William J.	50 Ulster Crescent, Edinburgh EH8 7JS [E-mail: will.farrell@freeuk.com]	0131-661 1026
Farrow, Edmund	14 Brunswick Terrace, Edinburgh EH7 5PG [E-mail: efsc18422@blueyonder.co.uk]	0131-558 8210
Kerrigan, Herbert A. MA LLB QC	Airdene, 20 Edinburgh Road, Dalkeith EH22 1IY [E-mail: kerriganqc@btconnect.com]	0131-660 3007
Kinnear, Dr Malcolm	25 Thorburn Road, Edinburgh EH13 0BH [E-mail: andrewk@kinnear25.fsnet.co.uk]	0131-441 3150
MacFarlane, Helen (Mrs)	5/5 Moat Drive, Edinburgh EH14 1NU [E-mail: helen@butterflytrust.org.uk]	0131-444 1709
McPherson, Alistair	77 Bonaly Wester, Edinburgh EH13 0RQ [E-mail: amjhmcpherson@blueyonder.co.uk]	0131-478 5384
Pearce, Martin	4 Corbiehill Avenue, Edinburgh EH4 5DR [E-mail: martin.j.pearce@blueyonder.co.uk]	0131-336 4864
Sheriffs, Irene (Mrs)	22/2 West Mill Bank, Edinburgh EH13 0QT	0131-466 9530
Wyllie, Anne (Miss)	46 Jordan Lane, Edinburgh EH10 4QX	0131-447 9035

2. WEST LOTHIAN

Beatson, David	'Schiefer Hof', Keepscaith Farm, Longridge, Bathgate EH47 9AL [E-mail: ireneagape@tiscali.co.uk]	01501 740494
Blackwood, Michael	Inshaig Cottage, Hatton, Kirknewton EH27 8DZ	0131-333 1448
Coyle, Charlotte (Mrs)	28 The Avenue, Whitburn EH47 0DA	01501 740687
Elliott, Sarah (Miss)	105 Seafield, Bathgate EH47 7AW	01506 654950
Galloway, Brenda (Miss)	Lochend, St Ninian's Road, Linlithgow EH49 7BN	01506 842028
Notman, Jean G.S. (Miss)	31 South Loch Park, Bathgate EH48 2QZ	01506 633820
Scoular, Iain W.	'The Wee Hoose', Ecclesmachan Road, Uphall, Broxburn EH52 6JP [E-mail: iain@iwsconsultants.com]	01506 855794
Wilkie, David	53 Goschen Place, Broxburn EH52 5JH	01506 854777

3. LOTHIAN

Name	Address	Telephone
Cannon, S. Christopher MA	Briarwood, Winterfield Place, Belhaven, Dunbar EH42 1QQ	01368 864991
Evans, W. John IEng MIIE(Elec)	Edenwood, 29 Smileyknowes Court, North Berwick EH39 4RG [E-mail: jevans7is@hotmail.com]	01620 894309

Gibson, C.B. Stewart — 27 King's Avenue, Longniddry EH32 0QN — 01875 853464

Herkes, Chistine W.S. (Mrs) — Viewfield, 224 Galashiels Road, Stow Galashiels TD1 2RA [E-mail: stewar.gibson27@tiscali.co.uk] [E-mail: herkesc@aol.com] — 01578 730413

Hogg, David MA — 82 Eskhill, Penicuik EH26 8DQ — 01968 676350

Johnston, June E. (Ms) BSc MEd BD — 49 Braeside Road South, Gorebridge EH23 4DL [E-mail: david@hoggdavid.wanadoo.co.uk] — 01875 823086
Lyall, George JP — Mossgiel, 13 Park Road, Bonnyrigg EH19 2AW — 0131-663 9343

Millan, Mary (Mrs) — 33 Polton Vale, Loanhead EH20 9DF [E-mail: george.lyall@bigfoot.com] — 0131-440 1624

Trevor, A. Hugh MA MTh — 29A Fidra Road, North Berwick EH39 4NE [E-mail: marymillan@fsmail.net] — 01620 894924

Yeoman, Edward T.N. FSAScot — 75 Newhailes Crescent, Musselburgh EH21 6EF [E-mail: htrevor@talktalk.net] — 0131-653 2291

4. MELROSE AND PEEBLES

Butcher, John W. — 'Sandal', 13 Ormiston Grove, Melrose TD6 9SR — 01896 822339
Cashman, Margaret D. (Mrs) — 38 Abbotsford Road, Galashiels TD1 3HR — 01896 752711
Selkirk, Frances (Mrs) — 2 The Glebe, Ashkirk, Selkirk TD7 4PJ — 01750 32204

5. DUNS

Deans, M. (Mrs) BA — 10 The Granary, Love Lane, Berwick-upon-Tweed TD15 1AR — 01289 307699
Elphinston, Enid (Mrs) — The Hollies, Woodlands, Foulden, Berwick-upon-Tweed TD15 1UH — 01289 386359
Landale, Alison (Mrs) — Green Hope, Duns TD11 3SG — 01361 890242

6. JEDBURGH

Findlay, Elizabeth (Mrs) — 2 Hendersons Court, Kelso TD5 7BG — 01573 226641

Knox, Dagmar (Mrs) — 3 Stichill Road, Ednam, Kelso TD5 7QQ [E-mail: elizabeth@findlay8124.fsword.co.uk] — 01573 224883

Thomson, Robert R. — 34/36 Fisher Avenue, Hawick TD9 9NB [E-mail: dagmar@knox-riding.wanadoo.co.uk] — 01450 373851

7. ANNANDALE AND ESKDALE

Boncey, David — Redbrae, Beattock, Moffat DG10 9RF — 01683 300613

Brown, Martin J. — Lochhouse Farm, Beattock, Moffat DG10 9SG [E-mail: boncey@free.uk.com] — 01683 300451

Brown, S. Jeffrey BA — Skara Brae, 8 Ballplay Road, Moffat DG10 9JU [E-mail: martin@lochhousefarm.com] — 01683 220475
Chisholm, Dennis A.G. MA BSc — Moss-side, Hightae, Lockerbie DG11 1JR — 01387 811803
Dodds, Alan — Trinco, Battlehill, Annan DG12 6SN — 01461 201235

Jackson, Susan (Mrs) — 48 Springbells Road, Annan DG12 6LQ [E-mail: alandodds46@btinternet.com] [E-mail: shjackson@supanet.com] — 01461 204159

Morton, Andrew A. BSc — 19 Sherwood Park, Lockerbie DG11 2DX — 01576 203164
[E-mail: andrew_a_morton@btinternet.com]

Saville, Hilda A. (Mrs) — 32 Crosslaw Burn, Moffat DG10 9LP — 01683 222854
[E-mail: qjhnic62@sky.com]

8. DUMFRIES AND KIRKCUDBRIGHT

Carroll, J. Scott — 17 Downs Place, Heathhall, Dumfries DG1 3RF — 01387 265350
Greer, Kathleen (Mrs) MEd — 10 Watling Street, Dumfries DG1 1HF — 01387 256113
Ogilvie, D.W. MA FSAScot — Lingerwood, 2 Nelson Street, Dumfries DG2 9AY — 01387 264267
Paterson, Ronald M. (Dr) — Mirkwood, Ringford, Castle Douglas DG7 2AL — 01557 820202
Piggins, Janette (Mrs) — Cleugh Wood, Dalbeattie DG5 4PF — 01387 780655
Wallace, Mhairi (Mrs) — The Manse, Twynholm, Kirkcudbright DG6 4NY — 01557 860381

9. WIGTOWN AND STRANRAER

Connery, Graham — Skellies Knowe, West Ervie, Stranraer DG9 — 01776 854277
Harvey, Joyce (Mrs) — 4A Allanfield Place, Newton Stewart DG8 6BS — 01671 403693
McQuistan, Robert — Old School House, Carsluith, Newton Stewart DG8 7DT — 01671 820327
Williams, Roy — 120 Belmont Road, Stranraer DG9 7BG

10. AYR

Anderson, James (Dr) BVMS PhD DVM FRCPath FIBiol MRCVS — 67 Henrietta Street, Girvan KA26 9AN — 01465 710059
Cuthbert, Helen (Miss) MA MSc — 63 Haining Avenue, Kilmarnock KA1 3QN — 01563 550403
Jamieson, Iain — 2 Whinfield Avenue, Prestwick KA9 2BH — 01242 476898
Morrison, James — 27 Monkton Road, Prestwick KA9 1AP — 01292 479313
Murphy, Ian — 56 Lamont Crescent, Cumnock KA18 3DU — 01290 423675
Rione, Elizabeth (Mrs) — Monkwood Mains, Minishant, Maybole KA19 8EY — 01292 443440

11. IRVINE AND KILMARNOCK

Bircham, James — 8 Holmlea Place, Kilmarnock KA1 1UU — 01563 532287
Crosbie, Shona (Mrs) — 4 Campbell Street, Darvel KA17 0PA — 01560 322229
Findlay, Elizabeth (Mrs) — 19 Keith Place, Kilmarnock KA3 7NS — 01563 528084
Hamilton, Margaret A. (Mrs) — 59 South Hamilton Street, Kilmarnock KA1 2DT — 01563 534431
Jamieson, John BSc(Hons) DEP AFBPSS — 22 Moorfield Avenue, Kilmarnock KA1 1TS — 01563 534065
Lightbody, Hunter B. — 36 Rannoch Place, Irvine KA12 9NQ — 01294 273955
McAllister, Anne C. (Mrs) — 39 Bowes Rigg, Stewarton KA3 5EN — 01560 483191
McLean, Donald — 1 Four Acres Drive, Kilmaurs, Kilmarnock KA3 2ND — 01563 381475
MacTaggart, Elspeth (Miss) — 21 Scargie Road, Kilmarnock KA3 1QR — 01563 527713
Mills, Catherine (Mrs) — 59 Crossdene Road, Crosshouse, Kilmarnock KA2 0JU — 01563 535305
Raleigh, Gavin — 21 Landsborough Drive, Kilmarnock KA3 1RY — 01563 520836
Scott, William BA DipEd — 6 Elgin Avenue, Stewarton, Kilmarnock KA3 3HJ — 01560 484273
Storm, Iain — 17 Kilwinning Road, Irvine KA12 8RR — 01294 277647
Wilson, Robert L.S. MA BD — 57 West Woodstock Street, Kilmarnock KA1 2JH — 01563 526658

12. ARDROSSAN

Barclay, Elizabeth (Mrs)	2 Jacks Road, Saltcoats KA21 5NT	01294 471855
Currie, Archie BD	55 Central Avenue, Kilbirnie KA25 6JP	01505 681474
Hunter, Jean C.Q. (Mrs) BD	The Manse, Lamlash, Brodick, Isle of Arran KA27 8LE	01770 860380
McCool, Robert	17 McGregor Avenue, Stevenston KA20 4BA	01294 466548
Mackay, Brenda H. (Mrs)	19 Eglinton Square, Ardrossan KA22 8LN	01294 464491
Nimmo, M. (Mrs)	12 Muirfield Place, Kilwinning KA13 6NL	01294 553718
Ross, Magnus BA MEd	39 Beachway, Largs KA30 8QH	01475 689572
Smith, N. (Mrs)	5 Kames Street, Millport, Isle of Cumbrae KA28 0BN	01475 530747
Spencer, P. (Mrs)	43 Gateside Street, Largs KA30 9LH	01475 686293

13. LANARK

Allan, Robert	59 Jennie Lee Drive, Overtown, Wishaw ML2 0EE	01698 376738
Grant, Alan	25 Moss-side Avenue, Carluke ML8 5UG	01555 771419
Kerr, Sheilah I. (Mrs)	Dunvegan, 29 Wilsontown Road, Forth, Lanark ML11 8ER	01555 812214
Love, William	30 Barmore Avenue, Carluke ML8 4FE	01555 751243

14. GREENOCK AND PAISLEY

Banks, Russell	18 Aboyne Drive, Paisley PA2 7SJ [E-mail: cbanks25@aol.com]	0141-884 6925
Campbell, Tom BA DipCPC	100 Craigielea Road, Renfrew PA4 8NJ [E-mail: thomas.campbell1180@ntlworld.co.uk]	0141-886 2503
Davey, Charles L.	16 Divert Road, Gourock PA19 1DT [E-mail: charles.davey@talktalk.net]	01475 631544
Glenny, John C.	49 Cloch Road, Gourock PA19 1AT [E-mail: jacklizg@aol.com]	01475 636415
Hood, Eleanor (Mrs)	12 Clochoderick Avenue, Kilbarchan, Johnstone PA10 2ES [E-mail: eleanor.hood.kilbarchan@ntlworld.com]	01505 704208
Jamieson, J.A.	148 Finnart Street, Greenock PA16 8HY	01475 729531
McFarlan, Elizabeth (Miss)	20 Fauldswood Crescent, Paisley PA2 9PA [E-mail: elizabeth.mcfarlan@ntlworld.com]	01505 358411
McHugh, Jack	'Earlshaugh', Earl Place, Bridge of Weir PA11 3HA [E-mail: jrmchugh@btinternet.com]	01505 612789
Marshall, Leon M.	Glenisla, Gryffe Road, Kilmacolm PA13 4BA [E-mail: lm@stevenson-kyles.co.uk]	01505 872417
Maxwell, Margaret (Mrs) BD	2 Grants Avenue, Paisley PA2 6AZ [E-mail: sandra1.maxwell@virgin.net]	0141-884 3710
Noonan, Pam (Mrs)	18 Woodburn Place, Houston, Johnstone PA6 7NA	01505 326254
Orry, Geoff	'Rhu Ellan', 4 Seaforth Crescent, Barrhead, Glasgow G78 1PL	0141-881 9748
Robertson, William	69 Colinbar Circle, Barrhead, Glasgow G78 2BG	0141-571 4338
Shaw, Ian	The Grove, 8 Commercial Road, Barrhead, Glasgow G78 1AJ	0141-881 2038

16. GLASGOW

Adams, Mary	44 Springcroft Crescent, Glasgow G69 6SB	0141-771 1957
Birchall, Edwin R.	11 Sunnybank Grove, Clarkston, Glasgow G76 7SU	0141-638 4332

Name	Address	Telephone
Callander, Thomas M.S.	31 Dalkeith Avenue, Bishopbriggs, Glasgow G64 2HQ	0141-563 6955
Campbell, Jack T. BD BEd	40 Kenmure Avenue, Bishopbriggs, Glasgow G64 2DE	0141-563 5837
Dickson, Hector	'Gwito', 61 Whitton Drive, Giffnock, Glasgow G46 6EF	0141-637 0080
Fullarton, Andrew	225 Aros Drive, Glasgow G52 1TJ	0141-883 9518
Galbraith, Iain B.	Beechwood, Overton Road, Alexandria G83 0LJ	01389 753563
Gibson, James N.	153 Peveril Avenue, Glasgow G41 3SF	0141-632 4162
Hunt, Roland BSc PhD CertEd	4 Flora Gardens, Bishopbriggs, Glasgow G64 1DS	0141-548 3658 (Daytime – Mon–Fri) 0141-563 3257 (Evenings and weekends)
McColl, John	53 Aberfoyle Street, Glasgow G31 3RP	0141-554 9881
McFarlane, Robert	25 Avenel Road, Glasgow G13 2PB	0141-954 5540
McLaughlin, Cathy (Mrs)	8 Lamlash Place, Glasgow G33 3XH	0141-774 2483
MacLeod, John	2 Shuna Place, Newton Mearns, Glasgow G77 6TN	0141-639 6862
Phillips, John B.	2/3, 30 Handel Place, Glasgow G5 0TP [E-mail: johnphillips@fish.co.uk]	0141-429 7716
Robertson, Adam	423 Amulree Street, Glasgow G32 7SS	0141-573 6662
Stuart, Alex	107 Baldorran Crescent, Cumbernauld, Glasgow G68 9EX	01236 727710
Tindall, Margaret (Mrs)	23 Ashcroft Avenue, Lennoxtown, Glasgow G65 7EN [E-mail: margarettindall@aol.com]	01360 310911
Wilson, George A.	46 Maxwell Drive, Garrowhill, Baillieston, Glasgow G69 6LS	0141-771 3862

17. HAMILTON

Anderson, Malcolm	5 Anford Place, Blantyre, Glasgow G72 0NR [E-mail: andersoncalvin1@aol.com]	01698 820510
Beattie, Richard	4 Bent Road, Hamilton ML3 6QB	01698 420806
Bell, Sheena	2 Langdale, East Kilbride, Glasgow G74 4RP	01355 248217
Clemenson, Anne	25 Dempsey Road, Lochview, Bellshill ML4 2UF [E-mail: aclemenson@msn.com]	01698 291019
Cruickshanks, William	63 Progress Drive, Caldercruix, Airdrie ML6 7PU	01236 843352
Haggarty, Frank	46 Glen Road, Caldercruix, Airdrie ML6 7PZ	01236 842182
Hawthorne, William G. MBE	172 Main Street, Plains, Airdrie ML6 7JH	01236 842230
Hewitt, Samuel	3 Corrie Court, Earnock, Hamilton ML3 9XE	01698 457403
Hislop, Eric	1 Castlegait, Strathaven ML10 6FF	01357 520003
Keir, Dickson	46 Brackenhill Drive, Hamilton ML3 8AY	01698 457351
Leckie, Elizabeth	41 Church Street, Larkhall ML9 1EZ	01698 308933
McCleary, Isaac	719 Coatbridge Road, Bargeddie, Glasgow G69 7PH	0141-236 0158
MacMillan, Georgina	1 Darngaber Gardens, Quarter, Hamilton ML3 7XX	01698 424040
Queen, Leslie	60 Loch Assynt, East Kilbride, Glasgow G74 2DW	01355 233932
Robertson, Rowan	68 Townhead Road, Coatbridge ML5 2HU	01236 425703
Smith, Alexander (Reader Emeritus)	6 Coronation Street, Wishaw ML2 8LF	01698 385797
Stevenson, Thomas	34 Castle Wynd, Quarter, Hamilton ML3 7XD	01698 282263
White, Ian	21 Muirhead, Stonehouse, Larkhall ML9 3HG	01698 792772
Wilson, William (Reader Emeritus)	115 Chatelherault Crescent, Low Waters Estate, Hamilton ML3 9PL	01698 421856

18. DUMBARTON

Foster, Peter	The Forge, Colgrain Steading, Colgrain, Cardross, Dumbarton G82 5JL	01389 849200
Giles, Donald (Dr)	Levern House, Stuckenduff, Shandon, Helensburgh G84 8NW	01436 820565
Harold, Sandy	The Laurels, Risk Street, Clydebank G81 3LW	0141-952 3673
Hart, R.J.M. BSc	7 Kidston Drive, Helensburgh G84 8QA	01436 672039
McCutcheon, John	Flat 2/6 Parkview, Milton Brae, Milton, Dumbarton G82 2TT	01389 739034
Nutter, Margaret (Miss)	14 Balloch Road, Balloch, Alexandria G83 8SR	01436 754505
Rettie, Sara (Mrs)	86 Dennistoun Crescent, Helensburgh G84 7JF	01436 677984
Robertson, Ishbell (Miss)	81 Bonhill Road, Dumbarton G82 2EU	01389 763436

19. ARGYLL

Binner, Aileen (Mrs)	'Ailand', Connel, Oban PA37 1QX	01631 710264
Challis, John O.	Bay Villa, Strachur, Cairndow PA27 8DE	01369 860436
Elwis, Michael	Erray Farm, Tobermory, Mull PA75 6PS	01688 302331
Garrett, William E.	7 Creag Ghlas, Cairnbaan, Lochgilphead PA31 8UE	01546 606769
Goodison, Michael	Dalriada Cottage, Bridge of Awe, Taynuilt PA35 1HT	01866 822479
	[E-mail: dalriada@btinternet.com]	
Holden, Robert	Orsay, West Bank Road, Ardrishaig, Lochgilphead PA30 8HG	01546 603211
Logue, David	3 Braeface, Tayvallich, Lochgilphead PA31 8PN	01546 870647
McLellan, James A.	West Drimvore, Lochgilphead PA31 8SU	01546 606403
	[E-mail: james.mclellan@argyll-bute.gov.uk]	
Mitchell, James S.	4 Main Street, Port Charlotte, Isle of Islay PA48 7TX	01496 850650
Morrison, John L.	Tigh na Barnashaig, Tayvallich, Lochgilphead PA31 8PN	01546 870637
Ramsay, Matthew M.	Portnastorm, Carradale, Campbeltown PA28 6SB	01583 431381
	[E-mail: portnastorm@tiscali.co.uk]	
Roberts, John V.	20 Toberonochy, Isle of Luing, Oban PA34 4UE	01852 314301
		(Prefix 18001 Text, prefix 18002 Voice)
Sinclair, Margaret (Mrs)	2 Quarry Place, Furnace, Inveraray PA32 8XW	01499 500633
	[E-mail: margaret_sinclair@btinternet.com]	
Stather, Angela (Mrs)	9 Gartness Cottages, Ballygrant, Isle of Islay PA45 7QN	01496 840527
Stewart, Agnes (Mrs)	Creagdhu Mansions, New Quay Street, Campbeltown PA28 6BB	01586 552805
Thornhill, Christopher R.	4 Ardfern Cottages, Ardfern, Lochgilphead PA31 9QN	01852 500674

22. FALKIRK

Duncan, Lorna (Mrs) BA	Richmond, 28 Solway Drive, Head of Muir, Denny FK5 5NS	01324 813020
McDonald, Rhona	3 Carron View, Maddiston, Falkirk FK2 0NF	01324 870752
Mathers, S. (Mrs)	10 Ercall Road, Brightons, Falkirk FK2 0RS	01324 872253
O'Rourke, Edith (Mrs)	16 Achray Road, Cumbernauld, Glasgow G67 4JH	01236 732813
Sarle, Andrew BSc BD	114 High Station Road, Falkirk FK1 5LN	01324 621648
Stewart, Arthur MA	51 Bonnymuir Crescent, Bonnybridge FK4 1GD	01324 812667
Struthers, I.	7 McVean Place, Bonnybridge FK4 1QZ	01324 841145
	[E-mail: ivar.struthers@btinternet.com]	

23. STIRLING

Brown, Kathryn (Mrs)	1 Callendar Park Walk, Callendar Grange, Falkirk FK1 1TA	01324 617352
Durie, Alastair	25 Forth Place, Stirling FK8 1UD	01786 451029
Grier, Hunter	17 Station Road, Bannockburn, Stirling FK7 8LG	01786 815192
Kimmitt, Alan	111 Glasgow Road, Stirling FK7 0PF	01786 817014
Lamont, John BD	62 Parkdyke, Stirling FK7 9LS	01786 474515
Mack, Lynne (Mrs)	36 Middleton, Menstrie FK11 7HD	01259 761465
Ross, Alastair	7 Elm Court, Doune FK16 6JG	01786 841648
Tilly, Patricia	4 Innerdownie Place, Dollar FK14 7BY	01259 742094
Weir, Andrew (Dr)	16 The Oaks, Killearn, Glasgow G63 9SF	01360 550779

24. DUNFERMLINE

Adams, William	24 Foulford Street, Cowdenbeath KY4 0EQ	01383 510540
Arnott, Robert G.K.	25 Sealstrand, Dalgety Bay, Dunfermline KY11 5GH	01383 822293
Blane, David	10 Ordnance Road, Crombie, Dunfermline KY12 8JZ	01383 873002
Conway, Bernard	4 Centre Street, Kelty KY4 0DU	01383 830442
McCaffery, Joyce (Mrs)	79 Union Street, Cowdenbeath KY4 9SA	01383 515775
McDonald, Elizabeth (Mrs)	Parleyhill, Culross, Dunfermline KY12 8JD	01383 880231
Meiklejohn, Barry	40 Lilac Grove, Dunfermline KY11 8AP	01383 731550
Mitchell, Ian G. QC	17 Carlingnose Point, North Queensferry, Inverkeithing KY11 1ER	01383 416240

25. KIRKCALDY

Biernat, Ian	2 Formonthills Road, Glenrothes KY6 3BX	01592 741487
	[E-mail: ian.biernat@virgin.net]	
Weatherston, Catriona M.A. (Miss) BSc	'Cruachan', Church Road, Leven KY8 4JB	01333 424636
	[E-mail: weatherstoncatriona@mac.com]	

26. ST ANDREWS

Elder, Morag Anne (Ms)	5 Provost Road, Tayport DD6 9JE	01382 552218
Grant, Allan	6 Normandy Place, Rosyth KY11 2HJ	01383 428760
	[E-mail: allan75@btinternet.com]	
King, C.M. (Mrs)	8 Bankwell Road, Anstruther KY10 3DA	01333 310017
Kinnis, W.K.B. (Dr) (Reader Emeritus)	4 Dempster Court, St Andrews KY16 9EU	01334 476959
Smith, Elspeth (Mrs)	Whinstead, Dalgairn, Cupar KY15 4PH	01334 653269

27. DUNKELD AND MEIGLE

Carr, Graham	St Helens, Meigle Road, Alyth PH11 8EU	01828 632474
Ewart, Ellen (Mrs)	Caputh Manse, Caputh, Perth PH1 4JH	01738 710520
Howat, David	Lilybank Cottage, Newton Street, Blairgowrie PH10 6MZ	01250 874715
Macmartin, Duncan M.	Teallach, Old Crieff Road, Aberfeldy PH15 2DG	01887 820693
Peacock, Graham	7 Glenisla View, Alyth, Blairgowrie PH11 8LW	01828 633341
Templeton, Elizabeth (Mrs)	Milton of Pitgur Farmhouse, Dalcapon, Pitlochry PH9 0ND	01796 482232

28. PERTH

Begg, James — 8 Park Village, Turretbank Road, Crieff PH7 4JN — 01764 655907
[E-mail: Bjimmy37@aol.com]

Brown, Stanley — 14 Buchan Drive, Perth PH1 1NQ — 01738 628818
Chappell, E. (Mrs) — Fiscal's House, Flat B, 1 South Street Perth PH2 8NJ — 01738 587808
[E-mail: emchappell@tesco.net]

Coulter, Hamish — 95 Cedar Drive, Perth PH1 1RW — 01738 636761
[E-mail: hamishscoulter@btinternet.com]

Davidson, Andrew — 95 Needless Road, Perth PH2 0LD — 01738 620839
[E-mail: a.r.davidson.91@cantab.net]

Hastings, W.P. — 5 Craigroyston Road, Scone, Perth PH2 6NB — 01738 560498
Laing, John — 10 Graybank Road, Perth PH2 0GZ — 01738 623888
[E-mail: laing_middlechurch@hotmail.com]

Livingstone, Alan — Meadowside, Lawmuir, Methven, Perth PH1 3SZ — 01738 840682
Michie, Margaret (Mrs) — 3 Loch Leven Court, Wester Balgedie. Kinross KY13 9NE — 01592 840602
[E-mail: margaretmichie@balgedie.freeserve.co.uk]

Ogilvie, Brian — 67 Whitecraigs, Kinnesswood, Kinross KY13 9JN — 01592 840823
[E-mail: brianj.ogilvie1@btopenworld.com]

Packer, Joan (Miss) — 11 Moredun Terrace, Perth PH2 0DA — 01738 623873
Thorburn, Susan (Mrs) MTh — 3 Daleally Cottages, St Madoes Road, Errol, Perth PH2 7TJ
[E-mail: s_thor2@yahoo.com]

Wilkie, Robert — 24 Huntingtower Road, Perth PH1 2JS — 01738 628301
Yellowlees, Deirdre (Mrs) — Ringmill House, Gannochy Farm, Perth PH2 7JH — 01738 633773
[E-mail: d.yellowlees@btinternet.com]

29. DUNDEE

Bell, Stephen (Dr) — 10 Victoria Street, Newport-on-Tay DD6 8DJ — 01382 542315
[E-mail: stephen.bell@dundeepresbytery.org.uk]

Brown, Isobel (Mrs) — 10 School Wynd, Muirhead, Dundee DD2 5LW — 01382 580545
Brown, Janet (Miss) — G2, 6 Baxter Park Terrace, Dundee DD4 6NL — 01382 453066
[E-mail: janet.brown@dundeepresbytery.org.uk]

Owler, Harry G. (Emeritus) — 43 Brownhill Road, Dundee DD2 4LH — 01382 622902
Ramsay, T. — 6 Inchcape Road, Broughty Ferry, Dundee DD5 2LP — 01382 778915
Rodgers, Mary (Mrs) — 12 Balmerino Road, Dundee DD4 8RN — 01382 500291
Simpson, Webster — 51 Wemyss Crescent, Monifieth, Dundee DD5 4RA — 01382 535218
Webster, Charles A. — 16 Bath Street, Broughty Ferry, Dundee DD5 2BY — 01382 739520
[E-mail: charles_webster@dundeepresbytery.org.uk]
Woodley, Alan G. (Dr) — 67 Marlee Road, Broughty Ferry, Dundee DD5 3UT — 01382 739820
[E-mail: alan.woodley@dundeepresbytery.org.uk]
Xenophontos-Hellen, Tim — 23 Ancrum Drive, Dundee DD2 2JG — 01382 660355
[E-mail: tim.xenophontos-hellen@dundeepresbytery.org.uk]

30. ANGUS

Anderson, Gordon — 33 Grampian View, Ferryden, Montrose DD10 9SU — 01674 674915
Beedie, A.W. — 62 Newton Crescent, Arbroath DD11 3JZ — 01241 875001

Davidson, P.I. — 95 Bridge Street, Montrose DD10 8AF — 01674 674098
Edwards, Dougal — 25 Mackenzie Street, Carnoustie DD7 6HD — 01241 852666
Gray, Ian — 'The Mallards', 15 Rossie Island Road, Montrose DD10 9NH — 01674 677126
Gray, Linda (Mrs) — 8 Inchgarth Street, Forfar DD8 3LY — 01307 464039
Ironside, Colin (Emeritus) — 21 Tailyour Crescent, Montrose DD10 9BL — 01674 673959
Leslie Melville, Ruth (Hon. Mrs) — Little Deuchar, Fern, Forfar DD8 3RA — 01356 650279
Nicol, Douglas C. — Edenbank, 16 New Road, Forfar DD8 2AE — 01307 463264
Stevens, Peter J. BSc BA — 7 Union Street, Montrose DD10 8PZ — 01674 673710
Thompson, Anne — 22 Braehead Drive, Carnoustie DD7 7SX — 01241 852084
Wheat, M. — 16A South Esk Street, Montrose DD10 8BJ — 01674 676083

31. ABERDEEN

Anderson, William — 1 Farepark Circle, Westhill, Skene AB32 6WJ — 01224 740017
(attached to the congregations of Cove and St Nicholas Kincorth)
Gray, Peter PhD — 165 Countesswells Road, Aberdeen AB15 7RA — 01224 318172
Morgan, Richard — 73A Bon-Accord Street, Aberdeen AB11 6ED — 01224 210270
Sinton, George P. (Emeritus) FIMLS — 12 North Donside Road, Bridge of Don, Aberdeen AB23 8PA — 01224 702273

32. KINCARDINE AND DEESIDE

Atkins, Sally (Mrs) — 9 Feugh View, Strachan, Banchory AB31 6NF — 01330 850434
Broere, Teresa (Mrs) — 3 Balnastraid Cottages, Dinnet, Aboyne AB34 5NE — 01339 880058
Coles, Stephen — 43 Mearns Walk, Laurencekirk AB30 1FA — 01561 378400
Harris, Michael — The Gables, Netherley Park, Netherley, Stonehaven AB39 3QM — 01569 731091
McCafferty, W. John — Lynwood, Cammachmore, Stonehaven AB39 3NR — 01569 730281
[E-mail: john.mccafferty@psfm.com]
McLuckie, John — 7 Monaltrie Close, Ballater AB35 5PT — 01339 755489
[E-mail: j-r-mcluckie@supanet.com]
Middleton, Robbie (Capt.) — 7 St Ternan's Road, Newtonhill, Stonehaven AB39 2PF — 01569 730852
Platt, David — 2 St Michael's Road, Newtonhill, Stonehaven AB39 3RW — 01569 730465
Simpson, Elizabeth (Mrs) — 33 Golf Road, Ballater AB35 5QX — 01339 755597
[E-mail: connemara33@yahoo.com]

33. GORDON

Doak, Alan B. — 17 Chievres Place, Ellon AB41 9WH — 01358 721819
Findlay, Patricia (Mrs) — Douglas View, Tullynessle, Alford AB33 8QR — 01975 562379
Mitchell, Jean (Mrs) — 6 Cowgate, Oldmeldrum, Inverurie AB51 0EN — 01651 872745
Rennie, Lyall — Dunisla, Oyne, Insch AB52 6QU — 01464 851587
Robb, Margaret (Mrs) — Chrislouan, Keithhall, Inverurie AB51 0LN — 01651 882310
Robertson, James Y. — 1 Nicol Road, Kintore, Inverurie AB51 0QA — 01467 633001
Sutherland, Susan (Mrs) — 53 Westhill Grange, Westhill, Skene AB32 6QJ — 01224 741889

34. BUCHAN

Allen, Sena (Mrs)	88 Kirk Street, Peterhead AB42 1RY [E-mail: sama@allen159.fsnet.co.uk]	01779 477327
Armitage, Rosaline (Mrs)	Whitecairn, Blackhills, Peterhead AE42 3LR [E-mail: r.r.armitage@uwclub.net]	01779 477267
Brown, Lillian (Mrs)	45 Main Street, Aberchirder, Huntly AB54 7ST	01466 780330
Davidson, James	19 Great Stuart Street, Peterhead AB42 1JX	01779 470242
Forsyth, Alicia (Mrs)	Rothie Inn Farm, Rothienorman, Inve'urie AB51 8YH [E-mail: amf@rothie518.fsnet.co.uk]	01651 821359
Givan, James	Zimra, Longmanhill, Banff AB45 3RP [E-mail: jim.givan@btopenworld.com]	01261 833318
Higgins, Scott	St Ninian's, Manse Terrace, Turriff AB53 4BA [E-mail: mhairiandscott@btinternet.com]	01888 569103
Lumsden, Vera (Mrs)	8 Queen's Crescent, Portsoy, Banff AB45 2PX [E-mail: ivsd@lumsden77.freeserve.co.uk]	01261 842712
McColl, John	East Cairnchina, Lonmay, Fraserburgh AB43 8RH [E-mail: info@solomonsfolly.co.uk]	01346 532558
Macnee, Anthea (Mrs)	Kingsville, Strichen, Fraserburgh AB43 6SQ	01771 637941
Mair, Dorothy (Miss)	53 Dennyduff Road, Fraserburgh AB43 9LY [E-mail: dorothymair1@aol.com]	01346 513879
Michie, William	34 Seafield Street, Whitehills, Banff AB45 2NR [E-mail: b.michie@dsl.pipex.com]	01261 861439
Noble, John	44 Henderson Park, Peterhead AB42 2WR [E-mail: john_m_noble@hotmail.co.uk]	01779 472522
Ogston, Norman	Rowandale, 6 Rectory Road, Turriff AB53 4SU [E-mail: norman.ogston@virgin.net]	01888 560342
Simpson, Andrew C.	10 Wood Street, Banff AB45 1JX [E-mail: andy.louise1@btinternet.com]	01261 812538
Smith, Ian M.G. MA	Chomriach, 2 Hill Street, Cruden Bay, Peterhead AB42 0HF	01779 812698
Smith, Jenny (Mrs)	5 Seatown Place, Cairnbulg, Fraserburgh AB43 8WP [E-mail: jennyfsmith@hotmail.com]	01346 582980
Sneddon, Richard	8 School Road, Peterhead AB42 2BE [E-mail: CARICHCARICH@aol.com]	01779 480803
Stewart, William	Denend, Strichen AB43 6RN [E-mail: clan@wmsjas.freeserve.co.uk]	01771 637256
Williams, Paul	20 Soy Burn Gardens, Portsoy AB45 2QG [E-mail: paul.williams447@virgin.net]	01261 842338
Yule, Joseph	5 Staffa Street, Peterhead AB42 1NF	01779 476400

35. MORAY

Benson, F. Stewart	8 Springfield Court, Forres IV36 3WY	01309 671525
Carson, John	2 Woodside Drive, Forres IV36 2UF	01309 674541
Finnie, Les	83 Robertson Road, Lhanbryde, Elgin IV30 8JQ	01343 842789
Forbes, Jean (Mrs)	Greenmoss, Drybridge, Buckie AB56 5JB	01542 831646

36. ABERNETHY

Bardgett, Alison (Mrs)	Tigh an Iasgair, Street of Kincardine, Boat of Garten PH24 3BY [E-mail: alison@bardgett.plus.com]	01479 831751
Duncanson, Mary (Mrs)	Falas-an-Duin, Catlodge, Laggan, Newtonmore PH20 1BS [E-mail: maryb@mduncanson.freeserve.co.uk]	01528 544399

37. INVERNESS

Archer, Morven (Mrs)	42 Firth View Drive, Inverness IV3 8QE	01463 237840
Barry, Dennis	50 Holm Park, Inverness IV2 4XU	01463 225883
Cazaly, Leonard	9 Moray Park, Culloden, Inverness IV2 4SX	01463 794469
Cook, Arnett D.	128 Laurel Avenue, Inverness IV3 5RS	01463 242586
Davidson, Margaret (Mrs)	11 Souters Rise, Nairn IV12 5BU	01667 859838
Ogston, Jean (Mrs)	Roselynn, Croyard Road, Beauly IV4 7DJ	01463 782260
Robertson, Hendry	'Park House', 51 Glenurquhart Road, Inverness IV3 5PB	01463 231858
Robertson, Stewart J.H.	27 Towerhill Drive, Inverness IV2 5FD	01463 793144
Roden, Vivien (Mrs)	15 Oldmill Road, Tomatin, Inverness IV13 7YW	01808 511355

38. LOCHABER

Chalkley, Andrew BSc	2 Telford Place, Claggan, Fort William PH33 6QG [E-mail: andrew.chalkley@btinternet.com]	01397 700271
Dick, Robert MA	8 Lanark Place, Fort William PH33 6UD	01397 704833
Fraser, John A. BA	26 Clunes Avenue, Caol, Fort William PH33 7BJ [E-mail: john.afraser@btopenworld.com]	01397 703467
Maitland, John	St Monance, Ardgour, Fort William PH33 7AA	01855 841267
Walker, Eric	Tigh a' Chlamm, Inverroy, Roy Bridge PH31 4AQ [E-mail: line15@btinternet.com]	01397 712028
Walker, Pat (Mrs)	Tigh a' Chlamm, Inverroy, Roy Bridge PH31 4AQ [E-mail: pw-15@tiscali.co.uk]	01397 712028

39. ROSS

Finlayson, Michael R.	Amberlea, Evanton, Dingwall IV16 9UY	01349 830598
Gilbertson, Ian	Firth View, Craigrory, North Kessock, Inverness IV1 1XH	01463 731538
Gunstone, Ronald	20 Bellfield Road, North Kessock, Inverness IV1 3XU	01463 731337
Jamieson, Patricia A. (Mrs)	7 Craig Avenue, Tain IV19 1JP	01862 893154
McCreadie, Frederick	Highfield, Highfield Park, Conon Bridge, Dingwall IV7 8AP	01349 862171
Riddell, Keith	2 Station Cottages, Fearn, Tain IV20 1RR [E-mail: shirleyriddell@yahoo.co.uk]	01862 832867

40. SUTHERLAND

Bruce, Dorothy (Mrs)	Eastwood, Altass, Rosehall, by Lairg IV27 4EU	01549 441285
Innes, Derek	Hill Cottage, Lairg Muir, Lairg IV27 4ED	01549 402215

Stobo, Mary (Mrs) — Druim-an-Sgairnich, Lower Gledfield, Ardgay IV24 3BG
Weidner, Karl — St Vincent Road, Tain IV19 1JR — 01863 766868 / 01862 894202

41. CAITHNESS
Duncan, Esme (Miss) — Avalon, Upper Warse, Canisbay, Wick KW1 4YD — 01955 611455
[E-mail: esmeduncan@btinternet.com]
Stewart, Heather (Mrs) — Burnthill, Thrumster, Wick KW1 5AX — 01955 651717
[E-mail: heatherburnthill@btopenworld.com]

42. LOCHCARRON – SKYE
Mackenzie, Hector — 53 Strath, Gairloch IV21 2DB — 01445 712433
Macrae, D.E. — Nethania, 52 Strath, Gairloch IV21 2DB — 01445 712235
[E-mail: Dmgai~@aol.com]
Ross, R. Ian — St Conal's, Inverinate, Kyle IV40 8HB — 01599 511371

43. UIST
Browning, Margaret — 1 Middlequarter, Sollar, Lochmaddy, Isle of North Uist HS6 — 01876 560392
Lines, Charles — Flat 1/02, 8 Queen Margaret Road, Glasgow G20 6DP — 0141-946 2142
MacAulay, John — Flodabay, Isle of Harris HS3 3HA — 01859 530340
MacNab, Ann (Mrs) — Druim Skilivat, Scolpaig, Lochmaddy, Isle of North Uist HS6 5DH — 01876 510701
MacSween, John — 5 Scott Road, Tarbert, Isle of Harris HS3 3DL — 01859 502338
Taylor, Hamish — Tigh na Tobair, Flodabay, Isle of Harris HS3 3HA — 01859 530310

44. LEWIS
Forsyth, William — 1 Berisay Place, Stornoway, Isle of Lewis HS1 2TF — 01851 702332
McAlpin, Robert J.G. MA FEIS — 42A Upper Coll Back, Isle of Lewis HS2 0LS — 01851 820288
Murray, Angus — 4 Ceann Chilleagraidh, Stornoway, Isle of Lewis HS1 2UJ — 01851 703550

45. ORKNEY
Robertson, Johan (Mrs) — Old Manse, Eday, Orkney KW17 2AA — 01857 622251
Steer, John — Beckington, Hillside Road, Stromness, Orkney KW16 3AH — 01856 850815

46. SHETLAND
Christie, William C. — 11 Fullaburn, Bressay, Shetland ZE2 9ET — 01595 820244
Greig, Diane (Mrs) MA — The Manse, Sandwick, Shetland ZE2 9HW — 01950 431244
Harrison, Christine (Mrs) BA — Gerdavatn, Baltasound, Unst, Shetland ZE2 9DY — 01957 711578
Jamieson, Ian MA — Linksview, Ringesta, Quendale, Shetland ZE2 9JD — 01950 460477
Laidlay, Una (Mrs) — 5 Bells Road, Lerwick, Shetland ZE1 0QB — 01595 695147
Smith, M. Beryl (Mrs) DCE MSc — Vakterlee, Cumliewick, Sandwick, Shetland ZE2 9HH — 01950 431280

47. ENGLAND
Dick, R.G. — Duneagle, Church Road, Sparkford, Somerset — 01963 40475
Green, Peter (Dr) — Samburu Cottage, Russells Green Road, Ninfield, East Sussex — 01424 892033
Mackay, Donald (Reader Emeritus) — 90 Hallgarth Street, Elvet, Durham DH1 3AS — 0191-383 2110
Menzies, Rena (Mrs) — 49 Elizabeth Avenue, St Brelade's, Jersey JE3 8GR — 01534 741095

48. EUROPE
Ross, David
URB El Campanario, EDF Granada, Esc 14, Baja B, Ctra Cadiz N-340, Km 168, 29680 Estepona, Malaga, Spain [E-mail: rosselcampanario@yahoo.co.uk]
(Tel/Fax) 0034 952 88 26 34

49. JERUSALEM
Zielinski, Jennifer C. (Mrs)
PO Box 104, Tiberias 14100, Israel [E-mail: scottie2@netvision.net.il]
(Tel) 00972 4 671 0710
(Fax) 00972 4 671 0711

LIST O – REPRESENTATIVES ON COUNCIL EDUCATION COMMITTEES

COUNCIL	NAME	ADDRESS	TEL
ABERDEEN CITY	Mr David Yacamini	29 Rubislaw Park Crescent, Aberdeen AB15 8BT [E-mail: jeananddave.yacamini@googlemail.com]	01224 316128
ABERDEENSHIRE	Mr Alexander Corner	4 Bain Road, Mintlaw, Peterhead AB42 5EW [E-mail: sandycorner@hotmail.com]	01771 622562
ANGUS	Mr David Adams	Glebe House, Farnell, by Brechin DD9 6UH	01674 820227
ARGYLL and BUTE	Miss Fiona Fisher	2 Nursery Cottages, Kilmun, Dunoon PA23 8SE [E-mail: fionae@tiscali.co.uk]	01369 840766
BORDERS	Mr Graeme Donald	1 Upper Loan Park, Lauder TD2 6TR [E-mail: graeme.donald@btopenworld.com]	01578 722422
CLACKMANNAN	Rev. Mairi Lovett	The Manse, 7 Long Row, Menstrie FK11 7BA [E-mail: mairi@kanyo.co.uk]	01259 761461
DUMFRIES and GALLOWAY	Mr Robert McQuistan	Kirkdale Schoolhouse, Carsluith, Newton Stewart DG8 7DT [E-mail: mcquistan@quista.net]	01387 722165
DUNDEE	Rev. James L. Wilson	53 Old Craigie Road, Dundee DD4 7JD [E-mail: R3VJW@aol.com]	01382 459249
EAST AYRSHIRE	Mr William McGregor	25 Blackburn Drive, Ayr KA7 2XW [E-mail: Bill.McGregor@east-ayrshire-gov.uk]	01292 293918
EAST DUNBARTONSHIRE	Mrs Barbara Jarvie	18 Cannerton Crescent, Milton of Campsie, Glasgow G66 8DR [E-mail: bj@bjarvie.fsnet.co.uk]	01360 319729
EAST LOTHIAN	Mrs Marjorie K. Goldsmith	20 St Lawrence, Haddington EH41 3RL	01620 823249
EAST RENFREWSHIRE	Rev. Maureen Leitch	14 Maxton Avenue, Barrhead, Glasgow G78 1DY [E-mail: maureen.leitch@ntlworld.com]	0141-881 1462
EDINBURGH CITY	Mr A. Craig Duncan	2 East Barnton Gardens, Edinburgh EH4 6AR [E-mail: acraigduncan@aol.com]	0131-336 4432

Council	Representative	Address	Telephone
EDINBURGH SCRUTINY PANEL	Dr J. Mitchell Manson	17 Huntingdon Place, Edinburgh EH7 4AX [E-mail: MitchellManson@aol.com]	0131-557 1933
FALKIRK	Mrs Margaret Coutts	34 Pirleyhill Gardens, Falkirk FK1 5NB [E-mail: margaret.coutts1@tiscali.co.uk]	01324 628732
FIFE	Rev. Alistair G. McLeod	13 Greenmantle Way, Glenrothes KY6 2QG [E-mail: aagm@talktalk.net]	01592 744558
GLASGOW CITY	Rev. Graham Cartlidge	5 Briar Grove, Newlands, Glasgow G43 2TG [E-mail: g.cartlidge@ntlworld.com]	0141-637 3228
GLASGOW CITY SCRUTINY PANEL	Rev. David A. Keddie	21 Ilay Road, Bearsden, Glasgow G61 1QG [E-mail: revked@hotmail.com]	0141-942 5173
HIGHLAND	Rev. Alexander Glass	Craigton, Tulloch Avenue, Dingwall IV15 9LH	01349 863258
INVERCLYDE	Rev. William Douglas Hamilton	67 Forsyth Street, Greenock PA16 8SX [E-mail: revwdhamilton@hotmail.com]	01475 724003
MIDLOTHIAN	Mr Paul Hayes	Kingsway Management Services Ltd, 127 Deanburn, Penicuik EH26 0JA [E-mail: paul.hayes@basilicon.com]	
MORAY	Mrs Alexandra Rose MacLennan	The Old Steading, Wester Golford, Auldearn, Nairn IV12 5QQ [E-mail: ian.maclennan3@btinternet.com]	01309 641342
NORTH AYRSHIRE	Mr John S. Scott	2 West Lynn, Dalry KA24 4LJ [E-mail: scott.lynn1@btopenworld.com]	
NORTH LANARKSHIRE	Mr Alistair H. MacLeod	21 Cairnhill Avenue, Airdrie ML6 9HQ [E-mail: alistairmacleod@blueyonder.co.uk]	01236 754760
ORKNEY	Mrs Carole Macnaughton	The Cathedral Manse, Berstane Road, Kirkwall, Orkney KW15 1NA [E-mail: fmacnaug@fish.co.uk]	01856 873312
PERTH and KINROSS	Mrs Hilary Spencer Bridge	House of Cardean, Meigle, Blairgowrie PH12 8RB [E-mail: hilary.bridge@btinternet.com]	01828 640452
RENFREWSHIRE	Mr George Hamilton	33 St Ninian's Road, Paisley PA2 6TP	0141-840 2233
SHETLAND	Rev. Tom Macintyre	The Rock, Whiteness, Shetland ZE2 9LJ [E-mail: the2macs.macintyre@btinternet.com]	
SOUTH AYRSHIRE	Rev. Dr John Lochrie	The Manse, Colmonell, Girvan KA26 0SA	01465 881224
SOUTH LANARKSHIRE	Mrs Marion Dickie	2 Murchison Drive, East Kilbride, Glasgow G75 8HF [E-mail: marion.ekmc.wpc@ukgateway.net]	
STIRLING	Mrs Joan Kerr	36 Strathallan Court, Bridge of Allan, Stirling FK9 4BW	01786 834939
WEST DUNBARTONSHIRE	Miss Sheila Rennie	128 Dunbuie Avenue, Dumbarton G82 2JW [E-mail: sheila_rennie@tiscali.co.uk]	01389 763246
WEST LOTHIAN	Rev. Dr Robert A. Anderson	The Manse, 5 MacDonald Gardens, Blackburn, Bathgate EH47 7RE [E-mail: robertanderson307@btinternet.com]	01506 652825
WESTERN ISLES	Rev. Andrew W.F. Coghill	Leurbost, Lochs, Isle of Lewis HS2 9NS [E-mail: andcoghill@aol.com]	01851 860243

LIST P – RETIRED LAY AGENTS

Forrester, Arthur A.	158 Lee Crescent North, Bridge of Don, Aberdeen AB22 8FR
Scott, John W.	15 Manor Court, Forfar DD8 1BR
Shepherd, Dennis	Mission House, Norby, Sandness, Shetland ZE2 9PL

LIST Q – MINISTERS ORDAINED FOR SIXTY YEARS AND UPWARDS

Until 1992, the *Year Book* contained each year a list of those ministers who had been ordained 'for fifty years and upwards'. For a number of reasons, that list was thereafter discontinued. The current Editor was encouraged to reinstate such a list, and the edition for 2002 included the names of those ordained for sixty years and upwards. With ministers, no less than the rest of society, living longer, it was felt reasonable to proceed on that basis. Correspondence made it clear that this list was welcomed, and it has been included in an appropriately revised form each year since then. Again this year, an updated version is offered following the best enquiries that could be made. The date of ordination is given in full where it is known.

1932	14 August	Thomas Mackenzie Donn (Duthil)
1938	29 June	George Alestair Alison Bennett (Strathkinness)
	13 October	Robert Hamilton (Kelso: Old)
1939	2 June	David Noel Fisher (Glasgow: Sherbrooke St Gilbert's)
	27 October	James Scott Marshall (Associate Minister: Leith South)
	12 November	Alexander McRae Houston (Tibbermore)
	18 November	David Sloan Walker (Makerstoun with Smailholm with Stichill, Hume and Nenthorn)
	10 December	Wellesley Grahame Bailey (Ladykirk with Whitsome)
	22 December	Alastair McRae Rennie (Kincardine Croick and Edderton)
1940	24 February	James Johnstone Turnbull (Arbirlot with Colliston)
	22 March	Donald MacKellar Leitch Urie (Kincardine O'Neil)
	29 May	Norman McGathan Bowman (Edinburgh: St Mary's)
	14 July	Nigel Ross MacLean (Perth: St Paul's)
	21 August	Donald MacFarlane (Inverness: East)
1941	29 May	Harry Galbraith Miller (Iona and Ross of Mull)
	6 June	Thomas Williamson (Dyke with Edinkillie)
	3 July	Donald William MacKenzie (Auchterarder: The Barony)

1942	2 January	James Gilbert Morrison (Rotterdam)
	4 February	Robert Macbean Gilmour (Kiltarlity)
	15 April	Frank Haughton (Kirkintilloch: St Mary's)
	5 July	Norman Christopher Macrae (Loanhead)
	22 November	Robert Gray (Stonehaven: Fetteresso)
	24 December	James Bews (Dundee: Craigiebank)
1943	11 May	Leon David Levison (Ormiston with Pencaitland)
	2 June	Duncan Finlayson (Morvern)
	3 September	George Cooper (Delting with Nesting and Lunnasting)
	1 October	Alick Hugh McAulay (Bellie with Speymouth)
	7 October	Hugh Talman (Polmont: Old)
	28 November	David Hutchison Whiteford (Gullane)
1944	3 January	Magnus William Cooper (Kirkcaldy: Abbotshall)
	21 June	Denis Macdonald Duncan (Editor: *The British Weekly*)
	12 July	James Kirk Porteous (Cupar: St John's)
	10 November	Alexander Spence (Elgin: St Giles': Associate)
1945	24 January	Thomas Morton (Rutherglen: Stonelaw)
	4 February	James Shirra (St Martin's with Scone New)
	20 April	Thomas Lithgow (Banchory-Devenick with Maryculter)
	5 May	Robert Stockbridge Whiteford (Shapinsay)
	27 June	Ian Arthur Girdwood Easton (University of Strathclyde)
	4 July	Douglas Lister (Largo and Newburn)
	1 August	John Walter Evans (Elgin: High)
	5 August	Richard Anderson Baigrie (Kirkurd with Newlands)
	4 September	John Paul Tierney (Peterhead West: Associate)
	5 September	Allan MacInnes Macleod (Gordon: St Michael's with Legerwood with Westruther)
1946	11 April	James Martin (Glasgow: High Carntyne)
	19 May	John McClymont Frew (Glasgow: Dennistoun)
	6 June	Robert McLachlan Wilson (University of St Andrews)
	23 June	Ian Masson Fraser (Selly Oak Colleges)
	18 September	John Wilkinson (Kikuyu)
	25 September	Frederick John Marshall (Bermuda)
	3 October	John Henry Whyte (Gourock: Ashton)
	13 November	Ian Bruce Doyle (Department of National Mission)
	18 December	Ronald Neil Grant Murray (Pardovan and Kingscavil with Winchburgh)
1947	23 January	Peter George Thomson (Irvine: Fullarton)
	22 June	James Alexander Robertson Mackenzie (Largo: St David's)
	24 July	James Alexander Wemyss Smith (Garvock St Cyrus)

27 November	William Duncan Crombie (Glasgow: Calton New with Glasgow: St Andrew's)
10 December	Robert James Stuart Wallace (Foveran)
1948	
February	James Philip (Edinburgh: Holyrood Abbey)
31 March	Gilbert Mollison Mowat (Dundee: Albany-Butterburn)
20 April	Andrew Kerr (Kilbarchan: West)
9 June	Hamish Stewart Duncan MacNab (Kilrenny)
6 July	Alexander Chestnut (Greenock: St Mark's Greenbank)
21 August	David William Norwood (Lisbon)
8 September	David Stuart Forsyth (Belhelvie)
6 October	George Davidson Wilkie (Kirkcaldy: Viewforth)
22 December	Henry Hutchison (Carmunnock)

LIST R – DECEASED MINISTERS

The Editor has been made aware of the following ministers who have died since the publication of the previous volume of the *Year Book*.

Aitken, Andrew John	(Glasgow: Tollcross Central with Park)
Baillie, David Robert	(Crawford with Lowther)
Bates, John Powers	(Dumfries: St Michael's and South)
Beattie, John Algie	(Dalmuir Overtoun)
Bell, Robert Patterson	(Ballantrae)
Birnie, Charles John	(Aberdour and Tyrie)
Black, John McLachlan	(Coatbridge: Blairhill Dundyvan)
Bruce, Arthur William	(Fortingall and Glenlyon)
Carrie, John Gilbert	(Edinburgh: Dalmeny with Edinburgh: Queensferry)
Coley, Richard	(Glasgow: Victoria Tollcross)
Craig, John Wilson	(Edinburgh: St Stephen's Comely Bank)
Craig, Neil Douglas	(Dalbeattie: Craignair with Urr)
Dawes, Peter Martin	(Chapelhall)
Elder, Albert Brown	(Dumfries: St Michael's and South)
Fauchelle, Ian Donald	(Zimbabwe and New Zealand)
Fulton, Frederick Haslehurst	(Clunie, Lethendy and Kinloch)
Hardy, Graham Wilberforce	(Edinburgh: Palmerston Place)
Harkes, George	(Cumbernauld: Old)
Hill, Arthur Thomas	(Ormiston with Prestonpans: Grange)
Hughes, Owain Tudor	(Guernsey: St Andrew's in the Grange)
Hutcheson, James Murray	(Glasgow: Possilpark)
Innes, David James	(Kirkwall: East)

Jones, William (Kirriemuir: St Andrew's)
Keith, Donald (Penpont, Keir and Tynron with Thornhill)
Liddell, Matthew (Glasgow: St Paul's (Outer High) and St David's (Ramshorn))
McCormick, William Cadzow (Glasgow: Maryhill Old)
Macdonald, Alexander (Cross Ness)
MacDonald, Kenneth (Associate: Applecross with Lochcarron)
MacKechnie, John Macgregor (Kilchrenan and Dalavich)
McLeod, Roderick (Lochwinnoch)
McMahon, Robert James (Crossford with Kirkfieldbank)
MacPhee, Duncan Primrose (Associate: Braemar with Crathie)
MacSween, Norman (Kinloch)
Matheson, James Gunn (Portree)
Mirrilees, James Brown (Aberdeen: High Hilton)
Moffett, James Robert (Paisley: St Matthew's)
Monro, George Douglas (Yester)
Nelson, John (Crawford with Wanlockhead and Leadhills)
Ord, James Kennedy (Condorrat)
Philp, Robert Anderson (Stepps: St Andrew's)
Pogue, Victor Charles (Baird Research Fellow)
Portchmouth, Roland John (Bendochy)
Pyper, James Stewart (Greenock: St George's North)
Reid, William Scott (Edinburgh: London Road)
Remnie, Donald Blair (Industrial Chaplain)
Ross, Andrew Christian (The University of Edinburgh)
Russell, Archibald (Duror with Glencoe)
Sanderson, William Roy (Stenton with Whittingehame)
Sim, John Geddes (Kirkcaldy: Old)
Skakle, George Scott (Aberdeen: Powis)
Skinner, Silvester (Lumphanan)
Smart, Geoffrey Howard (Falkirk: Laurieston with Redding and Westquarter)
Stoddart, David Lewis (Lagan with Newtonmore)
Swan, Andrew (Greenock: St Margaret's)
Taylor, Alexander Thomas Hain (Dunoon: Old and St Cuthbert's)
Torrance, Thomas Forsyth (The University of Edinburgh)
Watt, William George (Aberdeen: South of St Nicholas Kincorth)

SECTION 7

Legal Names and Scottish Charity Numbers for Individual Congregations

EXPLANATORY NOTE:

To comply with the requirements of the Scottish Charity Register, the names of congregations in all of the Scottish Presbyteries must be updated. In the pages that follow, these 'Legal Names' are shown together with the appropriate Scottish Charity Numbers. The Presbyteries of Greenock and Paisley (14), Glasgow (16), Argyll (19), Aberdeen (31) and Inverness (37) have not yet completed all the stages of this process. Their entries are therefore repeated as in last year's publication.

SCOTTISH CHARITY NUMBER

1.
NEW LEGAL NAME
Presbytery of Edinburgh

SC018012	Balerno Church of Scotland
SC001554	Edinburgh Currie Kirk (Church of Scotland)
SC010971	Dalmeny Parish Church of Scotland
SC018321	Albany Deaf Church, Edinburgh (Church of Scotland)
SC014757	Edinburgh Barclay Church of Scotland
SC008756	Blackhall St Columba's Church of Scotland, Edinburgh
SC011625	Bristo Memorial Church of Scotland, Craigmillar, Edinburgh
SC012642	Edinburgh: Broughton St Mary's Parish Church (Church of Scotland)
SC015251	Canongate Parish Church of Scotland, Edinburgh
SC004783	Carrick Knowe Parish Church of Scotland, Edinburgh
SC010313	Colinton Parish Church of Scotland, Edinburgh
SC015982	Colinton Mains Parish Church of Scotland, Edinburgh
SC014719	Edinburgh: Corstorphine Craigsbank Parish Church (Church of Scotland)
SC016009	Corstorphine Old Parish Church, Church of Scotland, Edinburgh
SC006300	Edinburgh: Corstorphine St Anne's Parish Church (Church of Scotland)
SC016557	Edinburgh: Corstorphine St Ninian's Parish Church (Church of Scotland)
SC003466	Edinburgh: Craigentinny St Christopher's Parish Church of Scotland
SC010545	Craiglockhart Parish Church, Edinburgh (Church of Scotland)
SC017061	Craigmillar Park Church of Scotland, Edinburgh
SC003430	Cramond Kirk, Edinburgh (Church of Scotland)
SC009470	Davidsons Mains Parish Church of Scotland, Edinburgh
SC001692	Dean Parish Church, Edinburgh – The Church of Scotland
SC005744	Drylaw Parish Church of Scotland, Edinburgh
SC016610	Duddingston Kirk (Church of Scotland), Edinburgh
SC015967	Fairmilehead Parish Church of Scotland, Edinburgh
SC011155	Edinburgh Gilmerton Church of Scotland
SC009146	Gorgie Parish Church of Scotland, Edinburgh
SC011985	Granton Parish Church of Scotland, Edinburgh
SC011325	Edinburgh Greenbank Parish Church of Scotland
SC009749	Edinburgh Greenside Church of Scotland
SC003761	Edinburgh: Greyfriars Tolbooth and Highland Kirk (Church of Scotland)
SC003565	St Giles' Cathedral, Edinburgh (Church of Scotland)
SC012562	Holy Trinity Church of Scotland, Edinburgh
SC000052	Holyrood Abbey Parish Church of Scotland, Edinburgh
SC015442	Inverleith Church of Scotland, Edinburgh
SC005197	Edinburgh Juniper Green Parish Church of Scotland
SC004950	Kaimes: Lockhart Memorial Church of Scotland, Edinburgh
SC014430	Kirk o' Field Parish Church, Edinburgh (Church of Scotland)
SC004932	Edinburgh Leith North Parish Church of Scotland

SC004695	South Leith Parish Church of Scotland, Edinburgh
SC012680	Leith St Andrews Church of Scotland, Edinburgh
SC008572	Edinburgh: Leith St Serf's Parish Church of Scotland
SC010072	Edinburgh: Leith St Thomas' Junction Road Parish Church of Scotland
SC008710	Wardie Parish Church of Scotland, Edinburgh
SC011602	Edinburgh: Liberton Kirk (Church of Scotland)
SC008891	Liberton Northfield Parish Church of Scotland, Edinburgh
SC000896	London Road Church of Scotland, Edinburgh
SC009338	Marchmont St Giles Parish Church of Scotland, Edinburgh
SC000785	Mayfield Salisbury Parish (Edinburgh) Church of Scotland
SC034396	Morningside Parish Church of Scotland, Edinburgh
SC015552	Edinburgh: Morningside United Church
SC000871	Muirhouse Parish Church of Scotland, Edinburgh
SC005198	Edinburgh Murrayfield Parish Church of Scotland
SC000963	New Restalrig Church of Scotland, Edinburgh
SC019117	Newhaven Church of Scotland, Edinburgh
SC006457	The Old Kirk of Edinburgh (Church of Scotland)
SC004291	Edinburgh: Palmerston Place Church of Scotland
SC007277	Edinburgh: Pilrig St Paul's Church of Scotland
SC004183	Polwarth Parish Church, Edinburgh (Church of Scotland)
SC002328	Edinburgh: Portobello Old Parish Church of Scotland
SC007372	Edinburgh: Portobello St James' Parish Church of Scotland
SC011728	St Philip's Church of Scotland: Edinburgh
SC014499	Priestfield Parish Church of Scotland, Edinburgh
SC014027	Church of Scotland, Reid Memorial Church, Edinburgh
SC009035	Richmond Craigmillar Parish Church of Scotland, Edinburgh
SC030896	Slateford Longstone Parish Church of Scotland, Edinburgh
SC003470	The Parish Church of St Andrew and St George, Edinburgh (Church of Scotland)
SC002748	Edinburgh: St Andrew's Clermiston Church of Scotland
SC009379	St Catherine's Argyle Parish Church of Scotland Edinburgh
SC013227	St Colms Parish Church of Scotland, Edinburgh
SC010592	St Cuthberts Parish Church of Scotland, Edinburgh
SC004746	St Davids Broomhouse Church of Scotland, Edinburgh
SC008990	St Georges West Church of Scotland, Edinburgh
SC030819	St John's Oxgangs Church of Scotland: Edinburgh
SC004779	St Margaret's Church of Scotland: Edinburgh
SC013918	St Martins Church of Scotland, Portobello, Edinburgh
SC009038	St Michaels Parish Church of Scotland, Edinburgh
SC007068	Edinburgh: St Nicholas' Sighthill Parish Church of Scotland

SC004487	St Stephen's Comely Bank Church of Scotland, Edinburgh
SC010004	Stenhouse St Aidan's Parish Church of Scotland: Edinburgh
SC002499	Stockbridge Parish Church of Scotland, Edinburgh
SC009274	Tron Kirk, Moredun, Edinburgh (Church of Scotland)
SC015373	Edinburgh Viewforth Church of Scotland
SC013924	Kirkliston Parish Church of Scotland
SC002329	Queensferry Parish Church of Scotland
SC001169	Ratho Church of Scotland

2.   **Presbytery of West Lothian**

SC013100	Abercorn Parish Church of Scotland
SC000791	Armadale Parish Church of Scotland
SC007454	Avonbridge Parish Church of Scotland
SC001881	Boghall Parish Church of Scotland, Bathgate
SC007418	Bathgate High Parish Church of Scotland
SC016755	St John's Parish Church of Scotland, Bathgate
SC024154	Blackburn and Seafield Parish Church of Scotland
SC006811	Blackridge Parish Church of Scotland
SC000800	Breich Valley Parish Church of Scotland
SC017180	Broxburn Parish Church of Scotland
SC016313	Fauldhouse St Andrews Parish Church of Scotland
SC007601	Harthill St Andrew's Parish Church of Scotland
SC013461	Kirk of Calder Parish (Church of Scotland)
SC006973	Kirknewton & East Calder Parish Church of Scotland
SC016185	St Michaels Parish Church of Scotland: Linlithgow
SC011348	St Ninians Craigmailen Parish Church of Scotland, Linlithgow
SC011826	Livingston Old Parish Church of Scotland
SC026230	Pardovan, Kingscavil and Winchburgh Parish Church of Scotland
SC017373	Polbeth Harwood Parish Church of Scotland
SC006336	Strathbrock Parish Church of Scotland, Uphall
SC021516	Torphichen Parish Church of Scotland
SC024255	Uphall South Parish Church of Scotland
SC004703	West Kirk of Calder (Church of Scotland)
SC003362	Brucefield Parish Church of Scotland, Whitburn
SC001053	Whitburn South Parish Church of Scotland

3.   **Presbytery of Lothian**

SC004580	Aberlady Parish Church (Church of Scotland)
SC009401	Athelstaneford Parish Church (Church of Scotland)
SC007231	Belhaven Parish Church (Church of Scotland)
SC032180	Bilston Parish Church (Church of Scotland)
SC003230	Bolton and Saltoun Parish Church (Church of Scotland)
SC003482	Bonnyrigg Parish Church (Church of Scotland)
SC015775	Borthwick Parish Church (Church of Scotland)
SC004630	Cockenzie and Port Seton: Chalmers Memorial Parish Church (Church of Scotland)
SC007052	Cockenzie and Port Seton: Old Parish Church (Church of Scotland)
SC013139	Cockpen and Carrington Parish Church (Church of Scotland)
SC006926	Cranstoun, Crichton and Ford Parish Church (Church of Scotland)
SC008958	Dalkeith: St John's and King's Park Parish Church (Church of Scotland)

SC014158	Dalkeith: St Nicholas Buccleuch Parish Church (Church of Scotland)
SC004533	Dirleton Parish Church (Church of Scotland)
SC000455	Dunbar Parish Church (Church of Scotland)
SC014299	Dunglass Parish Church (Church of Scotland)
SC007860	Fala and Soutra Parish Church (Church of Scotland)
SC014972	Garvald and Morham Parish Church (Church of Scotland)
SC005996	Gladsmuir Parish Church (Church of Scotland)
SC030433	Glencorse Parish Church (Church of Scotland)
SC004673	Gorebridge Parish Church (Church of Scotland)
SC005237	Gullane Parish Church (Church of Scotland)
SC010614	Haddington: St Mary's Parish Church (Church of Scotland)
SC022183	Haddington: West Parish Church (Church of Scotland)
SC014364	Howgate Parish Church (Church of Scotland)
SC016765	Humbie Parish Church (Church of Scotland)
SC015878	Lasswade Parish Church (Church of Scotland)
SC014420	Loanhead Parish Church (Church of Scotland)
SC016556	Longniddry Parish Church (Church of Scotland)
SC004722	Musselburgh: Northesk Parish Church (Church of Scotland)
SC000129	Musselburgh: St Andrew's High Parish Church (Church of Scotland)
SC001726	Musselburgh: St Clement's and St Ninian's Parish Church (Church of Scotland)
SC013559	Musselburgh: St Michael's Inveresk Parish Church (Church of Scotland)
SC035087	Newbattle Parish Church (Church of Scotland)
SC030879	Newton Parish Church (Church of Scotland)
SC004761	Abbey Church, North Berwick, Church of Scotland
SC006421	St Andrew Blackadder, Church of Scotland, North Berwick
SC014810	Ormiston Parish Church (Church of Scotland)
SC004871	Pencaitland Parish Church (Church of Scotland)
SC010902	Penicuik: North Parish Church (Church of Scotland)
SC005838	Penicuik: St Mungo's Parish Church (Church of Scotland)
SC011871	Penicuik: South Parish Church (Church of Scotland)
SC031191	Prestonpans: Prestongrange Parish Church (Church of Scotland)
SC004927	Rosewell Parish Church (Church of Scotland)
SC005457	Roslin Parish Church (Church of Scotland)
SC008667	Spott Parish Church (Church of Scotland)
SC017423	Tranent Parish Church (Church of Scotland)
SC012277	Traprain Parish Church (Church of Scotland)
SC000494	Whitekirk and Tyninghame Parish Church (Church of Scotland)
SC015414	Yester Parish Church (Church of Scotland)

4.   **Presbytery of Melrose and Peebles**

SC010768	Ashkirk Parish Church of Scotland
SC006480	Bowden and Melrose Church of Scotland
SC030062	Broughton, Glenholm and Kilbucho Church of Scotland
SC016990	Caddonfoot Parish Church of Scotland
SC001340	Carlops Parish Church of Scotland
SC009892	Channelkirk and Lauder Church of Scotland
SC003895	Earlston Parish Church of Scotland
SC010081	Eddleston Parish Church of Scotland
SC010389	Old Parish and St Paul's Church of Scotland: Galashiels

SC001386	Galashiels Trinity Church of Scotland
SC034662	Ettrick and Yarrow Parish (Church of Scotland)
SC000281	St John's Church of Scotland: Galashiels
SC001100	Innerleithen, Traquair and Walkerburn Parish Church of Scotland
SC021456	Lyne & Manor Church of Scotland
SC013481	Maxton and Mertoun Parish Church of Scotland
SC000575	Newtown Church of Scotland
SC013316	Peebles Old Parish Church of Scotland
SC009159	Church of Scotland St Andrews Leckie Parish: Peebles
SC010210	St Boswells Parish Church of Scotland
SC000228	Stow St Mary of Wedale & Heriot Church of Scotland
SC004728	Skirling Church of Scotland
SC001866	Stobo and Drumelzier Church of Scotland
SC013564	Tweedsmuir Kirk Church of Scotland
SC003938	St Andrews Parish Church of Scotland: West Linton
SC018087	Kirkurd and Newlands Parish Church of Scotland
SC014883	Selkirk Parish Church of Scotland

5.   Presbytery of Duns

SC001208	Church of Scotland: Ayton and Burnmouth Parish Church
SC000867	St Andrew's Wallace Green and Lowick Church of Scotland, Berwick-upon-Tweed
SC000246	Bonkyl & Preston Church of Scotland
SC006722	Chirnside Church of Scotland
SC009185	The Church of Scotland, Coldingham Priory
SC001456	Coldstream Parish Church of Scotland
SC005161	Duns Parish Church of Scotland
SC000031	Eccles Parish Church of Scotland
SC007567	Edrom & Allanton Church of Scotland
SC006499	The Church of Scotland, Eyemouth Parish Church
SC002789	Fogo & Swinton Church of Scotland
SC024535	Church of Scotland: Foulden and Mordington Parish Church
SC022349	Gordon St Michael's Church of Scotland
SC016400	Church of Scotland: Grantshouse, Houndwood and Reston Parish Church
SC013136	Greenlaw Parish, Church of Scotland
SC002216	Hutton, Fishwick and Paxton Church of Scotland
SC010680	Langton and Lammermuir Kirk, Church of Scotland
SC009995	Ladykirk Parish Church (Church of Scotland)
SC004582	Legerwood Parish, Church of Scotland
SC005115	Leitholm Parish Church (Church of Scotland)
SC004903	Westruther Parish, Church of Scotland
SC001611	Whitsome Church (Church of Scotland)

6.   Presbytery of Jedburgh

SC016457	Ale & Teviot United Church of Scotland
SC004550	Cavers and Kirkton Parish Church (Church of Scotland)
SC004517	Hawick Burnfoot Church of Scotland
SC005574	St Mary's & Old Parish Church of Scotland, Hawick
SC005191	Teviot and Roberton Church of Scotland
SC013892	Trinity Parish Church, Hawick (Church of Scotland)
SC017381	Wilton Parish Church of Scotland
SC012830	Hobkirk & Southdean Parish Church of Scotland
SC004530	Jedburgh Old and Trinity Parish Church of Scotland

SC000958	Kelso Country Churches (Church of Scotland)
SC014039	Kelso North and Ednam Parish Church of Scotland
SC010009	Kelso Old & Sprouston Parish Church of Scotland
SC003023	Linton, Morebattle, Hownam and Yetholm Parish Church of Scotland
SC010593	Oxnam Parish Church of Scotland
SC034629	Ruberslaw Parish Church of Scotland
SC006917	Teviothead Parish Church of Scotland

7.   Presbytery of Annandale and Eskdale

SC010555	Annan Old Parish Church of Scotland
SC010891	St Andrews Parish Church of Scotland, Annan
SC013947	Applegarth, Sibbaldbie & Johnstone Church of Scotland
SC012516	Brydekirk Parish Church of Scotland
SC000717	Canonbie Parish Church of Scotland
SC006344	Dalton Parish Church of Scotland
SC004542	Dornock Parish Church of Scotland
SC016747	Gretna Old, Gretna St Andrew's, Half Morton and Kirkpatrick Fleming Parish Church of Scotland
SC022170	Hightae Parish Church of Scotland
SC013467	Hoddom Church of Scotland
SC005701	Kirkpatrick Juxta Church of Scotland
SC012479	Kirtle-Eaglesfield Church of Scotland
SC011946	Langholm Eskdalemuir Ewes and Westerkirk Church of Scotland
SC006519	Liddesdale Parish Church of Scotland
SC004644	Lochmaben Church of Scotland
SC007116	Lockerbie Dryfesdale, Hutton and Corrie Church of Scotland
SC000722	Middlebie Church of Scotland
SC012236	St Andrews Church of Scotland, Moffat
SC001060	St Mungo Parish Church of Scotland, Lockerbie
SC013190	Tundergarth Church of Scotland
SC007536	Wamphray Church of Scotland
SC013922	Waterbeck Church of Scotland

8.   Presbytery of Dumfries and Kirkcudbright

SC016850	Auchencairn & Rerrick Church of Scotland
SC016053	Balmaclellan & Kells Church of Scotland
SC000498	Balmaghie Church of Scotland
SC004450	Borgue Parish Church of Scotland
SC003844	Buittle & Kelton Church of Scotland
SC008648	Caerlaverock Parish Church of Scotland
SC015242	Carsphairn Church of Scotland
SC011037	Castle Douglas Parish Church of Scotland
SC005624	Closeburn Parish Church of Scotland
SC009384	Colvend Southwick & Kirkbean Church of Scotland
SC007152	Corsock & Kirkpatrick Durham Church of Scotland
SC014901	Crossmichael & Parton Church of Scotland
SC013341	Cummertrees Parish Church of Scotland
SC002443	Dalbeattie Parish Church of Scotland
SC013121	Dalry Kirkcudbrightshire Church of Scotland
SC010748	Dumfries Northwest Church of Scotland
SC006404	St George's Church of Scotland, Dumfries
SC009432	St Mary's-Greyfriars' Parish Church, Dumfries (Church of Scotland)
SC016201	St Michael's & South Church of Scotland, Dumfries
SC000973	Troqueer Parish Church of Scotland, Dumfries
SC016060	Dunscore Parish Church of Scotland
SC014783	Durisdeer Church of Scotland
SC000961	Gatehouse of Fleet Parish Church of Scotland
SC014663	Glencairn & Moniaive Parish Church of Scotland

SC033058	Irongray Lochrutton & Terregles Parish Church of Scotland
SC014150	Kirkconnel Parish Church of Scotland
SC005883	Kirkcudbright Parish Church of Scotland
SC002286	Kirkgunzeon Church of Scotland
SC010508	Kirkmahoe Parish Church of Scotland
SC030785	Kirkmichael Tinwald & Torthorwald Church of Scotland
SC014590	Lochend and New Abbey Church of Scotland
SC015925	Maxwelltown West Church of Scotland, Dumfries
SC001144	Mouswald Church of Scotland
SC015087	Penpont Keir & Tynron Church of Scotland
SC015399	Ruthwell & Mount Kedar Church of Scotland
SC000845	St Bride's Parish Church of Scotland: Sanquhar
SC004475	Tarff & Twynholm Church of Scotland
SC012722	Thornhill Parish Church of Scotland
SC014465	Urr Parish Church of Scotland

9.   **Presbytery of Wigtown and Stranraer**

SC003122	Ervie-Kirkcolm Church of Scotland
SC001705	Glasserton and the Isle of Whithorn Church of Scotland
SC007375	Inch Church of Scotland
SC007136	Kirkcowan Parish Church (Church of Scotland)
SC001946	Kirkinner Church of Scotland
SC010150	Kirkmabreck Church of Scotland
SC007708	Kirkmaiden Parish Church (Church of Scotland)
SC009412	Leswalt Parish Church (Church of Scotland)
SC003300	Mochrum Church of Scotland
SC006014	Monigaff Church of Scotland
3C006316	New Luce Church of Scotland
SC005302	Old Luce Church of Scotland
SC031847	Parish of Penninghame (Church of Scotland)
SC015452	Portpatrick Parish Church (Church of Scotland)
SC010621	Sorbie Parish Church of Scotland
SC007346	Stoneykirk Parish Church (Church of Scotland)
SC017312	High Kirk of Stranraer (Church of Scotland)
SC002247	Stranraer: St Ninian's Parish Church (Church of Scotland)
SC009905	Town Kirk of Stranraer (Church of Scotland)
SC016881	Whithorn: St Ninian's Priory Church of Scotland
SC014552	Wigtown Parish Church (Church of Scotland)

10.   **Presbytery of Ayr**

SC012456	Alloway Parish Church of Scotland
SC013225	Annbank Parish Church of Scotland
SC008536	Ballantrae Parish Church of Scotland
SC006707	Auchinleck Parish Church of Scotland
SC001792	Castlehill Parish Church of Scotland: Ayr
SC031474	Dalmellington Parish Church of Scotland
SC001994	Newton-on-Ayr Parish Church of Scotland
SC001757	St Andrew's Parish Church of Scotland: Ayr
SC009336	St James' Parish Church of Scotland: Ayr
SC016860	St Leonard's Parish Church of Scotland: Ayr
SC018489	Wallacetown Parish Church of Scotland: Ayr
SC015366	Barr Parish Church of Scotland
SC013689	Catrine Parish Church of Scotland
SC005283	Coylton Parish Church (Church of Scotland)
SC002633	Craigie Parish Church of Scotland: Kilmarnock
SC017520	Crosshill Parish Church (Church of Scotland)
SC012591	Dailly Parish Church of Scotland
SC013503	Dalrymple Parish Church (Church of Scotland)

SC008482	Dundonald Church of Scotland
SC008226	Fisherton Church of Scotland
SC007347	Girvan: North Parish Parish Church of Scotland
SC010381	Girvan South Parish Church of Scotland
SC031952	Kirkmichael Parish Church of Scotland: Maybole
SC000213	Kirkoswald Parish Church of Scotland
SC007714	Mauchline Parish Church of Scotland
SC014055	Lugar Parish Church of Scotland
SC004906	St Quivox Parish Church: Ayr (Church of Scotland)
SC014794	New Cumnock Parish Church (Church of Scotland)
SC010606	Muirkirk Parish Church of Scotland
SC003164	Maybole Parish Church of Scotland
SC034504	Church of Scotland Cumnock Trinity Church
SC000130	Ochiltree Parish Church of Scotland
SC006025	Old Cumnock Old Church of Scotland
SC001940	Kingcase Parish Church of Scotland: Prestwick
SC011750	St Nicholas Parish Church of Scotland: Prestwick
SC007403	Prestwick South Church of Scotland
SC004271	Monkton & Prestwick North Parish Church of Scotland
SC014381	St Colmon (Arnsheen Barrhill and Colmonell) Church of Scotland
SC015899	Sorn Parish Church of Scotland
SC035601	Stair Parish Church (Church of Scotland)
SC013366	Straiton (St Cuthbert's) Parish Church of Scotland: Maybole
SC014767	Tarbolton Parish Church of Scotland
SC030714	Drongan: The Schaw Kirk (Church of Scotland)
SC007246	Troon Old Parish Church of Scotland
SC003477	Portland Parish Church of Scotland: Troon
SC015019	Troon St Meddan's Parish Church of Scotland
SC016648	The Auld Kirk of Ayr Church of Scotland
SC008562	Patna Waterside Parish Church of Scotland
SC002144	Symington Parish Church of Scotland
SC014338	Ayr St Columba Church of Scotland

11.   **Presbytery of Irvine and Kilmarnock**

SC011414	Crosshouse Parish Church (Church of Scotland)
SC012014	Darvel Parish Church of Scotland
SC008684	Dreghorn & Springside Parish Church of Scotland
SC000447	Dunlop Church of Scotland
SC010062	Fenwick Parish Church (Church of Scotland)
SC010370	Galston Parish Church of Scotland
SC001084	Hurlford Church of Scotland
SC005491	Girdle Toll Church of Scotland, Irvine New Town
SC008725	Fullarton Parish Church (Church of Scotland), Irvine
SC002299	Mure Parish Church of Scotland, Irvine
SC008345	Irvine Old Parish Church of Scotland
SC002469	Relief Church of Scotland, Irvine
SC010167	St Andrews Church of Scotland: Irvine
SC006920	Grange Church of Scotland, Kilmarnock
SC008154	Kilmarnock: Henderson Parish Church of Scotland
SC001059	Howard St Andrews Church of Scotland, Kilmarnock
SC031334	Laigh West High Kirk, Kilmarnock, Church of Scotland
SC008405	Old High Kirk of Kilmarnock (Church of Scotland)
SC006040	Kilmarnock Riccarton Church of Scotland

SC029057	Kilmarnock: Shortlees Parish Church of Scotland
SC033107	St Johns Parish Church of Scotland – Onthank: Kilmarnock
SC001324	St Kentigern's Parish Church of Scotland: Kilmarnock
SC006345	St Marnock's Parish Church of Scotland, Kilmarnock
SC012430	Kilmarnock: St Ninian's Bellfield Church of Scotland
SC009036	St Maurs Glencairn Church of Scotland, Kilmaurs
SC013880	Loudoun Church of Scotland, Newmilns
SC015890	John Knox Parish Church of Scotland, Stewarton
SC013595	St Columba's Parish Church of Scotland, Stewarton

12.   Presbytery of Ardrossan

SC004736	Ardrossan Park Parish Church of Scotland
SC002350	Ardrossan Barony St John's Church of Scotland
SC004660	Beith High Parish Church of Scotland
SC005680	Beith Trinity Church of Scotland
SC012017	Brodick Church of Scotland
SC005030	Corrie Parish Church of Scotland
SC004919	Cumbrae Parish Church of Scotland
SC013170	Dalry St Margaret's Parish Church of Scotland
SC006882	Dalry Trinity Church of Scotland
SC017304	Fairlie Parish Church of Scotland
SC012902	Fergushill Church of Scotland
SC016024	Kilbirnie Auld Kirk (Church of Scotland)
SC013750	St Columbas Parish Church of Scotland: Kilbirnie
SC023602	Kilmory Parish Church of Scotland
SC016499	Kilwinning Mansefield Trinity Church of Scotland
SC001856	Kilwinning Old Parish Church of Scotland
SC015072	Lamlash Church of Scotland
SC002782	Largs Clark Memorial Church of Scotland
SC002294	The Church of Scotland, Largs: St Columba's Parish Church
SC009048	Largs St John's Church of Scotland
SC009377	Lochranza & Pirnmill Church of Scotland
SC023003	Saltcoats New Trinity Parish Church of Scotland
SC003299	Saltcoats North Parish Church of Scotland
SC002905	Saltcoats St Cuthberts Parish Church of Scotland
SC005323	Shiskine Church of Scotland
SC015397	Stevenston Ardeer Parish Church of Scotland
SC009848	Stevenston High Church of Scotland
SC000452	Stevenston Livingstone Parish Church of Scotland
SC004565	West Kilbride Overton Church of Scotland
SC013464	St Andrews Church West Kilbride Church of Scotland
SC014005	Whiting Bay & Kildonan Church of Scotland

13.   Presbytery of Lanark

SC000333	Biggar Parish Church of Scotland
SC000603	Blackmount Parish Church (Church of Scotland)
SC017001	Cairngryffe Parish Church (Church of Scotland)
SC026539	Kirkton Parish Church, Carluke (Church of Scotland)
SC013968	St Andrews Parish Church of Scotland: Carluke
SC004066	St Johns Church of Scotland: Carluke

SC016360	Carnwath Parish Church of Scotland
SC028124	Carstairs & Carstairs Junction Church of Scotland
SC016493	Coalburn Parish Church (Church of Scotland)
SC014659	Crossford Church of Scotland
SC018252	Culter Parish Church (Church of Scotland)
SC003080	Forth St Paul's Parish Church (Church of Scotland)
SC017506	Glencaple Parish Church (Church of Scotland)
SC011211	Kirkfieldbank Parish Church (Church of Scotland)
SC014451	Kirkmuirhill Parish Church (Church of Scotland)
SC016504	Greyfriars Parish Church, Lanark (Church of Scotland)
SC011368	St Nicholas Parish Church, Lanark (Church of Scotland)
SC013217	Law Parish Church (Church of Scotland)
SC006516	Lesmahagow Abbeygreen (Church of Scotland)
SC017014	Lesmahagow Old Parish Church (Church of Scotland)
SC016304	Libberton & Quothquan Parish Church (Church of Scotland)
SC034654	Lowther Parish Church (Church of Scotland)
SC009095	Symington Parish Church (Church of Scotland)
SC001718	The Douglas Valley Church (Church of Scotland)

14. Presbytery of Greenock and Paisley

Barrhead: Arthurlie	SC015730
Barrhead: Bourock	SC016467
Barrhead: South and Levern	SC007776
Bishopton	SC006109
Bridge of Weir: Freeland	SC002293
Bridge of Weir: St Machar's Ranfurly	SC003766
Caldwell	SC008214
Elderslie Kirk	SC015701
Erskine	SC017177
Gourock: Old Gourock and Ashton	SC007324
Gourock: St John's	SC006412
Greenock: Ardgowan	SC010818
Greenock: East End	SC037023
Greenock: Finnart St Paul's	SC014076
Greenock: Mount Kirk	SC008357
Greenock: Old West Kirk	SC004855
Greenock: St George's North	SC015301
Greenock: St Luke's	SC005106
Greenock: St Margaret's	SC016711
Greenock: St Ninian's	SC008059
Greenock: Wellpark Mid Kirk	SC001043
Greenock: Westburn	SC005106
Houston and Killellan	SC012822
Howwood	SC003487
Inchinnan	SC011778
Inverkip	SC001079
Johnstone: High	SC009588
Johnstone: St Andrew's Trinity	SC011696
Johnstone: St Paul's	SC011747
Kilbarchan: East	SC012123
Kilbarchan: West	SC017140
Kilmacolm: Old	SC009291
Kilmacolm: St Columba	SC007992
Langbank	SC015085
Linwood	SC020972
Lochwinnoch	SC014518
Neilston	SC035155
Paisley: Abbey	SC007633
Paisley: Castlehead	SC003906
Paisley: Glenburn	SC006718

Paisley: Laigh Kirk	SC006437	Glasgow: Easterhouse St George's and St Peter's	SC003021
Paisley: Lylesland	SC012648	Glasgow: Eastwood	SC000277
Paisley: Martyrs'	SC011798	Glasgow: Gairbraid	SC030168
Paisley: Oakshaw Trinity	SC005362	Glasgow: Gardner Street	SC009218
Paisley: Sandyford (Thread Street)	SC003497	Glasgow: Garthamlock and Craigend East	SC016862
Paisley: Sherwood Greenlaw	SC007484	Glasgow: Gorbals	SC002214
Paisley: St Columba Foxbar	SC005770	Glasgow: Govan Old	SC013596
Paisley: St James'	SC000949	Glasgow: Govanhill Trinity	SC012752
Paisley: St Luke's	SC000558	Glasgow: High Carntyne	SC006729
Paisley: St Mark's Oldhall	SC011210	Glasgow: Hillington Park	SC002614
Paisley: St Ninian's Ferguslie	SC004753	Glasgow: Househillwood St Christopher's	SC007798
Paisley: Wallneuk North	SC012650	Glasgow: Hyndland	SC002398
Port Glasgow: Hamilton Bardrainney	SC005421	Glasgow: Ibrox	SC009841
Port Glasgow: St Andrew's	SC009018	Glasgow: John Ross Memorial (for Deaf People)	SC027651
Port Glasgow: St Martin's	SC002410	Glasgow: Jordanhill	SC015683
Renfrew: North	SC006605	Glasgow: Kelvin Stevenson Memorial	SC014414
Renfrew: Old	SC004411	Glasgow: Kelvinside Hillhead	SC006629
Renfrew: Trinity	SC003785	Glasgow: Kenmuir Mount Vernon	SC008980
Skelmorlie and Wemyss Bay	SC003309	Glasgow: King's Park	SC017040
		Glasgow: Kinning Park	SC014895
16. Presbytery of Glasgow		Glasgow: Knightswood St Margaret's	SC007757
Banton	SC017638	Glasgow: Langside	SC007055
Bishopbriggs: Kenmure	SC012329	Glasgow: Lansdowne	SC015778
Bishopbriggs: Springfield	SC005642	Glasgow: Linthouse St Kenneth's	SC005923
Broom	SC003290	Glasgow: Lochwood	SC002161
Burnside Blairbeth	SC006633	Glasgow: Martyrs', The	SC009428
Busby	SC016612	Glasgow: Maryhill	SC002102
Cadder	SC015193	Glasgow: Merrylea	SC004016
Cambuslang: Flemington Hallside	SC006638	Glasgow: Mosspark	SC013281
Cambuslang: Old	SC000061	Glasgow: Mount Florida	SC010138
Cambuslang: St Andrew's	SC023596	Glasgow: New Govan	SC004153
Cambuslang: Trinity St Paul's	SC011456	Glasgow: Newlands South	SC000042
Campsie	SC000835	Glasgow: North Kelvinside	SC003264
Chryston	SC006752	Glasgow: Partick South	SC008315
Eaglesham	SC006377	Glasgow: Partick Trinity	SC007632
Fernhill and Cathkin	SC001077	Glasgow: Penilee St Andrew's	SC022874
Gartcosh	SC007541	Glasgow: Pollokshaws	SC006683
Giffnock: Orchardhill	SC009774	Glasgow: Pollokshields	SC013690
Giffnock: South	SC007807	Glasgow: Possilpark	SC003241
Giffnock: The Park	SC002965	Glasgow: Priesthill and Nitshill	SC015858
Glasgow: Anderston Kelvingrove	SC014631	Glasgow: Queen's Park	SC001575
Glasgow: Baillieston Mure Memorial	SC002220	Glasgow: Renfield St Stephen's	SC011423
Glasgow: Baillieston St Andrew's	SC005625	Glasgow: Robroyston	SC032401
Glasgow: Balshagray Victoria Park	SC000885	Glasgow: Ruchazie	SC003149
Glasgow: Barlanark Greyfriars	SC025730	Glasgow: Ruchill	SC014538
Glasgow: Battlefield East	SC008946	Glasgow: Sandyford Henderson Memorial	SC002155
Glasgow: Blawarthill	SC006410	Glasgow: Sandyhills	SC009460
Glasgow: Bridgeton St Francis in the East	SC012535	Glasgow: Scotstoun	SC030418
Glasgow: Broomhill	SC007820	Glasgow: Shawlands	SC012969
Glasgow: Calton Parkhead	SC006958	Glasgow: Sherbrooke St Gilbert's	SC015155
Glasgow: Cardonald	SC010265	Glasgow: Shettleston Old	SC001070
Glasgow: Carmunnock	SC011224	Glasgow: South Carntyne	SC010899
Glasgow: Carmyle	SC000532	Glasgow: South Shawlands	SC005196
Glasgow: Carntyne Old	SC009154	Glasgow: Springburn	SC004397
Glasgow: Carnwadric	SC030150	Glasgow: St Andrew's East	SC009600
Glasgow: Castlemilk East	SC015309	Glasgow: St Columba	SC006342
Glasgow: Castlemilk West	SC009813	Glasgow: St David's Knightswood	SC017297
Glasgow: Cathcart Old	SC002727	Glasgow: St Enoch's Hogganfield	SC004918
Glasgow: Cathcart Trinity	SC033802	Glasgow: St George's Tron	SC004931
Glasgow: Cathedral (High or St Mungo's)	SC013966	Glasgow: St James' (Pollok)	SC013313
Glasgow: Colston Milton	SC012939	Glasgow: St John's Renfield	SC012920
Glasgow: Colston Wellpark	SC005709	Glasgow: St Luke's and St Andrew's	SC032738
Glasgow: Cranhill	SC009874	Glasgow: St Margaret's Tollcross Park	SC005764
Glasgow: Croftfoot	SC009761	Glasgow: St Nicholas' Cardonald	SC011527
Glasgow: Dennistoun Blackfriars	SC001093	Glasgow: St Paul's	SC016306
Glasgow: Dennistoun Central	SC008824	Glasgow: St Rollox	SC015459
Glasgow: Dennistoun New	SC008824	Glasgow: St Thomas' Gallowgate	SC006549
Glasgow: Drumchapel Drumry St Mary's	SC026241	Glasgow: Temple Anniesland	SC015579
Glasgow: Drumchapel St Andrew's	SC022128	Glasgow: Toryglen	SC009399
Glasgow: Drumchapel St Mark's	SC008954	Glasgow: Trinity Possil and Henry Drummond	SC009578
Glasgow: Eastbank	SC004642	Glasgow: Tron St Mary's	SC017015

Glasgow: Victoria Tollcross	SC004821
Glasgow: Wallacewell	SC008840
Glasgow: Wellington	SC000289
Glasgow: Whiteinch (New Charge Dev)	SC030362
Glasgow: Yoker	SC017408
Glenboig	SC002834
Greenbank	SC011453
Kilsyth: Anderson	SC009866
Kilsyth: Burns and Old	SC009912
Kirkintilloch: Hillhead	SC002424
Kirkintilloch: St Columba's	SC008735
Kirkintilloch: St David's Memorial Park	SC007427
Kirkintilloch: St Mary's	SC007260
Lenzie: Old	SC008935
Lenzie: Union	SC015287
Maxwell Mearns Castle	SC017317
Mearns	SC007125
Milton of Campsie	SC014735
Netherlee	SC015303
Newton Mearns	SC004219
Rutherglen: Old	SC006856
Rutherglen: Stonelaw	SC013558
Rutherglen: Wardlawhill	SC001080
Rutherglen: West	SC007585
Rutherglen: West and Wardlawhill	SC007585
Stamperland	SC003155
Stepps	SC014212
Thornliebank	SC008426
Torrance	SC016058
Twechar	SC011672
Williamwood	SC009939

SCOTTISH
CHARITY
NUMBER	**NEW LEGAL NAME**
17.	**Presbytery of Hamilton**
SC016464	Airdrie Broomknoll Parish Church of Scotland
SC011239	Airdrie Clarkston Parish Church of Scotland
SC014555	Airdrie Flowerhill Parish Church of Scotland
SC024357	Airdrie High Parish Church of Scotland
SC004083	Airdrie Jackson Parish Church of Scotland
SC011674	Airdrie New Monkland Parish Church of Scotland
SC002900	Airdrie St Columbas Parish Church of Scotland
SC004209	Bargeddie Parish Church of Scotland
SC012556	Bellshill Macdonald Memorial Parish Church of Scotland
SC006007	Bellshill Orbiston Parish Church of Scotland
SC008340	Bellshill West Parish Church of Scotland
SC005955	Blantyre St Andrew's Parish Church of Scotland
SC004084	Blantyre Livingstone Memorial Parish Church of Scotland
SC018492	Blantyre Old Parish Church of Scotland
SC012944	The New Wellwynd Parish Church of Scotland Airdrie
SC009819	Bothwell Parish Church of Scotland
SC003105	Coatbridge Clifton Parish Church of Scotland
SC015831	Calderbank Parish Church of Scotland
SC030492	Caldercruix and Longriggend Parish Church of Scotland
SC036085	Carfin Parish Church of Scotland
SC008486	Chapelhall Parish Church of Scotland
SC011817	Chapelton Parish Church of Scotland
SC017084	Cleland Parish Church of Scotland
SC009704	Coatbridge Blairhill Dundyvan Parish Church of Scotland
SC006854	Coatbridge Calder Parish Church of Scotland
SC016362	Coatbridge Middle Parish Church of Scotland

SC010236	Coatbridge Old Monkland Parish Church of Scotland
SC008809	Coatbridge Townhead Parish Church of Scotland
SC013521	Coatbridge St Andrew's Parish Church of Scotland
SC016156	Dalserf Parish Church of Scotland
SC007396	East Kilbride Claremont Parish Church of Scotland
SC030300	East Kilbride Greenhills Parish Church of Scotland
SC016751	East Kilbride Moncreiff Parish Church of Scotland
SC000609	East Kilbride Old Parish Church of Scotland
SC008332	East Kilbride South Parish Church of Scotland
SC000250	East Kilbride West Kirk Church of Scotland
SC001857	East Kilbride Westwood Parish Church of Scotland
SC014716	Glassford Parish Church of Scotland
SC012692	East Kilbride Mossneuk Parish Church of Scotland
SC018154	Greengairs Parish Church of Scotland
SC015042	Hamilton Burnbank Parish Church of Scotland
SC006611	Cadzow Parish Church of Scotland, Hamilton
SC011571	Hamilton Gilmour & Whitehill Parish Church of Scotland
SC005376	Hamilton Hillhouse Parish Church of Scotland
SC014508	Hamilton North Parish Church of Scotland
SC010855	Hamilton Old Parish Church of Scotland
SC007145	Hamilton St Andrew's Parish Church of Scotland
SC008779	Hamilton St John's Parish Church of Scotland
SC022166	Hamilton South Parish Church of Scotland
SC007051	Hamilton Trinity Parish Church of Scotland
SC008451	Hamilton West Parish Church of Scotland
SC012888	Holytown Parish Church of Scotland
SC013309	Chalmers Parish Church of Scotland Larkhall
SC002870	St Machan's Parish Church of Scotland Larkhall
SC008611	Trinity Parish Church of Scotland, Larkhall
SC034242	Church of Scotland Stewartfield New Charge Development East Kilbride
SC008810	Motherwell Crosshill Parish Church of Scotland
SC016821	Motherwell North Parish Church of Scotland
SC008601	Motherwell South Parish Church of Scotland
SC010924	Motherwell St Margaret's Parish Church of Scotland
SC012233	Motherwell St Marys Parish Church of Scotland
SC005427	Newarthill Parish Church of Scotland
SC006540	Bonkle Parish Church of Scotland
SC001381	Newmains Coltness Memorial Parish Church of Scotland
SC004688	New Stevenston Wrangholm Parish Church of Scotland
SC007360	Overtown Parish Church of Scotland
SC009689	Quarter Parish Church of Scotland
SC015503	Motherwell Dalziel St Andrew's Parish Church of Scotland
SC016435	Strathaven West Parish Church of Scotland
SC013269	Kirk o' Shotts Parish Church of Scotland
SC003239	Stonehouse St Ninian's Parish Church of Scotland
SC001956	Strathaven Avendale Old and Drumclog Memorial Parish Church of Scotland
SC015591	Strathaven East Parish Church of Scotland
SC001020	Strathaven Rankin Parish Church of Scotland
SC010039	Uddingston Burnhead Parish Church of Scotland

SC006538	Shotts Calderhead – Erskine Parish Church of Scotland	Dunoon: St John's	SC003216
		Dunoon: The High Kirk	SC017524
SC009991	Uddingston Viewpark Parish Church of Scotland	Gigha and Cara	SC002567
		Glassary, Kilmartin and Ford	SC002121
SC013037	Cambusnethan North Parish Church of Scotland, Wishaw	Glenaray and Inveraray	SC016665
		Glenorchy and Innishael	SC003179
SC011532	Wishaw Cambusnethan Old and Morningside Parish Church of Scotland	Innellan	SC013247
		Iona	SC036399
SC013841	Wishaw Craigneuk and Belhaven Church of Scotland	Jura	SC002925
		Kilarrow	SC009853
SC011253	Wishaw Old Parish Church of Scotland	Kilberry	SC006941
SC012529	Wishaw St Marks Parish Church of Scotland	Kilbrandon and Kilchattan	SC017005
SC016893	Uddingston Old Parish Church of Scotland	Kilcalmonell	SC006948
SC010775	South Wishaw Parish Church of Scotland	Kilchoman	SC013203
		Kilchrenan and Dalavich	SC009417

18.   **Presbytery of Dumbarton**

SC001268	Alexandria Parish Church of Scotland	Kildalton and Oa	SC006032
SC008929	Arrochar Parish Church of Scotland	Kilfinan	SC003483
SC006355	Baldernock Parish Church of Scotland	Kilfinichen and Kilvickeon and the Ross of Mull	SC013473
SC037739	Bearsden: Baljaffray Parish Church of Scotland	Killean and Kilchenzie	SC016020
		Kilmeny	SC015317
SC009748	Killermont Parish Church (Church of Scotland) Bearsden	Kilmodan and Colintraive	SC021449
		Kilmore and Oban	SC011171
SC012997	New Kilpatrick Parish Church of Scotland	Kilmun (St Munn's)	SC001694
SC009082	Bearsden Cross Parish Church of Scotland	Kilninver and Kilmelford	SC002458
SC004489	Westerton Fairlie Memorial Parish Church of Scotland, Bearsden	Kirn	SC001976
		Kyles	SC014928
SC000886	Bonhill Church of Scotland	Lismore	SC030972
SC003494	Cardross Parish Church of Scotland	Lochgilphead	SC016311
SC004596	Abbotsford, Church of Scotland, Clydebank	Lochgoilhead and Kilmorich	SC006458
SC005108	Faifley Parish Church of Scotland, Clydebank	Muckairn	SC013377
SC015005	Kilbowie St Andrews Church of Scotland, Clydebank	Mull, Isle of, Kilninian and Kilmore	SC025506
		North Knapdale	SC001002
SC013242	Radnor Park Church of Scotland, Clydebank	Portnahaven	SC004086
SC003077	St Cuthberts Parish Church of Scotland: Clydebank	Rothesay: Trinity	SC006420
		Saddell and Carradale	SC002609
SC001725	Craigrownie Parish Church of Scotland	Salen and Ulva	SC026099
SC013599	Dalmuir Barclay Church of Scotland	Sandbank	SC006657
SC002937	Riverside Parish Church of Scotland, Dumbarton	Skipness	SC004280
		South Knapdale	SC010782
SC006235	St Andrews Church of Scotland: Dumbarton	Southend	SC005484
SC010474	West Kirk, Dumbarton (Church of Scotland)	Strachur and Strachlachlan	SC001767
SC008854	Duntocher Trinity Parish Church of Scotland	Strathfillan	SC004088
SC016699	Garelochhead Parish Church of Scotland	Strone and Ardentinny	SC003410
SC007801	Park Church of Scotland, Helensburgh	Tarbert	SC002622
SC014837	St Columba Church of Scotland, Helensburgh	The United Church of Bute	SC030563
SC012053	West Kirk of Helensburgh (Church of Scotland)	Tiree	SC000878
		Tobermory	SC002878
SC012346	Jamestown Parish Church of Scotland	Torosay and Kinlochspelvie	SC003909
SC002145	Kilmaronock Gartocharn Church of Scotland	Toward	SC015531
SC017192	Luss Parish Church of Scotland		
SC009913	Cairns Church of Scotland, Milngavie		
SC003870	St Lukes Church of Scotland: Milngavie		
SC002737	St Pauls Parish Church of Scotland: Milngavie		
SC011630	Old Kilpatrick Bowling Parish Church of Scotland		
SC014833	Renton Trinity Parish Church of Scotland		
SC010086	Rhu and Shandon Parish Church of Scotland		
SC001510	Rosneath St Modans Church of Scotland		

SCOTTISH CHARITY NUMBER	NEW LEGAL NAME
22.	**Presbytery of Falkirk**
SC029326	Cumbernauld Abronhill Church of Scotland
SC011038	Airth Parish Church of Scotland
SC008191	Bo'ness Old Kirk (Church of Scotland)
SC015225	Bonnybridge St Helen's Parish Church of Scotland
SC001385	Brightons Parish Church of Scotland
SC014816	Camelon Parish Church, Church of Scotland
SC011839	Cumbernauld: Condorrat Parish Church of Scotland
SC000877	Cumbernauld Old Parish Church of Scotland
SC016255	Denny Old Parish Church of Scotland
SC007072	Denny Westpark Church of Scotland
SC002943	Dunipace Parish Church of Scotland
SC000652	Falkirk Old & St Modan's Parish Church of Scotland
SC000775	Grangemouth Abbotsgrange Church of Scotland

19. Presbytery of Argyll

Appin	SC015795
Ardchattan	SC000680
Ardrishaig	SC010713
Campbeltown: Highland	SC002493
Campbeltown: Lorne and Lowland	SC011686
Coll	SC035582
Colonsay and Oronsay	SC031271
Connel	SC006738
Craignish	SC003718
Cumlodden, Lochfyneside and Lochgair	SC016097

SC014536	Haggs Parish Church of Scotland
SC004564	Cumbernauld Kildrum Parish Church of Scotland
SC001603	Grangemouth, Kirk of the Holy Rood, Church of Scotland
SC006456	Larbert East Church of Scotland
SC000445	Larbert Old Church of Scotland
SC012251	Larbert West Parish Church of Scotland
SC007383	Laurieston Parish Church of Scotland
SC003421	Polmont Old Parish Church of Scotland
SC008787	Redding & Westquarter Church of Scotland
SC013602	Slamannan Parish Church of Scotland
SC005066	St Andrews West Church of Scotland, Falkirk
SC002263	Stenhouse & Carron Parish Church of Scotland: Stenhousemuir
SC013114	Grangemouth Zetland Parish Church of Scotland
SC036366	St Mungo's Church of Scotland, Cumbernauld
SC007546	The Church of Scotland Falkirk Erskine Parish Church
SC002512	Blackbraes & Shieldhill Parish Church of Scotland
SC007665	St James Church of Scotland, Falkirk
SC016991	Grahamston United Church
SC011448	St Andrew's Church of Scotland, Bo'ness
SC007571	Muiravonside Parish Church of Scotland
SC009754	Bothkennar & Carronshore Parish Church (Church of Scotland)
SC007811	Carriden Parish Church of Scotland
SC004142	Bainsford Parish Church of Scotland, Falkirk

23.   **Presbytery of Stirling**

SC001308	Aberfoyle Parish Church of Scotland
SC002898	Alloa North Church of Scotland
SC007821	St Mungo's Parish Church of Scotland, Alloa
SC007605	Alloa West Church of Scotland
SC000006	Alva Parish Church of Scotland
SC005335	Balfron Church of Scotland
SC012316	Balquhidder Parish Church of Scotland
SC002953	Allan Church of Scotland, Bannockburn
SC011345	Bannockburn Ladywell Church of Scotland
SC015171	Bridge of Allan Parish Church of Scotland
SC012927	Buchanan Parish Church of Scotland
SC000833	Buchlyvie Church of Scotland
SC000396	Callander Kirk Church of Scotland
SC019113	Cambusbarron Parish Church of Scotland Bruce Memorial
SC002324	Clackmannan Parish Church of Scotland
SC016296	Cowie and Plean Church of Scotland
SC009713	Dollar Parish Church of Scotland
SC004824	Drymen Church of Scotland
SC004454	Dunblane Cathedral Church of Scotland
SC005185	Dunblane: St Blane's Church of Scotland
SC028465	Fallin Parish Church of Scotland
SC012537	Fintry Church of Scotland
SC012154	Gargunnock Parish Church of Scotland
SC009788	Gartmore Parish Church of Scotland
SC003028	Glendevon Parish Church of Scotland
SC012140	Killearn Kirk (Church of Scotland)
SC012031	Killin & Ardeonaig Parish Church of Scotland
SC012031	Kilmadock Parish Church of Scotland, Doune
SC000802	Kincardine in Menteith Church of Scotland, Blair Drummond
SC004286	Kippen Parish Church of Scotland
SC014031	Lecropt Kirk Parish Church of Scotland
SC001298	Logie Kirk Stirling (Church of Scotland)
SC004778	Menstrie Parish Church of Scotland
SC009418	Muckhart Parish Church of Scotland
SC028719	Norrieston Parish Church of Scotland
SC001864	Port of Menteith Church of Scotland

SC018155	Sauchie and Coalsnaughton Parish Church of Scotland
SC001414	Allan Park South Church of Scotland, Stirling
SC011473	Church of the Holy Rude, Stirling (Church of Scotland)
SC011795	Stirling North Parish Church of Scotland
SC013444	St Columba's Church of Scotland Stirling
SC005432	St Marks Parish Church of Scotland: Stirling
SC016320	St Ninians Old Parish Church of Scotland, Stirling
SC007533	Viewfield Erskine Church of Scotland, Stirling
SC007261	Strathblane Parish Church of Scotland
SC016570	Tillicoultry Parish Church of Scotland
SC005918	St Serfs Church of Scotland, Tullibody

24.   **Presbytery of Dunfermline**

SC005851	St Fillans Church of Scotland: Aberdour
SC031695	Beath and Cowdenbeath North Church of Scotland
SC012892	Cairneyhill Parish Church of Scotland
SC010676	Carnock and Oakley Church of Scotland
SC003799	Cowdenbeath Trinity Church of Scotland
SC015149	Culross & Torryburn Church of Scotland
SC020926	Dalgety Parish Church of Scotland
SC016883	The Abbey Church of Dunfermline (Church of Scotland)
SC035690	Dunfermline East Church of Scotland
SC011659	Dunfermline Gillespie Memorial Church of Scotland
SC013226	Dunfermline North Parish Church of Scotland
SC007302	St Andrew's Erskine Church of Scotland, Dunfermline
SC007799	Dunfermline St Leonard's Parish Church of Scotland
SC007080	Dunfermline St Margaret's Parish Church of Scotland
SC007453	St Ninians Church of Scotland: Dunfermline
SC008085	Dunfermline Townhill & Kingseat Parish Church of Scotland
SC000968	Inverkeithing Parish Church of Scotland
SC011004	Kelty Church of Scotland
SC002435	Limekilns Church of Scotland
SC032353	Lochgelly and Benarty St Serf's Parish Church of Scotland
SC007414	North Queensferry Church of Scotland
SC013620	Rosyth Parish Church of Scotland
SC013688	Saline & Blairingone Parish Church of Scotland
SC002951	Tulliallan & Kincardine Parish Church of Scotland

25.   **Presbytery of Kirkcaldy**

SC031143	Auchterderran: St Fothads Parish Church of Scotland
SC025310	Auchtertool Kirk (Church of Scotland)
SC009495	Buckhaven Parish Church of Scotland
SC016418	Burntisland Parish Church of Scotland
SC008991	Dysart Kirk (Church of Scotland)
SC007397	Glenrothes Christ's Kirk (Church of Scotland)
SC016386	St Columba's Parish Church of Scotland, Glenrothes
SC009845	St Margaret's Parish Church of Scotland: Glenrothes
SC002472	St Ninian's Parish Church of Scotland: Glenrothes
SC009342	Innerleven East Parish Church of Scotland: Methil
SC016733	Kennoway, Windygates and Balgonie: St Kenneth's Church of Scotland
SC007848	Kinghorn Parish Church of Scotland
SC012030	Kinglassie Parish Church of Scotland

SC002586	Abbotshall Parish Church of Scotland, Kirkcaldy
SC012039	Linktown Church of Scotland, Kirkcaldy
SC002858	Pathhead Parish Church of Scotland, Kirkcaldy
SC011722	St Andrew's Parish Church of Scotland, Kirkcaldy
SC031064	St Bryce Kirk, Church of Scotland, Kirkcaldy
SC005628	St John's Parish Church of Scotland, Kirkcaldy
SC012756	Templehall Parish Church of Scotland, Kirkcaldy
SC015807	Torbain Parish Church of Scotland, Kirkcaldy
SC004264	Viewforth Parish Church of Scotland, Kirkcaldy
SC014025	Trinity Church of Scotland, Leslie
SC031969	Leven Parish Church of Scotland
SC005820	Markinch Parish Church of Scotland
SC009581	Methil Parish Church of Scotland
SC007949	Methilhill and Denbeath Parish Church of Scotland
SC003417	Thornton Parish Church of Scotland
SC006847	Wemyss Parish Church of Scotland

26.   **Presbytery of St Andrews**

SC004848	Abdie & Dunbog Parish Church of Scotland
SC012986	Anstruther Parish Church of Scotland
SC005402	Auchtermuchty Parish Church of Scotland
SC002542	Balmerino Parish Church of Scotland
SC001108	Boarhills and Dunino Parish Church of Scotland.
SC005565	Cameron Parish Church (Church of Scotland)
SC016744	Carnbee Church of Scotland
SC000181	Cellardyke Parish Church of Scotland
SC017442	Ceres, Kemback & Springfield Church of Scotland
SC001601	Crail Parish Church of Scotland
SC001907	Creich, Flisk and Kilmany Church of Scotland
SC013123	Cupar Old & St Michael of Tarvit Parish Church (of Scotland)
SC031896	St John's Parish Church of Scotland, Cupar
SC015721	Dairsie Parish Church of Scotland
SC015226	Edenshead and Strathmiglo Church of Scotland
SC003163	Elie Parish Church of Scotland
SC012247	Falkland Parish Church of Scotland
SC016622	Freuchie Parish Church of Scotland
SC005381	Howe of Fife Parish Church (Church of Scotland)
SC012750	Kilconquhar & Colinsburgh Church of Scotland
SC002653	Kilrenny Parish Church of Scotland
SC012192	Kingsbarns Parish Church of Scotland
SC003465	Largo & Newburn Parish Church of Scotland
SC013075	Largo St David's Church of Scotland
SC009474	Largoward Church of Scotland
SC015677	Leuchars: St Athernase Church of Scotland
SC015182	Monimail Parish (Church of Scotland)
SC004607	Newburgh Parish Church of Scotland
SC006758	Newport-on-Tay Church of Scotland
SC015271	Pittenweem Church of Scotland
SC017173	The Parish Church of the Holy Trinity, St Andrews (Church of Scotland).
SC014034	St Andrews Hope Park (Church of Scotland)
SC014986	Martyrs Church, St Andrews (Church of Scotland)
SC013586	St Andrews: St Leonard's Parish Church of Scotland Congregation
SC005556	St Monans Church of Scotland
SC014710	Strathkinness Parish Church of Scotland

SC008659	Tayport Parish Church of Scotland
SC006447	Wormit Parish Church of Scotland

27.   **Presbytery of Dunkeld and Meigle**

SC007899	Aberfeldy Parish Church of Scotland
SC028023	Amulree and Strathbraan Parish Church of Scotland
SC001465	Dull and Weem Parish Church of Scotland
SC000540	Alyth Parish Church of Scotland
SC000098	Ardler Kettins & Meigle Parish Church of Scotland
SC004358	Bendochy Parish Church of Scotland
SC014438	Coupar Angus Abbey Church of Scotland
SC013516	Blair Atholl and Struan Church of Scotland
SC001984	Tenandry Parish Church of Scotland
SC033757	Blairgowrie Parish Church of Scotland
SC011351	Braes of Rannoch Church of Scotland
SC006570	Foss and Rannoch Church of Scotland
SC001957	Caputh and Clunie Church of Scotland
SC009251	Kinclaven Church of Scotland
SC009867	Dunkeld Parish Church of Scotland
SC003310	Fortingall & Glenlyon Church of Scotland
SC006260	Kenmore and Lawers Church of Scotland
SC004275	Grantully Logierait & Strathtay Church of Scotland
SC008021	Kirkmichael Straloch & Glenshee Church of Scotland
SC000323	Rattray Parish Church of Scotland
SC008361	Pitlochry Church of Scotland

28.   **Presbytery of Perth**

SC000586	Abernethy and Dron and Arngask Church of Scotland
SC005203	Almondbank Tibbermore Parish Church of Scotland
SC000139	Ardoch Parish Church of Scotland
SC001688	Auchterarder Parish Church of Scotland
SC010247	Auchtergaven and Moneydie Parish Church of Scotland
SC005594	Blackford Parish Church of Scotland
SC007283	Cargill Burrelton Parish Church of Scotland
SC003168	Cleish Parish Church of Scotland
SC009031	Collace Church of Scotland
SC001878	Comrie Parish Church of Scotland
SC004304	Crieff Parish Church of Scotland
SC009638	Dunbarney and Forgandenny Parish Church (Church of Scotland)
SC010311	St Fillans Dundurn Parish Church of Scotland
SC015895	Errol Parish Church of Scotland
SC013157	Fossoway St Serf's & Devonside Parish Church of Scotland
SC002209	Fowlis Wester, Madderty and Monzie Parish Church of Scotland
SC009632	Gask Parish Church of Scotland
SC010838	Kilspindie & Rait Parish Church of Scotland
SC012555	Kinross Parish Church of Scotland
SC010807	Methven and Logiealmond Church of Scotland
SC004984	Muthill Parish Church of Scotland
SC015523	Orwell and Portmoak Parish Church of Scotland
SC001330	Perth: Craigie Parish Church of Scotland
SC007509	Kinnoull Parish Church of Scotland, Perth
SC002467	Perth: Letham St Mark's Church of Scotland
SC006021	Perth: Moncreiffe Parish Church (Church of Scotland)
SC013014	Perth North, Church of Scotland
SC011113	Perth Riverside Church of Scotland
SC017132	St John's Kirk of Perth (Church of Scotland)
SC002919	Perth St Leonard's-in-the-Fields & Trinity Church of Scotland

SC016829	Perth: St Matthew's Church of Scotland
SC010629	Redgorton and Stanley Parish Church – Church of Scotland
SC007094	Scone New Church of Scotland
SC001244	Scone Old Parish Church of Scotland
SC014964	St Madoes and Kinfauns Church of Scotland, Glencarse
SC020000	St Martin's Church of Scotland Perth
SC030799	The Church of Scotland: The Stewartry of Strathearn
SC000004	Trinity Gask and Kinkell Church (Church of Scotland)

29.   Presbytery of Dundee

SC007847	Abernyte Parish Church of Scotland
SC016717	Auchterhouse Parish Church of Scotland
SC017449	Dundee: Balgay Parish Church of Scotland
SC007031	Broughty Ferry New Kirk (Church of Scotland)
SC003677	Dundee: Camperdown Parish Church of Scotland
SC021763	Chalmers-Ardler Parish Church of Scotland, Dundee
SC012089	Dundee: Clepington and Fairmuir Parish Church (of Scotland)
SC016701	Dundee: Craigiebank Parish Church of Scotland
SC005707	Dundee: Downfield South Church of Scotland
SC010030	Dundee Douglas and Mid Craigie Church of Scotland
SC033313	Dundee Lochee Parish Church of Scotland
SC017136	Dundee: West Church of Scotland
SC002792	Fowlis & Liff Parish Church of Scotland
SC009839	Inchture & Kinnaird Parish Church of Scotland
SC009454	Invergowrie Parish Church of Scotland
SC009115	Dundee: Logie & St John's (Cross) Church of Scotland
SC012230	Longforgan Parish Church of Scotland
SC001085	Lundie and Muirhead Parish Church of Scotland
SC013884	Dundee: Mains Parish Church of Scotland
SC020742	Fintry Parish Church of Scotland, Dundee
SC013162	Dundee: Meadowside St Paul's Church of Scotland
SC004496	Dundee: Menzieshill Parish Church of Scotland
SC014775	Monikie & Newbigging Church of Scotland
SC012137	Murroes & Tealing Parish Church of Scotland
SC011775	Dundee: St Andrew's Parish Church of Scotland
SC000723	St David's High Kirk Dundee (Church of Scotland)
SC005210	St James Church of Scotland: Broughty Ferry
SC000088	St Luke's and Queen Street Church of Scotland: Broughty Ferry
SC011017	Barnhill St Margaret's Parish Church of Scotland
SC002198	Dundee Parish Church (St Mary's) Church of Scotland
SC003714	St Stephen's & West Parish Church of Scotland: Broughty Ferry
SC000384	Stobswell Parish Church of Scotland: Dundee
SC018015	Strathmartine Church of Scotland: Dundee
SC011021	Dundee: Trinity Parish Church of Scotland
SC000316	Dundee: Whitfield Parish Church of Scotland
SC014314	The Steeple Church: Dundee (Church of Scotland)
SC013282	Monifieth Panmure Parish Church of Scotland

SC008965	Monifieth: St Rule's Parish Church of Scotland
SC015950	Monifieth: South Parish Church of Scotland

30.   Presbytery of Angus

SC018944	Aberlemno Parish Church of Scotland
SC002545	Barry Parish Church of Scotland
SC008630	Brechin Gardner Memorial Church of Scotland
SC015146	Carnoustie Church of Scotland
SC001293	Colliston Church of Scotland
SC007997	Farnell Parish Church of Scotland
SC000572	Dun and Hillside Church of Scotland
SC013105	Edzell Lethnot Glenesk Church of Scotland
SC009017	Inchbrayock Parish Church of Scotland
SC031461	The Isla Parishes Church of Scotland
SC013352	Newtyle Church of Scotland
SC017413	Arbirlot Parish Church of Scotland
SC006482	Arbroath West Kirk Church of Scotland
SC011361	Arbroath Knox's Parish Church of Scotland
SC005478	Arbroath: St Andrew's Church of Scotland
SC017424	Carmyllie Parish Church of Scotland
SC004594	Carnoustie Panbride Church of Scotland
SC003833	Dunnichen, Letham and Kirkden Church of Scotland
SC016937	Eassie and Nevay Church of Scotland
SC004921	Forfar East and Old Parish Church of Scotland
SC002417	Forfar Lowson Memorial Parish Church of Scotland
SC010332	Brechin Cathedral Church of Scotland
SC005085	Friockheim and Kinnell Parish Church of Scotland
SC017785	Inverkeilor and Lunan Church of Scotland
SC004395	Kirriemuir St Andrew's Parish Church of Scotland
SC015123	The Glens and Kirriemuir Old Parish Church of Scotland
SC009016	Montrose Melville South Church of Scotland
SC009934	Montrose: Old and St Andrew's Church of Scotland
SC003049	Arbroath St Vigeans Church of Scotland
SC006317	Oathlaw Tannadice Church of Scotland
SC001506	Forfar St Margaret's Church of Scotland
SC013052	Arbroath Old and Abbey Church of Scotland
SC011205	Glamis, Inverarity and Kinnettles Parish Church of Scotland
SC017327	Guthrie and Rescobie Church of Scotland
SC003236	Fern, Careston and Menmuir Church of Scotland

31. Presbytery of Aberdeen

Aberdeen: Beechgrove	SC010643
Aberdeen: Bridge of Don Oldmachar	SC025324
Aberdeen: Cove	SC032413
Aberdeen: Craigiebuckler	SC017158
Aberdeen: Denburn	SC001962
Aberdeen: Ferryhill	SC010756
Aberdeen: Garthdee	SC022497
Aberdeen: Gilcomston South	SC013916
Aberdeen: High Hilton	SC003789
Aberdeen: Holburn Central	SC004461
Aberdeen: Holburn West	SC013318
Aberdeen: Mannofield	SC001680
Aberdeen: Mastrick	SC013459
Aberdeen: Middlefield	SC031459
Aberdeen: Midstocket	SC010643
Aberdeen: New Stockethill (New Charge Dev)	SC030587
Aberdeen: Northfield	SC034441
Aberdeen: Queen Street	SC014117
Aberdeen: Queen's Cross	SC002019
Aberdeen: Rosemount	SC008188

Aberdeen: Rubislaw	SC015841
Aberdeen: Ruthrieston South	SC003976
Aberdeen: Ruthrieston West	SC013020
Aberdeen: South Holburn	SC017516
Aberdeen: St Columba's Bridge of Don	SC027440
Aberdeen: St George's Tillydrone	SC024795
Aberdeen: St John's Church for Deaf People	SC021283
Aberdeen: St Machar's Cathedral	SC008157
Aberdeen: St Mark's	SC015451
Aberdeen: St Mary's	SC018173
Aberdeen: St Nicholas Kincorth, South of	SC016043
Aberdeen: St Nicholas Uniting, Kirk of	SC008689
Aberdeen: St Ninian's	SC013146
Aberdeen: St Stephen's	SC014120
Aberdeen: Summerhill	SC007076
Aberdeen: Torry St Fittick's	SC009020
Aberdeen: Woodside	SC001966
Bucksburn Stoneywood	SC017404
Cults	SC017517
Cults: East	SC014009
Cults: West	SC017517
Dyce	SC016950
Kingswells	SC006865
Newhills	SC011204
Peterculter	SC001452

SCOTTISH CHARITY NUMBER	NEW LEGAL NAME
32.	**Presbytery of Kincardine and Deeside**
SC016449	Aberluthnott Church of Scotland
SC014112	Aboyne/Dinnet Parish Church of Scotland
SC009239	Arbuthnott, Bervie and Kinneff (Church of Scotland)
SC011251	Banchory-Ternan East Church of Scotland
SC003306	Banchory-Ternan West Parish Church of Scotland
SC013648	Banchory Devenick & Maryculter-Cookney Parish Church of Scotland
SC018517	Birse & Feughside Church of Scotland
SC012075	Braemar and Crathie Parish, The Church of Scotland
SC015856	Parish of Cromar Church of Scotland
SC033779	Drumoak-Durris Church of Scotland
SC005522	Glenmuick (Ballater) Parish Church of Scotland
SC007436	Kinneff Church of Scotland
SC014830	Laurencekirk Church of Scotland
SC011997	Mearns Coastal Parish Church of Scotland
SC012967	Mid Deeside Parish, Church of Scotland
SC005679	Newtonhill Parish Church (Church of Scotland)
SC007420	Portlethen Parish Church of Scotland
SC013165	Stonehaven Dunnottar Church of Scotland
SC011191	Stonehaven Fetteresso Church of Scotland
SC016565	Stonehaven South Church of Scotland
SC016193	West Mearns Parish Church of Scotland
33.	**Presbytery of Gordon**
SC010960	Barthol Chapel Church of Scotland
SC016387	Belhelvie Church of Scotland
SC000935	Insch-Leslie-Premnay-Oyne Church of Scotland
SC004050	Blairdaff and Chapel of Garioch Church of Scotland
SC003429	Cluny Church of Scotland
SC010911	Culsalmond and Rayne Church of Scotland
SC030817	Cushnie and Tough Parish Church of Scotland
SC003254	Daviot Parish Church of Scotland
SC003215	Echt Parish Church of Scotland
SC008819	Ellon Parish Church of Scotland

SC003115	Fintray Kinellar Keithhall Church of Scotland
SC011701	Foveran Church of Scotland
SC007979	Howe Trinity Parish Church of Scotland
SC001405	Huntly Cairnie Glass Church of Scotland
SC008791	St Andrews Parish Church of Scotland Inverurie
SC016907	Inverurie West Church of Scotland
SC014790	Kemnay Parish Church of Scotland
SC001406	Kintore Parish Church of Scotland
SC015960	Meldrum & Bourtie Parish Church of Scotland
SC016542	Methlick Parish Church of Scotland
SC009556	Midmar Parish Church of Scotland
SC004525	Monymusk Parish Church of Scotland
SC024017	Newmachar Parish Church of Scotland
SC007582	Parish of Noth Church of Scotland
SC009462	Skene Parish Church of Scotland
SC017161	Tarves Parish Church of Scotland
SC006056	Udny & Pitmedden Church of Scotland
SC014679	Upper Donside Parish Church of Scotland
SC000534	Strathbogie Drumblade Church of Scotland Huntly
34.	**Presbytery of Buchan**
SC007197	Aberdour Church of Scotland
SC017101	Auchaber United Parish Church of Scotland
SC009168	Auchterless Parish Church of Scotland
SC015501	Banff Parish Church of Scotland
SC006889	Crimond Parish Church of Scotland
SC006408	Cruden Parish Church of Scotland
SC012985	Deer Parish Church of Scotland
SC000522	Fordyce Parish Church of Scotland
SC013119	Fraserburgh Old Church of Scotland
SC005714	Fraserburgh South Church of Scotland
SC016334	Fraserburgh West Parish Church of Scotland
SC001475	Fyvie Church of Scotland
SC012282	Gardenstown Church of Scotland
SC000375	Inverallochy and Rathen East Parish Church of Scotland
SC015077	King Edward Parish Church of Scotland
SC008873	Longside Parish Church of Scotland
SC008813	Lonmay Parish Church of Scotland
SC015786	Macduff Parish Church of Scotland
SC009773	Maud & Savoch Church of Scotland
SC010291	Monquhitter & New Byth Parish Church of Scotland
SC007917	New Deer St Kane's Church of Scotland
SC001107	Marnoch Church of Scotland
SC014620	New Pitsligo Parish Church of Scotland
SC001971	Ordiquhill & Cornhill Church of Scotland
SC011147	Peterhead Old Parish Church of Scotland
SC010841	Peterhead St Andrews Church of Scotland
SC009990	Peterhead Trinity Parish Church of Scotland
SC005498	Pitsligo Parish Church of Scotland
SC015604	Rathen West Parish Church of Scotland
SC032016	Rothienorman Parish Church of Scotland
SC000710	St Fergus Parish Church of Scotland
SC024874	Sandhaven Parish Church of Scotland
SC007273	Strichen and Tyrie Parish Church of Scotland
SC015620	St Andrews Parish Church of Scotland, Turriff
SC007470	Turriff St Ninians and Forglen Parish Church of Scotland
SC002085	Whitehills Parish Church of Scotland
35.	**Presbytery of Moray**
SC001336	Aberlour Parish Church of Scotland
SC010330	Alves & Burghead Parish Church of Scotland
SC005310	Bellie Parish Church of Scotland
SC016720	Birnie and Pluscarden Church of Scotland
SC001235	Buckie North Church of Scotland
SC005608	Buckie South & West Church of Scotland
SC011231	Cullen & Deskford Church of Scotland

SC015881	St Michael's Parish Church of Scotland, Dallas
SC004853	Duffus Spynie & Hopeman Church of Scotland
SC000585	Dyke Parish Church of Scotland
SC009986	Edinkillie Church of Scotland
SC005240	Elgin High Church of Scotland
SC015164	St Giles & St Columbas Church of Scotland, Elgin
SC015093	Enzie Parish Church of Scotland
SC010045	Findochty Parish Church of Scotland
SC000711	St Laurence Parish Church of Scotland, Forres
SC005094	St Leonard's Church of Scotland, Forres
SC033804	Keith North Newmill Boharm & Rothiemay Church of Scotland
SC031791	Kirk of Keith: St Rufus, Botriphnie and Grange (Church of Scotland)
SC014557	Kinloss & Findhorn Parish Church of Scotland
SC014428	Knockando Elchies & Archiestown Parish Church of Scotland
SC009793	St Gerardine's High Church of Scotland, Lossiemouth
SC000880	St James Church of Scotland: Lossiemouth
SC010193	Mortlach and Cabrach Church of Scotland
SC014485	Portknockie Parish Church of Scotland
SC022567	Rafford Parish Church of Scotland
SC015906	Rathven Parish Church of Scotland
SC016116	Rothes Parish Church of Scotland
SC007113	Speymouth Parish Church of Scotland
SC008850	St Andrews Lhanbryd & Urquhart Parish Church of Scotland, Elgin

	36. Presbytery of Abernethy
SC003652	Abernethy Church of Scotland
SC002884	Cromdale & Advie Church of Scotland
SC010001	Grantown-on-Spey Church of Scotland
SC001064	Duthil Church of Scotland
SC014015	Dulnain Bridge Church of Scotland
SC021546	Kingussie Church of Scotland
SC003282	Rothiemurchus & Aviemore Church of Scotland
SC001802	Tomintoul, Glenlivet and Inveravon Church of Scotland
SC000043	Alvie and Insh Church of Scotland
SC008346	Boat of Garten & Kincardine Church of Scotland
SC008016	Laggan Church of Scotland
SC005490	Newtonmore Church of Scotland

37. Presbytery of Inverness

Ardclach	SC012321
Ardersier	SC015446
Auldearn and Dalmore	SC026653
Cawdor	SC001695
Croy and Dalcross	SC013601
Culloden: The Barn	SC000662
Daviot and Dunlichity	SC003301
Dores and Boleskine	SC013579
Inverness: Crown	SC018159
Inverness: Dalneigh and Bona	SC011773
Inverness: East	SC016866
Inverness: Hilton	SC016775
Inverness: Inshes	SC005553
Inverness: Kinmylies	SC020888
Inverness: Ness Bank	SC010870
Inverness: Old High St Stephen's	SC035073
Inverness: St Columba High	SC008109
Inverness: Trinity	SC015432
Kilmorack and Erchless	SC008121
Kiltarlity	SC014918

Kirkhill	SC003866
Moy, Dalarossie and Tomatin	SC015653
Nairn: Old	SC000947
Nairn: St Ninian's	SC015361
Petty	SC004952
Urquhart and Glenmoriston	SC016627

SCOTTISH CHARITY NUMBER	NEW LEGAL NAME
38.	**Presbytery of Lochaber**
SC002916	Acharacle Parish Church of Scotland
SC008222	Ardgour and Kingairloch Parish Church of Scotland
SC030394	Ardnamurchan Parish Church of Scotland
SC021584	North West Lochaber Church of Scotland
SC018259	Duror Parish Church of Scotland
SC022635	Fort Augustus Parish Church of Scotland
SC013279	Fort William Duncansburgh MacIntosh Parish Church of Scotland
SC005211	Glencoe St Munda's Parish Church of Scotland
SC023413	Glengarry Parish Church of Scotland
SC005687	Kilmallie Parish Church of Scotland
SC014745	Kilmonivaig Parish Church of Scotland
SC030288	Kinlochleven Parish Church of Scotland
SC015532	Morvern Parish Church of Scotland
SC006700	Nether Lochaber Parish Church of Scotland
SC008982	Strontian Parish Church of Scotland

39.	**Presbytery of Ross**
SC015227	Alness Parish Church of Scotland
SC003921	Avoch Parish Church of Scotland
SC011897	Contin Parish Church of Scotland
SC006666	Cromarty Parish Church of Scotland
SC001167	Dingwall Castle Street Church of Scotland
SC001056	Dingwall St Clements Parish Church of Scotland
SC009309	Fearn Abbey & Nigg Church of Scotland
SC012675	Ferintosh Parish Church of Scotland
SC003499	Fodderty & Strathpeffer Parish Church of Scotland
SC004472	Fortrose & Rosemarkie Parish Church of Scotland
SC010964	Invergordon Church of Scotland
SC010319	Killearnan Parish Church of Scotland
SC013375	Kilmuir & Logie Easter Church of Scotland
SC009180	Kiltearn Parish Church of Scotland
SC014467	Knockbain Parish Church of Scotland
SC015631	Lochbroom & Ullapool Church of Scotland
SC013643	Resolis & Urquhart Church of Scotland
SC010093	Rosskeen Parish Church of Scotland
SC012425	Tain Parish Church of Scotland
SC021420	Tarbat Parish Church of Scotland
SC009902	Urray & Kilchrist Church of Scotland

40.	**Presbytery of Sutherland**
SC016038	Altnaharra & Farr Church of Scotland
SC010171	Assynt & Stoer Parish Church of Scotland
SC004973	Clyne Church of Scotland
SC003840	Creich Parish Church of Scotland
SC000315	Dornoch Cathedral (Church of Scotland)
SC005079	Durness & Kinlochbervie Church of Scotland
SC007326	Eddrachillis Parish Church of Scotland
SC004560	Golspie (St Andrews) Church of Scotland
SC004056	Kildonan & Loth Helmsdale Church of Scotland
SC016877	Kincardine Croick & Edderton Church of Scotland
SC020871	Lairg Church of Scotland
SC014066	Melness & Tongue Church of Scotland

SC010035	Rogart Church of Scotland
SC017558	Rosehall Church of Scotland

41.   **Presbytery of Caithness**

SC001363	Bower Church of Scotland
SC032164	Canisbay Parish Church of Scotland
SC030261	Dunnet Church of Scotland
SC008544	Halkirk & Westerdale Church of Scotland
SC010874	Keiss Parish Church of Scotland
SC034424	The Parish of Latheron Church of Scotland
SC010296	Olrig Church of Scotland
SC001815	North Coast Parish Church of Scotland
SC016691	Thurso St Peter's & St Andrew's Church of Scotland
SC007248	Thurso West Church of Scotland
SC003365	Watten Church of Scotland
SC013840	Wick Bridge Street Church of Scotland
SC011338	Wick Old Parish Church of Scotland
SC001291	Pulteneytown & Thrumster Church of Scotland

42.   **Presbytery of Lochcarron – Skye**

SC032334	Applecross, Lochcarron and Torridon Church of Scotland
SC022592	Bracadale and Duirinish Church of Scotland
SC015448	Gairloch and Dundonnell Church of Scotland
SC017510	Glenelg and Kintail Church of Scotland
SC014072	Kilmuir and Stenscholl Church of Scotland
SC016505	Lochalsh Church of Scotland
SC000416	Portree Church of Scotland
SC030117	Snizort Church of Scotland
SC001285	Strath and Sleat Church of Scotland

43.   **Presbytery of Uist**

SC003980	Barra Church of Scotland
SC002191	Benbecula Church of Scotland
SC016358	Berneray and Lochmaddy Church of Scotland
SC016461	Carinish Church of Scotland
SC030955	Kilmuir and Paible Church of Scotland
SC001770	Manish-Scarista Church of Scotland
SC031790	South Uist Church of Scotland
SC002622	Tarbert Church of Scotland

44.   **Presbytery of Lewis**

SC006563	Barvas Church of Scotland
SC032250	Carloway Church of Scotland
SC000991	Cross Ness Church of Scotland
SC008004	Kinloch Church of Scotland
SC014492	Knock Church of Scotland
SC024236	Lochs Crossbost Parish Church of Scotland
SC008746	Lochs-in-Bernera Church of Scotland
SC010164	Stornoway High Church of Scotland

SC000753	Martins Memorial Church of Scotland, Stornoway
SC006777	St Columba Old Parish Church of Scotland, Stornoway
SC007879	Uig Parish Church of Scotland

45.   **Presbytery of Orkney**

SC035048	Birsay Harray & Sandwick Church of Scotland
SC019770	East Mainland Church of Scotland
SC005404	Eday Church of Scotland
SC005062	Evie Church of Scotland
SC013330	Firth Church of Scotland
SC016203	Flotta Parish Church of Scotland
SC023194	Hoy & Walls Parish Church of Scotland
SC018002	Kirkwall East Church, Church of Scotland
SC005322	Kirkwall St Magnus Cathedral (Church of Scotland)
SC030098	North Ronaldsay Parish Church of Scotland
SC016221	Orphir Church of Scotland
SC013661	Papa Westray Church of Scotland
SC016806	Rendall Church of Scotland
SC001078	Rousay Church of Scotland
SC000271	Sanday Church of Scotland
SC006097	Shapinsay Church of Scotland
SC003298	South Ronaldsay & Burray Church of Scotland
SC008306	Stenness Church of Scotland
SC003099	Stromness Church of Scotland
SC006572	Moncur Memorial Church of Scotland, Stronsay
SC025053	Westray Parish Church of Scotland

46.   **Presbytery of Shetland**

SC030483	Burra Church of Scotland
SC029873	Delting Parish Church (Church of Scotland)
SC015253	Dunrossness and St Ninian's Parish Church (incl. Fair Isle) (Church of Scotland)
SC038365	Fetlar Church of Scotland
SC017535	Lerwick and Bressay Parish Church (Church of Scotland)
SC031996	Nesting and Lunnasting Church of Scotland
SC002341	Northmavine Parish Church of Scotland
SC012345	Sandsting and Aithsting Parish Church of Scotland
SC014545	Sandwick, Cunningsburgh and Quarff Church of Scotland
SC030748	St Paul's Church of Scotland Walls: Shetland
SC032982	Tingwall Parish Church of Scotland
SC007954	Unst Church of Scotland
SC000293	Whalsay and Skerries Parish Church of Scotland
SC020628	Yell Parish Church of Scotland

www.worldexchange.org.uk

ST COLM'S INTERNATIONAL HOUSE

23 Inverleith Terrace, Edinburgh EH3 5NS
T: 0131 315 4444   E: we@stcolms.org

SECTION 8

Church Buildings: Ordnance Survey National Grid References

The Churches are listed in the order in which they appear in the Presbytery Lists in the *Year Book*.

1. Presbytery of Edinburgh
Albany Deaf Church of Edinburgh, at Greenside
    NT263745
Balerno, NT163664
Barclay, NT249726
Blackhall St Columba's, NT219727
Bristo Memorial Craigmillar, NT287716
Broughton St Mary's, NT256748
Canongate, NT265738
Carrick Knowe, NT203721
Colinton, NT216692
Colinton Mains, NT233692
Corstorphine Craigsbank, NT191730
Corstorphine Old, NT201728
Corstorphine St Anne's, NT204730
Corstorphine St Ninian's, NT198730
Craigentinny St Christopher's, NT292748
Craiglockhart, NT244705
Craigmillar Park, NT269714
Cramond, NT190768
Currie, NT183676
Dalmeny, NT144775
Davidson's Mains, NT207752
Dean, NT238742
Drylaw, NT221754
Duddingston, NT284726
Fairmilehead, NT248683
Gilmerton, NT283686
Gorgie, NT237729
Granton, NT237766
Greenbank, NT243702
Greenside, NT263745
Greyfriars Tolbooth and Highland, NT256734
High (St Giles'), NT257736
Holyrood Abbey, NT274744
Holy Trinity, NT210700
Inverleith, NT243759
Juniper Green, NT199687
Kaimes Lockhart Memorial, NT277684
Kirkliston, NT125744
Kirk o' Field, NT263732
Leith North, NT263765
Leith St Andrew's, NT273757
Leith St Serf's, NT248761
Leith St Thomas' Junction Road, NT267761
Leith South, NT271761
Leith Wardie, NT246768
Liberton, NT275700
Liberton Northfield, NT280699
London Road, NT268745
Marchmont St Giles', NT256718
Mayfield Salisbury, NT266717
Morningside, NT246707
Morningside United, NT245719
Muirhouse St Andrew's, NT215763
Murrayfield, NT237733
Newhaven, NT254769
New Restalrig, NT284742
Old Kirk, NT220760
Palmerston Place, NT241734
Pilrig St Paul's, NT266752
Polwarth, NT236719
Portobello Old, NT309738
Portobello St James', NT303738
Portobello St Philip's Joppa, NT313736
Priestfield, NT271721
Queensferry, NT130782
Ratho, NT138710

Reid Memorial, NT261710
Richmond Craigmillar, NT296717
St Andrew's and St George's, NT255741
St Andrew's Clermiston, NT201746
St Catherine's Argyle, NT257721
St Colm's, NT237729
St Cuthbert's, NT248736
St David's Broomhouse, NT203714
St George's West, NT245736
St John's Oxgangs, NT237687
St Margaret's, NT284745
St Martin's, NT305726
St Michael's, NT234722
St Nicholas' Sighthill, NT194707
St Stephen's Comely Bank, NT241748
Slateford Longstone, NT213707
Stenhouse St Aidan's, NT218716
Stockbridge, NT247748 (St Stephen's NT249746)
Tron Moredun, NT294697
Viewforth, NT244725

2. Presbytery of West Lothian
Abercorn, NT082792
Armadale, NS935684
Avonbridge, NS910730
Bathgate: Boghall, NS996686
Bathgate: High, NS976691
Bathgate: St John's, NS977687
Blackburn and Seafield, NS991655
Blackridge, NS897671
Breich Valley, NS968622
Broxburn, NT085723
Fauldhouse: St Andrew's, NS936607
Harthill: St Andrew's, NS907647
Kirknewton and East Calder:
Kirknewton, NT106670
East Calder, NT086678
Kirk of Calder, NT074673, Midcalder
Linlithgow: St Michael's, NT002773
Linlithgow: St Ninian's Craigmailen, NS994771
Livingston Ecumenical Church:
    Carmondean, Knightsridge, Craigshill (St Columba's),
        NT063681
    Ladywell (St Paul's), NT054682
    Dedridge and Murieston: Lanthorn Centre, Dedridge,
        NT050663
Livingston: Old, NT037669
    Deans, NT021686
Pardovan, Kingscavil and Winchburgh:
    Pardovan, NT047770
    Kingscavil, NT030764
    Winchburgh, NT087750
Polbeth Harwood, NT017628
Strathbrock, NT060722
    Ecclesmachan, NT059737
Torphichen, NS969725
Uphall: South, NT061718
West Kirk of Calder, NT014629
Whitburn: Brucefield, NS948650
Whitburn: South, NS947646

3. Presbytery of Lothian
Aberlady, NT462799
Athelstaneford, NT533774
Belhaven, NT668787
Bilston, NT262647
Bolton and Saltoun:
    Bolton, NT507701
    Saltoun, NT474678
Bonnyrigg, NT307654
Borthwick, NT359596

Cockenzie and Port Seton: Chalmers Memorial, NT403757
Cockenzie and Port Seton: Old, NT401758
Cockpen and Carrington, NT319642
Cranston, Crichton and Ford, NT386656
Dalkeith: St John's and King's Park, NT330670
Dalkeith: St Nicholas' Buccleuch, NT333674
Dirleton, NT513842
Dunbar, NT682786
Dunglass:
    Cockburnspath, NT772710
    Innerwick, NT721739
    Oldhamstocks, NT738707
Fala and Soutra, NT438609
Garvald and Morham:
    Garvald, NT591709
    Morham, NT557726
Gladsmuir, NT457733
Glencorse, NT247627
Gorebridge, NT343619
Gullane, NT480827
Haddington: St Mary's, NT519736
Haddington: West, NT512739
Howgate, NT248580
Humbie, NT461637
Lasswade, NT305661
Loanhead, NT278654
Longniddry, NT442763
Musselburgh: Northesk, NT340727
Musselburgh: St Andrew's High, NT345727
Musselburgh: St Clement's and St Ninian's, NT360727
    Wallyford, NT368722
Musselburgh: St Michael's Inveresk, NT344721
Newbattle, NT331661:
    Newtongrange, NT334643
    Easthouses, NT348652
Newton, NT315693
North Berwick: Abbey, NT551853
North Berwick: St Andrew Blackadder, NT553853
Ormiston, NT414693
Pencaitland, NT443690
Penicuik: North, NT234603
Penicuik: St Mungo's, NT237599
Penicuik: South, NT236595
Prestonpans: Prestongrange, NT388746
Rosewell, NT288624
Roslin, NT673755
Spott, NT673755
Tranent, NT403734
Traprain, Prestonkirk, NT592778:
    Stenton, NT641753
    Whittingehame, NT603737
Whitekirk and Tyninghame, NT596815
Yester, NT535681

4. Presbytery of Melrose and Peebles
Ashkirk, NT466220
Bowden and Melrose:
    Bowden, NT554301
    Melrose, NT544344
Broughton, Glenholm and Kilbucho, NT111368
Caddonfoot, NT459348
Carlops, NT161559
Channelkirk and Lauder:
    Channelkirk, NT259145
    Lauder, NT531475
Earlston, NT581388
Eddleston, NT244472
Ettrick and Yarrow:
    Ettrick, NT259145
    Yarrow, NT356278
    Kirkhope, NT390244

Galashiels: Old and St Paul's, NT490362
Galashiels: St John's, NT509357
Galashiels: Trinity, NT491363
Innerleithen, Traquair and Walkerburn:
    Innerleithen, NT332369
    Traquair, NT320335
    Walkerburn, NT364373
Kirkurd and Newlands, NT162467
Lyne and Manor:
    Lyne, NT192405
    Manor, NT220380
Maxton and Mertoun:
    Maxton, NT610303
    Mertoun, NT615318
Newtown, NT315693
Peebles: Old, NT246406
Peebles: St Andrew's Leckie, NT253404
St Boswells, NT594310
Selkirk, NT472287
Skirling, NT075390
Stobo and Drumelzier:
    Stobo, NT183377
    Drumelzier, NT135343
Stow: St Mary of Wedale and Heriot:
    Stow: St Mary of Wedale, NT459444
    Heriot, NT390526
Tweedsmuir, NT101245
West Linton: St Andrew's, NT149516

5. Presbytery of Duns
Aytoun and Burnmouth:
    Aytoun, NT927609
    Burnmouth, NT956610
Berwick-upon-Tweed: St Andrew's Wallace Green and
    Lowick, NT999532
Bonkyl and Preston, NT808596
Chirnside, NT869561
Coldingham and St Abb's, NT904659
Coldstream, NT843398
Duns, NT786539
Eccles, NT764413
Edrom: Allanton, NT826558
Eyemouth, NT943640
Fogo and Swinton:
    Fogo, NT773492
    Swinton, NT838477
Foulden and Mordington, NT931558
Gordon: St Michael's, NT645432
Grantshouse and Houndwood and Reston:
    Reston, NT878621
    Grantshouse congregation meets in village hall
Greenlaw, NT712462
Hutton and Fishwick and Paxton:
    Hutton, NT907540
    Fishwick and Paxton, NT934532
Kirk of Lammermuir and Langton and Polwarth:
    Abbey St Bathan's NT758623
    Cranshaws NT758623
    Longformacus NT694573
Ladykirk, NT889477
Legerwood, NT594434
Leitholm, NT791441
Westruther, NT633502
Whitsome, NT861504

6. Presbytery of Jedburgh
Ale and Teviot United:
    Ancrum, NT627246
    Eckford, NT706270
    Crailing, NT682250
    Lilliesleaf, NT539253

Cavers and Kirkton:
  Cavers, NT538159
  Kirkton, NT541140
Hawick: Burnfoot, NT510162
Hawick: St Mary's and Old, NT502143
Hawick: Teviot and Roberton:
  Hawick: Teviot, NT501144
  Roberton, NT432142
Hawick: Trinity, NT505147
Hawick: Wilton, NT504153
Hobkirk and Southdean:
  Hobkirk, NT587109
  Southdean, NT631092
Jedburgh: Old and Trinity, NT651203
Kelso Country Churches:
  Makerstoun, NT669331
  Roxburgh, NT700307
  Smailholm, NT649364
  Stichill, NT711383
Kelso North and Ednam:
  Kelso: North, NT727341
  Ednam, NT737372
Kelso: Old and Sprouston:
  Kelso: Old, NT729339
  Sprouston, NT737372
Linton, Morebattle, Hownam and Yetholm:
  Linton NT773267
  Hoselaw, NT802318
  Morebattle, NT772250
  Hownam, NT778193
  Yetholm, NT826281
Oxnam, NT701190
Ruberslaw:
  Bedrule, NT599179
  Denholm, NT569186
  Minto, NT557201
Teviothead, NT403052

7. Presbytery of Annandale and Eskdale
Annan: Old, NY197666
Annan: St Andrew's, NY193665
Applegarth, Sibbaldbie and Johnstone, NY104843
Brydekirk, NY183705
Canonbie United, NY395763
Dalton, NY114740
Dornock, NY231660
Gretna: Old, Gretna: St Andrew's, Half Morton and
    Kirkpatrick Fleming:
  Gretna: Old, NY319680
  Gretna: St Andrew's, NY317670
  Half Morton and Kirkpatrick Fleming, NY177701
Hightae, NY090793
Hoddam, NY192745
Hutton and Corrie, NY171908
Kirkpatrick Juxta, NT083009
Kirtle-Eaglesfield:
  Kirtle NY237726
  Eaglesfield NY233743
Langholm Eskdalemuir Ewes and Westerkirk:
  Langholm, NY362844
  Eskdalemuir, NY253979
  Ewes, NY369908:
  Westerkirk, NY312903
Liddesdale:
  Castleton, NY482877
  Saughtree, NY562968
Lochmaben, NY084823
Lockerbie: Dryfesdale, NY135818
Middlebie, NY214762
Moffat: St Andrew's, NT075051
St Mungo, NY143771

The Border Kirk, Carlisle, Longtown
Tundergarth, NY175808
Wamphray, NY131965
Waterbeck, NY248777

8. Presbytery of Dumfries and Kirkcudbright
Auchencairn and Rerrick:
  Auchencairn, NX799512:
  Rerrick, NX748474
Balmaclellan and Kells:
  Balmaclellan, NX651791
  Kells, NX632784
Balmaghie, NX722663
Borgue, NX629483:
  Kirkandrews, NX601481
Buittle and Kelton:
  Buittle, NX808599
  Kelton, NX758603
Caerlaverock, Glencaple, NX996688
Carsphairn, NX563932
Castle Douglas, NX697699
Closeburn, NX904923
Colvend, Southwick and Kirkbean:
  Colvend, NX862541
  Southwick, NX906569
  Kirkbean, NX980592
Corsock and Kirkpatrick Durham:
  Corsock, NX762760
  Kirkpatrick Durham, NX786699
Crossmichael and Parton:
  Crossmichael, NX729670
  Parton, NX697699
Cummertrees, NY140664
Dalbeattie, NX831611
Dalry, NX618813
Dumfries: Maxwelltown West, NX967760
Dumfries: North West:
  Holywood, NX955796
Dumfries: Lincluden, NX964773
Dumfries: Lochside, NX958774
Dumfries: St George's, NX971764
Dumfries: St Mary's-Greyfriars, NX975763
Dumfries: St Michael's and South, NX975757
Dumfries: Troqueer, NX974475
Dunscore, NX867843
Durisdeer, NS894038
Gatehouse of Fleet, NX602566
Glencairn and Moniaive:
  Glencairn, NX809904
  Moniaive, NX777910
Irongray, Lochrutton and Terregles:
  Irongray, NX915794
  Terregles, NX931771
Kirkconnel, NS728123
Kirkcudbright, NX683509
Kirkgunzeon, NX866667
Kirkmahoe, NX874815:
  Dalswinton, NX942850
Kirkmichael, Tinwald and Torthorwald:
  Kirkmichael, NY005884
  Tinwald, NY003816
  Torthorwald, NY035783
Lochend and New Abbey, NX965660
Mouswald, NY064727
Penpont, Keir and Tynron, NX849944
Ruthwell, NY101683
Sanquhar: St Bride's, NS779102
Tarff and Twynholm: Twynholm, NX664542
Thornhill, NX883957
Urr, NX817658

9. Presbytery of Wigtown and Stranraer
Ervie Kirkcolm, NX002687
Glasserton and Isle of Whithorn:
 Glasserton, NX421381
 Isle of Whithorn, NX478363
Inch, NX101603
Kirkcowan, NX327610
Kirkinner, NX423514
Kirkmabreck, NX423514
Kirkmaiden, NX139324:
 Drummore, NX135376
Leswalt, NX020638
Mochrum, NX347463
Monigaff, NX410666
New Luce, NX175645
Old Luce, NX197574
Penninghame, NX410654:
 Bargrennan, NX349766
Portpatrick, NX002544
Sorbie, NX468463
Stoneykirk:
 Sandhead NX097500
 Ardwell, NX011467
Stranraer: High Kirk, NX057609
Stranraer: St Ninian's, NX060607
Stranraer: Town Kirk, NX064606
Whithorn: St Ninian's Priory, NX444403
Wigtown, NX436555

10. Presbytery of Ayr
Alloway, NS332180
Annbank, NS407243
Auchinleck, NS552216
Ayr: Auld Kirk of Ayr, NS339219
Ayr: Castlehill, NS347203
Ayr: Newton on Ayr, NS339224
Ayr: St Andrew's, NS338213
Ayr: St Columba, NS337209
Ayr: St James', NS342204
Ayr: St Leonard's, NS338204
Ayr: St Quivox:
 Auchincruive, NS375241
 Dalmilling, NS363229
Ayr: Wallacetown, NS342220
Ballantrae, NX038825:
 Glenapp, NX075746
Barr, NX275941
Catrine, NS528260
Coylton, NS422198
Craigie, NS427323
Crosshill, NS327068
Dailly, NS271016
Dalmellington, NS481061:
 Bellsbank, NS480046
Dalrymple, NS358144
Drongan: The Schaw Kirk, NS441185
Dundonald, NS366343
Fisherton, NS275175
Girvan: North (Old and St Andrew's), NX187982
Girvan: South, NX183977
Kirkmichael, NS345090
Kirkoswald, NS240073
Lugar, NS591213
Mauchline, NS498272
Maybole, worshipping in Maybole Baptist Church,
 NS299099
Monkton and Prestwick: North, NS353263
Muirkirk, NS701278
New Cumnock, NS617135
Ochiltree, NS504212
Old Cumnock: Old, NS568202

Old Cumnock: Trinity, NS567200:
 Netherthird NS578187
Patna: Waterside, NS412106
Prestwick: Kingcase, NS348243
Prestwick: St Nicholas', NS351256
Prestwick: South, NS351259
St Colmon (Arnsheen Barrhill and Colmonell):
 Colmonell NX144857
 Barrhill congregation meets in community centre
Sorn, NS550268
Stair, NS439236
Straiton: St Cuthbert's, NS381049
Symington, NS384314
Tarbolton, NS430272
Troon: Old, NS321309
Troon: Portland, NS323308
Troon: St Meddan's, NS323309

11. Presbytery of Irvine and Kilmarnock
Crosshouse, NS395384
Darvel, NS563375
Dreghorn and Springside, NS352383
Dunlop, NS405494
Fenwick, NS465435
Galston, NS500367
Hurlford, NS454372
Irvine: Fullarton, NS316389
Irvine: Girdle Toll, NS341409
Irvine: Mure, NS319390
Irvine: Old, NS322387
Irvine: Relief Bourtreehill, NS344392
Irvine: St Andrew's, NS325399
Kilmarnock: Grange, NS425379
Kilmarnock: Henderson, NS431380
Kilmarnock: Howard St Andrew's, NS426378
Kilmarnock: Laigh West High, NS428379
Kilmarnock: Old High Kirk, NS430382
Kilmarnock: Riccarton, NS428364
Kilmarnock: St John's Onthank, NS433399
Kilmarnock: St Kentigern's, NS448388
Kilmarnock: St Marnock's, NS427377
Kilmarnock: St Ninian's Bellfield, NS
Kilmarnock: Shortlees, NS428353
Kilmaurs: St Maur's Glencairn, NS415408
Newmilns: Loudoun, NS553373
Stewarton: John Knox, NS421460
Stewarton: St Columba's, NS419457
Ayrshire Mission to the Deaf, Kilmarnock, NS430377

12. Presbytery of Ardrossan
Ardrossan: Barony St John's, NS231420
Ardrossan: Park, NS233412
Beith: High, NS350539
Beith: Trinity, NS351544
Brodick, NS012359
Corrie, NS024437
Cumbrae, NS160550
Dalry: St Margaret's, NS291496
Dalry: Trinity, NS292494
Fairlie, NS209556
Fergushill, NS337430
Kilbirnie: Auld Kirk, NS315536
Kilbirnie: St Columba's, NS314546
Kilmory, NR700449
Kilwinning: Mansefield Trinity, NS290432
Kilwinning: Old, NS303433
Lamlash, NS026309
Largs: Clark Memorial, NS202593
Largs: St Columba's, NS203596
Largs: St John's, NS201593
Lochranza and Pirnmill:

Lochranza, NR937503
Pirnmill, NR873443
Saltcoats: New Trinity, NS246414
Saltcoats: North, NS252423
Saltcoats: St Cuthbert's, NS244418
Shiskine, NR910295
Stevenston: Ardeer, NS269411
Stevenston: High, NS266422
Stevenston: Livingston, NS268416
West Kilbride: Overton, NS203481
West Kilbride: St Andrew's, NS207484
Whiting Bay and Kildonan, NS047273

13. Presbytery of Lanark
Biggar, NT040379
Black Mount, NT101464
Cairngryffe, NS923384
Carluke: Kirkton, NS844503
Carluke: St Andrew's, NS584508
Carluke: St John's, NS847503
Carnwath, NS976465:
    Auchengray NS995540
    Tarbrax NT025549
Carstairs and Carstairs Junction (The United Church):
    Carstairs NS938461
    Carstairs Junction NS954450
Coalburn, NS813354
Crossford, NS827466
Culter, NT027342
Forth: St Paul's, NS942538
Glencaple, NS930234
Kirkfieldbank, NS866438
Kirkmuirhill, NS799429
Lanark: Greyfriars, NS880437
Lanark: St Nicholas', NS881437
Law, NS821527
Lesmahagow: Abbeygreen, NS813402
Lesmahagow: Old, NS814399
Libberton and Quothquan, NS992428
Lowther, NS885148
Symington, NS999352
The Douglas Valley Church:
    Douglas NS835310
    Douglas Water and Rigside NS873347

14. Presbytery of Greenock and Paisley
Barrhead: Arthurlie, NS501588
Barrhead: Bourock, NS499589
Barrhead: South and Levern, NS501588
Bishopton, NS445721
Bridge of Weir: Freeland, NS387656
Bridge of Weir: St Machar's Ranfurly, NS392653
Caldwell, NS435552
Elderslie Kirk, NS441631
Erskine, NS466707
Gourock: Old Gourock and Ashton, NS243725
Gourock: St John's, NS246778
Greenock: Ardgowan, NS271768
Greenock: East End
Greenock: Finnart St Paul's, NS265774
Greenock: Mount Kirk, NS271759
Greenock: Old West Kirk, NS279762
Greenock: St Margaret's, NS255764
Greenock: St Ninian's, NS242765
Greenock: Wellpark Mid Kirk, NS279762
Greenock: Westburn, NS273763
Houston and Killellan, NS410671
Howwood, NS396603
Inchinnan, NS479689
Inverkip, NS207720
Johnstone: High, NS426630

Johnstone: St Andrew's Trinity, NS424626
Johnstone: St Paul's, NS428624
Kilbarchan: East, NS403633
Kilbarchan: West, NS401632
Kilmacolm: Old, NS359670
Kilmacolm: St Columba, NS401632
Langbank, NS380734
Linwood, NS432645
Lochwinnoch, NS353587
Neilston, NS480574
Paisley: Abbey, NS486640
Paisley: Castlehead, NS476636
Paisley: Glenburn, NS473617
Paisley: Laigh Kirk, NS483634
Paisley: Lylesland, NS488626
Paisley: Martyrs', NS474639
Paisley: Oakshaw Trinity, NS480641
Paisley: St Columba Foxbar, NS458622
Paisley: St James', NS477644
Paisley: St Luke's, NS482632
Paisley: St Mark's Oldhall, NS511640
Paisley: St Ninian's Ferguslie, NS464644
Paisley: Sandyford (Thread Street), NS493657
Paisley: Sherwood Greenlaw, NS492642
Paisley: Wallneuk North, NS486643
Port Glasgow: Hamilton Bardrainney, NS337733
Port Glasgow: St Andrew's, NS329745
Port Glasgow: St Martin's, NS306747
Renfrew: North, NS508678
Renfrew: Old, NS509676
Renfrew: Trinity, NS505674
Skelmorlie and Wemyss Bay, NS192681

16. Presbytery of Glasgow
Banton, NS752788
Bishopbriggs: Kenmure, NS604698
Bishopbriggs: Springfield, NS615702
Broom, NS554563
Burnside Blairbeth:
    Burnside NS622601
    Blairbeth NS616603
Busby, NS577563
Cadder, NS616723
Cambuslang: Flemington Hallside, NS663595
Cambuslang Parish, NS646600
Campsie, NS629777
Chryston, NS688702
Eaglesham, NS592518
Fernhill and Cathkin, NS624594
Gartcosh, NS698682
Giffnock: Orchardhill, NS563587
Giffnock: South, NS559593
Giffnock: The Park, NS559593
Glenboig, NS723687
Greenbank, NS574568
Kilsyth: Anderson, NS717782
Kilsyth: Burns and Old, NS716778
Kirkintilloch: Hillhead, NS663730
Kirkintilloch: St Columba's, NS664733
Kirkintilloch: St David's Memorial Park, NS654739
Kirkintilloch: St Mary's, NS654739
Lenzie: Old, NS655720
Lenzie: Union, NS654722
Maxwell Mearns Castle, NS553553
Mearns, NS551556
Milton of Campsie, NS652768
Netherlee, NS557590
Newton Mearns, NS537557
Rutherglen: Old, NS613617
Rutherglen: Stonelaw, NS617612
Rutherglen: West and Wardlawhill, NS609618

Stamperland, NS576581
Stepps, NS657686
Thornliebank, NS546588
Torrance, NS620744
Twechar, NS700753
Williamwood, NS576576
Glasgow: Anderston Kelvingrove, NS577655
Glasgow: Baillieston Mure Memorial, NS673643
Glasgow: Baillieston St Andrew's, NS681639
Glasgow: Balshagray Victoria Park, NS549671
Glasgow: Barlanark Greyfriars, NS667649
Glasgow: Battlefield East, NS586613
Glasgow: Blawarthill, NS522683
Glasgow: Bridgeton St Francis in the East, NS614639
Glasgow: Broomhill, NS549674
Glasgow: Calton Parkhead, NS624638
Glasgow: Cardonald, NS526639
Glasgow: Carmunnock, NS599575
Glasgow: Carmyle, NS649618
Glasgow: Carnwadric, NS544599
Glasgow: Castlemilk East, NS607597
Glasgow: Castlemilk West, NS596594
Glasgow: Cathcart Old, NS587606
Glasgow: Cathcart Trinity, NS582604
Glasgow: Cathedral (High or St Mungo's), NS603656
Glasgow: Colston Milton, NS592697
Glasgow: Colston Wellpark, NS606692
Glasgow: Cranhill, NS643658
Glasgow: Croftfoot, NS603602
Glasgow: Dennistoun New, NS613652
Glasgow: Drumchapel Drumry St Mary's, NS515709
Glasgow: Drumchapel St Andrew's, NS523707
Glasgow: Drumchapel St Mark's, NS522709
Glasgow: Easterhouse St George's and St Peter's, NS678657
Glasgow: Eastwood, NS558607
Glasgow: Gairbraid, NS568688
Glasgow: Gardner Street, NS558667
Glasgow: Garthamlock and Craigend East, NS658667
Glasgow: Gorbals, NS587641
Glasgow: Govan and Linthouse, NS555658
Glasgow: Govanhill Trinity, NS587627
Glasgow: High Carntyne, NS636653
Glasgow: Hillington Park, NS534659
Glasgow: Househillwood St Christopher's, NS534616
Glasgow: Hyndland, NS559675
Glasgow: Ibrox, NS560642
Glasgow: John Ross Memorial Church for Deaf People, NS588644
Glasgow: Jordanhill, NS544682
Glasgow: Kelvin Stevenson Memorial, NS576673
Glasgow: Kelvinside Hillhead, NS567673
Glasgow: Kenmuir Mount Vernon, NS655626
Glasgow: King's Park, NS601608
Glasgow: Kinning Park, NS568644
Glasgow: Knightswood St Margaret's, NS536694
Glasgow: Langside, NS582614
Glasgow: Lansdowne, NS576669
Glasgow: Lochwood, NS685663
Glasgow: Martyrs', The, NS597657
Glasgow: Maryhill, NS653695
Glasgow: Merrylea, NS575603
Glasgow: Mosspark, NS544633
Glasgow: Mount Florida, NS587614
Glasgow: Newlands South, NS573611
Glasgow: North Kelvinside, NS573682
Glasgow: Partick South, NS559665
Glasgow: Partick Trinity, NS563668
Glasgow: Penilee St Andrew's, NS518647
Glasgow: Pollokshaws, NS561612
Glasgow: Pollokshields, NS569615
Glasgow: Possilpark, NS592677

Glasgow: Priesthill and Nitshill:
  Priesthill, NS531607
  Nitshill, NS522603
Glasgow: Queen's Park, NS579625
Glasgow: Renfield St Stephen's, NS582659
Glasgow: Robroyston, NS638688
Glasgow: Ruchazie, NS643662
Glasgow: Ruchill, NS573683
Glasgow: St Andrew's East, NS619656
Glasgow: St Columba, NS583657
Glasgow: St David's Knightswood, NS528689
Glasgow: St Enoch's Hogganfield, NS629660
Glasgow: St George's Tron, NS590655
Glasgow: St James' (Pollok), NS530626
Glasgow: St John's Renfield, NS558683
Glasgow: St Luke's and St Andrew's, NS602646
Glasgow: St Margaret's Tollcross Park, NS637631
Glasgow: St Nicholas' Cardonald, NS524646
Glasgow: St Paul's, NS631671
Glasgow: St Rollox, NS630668
Glasgow: St Thomas' Gallowgate, NS614646
Glasgow: Sandyford Henderson Memorial, NS570659
Glasgow: Sandyhills, NS658638
Glasgow: Scotstoun, NS533676
Glasgow: Shawlands, NS572621
Glasgow: Sherbrooke St Gilbert's, NS561636
Glasgow: Shettleston New, NS647642
Glasgow: Shettleston Old, NS649639
Glasgow: South Carntyne, NS630652
Glasgow: South Shawlands, NS569615
Glasgow: Springburn, NS607677
Glasgow: Temple Anniesland, NS547699
Glasgow: Toryglen, NS602615
Glasgow: Trinity Possil and Henry Drummond, NS593687
Glasgow: Tron St Mary's, NS618676
Glasgow: Victoria Tollcross, NS637631
Glasgow: Wellington, NS570667
Glasgow: Whiteinch, NS540668
Glasgow: Yoker, NS511689

17. Presbytery of Hamilton
Airdrie: Broomknoll, NS761653
Airdrie: Clarkston, NS783661
Airdrie: Flowerhill, NS765655
Airdrie: High, NS760658
Airdrie: Jackson, NS782647
Airdrie: New Monkland, NS753678
Airdrie: St Columba's, NS766665
Airdrie: The New Wellwynd, NS759644
Bargeddie, NS692648
Bellshill: Macdonald Memorial, NS738602
Bellshill: Orbiston, NS729593
Bellshill: West, NS727603
Blantyre: Livingstone Memorial, NS687577
Blantyre: Old, NS679565
Blantyre: St Andrew's, NS699562
Bothwell, NS705586
Calderbank, NS770631
Caldercruix and Longriggend, NS819677
Carfin, NS772584
Chapelhall, NS783627
Chapelton, NS685485
Cleland, NS797581
Coatbridge: Blairhill Dundyvan, NS726650
Coatbridge: Calder, NS738639
Coatbridge: Clifton, NS737652
Coatbridge: Middle, NS723646
Coatbridge: Old Monkland, NS718633
Coatbridge: St Andrew's, NS733653
Coatbridge: Townhead, NS718664

Dalserf, NS800507:
  Ashgill, NS783503
East Kilbride: Claremont, NS653543
East Kilbride: Greenhills, NS616525
East Kilbride: Moncreiff, NS647555
East Kilbride: Mossneuk, NS607532
East Kilbride: Old, NS635545
East Kilbride: South, NS633537
East Kilbride: Stewartfield, meets in a community centre at
  NS643561
East Kilbride: West, NS634547
East Kilbride: Westwood, NS618537
Glasford, NS726470
Greengairs, NS783705
Hamilton: Burnbank, NS699562
Hamilton: Cadzow, NS723550
Hamilton: Gilmour and Whitehill, NS704563:
  Whitehill, NS706568
Hamilton: Hillhouse, NS696554
Hamilton: North, NS719558
Hamilton: Old, NS723555
Hamilton: St Andrew's, NS723551
Hamilton: St John's, NS724523
Hamilton: South, NS717558
Hamilton: Trinity, NS711543
Hamilton: West, NS712558
Holytown, NS713608
Kirk o' Shotts, NS843629
Larkhall: Chalmers, NS763499
Larkhall: St Machan's, NS763511
Larkhall: Trinity, NS762513
Motherwell: Crosshill, NS756566
Motherwell: Dalziel St Andrew's, NS752571
Motherwell: North, NS741577
Motherwell: St Margaret's, NS769549
Motherwell: St Mary's, NS750566
Motherwell: South, NS757560
Newarthill, NS781597
Newmains: Bonkle, NS837571
Newmains: Coltness Memorial, NS819557
New Stevenston: Wrangholm Kirk, NS760596
Overtown, NS801527
Quarter, NS722512
Shotts: Calderhead Erskine, NS877600
Stonehouse: St Ninian's, NS752467
Strathaven: Avendale Old and Drumclog: Avendale Old,
  NS701443:
  Drumclog, NS640389
Strathaven: East, NS702446
Strathaven: Rankin, NS701406
Strathaven: West, 700444
Uddingston: Burnhead, NS717614
Uddingston: Old, NS696603
Uddingston: Viewpark, NS702616
Wishaw: Cambusnethan North, NS808554
Wishaw: Cambusnethan Old, NS806553
Wishaw: Craigneuk and Belhaven, NS773561
Wishaw: Old, NS796552
Wishaw: St Mark's, NS801566
Wishaw: South Wishaw, NS797548

18. Presbytery of Dumbarton
Alexandria, NS389798
Arrochar, NM296037
Baldernock, NS577751
Bearsden: Baljaffray, NS534732
Bearsden: Cross, NS427721
Bearsden: Killermont, NS557713
Bearsden: New Kilpatrick, NS543723
Bearsden: Westerton Fairlie Memorial, NS543706
Bonhill, NS395796

Cardross, NS345775
Clydebank: Abbotsford, NS498703
Clydebank: Faifley, NS502732
Clydebank: Kilbowie St Andrew's, NS497702
Clydebank: Radnor Park, NS495713
Clydebank: St Cuthbert's, NS511704
Craigrownie, NS225808
Dalmuir: Barclay, NS479715
Dumbarton: Riverside, NS398752
Dumbarton: St Andrew's, NS407764
Dumbarton: West Kirk, NS390750
Duntocher, NS494727
Garelochhead, NS239912
Helensburgh: Park, NS300823
Helensburgh: St Columba, NS297825
Helensburgh: The West Kirk, NS295825
Jamestown, NS397813
Kilmaronock and Gartocharn:
  Kilmaronock, NS452875
  Gartocharn, NS428864
Luss, NS361929
Milngavie: Cairns, NS556748
Milngavie: St Luke's, NS543747
Milngavie: St Paul's, NS557745
Old Kilpatrick Bowling, NS463731
Renton: Trinity, NS390780
Rhu and Shandon, NS267841
Rosneath: St Modan's, NS255832

19. Presbytery of Argyll
Appin, NM938459
Ardchattan, NM944360
Ardrishaig, NR854852
Campbeltown: Highland, NR720201
Campbeltown: Lorne and Lowland, NR718206
Coll, NM223573
Colonsay and Oronsay, NR890941
Connel, NM914343
Craignish, NM805042
Cumlodden, Lochfyneside and Lochgair:
  Cumlodden, NS014994
  Lochfyneside, NR979962
  Lochgair, NR922905
Dunoon: St John's, NS172769
Dunoon: The High Kirk, NS173769
Gigha and Cara, NR643481
Glassary, Kilmartin and Ford:
  Glassary, NR834988
  Kilmartin, NR836993
  Ford, NM869037
Glenaray and Inveraray, NN095085
Glenorchy and Innishael, NN168275
Innellan, NS151707
Iona, NM285243
Jura, NR527677
Kilarrow, NR312596
Kilberry, NR741620
Kilbrandon and Kilchattan:
  Kilbrandon, NM758155
  Kilchattan, NM743014
Kilcalmonell, NR763561
Kilchoman, NR255588
Kilchrenan and Dalavich:
  Kilchrenan, NN037229
  Dalavich, NM968124
Kildalton and Oa, NR257594
Kilfinan, NR934789
Kilfinichen and Kilvickeon and the Ross of Mull
  Kilfinichen and Kilvickeon, NM383218
  The Ross of Mull, NM316232
Killean and Kilchenzie, NR681418

Kilmeny, NR353636
Kilmodan and Colintraive:
  Kilmodan, NR995842
  Colintraive, NS045735
Kilmore and Oban:
  Kilmore, NM862295
  Oban, Old NM861296
  Corran Esplanade, NM956306
Kilmun (St Munn's), NS166821
Kilninver and Kilmelford:
  Kilninver, NM825217
  Kilmelford, NM849130
Kirn, NS184783
Kyles, Kames and Kilbride, NR973713:
  Tighnabruaich, NR980730
Lismore, NM861435
Lochgilphead, NR863882
Lochgoilhead and Kilmorich:
  Lochgoilhead, NN198015
  Kilmorich, NN181108
Muckairn, NN005310
Mull, Isle of, Kilninian and Kilmore, NM432517
North Knapdale, Kilmichael Inverlussa, NR776859:
  Bellanoch, NR797923
Portnahaven, NR168523
Rothesay: Trinity, NS089645
Saddell and Carradale, NR796376
Salen and Ulva, Salen, NM573431
Sandbank, NS163803
Skipness, NR899577
South Knapdale, NR781775
Southend, NR698094
Strachur and Strathlachlan:
  Strachur, NN096014
  Strathlachlan, NS022958
Strathfillan, Crianlarich, NN387252:
  Bridge of Orchy, NN297395
Strone and Ardentinny:
  Strone, NS193806
  Ardentinny, NS188876
Tarbert, NR863686
The United Church of Bute, NS086637
Tiree:
  Heylipol, NM964432
  Kirkapol, NM041468
Tobermory, NM504554
Torosay and Kinlochspelvie, NM721367
Toward, NS135679:
  Inverchaolain, NS091753

22. Presbytery of Falkirk
Airth, NS898878
Blackbraes and Shieldhill, NS899769
Bo'ness: Old, NS994813
Bo'ness: St Andrew's, NT007813
Bonnybridge: St Helen's, NS821804
Bothkennar and Carronshore, NS703834
Brightons, NS928778
Carriden, NT019812
Cumbernauld: Abronhill, NS781748
Cumbernauld: Condorrat, NS732730
Cumbernauld: Kildrum, NS767747
Cumbernauld: Old, NS764760
Cumbernauld: St Mungo's, NS757745
Denny: Dunipace, NS807833
Denny: Old, NS812828
Denny: Westpark, NS809828
Falkirk: Bainsford, NS887814
Falkirk: Camelon, NS873804
Falkirk: Erskine, NS884798
Falkirk: Grahamston United, NS889807

Falkirk: Laurieston, NS913794
Falkirk: Old and St Modan's, NS887800
Falkirk: St Andrew's West, NS887801
Falkirk: St James', NS893806
Grangemouth: Abbotsgrange, NS927821
Grangemouth: Kirk of the Holy Rood, NS931805
Grangemouth: Zetland, NS931818
Haggs, NS791789
Larbert: East, NS871829
Larbert: Old, NS856822
Larbert: West, NS863827
Muiravonside, NS956770
Polmont: Old, NS937793
Redding and Westquarter, NS921786
Slamannan, NS856730
Stenhouse and Carron, NS876831

23. Presbytery of Stirling
Aberfoyle, NN518005
Alloa: North, NS883932
Alloa: St Mungo's, NS886929
Alloa: West, NS884927
Alva, NS882970
Balfron, NS547893
Balquhidder, NN536209
Bannockburn: Allan, NS810903
Bannockburn: Ladywell, NS803907
Bridge of Allan, NS791974
Buchanan, NS443903
Buchlyvie, NS577939
Callander, NN629077
Cambusbarron: The Bruce Memorial, NS778924
Clackmannan, NS910918
Cowie and Plean:
  Cowie, NS837892
  Plean, NS836867
Dollar, NS964980
Drymen, NS474881
Dunblane: Cathedral, NN782014
Dunblane: St Blane's, NN783014
Fallin, NS844913
Fintry, NS627862
Gargunnock, NS707943
Gartmore, NS521971
Glendevon, NN979051
Killearn, NS523861
Killin and Ardeonaig, NN571330:
  Morenish, NO607356
Kincardine-in-Menteith, NS719988
Kippen, NS652849
Lecropt, NS781979
Logie, NS829968
Menstrie, NS849969
Muckhart, NO001010
Norrieston, NN670001
Port of Menteith, NS583011
Sauchie and Coalsnaughton, Sauchie, NS879945
Stirling: Allan Park South, NS755933
Stirling: Church of the Holy Rude, NS792937
Stirling: North, NS802920
Stirling: St Columba's, NS796930
Stirling: St Mark's, NS791948
Stirling: St Ninian's Old, NS795936
Stirling: Viewfield, NS795938
Strathblane, NS557797
Tillicoultry, NS923968
Tullibody: St Serf's, NS860954

24. Presbytery of Dunfermline
Aberdour: St Fillan's, NT193855
Beath and Cowdenbeath: North:

Beath NT153922
Cowdenbeath North, NT166925
Mossgreen and Crossgates, NT192903
Cairneyhill, NO052863
Carnock and Oakley:
  Carnock, NT043890
  Oakley, NT025890
Cowdenbeath: Trinity:
  Cowdenbeath, NT157908
  Crossgates, NT145893
Culross and Torryburn:
  Culross, NS989863
  Torryburn, NT027861
  Valleyfield, NT003866
Dalgety, NT155836
Dunfermline: Abbey, NT155836
Dunfermline: Gillespie Memorial, NT090876
Dunfermline: North, NT086879
Dunfermline: St Andrew's Erskine, NT107884
Dunfermline: St Leonard's, NT096869
Dunfermline: St Margaret's, NT114878
Dunfermline: St Ninian's, NT113868
Dunfermline: St Paul's East
Dunfermline: Townhill and Kingseat, NT098885
Inverkeithing, NT131830
Kelty, NT144942
Limekilns, NT078833
Lochgelly and Benarty: St Serf's:
  Lochgelly, NT186933
  Benarty: St Serf's, NT193777
North Queensferry, NT132808
Rosyth, NT113842
Saline and Blairingone, NT023924
Tulliallan and Kincardine, NS933879

25. Presbytery of Kirkcaldy
Auchterderran: St Fothad's, NT214960, Cardenden,
Auchtertool, NT207902
Buckhaven, NT358981
Burntisland, NT234857
Dysart, NT302931
Glenrothes: Christ's Kirk, NO275023
Glenrothes: St Columba's, NO270009
Glenrothes: St Margaret's, NO285002
Glenrothes: St Ninian's, NO257007
Innerleven: East, NO372003
Kennoway, Windygates and Balgonie: St Kenneth's:
  Kennoway, NO350023
  Windygates, NO348006
  Balgonie: St Kenneth's, NO328007
Kinghorn, NT272869
Kinglassie, NT227985
Kirkcaldy: Abbotshall, NT274913
Kirkcaldy: Linktown, NT278910
Kirkcaldy: Pathhead, NT291928
Kirkcaldy: St Andrew's, NT278919
Kirkcaldy: St Bryce Kirk, NT280917 and NT279917
Kirkcaldy: St John's, NT289727
Kirkcaldy: Templehall, NT265934
Kirkcaldy: Torbain, NT259939
Kirkcaldy: Viewforth, NT294936
Leslie: Trinity, NO247015
Leven, NO383017
Markinch, NO297019
Methil, NO370994
Methilhill and Denbeath, NT357999
Thornton, NT289976
Wemyss and West Wemyss:
  Wemyss, NT340968
  West Wemyss, NT328949

26. Presbytery of St Andrews
Abdie and Dunbog:
  Abdie, NO257167
  Dunbog, NO288180
Anstruther, NO567037
Auchtermuchty, NO238117
Balmerino, NO368245:
  (Gauldry, NO379239)
Boarhills and Dunino
  Boarhills, NO562137
  Dunino NO541109
Cameron, NO484116
Carnbee, NO532065
Cellardyke, NO574037
Ceres, Kemback and Springfield:
  Ceres, NO399117
  Kemback, NO419151
  Springfield, NO342119
Crail, NO613080
Creich, Flisk and Kilmany
  Creich, NO328200
  Kilmany, NO388217
Cupar: Old and St Michael of Tarvit, NO380146
Cupar: St John's, NO373147
Dairsie, NO413173
Edenshead and Strathmiglo, Strathmiglo, NO217103
Elie, NO491001
Falkland, NO252074
Freuchie, NO283067
Howe of Fife:
  Ballingry, NT173977
  Collessie, NO287133
  Cults, NO347099
  Kettle, NO310083
  Ladybank, NO302102
Kilconquhar and Colinsburgh
  Kilconquhar, NO485020
  Colinsburgh, NO475034
Kilrenny, NO575049
Kingsbarns, NO593121
Largo and Newburn, NO423035
  Largo: St David's, NO419026
Largoward, NO469077
Leuchars: St Athernase, NO455214
Monimail, NO303142
Newburgh, NO234183
Newport-on-Tay, NO422280
Pittenweem, NO549026
St Andrews: Holy Trinity, NO509167
St Andrews: Hope Park, NO505167
St Andrews: Martyrs', NO510168
St Andrews: St Leonard's, NO502164
St Monans, NO523014
Strathkinness, NO460163
Tayport, NO458286
Wormit, NO403267

27. Presbytery of Dunkeld and Meigle
Aberfeldy, NN854491
Alyth, NO243488
Amulree and Strathbraan, NN899366
Ardler, Kettins and Meigle:
  Ardler, NO265419
  Kettins, NO283390
  Meigle, NO287446
Bendochy, NO218415
Blair Atholl, NN874654:
  Struan, NN808654
Blairgowrie, NO177454
Braes of Rannoch, NN507566
Caputh and Clunie, NO088401

Coupar Angus: Abbey, NO223398
Dull and Weem, NN844497
Dunkeld: Cathedral, NO024426:
  Little Dunkeld, NO028423
  Dowally, NO001480
Fortingall and Glenlyon:
  Fortingall, NN742471
  Glenlyon, NN588475
Foss and Rannoch:
  Foss, NN790561
  Rannoch, NN663585
Grantully, Logierait and Strathtay:
  Logierait, NN967520
  Strathtay, NN908532
Kenmore and Lawers, NN772454
Kinclaven, NO151385
Kirkmichael, Straloch and Glenshee
  Kirkmichael, NO181601
  Glenshee, NO109702
  Netherton Bridge, NO143552
Pitlochry, NO942581
Rattray, NO190457
Tenandry, NN911615

28. Presbytery of Perth
Abernethy and Dron and Arngask
  Abernethy, NO190164
  Arngask (Glenfarg), NO133104
Almondbank and Tibbermore, NO065264
Ardoch, NO839098
Auchterarder, NN948129
Auchtergaven and Moneydie, new church being built
Blackford, NN899092
Cargill Burrelton, NO202377
Cleish, NT095981
Collace, NO197320
Comrie, NN770221
Crieff, NN867219
Dunbarney and Forgandenny
  Dunbarney, NO130185
  Forgandenny, NO087183
Dundurn, NN697241
Errol, NO253230
Fossoway: St Serf's and Devonside, NO033001
Fowlis Wester, Madderty and Monzie:
  Fowlis Wester, NN928241
  Madderty, NN947217
  Monzie, NN879250
Gask, NO003203
Kilspindie and Rait, NO220258
Kinross, NO118023
Methven and Logiealmond, Methven, NO026260
Muthill, NN868171
Orwell and Portmoak:
  Orwell, NO121051
  Portmoak, NO183019
Perth: Craigie, NO116237
Perth: Kinnoull, NO118233
Perth: Letham St Mark's, NO095243
Perth: Moncreiffe, NO113218
Perth: North, NO116237
Perth: Riverside, NO110256
Perth: St John the Baptist's, NO119235
Perth: St Leonard's-in-the-Fields and Trinity, NO117232
Perth: St Matthew's, NO112231
Redgorton and Stanley, NO108330
St Madoes and Kinfauns, NO167223
St Martin's, NO154304
Scone: New, NO136262
Scone: Old, NO134256
The Stewartry of Strathearn

Aberdalgie and Dupplin, NO064194
Aberuthven, NN979155
Forteviot, NO050174
Dunning, NO019145
Trinity Gask and Kinkell, NN963183

29. Presbytery of Dundee
Abernyte, NO267311
Auchterhouse, NO342381
Dundee: Balgay, NO038309
Dundee: Barnhill St Margaret's, NO478316
Dundee: Broughty Ferry New Kirk, NO464309
Dundee: Broughty Ferry St James', NO460307
Dundee: Broughty Ferry St Luke's and Queen Street, NO457312
Dundee: Broughty Ferry St Stephen's and West, NO458309
Dundee: Camperdown, NO363320
Dundee: Chalmers Ardler, NO377333
Dundee: Clepington and Fairmuir
  Clepington, NO403316
  Fairmuir, NO397323
Dundee: Craigiebank, NO429315
Dundee: Douglas and Mid Craigie
  Douglas and Angus, NO444332
  Mid Craigie, NO428321
Dundee: Downfield South, NO389336
Dundee: Dundee St Mary's, NO401301
Dundee: Fintry, NO423334
Dundee: Lochee, NO377318
Dundee: Logie and St John's Cross, NO386299
Dundee: Mains, NO403337
Dundee: Meadowside St Paul's, NO402300
Dundee: Menzieshill, NO363309
Dundee: St Andrew's, NO404307
Dundee: St David's High Kirk:
  St David's North NO391318
  High Kirk, NO394313
Dundee: Steeple, NO402301
Dundee: Stobswell, NO411315
Dundee: Strathmartine, NO384343
Dundee: Trinity, NO410310
Dundee: West, NO395297
Dundee: Whitfield, NO435334
Fowlis and Liff
  Fowlis, NO322334
  Liff, NO333328
Inchture and Kinnaird:
  Inchture, NO281288
  Kinnaird, NO243287
Invergowrie, NO346304
Longforgan, NO309300
Lundie and Muirhead of Liff:
  Lundie, NO291366
  Muirhead of Liff, NO342345
Monifieth: Panmure, NO638414
Monifieth: St Rule's, NO495323
Monifieth: South, NO493324
Monikie and Newbigging:
  Monikie, NO518388
  Newbigging, NO498362
Murroes and Tealing, NO461351

30. Presbytery of Angus
Aberlemno, NO523555
Arbirlot, NO602406
Arbroath: Knox's, NO638414
Arbroath: Old and Abbey, NO644413
Arbroath: St Andrew's, NO643414
Arbroath: St Vigean's, NO583446
Arbroath: West Kirk
Barry, NO541346

Brechin: Cathedral, NO595601:
  Stracathro, NO617657
Brechin: Gardner Memorial, NO601602
Carmyllie, NO549426
Carnoustie, NO559546
Carnoustie: Panbride, NO572358
  Panbride NO570347
Collieston, NO604453
Dun and Hillside:
  Dun, NO664600
  Hillside, NO709609
Dunnichen, Letham and Kirkden:
  Dunnichen, NO510488
  Letham, NO528488
Eassie and Nevay, NO353474
Edzell Lethnot Glenesk:
  Edzell Lethnot NO599688
  Glenesk, NO497795
Farnell, NO627554
Fern Careston Menmuir:
  Fern, NO484616
  Careston, NO528603
  Menmuir, NO534643
Forfar: East and Old, NO457506
Forfar: Lowson Memorial, NO465509
Forfar: St Margaret's, NO454505
Friockheim Kinnell:
  Friockheim, NO592497
  Kinnell, NO609503
Glamis, Inverarity and Kinnettles:
  Glamis, NO386469
  Inverarity, NO460440
Guthrie and Rescobie:
  Guthrie, NO568505
  Rescobie, NO509521
Inchbrayock, NO714567
Inverkeilor and Lunan:
  Inverkeilor, NO664496
  Lunan, NO687516
Kirriemuir: St Andrew's, NO386535
Montrose: Melville South, NO713575
Montrose: Old and St Andrew's, NO715778
Newtyle, NO296413
Oathlaw and Tannadice:
  Oathlaw, NO476562
  Tannadice, NO475581
The Glens and Kirriemuir Old:
  Kirriemuir Old, NO386539
  Clova, NO327730
  Cortachy, NO396507
  Glen Prosen, NO328657
  Memus, NO427590
The Isla Parishes:
  Airlie, NO313515
  Glenisla, NO215604
  Kilry, NO246538
  Lintrathen, NO286546
  Ruthven, NO286489

31. Presbytery of Aberdeen
Aberdeen: Bridge of Don Oldmachar, NJ935104
Aberdeen: Cove
Aberdeen: Craigiebuckler, NJ907053
Aberdeen: Ferryhill, NJ939054
Aberdeen: Garthdee, NJ918034
Aberdeen: Gilcomston South, NJ935058
Aberdeen: High Hilton, NJ923078
Aberdeen: Holburn West, NJ926052
Aberdeen: Mannofield, NJ917045
Aberdeen: Mastrick, NJ902073
Aberdeen: Middlefield, NJ911088

Aberdeen: Midstocket, NJ919066
Aberdeen: New Stockethill, meets in community centre
Aberdeen: Northfield, NJ905083
Aberdeen: Queen Street, NJ943064
Aberdeen: Queen's Cross, NJ925058
Aberdeen: Rubislaw, NJ924058
Aberdeen: Ruthrieston West, NJ924042
Aberdeen: St Columba's Bridge of Don, NJ935104
Aberdeen: St George's Tillydrone, NJ931090
Aberdeen: St John's Church for Deaf People, NJ923087
Aberdeen: St Machar's Cathedral, NJ939008
Aberdeen: St Mark's, NJ937063
Aberdeen: St Mary's, NJ943081
Aberdeen: St Nicholas Kincorth, South of, NJ934033
Aberdeen: St Nicholas Uniting, Kirk of, NJ941063
Aberdeen: St Stephen's, NJ936074
Aberdeen: South Holburn, NJ930042
Aberdeen: Summerhill, NJ904063
Aberdeen: Torry St Fittick's, NJ947050
Aberdeen: Woodside, NJ924088
Bucksburn Stoneywood, NJ897096
Cults:
  Cults East, NJ890028
  Cults West NJ886026
Dyce, NJ887130
Kingswells, NJ869063
Newhills, NJ876095
Peterculter, NO594996

32. Presbytery of Kincardine and Deeside
Aberluthnott, NO687656:
  Luthermuir, NO655685
Aboyne, NO520985
  Dinnet, NO459986
Arbuthnott, NO801746
  Bervie, NO830727
Banchory-Devenick and Maryculter/Cookney:
  Banchory-Devenick, NK907024
  Maryculter/Cookney, NO857993
Banchory-Ternan: East, NO707958
Banchory-Ternan: West, NO693957
Birse and Feughside, NO625925
Braemar and Crathie:
  Braemar, NO150913
  Crathie, NO265949
Cromar, Coldstone, NJ436043:
  Coull, NJ512024
  Tarland, NJ485047
Drumoak-Durris:
  Drumoak, NO792993
  Durris, NO772965
Glenmuick (Ballater), NO369957
Kinneff, NO843763
Laurencekirk, NO718717
Mearns Coastal:
  Johnshaven, NO798672
  St Cyrus, NO750648
Mid Deeside:
  Kincardine O'Neil, NO594997
  Lumphanan, NJ580038
  Torphins, NJ626021
Newtonhill, NO911934
Portlethen, NO924966
Stonehaven: Dunnottar, NO863853
Stonehaven: Fetteresso, NO869864
Stonehaven South, NO872857
West Mearns:
  Fettercairn, NO651735
  Fordoun, NO726784
  Glenbervie, NO766807

33. Presbytery of Gordon
Barthol Chapel, NJ814339
Belhelvie, NJ957184
Blairdaff and Chapel of Garioch:
  Blairdaff, NJ704173
  Chapel of Garioch, NJ716242
Cluny, NJ685124
Culsalmond and Rayne
  Culsalmond, NJ648327
  Rayne, NJ698302
Cushnie and Tough:
  Cushnie, NJ530108
  Tough, NJ616129
Daviot, NJ750283
Drumblade, NJ588402
Echt, NJ739057
Ellon, NJ959304:
  Slains, NK042290
Fintray Kinellar Keithhall:
  Fintray, NJ841166
  Kinellar, NJ822145
  Keithhall, NJ803210
Foveran, NJ985241:
  Holyrood Chapel, NJ999253
Howe Trinity, NJ577151, Keig
Huntly Cairnie Glass:
  Huntly, NJ539398
  Cairnie, NJ490446
Huntly Strathbogie, NJ531399
Insch-Leslie-Premnay-Oyne, Insch, NJ631283
Inverurie: St Andrew's, NJ777211
Inverurie: West, NJ774215
Kemnay, NJ737162
Kintore, NJ793163
Meldrum and Bourtie
  Meldrum, NJ813273
  Bourtie, NJ804248
Methlick, NJ858372
Midmar, NJ699065
Monymusk, NJ684152
New Machar, NJ887194
Noth, Rhynie, NJ497272:
  Lumsden, NJ475220
  Kennethmont, NJ545288
Skene, NJ803077:
  Westhill, NJ833072
Tarves, NJ868312
Udny and Pitmedden:
  Udny, NJ880264
  Pitmedden, NJ893274
Upper Donside:
  Strathdon, NJ355127
  Towie, NJ440129
  Kildrummy, NJ473176

34. Presbytery of Buchan
Auchaber United, NJ632411:
  Forgue, NJ611451
Auchterless, NJ713415
Banff, NJ689638
Crimond, NK054568
Cruden, NK071366:
  Hatton, NK048377
Deer, NJ979477:
  Fetterangus, NJ987508
Fordyce, NJ554637:
  Portsoy, NJ587659
Fraserburgh: Old, NJ998671
Fraserburgh: South, NJ998666
Fraserburgh: West, NJ994667
Fyvie, NJ768377

Gardenstown, NJ801648
Inverallochy and Rathen: East:
  Inverallochy, NK054651
  Rathen: East, NK033623
King Edward, NJ716579
Longside, NK037473
Lonmay, NK038602
Macduff, NJ701643
Marnoch, NJ628527
Maud and Savoch, NJ927478
Monquhitter and New Byth:
  Monquhitter, NJ803506
  New Byth, NJ822538
New Deer: St Kane's, NJ886469
New Pitsligo, NJ880562
Ordiquhill and Cornhill:
  Ordiquhill, NJ565555
  Cornhill, NJ587583
Peterhead: Old, NK131462
Peterhead: St Andrew's, NK131465
Peterhead: Trinity, NK132463
Pitsligo, NJ929673
Rathen: West, NK000609
Rothienorman, NJ723357
St Fergus, NK093519
Sandhaven, NJ963675
Strichen and Tyrie:
  Strichen, NJ945554
  Tyrie, NJ930631
Turriff: St Andrew's, NJ729497
Turriff: St Ninian's and Forglen, NJ723500
Whitehills, NJ655653:
  Boyndie, NH642639

35. Presbytery of Moray
Aberlour, NJ264428
Alves and Burghead:
  Alves, NJ125616
  Burghead, NJ114688
Bellie, NJ345588
Birnie and Pluscarden:
  Birnie, NJ207587
  Pluscarden, NJ149573
Buckie: North, NJ417657
Buckie: South and West, NJ426654
Cullen and Deskford, NJ507664
Dallas, NJ122518
Duffus, Spynie and Hopeman:
  Duffus, NJ168687
  Spynie, NJ183642
  Hopeman, NJ144693
Dyke, NH990584
Edinkillie, NJ020466
Elgin: High, NJ215627
Elgin: St Giles' and St Columba's South:
  St Giles', NJ217628
  St Columba's South, NJ219623
Enzie, NJ397618
Findochty, NJ464682
Forres: St Laurence, NJ035588
Forres: St Leonard's, NJ035588
Keith: North, Newmill, Boharm and Rothiemay:
  Keith: North, NJ433507
  Newmill, NJ429527
  Boharm Rothiemay, NJ547483
Keith: St Rufus, Botriphnie and Grange:
  Keith: St Rufus, NJ430518
  Botriphnie, NJ375441
  Grange, NJ481515
Kinloss and Findhorn:
  Kinloss, NJ063617

Findhorn, NJ042642
Knockando, Elchies and Archiestown, NJ186429
Lossiemouth: St Gerardine's High, NJ233706
Lossiemouth: St James', NJ235707
Mortlach and Cabrach:
  Mortlach, NJ387268
  Cabrach, NJ387268
  Lower Cabrach, NJ382413
Portknockie, NJ488684
Rafford, NJ061564
Rathven, NJ444657
Rothes, NJ278492
St Andrew's-Lhanbryd and Urquhart, NJ256622
Speymouth, NJ337607

36. Presbytery of Abernethy

Abernethy, NJ007218:
  Nethy Bridge, NJ003203
Alvie, NH864093:
  Insh, NH837053
Boat of Garten and Kincardine:
  Boat of Garten, NH941190
  Kincardine, NH938155
Cromdale and Advie:
  Cromdale, NJ067289
  Advie, NJ127343
Dulnain Bridge, NH998249
Duthil, NH908225
Grantown-on-Spey, NJ032281
Kingussie, NH761007
Laggan, NN615943
Newtonmore, NN615993
Rothiemurchus and Aviemore:
  Rothiemurchus, NH903108
  Aviemore, NH896130
Tomintoul, Glenlivet and Inveraven:
  Tomintoul, NJ169185
  Inveraven, NJ183576

37. Presbytery of Inverness

Ardersier, NH781553
Auldearn and Dalmore, NH919556
Cawdor, NH844499
Croy and Dalcross, NH797498
Culloden: The Barn, NH719461
Daviot and Dunlichity:
  Daviot, NH722394
  Dunlichity, NH659327
Dores and Boleskine:
  Dores, NH601350
  Boleskine, NH507183
  Errogie, NH562227
Inverness: Crown, NH671452
Inverness: Dalneigh and Bona:
  Dalneigh, NH655450
  Bona, NH895377
Inverness: East
Inverness: Hilton, NH674436
Inverness: Inshes, NH688441
Inverness: Kinmylies, NH646446
Inverness: Ness Bank, NH664444
Inverness: Old High St Stephen's:
  Old High, NH665455
  St Stephen's, NH672449
Inverness: St Columba High, NH665453
Inverness: Trinity, NH662454
Kilmorack and Erchless, Beauly, NH525465:
  Struy, NH402402
Kiltarlity, NH513413
Kirkhill, NH553454
Moy, Dalarossie and Tomatin:

Moy, NH772342
Dalarossie, NH767242
Tomatin, NH803290
Nairn: Old, NH879564
Nairn: St Ninian's, NH883563
Petty, NH767502
Urquhart and Glenmoriston:
  Urquhart, NH509294
  Glenmoriston, NH419169

38. Presbytery of Lochaber

Note: Arisaig and the Small Isles and Mallaig and Knoydart
  parishes are now united as the parish of North West
  Lochaber. The churches in the parish are Arisaig, Canna,
  Eigg and Mallaig: St Columba.
Acharacle, NM674683
Ardgour, NN011642
  Kingairloch, NM862526
Ardnamurchan, NM488638
Arisaig and the Small Isles:
  Arisaig, NM661866
  Eigg, NM474886
Duror, NM993553
Fort Augustus, NH377090
Fort William: Duncansburgh MacIntosh, NN104741
Glencoe: St Munda's, NN083578
Glengarry, NH304012
  Tomdoun, NH154011
Kilmallie, Achnacarry, NN181873:
  Caol, NN106762
  Corpach, NN092770
Kilmonivaig, NN092770
Kinlochleven, NS187621
Mallaig: St Columba and Knoydart:
  Mallaig: St Columba, NM676967
  Knoydart, Canna, NG277054
Morvern, NM972538
Nether Lochaber, NN031614
Strontian, NN817617

39. Presbytery of Ross

Alness, NH647693
Avoch, NH701552
Contin, NH457557:
  Kinlochluichart, NH317622
Cromarty, NH786674
Dingwall: Castle Street, NH552588
Dingwall: St Clement's, NH548589
Fearn Abbey and Nigg:
  Fearn Abbey, NH837773
  Nigg, NH825736
Ferintosh, Conon Bridge, NH543556
Fodderty and Strathpeffer, NH482480
Fortrose and Rosemarkie:
  Fortrose, NH728568
  Rosemarkie, NH737576
Invergordon, NH707687
Killearnan, NH577494
Kilmuir and Logie Easter:
  Kilmuir, NH758732
  Logie Easter, NH779757
Kiltearn, NH607662
Knockbain, NH647530:
  Kessock, NH655479
Lochbroom and Ullapool:
  Lochbroom, NH177848
  Ullapool, NH130942
Resolis and Urquhart
Rosskeen, NH658697
Tain, NH780820
Tarbat, NH917846

Urray and Kilchrist:
  Urray, NH509524
  Muir of Ord, NH528507

40. Presbytery of Sutherland
Altnaharra and Farr:
  Altnaharra, NC568355
  Farr, NC708622
  Strathnaver, NC694439
Assynt and Stoer, Lochinver, NC093225
Clyne, NC905044
Creich, Bonar Bridge, NH611917
Dornoch Cathedral, NH797897
Durness and Kinlochbervie:
  Durness, NC404669
  Kinlochbervie, NC221564
Eddrachillis, Scourie, NC151443
Golspie, NC837003
Kildonan and Loth Helmsdale, Helmsdale,
  ND029155
Kincardine, Croick and Edderton:
  Ardgay, NH595910
  Croick, NH457915
  Edderton, NH710847
Lairg, NC583065
Melness and Tongue:
  Melness, NC586634
  Tongue, NC591570
Rogart, Pitfure, NC710038:
  St Callan's, NC715038
Rosehall, NC484013

41. Presbytery of Caithness
Bower, ND238622
Canisbay, ND343728
Dunnet, ND220712
Halkirk and Westerdale:
  Halkirk, ND131594
  Westerdale, ND128517
Keiss, ND348611
Olrig, ND191682
The North Coast Parish:
  Halladale, NC893558
  Reay, NC967648
  Strathy NC830657
The Parish of Latheron:
  Latheron, ND197333
  Dunbeath, ND157295
Thurso: St Peter's and St Andrew's, ND117682
Thurso: West, ND114681
Watten, ND243547
Wick: Bridge Street, ND363509
Wick: Old, ND362512
Wick: Pulteneytown and Thrumster:
  Pulteneytown, ND365504
  Thrumster, ND333447

42. Presbytery of Lochcarron – Skye
Applecross, Lochcarron and Torridon:
  Applecross, NG711417
  Lochcarron, NG893391
  Torridon, NG864572
Bracadale and Duirinish:
  Bracadale, NG344383
  Carbost, NG380313
  Duirinish, NG251479
Gairloch and Dundonnell:
  Gairloch, NG801771
  Aultbea, NG869886
  Dundonnell, NH019919
  Kinlochewe, NH030619

Glenelg and Kintail:
  Glenelg, NG813193
  Glenshiel, NG900214
  Kintail, NG930213
Kilmuir and Stenscholl:
  Kilmuir, NC389692 or NC389694
  Stenscholl NG657069
Lochalsh, NG761277:
  Kirkton, NG829272
  Plockton, NG801331
  Stromeferry, NG863346
Portree, NG482436
Snizort, NG420517:
  Arnisort, NG348532
Strath and Sleat:
  Broadford, NG642235
  Elgol, NG523143
  Isleornsay, NG699128
  Kilmore, NG657069
  Kyleakin, NG751263

43. Presbytery of Uist
Barra, NF670034
Benbecula, NF800519, NF770528
Berneray and Lochmaddy:
  Berneray, NF921819
  Lochmaddy, NF918684
Carinish, NF820604:
  Clachan, NF811637
Kilmuir and Paible:
  Kilmuir, NF708927
  Bayhead, NF749684
Manish-Scarista, Scaristabeg, NG007927
South Uist:
  Howmore, NF758364
  Iochdar, NF787463
Tarbert, NG159998

44. Presbytery of Lewis
Barvas, NB360494
Carloway, NB206424
Cross Ness, NB506619
Kinloch, NB159367
Knock, NB486319
Lochs-Crossbost, NB382255
Lochs-in-Bernera, NB159366
Stornoway: High, NB427330
Stornoway: Martin's Memorial, NB424327
Stornoway: St Columba, NB426330
Uig, NB087347

45. Presbytery of Orkney
Birsay, Harray and Sandwick
  Harray, HY314179
  Sandwick, HY246207
East Mainland, HY503109
Eday, HY562328
Evie, HY368255
Firth, HY359138
Flotta, ND366931
Hoy and Walls, ND312908
Kirkwall: East, HY486516
Kirkwall: St Magnus Cathedral, HY449108
North Ronaldsay, congregation meets in community school,
  HY758532
Orphir, HY343059
Papa Westray, HY496516
Rendall, HY393206
Rousay, HY442278
Sanday, HY690412, HY659408
Shapinsay, HY503178

South Ronaldsay and Burray, St Margaret's Hope,
  HY449934
  St Peter's Eastside, HY472908
Stenness, HY311125
Stromness, HY254090
Stronsay: Moncur Memorial, HY654252
Westray, HY457462

46. Presbytery of Shetland
Burra Isle, HU371330
Delting, Brae, HU359673
  Togon, HU404637
  Mossbank, HU451753
  Muckle Roe, HU342647
Dunrossness and St Ninian's inc. Fair Isle, Bigton,
  HU384213
  Bobban, HU391151
Fetlar, HU607905
Lerwick and Bressay
  Lerwick, HU478411
  Gulberwick, HU443389
  Bressay, HU493410
Nesting and Lunnasting:
  Nesting, HU487578

Lunna, HU486690
Northmavine, Hillswick, HU282771:
  North Roe, HU365895
  Ollaberry, HU366806
Sandsting and Aithsting, Aithsting HU345556
Sandwick, Cunningsburgh and Quarff, Sandwick, HU432237
Tingwall, Scalloway, HU365895:
  Veensgarth, HU419437
  Weisdale, HU345556
Unst, Baltasound, HP614088:
  Haroldswick, HP636126
Walls and Sandness:
  Walls, HU240493
  Mid Walls, HU220502
  Sandness, HU195571
  Papa Stour, HU177600
  Foula, HT969378
Whalsay and Skerries, Whalsay, HU555654
Yell:
  Cullivoe, HP544021:
  Hamnavoe, HU494804
  Mid Yell, HU515907
  West Sandwick, HU449879

SECTION 9

Congregational
Statistics
2007

CHURCH OF SCOTLAND
Comparative Statistics: 1967–2007

	2007	1997	1987	1977	1967
Communicants	489,118	660,954	838,659	1,002,945	1,220,023
Elders	38,534	44,922	46,808	48,454	48,373

NOTES ON CONGREGATIONAL STATISTICS

Com   Number of communicants at 31 December 2007.

Eld   Number of elders at 31 December 2007.

G   Membership of the Guild including Young Woman's Group and others as recorded on the 2007 annual return submitted to the Guild Office.

In 07   Ordinary General Income for 2007. Ordinary General Income consists of members' offerings, contributions from congregational organisations, regular fund-raising events, income from investments, deposits and so on. This figure does not include extraordinary or special income, or income from special collections and fund-raising for other charities.

M&M   Final amount allocated to congregations after allowing for Presbytery-approved amendments up to 31 December 2007, but before deducting stipend endowments and normal allowances given for stipend purposes in a vacancy.

–18   This figure shows 'the number of children and young people aged 17 years and under who are involved in the life of the congregation'.

(NB: Figures may not be available for new charges created or for congregations which have entered into readjustment late in 2007 or during 2008. Figures might also not be available for congregations which failed to submit the appropriate schedule.)

Congregation	Com	Eld	G	In 07	M&M	–18
1. Edinburgh						
Albany Deaf Church of Edinburgh	119	8	–	–	–	–
Balerno	752	60	49	114,328	61,012	48
Barclay	282	28	–	123,274	73,248	45
Blackhall St Columba's	1,019	90	43	186,079	95,559	69
Bristo Memorial Craigmillar	123	6	22	84,934	15,824	25
Broughton St Mary's	261	29	–	59,833	42,473	74
Canongate	395	51	–	93,394	49,234	20
Carrick Knowe	496	49	77	62,307	40,383	180
Colinton	990	85	–	213,425	109,269	298
Colinton Mains	202	16	–	50,434	30,102	60
Corstorphine Craigsbank	609	38	–	95,984	67,528	72
Corstorphine Old	536	57	56	82,549	61,234	13
Corstorphine St Anne's	451	51	50	74,913	59,648	55
Corstorphine St Ninian's	859	76	46	168,880	97,207	52
Craigentinny St Christopher's	123	11	–	32,592	14,554	28
Craiglockhart	531	56	41	222,102	84,507	389
Craigmillar Park	287	19	32	97,744	57,572	33
Cramond	1,259	102	22	244,463	121,216	72
Currie	725	58	80	150,623	91,350	86
Dalmeny	116	9	–	16,222	13,277	–
Queensferry	759	58	69	83,588	38,865	120
Davidson's Mains	760	61	58	207,230	101,,472	150
Dean	221	24	–	65,167	41,609	16
Drylaw	167	17	–	21,113	8,999	–
Duddingston	866	60	43	109,380	61,085	200
Fairmilehead	818	60	40	98,315	64,617	469
Gilmerton	–	–	–	2,664	–	–
Gorgie	283	34	–	88,331	54,473	84
Granton	318	26	–	–	26,855	15
Greenbank	920	94	51	256,823	119,057	142
Greenside	204	36	–	–	35,526	36
Greyfriars Tolbooth and Highland Kirk	394	51	12	126,780	74506	24
High (St Giles')	571	37	–	274,735	108,667	8
Holyrood Abbey	258	30	–	131,212	88,837	38
Holy Trinity	209	21	–	135,309	46,410	56
Inverleith	334	39	–	70,175	63,254	11
Juniper Green	399	27	–	87,136	60,716	70
Kaimes Lockhart Memorial	85	–	9	–	10,725	–
Kirkliston	336	41	51	79,804	44,740	46
Kirk o' Field	177	–	–	33,595	31,455	–
Leith North	412	47	–	79,510	61,490	238
Leith St Andrew's	253	30	–	59,896	36,522	136
Leith St Serf's	295	29	16	69,515	42,501	23
Leith St Thomas' Junction Road	241	23	–	57,104	32,010	25
Leith South	489	75	–	127,626	54,935	105
Leith Wardie	565	64	35	129,400	75,550	117

Congregation	Com	Eld	G	In 07	M&M	–18
Liberton	840	84	61	158,452	85,425	85
Liberton Northfield	271	10	35	64,299	27,562	35
London Road	330	29	37	50,594	36,008	34
Marchmont St Giles'	257	41	27	59,156	60,132	40
Mayfield Salisbury	659	70	25	228,379	119,050	74
Morningside	708	93	24	168,702	90,956	29
Morningside United	243	41	–	96,532	–	40
Muirhouse St Andrew's	56	7	–	14,926	328	67
Murrayfield	537	67	–	168,248	70,532	30
Newhaven	233	18	43	72,434	48,184	116
New Restalrig	260	16	16	–	68,862	43
Old Kirk	138	14	–	23,973	14,040	18
Palmerston Place	463	50	–	–	97,374	117
Pilrig St Paul's	296	28	23	62,120	33,347	31
Polwarth	245	20	19	92,724	56,017	109
Portobello Old	364	39	34	73,296	45,994	126
Portobello St James'	369	34	–	55,950	39,662	8
Portobello St Philip's Joppa	618	61	82	147,749	82,268	143
Priestfield	201	20	22	63,518	42,716	13
Ratho	217	20	19	44,020	25,149	35
Reid Memorial	356	22	–	95,938	63,787	20
Richmond Craigmillar	107	8	–	14,040	8,559	7
St Andrew's and St George's	335	38	–	202,779	96,858	9
St Andrew's Clermiston	294	21	–	47,910	30,281	15
St Catherine's Argyle	253	29	13	142,033	80,872	140
St Colm's	135	16	24	23,295	24,146	8
St Cuthbert's	403	54	–	165,694	109,726	12
St David's Broomhouse	176	14	–	41,008	26,862	28
St George's West	164	34	–	66,866	67,204	7
St John's Oxgangs	293	24	41	43,472	17,966	15
St Margaret's	409	35	20	46,802	37,530	90
St Martin's	111	12	–	15,314	4,280	80
St Michael's	418	38	–	55,932	36,352	10
St Nicholas' Sighthill	455	30	22	61,429	36,045	35
St Stephen's Comely Bank	399	23	44	112,045	64,518	100
Slateford Longstone	278	25	44	–	34,219	25
Stenhouse St Aidan's	192	10	–	22,888	19,941	25
Stockbridge	324	34	22	85,621	49,704	30
Tron Moredun	138	15	–	–	3,873	22
Viewforth	204	25	–	45,958	41,981	20

2. West Lothian

Congregation	Com	Eld	G	In 07	M&M	–18
Abercorn	81	10	9	14,105	9,679	–
Pardovan, Kingscavil and Winchburgh	300	28	15	42,391	30,219	48
Armadale	616	45	38	–	40,161	190
Avonbridge	89	8	10	12,719	6,042	20
Torphichen	269	17	–	–	22,475	36
Bathgate: Boghall	284	35	20	64,526	34,948	74

Congregation	Com	Eld	G	In 07	M&M	–18
Bathgate: High.	543	42	38	80,788	52,984	89
Bathgate: St David's	–	–	16	–	29,010	–
Bathgate: St John's	363	23	35	57,315	34,447	111
Blackburn and Seafield	503	44	–	57,271	34,400	100
Blackridge	94	7	–	22,828	9,743	–
Harthill: St Andrew's.	261	15	45	67,847	33,222	103
Breich Valley	223	11	26	24,718	20,503	31
Broxburn	492	37	36	66,256	35,575	145
Fauldhouse: St Andrew's.	240	10	15	42,603	30,690	6
Kirknewton and East Calder	360	43	24	109,981	52,068	101
Kirk of Calder	646	45	25	78,052	46,346	70
Linlithgow: St Michael's	1,477	102	56	287,422	120,941	366
Linlithgow: St Ninian's Craigmailen	493	49	72	72,993	44,783	113
Livingston Ecumenical Parish.	771	58	–	–	–	230
Livingston: Old	446	35	27	78,584	47,978	54
Polbeth Harwood.	219	31	–	26,562	14,329	6
West Kirk of Calder	323	25	48	41,665	33,393	26
Strathbrock	345	39	20	105,094	63,529	100
Uphall: South.	219	26	–	57,733	27,072	71
Whitburn: Brucefield.	454	29	20	–	43,178	50
Whitburn: South	419	34	35	63,541	45,572	100

3. Lothian

Congregation	Com	Eld	G	In 07	M&M	–18
Aberlady	294	28	–	35,070	22,536	35
Gullane	439	36	39	63,429	35,117	30
Athelstaneford	214	16	–	21,161	12,583	15
Whitekirk and Tyninghame	154	13	–	–	21,961	19
Belhaven	746	34	56	75,933	39,801	100
Spott.	103	5	–	10,859	2,695	8
Bilston	103	6	17	10,437	2,266	–
Glencorse.	334	15	–	26,187	15,616	11
Roslin.	274	8	–	26,997	15,698	–
Bolton and Saltoun	159	15	15	28,990	12,156	6
Humbie	88	9	10	14,841	8,325	12
Yester.	210	21	14	26,481	15,202	14
Bonnyrigg	798	71	48	–	64,944	48
Borthwick	66	7	–	16,882	7,503	18
Cranstoun, Crichton and Ford.	256	23	–	44,790	27,635	70
Fala and Soutra	72	6	14	14,802	7,429	3
Cockenzie and Port Seton: Chalmers Memorial.	274	42	45	72,411	38,315	40
Cockenzie and Port Seton: Old.	443	17	31	–	15,594	23
Cockpen and Carrington	328	23	48	41,042	20,025	40
Lasswade	278	18	–	19,088	17,447	–
Rosewell	130	9	–	10,449	7,068	–
Dalkeith: St John's and King's Park	550	43	29	84,657	48,461	69
Dalkeith: St Nicholas' Buccleuch	457	29	–	53,262	29,306	20
Dirleton	253	16	16	–	21,774	2
North Berwick: Abbey	338	30	52	75,863	34,415	58

Congregation	Com	Eld	G	In 07	M&M	–18
Dunbar	800	22	39	98,577	52,547	30
Dunglass	350	17	17	28,320	18,701	1
Garvald and Morham	53	8	–	15,302	4,924	23
Haddington: West	499	31	51	65,182	36,818	50
Gladsmuir	207	15	–	22,770	12,896	–
Longniddry	421	38	37	74,092	46,432	58
Gorebridge	467	16	–	78,639	38,976	40
Haddington: St Mary's	637	63	–	115,440	80,089	61
Howgate	47	5	7	16,506	7,459	12
Penicuik: South	173	15	–	105,646	57,214	40
Loanhead	364	30	41	52,083	32,501	60
Musselburgh: Northesk	393	33	48	69,511	40,014	102
Musselburgh: St Andrew's High	369	35	27	60,127	35,912	18
Musselburgh: St Clement's and St Ninian's	360	28	–	37,030	20,425	15
Musselburgh: St Michael's Inveresk	504	33	23	–	39,152	24
Newbattle	617	35	42	62,334	37,085	229
Newton	158	7	16	14,292	9,968	–
North Berwick: St Andrew Blackadder	680	42	29	109,397	63,963	146
Ormiston	179	8	26	34,982	16,803	–
Pencaitland	265	10	12	69,547	33,640	50
Penicuik: North	616	36	–	83,366	55,520	97
Penicuik: St Mungo's	446	26	30	64,132	37,937	5
Prestonpans: Prestongrange	373	37	29	45,829	32,604	20
Tranent	281	12	23	51,065	29,820	32
Traprain	498	30	30	62,256	44,681	5

4. Melrose and Peebles

Ashkirk	63	6	–	6,549	2,798	3
Selkirk	564	24	25	65,395	42,437	10
Bowden and Melrose	954	55	55	–	88,201	40
Broughton, Glenholm and Kilbucho	171	13	28	17,485	8,993	8
Skirling	85	8	–	9,271	3,800	9
Stobo and Drumelzier	97	9	–	12,376	9,122	5
Tweedsmuir	41	6	–	7,540	3,040	11
Caddonfoot	225	18	–	25,450	8,106	9
Galashiels: Trinity	892	48	50	69,318	53,352	12
Carlops	69	14	–	17,061	5,263	–
Kirkurd and Newlands	109	11	14	18,680	9,613	–
West Linton: St Andrew's	245	21	–	43,220	20,048	–
Channelkirk and Lauder	442	27	17	38,630	27,849	17
Earlston	498	16	12	52,029	29,624	30
Eddleston	118	8	10	12,914	5,162	15
Peebles: Old	614	48	–	97,021	58,034	115
Ettrick and Yarrow	200	20	–	30,445	23,143	15
Galashiels: Old and St Paul's	331	22	28	71,197	41,072	36
Galashiels: St John's	258	19	–	47,374	23,180	94
Innerleithen, Traquair and Walkerburn	458	33	51	68,589	44,882	68
Lyne and Manor	114	11	–	34,933	14,228	20

Congregation	Com	Eld	G	In 07	M&M	–18
Maxton and Mertoun	151	12	–	17,361	13,291	10
Newtown	182	11	–	13,187	6,530	–
St Boswells	288	24	27	36,978	21,129	–
Peebles: St Andrew's Leckie	686	39	–	102,320	56,708	70
Stow: St Mary of Wedale and Heriot	198	17	–	35,686	22,832	30

5. Duns

Ayton and Burnmouth	191	12	–	18,499	10,453	18
Grantshouse and Houndwood and Reston	117	10	11	11,138	8,770	12
Berwick-upon-Tweed: St Andrew's						
Wallace Green and Lowick	457	32	38	53,292	36,346	15
Bonkyl and Preston	87	8	–	8,620	3,902	–
Chirnside	319	16	18	22,827	17,438	–
Edrom: Allanton	81	9	–	7,995	3,648	–
Coldingham and St Abb's	85	6	18	27,949	16,871	10
Eyemouth	280	22	43	39,224	23,261	9
Coldstream	410	28	18	42,764	25,362	13
Eccles	93	10	17	8,043	5,103	5
Duns	511	27	40	53,463	31,495	40
Fogo and Swinton	132	5	–	10,726	6,771	2
Ladykirk	30	6	11	9,781	5,304	–
Leitholm	87	8	–	15,588	3,458	2
Whitsome	48	4	10	4,633	2,974	–
Foulden and Mordington	98	11	9	4,876	5,106	–
Hutton and Fishwick and Paxton	68	8	12	9,480	7,601	2
Gordon: St Michael's	70	7	–	–	7,418	4
Greenlaw	126	9	15	19,142	11,187	8
Legerwood	67	7	–	8,599	2,917	6
Westruther	46	6	10	6,936	2,758	7
Kirk of Lammermuir and Langton and Polwarth	183	14	25	43,754	25,185	4

6. Jedburgh

Ale and Teviot United	485	34	25	47,094	33,556	20
Cavers and Kirkton	145	8	–	8,776	7,072	–
Hawick: Trinity	831	30	53	50,672	32,893	80
Hawick: Burnfoot	129	13	13	26,940	12,204	101
Hawick: St Mary's and Old	560	24	42	39,270	26,775	115
Hawick: Teviot and Roberton	356	10	8	47,650	36,844	41
Hawick: Wilton	424	25	35	45,516	27,282	28
Teviothead	78	6	11	5,680	2,744	5
Hobkirk and Southdean	180	15	15	10,292	13,970	–
Ruberslaw	306	23	20	28,652	21,715	1
Jedburgh: Old and Trinity	803	28	45	79,835	56,303	–
Kelso Country Churches	219	19	18	25,203	24,596	–
Kelso: North and Ednam	1,297	71	49	121,568	70,657	38
Kelso: Old and Sprouston	618	37	–	50,574	35,515	14
Linton, Morebattle, Hownam and Yetholm	475	29	41	59,640	36,919	–
Oxnam	110	7	–	8,331	2,937	7

Congregation	Com	Eld	G	In 07	M&M	–18
7. Annandale and Eskdale						
Annan: Old	422	38	49	74,792	41,417	50
Dornock	154	15	–	–	6,403	35
Annan: St Andrew's	758	39	84	64,478	39,254	98
Brydekirk	62	4	–	6,897	2,538	12
Applegarth, Sibbaldbie and Johnstone	196	12	20	10,504	8,567	–
Lochmaben	544	23	44	64,816	25,758	20
Canonbie United	139	13	–	23,558	–	18
Liddesdale	150	10	19	37,334	24,070	31
Dalton	119	7	8	14,624	7,269	8
Hightae	90	8	13	14,930	4,793	42
St Mungo	137	10	14	14,884	8,472	9
Gretna: Old, Gretna: St Andrew's and Half Morton						
and Kirkpatrick Fleming	397	29	31	–	24,339	25
Hoddam	147	8	–	9,399	6,393	–
Kirtle-Eaglesfield	91	10	17	13,150	6,656	–
Middlebie	101	–	15	–	3,753	–
Waterbeck	69	–	–	4,213	1,748	–
Hutton and Corrie	76	–	–	–	8,450	–
Tundergarth	58	7	13	9,044	2,609	–
Kirkpatrick Juxta	159	10	–	12,292	7,598	–
Moffat: St Andrew's	489	45	39	79,717	41,575	40
Wamphray	58	5	–	7,404	2,238	2
Langholm Eskdalemuir Ewes and Westerkirk	550	29	59	–	29,413	35
Lockerbie: Dryfesdale	829	–	47	48,916	30,237	–
The Border Kirk	368	45	50	62,002	31,111	33
8. Dumfries and Kirkcudbright						
Auchencairn and Rerrick	88	10	–	11,138	6,336	1
Buittle and Kelton	210	17	16	35,069	14,898	12
Balmaclellan and Kells	138	10	15	18,586	12,205	7
Carsphairn	110	10	–	9,050	4,070	7
Dalry	170	12	21	12,427	6,197	12
Balmaghie	114	7	13	13,866	7,525	–
Tarff and Twynholm	192	16	28	24,599	17,898	11
Borgue	53	6	11	2,644	2,422	5
Gatehouse of Fleet	320	23	28	53,179	30,199	6
Caerlaverock	162	8	–	9,759	4,759	18
Dumfries: St Mary's-Greyfriars	820	56	50	69,981	46,757	13
Castle Douglas	515	35	48	59,836	38,258	24
Closeburn	246	14	–	21,402	15,099	20
Durisdeer	164	8	21	19,453	12,419	10
Colvend, Southwick and Kirkbean	346	28	25	71,238	42,260	–
Corsock and Kirkpatrick Durham	129	15	24	19,466	14,489	12
Crossmichael and Parton	180	13	16	20,254	12,293	12
Cummertrees	49	4	–	6,212	3,338	–
Mouswald	80	8	13	–	6,193	–
Ruthwell	98	8	14	10,720	7,844	12

Congregation	Com	Eld	G	In 07	M&M	–18
Dalbeattie.	629	37	57	54,376	33,080	40
Urr	205	11	–	15,926	11,855	18
Dumfries: Lincluden and Holywood.	261	19	–	–	17,736	–
Dumfries: Lochside.	336	18	25	–	12,619	40
Dumfries: Maxwelltown West.	666	46	50	79,430	38,100	118
Dumfries: St George's.	556	48	45	89,172	45,100	81
Dumfries: St Michael's and South	925	51	35	83,416	45,100	118
Dumfries: Troqueer.	382	28	23	87,500	52,697	54
Dunscore	262	24	16	34,977	18,076	26
Glencairn and Moniaive	207	11	–	–	16,077	7
Irongray, Lochrutton and Terregles.	502	32	20	–	26,331	–
Kirkconnel.	343	12	12	47,098	31,436	8
Kirkcudbright	634	37	–	77,897	46,524	30
Kirkgunzeon	55	9	–	6,538	2,382	–
Kirkmahoe.	359	15	31	25,224	17,322	15
Kirkmichael, Tinwald and Torthorwald	548	41	35	59,589	43,373	30
Lochend and New Abbey	263	19	17	23,944	15,505	10
Penpont, Keir and Tynron	180	11	–	18,166	15,660	30
Thornhill	255	17	18	23,894	18,043	–
Sanquhar: St Bride's	488	28	25	39,662	26,257	32

9. Wigtown and Stranraer

Ervie Kirkcolm	251	17	–	25,725	12,391	26
Leswalt	300	14	16	29,297	15,179	18
Glasserton and Isle of Whithorn	118	9	–	22,000	9,331	–
Whithorn: St Ninian's Priory	339	15	23	27,287	17,595	–
Inch	257	18	14	18,061	12,072	18
Stranraer: Town Kirk.	679	46	–	61,831	50,619	84
Kirkcowan	150	8	–	21,698	15,965	–
Wigtown	222	12	11	30,783	22,943	32
Kirkinner	170	6	16	11,658	7,878	–
Sorbie.	147	10	9	14,499	9,523	20
Kirkmabreck	171	8	21	18,470	13,294	10
Monigaff	407	26	–	32,497	19,957	30
Kirkmaiden	228	20	14	21,297	17,059	20
Stoneykirk	377	26	18	39,644	22,072	20
Mochrum.	280	21	32	91,111	17,828	15
New Luce	105	9	–	11,443	5,419	14
Old Luce	169	11	34	40,450	22,958	28
Penninghame.	547	26	29	60,738	44,576	14
Portpatrick.	245	10	30	15,540	12,450	20
Stranraer: St Ninian's	434	22	24	42,276	24,608	–
Stranraer: High Kirk	613	37	32	68,972	39,419	66

10. Ayr

Alloway	1,263	95	28	219,355	110,004	145
Annbank	297	20	24	28,224	19,366	11
Tarbolton	526	32	28	44,180	28,051	12

Congregation	Com	Eld	G	In 07	M&M	–18
Auchinleck.	381	20	31	–	24,672	25
Catrine	150	14	29	19,354	12,079	–
Ayr: Auld Kirk of Ayr	636	–	37	88,173	62,534	–
Ayr: Castlehill	688	41	66	–	54,692	196
Ayr: Newton on Ayr.	365	–	58	110,672	65,527	261
Ayr: St Andrew's	492	34	14	77,262	52,809	80
Ayr: St Columba.	1,441	147	63	211,211	104,033	112
Ayr: St James'	446	34	59	64,481	39,105	395
Ayr: St Leonard's	608	–	37	75,561	48,064	–
Ayr: St Quivox.	376	33	21	47,960	36,817	20
Ayr: Wallacetown	365	25	33	49,933	27,253	9
Ballantrae.	270	23	40	34,827	27,559	15
Barr	73	–	–	3,360	2,915	–
Dailly.	178	12	16	14,651	9,955	4
Girvan: South	327	26	32	33,979	20,621	15
Coylton	324	19	–	48,234	12,813	110
Drongan: The Schaw Kirk.	245	22	19	37,652	10,737	100
Craigie.	126	8	–	14,486	7,095	15
Symington	375	21	27	52,577	36,091	15
Crosshill.	192	10	23	17,359	10,720	10
Dalrymple	262	15	–	25,697	17,159	–
Dalmellington	298	26	69	48,019	32,091	100
Patna: Waterside	159	–	–	29,592	12,079	–
Dundonald.	518	47	47	–	47,998	82
Fisherton	141	9	10	18,163	8,005	1
Kirkoswald	256	14	14	31,907	21,099	12
Girvan: North (Old and St Andrew's).	943	63	–	67,864	49,154	105
Kirkmichael.	225	18	22	21,692	12,453	14
Straiton: St Cuthbert's.	166	13	16	16,054	8,939	20
Lugar.	166	11	21	–	8,511	–
Old Cumnock: Old	397	17	42	60,225	28,825	68
Mauchline	575	28	61	74,327	48,695	125
Maybole.	583	–	32	60,470	32,576	–
Monkton and Prestwick: North.	473	39	43	101,488	62,849	63
Muirkirk.	213	16	25	34,942	14,110	9
Sorn.	161	12	20	20,735	16,276	7
New Cumnock.	588	36	49	58,977	36,773	144
Ochiltree	267	23	20	32,037	16,575	26
Stair	226	–	12	23,798	17,171	–
Old Cumnock: Trinity.	398	20	40	40,567	30,626	13
Prestwick: Kingcase	774	84	64	120,926	68,164	280
Prestwick: St Nicholas'.	794	–	77	103,472	63,233	–
Prestwick: South	352	35	44	84,370	52,358	100
St Colmon (Arnsheen Barrhill and Colmonell)	280	16	–	17,435	13,954	–
Troon: Old.	1,185	–	–	135,270	90,365	–
Troon: Portland	692	–	45	128,210	69,793	–
Troon: St Meddan's	1,065	112	69	161,189	98,418	80

Congregation	Com	Eld	G	In 07	M&M	–18
11. Irvine and Kilmarnock						
Crosshouse.	314	30	23	–	19,826	17
Darvel	540	37	59	46,721	26,617	12
Dreghorn and Springside.	613	57	39	67,877	45,772	18
Dunlop.	409	37	40	57,856	34,670	35
Fenwick.	383	24	23	65,558	38,602	30
Galston.	776	67	77	110,702	74,120	94
Hurlford.	538	24	40	58,359	39,078	20
Irvine: Fullarton.	461	35	55	108,776	65,971	135
Irvine: Girdle Toll	187	18	26	41,112	22,672	95
Irvine: Mure.	428	29	30	83,752	46,822	62
Irvine: Old.	502	30	20	90,529	61,480	–
Irvine: Relief Bourtreehill.	334	27	33	46,962	27,340	18
Irvine: St Andrew's	316	19	33	40,518	29,039	20
Kilmarnock: Grange	394	33	50	64,135	38,569	30
Kilmarnock: Henderson	580	60	62	120,650	74,438	28
Kilmarnock: Howard St Andrew's	395	35	32	63,493	50,873	5
Kilmarnock: Laigh West High	897	70	59	131,469	97,009	191
Kilmarnock: Old High Kirk	210	17	20	52,115	27,805	22
Kilmarnock: Riccarton	327	32	32	67,900	39,230	95
Kilmarnock: St John's Onthank	277	27	26	51,021	26,499	75
Kilmarnock: St Kentigern's.	288	26	–	55,978	30,624	153
Kilmarnock: St Marnock's	745	81	–	114,505	73,880	338
Kilmarnock: St Ninian's Bellfield.	219	18	23	30,046	18,670	36
Kilmarnock: Shortlees.	117	12	–	29,466	18,150	–
Kilmaurs: St Maur's Glencairn	331	20	26	48,931	34,232	23
Newmilns: Loudoun	347	9	–	85,371	52,809	45
Stewarton: John Knox.	270	36	21	73,137	46,718	60
Stewarton: St Columba's.	494	42	45	74,046	47,283	52
12. Ardrossan						
Ardrossan: Barony St John's.	339	23	37	44,300	31,199	20
Ardrossan: Park.	457	36	38	60,780	40,195	105
Beith: High	803	74	22	57,110	37,196	40
Beith: Trinity.	243	32	32	48,264	27,220	25
Brodick	206	19	–	41,862	21,877	12
Corrie.	74	8	–	17,529	6,550	6
Lochranza and Pirnmill.	63	10	12	13,790	7,327	3
Shiskine.	70	9	13	21,269	8,155	11
Cumbrae	291	24	56	51,932	29,809	62
Dalry: St Margaret's	832	51	32	104,578	56,691	145
Dalry: Trinity.	246	22	46	87,985	48,357	62
Fairlie.	271	–	56	74,950	36,759	24
Fergushill.	49	5	–	6,297	1,876	9
Kilbirnie: Auld Kirk	451	37	20	43,676	30,506	12
Kilbirnie: St Columba's.	608	42	30	64,460	37,307	114
Kilmory.	49	8	–	13,183	3,569	8
Kilwinning: Mansefield Trinity.	254	17	42	45,449	16,000	–

Congregation	Com	Eld	G	In 07	M&M	–18
Kilwinning: Old	728	51	75	90,184	49,352	30
Lamlash	120	16	30	32,762	14,849	–
Largs: Clark Memorial	941	91	51	111,735	69,609	42
Largs: St Columba's	485	48	57	120,329	57,398	41
Largs: St John's	884	52	85	164,627	82,650	104
Saltcoats: New Trinity	327	48	23	59,595	41,592	19
Saltcoats: North	347	26	38	55,761	31,852	98
Saltcoats: St Cuthbert's	500	47	22	91,350	57,479	140
Stevenston: Ardeer	316	23	31	37,629	20,344	80
Stevenston: Livingstone	364	44	39	46,082	23,955	14
Stevenston: High	272	28	48	81,967	44,028	28
West Kilbride: Overton	340	29	33	50,149	35,107	150
West Kilbride: St Andrew's	597	53	24	–	49,017	31
Whiting Bay and Kildonan	118	13	–	39,522	22,724	23

13. Lanark

Congregation	Com	Eld	G	In 07	M&M	–18
Biggar	640	39	52	72,483	48,142	32
Black Mount	72	7	15	12,158	7,570	6
Culter	94	10	–	12,134	6,170	6
Libberton and Quothquan	89	12	–	10,609	3,646	12
Cairngryffe	175	15	20	24,054	21,167	20
Symington	242	19	25	39,358	17,800	14
Carluke: Kirkton	828	53	27	116,482	62,000	300
Carluke: St Andrew's	340	16	15	56,369	29,000	39
Carluke: St John's	786	46	34	–	52,500	30
Carnwath	327	17	26	40,784	26,231	–
Carstairs and Carstairs Junction	312	20	34	30,664	24,759	25
Coalburn	157	8	18	17,448	7,990	7
Lesmahagow: Old	612	26	25	74,533	33,135	40
Crossford	195	9	–	31,563	15,716	17
Kirkfieldbank	124	8	19	18,985	8,683	–
Forth: St Paul's	405	27	50	46,641	29,892	28
Glencaple	214	12	20	25,006	22,796	15
Lowther	41	5	–	6,830	2,606	4
Kirkmuirhill	322	21	51	107,305	65,000	80
Lanark: Greyfriars	826	45	38	86,594	50,775	230
Lanark: St Nicholas'	567	51	37	93,698	54,138	135
Law	178	19	37	–	21,118	150
Lesmahagow: Abbeygreen	232	16	2	90,843	49,799	65
The Douglas Valley Church	406	27	43	53,521	24,100	10

14. Greenock and Paisley

Congregation	Com	Eld	G	In 07	M&M	–18
Barrhead: Arthurlie	332	33	26	88,255	49,760	86
Barrhead: Bourock	493	50	57	86,319	50,105	270
Barrhead: South and Levern	442	32	26	82,884	46,825	185
Bishopton	822	57	–	95,352	55,354	110
Bridge of Weir: Freeland	426	53	–	112,480	70,795	60
Bridge of Weir: St Machar's Ranfurly	470	42	34	94,899	50,340	30

Congregation	Com	Eld	G	In 07	M&M	–18
Caldwell	255	16	–	64,177	35,637	49
Elderslie Kirk	590	57	59	116,501	63,261	160
Erskine	363	34	72	–	63,786	301
Gourock: Old Gourock and Ashton	853	70	48	129,041	80,258	250
Gourock: St John's	655	73	20	106,977	62,443	332
Greenock: Ardgowan	452	47	31	83,809	54,796	221
Greenock: East End	–	–	–	12,160	–	16
Greenock: Finnart St Paul's	382	30	–	66,438	48,903	90
Greenock: Mount Kirk	345	42	20	61,950	43,481	170
Greenock: Old West Kirk	354	28	36	73,395	52,014	18
Greenock: St Margaret's	178	21	21	27,897	16,750	22
Greenock: St Ninian's	246	22	–	25,741	13,146	98
Greenock: Wellpark Mid Kirk	604	45	32	75,121	53,032	159
Greenock: Westburn	982	109	51	154,963	110,255	226
Houston and Killellan	736	54	59	154,309	78,346	350
Howwood	218	13	24	52,698	30,455	23
Inchinnan	376	41	31	67,056	43,030	175
Inverkip	405	29	37	78,713	33,147	95
Johnstone: High	310	39	36	84,951	54,689	40
Johnstone: St Andrew's Trinity	248	31	36	45,792	29,182	132
Johnstone: St Paul's	531	75	26	86,877	48,041	35
Kilbarchan: East	383	42	29	76,810	41,483	65
Kilbarchan: West	460	48	34	93,446	69,254	54
Kilmacolm: Old	551	48	–	122,712	75,537	50
Kilmacolm: St Columba	562	29	23	111,119	67,578	50
Langbank	148	15	–	33,750	21,345	12
Linwood	475	38	26	62,480	41,408	22
Lochwinnoch	155	14	–	–	22,741	222
Neilston	644	47	27	–	60,718	40
Paisley: Abbey	778	58	–	152,583	76,030	128
Paisley: Castlehead	266	29	15	58,115	36,079	24
Paisley: Glenburn	267	22	–	46,531	28,623	35
Paisley: Laigh Kirk	423	67	84	78,192	46,138	48
Paisley: Lylesland	439	62	50	81,608	52,669	40
Paisley: Martyrs'	472	56	–	–	49,275	45
Paisley: Oakshaw Trinity	627	100	48	146,522	–	50
Paisley: St Columba Foxbar	222	29	23	37,845	26,633	145
Paisley: St James'	366	36	–	63,361	30,806	37
Paisley: St Luke's	273	32	–	–	34,678	9
Paisley: St Mark's Oldhall	597	61	98	118,824	66,947	240
Paisley: St Ninian's Ferguslie	47	–	–	16,452	–	25
Paisley: Sandyford (Thread Street)	292	21	18	49,087	31,315	12
Paisley: Sherwood Greenlaw	726	92	47	149,917	73,556	60
Paisley: Wallneuk North	467	52	–	–	40,798	25
Port Glasgow: Hamilton Bardrainney	305	19	22	43,410	27,093	33
Port Glasgow: St Andrew's	642	65	45	–	52,171	303
Port Glasgow: St Martin's	171	16	–	–	11,723	13
Renfrew: North	683	64	36	106,625	63,524	140

Congregation	Com	Eld	G	In 07	M&M	–18
Renfrew: Old	575	41	47	86,587	52,082	–
Renfrew: Trinity	368	29	57	77,149	50,889	–
Skelmorlie and Wemyss Bay	391	27	–	69,814	45,391	20

16. Glasgow

Banton	83	12	–	14,166	7,810	19
Twechar	74	14	–	17,134	5,770	10
Bishopbriggs: Kenmure	334	23	53	77,192	49,666	150
Bishopbriggs: Springfield	890	51	93	105,093	65,252	182
Broom	780	63	35	150,412	87,156	75
Burnside Blairbeth	713	56	85	252,861	118,835	291
Busby	329	43	30	66,143	39,918	45
Cadder	872	85	66	148,132	95,765	210
Cambuslang: Flemington Hallside	289	16	23	38,902	19,024	147
Cambuslang: Old	366	49	41	64,984	51,630	18
Cambuslang: St Andrew's	377	37	–	69,906	46,468	70
Cambuslang: Trinity St Paul's	298	20	–	78,051	47,178	47
Campsie	200	17	20	–	35,404	112
Chryston	672	39	25	178,751	88,992	98
Eaglesham	652	52	65	121,443	70,571	160
Fernhill and Cathkin	307	25	44	44,648	27,234	125
Gartcosh	146	9	8	17,539	10,578	60
Glenboig	134	–	12	13,534	6,370	7
Giffnock: Orchardhill	503	50	29	168,720	103,367	323
Giffnock: South	931	96	51	200,779	109,254	120
Giffnock: The Park	305	31	–	60,566	34,694	115
Greenbank	1,030	80	54	216,125	120,616	280
Kilsyth: Anderson	406	21	60	87,316	56,671	129
Kilsyth: Burns and Old	476	37	45	72,559	48,287	98
Kirkintilloch: Hillhead	123	8	16	–	9,026	45
Kirkintilloch: St Columba's	533	50	49	89,719	53,612	120
Kirkintilloch: St David's Memorial Park	699	58	34	135,757	78,157	129
Kirkintilloch: St Mary's	781	68	65	136,012	74,803	100
Lenzie: Old	484	46	–	107,480	54,797	44
Lenzie: Union	766	72	87	163,884	97,285	251
Maxwell Mearns Castle	302	29	–	160,296	89,518	228
Mearns	917	45	–	171,512	95,658	51
Milton of Campsie	365	46	35	56,725	36,629	148
Netherlee	803	79	56	200,083	114,555	401
Newton Mearns	700	57	24	124,853	76,575	148
Rutherglen: Old	364	31	–	56,351	37,227	70
Rutherglen: Stonelaw	412	43	43	128,643	75,849	45
Rutherglen: West and Wardlawhill	562	57	76	135,939	71,287	118
Stamperland	416	28	28	76,288	49,363	230
Stepps	379	27	18	–	33,632	160
Thornliebank	225	16	48	48,956	32,642	70
Torrance	312	15	–	87,018	34,909	173
Williamwood	499	74	37	–	78,226	257

Congregation	Com	Eld	G	In 07	M&M	–18
Glasgow: Anderston Kelvingrove	66	10	11	–	14,379	–
Glasgow: Baillieston Mure Memorial	507	35	105	91,031	53,068	265
Glasgow: Baillieston St Andrew's	386	26	48	68,434	39,425	121
Glasgow: Balshagray Victoria Park	276	37	28	97,661	52,723	60
Glasgow: Barlanark Greyfriars	161	21	20	36,974	19,678	182
Glasgow: Battlefield East	146	12	29	40,409	26,058	3
Glasgow: Blawarthill	189	19	33	–	17,603	96
Glasgow: Bridgeton St Francis in the East	98	17	9	33,959	19,638	30
Glasgow: Broomhill	591	65	47	145,310	85,046	140
Glasgow: Calton Parkhead	96	12	–	19,525	14,715	20
Glasgow: Cardonald	464	45	86	123,795	79,261	226
Glasgow: Carmunnock	341	28	33	50,314	35,862	50
Glasgow: Carmyle	115	6	23	–	12,253	39
Glasgow: Kenmuir Mount Vernon	152	10	34	51,648	28,641	90
Glasgow: Carnwadric	139	17	28	29,861	16,626	55
Glasgow: Castlemilk East	152	9	14	29,417	19,249	15
Glasgow: Castlemilk West	126	17	12	23,850	13,283	37
Glasgow: Cathcart Old	308	47	47	83,127	54,198	460
Glasgow: Cathcart Trinity	526	64	60	197,509	98,841	88
Glasgow: Cathedral (High or St Mungo's)	420	55	–	112,581	60,826	16
Glasgow: Colston Milton	103	17	–	25,063	15,206	70
Glasgow: Colston Wellpark	178	13	–	–	21,095	63
Glasgow: Cranhill	33	7	–	13,725	2,642	40
Glasgow: Croftfoot	320	46	37	77,329	49,569	31
Glasgow: Dennistoun New	334	39	42	–	64,314	160
Glasgow: Drumchapel Drumry St Mary's	94	12	–	7,865	1,855	15
Glasgow: Drumchapel St Andrew's	404	45	–	51,628	33,328	22
Glasgow: Drumchapel St Mark's	71	10	–	13,360	1,268	5
Glasgow: Easterhouse St George's and St Peter's	72	9	–	–	128	15
Glasgow: Eastwood	333	51	42	93,601	55,909	21
Glasgow: Gairbraid	212	18	17	34,000	25,256	20
Glasgow: Gardner Street	38	8	–	35,027	29,885	3
Glasgow: Garthamlock and Craigend East	85	14	–	–	2,255	85
Glasgow: Gorbals	95	12	–	28,056	15,593	9
Glasgow: Govan Old	143	29	22	–	30,076	38
Glasgow: Govanhill Trinity	127	17	20	25,363	19,009	4
Glasgow: High Carntyne	371	41	76	75,506	52,000	144
Glasgow: Hillington Park	363	32	45	68,997	42,873	145
Glasgow: Househillwood St Christopher's	125	9	22	–	9,850	56
Glasgow: Hyndland	282	40	30	101,779	58,204	33
Glasgow: Ibrox	213	16	26	–	32,260	99
Glasgow: John Ross Memorial (for Deaf People)	68	8	–	–	–	–
Glasgow: Jordanhill	624	78	35	178,880	95,619	192
Glasgow: Kelvin Stevenson Memorial	157	29	21	37,793	27,276	102
Glasgow: Kelvinside Hillhead	169	23	–	65,940	42,135	97
Glasgow: King's Park	741	78	53	158,985	94,038	214

Congregation	Com	Eld	G	In 07	M&M	–18
Glasgow: Kinning Park	146	15	15	34,031	22,822	12
Glasgow: Knightswood St Margaret's	642	43	34	59,955	36,268	135
Glasgow: Langside	222	41	17	57,311	34,281	150
Glasgow: Lansdowne	101	12	–	6,800	6,595	5
Glasgow: Linthouse St Kenneth's	81	15	10	–	17,906	46
Glasgow: Lochwood	72	4	10	–	4,857	55
Glasgow: Martyrs', The	117	5	–	15,223	15,335	7
Glasgow: Maryhill	185	14	18	40,490	24,602	204
Glasgow: Merrylea	404	67	40	85,771	56,326	160
Glasgow: Mosspark	200	37	41	58,039	40,886	82
Glasgow: Mount Florida	271	33	39	102,607	59,064	154
Glasgow: New Govan	81	17	21	–	37,682	58
Glasgow: Newlands South	595	75	32	177,768	105,005	27
Glasgow: North Kelvinside	62	4	22	33,999	21,219	10
Glasgow: Partick South	178	33	32	62,095	38,376	135
Glasgow: Partick Trinity	178	25	–	62,368	27,685	65
Glasgow: Penilee St Andrew's	154	25	–	–	23,719	138
Glasgow: Pollokshaws	162	23	30	41,893	25,583	48
Glasgow: Pollokshields	272	41	47	–	72,395	45
Glasgow: Possilpark	175	18	21	30,367	18,871	56
Glasgow: Priesthill and Nitshill	124	18	16	33,608	19,708	25
Glasgow: Queen's Park	227	31	37	84,215	58,363	67
Glasgow: Renfield St Stephen's	166	27	34	83,185	45,661	12
Glasgow: Robroyston	67	–	–	7,883	–	26
Glasgow: Ruchazie	69	6	–	7,878	7,162	105
Glasgow: Ruchill	82	22	–	–	32,026	10
Glasgow: St Andrew's East	114	18	23	36,452	24,214	28
Glasgow: St Columba	136	–	11	–	22,173	–
Glasgow: St David's Knightswood	454	30	43	107,437	60,683	40
Glasgow: St Enoch's Hogganfield	202	–	35	37,603	27,460	–
Glasgow: St George's Tron	409	28	–	167,355	126,944	50
Glasgow: St James' (Pollok)	165	29	21	47,325	33,213	78
Glasgow: St John's Renfield	422	50	–	158,374	89,320	160
Glasgow: St Luke's and St Andrew's	77	9	10	–	11,961	–
Glasgow: St Margaret's Tollcross Park	144	4	–	30,464	16,995	8
Glasgow: St Nicholas' Cardonald	327	31	11	62,101	38,875	338
Glasgow: St Paul's	56	7	–	–	3,265	12
Glasgow: St Rollox	110	11	–	36,235	13,383	6
Glasgow: St Thomas' Gallowgate	36	8	–	–	3,235	10
Glasgow: Sandyford Henderson Memorial	195	26	19	151,470	71,365	50
Glasgow: Sandyhills	333	28	59	–	47,572	31
Glasgow: Scotstoun	254	12	–	78,023	45,008	65
Glasgow: Shawlands	406	28	43	98,817	64,649	23
Glasgow: Sherbrooke St Gilbert's	389	49	30	140,425	77,789	115
Glasgow: Shettleston New	259	35	42	97,868	45,010	72
Glasgow: Shettleston Old	207	18	22	34,832	28,910	76
Glasgow: South Carntyne	75	8	–	29,361	14,636	45
Glasgow: South Shawlands	213	28	–	68,778	36,156	142

Congregation	Com	Eld	G	In 07	M&M	–18
Glasgow: Springburn	275	40	25	63,913	44,023	132
Glasgow: Temple Anniesland	387	28	61	90,531	53,252	124
Glasgow: Toryglen	125	12	–	19,927	9,019	22
Glasgow: Trinity Possil and Henry Drummond	106	7	–	55,323	30,506	15
Glasgow: Tron St Mary's	142	21	–	33,988	23,801	170
Glasgow: Victoria Tollcross	139	16	20	–	14,851	112
Glasgow: Wallacewell	126	15	23	38,776	19,662	–
Glasgow: Wellington	249	29	–	83,569	58,664	25
Glasgow: Whiteinch	31	–	–	55,750	–	–
Glasgow: Yoker	100	12	–	24,698	16,718	4

17. Hamilton

Congregation	Com	Eld	G	In 07	M&M	–18
Airdrie: Broomknoll	329	39	34	66,308	39,268	198
Calderbank	130	9	17	24,690	9,510	11
Airdrie: Clarkston	420	34	32	57,233	41,374	119
Airdrie: Flowerhill	705	62	21	131,478	57,332	228
Airdrie: High	403	27	–	65,696	32,855	100
Airdrie: Jackson	321	45	21	61,851	38,709	73
Airdrie: New Monkland	343	25	22	51,085	19,297	119
Greengairs	139	8	–	21,264	12,166	–
Airdrie: St Columba's	236	6	–	–	9,824	50
Airdrie: The New Wellwynd	719	83	35	126,272	61,708	52
Bargeddie	136	11	–	69,212	35,675	17
Bellshill: Macdonald Memorial	281	22	20	42,302	25,821	18
Bellshill: Orbiston	231	21	16	17,324	8,800	12
Bellshill: West	760	55	40	67,660	42,439	50
Blantyre: Livingstone Memorial	275	21	27	59,624	29,767	130
Blantyre: Old	338	18	24	41,211	35,158	53
Blantyre: St Andrew's	270	24	25	65,632	39,949	46
Bothwell	525	58	46	114,205	76,791	150
Caldercruix and Longriggend	225	12	17	54,528	32,467	15
Carfin	50	8	–	9,773	3,074	–
Newarthill	430	32	18	–	30,981	173
Chapelhall	287	23	39	40,148	22,105	77
Chapelton	197	15	23	26,368	15,736	25
Strathaven: Rankin	572	63	43	82,762	51,848	160
Cleland	218	21	–	26,329	16,105	19
Coatbridge: Blairhill Dundyvan	371	28	32	59,452	38,183	119
Coatbridge: Calder	443	29	35	58,883	36,094	89
Coatbridge: Clifton	220	23	22	–	31,995	6
Coatbridge: Middle	378	33	37	49,385	31,550	163
Coatbridge: Old Monkland	318	21	26	59,302	29,853	65
Coatbridge: St Andrew's	665	61	37	102,194	57,278	235
Coatbridge: Townhead	331	20	30	50,135	32,647	130
Dalserf	249	18	26	70,054	42,243	48
East Kilbride: Claremont	718	84	34	–	63,099	235
East Kilbride: Greenhills	173	14	35	41,097	14,685	18
East Kilbride: Moncreiff	819	72	52	121,265	70,184	250

Congregation	Com	Eld	G	In 07	M&M	–18
East Kilbride: Mossneuk	263	19	–	41,077	20,000	260
East Kilbride: Old	688	66	51	98,858	58,173	155
East Kilbride: South	375	43	44	81,953	58,441	40
East Kilbride: Stewartfield	–	–	–	10,227	–	–
East Kilbride: West	544	36	69	74,269	39,343	200
East Kilbride: Westwood	678	41	130	80,659	51,702	25
Glasford	177	7	23	21,092	10,424	–
Strathaven: East	290	32	36	52,079	27,421	40
Hamilton: Burnbank	113	12	–	28,169	15,258	7
Hamilton: North	139	29	25	35,287	21,769	19
Hamilton: Cadzow	700	66	66	105,148	68,866	153
Hamilton: Gilmour and Whitehill	175	26	–	31,148	23,900	–
Hamilton: Hillhouse	435	50	32	88,588	54,807	52
Hamilton: Old	561	66	38	126,088	79,692	71
Hamilton: St Andrew's	333	34	30	59,102	39,005	126
Hamilton: St John's	584	55	57	116,963	74,942	215
Hamilton: South	277	31	32	52,155	35,522	32
Quarter	102	12	19	24,807	9,762	19
Hamilton: Trinity	318	28	–	47,699	27,839	112
Hamilton: West	374	32	–	69,598	42,772	25
Holytown	314	19	38	41,515	28,409	84
New Stevenston: Wrangholm Kirk	181	11	19	37,080	24,832	55
Kirk o' Shotts	198	20	11	28,817	17,765	20
Larkhall: Chalmers	152	15	25	35,965	22,621	25
Larkhall: St Machan's	565	53	49	100,406	56,504	81
Larkhall: Trinity	310	23	33	48,934	30,602	115
Motherwell: Crosshill	464	54	56	80,062	49,024	108
Motherwell: Dalziel St Andrew's	582	74	60	133,168	70,172	200
Motherwell: North	207	28	43	44,569	28,388	250
Motherwell: St Margaret's	366	19	21	–	26,446	197
Motherwell: St Mary's	907	99	85	117,322	60,466	280
Motherwell: South	546	66	80	97,955	75,916	56
Newmains: Bonkle	162	17	–	40,401	17,511	15
Newmains: Coltness Memorial	229	27	26	65,629	29,461	103
Overtown	292	30	43	45,073	28,361	170
Shotts: Calderhead Erskine	529	49	35	89,051	48,193	35
Stonehouse: St Ninian's	434	47	47	77,061	49,724	25
Strathaven: Avendale Old and Drumclog	748	60	68	–	78,078	98
Strathaven: West	223	18	28	43,361	28,607	44
Uddingston: Burnhead	274	26	11	37,899	28,209	85
Uddingston: Old	690	63	72	114,981	72,480	159
Uddingston: Viewpark	466	50	36	84,177	40,825	275
Wishaw: Cambusnethan North	524	39	–	80,177	48,965	140
Wishaw: Cambusnethan Old and Morningside	537	48	22	79,279	55,074	170
Wishaw: Craigneuk and Belhaven	216	26	27	45,024	29,374	13
Wishaw: Old	347	35	–	43,519	27,791	82
Wishaw: St Mark's	452	37	43	67,542	46,598	208
Wishaw: South Wishaw	580	35	61	99,517	63,474	32

Congregation	Com	Eld	G	In 07	M&M	–18
18. Dumbarton						
Alexandria	419	40	25	68,661	40,831	40
Arrochar	63	–	16	16,849	6,759	57
Luss	93	–	19	36,318	12,635	–
Baldernock	228	19	–	44,925	27,008	19
Bearsden: Baljaffray	331	31	73	56,713	33,764	133
Bearsden: Cross	1,028	115	42	199,816	126,609	96
Bearsden: Killermont	695	69	69	158,875	85,820	210
Bearsden: New Kilpatrick	1,670	125	119	290,710	163,205	170
Bearsden: Westerton Fairlie Memorial	452	48	44	79,114	54,212	55
Bonhill	895	58	–	74,091	48,748	125
Cardross	435	34	32	90,052	59,771	40
Clydebank: Abbotsford	322	23	–	49,925	33,971	26
Clydebank: Faifley	221	18	38	38,541	20,509	16
Clydebank: Kilbowie St Andrew's	305	21	32	45,170	31,299	113
Clydebank: Radnor Park	228	29	31	45,994	31,315	–
Clydebank: St Cuthbert's	129	17	24	29,140	14,008	8
Duntocher	293	33	25	53,746	31,651	–
Craigrownie	222	23	20	36,909	24,682	22
Rosneath: St Modan's	150	11	26	26,634	15,212	13
Dalmuir: Barclay	277	17	28	40,812	24,037	64
Dumbarton: Riverside	657	82	76	115,710	71,928	389
Dumbarton: St Andrew's	144	29	12	32,043	18,699	12
Dumbarton: West Kirk	328	45	18	–	33,294	40
Garelochhead	179	19	–	57,625	33,189	91
Helensburgh: Park	449	47	31	81,437	52,804	18
Helensburgh: St Columba	540	49	38	88,997	65,436	61
Helensburgh: The West Kirk	606	52	46	141,544	74,570	45
Jamestown	382	–	24	52,286	34,719	–
Kilmaronock Gartocharn	266	11	–	29,151	19,422	12
Milngavie: Cairns	658	55	–	124,747	71,342	49
Milngavie: St Luke's	397	39	28	70,189	41,657	43
Milngavie: St Paul's	1,096	92	92	215,788	110,531	104
Old Kilpatrick Bowling	305	28	28	48,801	32,448	167
Renton: Trinity	279	25	–	30,908	22,663	12
Rhu and Shandon	288	30	44	77,868	51,141	35
19. Argyll						
Appin	84	14	20	26,100	9,404	12
Lismore	56	8	10	–	5,431	11
Ardchattan	139	12	10	18,433	10,627	14
Ardrishaig	170	26	27	33,413	25,308	23
South Knapdale	39	6	–	–	2,650	1
Campbeltown: Highland	462	35	26	55,683	32,552	10
Campbeltown: Lorne and Lowland	907	61	62	83,419	50,229	65
Coll	15	3	–	2,959	913	–
Connel	148	24	18	48,948	25,002	18
Colonsay and Oronsay	16	2	–	3,800	3,162	–

Congregation	Com	Eld	G	In 07	M&M	–18
Craignish	41	–	–	9,729	4,704	–
Kilbrandon and Kilchattan	90	–	–	22,628	12,485	–
Kilninver and Kilmelford	58	6	–	11,033	5,593	2
Cumlodden, Lochfyneside and Lochgair	96	14	13	–	11,878	10
Dunoon: St John's	234	28	23	34,743	27,437	25
Sandbank	147	–	–	17,406	10,991	–
Dunoon: The High Kirk	396	36	43	–	35,981	19
Innellan	106	12	–	25,763	12,956	13
Toward	112	11	–	21,405	9,709	23
Gigha and Cara	38	–	–	8,771	3,811	24
Glassary, Kilmartin and Ford	115	10	–	20,081	14,046	–
North Knapdale	70	10	–	30,742	21,333	4
Glenaray and Inveraray	116	14	11	17,357	16,380	–
Glenorchy and Innishael	79	6	–	9,799	3,514	–
Strathfillan	47	12	–	10,571	3,972	–
Iona	23	–	–	5,320	2,897	–
Kilfinichen and Kilvickeon and the Ross of Mull	33	–	–	11,042	4,305	–
Jura	44	–	–	14,333	5,725	–
Kilarrow	94	–	11	30,911	18,092	–
Kilberry	12	–	–	1,058	484	–
Tarbert	167	–	25	33,767	22,162	–
Kilcalmonell	56	7	10	7,991	2,781	7
Killean and Kilchenzie	170	11	20	23,713	19,663	18
Kilchoman	91	10	–	17,917	17,005	14
Kilmeny	41	6	–	11,407	3,744	21
Portnahaven	23	4	15	5,920	2,107	–
Kilchrenan and Dalavich	35	4	8	8,894	7,386	–
Muckairn	130	18	11	25,354	11,248	18
Kildalton and Oa	122	–	13	36,787	20,321	–
Kilfinan	30	–	9	4,864	1,891	–
Kilmodan and Colintraive	139	–	–	20,932	12,403	–
Kyles	165	17	22	27,281	14,510	2
Kilmore and Oban	594	56	50	91,993	53,561	39
Kilmun (St Munn's)	116	11	24	15,649	8,862	4
Strone and Ardentinny	117	10	14	21,695	15,537	8
Kirn	359	31	15	74,009	46,858	8
Lochgilphead	217	–	16	28,110	19,696	–
Lochgoilhead and Kilmorich	103	–	15	28,700	18,737	–
Mull, Isle of, Kilninian and Kilmore	28	4	–	10,669	5,463	–
Salen and Ulva	43	6	–	13,398	4,476	2
Tobermory	73	14	–	24,486	9,407	10
Torosay and Kinlochspelvie	25	5	–	6,674	2,463	2
Rothesay: Trinity	456	42	38	61,696	36,668	43
Saddell and Carradale	218	14	29	34,446	18,518	19
Skipness	30	3	–	6,541	2,639	5
Southend	248	14	23	–	20,488	20
Strachur and Strachlachlan	137	19	15	33,112	23,504	10

Congregation	Com	Eld	G	In 07	M&M	–18
The United Church of Bute	641	43	50	67,410	53,002	49
Tiree	99	10	22	18,501	13,054	4

22. Falkirk

Congregation	Com	Eld	G	In 07	M&M	–18
Airth	157	8	18	–	28,647	51
Blackbraes and Shieldhill	176	14	13	23,191	15,321	8
Muiravonside	211	18	12	29,431	22,221	–
Bo'ness: Old	445	37	33	66,345	38,313	89
Bo'ness: St Andrew's	560	31	–	75,786	45,420	103
Bonnybridge: St Helen's	354	17	32	50,809	37,116	30
Bothkennar and Carronshore	270	30	–	33,008	22,279	8
Brightons	725	38	53	110,327	63,790	244
Carriden	502	49	22	48,014	33,425	11
Cumbernauld: Abronhill	293	34	37	60,035	31,574	319
Cumbernauld: Condorrat	446	33	28	68,705	37,624	95
Cumbernauld: Kildrum	364	40	–	59,340	26,983	220
Cumbernauld: Old	447	41	–	66,481	43,318	112
Cumbernauld: St Mungo's	308	28	–	51,710	20,828	91
Denny: Dunipace	401	36	16	63,418	35,816	81
Denny: Old	448	61	25	61,049	40,743	100
Denny: Westpark	627	52	42	68,381	50,740	90
Falkirk: Bainsford	307	–	–	–	25,325	–
Falkirk: Camelon	384	26	24	82,748	57,505	24
Falkirk: Erskine	499	43	40	80,712	49,443	26
Falkirk: Grahamston United	429	44	37	63,557	–	68
Falkirk: Laurieston	256	19	33	–	24,617	17
Redding and Westquarter	189	13	35	30,235	13,730	10
Falkirk: Old and St Modan's	708	50	26	115,738	70,132	105
Falkirk: St Andrew's West	562	39	–	–	66,676	60
Falkirk: St James'	276	25	15	36,385	22,329	54
Grangemouth: Abbotsgrange	670	64	32	65,171	38,326	136
Grangemouth: Kirk of the Holy Rood	627	50	–	59,167	38,452	84
Grangemouth: Zetland	868	76	75	108,182	69,226	199
Haggs	295	30	20	–	27,667	74
Larbert: East	668	43	43	98,556	55,836	147
Larbert: Old	630	37	18	97,930	60,397	210
Larbert: West	507	40	41	86,022	48,038	205
Polmont: Old	447	31	72	77,905	46,888	130
Slamannan	252	–	–	–	21,204	–
Stenhouse and Carron	451	–	24	79,129	51,370	–

23. Stirling

Congregation	Com	Eld	G	In 07	M&M	–18
Aberfoyle	129	12	26	22,453	12,829	29
Port of Menteith	66	8	–	14,065	4,371	7
Alloa: North	274	17	20	46,742	31,145	21
Alloa: St Mungo's	597	46	48	66,273	44,992	22
Alloa: West	222	14	40	50,789	28,063	7
Alva	584	53	31	75,576	42,919	124

Congregation	Com	Eld	G	In 07	M&M	–18
Balfron	164	18	20	67,958	39,790	25
Fintry	144	12	20	28,634	10,918	2
Balquhidder	94	5	–	14,886	13,909	8
Killin and Ardeonaig	153	8	12	24,738	17,509	9
Bannockburn: Allan	458	34	–	73,127	35,143	58
Bannockburn: Ladywell	476	39	19	–	24,617	10
Bridge of Allan	789	51	53	112,237	86,706	72
Buchanan	98	9	–	25,072	12,946	16
Drymen	289	22	22	56,506	31,579	58
Buchlyvie	231	12	17	27,903	15,408	14
Gartmore	79	11	–	17,475	11,773	8
Callander	667	50	44	116,617	70,533	95
Cambusbarron: The Bruce Memorial	374	25	–	–	25,142	36
Clackmannan	493	29	43	71,414	50,561	42
Cowie and Plean	230	9	9	30,623	17,963	–
Fallin	259	8	–	38,437	26,780	70
Dollar	644	45	53	101,663	58,448	45
Glendevon	49	3	–	8,053	2,053	–
Muckhart	130	8	–	15,627	10,112	11
Dunblane: Cathedral	976	87	56	226,078	108,924	297
Dunblane: St Blane's	392	36	36	103,291	58,169	20
Gargunnock	175	14	–	32,931	15,608	12
Kilmadock	107	14	–	10,726	7,726	6
Kincardine-in-Menteith	96	8	–	13,525	6,495	22
Killearn	489	40	45	84,596	47,684	43
Kippen	305	–	24	30,648	23,273	–
Norrieston	133	13	13	17,037	11,960	4
Lecropt	244	15	21	44,007	29,787	12
Logie	580	53	42	92,989	61,396	58
Menstrie	392	30	26	65,601	41,094	28
Sauchie and Coalsnaughton	786	37	29	64,336	43,527	18
Stirling: Allan Park South	229	41	29	47,240	27,776	22
Stirling: Church of the Holy Rude	229	31	–	35,157	26,991	–
Stirling: North	528	37	25	70,052	35,499	50
Stirling: St Columba's	546	67	–	–	58,101	85
Stirling: St Mark's	260	9	–	31,785	24,857	–
Stirling: St Ninians Old	793	57	–	83,744	55,718	93
Stirling: Viewfield	404	22	33	55,493	42,305	20
Strathblane	199	26	37	72,347	48,306	42
Tillicoultry	794	56	52	91,620	58,446	112
Tullibody: St Serf's	469	19	30	–	43,317	75

24. Dunfermline

Aberdour: St Fillan's	409	27	–	72,111	43,300	40
Beath and Cowdenbeath: North	211	17	21	49,337	26,000	36
Cairneyhill	187	18	–	25,984	12,500	30
Limekilns	316	51	–	63,489	47,700	23
Carnock and Oakley	222	18	15	53,824	30,900	17

Congregation	Com	Eld	G	In 07	M&M	–18
Cowdenbeath: Trinity	423	25	19	56,249	31,000	68
Culross and Torryburn	261	20	–	45,357	28,500	–
Dalgety	613	37	29	120,418	64,000	170
Dunfermline: Abbey	771	70	–	128,323	77,000	200
Dunfermline: Gillespie Memorial	338	64	20	126,984	68,000	65
Dunfermline: North	218	16	–	34,599	22,100	24
Dunfermline: St Andrew's Erskine	229	26	19	41,747	21,100	175
Dunfermline: St Leonard's	483	42	25	70,043	35,000	58
Dunfermline: St Margaret's	400	47	28	55,731	35,100	24
Dunfermline: St Ninian's	318	43	41	41,842	25,500	58
Dunfermline: St Paul's East	–	4	–	8,016	–	48
Dunfermline: Townhill and Kingseat	381	32	36	64,285	39,700	30
Inverkeithing	373	25	–	64,207	37,400	105
North Queensferry	76	8	–	22,257	8,500	18
Kelty	378	–	45	79,799	37,500	–
Lochgelly and Benarty: St Serf's	530	46	–	58,494	34,700	25
Rosyth	293	19	–	38,201	23,000	20
Saline and Blairingone	176	13	25	43,522	31,200	19
Tulliallan and Kincardine	551	49	40	57,137	31,000	25

25. Kirkcaldy

Congregation	Com	Eld	G	In 07	M&M	–18
Auchterderran: St Fothad's	376	23	11	34,056	27,908	18
Kinglassie	175	12	–	–	12,518	13
Auchtertool	78	7	–	10,540	2,880	8
Kirkcaldy: Linktown	381	39	25	49,367	35,462	25
Buckhaven	216	23	–	33,762	20,197	10
Burntisland	523	39	49	48,948	46,590	16
Dysart	364	31	18	56,017	29,003	28
Glenrothes: Christ's Kirk	305	24	43	58,392	20,087	20
Glenrothes: St Columba's	586	32	20	–	36,559	47
Glenrothes: St Margaret's	376	32	34	61,223	37,269	80
Glenrothes: St Ninian's	293	42	12	61,927	41,067	20
Innerleven: East	123	7	17	28,220	14,223	77
Kennoway, Windygates and Balgonie: St Kenneth's	723	48	74	79,699	38,074	44
Kinghorn	443	29	–	68,012	45,366	50
Kirkcaldy: Abbotshall	647	60	–	78,105	51,414	24
Kirkcaldy: Pathhead	558	48	58	87,678	56,479	131
Kirkcaldy: St Andrew's	261	24	29	46,644	28,448	8
Kirkcaldy: St Bryce Kirk	680	38	34	83,235	59,000	38
Kirkcaldy: St John's	368	43	51	72,288	43,078	14
Kirkcaldy: Templehall	249	20	21	48,313	24,098	12
Kirkcaldy: Torbain	255	35	25	37,395	23,867	26
Kirkcaldy: Viewforth	326	12	–	34,249	19,526	4
Thornton	202	9	–	19,673	11,799	2
Leslie: Trinity	274	21	31	38,572	18,471	5
Leven	702	44	37	105,817	53,363	46
Markinch	604	40	31	81,634	41,888	24
Methil	333	25	30	–	23,330	9

Congregation	Com	Eld	G	In 07	M&M	–18
Methilhill and Denbeath	236	19	67	30,940	15,845	16
Wemyss	135	10	24	24,283	19,877	13

26. St Andrews

Abdie and Dunbog	175	21	–	17,448	12,092	12
Newburgh	261	14	–	22,849	14,858	20
Anstruther	342	30	–	45,257	28,143	21
Auchtermuchty	304	21	23	34,880	19,401	25
Balmerino	152	13	21	26,287	17,213	5
Wormit	284	18	37	31,360	17,642	18
Boarhills and Dunino	162	6	–	21,466	11,779	–
St Andrews: Martyrs'	274	19	25	33,666	27,743	–
Cameron	92	12	14	18,323	9,419	25
St Andrews: St Leonard's	590	49	23	123,302	68,418	25
Carnbee	109	14	20	21,782	9,377	9
Pittenweem	300	18	25	28,942	20,130	15
Cellardyke	299	24	49	44,497	22,368	12
Kilrenny	125	11	16	22,583	15,509	15
Ceres, Kemback and Springfield	463	49	31	58,645	67,987	29
Crail	425	33	51	50,356	34,321	16
Kingsbarns	97	10	–	17,315	8,633	–
Creich, Flisk and Kilmany	119	12	17	19,155	14,032	5
Monimail	107	14	–	20,243	14,636	19
Cupar: Old and St Michael of Tarvit	642	45	22	–	64,846	98
Cupar: St John's	795	42	45	68,772	42,506	42
Dairsie	120	6	16	16,611	9,405	3
Edenshead and Strathmiglo	203	13	18	29,982	16,031	9
Elie	378	29	67	59,978	47,853	10
Kilconquhar and Colinsburgh	209	17	–	34,168	22,892	18
Falkland	300	19	–	36,027	20,896	10
Freuchie	236	12	28	27,442	14,579	9
Howe of Fife	712	33	–	51,011	41,255	36
Largo and Newburn	288	18	–	46,314	22,791	19
Largo: St David's	190	17	42	35,330	16,997	7
Largoward	87	6	–	12,331	4,583	11
St Monans	294	13	43	56,802	32,528	70
Leuchars: St Athernase	494	25	40	61,697	36,621	15
Newport-on-Tay	384	42	–	70,155	47,564	76
St Andrews: Holy Trinity	517	44	54	80,532	49,766	80
St Andrews: Hope Park	686	84	40	127,394	78,611	35
Strathkinness	123	11	11	19,049	13,348	–
Tayport	452	34	29	41,874	31,224	26

27. Dunkeld and Meigle

Aberfeldy	251	17	15	33,247	25,914	178
Amulree and Strathbraan	22	3	–	–	2,525	–
Dull and Weem	106	10	17	15,392	9,999	13
Alyth	800	36	46	73,580	48,432	12

Congregation	Com	Eld	G	In 07	M&M	–18
Ardler, Kettins and Meigle	459	27	45	43,989	33,501	30
Bendochy	88	11	–	20,979	9,441	5
Coupar Angus: Abbey	342	29	14	46,750	30,993	88
Blair Atholl and Struan	145	20	17	21,139	17,718	12
Tenandry	72	9	–	20,592	10,256	5
Blairgowrie	965	53	47	98,406	59,950	24
Braes of Rannoch	35	8	–	15,228	7,848	–
Foss and Rannoch	116	16	23	–	15,340	3
Caputh and Clunie	188	28	13	25,429	18,720	18
Kinclaven	159	16	11	19,556	10,681	–
Dunkeld	428	29	23	85,878	68,505	30
Fortingall and Glenlyon	48	10	–	15,281	11,094	4
Kenmore and Lawers	95	8	24	28,330	19,204	30
Grantully, Logierait and Strathtay	159	15	12	35,955	25,376	18
Kirkmichael, Straloch and Glenshee	141	11	–	12,992	10,779	8
Rattray	466	23	28	37,015	22,345	11
Pitlochry	473	39	25	83,971	50,806	41

28. Perth

Abernethy and Dron and Arngask	379	27	34	–	29,959	33
Almondbank Tibbermore	327	24	46	40,203	24,632	45
Ardoch	179	16	36	31,174	18,126	12
Blackford	104	15	–	22,763	8,067	–
Auchterarder	686	37	47	87,499	53,321	70
Auchtergaven and Moneydie	510	20	30	40,392	27,005	79
Cargill Burrelton	335	16	37	37,188	29,140	7
Collace	127	9	14	17,648	10,702	15
Cleish	258	19	18	55,203	37,881	34
Fossoway: St Serf's and Devonside	254	21	–	38,262	23,683	41
Comrie	472	29	30	70,445	37,136	16
Dundurn	63	6	–	14,103	7,502	–
Crieff	928	56	50	96,591	53,036	83
Dunbarney and Forgandenny	621	36	45	60,825	36,553	23
Errol	297	18	21	32,918	22,787	35
Kilspindie and Rait	70	6	–	–	6,040	9
Fowlis Wester, Madderty and Monzie	325	34	13	48,763	23,895	26
Gask	130	13	14	15,795	13,769	8
Methven and Logiealmond	335	25	18	–	17,708	–
Kinross	643	34	40	79,975	48,482	115
Muthill	301	22	15	31,698	26,113	20
Trinity Gask and Kinkell	62	5	–	11,919	3,110	–
Orwell and Portmoak	514	45	26	67,396	40,812	37
Perth: Craigie	647	33	35	56,265	35,400	18
Perth: Kinnoull	463	37	28	–	38,438	50
Perth: Letham St Mark's	606	–	30	90,678	46,211	65
Perth: Moncreiffe	171	12	–	–	11,460	726
Perth: North	1,240	99	25	215,819	117,193	42
Perth: Riverside	70	–	–	31,678	–	27

Congregation	Com	Eld	G	In 07	M&M	–18
Perth: St John the Baptist's	710	38	–	110,843	63,240	–
Perth: St Leonard's-in-the-Fields and Trinity	570	78	–	–	63,891	13
Perth: St Matthew's	901	55	36	101,702	63,845	49
Redgorton and Stanley	406	34	30	35,935	24,804	47
St Madoes and Kinfauns	347	28	28	30,697	21,365	40
St Martin's	187	6	16	9,097	5,750	9
Scone: New	549	37	62	63,174	39,278	36
Scone: Old	638	36	39	64,252	40,244	44
The Stewartry of Strathearn	492	36	16	57,137	36,962	49

29. Dundee

Congregation	Com	Eld	G	In 07	M&M	–18
Abernyte	89	10	–	13,088	8,028	14
Inchture and Kinnaird	237	25	–	28,609	16,453	10
Longforgan	221	–	29	36,348	19,194	–
Auchterhouse	160	–	21	26,448	15,743	–
Murroes and Tealing	324	18	19	38,058	16,220	25
Dundee: Balgay	498	43	31	81,482	47,060	67
Dundee: Barnhill St Margaret's	830	64	60	114,271	75,593	33
Dundee: Broughty Ferry New Kirk	1,014	74	53	114,168	86,203	43
Dundee: Broughty Ferry St James'	242	–	34	57,993	29,971	–
Dundee: Broughty Ferry St Luke's and Queen Street	513	53	40	81,602	54,346	45
Dundee: Broughty Ferry St Stephen's and West	346	24	–	38,647	24,049	12
Dundee: Camperdown	178	16	13	32,037	19,480	8
Dundee: Chalmers Ardler	241	19	25	71,751	42,538	125
Dundee: Clepington and Fairmuir	469	–	–	56,216	33,358	–
Dundee: Craigiebank	275	21	–	48,179	33,380	12
Dundee: Douglas and Mid Craigie	–	–	22	35,639	17,134	–
Dundee: Downfield South	373	–	34	68,815	37,196	–
Dundee: Dundee (St Mary's)	644	55	34	74,500	62,241	20
Dundee: Lochee	717	49	36	81,563	49,280	258
Dundee: Logie and St John's Cross	353	20	27	121,377	64,755	65
Dundee: Mains	152	–	–	15,251	12,172	–
Dundee: Mains of Fintry	137	–	–	50,904	28,728	–
Dundee: Meadowside St Paul's	538	–	33	71,056	45,924	–
Dundee: Menzieshill	399	–	–	44,672	28,163	–
Dundee: St Andrew's	685	70	30	–	65,376	24
Dundee: St David's High Kirk	387	48	45	62,805	33,962	57
Dundee: Steeple	343	35	–	123,345	68,650	30
Dundee: Stobswell	553	–	–	68,608	48,816	–
Dundee: Strathmartine	406	35	35	–	38,293	9
Dundee: Trinity	629	52	31	50,389	33,606	89
Dundee: West	424	–	25	77,124	45,973	–
Dundee: Whitfield	–	–	–	14,487	–	–
Fowlis and Liff	152	14	12	19,079	22,894	17
Lundie and Muirhead of Liff	344	34	–	45,767	21,849	–
Invergowrie	449	53	57	59,092	38,054	118
Monifieth: Panmure	420	33	–	55,570	29,149	49
Monifieth: St Rule's	588	31	41	51,563	36,103	12

Congregation	Com	Eld	G	In 07	M&M	–18
Monifieth: South	370	23	37	47,366	31,408	139
Monikie and Newbigging	245	18	–	23,917	20,290	2

30. Angus

Congregation	Com	Eld	G	In 07	M&M	–18
Aberlemno	196	12	–	19,803	12,776	17
Guthrie and Rescobie	230	12	14	21,633	12,787	15
Arbirlot	216	14	–	19,051	12,642	16
Carmyllie	131	13	12	19,389	14,284	6
Arbroath: Knox's	384	26	37	40,472	24,969	2
Arbroath: St Vigeans	643	49	–	63,006	42,859	26
Arbroath: Old and Abbey	652	43	39	93,698	58,366	75
Arbroath: St Andrew's	804	50	27	147,886	63,301	160
Arbroath: West Kirk	989	81	58	92,148	65,057	98
Barry	233	15	12	28,223	17,633	6
Carnoustie	450	34	30	77,683	44,041	35
Brechin: Cathedral	952	49	16	–	48,840	16
Brechin: Gardner Memorial	558	36	12	42,349	32,240	6
Carnoustie: Panbride	756	35	–	64,440	38,953	55
Colliston	195	10	12	19,935	10,901	12
Friockheim Kinnell	225	17	23	18,583	12,987	14
Inverkeilor and Lunan	199	11	21	22,965	14,512	–
Dun and Hillside	463	41	29	–	27,177	40
Dunnichen, Letham and Kirkden	356	17	30	40,731	26,282	18
Eassie and Nevay	60	7	–	9,137	5,730	–
Newtyle	294	16	50	25,520	19,049	18
Edzell Lethnot Glenesk	450	26	34	41,223	31,695	12
Fern Careston Menmuir	127	9	–	15,679	11,869	4
Farnell	110	11	–	4,694	7,765	–
Forfar: East and Old	1,292	49	44	83,666	65,463	75
Forfar: Lowson Memorial	973	35	25	78,378	44,206	105
Forfar: St Margaret's	909	37	25	67,783	49,656	70
Glamis, Inverarity and Kinettles	418	26	–	42,042	28,963	26
Inchbrayock	206	11	–	47,003	20,787	2
Montrose: Melville South	339	16	–	36,301	21,499	–
Kirriemuir: St Andrew's	385	31	45	82,348	32,577	15
Oathlaw Tannadice	178	8	–	18,327	14,124	20
Montrose: Old and St Andrew's	935	53	47	–	69,018	115
The Glens and Kirriemuir: Old	1,147	93	43	161,209	89,893	45
The Isla Parishes	293	23	17	–	23,038	20

31. Aberdeen

Congregation	Com	Eld	G	In 07	M&M	–18
Aberdeen: Bridge of Don Oldmachar	298	4	–	–	31,443	200
Aberdeen: Cove	57	6	–	15,088	–	24
Aberdeen: Craigiebuckler	828	66	60	–	58,762	130
Aberdeen: Ferryhill	490	49	34	87,527	46,868	15
Aberdeen: Garthdee	266	17	22	–	13,702	9
Aberdeen: Gilcomston South	334	26	–	192,931	77,252	55
Aberdeen: High Hilton	553	57	43	–	71,325	55

Congregation	Com	Eld	G	In 07	M&M	–18
Aberdeen: Holburn West	514	44	22	99,011	66,393	23
Aberdeen: Mannofield	1,510	122	67	178,149	112,654	214
Aberdeen: Mastrick	398	18	19	54,969	25,893	30
Aberdeen: Middlefield	167	9	–	10,713	1,105	20
Aberdeen: Midstocket	745	69	66	122,846	87,286	33
Aberdeen: New Stockethill	86	–	–	33,543	–	17
Aberdeen: Northfield	307	14	23	26,443	18,981	80
Aberdeen: Queen Street	879	59	47	73,574	65,856	40
Aberdeen: Queen's Cross	613	50	36	161,769	95,735	75
Aberdeen: Rubislaw	651	83	40	139,933	83,238	100
Aberdeen: Ruthrieston West	393	35	33	67,018	37,501	20
Aberdeen: St Columba's Bridge of Don	362	25	–	84,851	54,514	274
Aberdeen: St George's Tillydrone	110	9	18	21,076	8,804	–
Aberdeen: St John's Church for Deaf People	105	6	–	–	–	1
Aberdeen: St Machar's Cathedral	631	44	–	96,354	65,199	34
Aberdeen: St Mark's	507	47	30	93,108	56,662	60
Aberdeen: St Mary's	495	55	20	56,660	28,766	80
Aberdeen: St Nicholas Kincorth, South of	460	31	30	55,392	37,546	70
Aberdeen: St Nicholas Uniting, Kirk of	484	55	17	97,684	–	4
Aberdeen: St Stephen's	249	27	16	65,365	34,065	46
Aberdeen: South Holburn	797	60	69	91,425	71,339	46
Aberdeen: Summerhill	169	21	–	28,426	16,377	24
Aberdeen: Torry St Fittick's	529	31	32	48,977	30,205	2
Aberdeen: Woodside	342	33	27	47,784	25,572	46
Bucksburn Stoneywood	555	–	24	–	33,083	–
Cults	855	68	57	148,714	77,612	40
Dyce	1,281	77	35	–	53,424	255
Kingswells	432	31	23	49,258	31,166	26
Newhills	902	44	63	101,949	59,979	170
Peterculter	693	51	–	100,478	55,178	163

32. Kincardine and Deeside

Aberluthnott	220	10	19	14,996	11,413	–
Laurencekirk	504	13	35	31,535	19,755	14
Aboyne and Dinnet	441	6	29	–	40,679	20
Cromar	261	10	–	–	13,213	4
Arbuthnott and Bervie	589	35	–	–	34,468	53
Banchory-Devenick and Maryculter/Cookney	231	19	14	54,197	28,675	50
Banchory-Ternan: East	636	48	34	88,307	49,317	127
Banchory-Ternan: West	638	42	37	111,369	53,825	50
Birse and Feughside	254	25	18	31,140	32,222	14
Braemar and Crathie	273	34	16	65,791	34,135	20
Drumoak-Durris	467	24	46	60,202	34,598	69
Glenmuick (Ballater)	340	27	26	47,933	30,053	–
Kinneff	145	5	–	–	4,268	–
Stonehaven: South	299	24	13	44,395	25,178	16
Mearns Coastal	318	28	62	29,048	23,327	–
Mid Deeside	794	51	26	55,151	45,705	24

Congregation	Com	Eld	G	In 07	M&M	–18
Newtonhill	391	14	20	28,209	21,418	146
Portlethen	501	17	–	58,781	40,737	177
Stonehaven: Dunnottar	840	27	21	78,942	45,070	21
Stonehaven: Fetteresso	928	40	38	165,078	73,897	164
West Mearns	545	21	51	44,342	32,979	29

33. Gordon

Barthol Chapel	98	10	10	10,629	2,563	19
Tarves	496	31	37	35,895	28,458	–
Belhelvie	379	36	23	72,463	35,704	72
Blairdaff and Chapel of Garioch	421	34	19	43,592	27,301	55
Cluny	205	10	10	22,473	15,504	15
Monymusk	125	6	–	17,984	9,249	21
Culsalmond and Rayne	234	7	–	10,332	7,641	21
Daviot	154	10	–	17,828	11,477	13
Cushnie and Tough	288	17	11	33,009	21,648	15
Drumblade	86	7	11	–	3,859	5
Huntly Strathbogie	776	41	30	64,163	37,510	108
Echt	273	14	12	25,179	17,663	24
Midmar	163	7	–	14,313	9,075	17
Ellon	1,727	95	–	132,037	75,743	38
Fintray Kinellar Keithhall	230	18	13	–	24,562	25
Foveran	362	20	–	–	21,294	30
Howe Trinity	673	31	45	49,763	31,000	35
Huntly Cairnie Glass	778	21	33	39,727	34,842	8
Insch-Leslie-Premnay-Oyne	548	40	40	30,653	33,998	8
Inverurie: St Andrew's	1,209	37	35	100,134	62,649	50
Inverurie: West	756	45	34	86,652	43,000	72
Kemnay	611	38	–	53,234	36,807	148
Kintore	864	49	31	–	63,143	125
Meldrum and Bourtie	539	35	42	62,348	40,252	44
Methlick	361	24	21	50,445	29,486	21
New Machar	486	25	28	51,258	30,000	60
Noth	339	12	–	20,747	16,905	15
Skene	1,515	100	58	145,950	81,172	187
Udny and Pitmedden	488	–	16	63,268	38,286	–
Upper Donside	437	21	–	42,523	25,809	43

34. Buchan

Aberdour	139	10	9	9,940	5,265	12
Pitsligo	130	11	–	–	11,380	30
Sandhaven	76	7	–	–	2,794	27
Auchaber United	165	12	11	13,243	12,163	14
Auchterless	202	19	18	25,438	13,655	11
Banff	755	33	26	74,470	58,864	167
King Edward	163	17	14	19,366	11,516	11
Crimond	258	12	–	18,140	12,483	–
Lonmay	171	12	12	10,174	7,591	–

Congregation	Com	Eld	G	In 07	M&M	–18
St Fergus	200	9	9	13,463	4,343	12
Cruden	481	32	31	56,766	34,937	35
Deer	833	35	22	49,806	31,414	17
Fordyce	508	27	33	53,507	40,925	16
Fraserburgh: Old	811	65	77	121,327	81,202	273
Fraserburgh: South	326	23	–	35,484	26,117	27
Inverallochy and Rathen: East	95	11	–	17,275	3,949	12
Fraserburgh: West	642	41	–	54,612	31,609	68
Rathen: West	110	10	–	7,645	2,944	7
Fyvie	387	24	37	39,167	27,951	24
Rothienorman	155	12	12	13,425	6,158	–
Gardenstown	70	11	31	54,067	29,774	60
Longside	553	25	–	54,780	33,194	118
Macduff	853	41	61	93,914	54,961	126
Marnoch	468	16	13	41,984	24,338	4
Maud and Savoch	239	19	22	25,637	15,206	9
New Deer: St Kane's	455	21	17	51,204	25,590	92
Monquhitter and New Byth	383	20	14	24,973	16,814	14
Turriff: St Andrew's	556	32	23	46,800	27,394	33
New Pitsligo	341	9	–	22,391	15,100	18
Strichen and Tyrie	605	22	31	48,070	25,242	30
Ordiquhill and Cornhill	158	11	10	10,628	7,205	19
Whitehills	304	20	38	33,471	18,223	15
Peterhead: Old	457	29	36	69,907	36,309	45
Peterhead: St Andrew's	564	37	35	62,777	32,478	20
Peterhead: Trinity	355	24	30	131,904	58,226	23
Turriff: St Ninian's and Forglen	950	41	44	75,074	46,953	100
35. Moray						
Aberlour	334	26	24	39,007	30,171	42
Alves and Burghead	161	18	43	–	14,698	15
Kinloss and Findhorn	94	17	11	18,196	11,806	4
Bellie	313	20	35	38,886	32,835	96
Speymouth	219	12	20	24,811	10,899	16
Birnie and Pluscarden	308	24	43	32,514	25,018	8
Elgin: High	669	45	–	75,786	48,816	66
Buckie: North	478	40	55	59,542	35,692	34
Buckie: South and West	316	30	31	39,126	23,760	214
Enzie	96	8	16	12,929	8,755	6
Cullen and Deskford	379	29	35	43,333	26,619	13
Dallas	60	7	12	9,434	8,776	10
Forres: St Leonard's	254	16	39	62,420	39,196	95
Rafford	78	5	–	–	5,158	–
Duffus, Spynie and Hopeman	347	38	28	50,611	31,096	10
Dyke	148	13	16	20,151	11,138	14
Edinkillie	90	13	–	15,393	12,162	3
Elgin: St Giles' and St Columba's South	1,231	96	49	132,057	81,873	145
Findochty	51	10	11	–	12,481	24

Congregation	Com	Eld	G	In 07	M&M	–18
Portknockie	85	9	26	30,281	11,658	50
Rathven	108	14	21	17,859	11,199	7
Forres: St Laurence	450	30	40	72,644	46,749	12
Keith: North, Newmill, Boharm and Rothiemay	657	55	30	49,516	54,684	132
Keith: St Rufus, Botriphnie and Grange	1,038	57	34	62,126	39,599	124
Knockando, Elchies and Archiestown	271	15	11	21,492	18,711	8
Rothes	323	20	24	29,447	19,198	20
Lossiemouth: St Gerardine's High	387	13	35	59,106	35,185	12
Lossiemouth: St James'	340	22	41	49,476	31,932	20
Mortlach and Cabrach	394	17	14	20,849	18,709	5
St Andrew's-Lhanbryd and Urquhart	483	43	26	52,185	41,834	46

36. Abernethy

Abernethy	163	20	–	40,979	22,876	86
Cromdale and Advie	94	2	–	11,162	8,444	7
Alvie and Insh	68	8	–	28,512	16,808	21
Boat of Garten and Kincardine	86	9	20	22,110	13,157	6
Duthil	73	8	16	9,938	4,016	12
Dulnain Bridge	35	5	–	10,861	8,274	–
Grantown-on-Spey	246	18	15	35,302	26,057	10
Kingussie	120	14	–	26,313	12,624	18
Laggan	35	5	–	19,149	6,567	10
Newtonmore	91	15	–	29,494	13,928	
Rothiemurchus and Aviemore	89	6	–	18,804	12,321	10
Tomintoul, Glenlivet and Inveraven	171	13	–	20,896	16,432	7

37. Inverness

Ardersier	64	11	11	17,558	9,426	14
Petty	72	12	11	20,033	9,686	17
Auldearn and Dalmore	80	6	15	16,691	5,954	80
Nairn: St Ninian's	251	20	33	45,540	25,240	43
Cawdor	180	18	–	31,083	18,020	12
Croy and Dalcross	57	11	9	11,687	5,889	7
Culloden: The Barn	347	21	18	76,557	42,153	150
Daviot and Dunlichity	61	7	–	18,446	10,843	13
Moy, Dalarossie and Tomatin	31	5	9	9,150	7,616	15
Dores and Boleskine	73	10	–	17,384	12,388	10
Inverness: Crown	650	67	74	144,768	75,435	121
Inverness: Dalneigh and Bona	286	19	29	94,651	53,081	50
Inverness: East	323	41	–	136,765	79,609	120
Inverness: Hilton	289	8	27	90,969	33,286	95
Inverness: Inshes	215	17	–	122,647	54,352	49
Inverness: Kinmylies	127	12	–	62,337	15,562	30
Inverness: Ness Bank	620	71	36	117,611	61,505	118
Inverness: Old High St Stephen's	526	59	–	119,578	69,499	67
Inverness: St Columba High	206	25	16	48,143	28,935	7
Inverness: Trinity	332	30	23	83,834	46,625	77
Kilmorack and Erchless	138	18	26	49,237	20,165	25

Congregation	Com	Eld	G	In 07	M&M	–18
Kiltarlity	35	6	–	14,696	11,504	–
Kirkhill	74	5	13	13,303	7,280	15
Nairn: Old	854	59	35	110,816	65,285	80
Urquhart and Glenmoriston	133	6	–	57,042	33,137	37

38. Lochaber

Acharacle	49	4	–	21,773	8,334	7
Ardnamurchan	20	5	–	7,272	2,740	5
Ardgour	55	7	10	13,922	8,025	9
Strontian	27	4	8	10,013	2,666	21
Arisaig and the Small Isles	65	8	18	14,475	6,209	12
Mallaig: St Columba and Knoydart	55	5	–	21,151	14,148	45
Duror	42	7	14	14,647	4,240	10
Glencoe: St Munda's	63	8	22	17,727	7,405	12
Fort Augustus	75	7	13	22,229	11,728	36
Glengarry	31	5	12	12,529	6,666	10
Fort William: Duncansburgh MacIntosh	465	38	31	104,337	66,780	92
Kilmonivaig	86	6	15	16,719	15,140	10
Kilmallie	162	10	25	–	29,444	14
Kinlochleven	66	8	20	18,813	10,089	29
Nether Lochaber	50	10	–	13,392	8,089	18
Morvern	45	6	10	9,662	6,701	6

39. Ross

Alness	92	12	–	37,068	20,837	38
Avoch	32	7	15	15,104	8,574	17
Fortrose and Rosemarkie	118	16	–	41,004	23,623	13
Contin	66	10	–	25,978	14,114	26
Cromarty	50	7	14	–	11,309	30
Dingwall: Castle Street	135	21	25	53,753	24,744	10
Dingwall: St Clement's	251	30	22	57,640	34,096	30
Fearn Abbey and Nigg	100	12	–	36,042	18,138	5
Tarbat	69	10	–	16,377	8,982	–
Ferintosh	191	24	31	50,150	28,527	49
Fodderty and Strathpeffer	135	17	21	35,323	18,160	32
Invergordon	165	13	–	51,738	28,712	49
Killearnan	132	20	–	29,649	21,311	30
Knockbain	59	11	–	19,151	11,738	2
Kilmuir and Logie Easter	80	11	29	26,985	18,464	14
Kiltearn	90	7	–	30,205	16,406	38
Lochbroom and Ullapool	55	5	10	27,003	20,420	11
Resolis and Urquhart	84	7	–	25,292	17,948	18
Rosskeen	133	11	22	49,661	27,474	41
Tain	155	11	19	59,304	33,609	200
Urray and Kilchrist	116	14	19	42,752	25,849	50

40. Sutherland

Altnaharra and Farr	32	2	–	11,314	6,657	3

Congregation	Com	Eld	G	In 07	M&M	–18
Assynt and Stoer	28	1	–	–	7,109	14
Clyne	73	9	–	22,112	11,760	5
Kildonan and Loth Helmsdale	42	6	–	–	4,238	8
Creich	26	7	13	15,583	10,640	–
Rosehall	21	3	–	7,878	3,665	4
Dornoch Cathedral	345	34	54	128,954	64,089	70
Durness and Kinlochbervie	33	3	10	17,323	12,275	11
Eddrachillis	17	2	–	15,677	7,461	5
Golspie	83	19	10	29,927	18,714	10
Kincardine Croick and Edderton	77	12	15	25,886	17,235	19
Lairg	51	6	19	24,979	11,042	11
Rogart	25	4	8	15,339	7,069	6
Melness and Tongue	47	7	–	14,624	10,275	6

41. Caithness

	Com	Eld	G	In 07	M&M	–18
Bower	36	6	10	14,951	4,641	–
Watten	45	4	–	12,600	7,144	24
Canisbay	44	3	16	16,858	6,619	25
Dunnet	18	3	–	–	2,837	–
Keiss	29	2	9	13,555	3,287	–
Halkirk and Westerdale	47	5	17	18,339	9,427	18
Olrig	53	3	8	8,977	4,090	14
The North Coast Parish	56	15	27		13,499	11
The Parish of Latheron	70	12	18	22,009	19,440	13
Thurso: St Peter's and St Andrew's	225	19	44	–	40,958	56
Thurso: West	264	25	38	50,216	37,657	35
Wick: Bridge Street	163	12	–	28,302	20,187	–
Wick: Old	208	40	32	53,145	40,485	17
Wick: Pulteneytown and Thrumster	241	16	23	–	32,434	275

42. Lochcarron – Skye

	Com	Eld	G	In 07	M&M	–18
Applecross, Lochcarron and Torridon	86	5	12	36,085	23,155	23
Bracadale and Duirinish	70	8	8	24,291	19,924	4
Gairloch and Dundonnell	97	5	–	66,442	44,752	30
Glenelg and Kintail	51	8	–	30,519	16,838	35
Kilmuir and Stenscholl	72	8	–	39,632	24,264	45
Lochalsh	74	10	24	41,087	25,194	25
Portree	95	7	–	55,570	32,613	30
Snizort	57	5	–	37,937	32,071	20
Strath and Sleat	192	14	14	93,737	48,794	76

43. Uist

	Com	Eld	G	In 07	M&M	–18
Barra	38	5	–	18,825	4,875	91
Benbecula	70	12	10	36,180	17,572	50
Berneray and Lochmaddy	57	4	13	33,708	17,462	6
Carinish	79	8	13	50,902	26,287	18
Kilmuir and Paible	32	4	–	35,816	21,269	45
Manish-Scarista	41	3	–	33,106	21,074	13

Congregation	Com	Eld	G	In 07	M&M	–18
South Uist	63	10	9	21,689	14,919	22
Tarbert	141	18	–	88,181	51,545	53
44. Lewis						
Barvas	88	8	–	61,900	35,761	36
Carloway	43	3	–	27,719	15,597	28
Cross Ness	70	10	–	65,251	22,207	42
Kinloch	42	7	–	30,345	16,275	24
Knock	56	2	–	47,017	27,967	14
Lochs-Crossbost	22	4	–	24,375	9,743	14
Lochs-in-Bernera	28	3	–	20,017	9,481	27
Stornoway: High	256	18	–	134,518	71,135	70
Stornoway: Martin's Memorial	154	10	17	75,986	31,927	80
Stornoway: St Columba	147	17	50	78,163	45,188	92
Uig	34	6	–	24,183	13,826	5
45. Orkney						
Birsay, Harray and Sandwick	354	29	49	44,673	28,304	41
East Mainland	275	21	22	17,713	20,496	15
Eday	6	1	–	3,148	821	–
Stronsay: Moncur Memorial	84	12	15	13,357	6,392	16
Evie	37	2	–	6,618	6,557	–
Firth	117	10	–	25,697	13,509	45
Rendall	53	–	14	8,263	5,421	–
Flotta	24	6	–	3,092	1,284	4
Hoy and Walls	64	13	13	–	1,990	7
Kirkwall: East	452	44	32	–	37,985	39
Kirkwall: St Magnus Cathedral	645	–	28	70,557	46,064	–
North Ronaldsay	15	–	–	–	979	–
Sanday	82	10	13	9,181	5,288	–
Orphir	123	12	16	18,700	10,764	14
Stenness	85	9	–	13,704	8,036	3
Papa Westray	10	4	–	4,694	1,905	4
Westray	69	16	24	19,675	11,067	35
Rousay	23	3	7	3,038	2,723	–
Shapinsay	59	8	–	4,919	2,870	7
South Ronaldsay and Burray	173	12	14	17,104	12,128	18
Stromness	366	26	26	43,816	35,790	20
46. Shetland						
Burra Isle	42	6	23	8,554	2,982	18
Tingwall	159	18	10	27,736	20,668	36
Delting	92	8	–	15,607	9,815	14
Northmavine	74	9	–	11,133	5,290	10
Dunrossness and St Ninian's inc. Fair Isle	69	18	–	17,809	9,603	67
Sandwick, Cunningsburgh and Quarff	120	10	27	26,497	14,287	36
Fetlar	19	5	–	1,453	875	–
Unst	127	10	17	18,784	9,573	4

Congregation	Com	Eld	G	In 07	M&M	–18
Yell	117	13	14	12,295	7,889	–
Lerwick and Bressay	–	–	10	72,049	44,769	–
Nesting and Lunnasting	40	5	19	7,351	5,785	–
Whalsay and Skerries	229	17	20	29,204	13,539	25
Sandsting and Aithsting	48	9	–	9,437	2,741	38
Walls and Sandness	41	12	5	8,227	2,852	12

47. England

Corby: St Andrew's	294	20	33	49,379	32,236	20
Corby: St Ninian's	284	20	10	38,772	28,245	6
Guernsey: St Andrew's in the Grange	226	24	–	51,439	34,914	24
Jersey: St Columba's	128	18	–	60,042	34,642	27
Liverpool: St Andrew's	37	5	5	21,584	8,641	8
London: Crown Court	254	35	9	–	52,693	28
London: St Columba's	1,105	45	–	–	125,958	115
Newcastle: St Andrew's	102	20	–	–	4,269	18

INDEX OF MINISTERS

NOTE: Ministers who are members of a Presbytery are designated 'A' if holding a parochial appointment in that Presbytery, or 'B' if otherwise qualifying for membership.

'A-1, A-2' etc. indicate the numerical order of congregations in the Presbyteries of Edinburgh, Glasgow and Hamilton.

Also included are:

(1) Ministers who have resigned their seat in Presbytery (List 6-H)

(2) Ministers who hold a Practising Certificate (List 6-I)

(3) Ministers serving overseas (List 6-K)

(4) Auxiliary Ministers (List 6-A)

(5) Ministers ordained for sixty years and upwards (List 6-Q)

(6) Ministers who have died since the publication of the last *Year Book* (List 6-R)

NB *For a list of the Diaconate, see List 6-G.*

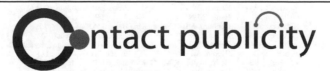

MacLeod, N.	Hamilton 17A-48	MacRae, G.	Stirling 23A	Maxton, R.M.	Falkirk 22B
MacLeod, N.	Kirkcaldy 25B	Macrae, Mrs J.	Lothian 3A	Maxwell, F.E.	Dumbarton 18A
McLeod, R.	List 6-R	MacRae, M.H.	Dunkeld/Meigle 27A	Maxwell, I.D.	Edinburgh 1A-39
MacLeod, R.	Argyll 19A	Macrae, N.C.	Lothian 3B	May, A.	Glasgow 16A-34
MacLeod, R.A.R.	St Andrews 26A	MacRae, N.I.	West Lothian 2B	Mayes, R.	Ayr 10A
MacLeod, R.N.	England 47B	MacRae, R.N.	Lochcarron/Skye 42A	Mayne, K.A.L.	G'ock/Paisley 14A
Macleod, W.	Lewis 44B	Macritchie, I.A.M.	Inverness 37B	Mead, J.M.	Wigtown/Stranraer 9A
MacLeod-Mair, A.T.	Glasgow 16A-44	McRoberts, T.D.	Moray 35A	Meager, P.	St Andrews 26B
McMahon, Miss E.J.	G'ock/Pais' 14A	MacSween, D.A.	Ross 39A	Mealyea, H.B.	Ayr 10A
McMahon, J.K.S.	Edinburgh 1B	MacSween, N.	List 6-R	Mehigan, A.	Moray 35A
MacMahon, Mrs J.P.H.	D'barton 18A	MacVicar, K.	Dunkeld/Meigle 27B	Meikle, Mrs A.A.	Lanark 13A
McMahon, R.J.	List 6-R	McWhirter, T.M.	Wigtown/Stran' 9A	Melrose, J.H.L.	Hamilton 17B
McMillan, C.D.	Dundee 29B	McWilliam, A.	Glasgow 16A-141	Melville, D.D.	Dunfermline 24B
McMillan, Mrs E.F.	Dundee 29A	McWilliam, T.M.	Ross 39B	Merchant, M.C.	Gordon 33A
Macmillan, G.	Edinburgh 1A-32	McWilliams, G.	Perth 28A	Messeder, L.	Dunfermline 24A
MacMillan, Mrs R.M.	Perth 28B	Mailer, C.	List 6-I	Middleton, J.R.H.	Edinburgh 1B
McMillan, S.	Dundee 29A	Main, A.	Aberdeen 31B	Middleton, P.	Edinburgh 1B
McMillan, W.J.	Buchan 34B	Main, A.W.A.	List 6-I	Mill, D.	Greenock/Paisley 14A
MacMillan, W.M.	Annan'/Eskdale 7B	Main, D.M.	Perth 28A	Millar, A.E.	Perth 28B
McMullin, J.A.	Falkirk 22B	Mair, J.	List 6-H	Millar, A.M.	Perth 28B
MacMurchie, F.L.	Edinburgh 1B	Mair, M.V.A.	Dundee 29B	Millar, J.L.	List 6-H
McNab, D.G.	Ayr 10A	Majcher, P.L.	England 47A	Millar, Mrs J.M.	Perth 28B
MacNab, H.S.D.	St Andrews 26B	Malcolm, A.	Inverness 37A	Millar, Miss M.R.M.	Argyll 19B
McNab, J.L.	Orkney 45A	Malcolm, M.	Glasgow 16A-11	Millar, P.W.	List 6-I
McNaught, N.A.	Ayr 10A	Malloch, P.R.M.	Stirling 23A	Miller, A.	Europe 48A
McNaught, S.M.	Kirkcaldy 25B	Malloch, R.J.	Dum'/K'cudbright 8A	Miller, C.W.	Dundee 29B
McNaughtan, J.	Irv'/K'marnock 11A	Mann, J.	Glasgow 16A-117	Miller, H.G.	Argyll 19B
McNaughton, D.J.H.	Perth 28B	Mann, J.T.	Sutherland 40A	Miller, Mrs I.B.	Lists 6-H and 6-I
Macnaughton, G.F.H.	Orkney 45A	Manners, S.	Edinburgh 1A-68	Miller, I.H.	Dumbarton 18A
Macnaughton, J.A.	Glasgow 16B	Manson, Mrs E.	G'ock/Paisley 14A	Miller, J.D.	Glasgow 16B
McNay, J.J.	Ardrossan 12A	Manson, I.A.	Europe 48A	Miller, J.G.	Dum'/Kirkcudbright 8B
Macnee, I.	Buchan 34A	Manson, J.A.	Lothian 3B	Miller, J.R.	Dum'/Kirkcudbright 8B
McNeil, J.N.R.	Stirling 23A	Manson, R.L.	West Lothian 2B	Miller, W.B.	Moray 35B
MacNeil, T.	Lewis 44A	Mappin, M.G.	Caithness 41B	Milliken, J.	Dum'/Kirkcudbright 8A
McNeill, C.C.	Europe 48D	Mair, I.	List 6-I	Milloy, A.M.	England 47B
McNicol, B.	Jedburgh 6B	Marsh, S.	Dum'/K'cudbright 8A	Mills, A.	List 6-I
McNidder, R.H.	Ayr 10B	Marshall, A.S.	West Lothian 2A	Mills, P.W.	England 47B
McPake, J.L.	Hamilton 17A-34	Marshall, Mrs F.	Argyll 19B	Milne, R.B.	Annandale/Eskdale 7A
McPake, J.M.	Edinburgh 1A-47	Marshall, F.J.	Greenock/Paisley 14B	Milroy, T.	Dundee 29B
McPhail, A.M.	Ayr 10B	Marshall, J.S.	List 6-H	Milton, E.G.	Angus 30B
McPhee, D.C.	Edinburgh 1B	Marshall, T.E.	Irv'/Kilmarnock 11A	Mirrilees, J.B.	List 6-R
MacPhee, D.P.	List 6-R	Marten, S.	Edinburgh 1A-48	Mitchell, A.B.	Stirling 23A
MacPherson, A.J.	Stirling 23A	Martin, A.M.	England 47B	Mitchell, D.	Argyll 19A
Macpherson, A.S.	Edinburgh 1B	Martin, D.N.	Buchan 34A	Mitchell, D.R.	Ardrossan 12B
Macpherson, C.C.R.	Edinburgh 1B	Martin, G.M.	Lochcarron/Skye 42B	Mitchell, J.	Lothian 3A
McPherson, D.	Inverness 37A	Martin, J.	Hamilton 17B	Mitchell, J.	Dundee 29B
McPherson, D.C.	Hamilton 17A-30	Martindale, J.P.F.	Glasgow 16B	Mitchell, Miss S.M.	Ayr 10B
Macpherson, D.J.	Annan'/Esk' 7B	Masih, M.	Hamilton 17A-38	Moffat, R.	Edinburgh 1A-78
MacPherson, G.C.	List 6-I	Massie, R.W.	Kin'/Deeside 32B	Moffat, T.	Glasgow 16B
Macpherson, J.	Sutherland 40A	Masson, J.D.	List 6-I	Moffett, J.R.	List 6-R
Macpherson, K.J.	Uist 43B	Mathers, D.L.	Falkirk 22B	Moir, I.A.	Edinburgh 1B
McPherson, S.M.	Edinburgh 1A-11	Matheson, I.G.	List 6-I	Moir, S.W.	Melrose/Peebles 4A
Macpherson, S.M.	Dunfermline 24B	Matheson, J.G.	List 6-R	Monro, G.D.	List 6-R
McPherson, W.	List 6-I	Mathew, J.G.	Moray 35A	Monteith, W.G.	Edinburgh 1B
MacQuarrie, D.A.	Lochaber 38A	Mathieson, A.R.	Edinburgh 1B	Montgomerie, Miss J.B.	Ab'deen 31B
McQuarrie, I.A.	Edinburgh 1A-10	Mathieson, Mrs F.M.	Edinburgh 1A-8	Montgomery, R.A.	G'ock/Paisley 14B
MacQuarrie, S.	Glasgow 16B	Mathieson, J.S.	Inverness 37A	Moodie, A.R.	List 6-I
McQuilken, J.E.	Perth 28B	Matthews, J.C.	Glasgow 16A-111	Moore, Miss A.A.	Hamilton 17A-12
MacRae, Mrs E.H.	Stirling 23A	Matthews, S.C.	Glasgow 16A-94	Moore, A.J.	Falkirk 22A

INDEX OF PARISHES AND PLACES

NOTE: Numbers on the right of the column refer to the Presbytery in which the district lies. Names in brackets are given for ease of identification. They may refer to the name of the parish, which may be different from that of the district, or they distinguish places with the same name, or they indicate the first named charge in a union.

INDEX OF DISCONTINUED PARISH AND CONGREGATIONAL NAMES

The following index updates and corrects the 'Index of Former Parishes and Congregations' printed in the previous edition of the *Year Book*. As before, it lists the parishes of the Church of Scotland and the congregations of the United Presbyterian Church (and its constituent denominations), the Free Church (1843–1900) and the United Free Church (1900–29) whose names have completely disappeared, largely as a consequence of union.

The observant will notice that this index appears this year under a different title. The hope is that this will make even more clear what the index does and does not contain. The introductory paragraphs to the index have from the outset contained a statement to the effect that this is *not* intended to offer 'a comprehensive guide to readjustment in the Church of Scotland'; that would require a considerably larger number of pages. Experience has shown, however, that there have been those who have been sufficiently misled by the apparent all-inclusiveness of the previous title to draw to the editor's attention the omission of this or that congregation whose name had been slightly altered – but not out of all recognition – as a result of union.

As was stated in previous years, the purpose of this index is to assist those who are trying to identify the present-day successor of some former parish or congregation whose name is now wholly out of use and which can therefore no longer be easily traced. Where the former name has not disappeared completely, and the whereabouts of the former parish or congregation may therefore be easily established by reference to the name of some existing parish, the former name has not been included in this index. The following examples will illustrate some of the criteria used to determine whether a name should be included or not:

- Where all the former congregations in a town have been united into one, as in the case of Melrose or Selkirk, the names of these former congregations have not been included; but, in the case of towns with more than one congregation, such as Galashiels or Hawick, the names of the various constituent congregations are listed.
- The same principle applies in the case of discrete areas of cities. For example, as Dundee: Lochee and Glasgow: Dennistoun New are now the only congregations in Lochee and Dennistoun respectively, there is no need to list Dundee: Lochee St Ninian's, Glasgow: Dennistoun South and any other congregations which had Lochee or Dennistoun in their names.
- Where a prefix such as North, Old, Little, Mid or the like has been lost but the substantive part of the name has been retained, the former name has not been included: it is assumed that someone searching for Little Dalton or Mid Yell will have no difficulty in connecting these with Dalton or Yell.
- Where the present name of a united congregation includes the names of some or all of its constituent parts, these former names do not appear in the list: thus, neither Glasgow: Anderston nor Glasgow: Kelvingrove appears, since both names are easily traceable to Glasgow: Anderston Kelvingrove.

Two other criteria for inclusion or exclusion may also be mentioned:

- Some parishes and congregations have disappeared, and their names have been lost, as a consequence of suppression, dissolution or secession. The names of rural parishes in this category have been included, together with the names of their Presbyteries to assist with identification, but those in towns and cities have not been included, as there will clearly be no difficulty in establishing the general location of the parish or congregation in question.
- Since 1929, a small number of rural parishes have adopted a new name (for example, Whitehills, formerly Boyndie). The former names of these parishes have been included, but it would have been too unwieldy to include either the vast numbers of such changes of name in towns and cities, especially those which occurred at the time of the 1900 and 1929 unions, or the very many older names of pre-Reformation parishes which were abandoned in earlier centuries (however fascinating a list of such long-vanished names as Fothmuref, Kinbathock and Toskertoun might have been).

In this index, the following abbreviations have been used:

C of S	Church of Scotland
FC	Free Church
R	Relief Church
RP	Reformed Presbyterian Church
UF	United Free Church
UP	United Presbyterian Church
US	United Secession Church

Name no longer used	Present name of parish
Abbey St Bathan's	Langton and Lammermuir Kirk
Abbotrule	charge suppressed: Presbytery of Jedburgh
Aberargie	charge dissolved: Presbytery of Perth
Aberchirder	Marnoch
Aberdalgie	The Stewartry of Strathearn
Aberdeen: Beechgrove	Aberdeen: Midstocket
Aberdeen: Belmont Street	Aberdeen: St Mark's
Aberdeen: Carden Place	Aberdeen: Queen's Cross
Aberdeen: Causewayend	Aberdeen: St Stephen's
Aberdeen: East	Aberdeen: St Mark's
Aberdeen: Gallowgate	Aberdeen: St Mary's
Aberdeen: Greyfriars	Aberdeen: Queen Street
Aberdeen: Hilton	Aberdeen: Woodside
Aberdeen: Holburn Central	Aberdeen: South Holburn
Aberdeen: John Knox Gerrard Street	Aberdeen: Queen Street
Aberdeen: John Knox's (Mounthooly)	Aberdeen: Queen Street
Aberdeen: King Street	Aberdeen: Queen Street
Aberdeen: Melville	Aberdeen: Queen's Cross
Aberdeen: Nelson Street	Aberdeen: Queen Street
Aberdeen: North	Aberdeen: Queen Street
Aberdeen: North of St Andrew	Aberdeen: Queen Street
Aberdeen: Pittodrie	Aberdeen: St Mary's
Aberdeen: Powis	Aberdeen: St Stephen's
Aberdeen: Ruthrieston (C of S)	Aberdeen: South Holburn
Aberdeen: Ruthrieston (FC)	Aberdeen: Ruthrieston West
Aberdeen: South (C of S)	Aberdeen: South of St Nicholas, Kincorth
Aberdeen: South (FC)	Aberdeen: St Mark's
Aberdeen: St Andrew's	Aberdeen: Queen Street
Aberdeen: St Columba's	Aberdeen: High Hilton
Aberdeen: St Mary's	Aberdeen: St Machar's Cathedral
Aberdeen: St Ninian's	Aberdeen: Midstocket
Aberdeen: Trinity (C of S)	Aberdeen: Kirk of St Nicholas Uniting
Aberdeen: Trinity (FC)	Aberdeen: St Mark's
Aberuthven	The Stewartry of Strathearn
Abington	Glencaple
Addiewell	Breich Valley
Afton	New Cumnock
Airdrie: West	Airdrie: New Wellwynd
Airlie	The Isla Parishes
Aldbar	Aberlemno
Aldcambus	Dunglass
Alford	Howe Trinity
Alloa: Chalmers	Alloa: North
Alloa: Melville	Alloa: North
Alloa: St Andrew's	Alloa: North
Altries	charge dissolved: Presbytery of Kincardine and Deeside
Altyre	Rafford
Alvah	Banff
Ancrum	Ale and Teviot United
Annan: Erskine	Annan: St Andrew's
Annan: Greenknowe	Annan: St Andrew's
Anwoth	Gatehouse of Fleet
Arbroath: East	Arbroath: St Andrew's
Arbroath: Erskine	Arbroath: West Kirk
Arbroath: High Street	Arbroath: St Andrew's
Arbroath: Hopemount	Arbroath: St Andrew's
Arbroath: Ladyloan	Arbroath: West Kirk
Arbroath: Princes Street	Arbroath: West Kirk

Name no longer used	Present name of parish
Arbroath: St Columba's	Arbroath: West Kirk
Arbroath: St Margaret's	Arbroath: West Kirk
Arbroath: St Ninian's	Arbroath: St Andrew's
Arbroath: St Paul's	Arbroath: St Andrew's
Ardallie	Deer
Ardclach	charge dissolved: Presbytery of Inverness
Ardwell	Stoneykirk
Arisaig	North West Lochaber
Ascog	The United Church of Bute
Auchindoir	Upper Donside
Auchmithie	Arbroath: St Vigean's
Auldcathie	Dalmeny
Aultbea	Gairloch and Dundonnell
Ayr: Cathcart	Ayr: St Columba
Ayr: Darlington New	Ayr: Auld Kirk of Ayr
Ayr: Darlington Place	Ayr: Auld Kirk of Ayr
Ayr: Lochside	Ayr: St Quivox
Ayr: Martyrs'	Ayr: Auld Kirk of Ayr
Ayr: Sandgate	Ayr: St Columba
Ayr: St John's	Ayr: Auld Kirk of Ayr
Ayr: Trinity	Ayr: St Columba
Ayr: Wallacetown South	Ayr: Auld Kirk of Ayr
Back	charge dissolved: Presbytery of Lewis
Badcall	Eddrachillis
Balbeggie	Collace
Balfour	charge dissolved: Presbytery of Dundee
Balgedie	Orwell and Portmoak
Baliasta	Unst
Ballachulish	Nether Lochaber
Ballater	Glenmuick
Ballingry	Lochgelly and Benarty: St Serf's
Balmacolm	Howe of Fife
Balmullo	charge dissolved: Presbytery of St Andrews
Balnacross	Tarff and Twynholm
Baltasound	Unst
Banchory-Ternan: North	Banchory-Ternan: West
Banchory-Ternan: South	Banchory-Ternan: West
Bandry	Luss
Bara	Garvald and Morham
Bargrennan	Penninghame
Barnweil	Tarbolton
Barrhead: Westbourne	Barrhead: Arthurlie
Barrock	Dunnet
Bearsden: North	Bearsden: Cross
Bearsden: South	Bearsden: Cross
Bedrule	Ruberslaw
Beith: Hamilfield	Beith: Trinity
Beith: Head Street	Beith: Trinity
Beith: Mitchell Street	Beith: Trinity
Belkirk	Liddesdale
Benholm	Mearns Coastal
Benvie	Fowlis and Liff
Berriedale	The Parish of Latheron
Binny	Linlithgow: St Michael's
Blackburn	Fintray Kinellar Keithhall
Blackhill	Longside
Blairlogie	congregation seceded: Presbytery of Stirling
Blanefield	Strathblane

Name no longer used	Present name of parish
Blantyre: Anderson	Blantyre: St Andrew's
Blantyre: Burleigh Memorial	Blantyre: St Andrew's
Blantyre: Stonefield	Blantyre: St Andrew's
Blyth Bridge	Kirkurd and Newlands
Boddam	Peterhead: Trinity
Bonhill: North	Alexandria
Bothwell: Park	Uddingston: Viewpark
Bourtreebush	Newtonhill
Bow of Fife	Monimail
Bowmore	Kilarrow
Boyndie	Whitehills
Brachollie	Petty
Braco	Ardoch
Braehead	Forth
Brechin: East	Brechin: Gardner Memorial
Brechin: Maison Dieu	Brechin: Cathedral
Brechin: St Columba's	Brechin: Gardner Memorial
Brechin: West	Brechin: Gardner Memorial
Breich	Breich Valley
Bridge of Teith	Kilmadock
Brora	Clyne
Bruan	The Parish of Latheron
Buccleuch	Ettrick and Yarrow
Burnhead	Penpont, Keir and Tynron
Cairnryan	charge dissolved: Presbytery of Wigtown and Stranraer
Cambuslang: Old	Cambuslang
Cambuslang: Rosebank	Cambuslang
Cambuslang: St Andrew's	Cambuslang
Cambuslang: St Paul's	Cambuslang
Cambuslang: Trinity	Cambuslang
Cambuslang: West	Cambuslang
Cambusmichael	St Martin's
Campbeltown: Longrow	Campbeltown: Lorne and Lowland
Campsail	Rosneath: St Modan's
Canna	North West Lochaber
Carbuddo	Guthrie and Rescobie
Cardenden	Auchterderran: St Fothad's
Carlisle	The Border Kirk
Carmichael	Cairngryffe
Carnoch	Contin
Carnousie	Turriff: St Ninian's and Forglen
Carnoustie: St Stephen's	Carnoustie
Carrbridge	Duthil
Carruthers	Middlebie
Castle Kennedy	Inch
Castleton	Liddesdale
Caterline	Arbuthnott, Bervie and Kinneff
Chapelknowe	congregation seceded: Presbytery of Annandale and Eskdale
Clatt	Noth
Clayshant	Stoneykirk
Climpy	charge dissolved: Presbytery of Lanark
Clola	Deer
Clousta	Sandsting and Aithsting
Clova	The Glens and Kirriemuir: Old
Clydebank: Bank Street	Clydebank: St Cuthbert's
Clydebank: Boquhanran	Clydebank: Kilbowie St Andrew's
Clydebank: Hamilton Memorial	Clydebank: St Cuthbert's
Clydebank: Linnvale	Clydebank: St Cuthbert's

Name no longer used	Present name of parish
Clydebank: St James'	Clydebank: Abbotsford
Clydebank: Union	Clydebank: Kilbowie St Andrew's
Clydebank: West	Clydebank: Abbotsford
Coatbridge: Cliftonhill	Coatbridge: Clifton
Coatbridge: Coatdyke	Coatbridge: Clifton
Coatbridge: Coats	Coatbridge: Clifton
Coatbridge: Dunbeth	Coatbridge: St Andrew's
Coatbridge: Gartsherrie	Coatbridge: St Andrew's
Coatbridge: Garturk	Coatbridge: Calder
Coatbridge: Maxwell	Coatbridge: St Andrew's
Coatbridge: Trinity	Coatbridge: Clifton
Coatbridge: Whifflet	Coatbridge: Calder
Cobbinshaw	charge dissolved: Presbytery of West Lothian
Cockburnspath	Dunglass
Coigach	charge dissolved: Presbytery of Lochcarron – Skye
Coldstone	Cromar
Collessie	Howe of Fife
Corgarff	Upper Donside
Cortachy	The Glens and Kirriemuir: Old
Coull	Cromar
Covington	Cairngryffe
Cowdenbeath: Cairns	Cowdenbeath: Trinity
Cowdenbeath: Guthrie Memorial	Beath and Cowdenbeath: North
Cowdenbeath: West	Cowdenbeath: Trinity
Craggan	Tomintoul, Glenlivet and Inveraven
Craig	Inchbrayock
Craigdam	Tarves
Craigend	Perth: Moncreiffe
Crailing	Ale and Teviot United
Cranshaws	Langton and Lammermuir Kirk
Crawford	Glencaple
Crawfordjohn	Glencaple
Cray	Kirkmichael, Straloch and Glenshee
Creetown	Kirkmabreck
Crofthead	Fauldhouse St Andrew's
Crombie	Culross and Torryburn
Crossgates	Cowdenbeath: Trinity
Cruggleton	Sorbie
Cuikston	Farnell
Culbin	Dyke
Cullicudden	Resolis and Urquhart
Cults	Howe of Fife
Cumbernauld: Baird	Cumbernauld: Old
Cumbernauld: Bridgend	Cumbernauld: Old
Cumbernauld: St Andrew's	Cumbernauld: Old
Dalgarno	Closeburn
Dalguise	Dunkeld
Daliburgh	South Uist
Dalkeith: Buccleuch Street	Dalkeith: St Nicholas Buccleuch
Dalkeith: West (C of S)	Dalkeith: St Nicholas Buccleuch
Dalkeith: West (UP)	Dalkeith: St John's and King's Park
Dalmeath	Huntly Cairnie Glass
Dalreoch	charge dissolved: Presbytery of Perth
Dalry: Courthill	Dalry: Trinity
Dalry: St Andrew's	Dalry: Trinity
Dalry: West	Dalry: Trinity
Deerness	East Mainland
Denholm	Ruberslaw

Name no longer used	Present name of parish
Denny: Broompark	Denny: Westpark
Denny: West	Denny: Westpark
Dennyloanhead	charge dissolved: Presbytery of Falkirk
Dolphinton	Black Mount
Douglas	The Douglas Valley Church
Douglas Water	The Douglas Valley Church
Dowally	Dunkeld
Drainie	Lossiemouth St Gerardine's High
Drumdelgie	Huntly Cairnie Glass
Dumbarrow	charge dissolved: Presbytery of Angus
Dumbarton: Bridgend	Dumbarton: West
Dumbarton: Dalreoch	Dumbarton: West
Dumbarton: High	Dumbarton: Riverside
Dumbarton: Knoxland	Dumbarton: Riverside
Dumbarton: North	Dumbarton: Riverside
Dumbarton: Old	Dumbarton: Riverside
Dumfries: Lincluden	Dumfries: Northwest
Dumfries: Lochside	Dumfries: Northwest
Dumfries: Maxwelltown Laurieknowe	Dumfries: Troqueer
Dumfries: Townhead	Dumfries: St Michael's and South
Dunbeath	The Parish of Latheron
Dunblane: East	Dunblane: St Blane's
Dunblane: Leighton	Dunblane: St Blane's
Dundee: Albert Square	Dundee: Meadowside St Paul's
Dundee: Baxter Park	Dundee: Trinity
Dundee: Broughty Ferry East	Dundee: Broughty Ferry New Kirk
Dundee: Broughty Ferry St Aidan's	Dundee: Broughty Ferry New Kirk
Dundee: Broughty Ferry Union	Dundee: Broughty Ferry St Stephen's and West
Dundee: Chapelshade (FC)	Dundee: Meadowside St Paul's
Dundee: Douglas and Angus	Dundee: Douglas and Mid Craigie
Dundee: Downfield North	Dundee: Strathmartine
Dundee: Hawkhill	Dundee: Meadowside St Paul's
Dundee: Martyrs'	Dundee: Balgay
Dundee: Maryfield	Dundee: Stobswell
Dundee: McCheyne Memorial	Dundee: West
Dundee: Ogilvie	Dundee: Stobswell
Dundee: Park	Dundee: Stobswell
Dundee: Roseangle	Dundee: West
Dundee: Ryehill	Dundee: West
Dundee: St Andrew's (FC)	Dundee: Meadowside St Paul's
Dundee: St Clement's Steeple	Dundee: Steeple
Dundee: St David's (C of S)	Dundee: Steeple
Dundee: St Enoch's	Dundee: Steeple
Dundee: St George's	Dundee: Meadowside St Paul's
Dundee: St John's	Dundee: West
Dundee: St Mark's	Dundee: West
Dundee: St Matthew's	Dundee: Trinity
Dundee: St Paul's	Dundee: Steeple
Dundee: St Peter's	Dundee: West
Dundee: Tay Square	Dundee: Meadowside St Paul's
Dundee: Victoria Street	Dundee: Stobswell
Dundee: Wallacetown	Dundee: Trinity
Dundee: Wishart Memorial	Dundee: Steeple
Dundurcas	charge suppressed: Presbytery of Moray
Duncaton	Glencaple
Dunfermline: Chalmers Street	Dunfermline: St Andrew's Erskine
Dunfermline: Maygate	Dunfermline: Gillespie Memorial
Dunfermline: Queen Anne Street	Dunfermline: St Andrew's Erskine

Name no longer used	Present name of parish
Dungree	Kirkpatrick Juxta
Duninald	Inchbrayock
Dunlappie	Brechin: Cathedral
Dunning	The Stewartry of Strathearn
Dunoon: Gaelic	Dunoon: St John's
Dunoon: Old	Dunoon: The High Kirk
Dunoon: St Cuthbert's	Dunoon: The High Kirk
Dunrod	Kirkcudbright
Dunsyre	Black Mount
Dupplin	The Stewartry of Strathearn
Ecclefechan	Hoddam
Ecclesjohn	Dun and Hillside
Ecclesmachan	Strathbrock
Ecclesmoghriodan	Abernethy and Dron and Arngask
Eckford	Ale and Teviot United
Edgerston	Jedburgh: Old and Trinity
Edinburgh: Abbey	Edinburgh: Greenside
Edinburgh: Abbeyhill	Edinburgh: Holyrood Abbey
Edinburgh: Arthur Street	Edinburgh: Kirk o' Field
Edinburgh: Barony	Edinburgh: Greenside
Edinburgh: Belford	Edinburgh: Palmerston Place
Edinburgh: Braid	Edinburgh: Morningside
Edinburgh: Bruntsfield	Edinburgh: Barclay
Edinburgh: Buccleuch	Edinburgh: Kirk o' Field
Edinburgh: Cairns Memorial	Edinburgh: Gorgie
Edinburgh: Candlish	Edinburgh: Polwarth
Edinburgh: Canongate (FC, UP)	Edinburgh: Holy Trinity
Edinburgh: Chalmers	Edinburgh: Barclay
Edinburgh: Charteris Memorial	Edinburgh: Kirk o' Field
Edinburgh: Cluny	Edinburgh: Morningside
Edinburgh: College	Edinburgh: Muirhouse St Andrew's
Edinburgh: College Street	Edinburgh: Muirhouse St Andrew's
Edinburgh: Cowgate (FC)	Edinburgh: Muirhouse St Andrew's
Edinburgh: Cowgate (R)	Edinburgh: Barclay
Edinburgh: Cowgate (US)	Edinburgh: Mayfield Salisbury
Edinburgh: Dalry	Edinburgh: St Colm's
Edinburgh: Davidson	Edinburgh: Stockbridge
Edinburgh: Dean (FC)	Edinburgh: Palmerston Place
Edinburgh: Dean Street	Edinburgh: Stockbridge
Edinburgh: Fountainhall Road	Edinburgh: Mayfield Salisbury
Edinburgh: Grange (C of S)	Edinburgh: Marchmont St Giles
Edinburgh: Grange (FC)	Edinburgh: St Catherine's Argyle
Edinburgh: Guthrie Memorial	Edinburgh: Greenside
Edinburgh: Haymarket	Edinburgh: St Colm's
Edinburgh: Henderson (C of S)	Edinburgh: Craigmillar Park
Edinburgh: Henderson (UP)	Edinburgh: Richmond Craigmillar
Edinburgh: Hillside	Edinburgh: Greenside
Edinburgh: Holyrood	Edinburgh: Holyrood Abbey
Edinburgh: Hope Park	Edinburgh: Mayfield Salisbury
Edinburgh: Hopetoun	Edinburgh: Greenside
Edinburgh: John Ker Memorial	Edinburgh: Polwarth
Edinburgh: Knox's	Edinburgh: Holy Trinity
Edinburgh: Lady Glenorchy's North	Edinburgh: Greenside
Edinburgh: Lady Glenorchy's South	Edinburgh: Holy Trinity
Edinburgh: Lady Yester's	Edinburgh: Greyfriars Tolbooth and Highland
Edinburgh: Lauriston	Edinburgh: Barclay
Edinburgh: Lochend	Edinburgh: St Margaret's
Edinburgh: Lothian Road	Edinburgh: Palmerston Place

Name no longer used	Present name of parish
Edinburgh: Mayfield North	Edinburgh: Mayfield Salisbury
Edinburgh: Mayfield South	Edinburgh: Craigmillar Park
Edinburgh: McCrie	Edinburgh: Kirk o' Field
Edinburgh: McDonald Road	Edinburgh: Broughton St Mary's
Edinburgh: Moray	Edinburgh: Holy Trinity
Edinburgh: Morningside High	Edinburgh: Morningside
Edinburgh: New North (C of S)	Edinburgh: Marchmont St Giles
Edinburgh: New North (FC)	Edinburgh: Greyfriars Tolbooth and Highland
Edinburgh: Newington East	Edinburgh: Kirk o' Field
Edinburgh: Newington South	Edinburgh: Mayfield Salisbury
Edinburgh: Nicolson Street	Edinburgh: Kirk o' Field
Edinburgh: North Morningside	Edinburgh: Morningside United
Edinburgh: North Richmond Street	Edinburgh: Richmond Craigmillar
Edinburgh: Pleasance (FC)	Edinburgh: Muirhouse St Andrew's
Edinburgh: Pleasance (UF)	Edinburgh: Kirk o' Field
Edinburgh: Prestonfield	Edinburgh: Priestfield
Edinburgh: Queen Street (FC)	Edinburgh: St Andrew's and St George's
Edinburgh: Queen Street (UP)	Edinburgh: Stockbridge
Edinburgh: Restalrig (C of S)	Edinburgh: St Margaret's
Edinburgh: Restalrig (FC)	Edinburgh: New Restalrig
Edinburgh: Rosehall	Edinburgh: Priestfield
Edinburgh: Roxburgh	Edinburgh: Kirk o' Field
Edinburgh: Roxburgh Terrace	Edinburgh: Kirk o' Field
Edinburgh: South Morningside	Edinburgh: Morningside
Edinburgh: St Bernard's	Edinburgh: Stockbridge
Edinburgh: St Bride's	Edinburgh: St Colm's
Edinburgh: St Columba's	Edinburgh: Greyfriars Tolbooth and Highland
Edinburgh: St David's (C of S)	Edinburgh: Viewforth
Edinburgh: St David's (FC)	Edinburgh: St David's Broomhouse
Edinburgh: St James' (C of S)	Edinburgh: Greenside
Edinburgh: St James' (FC)	Edinburgh: Inverleith
Edinburgh: St James' Place	Edinburgh: Greenside
Edinburgh: St John's	Edinburgh: Greyfriars Tolbooth and Highland
Edinburgh: St Luke's	Edinburgh: St Andrew's and St George's
Edinburgh: St Matthew's	Edinburgh: Morningside
Edinburgh: St Oran's	Edinburgh: Greyfriars Tolbooth and Highland
Edinburgh: St Oswald's	Edinburgh: Viewforth
Edinburgh: St Paul's	Edinburgh: Kirk o' Field
Edinburgh: St Stephen's (C of S)	Edinburgh: Stockbridge
Edinburgh: St Stephen's (FC)	Edinburgh: St Stephen's Comely Bank
Edinburgh: Tolbooth (C of S)	Edinburgh: Greyfriars Tolbooth and Highland
Edinburgh: Tolbooth (FC)	Edinburgh: St Andrew's and St George's
Edinburgh: Trinity College	Edinburgh: Holy Trinity
Edinburgh: Tynecastle	Edinburgh: Gorgie
Edinburgh: Warrender	Edinburgh: Marchmont St Giles
Edinburgh: West St Giles	Edinburgh: Marchmont St Giles
Eigg	North West Lochaber
Eilean Finain	Ardnamurchan
Elgin: Moss Street	Elgin: St Giles and St Columba's South
Elgin: South Street	Elgin: St Giles and St Columba's South
Ellem	Langton and Lammermuir Kirk
Elsrickle	Black Mount
Eshaness	Northmavine
Essie	Noth
Essil	Speymouth
Ethie	Inverkeilor and Lunan
Ettiltoun	Liddesdale
Ewes Durris	Langholm Eskdalemuir Ewes and Westerkirk

Name no longer used	Present name of parish
Falkirk: Graham's Road	Falkirk: Grahamston United
Farnua	Kirkhill
Ferryden	Inchbrayock
Fetterangus	Deer
Fettercairn	West Mearns
Fetternear	Blairdaff and Chapel of Garioch
Finzean	Birse and Feughside
Fochabers	Bellie
Forbes	Howe Trinity
Fordoun	West Mearns
Forfar: South	Forfar: St Margaret's
Forfar: St James'	Forfar: St Margaret's
Forfar: West	Forfar: St Margaret's
Forgan	Newport-on-Tay
Forgue	Auchaber United
Forres: Castlehill	Forres: St Leonard's
Forres: High	Forres: St Leonard's
Forteviot	The Stewartry of Strathearn
Forvie	Ellon
Foula	Walls and Sandness
Galashiels: East	Galashiels: Trinity
Galashiels: Ladhope	Galashiels: Trinity
Galashiels: South	Galashiels: Trinity
Galashiels: St Aidan's	Galashiels: Trinity
Galashiels: St Andrew's	Galashiels: Trinity
Galashiels: St Columba's	Galashiels: Trinity
Galashiels: St Cuthbert's	Galashiels: Trinity
Galashiels: St Mark's	Galashiels: Trinity
Galashiels: St Ninian's	Galashiels: Trinity
Galtway	Kirkcudbright
Gamrie	charge dissolved: Presbytery of Buchan
Garmouth	Speymouth
Gartly	Noth
Garvell	Kirkmichael, Tinwald and Torthorwald
Garvock	Mearns Coastal
Gauldry	Balmerino
Gelston	Buittle and Kelton
Giffnock: Orchard Park	Giffnock: The Park
Girthon	Gatehouse of Fleet
Girvan: Chalmers	Girvan: North (Old and St Andrew's)
Girvan: Trinity	Girvan: North (Old and St Andrew's)
Glasgow: Abbotsford	Glasgow: Gorbals
Glasgow: Albert Drive	Glasgow: Pollokshields
Glasgow: Auldfield	Glasgow: Pollokshaws
Glasgow: Baillieston Old	Glasgow: Baillieston St Andrew's
Glasgow: Baillieston Rhinsdale	Glasgow: Baillieston St Andrew's
Glasgow: Balornock North	Glasgow: Wallacewell
Glasgow: Barmulloch	Glasgow: Wallacewell
Glasgow: Barrowfield (C of S)	Glasgow: Bridgeton St Francis in the East
Glasgow: Barrowfield (RP)	Glasgow: St Luke's and St Andrew's
Glasgow: Bath Street	Glasgow: Renfield St Stephen's
Glasgow: Battlefield West	Glasgow: Langside
Glasgow: Bellahouston	Glasgow: Ibrox
Glasgow: Bellgrove	Glasgow: Dennistoun New
Glasgow: Belmont	Glasgow: Kelvinside Hillhead
Glasgow: Berkeley Street	Glasgow: Renfield St Stephen's
Glasgow: Blackfriars	Glasgow: Dennistoun New
Glasgow: Bluevale	Glasgow: Dennistoun New

Name no longer used	Present name of parish
Glasgow: Blythswood	Glasgow: Renfield St Stephen's
Glasgow: Bridgeton East	Glasgow: Bridgeton St Francis in the East
Glasgow: Bridgeton West	Glasgow: St Luke's and St Andrew's
Glasgow: Buccleuch	Glasgow: Renfield St Stephen's
Glasgow: Burnbank	Glasgow: Lansdowne
Glasgow: Calton New	Glasgow: St Luke's and St Andrew's
Glasgow: Calton Old	Glasgow: Calton Parkhead
Glasgow: Calton Relief	Glasgow: St Luke's and St Andrew's
Glasgow: Cambridge Street	Bishopbriggs: Springfield Cambridge
Glasgow: Candlish Memorial	Glasgow: Govanhill Trinity
Glasgow: Carntyne Old	Glasgow: Shettleston New
Glasgow: Cathcart South	Glasgow: Cathcart Trinity
Glasgow: Central	Glasgow: St Luke's and St Andrew's
Glasgow: Cessnock	Glasgow: Kinning Park
Glasgow: Chalmers (C of S)	Glasgow: St Luke's and St Andrew's
Glasgow: Chalmers (FC)	Glasgow: Gorbals
Glasgow: Claremont	Glasgow: Anderston Kelvingrove
Glasgow: College	Glasgow: Anderston Kelvingrove
Glasgow: Copland Road	Glasgow: Govan and Linthouse
Glasgow: Cowcaddens	Glasgow: Renfield St Stephen's
Glasgow: Cowlairs	Glasgow: Springburn
Glasgow: Crosshill	Glasgow: Queen's Park
Glasgow: Dalmarnock (C of S)	Glasgow: Calton Parkhead
Glasgow: Dalmarnock (UF)	Rutherglen: Old
Glasgow: Dean Park	Glasgow: Govan and Linthouse
Glasgow: Dowanhill	Glasgow: Partick Trinity
Glasgow: Dowanvale	Glasgow: Partick South
Glasgow: Drumchapel Old	Glasgow: Drumchapel St Andrew's
Glasgow: East Campbell Street	Glasgow: Dennistoun New
Glasgow: East Park	Glasgow: Kelvin Stevenson Memorial
Glasgow: Eastbank	Glasgow: Shettleston New
Glasgow: Edgar Memorial	Glasgow: St Luke's and St Andrew's
Glasgow: Eglinton Street	Glasgow: Govanhill Trinity
Glasgow: Elder Park	Glasgow: Govan and Linthouse
Glasgow: Elgin Street	Glasgow: Govanhill Trinity
Glasgow: Erskine	Glasgow: Langside
Glasgow: Fairbairn	Rutherglen: Old
Glasgow: Fairfield	Glasgow: Govan and Linthouse
Glasgow: Finnieston	Glasgow: Anderston Kelvingrove
Glasgow: Garnethill	Glasgow: Renfield St Stephen's
Glasgow: Garscube Netherton	Glasgow: Knightswood St Margaret's
Glasgow: Gillespie	Glasgow: St Luke's and St Andrew's
Glasgow: Gordon Park	Glasgow: Whiteinch
Glasgow: Grant Street	Glasgow: Renfield St Stephen's
Glasgow: Greenhead	Glasgow: St Luke's and St Andrew's
Glasgow: Hall Memorial	Rutherglen: Old
Glasgow: Hamilton Crescent	Glasgow: Partick South
Glasgow: Highlanders' Memorial	Glasgow: Knightswood St Margaret's
Glasgow: Hyndland (UF)	Glasgow: St John's Renfield
Glasgow: John Knox's	Glasgow: Gorbals
Glasgow: Johnston	Glasgow: Springburn
Glasgow: Jordanvale	Glasgow: Whiteinch
Glasgow: Kelvinhaugh	Glasgow: Anderston Kelvingrove
Glasgow: Kelvinside Botanic Gardens	Glasgow: Kelvinside Hillhead
Glasgow: Kelvinside Old	Glasgow: Kelvin Stevenson Memorial
Glasgow: Kingston	Glasgow: Carnwadric
Glasgow: Lancefield	Glasgow: Anderston Kelvingrove
Glasgow: Langside Avenue	Glasgow: Shawlands

Name no longer used	Present name of parish
Glasgow: Langside Hill	Glasgow: Battlefield East
Glasgow: Langside Old	Glasgow: Langside
Glasgow: Laurieston (C of S)	Glasgow: Gorbals
Glasgow: Laurieston (FC)	Glasgow: Carnwadric
Glasgow: London Road	Glasgow: Bridgeton St Francis in the East
Glasgow: Lyon Street	Glasgow: Renfield St Stephen's
Glasgow: Macgregor Memorial	Glasgow: Govan and Linthouse
Glasgow: Macmillan	Glasgow: St Luke's and St Andrew's
Glasgow: Milton	Glasgow: Renfield St Stephen's
Glasgow: Netherton St Matthew's	Glasgow: Knightswood St Margaret's
Glasgow: New Cathcart	Glasgow: Cathcart Trinity
Glasgow: Newhall	Glasgow: Bridgeton St Francis in the East
Glasgow: Newton Place	Glasgow: Partick South
Glasgow: Nithsdale	Glasgow: Queen's Park
Glasgow: Old Partick	Glasgow: Partick Trinity
Glasgow: Paisley Road	Glasgow: Kinning Park
Glasgow: Partick Anderson	Glasgow: Partick South
Glasgow: Partick East	Glasgow: Partick Trinity
Glasgow: Partick High	Glasgow: Partick South
Glasgow: Phoenix Park	Glasgow: Springburn
Glasgow: Plantation	Glasgow: Kinning Park
Glasgow: Pollok St Aidan's	Glasgow: St James' Pollok
Glasgow: Pollok Street	Glasgow: Kinning Park
Glasgow: Polmadie	Glasgow: Govanhill Trinity
Glasgow: Queen's Cross	Glasgow: Ruchill
Glasgow: Renfield (C of S)	Glasgow: Renfield St Stephen's
Glasgow: Renfield (FC)	Glasgow: St John's Renfield
Glasgow: Renfield Street	Glasgow: Renfield St Stephen's
Glasgow: Renwick	Glasgow: Gorbals
Glasgow: Robertson Memorial	Glasgow: The Martyrs'
Glasgow: Rockcliffe	Rutherglen: Old
Glasgow: Rockvilla	Glasgow: Possilpark
Glasgow: Rose Street	Glasgow: Langside
Glasgow: Rutherford	Glasgow: Dennistoun New
Glasgow: Shamrock Street	Glasgow: Renfield St Stephen's
Glasgow: Shawholm	Glasgow: Pollokshaws
Glasgow: Shawlands Cross	Glasgow: Shawlands
Glasgow: Shawlands Old	Glasgow: Shawlands
Glasgow: Sighthill	Glasgow: Springburn
Glasgow: Somerville	Glasgow: Springburn
Glasgow: Springbank	Glasgow: Lansdowne
Glasgow: St Clement's	Glasgow: Bridgeton St Francis in the East
Glasgow: St Columba Gaelic	Glasgow: Govan and Linthouse
Glasgow: St Cuthbert's	Glasgow: Ruchill
Glasgow: St Enoch's (C of S)	Glasgow: St Enoch's Hogganfield
Glasgow: St Enoch's (FC)	Glasgow: Anderston Kelvingrove
Glasgow: St George's (C of S)	Glasgow: St George's Tron
Glasgow: St George's (FC)	Glasgow: Anderston Kelvingrove
Glasgow: St George's Road	Glasgow: Renfield St Stephen's
Glasgow: St James' (C of S)	Glasgow: St James' Pollok
Glasgow: St James' (FC)	Glasgow: St Luke's and St Andrew's
Glasgow: St John's (C of S)	Glasgow: St Luke's and St Andrew's
Glasgow: St John's (FC)	Glasgow: St John's Renfield
Glasgow: St Kenneth's	Glasgow: Govan and Linthouse
Glasgow: St Kiaran's	Glasgow: Govan and Linthouse
Glasgow: St Mark's	Glasgow: Anderston Kelvingrove
Glasgow: St Mary's Partick	Glasgow: Partick South
Glasgow: St Matthew's (C of S)	Glasgow: Renfield St Stephen's

Name no longer used	Present name of parish
Glasgow: St Matthew's (FC)	Glasgow: Knightswood St Margaret's
Glasgow: St Ninian's	Glasgow: Gorbals
Glasgow: St Peter's	Glasgow: Anderston Kelvingrove
Glasgow: Steven Memorial	Glasgow: Ibrox
Glasgow: Strathbungo	Glasgow: Queen's Park
Glasgow: Summerfield	Rutherglen: Old
Glasgow: Summertown	Glasgow: Govan and Linthouse
Glasgow: Sydney Place	Glasgow: Dennistoun New
Glasgow: The Park	Giffnock: The Park
Glasgow: Titwood	Glasgow: Pollokshields
Glasgow: Tradeston	Glasgow: Gorbals
Glasgow: Trinity	Glasgow: St Luke's and St Andrew's
Glasgow: Trinity Duke Street	Glasgow: Dennistoun New
Glasgow: Tron St Anne's	Glasgow: St George's Tron
Glasgow: Union	Glasgow: Carnwadric
Glasgow: Victoria	Glasgow: Queen's Park
Glasgow: Wellfield	Glasgow: Springburn
Glasgow: Wellpark	Glasgow: Dennistoun New
Glasgow: West Scotland Street	Glasgow: Kinning Park
Glasgow: White Memorial	Glasgow: Kinning Park
Glasgow: Whitehill	Glasgow: Dennistoun New
Glasgow: Whitevale (FC)	Glasgow: St Thomas' Gallowgate
Glasgow: Whitevale (UP)	Glasgow: Dennistoun New
Glasgow: Wilton	Glasgow: Kelvin Stevenson Memorial
Glasgow: Woodlands	Glasgow: Wellington
Glasgow: Woodside	Glasgow: Lansdowne
Glasgow: Wynd (C of S)	Glasgow: St Luke's and St Andrew's
Glasgow: Wynd (FC)	Glasgow: Gorbals
Glasgow: Young Street	Glasgow: Dennistoun New
Glen Convinth	Kiltarlity
Glen Ussie	Fodderty and Strathpeffer
Glenapp	Ballantrae
Glenbervie	West Mearns
Glenbuchat	Upper Donside
Glenbuck	Muirkirk
Glencaple	Caerlaverock
Glendoick	St Madoes and Kinfauns
Glenfarg	Abernethy and Dron and Arngask
Glengairn	Glenmuick
Glengarnock	Kilbirnie: Auld Kirk
Glenisla	The Isla Parishes
Glenluce	Old Luce
Glenmoriston (FC)	Fort Augustus
Glenprosen	The Glens and Kirriemuir: Old
Glenrinnes	Mortlach and Cabrach
Glenshiel	Glenelg and Kintail
Glentanar	Aboyne and Dinnet
Gogar	Edinburgh: Corstorphine Old
Gordon	Monquhitter and New Byth
Graemsay	Stromness
Grangemouth: Dundas	Grangemouth: Abbotsgrange
Grangemouth: Grange	Grangemouth: Zetland
Grangemouth: Kerse	Grangemouth: Abbotsgrange
Grangemouth: Old	Grangemouth: Zetland
Greenloaning	Ardoch
Greenock: Augustine	Greenock: East End
Greenock: Cartsburn	Greenock: East End
Greenock: Cartsdyke	Greenock: East End

Name no longer used	Present name of parish
Greenock: Crawfordsburn	Greenock: East End
Greenock: Gaelic	Greenock: Westburn
Greenock: Greenbank	Greenock: Westburn
Greenock: Martyrs'	Greenock: Westburn
Greenock: Middle	Greenock: Westburn
Greenock: Mount Park	Greenock: Mount Kirk
Greenock: Mount Pleasant	Greenock: Mount Kirk
Greenock: North (C of S)	Greenock: Old West Kirk
Greenock: North (FC)	Greenock: Westburn
Greenock: Sir Michael Street	Greenock: Ardgowan
Greenock: South	Greenock: Mount Kirk
Greenock: South Park	Greenock: Mount Kirk
Greenock: St Andrew's	Greenock: Ardgowan
Greenock: St Columba's Gaelic	Greenock: Old West Kirk
Greenock: St George's	Greenock: Westburn
Greenock: St Luke's	Greenock: Westburn
Greenock: St Mark's	Greenock: Westburn
Greenock: St Thomas'	Greenock: Westburn
Greenock: The Old Kirk	Greenock: Westburn
Greenock: The Union Church	Greenock: Ardgowan
Greenock: Trinity	Greenock: Ardgowan
Greenock: Union Street	Greenock: Ardgowan
Greenock: West	Greenock: Westburn
Gress	Stornoway: St Columba
Guardbridge	Leuchars: St Athernase
Haddington: St John's	Haddington: West
Hamilton: Auchingramont North	Hamilton: North
Hamilton: Avon Street	Hamilton: St Andrew's
Hamilton: Brandon	Hamilton: St Andrew's
Hamilton: Saffronhall Assoc. Anti-Burgher	Hamilton: North
Hardgate	Urr
Hassendean	Ruberslaw
Hawick: East Bank	Hawick: Trinity
Hawick: Orrock	Hawick: St Mary's and Old
Hawick: St Andrew's	Hawick: Trinity
Hawick: St George's	Hawick: Teviot
Hawick: St George's West	Hawick: Teviot
Hawick: St John's	Hawick: Trinity
Hawick: St Margaret's	Hawick: Teviot
Hawick: West Port	Hawick: Teviot
Hawick: Wilton South	Hawick: Teviot
Haywood	Forth
Helensburgh: Old	Helensburgh: The West Kirk
Helensburgh: St Andrew's	Helensburgh: The West Kirk
Helensburgh: St Bride's	Helensburgh: The West Kirk
Heylipol	Tiree
Hillside	Unst
Hillswick	Northmavine
Hilton	Whitsome
Holm	East Mainland
Holywell	The Border Kirk
Holywood	Dumfries: Northwest
Hope Kailzie	charge suppressed: Presbytery of Melrose and Peebles
Horndean	Ladykirk
Howford	charge dissolved: Presbytery of Inverness
Howmore	South Uist
Hume	Kelso Country Churches
Huntly: Princes Street	Strathbogie Drumblade

Name no longer used	Present name of parish
Inchkenneth	Kilfinichen and Kilvickeon and the Ross of Mull
Inchmartin	Errol
Innerwick	Dunglass
Inverallan	Grantown-on-Spey
Inverchaolain	Toward
Inverkeithny	Auchaber United
Inverness: Merkinch St Mark's	Inverness: Trinity
Inverness: Queen Street	Inverness: Trinity
Inverness: St Mary's	Inverness: Dalneigh and Bona
Inverness: West	Inverness: Inshes
Irving	Gretna, Half Morton and Kirkpatrick Fleming
Johnshaven	Mearns Coastal
Johnstone: East	Johnstone: St Paul's
Johnstone: West	Johnstone: St Paul's
Kames	Kyles
Kearn	Upper Donside
Keig	Howe Trinity
Keith Marischal	Humbie
Keith: South	Keith: North, Newmill, Boharm and Rothiemay
Kelso: East	Kelso: North and Ednam
Kelso: Edenside	Kelso: North and Ednam
Kelso: St John's	Kelso: North and Ednam
Kelso: Trinity	Kelso: North and Ednam
Kennethmont	Noth
Kettle	Howe of Fife
Kilbirnie: Barony	Kilbirnie: Auld Kirk
Kilbirnie: East	Kilbirnie: St Columba's
Kilbirnie: West	Kilbirnie: St Columba's
Kilblaan	Southend
Kilblane	Kirkmahoe
Kilbride (Cowal)	Kyles
Kilbride (Dumfries and Kirkcudbright)	Sanquhar
Kilbride (Lorn)	Kilmore and Oban
Kilbride (Stirling)	Dunblane: Cathedral
Kilchattan Bay	The United Church of Bute
Kilchousland	Campbeltown: Highland
Kilcolmkill (Kintyre)	Southend
Kilcolmkill (Lochaber)	Morvern
Kildrummy	Upper Donside
Kilkerran	Campbeltown: Highland
Kilkivan	Campbeltown: Highland
Killintag	Morvern
Kilmacolm: St James'	Kilmacolm: St Columba
Kilmahew	Cardross
Kilmahog	Callander
Kilmarnock: Howard	Kilmarnock: St Andrew's and St Marnock's
Kilmarnock: King Street	Kilmarnock: St Andrew's and St Marnock's
Kilmarnock: Portland Road	Kilmarnock: St Andrew's and St Marnock's
Kilmarrow	Killean and Kilchenzie
Kilmichael (Inverness)	Urquhart and Glenmoriston
Kilmichael (Kintyre)	Campbeltown: Highland
Kilmoir	Brechin: Cathedral
Kilmore	Urquhart and Glenmoriston
Kilmoveonaig	Blair Atholl and Struan
Kilmun: St Andrew's	Strone and Ardentinny
Kilpheder	South Uist
Kilry	The Isla Parishes
Kilwinning: Abbey	Kilwinning: Old

Name no longer used	Present name of parish
Lanark: St Leonard's	Lanark: St Nicholas'
Largieside	Killean and Kilchenzie
Lassodie	Dunfermline: Townhill and Kingseat
Lathones	Largoward
Laurieston	Balmaghie
Laxavoe	Delting
Leadhills	Lowther
Leith: Bonnington	Edinburgh: Leith North
Leith: Claremont	Edinburgh: Leith St Andrew's
Leith: Dalmeny Street	Edinburgh: Pilrig St Paul's
Leith: Elder Memorial	Edinburgh: St John's Oxgangs
Leith: Harper Memorial	Edinburgh: Leith North
Leith: Kirkgate	Edinburgh: Leith South
Leith: South (FC)	Edinburgh: Leith St Andrew's
Leith: St Andrew's Place	Edinburgh: Leith St Andrew's
Leith: St John's	Edinburgh: St John's Oxgangs
Leith: St Nicholas	Edinburgh: Leith North
Leith: St Ninian's	Edinburgh: Leith North
Lemlair	Kiltearn
Lempitlaw	Kelso: Old and Sprouston
Leny	Callander
Leochel	Cushnie and Tough
Lesmahagow: Cordiner	Lesmahagow: Abbey Green
Lethendy	Caputh and Clunie
Lilliesleaf	Ale and Teviot United
Lindowan	Craigrownie
Linlithgow: East	Linlithgow: St Ninian's Craigmailen
Linlithgow: Trinity	Linlithgow: St Ninian's Craigmailen
Lintrathen	The Isla Parishes
Livingston: Tulloch	Livingston: Old
Livingston: West	Livingston: Old
Lochaline	Morvern
Lochcraig	Lochgelly and Benarty: St Serf's
Lochdonhead	Torosay and Kinlochspelvie
Lochearnhead	Balquhidder
Lochlee	Edzell Lethnot Glenesk
Lochryan	Inch
Logie (Dundee)	Fowlis and Liff
Logie (St Andrews)	charge dissolved: Presbytery of St Andrews
Logie Buchan	Ellon
Logie Mar	Cromar
Logie Pert	charge dissolved: Presbytery of Angus
Logie Wester	Ferintosh
Logiebride	Auchtergaven and Moneydie
Longcastle	Kirkinner
Longformacus	Langton and Lammermuir Kirk
Longnewton	Ale and Teviot United
Longridge	Breich Valley
Longtown	The Border Kirk
Luce	Hoddam
Lude	Blair Atholl and Struan
Lumphanan	Mid Deeside
Lumphinnans	Beath and Cowdenbeath: North
Lumsden	Upper Donside
Luncarty	Redgorton and Stanley
Lund	Unst
Lybster	The Parish of Latheron
Lynturk	Cushnie and Tough

Name no longer used	Present name of parish
Newseat	Rothienorman
Newton Stewart	Penninghame
Newtongrange	Newbattle
Nigg	charge dissolved: Presbytery of Aberdeen
Nisbet	Ale and Teviot United
North Bute	The United Church of Bute
Norwick	Unst
Ogston	Lossiemouth: St Gerardine's High
Old Cumnock: Crichton Memorial	Old Cumnock: Trinity
Old Cumnock: St Ninian's	Old Cumnock: Trinity
Old Cumnock: West	Old Cumnock: Trinity
Old Kilpatrick: Barclay	Dalmuir: Barclay
Oldhamstocks	Dunglass
Ollaberry	Northmavine
Olnafirth	Delting
Ord	Ordiquhill and Cornhill
Paisley: Canal Street	Paisley: Castlehead
Paisley: George Street	Paisley: Glenburn
Paisley: High	Paisley: Oakshaw Trinity
Paisley: Merksworth	Paisley: Wallneuk North
Paisley: Middle	Paisley: Castlehead
Paisley: Mossvale	Paisley: Wallneuk North
Paisley: New Street	Paisley: Glenburn
Paisley: North	Paisley: Wallneuk North
Paisley: Oakshaw West	Paisley: St Luke's
Paisley: Orr Square	Paisley: Oakshaw Trinity
Paisley: South	Paisley: St Luke's
Paisley: St Andrew's	Paisley: Laigh
Paisley: St George's	Paisley: Laigh
Paisley: St John's	Paisley: Oakshaw Trinity
Papa Stour	Walls and Sandness
Park	Kinloch
Pathhead	Ormiston
Pathstruie	The Stewartry of Strathearn
Pearston	Dreghorn and Springside
Peebles: West	Peebles: St Andrew's Leckie
Pennersaughs	Middlebie
Pentland	Lasswade and Rosewell
Persie	Kirkmichael, Straloch and Glenshee
Perth: Bridgend	Perth: St Matthew's
Perth: East	Perth: St Leonard's-in-the-Fields and Trinity
Perth: Knox's	Perth: St Leonard's-in-the-Fields and Trinity
Perth: Middle	Perth: St Matthew's
Perth: St Andrew's	Perth: Riverside
Perth: St Columba's	Perth: North
Perth: St Leonard's	Perth: North
Perth: St Stephen's	Perth: Riverside
Perth: West	Perth: St Matthew's
Perth: Wilson	Perth: St Matthew's
Perth: York Place	Perth: St Leonard's-in-the-Fields and Trinity
Peterhead: Charlotte Street	Peterhead: Trinity
Peterhead: East	Peterhead: St Andrew's
Peterhead: South	Peterhead: St Andrew's
Peterhead: St Peter's	Peterhead: Trinity
Peterhead: West Associate	Peterhead: Trinity
Pettinain	Cairngryffe
Pitcairn (C of S)	Redgorton and Stanley
Pitcairn (UF)	Almondbank Tibbermore

Name no longer used	Present name of parish
Pitlessie	Howe of Fife
Pitroddie	St Madoes and Kinfauns
Plockton	Lochalsh
Polmont South	Brightons
Polwarth	Langton and Lammermuir Kirk
Poolewe	Gairloch and Dundonnell
Port Bannatyne	The United Church of Bute
Port Ellen	Kildalton and Oa
Port Glasgow: Clune Park	Port Glasgow: St Andrew's
Port Glasgow: Newark	Port Glasgow: St Andrew's
Port Glasgow: Old	Port Glasgow: St Andrew's
Port Glasgow: Princes Street	Port Glasgow: St Andrew's
Port Glasgow: West	Port Glasgow: St Andrew's
Port Sonachan	Glenorchy and Inishail
Port William	Mochrum
Portobello: Regent Street	Edinburgh: Portobello Old
Portobello: Windsor Place	Edinburgh: Portobello Old
Portsoy	Fordyce
Prestonkirk	Traprain
Prinlaws	Leslie: Trinity
Quarrier's Mount Zion	Kilmacolm: St Columba
Raasay	Portree
Rathillet	Creich, Flisk and Kilmany
Rathmuriel	Noth
Reay	The North Coast Parish
Redcastle	Killearnan
Restenneth	Forfar: East and Old
Rhynd	Perth: Moncreiffe
Rhynie	Noth
Rickarton	charge dissolved: Presbytery of Kincardine and Deeside
Rigg	Gretna, Half Morton and Kirkpatrick Fleming
Rigside	The Douglas Valley Church
Rinpatrick	Gretna, Half Morton and Kirkpatrick Fleming
Roberton	Glencaple
Rosehearty	Pitsligo
Rossie	Inchture and Kinnaird
Rothesay: Bridgend	The United Church of Bute
Rothesay: Craigmore High	Rothesay: Trinity
Rothesay: Craigmore St Brendan's	The United Church of Bute
Rothesay: High	The United Church of Bute
Rothesay: New	The United Church of Bute
Rothesay: St James'	Rothesay: Trinity
Rothesay: St John's	The United Church of Bute
Rothesay: West	Rothesay: Trinity
Roxburgh	Kelso Country Churches
Rutherglen: East	Rutherglen: Old
Rutherglen: Greenhill	Rutherglen: Old
Rutherglen: Munro	Rutherglen: West and Wardlawhill
Ruthven (Angus)	The Isla Parishes
Ruthven (Gordon)	Huntly Cairnie Glass
Saltcoats: Erskine	Saltcoats: New Trinity
Saltcoats: Landsborough	Saltcoats: New Trinity
Saltcoats: Middle	Saltcoats: New Trinity
Saltcoats: South Beach	Saltcoats: St Cuthbert's
Saltcoats: Trinity	Saltcoats: New Trinity
Saltcoats: West	Saltcoats: New Trinity
Sandhead	Stoneykirk
Saughtree	Liddesdale

Name no longer used	Present name of parish
Saulseat	Inch
Scalloway	Tingwall
Scatsta	Delting
Sclattie	Blairdaff and Chapel of Garioch
Scone: Abbey	Scone: New
Scone: West	Scone: New
Scoonie	Leven
Scourie	Eddrachillis
Seafield	Portknockie
Sennick	Borgue
Seton	Tranent
Shawbost	Carloway
Shebster	The North Coast Parish
Sheuchan	Stranraer: High
Shieldaig	Applecross, Lochcarron and Torridon
Shiels	Belhelvie
Shottsburn	Kirk o' Shotts
Shurrery	The North Coast Parish
Simprin	Fogo and Swinton
Skerrols	Kilarrow
Skinnet	Halkirk and Westerdale
Slains	Ellon
Smailholm	Kelso Country Churches
Small Isles	North West Lochaber
South Ballachulish	charge dissolved: Presbytery of Lochaber
Spittal (Caithness)	Halkirk and Westerdale
Spittal (Duns)	charge dissolved: Presbytery of Duns
Springfield	Gretna, Half Morton and Kirkpatrick Fleming
St Andrew's (Orkney)	East Mainland
St Cyrus	Mearns Coastal
St Ola	Kirkwall: St Magnus Cathedral
Stenton	Traprain
Stewartfield	Deer
Stewarton: Cairns	Stewarton: St Columba's
Stewarton: Laigh	Stewarton: St Columba's
Stichill	Kelso Country Churches
Stirling: Craigs	Stirling: St Columba's
Stirling: North (FC)	Stirling: St Columba's
Stobhill	Gorebridge
Stockbridge	Dunglass
Stonehaven: North	Stonehaven: South
Stoneyburn	Breich Valley
Stornoway: James Street	Stornoway: Martin's Memorial
Stracathro	Brechin: Cathedral
Strachan	Birse and Feughside
Stranraer: Bellevilla	Stranraer: St Ninian's
Stranraer: Bridge Street	Stranraer: St Ninian's
Stranraer: Ivy Place	Stranraer: Town Kirk
Stranraer: Old	Stranraer: Town Kirk
Stranraer: St Andrew's	Stranraer: Town Kirk
Stranraer: St Margaret's	Stranraer: High
Stranraer: St Mark's	Stranraer: Town Kirk
Strathconon	Contin
Strathdeveron	Mortlach and Cabrach
Strathdon	Upper Donside
Stratherrick	Dores and Boleskine
Strathgarve	Contin
Strathglass	Kilmorack and Erchless

Name no longer used	Present name of parish
Strathmartine (C of S)	Dundee: Mains
Strathy	The North Coast Parish
Strowan	Comrie
Suddie	Knockbain
Tarfside	Edzell Lethnot Glenesk
Tarland	Cromar
Tarvit	Cupar: Old and St Michael of Tarvit
Temple	Gorebridge
Thankerton	Cairngryffe
The Bass	North Berwick: St Andrew Blackadder
Tighnabruaich	Kyles
Tongland	Tarff and Twynholm
Torphins	Mid Deeside
Torrance	East Kilbride: Old
Towie	Upper Donside
Trailflat	Kirkmichael, Tinwald and Torthorwald
Trailtrow	Cummertrees
Trefontaine	Langton and Lammermuir Kirk
Trossachs	Callander
Trumisgarry	Berneray and Lochmaddy
Tullibole	Fossoway: St Serf's and Devonside
Tullich	Glenmuick
Tullichetil	Comrie
Tullynessle	Howe Trinity
Tummel	Foss and Rannoch
Tushielaw	Ettrick and Yarrow
Uddingston: Aitkenhead	Uddingston: Viewpark
Uddingston: Chalmers	Uddingston: Old
Uddingston: Trinity	Uddingston: Old
Uig	Snizort
Uphall: North	Strathbrock
Uyeasound	Unst
Walston	Black Mount
Wandel	Glencaple
Wanlockhead	Lowther
Waternish	Bracadale and Duirinish
Wauchope	Langholm, Eskdalemuir, Ewes and Westerkirk
Waulkmill	Insch-Leslie-Premnay-Oyne
Weisdale	Tingwall
West Kilbride: Barony	West Kilbride: St Andrew's
West Kilbride: St Bride's	West Kilbride: St Andrew's
Wheelkirk	Liddesdale
Whitehill	New Pitsligo
Whiteness	Tingwall
Whittingehame	Traprain
Wick: Central	Wick: Pulteneytown and Thrumster
Wick: Martyrs'	Wick: Pulteneytown and Thrumster
Wick: St Andrew's	Wick: Pulteneytown and Thrumster
Wilkieston	Edinburgh: Ratho
Wilsontown	Forth
Wishaw: Chalmers	Wishaw: South Wishaw
Wishaw: Thornlie	Wishaw: South Wishaw
Wiston	Glencaple
Wolfhill	Cargill Burrelton
Wolflee	Hobkirk and Southdean
Woomet	Newton
Ythan Wells	Auchaber United

INDEX OF SUBJECTS

INDEX OF ADVERTISERS